Tolley's
Estate Planning

2016–17

by

Sharon McKie LLB(Hons), Solicitor (non-practising), CTA (Fellow)

and

Simon McKie MA(Oxon), FCA, CTA (Fellow), TEP

both of McKie & Co (Advisory Services) LLP

Members of the LexisNexis Group worldwide

United Kingdom	RELX (UK) Limited trading as LexisNexis, 1–3 Strand, London WC2N 5JR and 9–10 St Andrew Square, Edinburgh EH2 2AF
Australia	LexisNexis Butterworths, Chatswood, New South Wales
Austria	LexisNexis Verlag ARD Orac GmbH & Co KG, Vienna
Benelux	LexisNexis Benelux, Amsterdam
Canada	LexisNexis Canada, Markham, Ontario
China	LexisNexis China, Beijing and Shanghai
France	LexisNexis SA, Paris
Germany	LexisNexis GmbH, Dusseldorf
Hong Kong	LexisNexis Hong Kong, Hong Kong
India	LexisNexis India, New Delhi
Italy	Giuffrè Editore, Milan
Japan	LexisNexis Japan, Tokyo
Malaysia	Malayan Law Journal Sdn Bhd, Kuala Lumpur
New Zealand	LexisNexis NZ Ltd, Wellington
Singapore	LexisNexis Singapore, Singapore
South Africa	LexisNexis Butterworths, Durban
USA	LexisNexis, Dayton, Ohio

© 2016 RELX (UK) Limited.
Published by LexisNexis

ISBN for this volume: 9780754552611

Printed and bound in Great Britain by Hobbs the Printers Ltd, Totton, Hampshire

Visit LexisNexis at www.lexisnexis.co.uk

About the Authors

Sharon McKie is a Partner of McKie and Co (Advisory Services) LLP. She has specialised in private client taxation services since 1997, providing bespoke tax advice to private clients. She has developed a particular expertise in the management of complex tax litigation. She is a well-known authoress on capital tax planning issues and a member of the Succession Taxes Sub-Committee of the Chartered Institute of Taxation and is a former member of the Inheritance Tax & Trusts Sub-Committee of the Faculty of Taxation.

She was awarded the Chartered Institute of Taxation's Fellowship Medal for the best fellowship submission of the year in 2014.

Simon McKie is a Partner of McKie & Co (Advisory Services) LLP. He is a member of the Technical Committee of the Society of Trust and Estate Practitioners, and also a member of the Succession Taxes Sub-Committee and CGT and Investment Sub-Committee of the Chartered Institute of Taxation, and he is a former chairman of that Institute's Capital Taxes Sub-Committee. He is a former chairman of the Faculty of Taxation and of the Faculty's Inheritance Tax and Trusts Technical Sub-Committee. He is an established tax author and has written and lectured widely on taxation.

McKie & Co (Advisory Services) LLP provides expert advice on matters of private client taxation to solicitors, accountants and other advisers. It also provides advice directly to individuals, trusts, companies and other entities. It has won the 'Best Tax Consultancy Team' award in both the 2015 and 2012 Taxation Awards. In 2009/2010 it won the Society of Trust and Estate Practitioners' award for 'Boutique Firm of the Year'. The judges said: 'McKie & Co offers the highest level of specialist trust and tax service. Their broad experience and clear, logically ordered and positive advice was reflected in positive client references.' It was shortlisted again for this award in 2013 and 2016.

Preface

This year has seen an unprecedented volume of changes to the tax legislation of relevance to estate planning with the possibility of further significant changes in the near future. The many detailed changes to our text reflect the rapid rate of change in our tax system. This year's edition is based on the law in force at 31 August 2016. It does, however, include commentary on the legislative changes made in the Finance Act 2016, which received Royal Assent on 15 September 2016.

We are grateful for the enormous help we have received from our specialist contributors – from Ken Chapman in relation to insurance and pensions; from Simon Rylatt, Harriet Errington, Alexandra Hirst, Mark Lindley, Min Nolan, Fred Clark and Katie Male of Boodle Hatfield whose advice on matrimonial matters has been invaluable; from Andrew Green of Hampden Tax Consultants Ltd, who has given expert advice in relation to Lloyds Underwriters and from Gillian Arthur of Shepherd & Wedderburn who has given expert advice in relation to Scottish matters.

Our thanks are also due to the editorial staff at LexisNexis for entrusting us with this task and for their help and encouragement in bringing it to fruition.

Sharon McKie

Simon McKie

31 August 2016

Contents

Contents

Contents

Table of Statutes

Paragraph references printed in **bold** type indicate where the Statute is set out in part or in full.

Other Jurisdictions
Jersey

Table of Statutory Instruments

Paragraph references printed in **bold** type indicate where the Statutory Instrument is set out in part or in full

Table of Cases

C

G

H

I

J

K

L

M

N

O

P

Q

R

S

T

X

Y

Z

Decisions of the European Court of Justice are listed below numerically. These decisions are also included in the preceding alphabetical list.

Chapter 1

What is Estate Planning?

A science and an art

[1.1] This is a work on taxation but estate planning is not merely a sub-division of tax planning. Estate planning is planning to preserve, protect and devolve family wealth. If taxation did not exist, estate planning would still not be simple. An individual would still be faced with hard choices in protecting his wealth against investment risk and political interference and in balancing his children's need to gain experience in the management of wealth against the dangers of youthful improvidence.

In writing about taxation for estate planning, therefore, one needs always to keep in mind a variety of non-taxation considerations which define the problems to be solved as well as constraining the solutions.

One should take account of the client's wishes, expectations, opinions and prejudices and the nature of his relationships with his spouse, children, grandchildren and wider family. One needs to make informed guesses about the future; as to how his family relationships will develop, what will happen to his major assets, how he will want to live and how the political and economic environment will change.

Dealing with such subjective and uncertain matters, estate planning can never be either uniform or absolute; it is a bespoke and continuous service and not a retail product sold once and for all. The future becomes the present and then the past in ways which are never completely predictable. Our predictions must always be provisional; estate plans must be continually revised.

Perhaps it is only the saints who, in this life, are indifferent to protecting their wealth. The rest of mankind needs estate planning in some form. For many, the irreducible minimum is to make a will, to take some life insurance cover to protect one's dependants from the consequences of one's death and to write those insurance policies in trust so that the proceeds will be available to one's personal representatives before probate is granted. In addition, joint owners of property need to consider whether that property should be held as joint tenants or as tenants in common and members of pension schemes should ensure that the scheme trustees have been informed of their wishes for the application of death benefits. Readers of this book are, however, likely to advise clients who have estates far more complex than this which require tax planning which is similarly more complex than this bare minimum.

Estate planning is essential to anyone who owns significant assets, from the moderately prosperous to the very rich, although not all estate planning techniques will be appropriate to every level of wealth. We attempt to cover estate planning as it is relevant to every level of wealth, however one describes holders of such wealth. Those with very substantial assets are often described by such terms as 'High Net Worth Individuals' or HNWIs or the 'super rich'. We eschew such unlovely jargon for it disguises the many other ways in which persons to whom estate planning is suitable may be categorised. We keep in mind throughout, however, the differing characteristics of the moderately prosperous, the substantially wealthy and the very rich and **CHAPTER 24 A LIFETIME OF PLANNING**, gives an extended example of lifetime planning for a family with quite substantial assets.

Basic principles

[1.2] The basic principles of all estate planning, however, are simple.

First, one must determine the clients' objectives. In order to do so one needs to explore the nature of their wealth, their relationships with their family, their expectations for the future and their attitudes towards financial risk and the devolution of wealth.

Secondly, as most estate planning involves making gifts of some sort, one should determine whether they currently have, or expect to have, a surplus of wealth over required expenditure. We deliberately express it in that way because often one of the greatest barriers to estate planning is an over-emphasis by clients on the need to preserve capital and to spend only income. A man of eighty with an annual expenditure of only £40,000 may yet have an investment portfolio of £1m. Whatever view one takes of his life expectancy he does not need to hold on to all of his capital in order to be quite secure that he will be able to continue to maintain his expenditure for the rest of his life. Holding on to wealth too long is far commoner than giving away too much too early.

Thirdly, in making gifts one must determine the appropriate assets to be given away. For example, it may be useful to give assets which have the prospect of substantial future capital growth to younger family members. One must also determine the appropriate form of the gift; should it be absolute or in trust? In coming to these decisions one must avoid creating unnecessary administrative difficulties but be careful to consider the effect of the gift on the recipient. It is usually unwise, for example, to give absolute control of a family company to a child who is just 18.

Fourthly, although most estate planning will be directed towards avoiding particular tax charges, it is important to keep in mind the whole range of taxes which can apply to family wealth.

Fifthly, one should aim for the greatest possible flexibility so that one can adapt the chosen strategy to changes in circumstances and expectations.

Finally, whatever plan is adopted, one needs to review it formally at regular intervals to determine changes in the client's intentions and expectations for the future and to adapt the plan to those changes.

A hostile environment

[1.3] In designing and implementing tax planning steps, an adviser should recognise that he is now operating in a hostile environment. For some years the government and HMRC have conducted a campaign to vilify tax planners and tax planning and to blur the very clear dividing line between tax planning and tax evasion. HMRC's litigation strategy has seen the government refusing to make sensible compromises in disputes with taxpayers; instead choosing to litigate aggressively, considerably increasing the number of cases coming to the courts. At the same time, the government has taken, without adequate consultation, new powers for HMRC to obtain information, to enter and search premises, to impose penalties, to expose taxpayers' affairs to public scrutiny and to collect a purported tax liability whilst it is in dispute. In practice, these powers allow HMRC to inconvenience and penalise taxpayers of whose activities it disapproves whether or not they have failed to comply with their statutory duties.

There has been an alarming decline in the precision with which tax legislation is drafted. This has diminished the taxpayers' ability to determine the scope of the law by which they are taxed, a situation which is made worse by the decline in the standard of HMRC's guidance on the law. In many instances that guidance has been criticised by the professional bodies as positively misleading and as an improper attempt to substitute administrative fiat for the rule of law. In the courts, the decision in *Barclays Mercantile Business Finance Ltd v Mawson (Inspector of Taxes)* [2004] UKHL 51, [2005] 1 AC 684, [2005] 1 All ER 97, a laudable attempt to bring some conceptual clarity to the line of cases which began with *WT Ramsay Ltd v IRC* [1982] AC 300, [1981] 1 All ER 865, [1981] STC 174, has encouraged some of the judiciary to take liberties with the language of tax legislation. They have gone beyond construing the words of legislation in the light of Parliament's intention to substituting provisions which the court considers Parliament should have enacted for the words which it actually did enact. Other members of the judiciary continue to apply themselves to construing the words enacted by Parliament (see *Revenue & Customs Comrs v D'Arcy* [2007] EWHC 163 (Ch), [2008] STC 1329) and *Mayes v Revenue & Customs Comrs* [2011] EWCA Civ 407, [2011] STC 1269, [2011] NLJR 597. Hence the outcome of tax litigation has become heavily dependent upon which judge, or judges, is, or are, allocated to a particular case.

In recent years, tax planning has become a matter of popular debate migrating from newspapers' financial sections to the front page. Unfortunately, the public debate has been conducted by reference to a state of affairs which simply does not exist, fuelled by extravagant claims by 'research' organisations and charities about the amount of tax 'lost' through 'tax avoidance' and by journalists repeating the marketing claims of some of the few organisations still promoting artificial tax avoidance schemes. Politicians have used the proceedings of the Public Accounts Committee as an opportunity to garner media attention through inaccurate but easy soundbites until even HMRC's CEO, appearing before the Committee, was driven to point out that understanding the administration of a tax system ' . . . is a matter for the application of expert tax knowledge. I'm afraid this is something I think . . .

[HMRC] . . . do rather better than a tax committee'. In the UK, almost all major professional firms and banks ceased marketing artificial tax avoidance schemes many years ago because of the introduction in 2004 of the Disclosure of Tax Avoidance Schemes (DOTAS) rules (see CHAPTER 23 DISCLOSURE OF TAX AVOIDANCE SCHEMES). In 2013/14 (the latest year for which figures are available) HMRC estimated that tax lost through all tax avoidance was just 0.43% (down from 0.46% in 2012/13) of government revenues and that figure is likely to reduce significantly because it will include schemes implemented before the coming into force of the many new and increased powers which have been conferred on HMRC in recent years. Even if it were possible to squeeze all tax avoidance out of the tax system, which would require longstanding constitutional liberties to be abrogated, the effect on government revenues would be insignificant. What is more, the tax 'lost' through artificial schemes will only be a small part of the total for all tax avoided.

It is a fantasy to suggest, as some newspapers and other commentators have done, that wealthy individuals can reduce their tax liabilities to almost nothing by implementing pre-packaged tax avoidance schemes. In most cases concerning such schemes heard by the courts in recent years, the taxpayer has been unsuccessful (see, for example, *Eclipse Film Partners No 35 LLP v Commissioners for Her Majesty's Revenue and Customs* [2016] UKSC 24, [2016] 3 All ER 719, [2016] 1 WLR 1939, *UBS AG v Revenue and Customs Comrs* [2016] UKSC 13, [2016] 3 All ER 1, [2016] 1 WLR 1005; *DB Group Services (UK) Ltd v Revenue and Customs Comrs* [2016] UKSC 13, [2016] 3 All ER 1, [2016] 1 WLR 1005).

Imaginary though the problem of tax avoidance undoubtedly is, the furore in the national media has provided an atmosphere which has allowed a considerable expansion of HMRC's powers, most recently in the Finance Act 2016.

Of course these developments have disturbing implications for the essential freedoms and economic health of the nation but to the adviser they cause particular problems. He may not be able to determine how the law applies to particular transactions. Instead of relying entirely on the protection of the law he must calculate whether a particular course of action is likely to arouse the hostility of HMRC. He must consider what he must do where the law conflicts with HMRC's guidance on it. If he advises his client to take his case before the courts, he must ensure that the client understands that, however strong his case may appear to be, there will be a significant possibility of an adverse outcome.

An essential service

[1.4] If the current time is a difficult one for tax planning, however, it is also one in which such planning is absolutely necessary. The present government shows no sign of taking action to reduce public spending. Indeed, total government spending is budgeted to rise in all years over its planning horizon with the result that, in spite of the fact that the government intends to increase the money it appropriates in tax from £604.5bn in 2014/15 to £788.31bn, in 2020/21 even on its own assumptions it will not have reduced its annual spending to match its income until 2019/20 when total UK government debt will be over £1.7 trillion.

Whilst HMRC continues to caricature tax planning as a dishonest assault on the pockets of the many, it has resorted to strained constructions of the law amounting to artificial tax assessment in its efforts to maintain government revenues.

In a succession of penalty cases, taxpayers have successfully appealed against penalties which HMRC, applying a faulty and artificially restricted view of the relevant provisions, has imposed.

More than ever, clients need the knowledge and skill of their advisers to protect them from a department of government determined to maximise revenue in the short term regardless of the consequences for the long term integrity of the country's taxation system.

Chapter 2

The GAAR

The background

[2.1] The febrile nature of the media furore over tax avoidance which has raged since the world financial crash provided, in due course, a justification for the government's introduction of a General Anti-Avoidance Rule (the 'GAAR') in the Finance Act 2013 (which it has called, for presentational purposes, a General Anti-Abuse Rule). As the Society of Trust and Estate Practitioners has commented:

> 'The GAAR . . . will considerably increase the uncertainty of our tax law and decrease the ability of large numbers of taxpayers to predict with reasonable probability, the tax effects of their transactions with the result that it will inhibit and depress the UK economy.'

An adviser now has to consider the application of the GAAR in relation to any planning advice given to a client. Although Graham Aaronson QC, who produced the report for the government on the GAAR in 2011 on which the subsequent legislation was loosely based, said that ' . . . an anti-abuse rule which is targeted at contrived and artificial schemes will not apply to the centre ground of responsible tax planning . . . ', the GAAR is so widely drafted that it applies to much planning which many would consider to be standard practice.

Contrary to its original representations, the government has been unable to resist using the application of the GAAR as a condition for the imposition of draconian administrative provisions and penalties. For example, the application of the GAAR is relevant to the application of Accelerated Payment Notices (FA 2014, s 219), Conduct Notices to Promoters of Tax Avoidance Schemes (FA 2014, s 237) and the Code of Practice on Taxation for Banks (FA 2014, s 287(9), (10) and (11)).

Application

[2.2] The GAAR applies to income tax, capital gains tax, corporation tax, inheritance tax, SDLT, ATED, NIC and petroleum revenue tax (FA 2013, s 206). The application of a GAAR to inheritance tax poses particular difficulties because inheritance tax applies to transactions which are by their nature uncommercial and intended to confer a gratuitous benefit, and involves arrangements which must operate over many decades. For this reason Mr Aaronson had recommended that the GAAR should not apply to inheritance tax. Although he later said that his study group were 'quite happy to see the scope of the GAAR extended [to IHT]' he did not give a reason for this change of view and he reiterated that 'areas of taxation such as trusts can create particular difficulties . . . '. The government's decision that the GAAR should apply to inheritance tax was strongly criticised both by the CIOT and the STEP.

Purpose

[2.3] The claimed purpose of the GAAR is to 'counteract tax advantages arising from tax arrangements that are abusive' (FA 2013, s 206(1)). As we shall see, however, what are 'abusive arrangements' are given a statutory definition which bears little relationship to the meaning of the phrase in ordinary English. Tax arrangements are arrangements which 'having regard to all the circumstances, it would be reasonable to conclude that the obtaining of a tax advantage was the main purpose, or one of the main purposes, of the arrangements' (FA 2013, s 207).

Tax advantage

[2.4] A tax advantage is defined in FA 2013, s 208 as including:

'(a) relief or increased relief from tax,
(b) repayment or increased repayment of tax,
(c) avoidance or reduction of a charge to tax or an assessment to tax,
(d) avoidance of a possible assessment to tax,
(e) deferral of a payment of tax or advancement of a repayment of tax, and
(f) avoidance of an obligation to deduct or account for tax.'

HMRC in its Guidance states that 'this definition . . . is inclusive . . . and is intended to have a very wide meaning.' (para C2.2).

Arrangements

[2.5] For this purpose, 'arrangements' include any agreement, understanding, scheme, transaction or series of transactions (whether or not legally enforceable) (FA 2013, s 214). In the similar definition of arrangements for the purposes of the income tax provisions relating to settlements, the term 'arrangements' has been held to be of very wide meaning. (See for example *Burston v IRC (No 1)* [1945] 2 All ER 61, 28 TC 123, CA; *IRC v Prince-Smith* [1943] 1 All ER 434, 25 TC 84; *Young v Pearce; Young (Inspector of Taxes) v Scrutton* [1996] STC 743, 70 TC 331; *IRC v Pay* [1955] 36 TC 109, 34 ATC 223; *Crossland (Inspector of Taxes) v Hawkins* [1961] Ch 537, [1961] 2 All ER 812, CA; *Vandervell v IRC* [1967] 2 AC 291, [1967] 1 All ER 1, HL; *IRC v Watchtel* [1971] Ch 573, [1971] 1 All ER 296.) It is likely that the court will take a similarly wide view of its meaning in the GAAR.

It is clear that 'arrangements' in this context can include a single transaction.

Although FA 2013, s 207(1) is based on a familiar pattern of 'the standard "main purpose" rules embedded in some existing targeted anti-avoidance rules', it still raises difficult areas of construction.

Objective or subjective?

[2.6] Finance Act 2013, s 207(1) does not ask what are the purposes of the arrangements but whether 'it would be reasonable to conclude' that one of their main purposes was of the required sort. It is sometimes suggested that this wording imports an objective element into the test. If, however, the main purposes of the arrangements do not include the obtaining of a tax advantage, in what possible circumstances could it be 'reasonable to conclude' that they do? If they do, in what circumstances would it be reasonable to conclude that they do not? Surely only where one assumes a hypothetical person judging reasonableness who is not in possession of all the relevant facts. The section provides, however, that one is to have 'regard to all the circumstances'. So it is not clear why the draftsman has not merely provided that arrangements are tax arrangements if the obtaining of a tax advantage was one of their main purposes or their only main purpose.

Main purposes

[2.7] Finance Act 2013, s 207(1) raises the difficult question of when a purpose is a 'main purpose'. There is no definition found in the legislation. HMRC's view given in its *General Anti-Abuse Rule (GAAR) Guidance* states that 'these expressions are to be given their normal meaning as ordinary English words. They have to be applied objectively, having regard to the full context and facts' (para C3.4). The *Oxford English Dictionary* defines 'main' as 'principal, chief, pre-eminent' and specifically in relation to 'a quality, a condition, action etc' as meaning 'very great in degree, value etc; highly remarkable for a specified quality, very great or considerable of its kind'. It should be clear from this definition that there can only be more than one main purpose of arrangements where their main purposes may all fairly be described as chief or as very great in degree or highly remarkable, etc. Where one purpose is of greatly more importance than all the others, the absolute pre-eminence of one purpose precludes any other purpose from being a main purpose. One might, however, be cautious in the light of the Special Commissioner's decision in *Snell v Revenue & Customs Comrs* [2008] STC (SCD) 1094, which concerned the meaning of 'main purpose' in the 'transactions in securities legislation' now found in ITA 2007, s 684(1)(c). The Special Commissioner found that, although a sale was undertaken for a bona fide commercial purpose, it also had another main purpose of conferring a tax advantage. This, in spite of the fact that the tax benefit of the transaction was just 7% of the total transaction value.

Not a significant filter

[2.8] Most transactions undertaken for tax planning purposes will be tax arrangements under this definition because the obtaining of a tax advantage will usually be one of the main purposes of such transactions, particularly if the courts construe 'main' in this context with the width with which it was construed in *Snell v Revenue & Customs Comrs*. In its Guidance, HMRC states that 'it is likely that many transactions that would achieve some tax advantage will fall within this definition' (para C3.8). However, it goes on to say that this does not mean that all those transactions would fall to be counteracted by the GAAR (para C3.9).

The reasonableness test

[2.9] One has to consider FA 2013, s 207(2)–(6), which determine whether tax arrangements are 'abusive'. It is these subsections which determine the scope of the GAAR and whether it fulfils the government's stated objective that the GAAR must 'provide sufficient certainty about the tax treatment of transactions without resulting in undue costs for businesses and Her Majesty's Revenue and Customs' (Foreword to the June 2012 Consultation Document entitled *A General Anti-Abuse Rule*).

The legislation provides that:

'(2) Tax arrangements are "abusive" if they are arrangements the entering into or carrying out of which cannot reasonably be regarded as a reasonable course of action in relation to the relevant tax provisions, having regard to all the circumstances including:

  (a) whether the substantive results of the arrangements are consistent with any principles on which those provisions are based (whether express or implied) and the policy objectives of those provisions,
  (b) whether the means of achieving those results involves one or more contrived or abnormal steps, and
  (c) whether the arrangements are intended to exploit any shortcomings in those provisions.

(3) Where the tax arrangements form part of any other arrangements regard must also be had to those other arrangements.

(4) Each of the following is an example of something which might indicate that tax arrangements are abusive:

  (a) the arrangements result in an amount of income, profits or gains for tax purposes that is significantly less than the amount for economic purposes,
  (b) the arrangements result in deductions or losses of an amount for tax purposes that is significantly greater than the amount for economic purposes, and
  (c) the arrangements result in a claim for the repayment or crediting of tax (including foreign tax) that has not been, and is unlikely to be, paid,
  but in each case only if it is reasonable to assume that such a result was not the anticipated result when the relevant tax provisions were enacted.

(5) The fact that tax arrangements accord with established practice, and HMRC had, at the time the arrangements were entered into, indicated its acceptance of that practice, is an example of something which might indicate that the arrangements are not abusive.

(6) The examples given in subsections (4) and (5) are not exhaustive.'

The double reasonableness test

[2.10] Finance Act 2013, s 207(2) has been referred to as the 'double reasonableness rule', referring as it does to 'reasonably' and 'reasonable'. It is difficult to see, however, if one has 'regard to all the circumstances', how a course of action which is unreasonable could 'reasonably be regarded as reasonable' or how a course of action which is reasonable could 'reasonably be regarded as unreasonable'. That being so, surely the words 'cannot reasonably be regarded as a reasonable course of action' could be simplified to 'which is not a reasonable course of action' without any change of effect. There is, therefore, no double reasonableness requirement but simply a reasonableness test. Arrangements which are reasonable courses of action will not be abusive, and arrangements which are not, will be.

How is the taxpayer to determine what a court will consider to be reasonable?

All the circumstances

[2.11] In determining reasonableness one must have regard to all the circumstances and these will include items listed in s 207(2)(a)–(c). It is unlikely that the things listed would not be included in 'all the circumstances' in any event, so the list seems to have no practical effect. What the section does not tell us is how, in judging reasonableness, one is to have regard to the relevant circumstances.

Do the succeeding subsections provide any help in determining this?

At first sight, subsections (4) and (5) do help in identifying abusive arrangements because they list certain characteristics of tax arrangements that 'might indicate that tax arrangements are abusive'. The legislation, however, does not provide a means of determining whether arrangements are reasonable, and therefore abusive, or not. What is a reasonable course of action within s 207(2) and therefore what are abusive tax arrangements to which the GAAR applies will need to be determined by the courts developing a body of case law in future years. The GAAR does not provide any principles by which the reasonableness or otherwise of a course of action can be determined. It is a broad spectrum general anti-avoidance rule based upon a judicial discretion to determine reasonableness.

Counteracting tax advantages

[2.12] Finance Act 2013, s 209, provides that where there are tax arrangements that are abusive and the procedural requirements of FA 2013, Sch 43 have been complied with, the tax advantage arising from the arrangements is to be counteracted on a just and reasonable basis.

The counteraction may be made in respect of the tax in question or any other tax to which the GAAR applies (FA 2013, s 209(3)). An officer of HMRC must make, on a just and reasonable basis, such adjustments in respect of any tax to which the GAAR applies (FA 2013, s 209(3)). These adjustments may impose or increase a liability to tax in any case where there would be no liability or a smaller liability and tax is to be charged accordingly. This can be done by way of an assessment, modification of an assessment, amendment, disallowance of a claim or otherwise (FA 2013, s 209(5)).

Procedure

Notice of Counteraction

[2.13] Where a designated HMRC officer considers that a tax advantage has arisen to a taxpayer from abusive tax arrangements and that advantage ought to be counteracted under s 209, a written notice must be given to the taxpayer to that effect (FA 2013, Sch 43, para 3). The written notice must contain certain information and it may set out steps that the taxpayer may take to avoid the proposed counteraction. The taxpayer then has 45 days to submit written representations in response to the notice to the designated HMRC officer (FA 2013, Sch 43, para 4). That 45-day period may be extended at the written request of the taxpayer. If no written representations are made, the matter must be referred to the GAAR Advisory Panel. Where representations are made, a designated HMRC officer 'must consider them' (FA 2013, Sch 43, para 6).

Reference to the GAAR Advisory Panel

[2.14] If after considering the representations, the designated HMRC officer considers that the tax advantage ought to be counteracted, he must refer the matter to the GAAR Advisory Panel (FA 2013, Sch 43, para 6(2)) and certain specified information must be supplied to the panel. At the same time, a notice must be served on the taxpayer specifying that the matter is being referred (FA 2013, Sch 43, paras 8 and 9). The taxpayer then has 21 days (unless the period is extended) to send written representations to the GAAR Advisory Panel which should also be copied to the designated HMRC officer (FA 2013, Sch 43, para 9).

A sub-panel of three members must consider the matter referred to the Panel (FA 2013, Sch 43, para 10). The taxpayer and the designated HMRC officer may be asked to supply more information to the sub-panel as they request. The sub-panel must produce one opinion notice stating the joint opinion of all the members of the sub-panel or two or three opinion notices which taken together state the opinions of all the members (FA 2013, Sch 43, para 11). An opinion notice is the opinion of the members that either the entering into and carrying out of the arrangements is a reasonable course of action or it is not and they must give their reasons for the opinion (FA 2013, Sch 43, para 11(3)). It is strange that the Panel is not required to give an opinion on whether the arrangements are 'abusive', in the terms of the legislation, nor on whether the proposed counteraction is just and reasonable.

Having received the opinion of the GAAR Advisory Panel, the designated HMRC officer must, having considered it, give a written notice to the taxpayer setting out whether the tax advantage arising from the arrangements is to be counteracted under the GAAR (FA 2013, Sch 43, para 12). Where the GAAR does apply, HMRC must make just and reasonable adjustments. In an attempt to ensure that counteracting the abusive tax arrangements does not give rise to any element of double taxation, it is provided that a claim for consequential relieving adjustments may be made (FA 2013, s 210). Such a claim must be made within 12 months of the date on which the counteraction becomes final.

Proceedings before a court or tribunal

The burden of proof

[2.15] Finance Act 2013, s 211 makes provisions about proceedings before a court or tribunal in connection with the GAAR. The burden of proof is placed on HMRC to show:

'(a)   that there are tax arrangements that are abusive, and

(b)   that the adjustments made to counteract the tax advantages arising from the arrangements are just and reasonable.'

Section 211(2) provides that:

'In determining any issue in connection with the general anti-abuse rule, a court or tribunal must take into account:

(a)   HMRC's guidance about the general anti-abuse rule that was approved by the GAAR Advisory Panel at the time the tax arrangements were entered into, and

(b)   any opinion of the GAAR Advisory Panel about the arrangements (see paragraph 11 of Schedule 43).'

And section 211(3) provides that it may take into account:

'(a)   guidance, statements or other material (whether of HMRC, a Minister of the Crown or anyone else) that was in the public domain at the time the arrangements were entered into, and

(b)   evidence of established practice at that time.'

Although a court must or may take account of these materials, the legislation provides no means of determining how they are to be taken into account. What is more, this requirement and permission is contained in a procedural section separate from the definition of abusive tax transactions in section 207 and the counteraction provisions of section 209. So it is clear that the materials cannot modify the test under section 207 of whether the tax arrangements are 'abusive' nor modify the concept of what is 'just and reasonable' in section 209.

Finance Act 2016

Penalties

[2.16] The Finance Act 2016 has introduced a 60% penalty where a tax advantage has been counteracted under the GAAR provisions (FA 2016, s 158, new s 212A and Sch 43C into FA 2013).

Pooling and Binding

[2.17] It has also introduced a procedure under which HMRC may 'pool' and 'bind' sets of tax arrangements which, in its view, are equivalent to other arrangements ('lead arrangements') in respect of which a proposed counteraction notice has been issued under FA 2013, Sch 43 para 3. The result of HMRC doing so is that, in respect of the GAAR Advisory Panel, the arrangements may be dealt with by reference to the Lead Case (where the equivalent arrangements are pooled and bound to a lead case) or on a generic basis where arrangements are pooled but not bound (FA 2016, s 157 which inserts Schs 43A and 43B into FA 2013 and makes amendments to FA 2013 and other enactments).

Provisional Counteraction Notices

[2.18] Finance Act 2016 has also introduced a rather cumbersome machinery for HMRC to issue provisional counteraction notices which applies from the date of the Royal Assent to the Act regardless of when the tax arrangements were made. HMRC states that its purpose is to allow HMRC to make provisional counteractions under the GAAR within 'assessing time limits'. This, it seems, will allow it to issue Accelerated Payment Notices ('APNs') in respect of arrangements which it claims to fall within the scope of the GAAR without the bother of first having referred the arrangements to the GAAR Advisory Panel or of waiting to receive the Panel's opinion. If, in the event a full counteraction notice (under FA 2013, Sch 43), a pooling notice or binding notice (under Sch 43A) or a general referral notice (under Sch 43B) is not given, the amount paid under the APN will be repayable.

Implications for advisers

[2.19] The GAAR does not provide a sufficiently precise definition of the avoidance which is its target, to allow its application to be determined with reasonable certainty. Rather, it leaves the court to decide what is a reasonable course of action without providing the principles by which what is reasonable may be distinguished from what is unreasonable. In effect, the GAAR amounts to conferring a discretionary power on the courts to distinguish unacceptable tax planning from acceptable and to penalise it. Perhaps over many years the courts will develop a set of principles to remedy the legislation's lack. But in doing so they will be left with the very same problem which nobody has yet been able to solve: what distinguishes unacceptable tax planning from acceptable?

Although it is not possible to define tax avoidance with statutory precision, there are many tax planning schemes which one can recognise as being of a sort likely to raise the hostility of HMRC and the courts. Such tax planning rarely succeeds in the courts in any event and the advisor will be able to advise clients of the extreme improbability of its being successful in the future.

In respect of most routine tax planning, however, the advisor will not able to say, with any degree of practical probability, whether the GAAR will or will not apply, at least until a sufficient body of case law has built up to allow greater predictability. Almost all tax planning advice must be caveated on the basis that the GAAR might apply to it. HMRC's guidance is of little use in identifying the dividing line between arrangements which HMRC regards as falling within the GAAR and those which it does not. Advisors may try to lay off the risk resulting from the uncertainty of the GAAR's application by frequently referring to Counsel on the issue. Sensible Counsel, however, are themselves wary of giving unqualified opinions on the matter and one would not be acting in the interests of a client if one took an opinion from a less than cautious Counsel simply in order to protect oneself from a professional negligence action.

So the difficulties posed by the GAAR to those offering tax planning advice are very real. In practice, HMRC, because it had committed itself to the assertion that the GAAR will apply only to artificial and abusive schemes, has held it *in terrorem*, threatening to apply it only to those arrangements and taxpayers whom it is determined to defeat. As time goes on, however, HMRC may well find such a powerful and indiscriminate weapon too great a temptation to confine to a narrow target and use it in respect of an ever expanding class of ordinary tax planning arrangements.

Chapter 3

Lifetime Planning: An Overview

Introduction to lifetime planning

[3.1] The purpose of this chapter is to give a general outline of inheritance tax, the basic principles involved in lifetime estate planning and raise a number of matters which receive more detailed treatment in other chapters.

So: 'what is the primary purpose of lifetime planning?'. The traditional response is the mitigation of inheritance tax payable on a person's death'. In today's world, however, consideration also needs to be given to the mitigation of capital gains tax and, in some cases, income tax. It should be remembered that tax savings are not the only purpose of estate planning. Whilst the deceased's heirs will usually regard the inheritance tax payable on death as being most instrumental in reducing their share of the estate, the legal and other costs of winding up the estate, which can be considerable, have the same effect. Therefore, one aspect of lifetime planning should be to organise one's estate into a form which minimises the costs of administration after death.

Whilst one motive a client may have for passing assets to his children may be to take a proportion of his estate out of the inheritance tax charge on his death, there are other motives for doing so. These include the desire to give children a 'start in life', by helping them, for example, to buy a residence or a car or set up their own business; or the desire to help with the cost of educating the client's grandchildren. The client will therefore be seeking advice on the most tax efficient ways of making such gifts; in particular, ways which give rise to minimum inheritance tax, capital gains tax, stamp duty land tax or income tax liabilities.

These three aspects of lifetime planning — the general mitigation of the inheritance tax charge on death, tax efficient ways of giving and the general organisation of an estate — are the subject matter of this chapter. There is a clear overlap between the first and second of these because one of the most obvious ways of mitigating inheritance tax on death is by immediate lifetime gifts. Thus, whilst a client may have multiple motives for making a gift during his lifetime, the general principles involved will be the same and accordingly the second of these three aspects will be dealt with as part of the first.

Inheritance tax

The charge to tax

[3.2] Inheritance tax is charged on the value transferred by a chargeable transfer (IHTA 1984, s 1). A chargeable transfer is a transfer of value which is made by an individual which is not an exempt transfer (IHTA 1984, s 2).

A transfer of value is a disposition made by a person as a result of which the value of his estate is reduced and that reduction is the measure of the transfer (IHTA 1984, s 3). For this purpose no account is taken of the value of excluded property which ceases to form part of a person's estate as a result of a disposition (IHTA 1984, s 3(2)). Excluded property includes property situated outside the UK if the person beneficially entitled to it is domiciled outside the UK, which is discussed in CHAPTER 21 UK RESIDENTS WITH MULTI-JURISDICTIONAL AFFAIRS. So a disposition of foreign situs property by a person who is domiciled outside the UK is not a transfer of value.

Transactions deemed not to be transfers of value

[3.3] There are a number of classes of transactions which would otherwise be transfers of value which are specifically provided not to be so. The most important of these are the following:

- lifetime dispositions not intended to confer a gratuitous benefit on any person and which are either made in a transaction at arm's length between persons who are not connected with one another or are such as might be expected to be made in such a transaction (IHTA 1984, s 10);
- lifetime dispositions made by one party to a marriage (or civil partnership) in favour of the other or of a child of either party if they are:
  (a) for the maintenance of the other party;
  (b) for the maintenance, education or training of the child for a period ending not later than the later of:
  (i) the child's 18th birthday;
  (ii) the child ceasing to undergo full-time education or training (IHTA 1984, s 11).

It should be noted that these dispositions will not be transfers of value provided that they are made during the donor's lifetime. A gift under a will for the maintenance of a relative (not a spouse or civil partner) is not exempt.

Potentially exempt transfers

[3.4] A transfer of value by an individual which is a gift to another individual or into certain favoured trusts is exempt if it is made seven years or more before the death of the transferor. Therefore, between the time of the gift and the expiration of seven years or, if earlier, the death of the transferor, it will be uncertain whether or not the transfer is exempt. Such transfers are, therefore, referred to as potentially exempt transfers ('PETs'). These are discussed in detail in CHAPTER 4 LIFETIME PLANNING: MAKING GIFTS.

Exempt transfers

[3.5] Certain transfers of value are exempt transfers, some of the most important of which are listed below and considered in CHAPTER 4 LIFETIME PLANNING: MAKING GIFTS.

- Inter-Spouse Transfers —
  Transfers between spouses or civil partners are exempt except that transfers from an individual domiciled in a country of the UK to his spouse or civil partner who is not so domiciled are exempt only up to an aggregate limit of £325,000 unless an election to be treated as UK domiciled is made.
- Normal expenditure out of income —
  A transfer of value is an exempt transfer if:
  (a)   it is made as part of the normal expenditure of the transferor; *and*
  (b)   (taking one year with another) it was made out of his income; *and*
  (c)   after allowing for all transfers of value forming part of his normal expenditure, the transferor was left with sufficient income to maintain his usual standard of living.
- Gifts to charities —
  Transfers of value are exempt to the extent that the values transferred by them are attributable to property which is given to charities. In addition, where at least 10% of an estate passes on death to a charity, the rate of IHT on the taxable property, which would otherwise have been 40%, will be reduced to 36%.
- Annual exemption —
  The first £3,000 of aggregate transfers in any fiscal year is exempt. Any unused portion of the exemption from the preceding year may be brought forward and be added to the current year's exempt amount.

Deemed transfer of value on death

[3.6] On the death of a person, inheritance tax is charged as if immediately before his death he had made a transfer of value of an amount equal to the value of his estate at that time. In arriving at this value, however, certain changes occurring by reason of his death are deemed to affect that value.

Variations of dispositions under a will or intestacy within two years of the relevant death may be treated as taking effect on the death. Where an exit charge would otherwise occur in respect of relevant property settled by will on an event within two years of the testator's death, the event is treated as taking place under the will. This is discussed in detail in CHAPTER 19 POST-DEATH ESTATE PLANNING.

The scope of the charge on individuals

A person domiciled in a country of the UK

[3.7] Putting these rules together, therefore, an individual domiciled in the UK will be chargeable during his lifetime on all of his transfers of value except exempt transfers and gifts to individuals made seven years or more before his death. When he dies, he will be deemed to make a chargeable transfer immediately before his death of an amount equal to the value of his worldwide assets at that time, subject to any exemptions which may apply to the bequests under his will.

A person not domiciled in a country of the UK

[3.8] A person who is not domiciled or treated as domiciled in a country of the UK is subject to inheritance tax only on the value of his assets situated in the UK. Any assets situated abroad will not be subject to UK inheritance tax. The government has announced that legislation will be introduced with effect from 6 April 2017 to charge inheritance tax on UK residential property held through offshore structures by non-domiciliaries.

The scope of the charge on settlements

[3.9] There is a special regime for settlements; that is, loosely, where assets are held on trusts other than bare trusts. All settlements will be 'relevant property settlements' unless they fall into one of the categories of privileged trusts which are discussed in CHAPTER 6 CREATING SETTLEMENTS.

Transfers into settlement

[3.10] A transfer into a relevant property settlement will be a chargeable transfer.

The decennial charge

[3.11] The settlement itself is, in effect, treated as an individual taxable entity. The property in the settlement will be subject to a charge (the 'decennial charge') on each tenth anniversary of the settlement being made. The computation of that charge is complex but currently it cannot exceed 6% of the value of the relevant property in the settlement and will often be at 0%.

The exit charge

[3.12] Where property ceases to be relevant property either because it leaves a settlement or because the nature of the trusts over the property are changed, there is a charge to tax on that property (the 'Exit Charge'). Again, the computation of the charge is complex but because it is based on the rate of charge at the previous decennial (or in the first ten years, on another complex computation) it cannot be more than 6% and will normally be very much less than that.

Excluded property and settlements

[3.13] Section 3(2) provides that no account shall be taken of the value of excluded property which ceases to form part of a person's estate as a result of a disposition. Therefore, currently a transfer of non-UK situs assets to a trust will not be subject to UK inheritance tax. This is discussed in detail in CHAPTER 21 UK RESIDENTS WITH MULTI-JURISDICTIONAL AFFAIRS.

Rates of tax

The nil rate band

[3.14] Chargeable transfers made by an individual are charged at rates found by aggregating his chargeable transfers within the previous seven years. The first portion (the nil rate band) is charged at 0%. The nil rate band has been fixed in advance until 2020/21 at £325,000.

In addition to the nil rate band, for deaths after 5 April 2017 a residence nil rate amount will be available where a qualifying residential interest passes on death to a direct descendant. The maximum amount will be £100,000 in 2017/18, £125,000 in 2018/19, £150,000 in 2019/20 and £175,000 in 2020/21. This is discussed in more detail in CHAPTER 18 MAKING A WILL.

The transferable nil rate band

[3.15] Where a nil rate band is unused on a person's death it can be transferred to the estate of their spouse or civil partner provided a formal claim is made.

In order to know whether to claim the relief, one first has to determine whether there is an unused nil rate band and if so what proportion is unused. From 2017/18, the unused residence nil rate amount can be transferred to the surviving spouse or civil partner provided a claim is made. This is discussed in detail in CHAPTER 18 MAKING A WILL.

Rates on the excess over the nil rate band

[3.16] Tax is initially charged on immediately chargeable transfers in excess of the nil rate band at 20%. Tax on the death estate in excess of the nil rate band is charged at 40%, or 36% where 10% or more of the deceased's estate is left to charity. Where a person dies within three years of a chargeable gift, then the tax payable is recomputed either at the death rates in force at the date of the gift or, if the rates have been reduced, at the rates applicable at the date of death, and the additional tax, if any, becomes payable (IHTA 1984, s 7(1), (4), Sch 2). Similarly, where a person dies more than three years after the chargeable gift, taper relief is available. The tax is recomputed at the tapering percentages of either the death rates in force at the date of the gift or, if the rates are lower, the death rates in force at the date of death. Again, any additional tax becomes payable (IHTA 1984, s 7(4), Sch 2).

	Taper relief	Effective IHT rate
Within less than three years of death	100%	40%
Within less than four years of death	80%	32%
Within less than five years of death	60%	24%
Within less than six years of death	40%	16%
Within less than seven years of death	20%	8%

[**3.17**] Where the subject matter of the gift:

(a)   is still in the hands of the transferee or his spouse at the date of death and has a lower value at that date than at the date of the gift; or

(b)   has been sold on the open market before the death at a lower value,

then the additional tax payable on death is calculated by reference to the lower value (IHTA 1984, s 131). For this to apply, however, the gift must not comprise tangible movable property which are wasting assets (IHTA 1984, s 132).

Agricultural and business property relief ('APR' and 'BPR')

[**3.18**] To the extent that the value transferred by a transfer of value is attributable to the agricultural value of agricultural property or to the value of business property and various conditions are satisfied, the value transferred is treated as reduced by a percentage which is either 50% or 100%. These reliefs are discussed in details in CHAPTER 12 THE FAMILY BUSINESS and CHAPTER 13 THE FAMILY FARM.

Liabilities

[**3.19**] In determining the value of a person's estate, his liabilities at the date of valuation are to be taken into account unless they are specifically excluded from being taken into account. A liability which is an incumbrance on any property first reduces the value of that property. So where there is a loan on mortgage, the loan will be taken to reduce the value of the property on which it is secured subject to any restrictions on its deductibility. A liability to a person resident outside the UK which neither falls to be discharged (that is, to be repaid), in the UK nor is an incumbrance on property in the UK (to the extent that it is not taken to reduce the value of property subject to APR, BPR or woodlands relief) first reduces the value of property outside the UK. The place where a liability is to be repaid is first to be determined from the express provisions of the loan agreement. In the absence of such express provision, a debt is repayable where the creditor resides.

As mentioned above, certain liabilities will not be deductible in determining the value of a person's estate. The restriction on liabilities is discussed in **3.25**. In addition, a liability will only be deductible from an estate on death provided it is discharged out of the estate on or after death.

Anti-avoidance

[**3.20**] There are many complex anti-avoidance provisions within the inheritance tax code.

Gifts with reservation

[**3.21**] Perhaps the most important anti-avoidance provisions are the gifts with reservation provisions. Very loosely, these aim to prevent a person from making a gift of assets during his lifetime so as to reduce the inheritance tax chargeable on his death whilst continuing to enjoy the benefit of those assets. These provisions are discussed in detail in CHAPTER 4 LIFETIME PLANNING: MAKING GIFTS.

Pre-owned assets charge

[**3.22**] The pre-owned assets charge is an income tax charge which is imposed where a person enjoys some benefit from land or chattels which he has given away. This is discussed in detail in CHAPTER 4 LIFETIME PLANNING: MAKING GIFTS.

FA 1986 section 103

[**3.23**] There are anti-avoidance provisions in FA 1986, s 103 which, HMRC state, aim to prevent the deduction of artificial debts where the taxpayer has given away assets and has, in effect, borrowed them back. Where the conditions of FA 1986, s 103 are satisfied, the deduction of the liability is disallowed or reduced. This is discussed at **3.25**.

Mitigation of inheritance tax

[**3.24**] Broadly, inheritance tax may be mitigated in one of the following five ways.

(a)   Reducing the estate through immediate lifetime gifts, the intention being to take assets out of the inheritance tax charge on death. This is known as 'asset reduction'.

(b)   Reducing the estate through taking loans or otherwise incurring liabilities where the moneys borrowed or assets acquired in consideration of the liabilities are converted into relevant or excluded property or are the subject of gifts. This is known as 'liability offset'.

(c)   Converting assets of the estate which do not qualify for any form of inheritance tax relief into assets which do (for example, agricultural property or business assets), the intention being to reduce the value of the assets when calculating the inheritance tax charge on death. This is known as 'asset conversion'.

(d)   Freezing the value of assets in the estate so that any future growth in value will pass to the next generation, the intention being to take the 'growth element' out of the inheritance tax charge altogether. This is known as 'asset freezing'.

(e)   Converting capital assets of the estate into high income producing assets. This is known as 'conversion of capital assets'.

These five methods of mitigation will need to be measured against the General Anti-Abuse Rule ('the GAAR') which is discussed in detail in CHAPTER 2 THE GAAR.

As is to be expected, 'asset reduction' is the most popular method although there are a number of considerations to take into account before making a gift. It is for this reason that it has a Chapter of its own — CHAPTER 4 LIFETIME PLANNING: MAKING GIFTS.

In this Chapter we go on to discuss the other methods listed in (b) to (e) above.

Liability offset

[3.25] The second method by which the inheritance tax payable on death may be mitigated is by an individual taking out a loan. In valuing an individual's estate, all liabilities in existence at the time are taken into account (IHTA 1984, s 5(3)) subject to the various exceptions including those introduced by FA 2013 which are discussed below. The anti-avoidance provisions found in FA 1986, s 103 that are designed to prevent the artificial creation of liabilities must also be considered. Section 103 applies where consideration given by the creditor consisted of property derived from the deceased or other consideration given by a person who was at any time entitled to, or whose resources included at any time, property derived from the deceased. A liability of the transferor is only taken into account to the extent that it was incurred for consideration in money or money's worth (IHTA 1984, s 5(5)). As a general rule, debts are deducted against the value of the assets in the deceased's free estate except where the loan is secured against a property, in which case that liability is taken to reduce the value of the property (IHTA 1984, s 162(4)). Therefore an individual could borrow money secured against, for example, his home and then use the borrowed funds to make a gift of cash to a family member which would be a potentially exempt transfer and, provided he survived for seven years, would fall outside of his estate for inheritance tax purposes. The secured loan would reduce the value of the property against which it was secured thus reducing the inheritance tax payable on death.

It was the case that monies would be borrowed and used to acquire assets which would qualify for relief such as business property relief, agricultural property relief or woodlands relief. Again, the loan would reduce the value of the asset against which it was secured and relief would be available on the qualifying assets provided the requisite conditions were satisfied. Similarly, non-domiciled individuals would use the funds to acquire property situated outside the UK which would be excluded property and so not chargeable to inheritance tax. This type of planning, whilst not suitable for some clients, has played a part in many client's estate planning strategies.

Legislation introduced in FA 2013, however, restricts the deduction of liabilities depending upon the purpose of the loan or whether, on death, the loan is repaid. Essentially, there will be a restriction where:

(a)   the borrowed funds were used to acquire, maintain or enhance excluded property;

(b)   the borrowed funds were used to finance relevant balances on non-residents' foreign currency accounts — this restriction was introduced by FA 2014;

(c)   the borrowed funds were used to acquire, maintain or enhance assets that qualify for agricultural property relief, business property relief or woodlands relief;

(d)   on death, the liability is not repaid or discharged out of the estate.

It should be noted under (a) and (c) that the restrictions will only apply where the borrowed funds were used to acquire, maintain or enhance such assets. The restrictions do not apply if a client already has such assets in his estate. Where (d) above applies, the debt will still be deductible provided certain conditions are satisfied. These are that there is a real commercial reason why the liability is not discharged, it is not the purpose of leaving the loan outstanding to obtain a tax advantage and the deduction of the liability is not otherwise prevented.

Loan used to acquire excluded property

[3.26] Where borrowed funds are used to:

(a)   directly or indirectly to acquire excluded property; or
(b)   for the maintenance or enhancement of the value of any excluded property.

the borrowed moneys would be first deducted against those assets with any excess being deducted against any remaining chargeable assets.

As mentioned above, borrowed funds must be used for the acquisition of excluded property which normally should be relatively straightforward to identify. In addition, if such funds are used for the maintenance or enhancement of the value of such property that is also caught by the provisions. HMRC in its guidance state that the words should be given their normal meaning. HMRC then goes on to say that 'maintain' means 'to keep in good or proper order' and of 'enhance' it says means 'to improve or augment' (HMRC Inheritance Tax Manual, para 28012). The *Shorter Oxford English Dictionary* defines 'maintenance' as 'the action of keeping something in working order, in repair, etc; the keeping up of a building'. One might argue that this is a slightly lower level than HMRC's meaning, in which case certain expenditure to keep a building in working order would not fall within IHTA 1984, s 162A but expenditure to ensure it is in good order would be. 'Enhance' is defined in the *Shorter Oxford English Dictionary* as 'raise (a price or value); . . . of property: rise in price . . . improve in quality'.

Directly or indirectly

[3.27] The legislation will apply where funds are used directly or indirectly for the purchase, maintenance or enhancement of excluded property. It is apparent from HMRC's guidance at para 28013 that it takes a very broad view of the meaning of 'directly or indirectly'. There is no motive test and so the intention of the individual when taking out the loan is immaterial. It does not matter that, at the time the loan was taken out, the individual had no intention to acquire excluded property or use it for the enhancement or maintenance of such property. On the authority of *IRC v Stype Investment (Jersey) Limited 1983* (unreported) it is HMRC's view that any property into which the borrowed funds can be traced is subject to IHTA 1984, s 162A. It does not matter how many steps are attributed to the acquisition of the excluded property or the timescale involved. Each case, HMRC says, will depend on the facts. The only comfort that a taxpayer has is that 'it must be possible to reasonably attribute the acquisition of the excluded or relievable property to the borrowed funds before the deduction of the loan is disallowed' (HMRC Inheritance Tax Manual, para 28013). The Inheritance Tax Manual gives a number of examples of when, in HMRC's view, a loan is not deductible. What is clear is that where loans are taken out a comprehensive paper trail should be retained.

Example

Ganni is resident but not domiciled in the UK. He has a house in London but wishes to buy an estancia in Argentina for £1 million. He borrows £500,000 from a UK bank which is secured on his London house. The loan cannot be used to reduce the value of his UK home under IHTA 1984, s 162A. If he had used the funds to buy a property in Devon, the loan would reduce the value of his London home under IHTA 1984, s 162(4) because it was not used to acquire excluded property.

It should not be overlooked that IHTA 1984, s 162A will also apply to trustees of an excluded property trust.

Example

The trustees of an excluded property trust borrow £1 million secured against UK shares held by them. The £1 million is transferred to an offshore account which is excluded property. The liability will be disallowed.

Exceptions

[3.28] There are situations where a loan used to acquire, maintain or enhance the value of excluded property may be deducted (IHTA 1984, s 162A(2)). It may be deductible where the excluded property has been disposed of (in whole or in part) for full consideration in money or money's worth. The liability will be allowable to the extent that the consideration is now represented by assets that are subject to tax and was not used to finance either the acquisition of other excluded property or their enhancement or maintenance or to discharge any other borrowing which would be disallowable under IHTA 1984, s 162A.

Example

Bobby borrowed £2 million secured on his UK property to purchase a property in St Petersburg. At this stage the loan is not deductible. For family reasons, Bobby sells the St Petersburg property and uses the funds to buy a country home in the UK. The loan would now be deductible because the excluded property has been disposed of and replaced with assets chargeable to UK inheritance tax.

A loan will also be deductible where a property when it was acquired was excluded property, has not been disposed of and is no longer excluded property and is therefore subject to inheritance tax.

Sophie, who is domiciled in Cyprus, bought a property in Columbia for £500,000 by way of loan. Some years later she became deemed domiciled in the UK under IHTA 1984, s 267 with the result that the Columbian property formed part of her estate for UK inheritance tax purposes. The liability would, on her death, be deductible but only up to the value of the property now chargeable, namely the Columbian property (IHTA 1984, s 162A(3)).

Where the terms of a loan allow interest on the loan to accumulate instead of being repaid with the result that, on death, the liability is greater than the value of the property, a deduction is allowed up to the value of the property only and not on the greater amount.

Where the value of the liability is greater than the value of the asset acquired with the loan and that asset has not been disposed of and remains excluded property, the excess liability may be deducted under IHTA 1984, s 162A(4) provided that the excess was not as a result of one of the following:

(a)   arrangements, the main purpose, or one of the main purposes, of which is to secure a tax advantage;

(b)   an increase in the amount of the liability (whether due to the accrual of interest or otherwise). An example would be where interest has been added to the initial loan; or

(c)   a disposal, in whole or in part, of the property.

Arrangements are defined in IHTA 1984, s 162A(8) as 'any scheme, transaction or series of transactions, agreement or understanding, whether or not legally enforceable, and any associated operations'. A tax advantage is 'the avoidance or reduction of a charge to tax, or the avoidance of a possible determination in respect of tax'. Tax in this context means inheritance tax (IHTA 1984, s 272; FA 1986, s 100).

Where borrowed moneys are used to purchase excluded property which subsequently falls in value — for example, because of a move in the markets — the excess may be taken into account and deducted against other assets in the estate.

The restriction will also apply where borrowed funds were used to acquire assets which later become excluded property and have not been disposed of (IHTA 1984, s 162A(5)). The liability may only be taken into account to the extent that its value is greater than the assets acquired with the borrowed funds.

Alberto is non-UK domiciled and borrowed £2 million to buy some diamond jewellery for £3 million which he kept in the safe in his London property. His wife took the jewellery with her on a trip to the Cannes Film Festival. Whilst she was in Cannes, Alberto died. At the time of his death the diamonds would have been excluded property and so the liability of £2 million is therefore not allowable. If she had taken only half the jewellery, with a value of £1.5 million, a liability of £1 million would have been allowable.

Application of the rules

[3.29] IHTA 1984, s 162A applies to deaths and other chargeable events which occur after 16 July 2013 regardless of when the liability was incurred (FA 2013, Sch 36, para 5).

A liability is treated as having been incurred on the date that the agreement was made (FA 2013, Sch 36, para 5(3)). Where an existing loan agreement is varied, the additional liability is treated as having been incurred on the date that the agreement was varied (FA 2013, Sch 36, para 5(3)(A)). In most cases there will be a written loan agreement but in the event that there is not, HMRC states that the liability will be treated as incurred on the date the money is paid to the borrower (HMRC Inheritance Tax Manual, para 28011).

Loans used to finance non-residents' foreign currency accounts

[3.30] A liability which has been used to finance a relevant balance on a UK bank account denominated in a foreign currency held by a non-resident and non-domiciled individual will not be deductible for transfers of value made or treated as made after 16 July 2014 (IHTA 1984, s 162AA). Previously, such accounts were not taken into consideration in determining the value of a non-UK resident and a non-domiciled individual's estate under IHTA 1984, s 157 and nor were they included within the definition of excluded property. This meant that no inheritance tax was payable on such accounts and in addition the liability was deductible.

Application of the rules

[3.31] IHTA 1984, s 162AA, which relates specifically to relevant balances on UK foreign currency bank accounts, has effect in relation to transfers of value made or treated as made after 16 July 2014. This is discussed in more detail in CHAPTER 22 THE OVERSEAS CLIENT.

Acquisition of certain relievable property

Acquisition of assets qualifying for business property relief

[3.32] Where a liability is incurred to acquire assets that qualify for business property relief under IHTA 1984, s 104 or for the maintenance or enhancement of the value of those assets, IHTA 1984, s 162B(2) provides that the liability will be deducted first from the value of the assets qualifying for relief regardless of whether the liability is secured on other assets. Business property relief will be given on the net value of the asset after deduction of the liability. Where the liability has already been taken into account under IHTA 1984, s 110(b), section 162B does not apply.

Example

Brian borrows £300,000 secured against his house which he uses to buy shares in a company in which he is a director which qualify for business property relief. On his death, the shares have increased in value and IHTA 1984, s 162B applies because the liability has been incurred to acquire a relevant business asset. The liability will reduce the value of the shares subject to IHTA 1984, s 175A being met (see 3.37 below) with the excess of the value in the company shares over the liability being reduced by business property relief. In valuing his house on his death the liability will not be taken into account.

There is some concern amongst practitioners as to the interaction between IHTA 1984, s 162B and the spouse exemption under IHTA 1984, s 18. HMRC Inheritance Tax Manual at para 28020 gives the following example:

'Ian borrows £600,000, which is charged on his house and uses the money to buy shares in his son's company. At Ian's date of death, the shares are worth £800,000, the house £1m and his personal estate is worth £500,000. Under his Will, Ian leaves his house to his spouse with the residue to his son.

Assuming the liability meets the conditions of IHTA84/S175A, it is taken to reduce the value of the company shares before business relief is applied. As the liability has been taken into account under IHTA84/S162B, it cannot be taken against the value of the house under IHTA84/S162(4). The value of shares is reduced to nil through a combination of deducting the liability (£600,000) and business relief (£200,000). The liability has been taken into account against the shares, so the house passes to the spouse, free of the liability and qualifies for spouse or civil partner exemption. This leaves a chargeable estate of £500,000 that passes to the son.'

Some practitioners consider that this example is not correct because the spouse exemption will only be available on the value transferred which in HMRC's example is £400,000, and not the whole £1m value of the house because £600,000 of the value of the house must be used to discharge the liability. It is understood that STEP has written to HMRC seeking clarification on this point.

Acquisition of assets qualifying for agricultural property relief

[3.33] IHTA 1984, s 162B(3) and (4) are similar to those provisions discussed above in relation to assets qualifying for business property relief. Where borrowed moneys are used directly or indirectly to acquire assets that qualify for agricultural property relief under IHTA 1984, s 116 or to enhance or maintain the value of such assets then the liability will be deducted first from the value of those assets (IHTA 1984, s 162B(4)). Again, this will be the case even where the liability is secured on other assets. Agricultural property relief will then be given on the agricultural value of the asset after deduction of the liability.

Example

Marjorie borrows £500,000 to purchase some farmland adjoining her farm. On her death the value of her estate is £3 million, of which £1.5 million represents assets qualifying for relief. The liability of £500,000 reduces the agricultural value of the property on which relief is available to £1 million.

In the case where assets are acquired, some of which qualify for agricultural property relief and some of which do not, the apportionment of any loan at the date of death needs to be considered. HMRC accepts that there may be a number of approaches but seem to prefer the method of using the values at the date of acquisition (HMRC Inheritance Tax Manual, para 28021).

There will, of course, be situations where an asset qualifies for both agricultural and business property relief. IHTA 1984, s 114 provides that agricultural property relief applies to the agricultural value first and business property relief applies to any excess value on the agricultural value of the asset. Where the liability exceeds the agricultural value of the asset, there will be no agricultural property relief to be deducted against the estate. The balance of the liability can then be set against the non-agricultural value of the asset to determine the value of the asset which may qualify for business property relief.

Acquisition of assets qualifying for woodlands relief

[3.34] Where moneys are borrowed to acquire land, trees or underwood, to allow the planting of trees or underwood or the maintenance or enhancement of the value of the trees or underwood, the liability will be treated in the same way as discussed above (IHTA 1984, s 162B(5) and (6)).

Example

On 31 March 2013, Bradley borrowed £350,000, which was secured on his home in order to purchase woodlands, Brambly Wood, paying £350,000 in total. Under the terms of his will, he leaves his entire estate to his old school friend. When he dies in 2024 his estate comprises:

House	1,200,000	
Less: outstanding loan to purchase Brambly Wood	200,000	
		1,000,000
Land at Brambly Wood	200,000	
Standing timber at Brambly Wood	250,000	
		450,000
		1,450,000

His inheritance tax liability (assuming inheritance tax rates remain unchanged) is:

	£
Estate	1,450,000
Less: woodland relief under section 125(2)(a)	250,000
	1,200,000
Less: nil rate band	325,000
	875,000
Inheritance Tax payable	350,000

If Bradley had purchased the land six days later, IHTA 1984, s 162B would have applied to restrict the deduction of the loan. Where section 162B(5) applies, to the extent that the liability is attributable to financing the acquisition of timber the value of which is left out of account under IHTA 1984, s 125(2)(a), or the acquisition of the land on which it is grown, or the planting, maintenance or enhancement of the timber, the liability is first to reduce the value of the growing timber before their value is left out of account. The inheritance tax liability on Bradley's estate would have increased by £80,000 (£200,000 at 40%).

Application of the rules

[3.35] The provisions found in IHTA 1984, s 162B apply only to liabilities incurred after 5 April 2013.

Repayment of loans used to finance excluded property, relevant balances or certain relievable property

[3.36] IHTA 1984, s 162C will apply when a loan has been partially repaid. It is only the unpaid balance of the loan which will be affected by the provisions found in IHTA 1984, ss 162A, 162AA and 162B. The legislation also provides rules as to how repayments should be applied to a liability. The repayment is first applied to any part of the liability that was not attributable to excluded property, relievable property or relevant foreign currency balances then to any part used to finance relievable property, then to any part attributable to relevant balances and finally to any part used to finance excluded property.

There is a similar priority rule for partial repayment of the liability in cases other than on death. In such cases, IHTA 1984, s 157 does not apply so that any part of a liability attributable to financing a relevant balance on a foreign currency bank account is treated as repaid before any part which would be restricted or disallowed.

Discharge of liability after death

[3.37] IHTA 1984, s 175A imposes a restriction on the deductibility of liabilities from an estate where the liability is not repaid or discharged out of the estate. Where this is the case it may still be taken into account to reduce the value of the estate to the extent that:

(a)   there is a real commercial reason for the liability not being repaid;

(b)   the main purpose or one of the main purposes of leaving the liability or part of it undischarged is not to secure a tax advantage;

(c)   the liability is not prevented under any other provision of IHTA 1984 from being taken into account (IHTA 1984, s 175A(2)).

All three conditions must be met. In such a case the liability may be allowed as a deduction against the estate even if it is not repaid. IHTA 1984, s 175A(3) provides that there is a real commercial reason for a liability not being discharged where it is shown that:

(a)   the liability is to a person dealing at arm's length; or

(b)   if the liability were to a person dealing at arm's length, that person would not require the liability to be discharged.

The legislation does not, however, specify the time at which the 'real commercial reason' must exist, nor does it specify whether s 175A(3) is an exhaustive definition or not.

A 'tax advantage' is defined for the purposes of s 175A(2)(b) as:

(a)   a relief from tax or increased relief from tax;

(b)   a repayment of tax or increased repayment of tax;

(c)   the avoidance, reduction or delay of a charge to tax or an assessment to tax; or

(d)   the avoidance of a possible assessment to tax or determination in respect of tax.

For these purposes 'tax' includes income tax and capital gains tax whereas IHTA 1984, s 169B only relates to inheritance tax.

It is considered by many that IHTA 1984, s 175A was introduced to frustrate the home loan or double trust scheme. HMRC in its guidance at para 28029 states that:

> 'It is important to note here that whilst the liability may be part of wider arrangements that are aimed at securing a tax advantage, for example, a home loan or double trust scheme, you should only consider whether it is the non-repayment of the liability [that] gives rise to a tax advantage.'

There are specific provisions dealing with the situation where a liability is secured on property which passes to a spouse or civil partner. Where a liability is not taken into account in determining the value of a person's estate, the liability is not to be taken into account in determining the extent which the estate of any spouse or civil partner has increased (IHTA 1984, s 175A(4)).

Example

Jasmine makes a loan of £50,000 to her aunt to make a trip of a lifetime which is secured on her aunt and uncle's £1 million house. The loan is interest-free and repayable on demand. On her aunt's death her uncle is the sole beneficiary of her Will. The loan is not repaid as Jasmine is happy for it to remain outstanding until her uncle's death. The loan would not be left outstanding by an arm's length creditor and so under s 175A(2)(a) it would not be taken into account. As the liability is disallowed the chargeable value of the property is £1 million rather than £950,000. The spouse exemption of £1 million, however, is available.

Where a liability is partially repaid after death, the part repaid will be allowed as a deduction unless the unpaid portion meets the conditions of IHTA 1984, s 175A(2).

Where funds have been used to acquire excluded property, relevant balances on foreign currency bank accounts, relievable property and other assets and the liability is partially repaid, IHTA 1984, s 175A(7) sets out the priority of allocation against the assets of the estate.

As mentioned above, in order for a liability to be taken into account it must be discharged out of the estate or from excluded property owned by the deceased immediately before his death. This raises the question of what happens in the typical arrangement where a mortgage is repaid using the proceeds of an insurance policy which had been written in trust. The proceeds of the insurance policy fall outside the deceased's estate and therefore if the mortgage is repaid using those moneys the mortgage will not be deducted. If, however, the proceeds of the insurance policy were lent to the estate in order to repay the mortgage, it would seem that HMRC will accept that the liability has been discharged out of the estate (HMRC Inheritance Tax Manual, para 28028).

Where executors borrow money to repay a mortgage and secure the new loan on the property, HMRC accepts that the liability, ie the mortgage, has been repaid 'out of the estate'. It gives an example of this in its Inheritance Tax Manual at para 28028. This example goes on to provide that the beneficiary receives the property charged with the new debt. This may, however, cause an SDLT liability as a debt can comprise chargeable consideration in certain circumstances (FA 2003, Sch 4, para 8). FA 2003, Sch 3, para 3A provides, however, that where personal representatives distribute property subject to a secured debt, no SDLT is payable provided the only consideration given by the beneficiary is the assumption of that secured debt. Therefore the transfer of property by the executors subject to the original mortgage will not be subject to SDLT because the para 3A exemption will apply. The difficulty is that secured debt for these purposes means 'debt that, immediately after the death of the deceased person, is secured on the property'. New borrowing will have been secured during the administration of the estate and will not have been secured on the property immediately after death. The para 3A exemption will not be available and so SDLT may be payable. For executors who secure a new loan to repay the original liability, care needs to be taken to avoid such a charge if possible. It is understood that STEP has written to HMRC about this matter.

Double charge to inheritance tax

[3.38] A double charge to inheritance tax may arise where the settlor owes a debt to a settlement in which he has qualifying interest in possession unless that debt is subsequently repaid (or unless there is a commercial reason for the liability not subsequently being discharged). The double charge arises because the benefit of the debt forms part of his settled estate and unless it is repaid, that debt is not deductible from the assets of his free estate. The same issue applies where the deceased is owed a debt by the trustees of a settlement in which he has a qualifying interest in possession. It is understood that STEP has written to HMRC about this matter.

Application of the rules

[3.39] IHTA 1984, section 175A applies in relation to deaths and other chargeable events that occur after 16 July 2013. These rules may be said, therefore, to have an element of retrospection in as much as they apply to liabilities incurred before the passing of the Finance Act 2013. Section 175A(7) applies to transfers of value made after 16 July 2014.

Asset conversion

[3.40] The third basic way in which the inheritance tax payable on a person's death may be mitigated is by asset conversion. An estate comprising a portfolio of gilts and securities quoted on the Stock Exchange and a house worth in total (say) £500,000 will (at 2016/17 rates) suffer on death an inheritance tax charge of £70,000. If, however, that estate had solely comprised property which qualified for 50% agricultural property relief, the value of the estate for inheritance tax purposes would reduce to £250,000 and no tax would be chargeable.

This is an extreme example, but it illustrates the basic principle that in inheritance tax terms it is better for a wealthy client with surplus assets which he is not prepared to give away to invest those assets in commercially sound property which qualifies for some form of relief. The types of property most suitable for this exercise include the following.

(a) *Agricultural property*, tenanted or untenanted. See CHAPTER 13 THE FAMILY FARM.
(b) *Woodlands*. Provided the statutory rules are satisfied, full 100% business property relief should apply. Woodlands also have certain capital gains tax advantages for their owner. For a more detailed analysis, see CHAPTER 14 WOODLANDS.
(c) *Lloyd's underwriting assets*. Business property relief is available on a Lloyds' member's interest in Lloyds, whether the member is an individual, a member of a SLP or LLP or a shareholder in a company (NameCo). An individual member at Lloyd's may qualify for business property relief on his syndicate capacity, his funds at Lloyds comprising his Lloyd's deposit, his special reserve fund, his general (or personal) reserve and any assets which secure a guarantee or letter of credit issued by a bank up to the amount of the guaranteed sum and his open underwriting years. The relief will be subject to the overriding constraint that funds eligible for relief cannot be disproportionate to the level of underwriting as a whole. Business property relief is also available on the value of a member's interest in a Lloyd's SLP or LLP, and the ancillary trust fund assets supporting them, and on the value of shares in a NameCo. Business property relief is not available on external ancillary trust fund assets supporting a NameCo except to the extent that they also support the unlimited run-off of a converting member. For a more detailed consideration, see CHAPTER 18 MAKING A WILL.
(d) *Unquoted shares or securities in a company*. Rather than an individual trying to source a portfolio of suitable unquoted shares or securities on which business property relief will be available, there are a number of organisations that manage portfolios of suitable shares which qualify for relief in return for a management fee.
(e) *Sleeping partner in unincorporated business*. An individual not wishing to take an active role in a business may consider becoming a sleeping partner of an unincorporated business or a member of a limited liability partnership. Business property relief of 100% will be available.

It must be remembered that in order to qualify for business property relief, agricultural property relief or woodlands relief, the deceased must have satisfied various conditions, relating, for example, to the period of ownership of the assets in question.

One other device for converting assets not qualifying for relief into assets that do, although one which is extremely rare in practice, concerns shareholdings in publicly quoted companies. A controlling shareholding in a quoted company qualifies for 100% business property relief (IHTA 1984, s 105(1)(b)). A non-controlling holding does not qualify for any relief. If two or more individuals own shareholdings which together (but not separately) give control of a public trading company, they could transfer their shares to a newly formed unlisted holding company in return for shares in that company. The shares in the holding company would then qualify for 100% or 50% business property relief depending upon the size of the holding. Section 105(3) provides that business property relief will not apply to shares in companies whose only or main business is, *inter alia*, making or holding investments. However, under s 105(4)(b) the relief will still apply to the holding company of one or more trading subsidiaries.

It will be appreciated that the scope for the 'asset conversion' type of inheritance tax mitigation will be fairly limited. It is also a device to be used with care.

The use of loans

[3.41] Before 2013/14 individuals with a surplus of assets which they preferred not to realise and invest (either because they liked the existing investment or because to do so would give rise to a large chargeable gain) would borrow on the security of the non-qualifying assets and invest the borrowings in assets qualifying for relief.

This had the result that the loan would reduce the value of the non-qualifying assets on which the loan was secured and relief would be available on the qualifying assets provided the various conditions were satisfied.

As discussed in **3.25**, no deduction is now given for loans taken out after 5 April 2013 to finance the acquisition of such assets.

Asset freezing

[3.42] The fourth way of mitigating inheritance tax is by asset freezing.

Loans

[3.43] The simplest example of an asset freezing measure is making a loan to the persons one wishes to benefit from one's estate. This freezes the value of the debt due to the lender which forms part of the lender's estate; and any capital growth of the assets in which the borrower invests the proceeds of the loan falls outside the lender's estate. To ensure making the loan does not itself give rise to an inheritance tax charge, the loan is usually expressed to be interest free and repayable on demand, so that there is no immediate reduction in the value of the lender's estate.

A loan is a very effective, commonly used estate planning device. It is particularly attractive to moderately wealthy parents with some free capital who wish to help out their children but are reluctant to part completely with a part of their estate. The lender can always write off the loan over a period of time using his annual £3,000 exemption and may write it off completely by way of a potentially exempt transfer, if he later finds that he can do without the capital. (Whilst the loan and the subsequent release will undoubtedly amount to associated operations within IHTA 1984, s 268(1), s 268(3) will operate to prevent there being an overall chargeable transfer.)

Matters to consider

[3.44] Where the borrower uses the proceeds of the loan to purchase an asset which is not readily realisable, or which is only immediately realisable for a lower figure than its cost, and has no other liquid assets available to repay the loan and (for whatever reason) is not in a position to borrow funds commercially to do so, then although the loan is repayable on demand there is a possibility that it will not be repaid and therefore there may be an immediate reduction in the lender's estate.

It is possible that in those circumstances HMRC may argue that the failure to charge interest represents a waiver of interest and may seek to treat this as a succession of gifts made over the duration of the loan. Such an attempt would be entirely misconceived.

It is sometimes suggested that any income arising from the benefit of the loan in the borrower's hands will form part of the total income of the lender under the income tax settlement rules. This is, however, a difficult argument to sustain because, even if a straightforward loan can be regarded as a 'settlement' for the purposes of ITTOIA 2005, Pt 5 Ch 5, it is necessary first to identify the settled property and then to show that income arises from that property. As the lender is merely exchanging the property lent for a chose in action (namely his rights against the borrower), the settled property can only be either the chose in action, which does not give rise to any income, or the proceeds of the loan in the hands of the borrower in which the lender would seem to have no interest. Nevertheless, the risk of some form of attack from HMRC clearly exists (for example, see *IRC v Levy* [1982] STC 442, 56 TC 68 (Ch D)). HMRC may attempt to argue that the loan constitutes part of a wider 'arrangement' that the interest would not be paid. In such circumstances, it may seek to argue that any income earned from the capital lent constitutes assessable income in the hands of the lender. It is unlikely that HMRC would be successful in such an approach.

Another possible problem is the gifts with reservation provisions, but again it is difficult to see how a straightforward loan (even interest-free) could be regarded as a gift for the purposes of FA 1986, s 102. HMRC's view on this appears to be that the grant of an interest-free loan repayable on demand is not a transfer of value but it is a gift because there is a clear intention to confer bounty; the property disposed of being the interest foregone (see HMRC Inheritance Tax Manual, para 14317). That view is clearly incorrect. The lender cannot be said to have disposed of property which is the interest arising on the loan because that 'property' has never existed. Nor can the lender be said to have disposed of the income arising on the investment of the money lent because that income has never belonged to the lender.

One also has to consider the pre-owned assets charge under FA 2004, Sch 15 where a lender resides in a property purchased by another with money loaned to him by the lender. HMRC's view is that it does not regard the contribution condition set out in Sch 15, para 3(3) as being met. It is HMRC's view that since the outstanding debt will form part of his estate for inheritance tax purposes, it would not be reasonable to consider that the loan falls within the contribution condition and therefore not reasonably attributable to the consideration, even where the loan was interest free. HMRC says that it follows that the 'lender', in such an arrangement, would not be caught by a charge under Sch 15 (HMRC Inheritance Tax Manual, para 44005).

The loan may be made either to an individual or to a trust. However, great care is required where a loan is made by a settlor and the trustees invest in income-producing assets. Any repayment of the loan to the lender may give rise to an income tax liability under ITTOIA 2005, s 633. This is broadly to the extent of the amount repaid if the trustees then, or in the future, have any undistributed income.

Where there is a privileged trust with a life tenant and one or more remaindermen, an on-demand loan by the trustees to the remaindermen of assets in the trust fund will effectively freeze the value of those assets in the estate of the life tenant. It may be advisable to charge a modest level of interest on the loan as a means of countering the argument that there has been a partial termination of the life tenant's interest in possession.

Release of the loan

[3.45] As mentioned above a loan can be written off over a period of time taking advantage of the annual exemption and also the potentially exempt transfer provisions.

Where no consideration is given for the release of a loan, the release can only be effected by deed. For a deed to be validly executed, the intention that the instrument is a deed must be made clear in the document. The instrument must either be signed by the person making it in the presence of a witness or be signed at the direction of the person making it in the presence of two witnesses.

Sales of assets

[3.46] A sale is another, but less obvious, type of asset freezing measure. If a father sells his cottage in the country to his son at full market value, any future growth in value will accrue for the benefit of the son. If the father goes on to spend the sale proceeds over a period of time, rather than to retain and invest them, then so much the better as he is reducing his own estate as well. Should the father wish to continue to occupy the property, then the gifts with reservation provisions will not be a problem as the disposal of the cottage will have been by way of a sale for full consideration rather than by way of a gift. Care will need to be taken to ensure the sale of the property to the son is a transaction such as might be expected to be made at arm's length between unconnected parties if the father is to avoid a charge to income tax under the pre-owned assets regime. The disadvantage of the sale is that it could give rise to a capital gains tax charge for the father and also to a stamp duty land tax liability for the son.

Grants of option to purchase

[3.47] Another example of an asset freezing arrangement is the grant of an option to purchase property at its market value at the date of the grant. On the exercise of the option any increase in value in the property will flow through to the grantee free of inheritance tax. The grant of the option must be made for full consideration, otherwise the existence of the option will not be fully taken into account when valuing the property in the grantor's estate on his death or on an exercise of the option (IHTA 1984, s 163).

The grant of an option for consideration will be treated as a disposal of a chargeable asset (with a nil base cost) for capital gains tax purposes and may give rise to a chargeable gain (TCGA 1992, s 144(1)). A gain may arise on the exercise by reference to the unencumbered value of the asset where the parties are connected (TCGA 1992, s 18(7)). In addition, a stamp duty land tax charge may arise on the grant of the option. It should also be borne in mind that options over land are only valid for a period of 21 years (Perpetuities and Accumulations Act 1964, s 9(2)).

The grant should not be a gift with reservation for inheritance tax purposes because no benefit is received by the transferor from the subject matter of the gift (the option) nor does he receive any collateral benefit referable to the gift.

If an option is allowed to lapse without being exercised, this may result in a transfer of value for inheritance tax purposes (IHTA 1984, s 3(3)) which is not capable of constituting a potentially exempt transfer (IHTA 1984, s 3A(6)).

Other arrangements

[3.48] There are other more sophisticated types of asset freezing arrangement. Those involving companies and partnerships are dealt with in more detail in CHAPTER 12 THE FAMILY BUSINESS. One such arrangement for a company (now usually an investment company) involves the creation of two classes of shares, one of the original shareholders, and the other of which carries the excess value, which is given away. There is a similar arrangement involving the issue of deferred shares which is also dealt with in more detail in CHAPTER 12 THE FAMILY BUSINESS.

So far as partnerships are concerned, it is often the case that the entitlement of a retiring or deceased partner will be limited to the balance on his capital account plus his pro rata share of accrued profits. The effect of this is that any underlying growth in value of the partnership assets accrue for the benefit of the continuing partners, who will often be members of the next generation in a family.

Various insurance companies offer products designed to freeze the value of an estate at a given time. These products involve an individual making a capital investment which is treated as a potentially exempt transfer. The capital is invested in a single premium bond which consists of a capital fund and an income fund. The income fund provides annual amounts often referred to in the marketing literature as 'income' which, if it is 5% or less, will be free from income tax. For a more detailed explanation see CHAPTER 9 INSURANCE.

Conversion of capital assets

[3.49] The fifth basic method by which the inheritance tax payable on death may be mitigated is by the conversion of capital assets into income producing assets.

Where an individual has capital which he no longer requires or needs he may consider purchasing assets which produce income only for a given period of time. For example, income shares of a split capital investment trust which confer rights to receive dividends but not to assets on a winding up. As the pre-determined winding-up date approaches the market value of the income share decreases. Thus, the investor receives a stream of large income payments (which he uses for his living expenses) matched by a decrease in the capital value of his investments which reduces the inheritance tax liability on his estate.

This method now has a very limited application with the additional rate of income tax being 45% and inheritance tax and capital gains tax being at lower rates.

Lasting power of attorney

[3.50] A lasting power of attorney (an LPA) allows an individual to appoint another individual to make decisions on his behalf in the event that he is unable to do so during his lifetime. Otherwise the Court of Protection will appoint a deputy who could be a close relative or friend, a professional or indeed a local authority. Clearly it is more preferable for an individual to make his own choice as to the individual he would like to make decisions on his behalf and so it is advisable for every individual with the necessary mental capacity to make an LPA regardless of age.

Organisation of an estate

General

[3.51] The last topic to consider is the best way of organising an estate with a view to facilitating an easy and cost-effective administration after death. This aspect of estate planning should be kept in mind throughout the individual's lifetime and the following is a list of relevant points all of which are further considered in CHAPTER 18 MAKING A WILL.

Jointly held property

[3.52] Spouses and indeed unmarried individuals living together often hold property jointly either as beneficial joint tenants or as tenants in common. Where property is held as joint tenants, each joint tenant is entitled to the whole of the asset in equal shares and, on death, the deceased's share of the property automatically passes by survivorship to the surviving joint tenant. Under a tenancy in common, each joint owner owns a separate and distinct although undivided share of the property which on their death passes under the terms of their Will or intestacy. Where property is held jointly, it is common (particularly in relation to land) for there to be an express declaration of trust, although there are some situations where there is no such express declaration and so the court has to determine whether, on the facts, there is a constructive trust. Where a property is held by tenants in common it is usual for a declaration of trust to provide for the shares in which the property is held. Holding assets as joint tenants allows the assets to pass to the survivor automatically on the first death without the delay and expense of the personal representatives of the deceased having to transfer them to the survivor. Of course, the tax implications of holding property jointly during a person's lifetime need to be considered. The general rule is that in relation to income arising on joint property, tenants in common are entitled to the income in proportion to their capital entitlement and joint tenants are entitled in proportion to the number of joint tenants. There are, however, a number of exceptions to this rule. For tax purposes, there is a presumption that spouses and civil partners who are living together are beneficially entitled to income arising from jointly owned property in equal shares (ITA 2007, s 836). Yet there are certain types of income which are excluded from this rule (ITA 2007, s 836(3)). Where spouses or civil partners are beneficially entitled to income in unequal shares which correspond to their beneficial interests in the property from which it arises, spouses can give a joint declaration to HMRC. Notice may only be given within 60 days of the interest beginning (ITA 2007, s 837). Where there is to be an equal entitlement, this should be evidenced in writing as it is HMRC's practice to request this evidence (Trusts, Settlements and Estates Manual, para 9851).

Legislation provides that where spouses in England and Wales die in circumstances rendering it uncertain which of them survives the other, they will be deemed to die in order of seniority (Law of Property Act 1925, s 184). Whilst it is sensible for certain property to be held jointly, there may be a number of good reasons for vesting assets in the sole name of one of the spouses; for example, where the other is a sole trader or partner in a trading partnership.

Joint bank accounts

[3.53] Joint bank accounts, whilst practical, can cause difficulties in two areas: first, in determining the deceased's interest in the account on death, and second, in identifying the owner who has made a gift from the account. In *Matthews v Revenue & Customs Comrs* [2012] UKFTT 658 (TC), [2013]

SWTI 299, [2012] TC 2329 the deceased transferred money into an account held jointly with her son. HMRC claimed that the entire account was taxable under IHTA 1984, s 5(2) because the deceased had a power to appoint or dispose of the property as she saw fit. A reference was made to the comment made obiter in *Melville v IRC* [2001] EWCA Civ 1247, [2001] STC 1271 which recognised that there was the potential for double taxation on joint bank accounts where any holder can draw on the account so that the account is taxable on the death of each holder. In *Matthews*, the First-Tier Tribunal held that the entire sum was taxable under s 5(2) and that the gift with reservation rules applied. HMRC in its Inheritance Tax Manual at para 15042 state that it is not their practice to tax 'a share of the account that is greater than the share provided by the joint owner'; this is not a statement of law but of practice and so care should be taken when relying upon it.

There is no doubt that the application of inheritance tax to bank accounts 'can be particularly difficult' and so it is recommended that where there are joint bank accounts, a declaration is made as to the parties' intentions and details of the deposits and payments are kept.

The income tax consequences of joint bank accounts should be considered, as the case of *Bingham v Revenue & Customs Comrs* [2013] UKFTT 110 (TC), [2013] SFTD 689 illustrates. In that case, a father had transferred money into a bank account held jointly with his children and wife. The interest arising was apportioned between his wife and children. It was held that the father was assessable on all the interest arising as the settlor because the settlement provisions applied.

Foreign assets

[3.54] It is a costly procedure to register a UK grant of probate, or to take out a fresh grant, in a foreign jurisdiction in order to obtain title to foreign stocks and shares. Small holdings should therefore be liquidated if possible before death. If an individual makes investments abroad, either they should be registered in the name of a UK nominee company, which will avoid the need for a foreign grant, or he should be encouraged to consider indirect investment through a UK unit trust or investment company. The same problems will be encountered with a foreign holiday home and again can often be avoided by holding the property in the name of a nominee (which could be a UK incorporated limited company specially set up by the client for the purpose). See also **CHAPTER 20 UK DOMICILIARIES INVESTING ABROAD** for more on this aspect.

Life policies

[3.55] These should be inspected to see whether the proceeds are payable to the insured's estate or are held in trust. If the former, then unless the insured leaves the proceeds to his spouse and the spouse survives the insured, they will give rise to an inheritance tax charge on his death. Where the proceeds are intended for the spouse and/or children, the benefit of the policy should be put in trust for them during the insured's lifetime. New policies should similarly be settled on trust from the outset. The additional advantage of the trust is that the policy proceeds may be paid out immediately following the death (on production of the death certificate) without the need to wait for a grant. See also **CHAPTER 9 INSURANCE** for more on this aspect.

Pensions

[3.56] Where the individual has a right of nomination over a lump sum death benefit payable under a pension scheme, he should be sure to exercise the right to avoid the benefit falling into his estate on death and possibly being charged to inheritance tax. Where the benefit is payable under a discretionary trust, then he should make sure that the trustees are aware of his wishes as to their ultimate destination.

These lump sum death benefits can provide useful estate planning opportunities in that by directing the lump sums to his children and leaving his wife to inherit his free estate, an individual may leave all members of his family well provided for on his death without incurring any inheritance tax charge. Reference should also be made to **CHAPTER 10 PENSIONS** for more on this aspect.

Accident/death in service policies

[3.57] Similar considerations apply here. Where the individual has a right of nomination over the proceeds or may express wishes to trustees as to their destination, he should be sure to do so.

The will

[3.58] No client should ever die intestate. Not only is it usually more costly and more time consuming to obtain a grant of letters of administration rather than a grant of probate but also the trusts which can arise under the intestacy rules can be very costly to administer and they are unlikely to reflect the client's true wishes regarding the devolution of his estate. The statutory intestacy rules are found at **18.3**.

Chapter 4

Lifetime Planning: Making Gifts

[4.1] The aim of asset reduction is to reduce an individual's estate on death by making lifetime gifts. A lifetime gift will be either a potentially exempt transfer, a chargeable lifetime transfer or an exempt transfer. These are all discussed in this chapter. Typically one might say that an individual has to balance making a gift to reduce his estate on death to save inheritance tax against any potential capital gains tax liability on the disposal of an asset by way of gift. Making a gift might seem straightforward but there are a number of considerations to take into account before doing so.

First, the individual has to identify the asset to be given away. An individual may not wish to make a gift of an income-producing asset because he needs the income and so, alternatively, may choose a non-income producing asset. Where such an asset has an inherent capital gain, the gain will be brought into charge unless hold-over relief is available.

Secondly, the recipient of the gift needs to be determined. An individual may wish to make a gift to trustees to hold the asset on trust for the individual rather than making an absolute gift to them. This may be because there is concern that the ultimate beneficiary may not be responsible because, for example, the beneficiaries are minors or the individual making the gift wishes there to be some flexibility as to the benefits to be received in the future by a class of beneficiaries. There may also be tax reasons for making a gift to a relevant property trust and that is to obtain TCGA 1992, s 260 hold-over relief on the gain arising on a gift of assets which would not qualify for business assets hold-over relief under TCGA 1992, s 165.

In addition, an individual has to consider who should be responsible for paying the capital gains tax on the disposal and inheritance tax on the transfer should any be due.

When making a gift an individual has to bear in mind the anti-avoidance provisions which are discussed in this chapter.

Before considering any of these matters, however, the individual's mental capacity to make a gift must be determined. The common law test set out in *Re Beaney (Deceased)* [1978] 1WLR 770 is that an individual must have a high level of understanding of the fact that he is making a gift, the nature of that gift and its consequences. This test was confirmed as still being the appropriate test for capacity in *Estate of Joyce Smith (dec'd), Re, Kicks v Leigh* [2014] EWHC 3926 (Ch), [2015] 4 All ER 329, [2015] WTLR 579, despite the implementation of the Mental Capacity Act 2005.

Potentially exempt transfers

[4.2] Potentially exempt transfers enable an individual to make specified gifts of unlimited value which will escape tax completely if he survives for a period of seven years following the gift (IHTA 1984, s 3A). A gift will only be a potentially exempt transfer if it is made by an individual to:

(i)   another individual (including the creation of a transitional serial interest); or

(ii) the trustees of a disabled trust; or

(iii) the trustees of a bereaved minor's trust on the coming to the end of an immediate post-death interest.

A gift to most forms of settlement including a gift to an interest in possession trust (unless it falls within one of the special categories) will not be a potentially exempt transfer, instead it will be a lifetime chargeable transfer. The various types of trust are discussed in more detail in **CHAPTER 6 CREATING SETTLEMENTS**.

Although it is no longer possible for transfers into trust to be potentially exempt transfers, it will not necessarily be a problem for all. Where an individual is going to make a transfer equal to or below the nil rate band but considers because of family circumstances that a trust is required, there is no immediate difference between making a chargeable transfer or a potentially exempt transfer.

Example

Mary's estate is worth £1.9m. She is 81 years of age and wishes to settle the sum of £325,000 on interest in possession trusts for the benefit of her four grand-daughters. Mary will be excluded from benefiting under the terms of the trust. The money was settled on 1 October 2009. Mary is 'staunch' and outlives the seven-year period.

The transfer to the trust is a chargeable transfer which is taxed at 0%. As she survived the seven-year period there is no inheritance tax liability on that transfer.

If she had made an absolute gift to her granddaughters, there would have been no inheritance tax paid on the gift. Having survived for the requisite seven-year period the potentially exempt transfer would be fully exempt.

In the event that she had not survived the seven-year period the chargeable transfer would have remained a chargeable transfer and, if indeed she had made the potentially exempt transfer, it would have become chargeable. The latter situation would have resulted in the same consequences thus reducing the nil rate band available on death.

There has been some concern as to the extent of a PET in the situation where a gift of property is made and the value of the property received by the donee is less than the reduction in value of the donor's estate. This uncertainty is caused by IHTA 1984, s 3A(2)(a), which states that a transfer of value to another individual will be a PET to the extent that the value transferred is attributable to property which becomes part of the donee's estate or, so far as that value is not attributable to such property, then to the extent that the estate of the donee has increased, and so the difference in value would be an immediately chargeable transfer. Does this have the result that the transfer of value measured as the diminution in the transferor's estate will only be a PET to the extent that the donee's estate is increased by the transfer? Clearly it does not, but a change in the wording of the HMRC Inheritance Tax Manual discussing the issue suggested that HMRC might have adopted this view. In correspondence with the ICAEW, HMRC has confirmed that it is still their view that the entire diminution in the donor's estate constitutes a PET (HMRC Inheritance Tax Manual, para 4066).

Where the transferor dies within three years of the gift, inheritance tax at the full death rates is charged unless those rates have increased in which case the rates at the time of the transfer are used. Where the gift is made more than three years before the death, the rates are 'tapered' as follows.

	Taper relief	Effective IHT rate
Within less than three years of death	100%	40%
Within less than four years of death	80%	32%
Within less than five years of death	60%	24%
Within less than six years of death	40%	16%
Within less than seven years of death	20%	8%

In addition, when calculating the inheritance tax payable on the transferor's estate, any potentially exempt transfers and chargeable transfers will be aggregated with the value of his estate. This may increase the amount of tax payable on death.

The potentially exempt transfer is still very important in estate planning. It is possible to make gifts without any charge to inheritance tax at all provided the transferor survives for the necessary period. The risk of the transferor dying within this period may be insured against at rates which, depending upon the age and state of health of the transferor, are often only a small percentage of the potential tax liability. This is considered in more detail in CHAPTER 9 INSURANCE.

Gifts within the nil rate tax band

[4.3] No tax is payable until the cumulative total of all gifts made within any seven-year period exceeds £325,000.

Although unlimited tax-free gifts can be made by way of potentially exempt transfers, in some circumstances it may be preferable to make gifts within the nil rate band to a discretionary trust because of the flexibility which such trusts offer. This will allow further gifts to be made to the trust, or to another trust, seven years after the initial gift. Despite the Consultation Document 'Inheritance Tax: A Fairer Way of Calculating Trust Charges' published in June 2014 proposing that in calculating decennial and exit charges, all the settlements made by the same settlor will have, in aggregate, only one Settlement Nil Rate Band between them, this proposal was not implemented.

Gifts to relevant property trusts have a significant advantage over outright gifts. An election may be made under TCGA 1992, s 260 to hold-over any chargeable gain which would otherwise arise on the gift to a trust from which the settlor is excluded from benefiting, provided that there is no arrangement subsisting under which the settlor may acquire an interest in the settlement (TCGA 1992, s 169B(2)). The held-over gains may be brought back into charge if the settlor acquires an interest in the settlement or arrangements subsist under which the settlor will, or may, acquire such an interest within a defined period. The clawback period begins immediately following the disposal and ends six years after the end of the year of assessment in which the disposal was made (TCGA 1992, s 169C). In relation to gifts which are potentially exempt transfers, hold-over relief will only be available in relation to certain types of business assets (see **4.63**).

Exemptions and quasi-exemptions

[4.4] Because inheritance tax is charged by reference to the reduction in value of a person's estate (IHTA 1984, s 3(1)), any gift will *prima facie* give rise to a tax charge. There are, however, a number of important exemptions and, what could be termed, 'quasi-exemptions' which enable a person to reduce his estate without giving rise to an immediate tax charge.

Some of the exemptions only apply to transactions made in a person's lifetime whilst others apply both to lifetime transfers and transfers on death. The lifetime exemptions are set out in **4.5–4.14**.

These exemptions and quasi-exemptions will now each be considered in turn.

Annual exemption

[4.5] A person may make gifts of up to £3,000 each year completely free of inheritance tax (IHTA 1984, s 19). Unlike the potentially exempt transfer, this exemption applies regardless of the nature of the recipient of the gift. In addition, there is no requirement for survival by the transferor. If this exemption is wholly or partly unused in any year, it or the balance may be carried forward to the next year. However, if it is not used in that year it will be lost.

Example

> A transferor who makes a gift in year 1 of only £1,000 may make gifts within the annual exemption of up to £5,000 in year 2. If he only makes gifts of £3,000 in year 2, the £2,000 shortfall in year 1 will be lost forever.

It will be apparent that in the case of outright gifts either to an individual, or to trustees of privileged trusts, there is an overlap between this exemption and the potentially exempt transfer. Thus, a transferor who reasonably expects to survive for the next seven years need not limit himself to annual gifts of only £3,000. He could give away significantly more each year. The existence of the annual exemption will only become material if the transferor dies within seven years of one of these gifts.

Example

> A father gives his son £49,428 in each of years one to seven. If the father then dies at the end of year seven, all the previous gifts will become chargeable but only as to £46,428 of each, because the annual exemption will be available to exempt the first £3,000 of each gift. As the chargeable gifts amount to £324,996, which is within the 2016/17 nil rate tax band, the lifetime gifts will not give rise to any tax charge. They will, however, be aggregated with the value of the deceased's free estate in calculating the inheritance tax due on the death.

If in the above example the father had survived for seven years then the annual exemption is wasted on gifts that are subsequently exempt. To ensure that the annual exemption is fully utilised the father could have made a chargeable transfer before making a PET. The annual exemption is set against the first gift made. If two gifts are made on the same day, the annual exemption should be apportioned between them (see HMRC Inheritance Tax Manual, para 14143). Even with the existence of the potentially exempt transfer, the annual exemption is of importance.

The 'normal expenditure out of income' exemption

[4.6] This relief is generous in that there is no statutory limit as to the amount that can be relieved. This exemption applies to a gift if, or to the extent that, it is shown that:

(a)   the gift is made as part of the normal expenditure of the transferor;
(b)   taking one year with another, the gift is made out of his income; and
(c)   after allowing for all other gifts or dispositions forming part of his normal expenditure, the transferor is left with sufficient income to maintain his usual standard of living. (IHTA 1984, s 21).

This exemption must be claimed and will not apply automatically. Whether a gift will qualify for this exemption will be a question of fact in each case.

Made as part of normal expenditure

[4.7] There is no statutory definition of normal. HMRC adopts the dictionary definition of normal which includes 'standard, regular, typical, habitual or usual.' According to HMRC, 'normal' means 'normal for the transferor and not for the average person' (HMRC Inheritance Tax Manual, para 14241). So what may be 'normal expenditure' for a person with a net income of £150,000 is unlikely to be so for a person earning £30,000. On the other hand, a person who does earn £30,000 net, with no mortgage, wife, or children and a simple lifestyle may be able to make gifts, for example, to nieces and nephews, which qualify for this exemption to an extent which a person with a much higher income but with a wife and children and a high standard of living cannot.

To be normal, the gift does not necessarily have to be one of a series of regular payments but if not, it must be the type of payment which by its nature is likely to recur (as in the case of the examples given below). As it is essential that the gifts are made out of income, it is advisable that they are payments of cash.

The scope of IHTA 1984, s 21 was considered in the case of *Bennett v IRC* [1995] STC 54 (Ch D). The *Bennett* decision answered a number of key questions concerning the operation of the exemption. The term 'normal expenditure out of income' simply means expenditure which at the time it takes place accords with the settled pattern of expenditure adopted by the transferor. This pattern may be established in one of two ways, by reference to a sequence of payments by the transferor in the past, or by proof of some prior commitment or resolution adopted by him as regards future expenditure, and which he complied with thereafter.

The High Court affirmed that there is no fixed minimum period during which the expenditure must have been incurred. All that is necessary is for there to be evidence of a pattern of actual or intended regular payments, and that the payment in question falls within that category. This means that a single payment might qualify, provided sufficient resolution or commitment for future payments also exists. Where there is a commitment to make future expenditure the commitment must envisage that the payments will 'remain in place . . . for a sufficient period (barring unforeseen circumstances) . . . it need not be legally binding'. It is prudent for an individual to plan ahead. HMRC's approach is to test 'whether a gift is "normal" by considering all the relevant factors. These will include the frequency and amount, the nature of the gifts, the identity of those who received them and the reasons for the gifts' (HMRC Inheritance Tax Manual, para 14243). It is important that the pattern of such gifts is expected to continue for more than simply a *de minimis* period of time, barring unforeseen circumstances. This effectively precludes death bed schemes. HMRC considers that a reasonable period would normally be three to four years (HMRC Inheritance Tax Manual, para 14242) despite the court ruling that there was no minimum period. In HMRC's view, the amount of the expenditure does not have to be fixed but must be comparable in size, although small differences do not need to be queried (HMRC Inheritance Tax Manual, para 14243). If the details provided over a given period, however, do not illustrate normality, an individual may be asked to provide particulars over a longer period. This means that gifts to a discernible class, such as members of the same family could qualify. In the case of *Nadin v IRC* [1997] STC (SCD) 107, (SpC 112) the Special Commissioners held that irregular payments to close relatives did not constitute normal expenditure.

Of course, it is more difficult to illustrate a pattern where a single gift is involved. HMRC considers that the taxpayer must provide strong evidence in such cases that the gift was genuinely intended to be the first in a pattern and that there was 'a realistic expectation that further payments would be made'. A single gift by way of payment under a deed of covenant or other regular commitment, such as payment of the first of a series of premiums on a life policy, may be accepted as normal (HMRC Inheritance Tax Manual, para 14242).

Made out of income

[**4.8**] What does the phrase 'made out of income' mean? First, it is accepted that 'income' here, means income under the general meaning of that word, that is, income determined under normal accountancy principles, rather than amounts assessable to income tax under the Taxes Acts. HMRC's guidance (at HMRC Inheritance Tax Manual, para 14250) says:

> 'Income is not defined . . . but should be determined for each year in accordance with normal accountancy rules. It is not necessarily the same as income for income tax purposes.'

Thus, it will not include amounts of capital such as gains arising on the surrender of life insurance policies, receipts from a discounted gift scheme or amounts paid out from a lifetime care plan. It is HMRC's view that regular withdrawals of 5% of the premium from a single premium insurance bond are payments of capital and, as such, they do not fall within the description of income for the purposes of the IHTA 1984, s 21 exemption (HMRC Inheritance Tax Manual, para 14250).

In *McDowall (executors of McDowall, dec'd) v IRC* [2004] STC (SCD) 22, (SpC 382) the issue arose as to whether payments made by an attorney established a pattern of intended regular payments. It was held, in that particular case, that the attorney did not have the power to make the gifts. Had the gifts been valid, however, they would have been exempt under IHTA 1984, s 21.

HMRC does not consider that *McDowall* is authority that income which has not been reinvested retains its character, which is surprising considering that the Special Commissioners said: 'our inclination is to conclude that the payments were made out of retained income which remained income in character rather than capital; it was identifiably money which was essentially unspent income and which had been placed on deposit, but not invested in any more formal sense'.

HMRC will first look at the income of the year in which gifts were made to see if there was enough income available to make the gifts, before considering earlier years. With regard to income from previous years it is HMRC's view that it does not retain its character as income indefinitely. At some point it becomes capital, but there are no hard and fast rules about when this point is reached. HMRC states that: 'if there is no evidence to the contrary, we consider that income becomes capital after a period of two years . . . Each case will depend on its own facts but, in general, the longer the period of accumulation, the more likely it is that the income has become capital.' (HMRC Inheritance Tax Manual, para 14250).

The legislation recognises that income can fluctuate. IHTA 1984, s 21(1)(b) is satisfied if 'taking one year with another' the payment was made out of income. In its Inheritance Tax Manual, HMRC states that it 'may need to look at the income and expenditure over a number of years to see if the income test is satisfied.' It does warn that 'although income can be carried over from year to year in these circumstances, you should refer to Technical if the taxpayer wishes to carry forward more than two year's income' (HMRC Inheritance Tax Manual, para 14250).

Does the requirement that the transfer be 'made out of the [transferor's] income' require one to undertake a tracing exercise such as is required to determine whether there has been a remittance of foreign income or capital gains under the remittance basis? The decided cases do not specifically deal with the problem.

A counsel of perfection would be to segregate funds in the way in which, for example, a non-domiciliary segregates his offshore accounts so as to clearly identify the regular payments as being amounts of income. In practice, few people would care to have their use of money restricted in this way. If there is a surplus of income over revenue expenditure it is unlikely that HMRC would be successful in asserting that a gift from a bank account which, although it also contained capital, contained sufficient income to make the gift, did not come wholly within s 21(1)(b).

Sufficient income to maintain his usual standard of living

[4.9] How does one determine whether the transferor was 'left with sufficient income'? Of the three cases which have been decided on s 21, sub-section (c) was considered only in *Nadin v Inland Revenue Commissioners* [1997] STC (SCD) 107 (this was a case before the Special Commissioners which did not proceed to the High Court). In that case, in respect of certain years, the Special Commissioner found that the condition in sub-section (c) was not satisfied because the taxpayer's annual nursing home costs, personal expenditure and Income Tax exceeded her annual income. The decision does not record any argument on the construction of sub-section (c) except that the Appellant argued that capital sums on the sale of investments were income. What was not argued was whether sub-section (c) allows one to take into account the extent to which capital is available to supplement income and is actually applied to doing so.

HMRC assumes in its guidance, that the exemption will not apply to the extent that 'the transferor had to resort to capital to meet their normal living expenses' (HMRC Inheritance Tax Manual, para 14255). It is arguable, however, that if one had such a large amount of capital that, on the basis of the most conservative estimates, it would be sufficient to fund one's living expenses for one's lifetime, even a small amount of income would be sufficient to maintain one's usual standard of living. People in that position, therefore, would have sufficient income to maintain their usual standard of living even if all but a minimal part of their income were expended in making gifts.

There is no requirement that income is actually used for living expenses. A person may use their capital to meet their living expenses and use the income remaining, after making the gifts, for some other use. The transferor must be capable of maintaining their usual standard of living from their remaining income after making the gifts. This test is applied at the time of making the gift. Where payments have been made in fulfilment of an intention to make a series of payments out of income, and further payments are not made because of an unforeseen change in the payer's circumstances, the exemption will still apply to the payments actually made before the change.

Compliance

[4.10] It is advisable that all such payments are documented to provide evidence that they met the conditions of the exemption. The information retained should be the date of such a gift, the name of the transferee and the nature of his relationship with the transferor, a description of the gift (ie cash, the premiums paid on an insurance policy) and the value of the gift. Form IHT403 to the IHT Account form IHT400 provides a useful proforma of this information. It would seem that HMRC expects an IHT form IHT100 to be delivered in the situation where an inheritance tax liability would arise should the exemption be denied, its rationale being that the 'availability of the exemption can be agreed' (HMRC Inheritance Tax Manual, para 10652).

Uses

[4.11] Normal expenditure out of income is an important exemption, which can be used in the following ways.

(a)   Payments out of income by individuals.
      Individuals with large net incomes or surplus incomes can make regular gifts out of that income free of inheritance tax to members of their families or to family trusts.

(b)   A parent takes out a 10-year endowment policy on his life and declares himself a bare trustee of the policy for the benefit of his children. He pays all the premiums under the policy out of his income. On the maturity of the policy the beneficiaries under the trust benefit from the proceeds. If the premiums are paid direct to the life assurance company, such payments will not be potentially exempt if the amount of the premium is not fully reflected in the increased value of the policy. Provided the parent pays the premiums out of his income, however, and is able to maintain his usual standard of living, such payments should fall within the normal expenditure out of income exemption. If an alternative investment vehicle is required, there seems no reason why the same arrangement could not be set up by means of a regular monthly savings contract with a unit trust or an investment company, the units and shares themselves being held in trust for the next generation. The disadvantage of this alternative is that it will be necessary for the trustees to make annual returns of trust income.

(c)   Premiums on a life policy written in trust to fund all or part of any potential inheritance tax liability on lifetime transfers or on death.

(d)   Annuities paid gratuitously by partners out of their trading profits to a retired partner or the spouse of a deceased partner.

(e)   Where the nil rate band has already been utilised, payments out of income could be made to fund a discretionary trust.

It should be noted that the exemption does not apply where a policy is taken out in conjunction with the purchase of an annuity on the individual's life (IHTA 1984, s 21(2)).

Regular gifts out of income may also be made to help the transferee of an earlier chargeable gift pay the inheritance tax due where there is a facility to pay the tax by annual instalments – see **4.58** and **4.73** below.

This exemption can be used to pass assets down to the next generation on a regular basis whilst still preserving the £3,000 annual exemption for other gifts. Ideally, both exemptions should be used in tandem.

It should be remembered that it is HMRC's view that although a transfer qualifies for the normal expenditure out of income exemption, it can still be subject to tax as a gift with reservation (HMRC Inheritance Tax Manual, para 14231).

Small gifts

[4.12] Gifts of up to £250 can be made to any one person in any one year free of inheritance tax (IHTA 1984, s 20). This exemption cannot be used in conjunction with another exemption, eg the annual exemption. It will be lost if the total annual gifts to any one person exceed £250. The gifts must be outright and therefore cannot be made to trustees. In an estate planning context the exemption is '*de minimis*'.

Gifts in consideration of marriage or registration of a civil partnership

[4.13] Gifts below a certain value that are made 'in consideration of marriage or of the registration of a civil partnership' are exempt from inheritance tax. A gift in consideration of marriage or civil partnership is not defined in the legislation. In the case of *IRC v Rennell (Lord)* [1964] AC 173, [1963] 1 All ER 803, HL, which was an estate duty case, the House of Lords held that a gift had to satisfy three conditions to be accepted as 'made in consideration of marriage'. The conditions are that:

- the gift must be made on the occasion of the marriage or civil partnership;
- it must be conditional on the marriage or civil partnership taking place; and
- the gift must be made by a person for the purpose of, or with a view to encouraging or facilitating, the marriage or civil partnership.

Parents may each give outright gifts in consideration of marriage or of the registration of a civil partnership of up to £5,000 to the parties to the marriage or civil partnership completely free of inheritance tax. Grandparents and great grandparents may similarly make outright gifts of up to £2,500. Other persons may make such gifts of up to £1,000 (IHTA 1984, s 22).

The exemption applies not only to outright gifts but also to gifts into a settlement. The beneficiaries of such a settlement must, however, be limited to those persons specified in IHTA 1984, s 22(4) to which special reference should be made by anyone wishing to create such a settlement. Care should therefore be taken when defining the beneficiaries of such a trust.

To ensure that the gifts are made 'in consideration of the marriage or civil partnership', they must be made either before or at the date of the marriage or civil partnership. The gifts should also be accompanied by a suitable letter evidencing the fact that the gift is conditional on the marriage or civil partnership taking place. HMRC states in its Inheritance Tax Manual at para 14201 that gifts made after the marriage or civil partnership will not qualify for the exemption unless made in the fulfilment of a binding promise made before the marriage or civil partnership.

Gifts for maintenance of family

[4.14] Although not an exemption, IHTA 1984, s 11 provides that the following dispositions will not be transfers of value:

(a) a disposition by one party to a marriage or civil partnership in favour of the other party for his or her maintenance;

(b) a disposition by one party to a marriage or civil partnership in favour of a child of either party for the maintenance, education or training of the child and made up to the later of the year in which the child attains 18 or ceases full-time education or training. These provisions are important in that they exempt all expenditure by parents on the education of their children;

(c) a disposition in favour of a child who is not in the care of his parent for his maintenance, education or training and made up to the later of the year in which the child attains 18 or ceases full-time education or training. Gifts made to such a child who is over 18 are only exempt if they are made by a person in whose care the child has been for substantial periods prior to attaining 18;

(d) a disposition in favour of an illegitimate child of the transferor for his maintenance, education or training and made up to the later of the year in which he attains 18 or ceases full-time education or training; and

(e) a disposition in favour of a 'dependent relative' which constitute reasonable provision for his or her care or maintenance. Unlike the situation with a spouse or civil partner and children, the provision must be both for 'care' or 'maintenance', and it must also be reasonable. These terms are not defined in the legislation but it is HMRC's view that 'care' 'seems to suggest the provision of services, whether privately or in an institution'. HMRC considers that 'reasonable' is an 'amount as is reasonably necessary for the purpose of providing care and maintenance (but no more), having regard to the financial and other circumstances of the transferor and the relative and the degree of incapacity [or] infirmity of the [relative]' (HMRC Inheritance Tax Manual, para 4177). HMRC considers that the incapacity needs to be both physical and financial (HMRC Inheritance Tax Manual, para 4179). A 'dependent relative' is defined as any relative of the transferor or of his spouse or civil partner who is incapacitated by old age or infirmity from maintaining himself; or his mother or father or his spouse's or civil partner's mother or father.

Traditionally, HMRC has argued that IHTA 1984, s 11 only applied to income expenditure and did not apply to a gift of capital. In *McKelvey (personal representative of McKelvey, decd) v Revenue & Customs Comrs* [2008] STC (SCD) 944, [2008] SWTI 1752 it was held that the exemption could extend to a gift of capital in appropriate circumstances. The deceased ('D') lived with her mother ('M') who was in poor health. D had been diagnosed with cancer. She transferred two properties to M to provide for her maintenance, the intention was that the properties be sold, when necessary, to meet the costs of M's nursing care. In the meantime M had had the benefit of the rental income. The properties were not sold because of M's refusal to accept paid care. HMRC sought tax on the basis that the transfers were PETs. D's executors appealed arguing that the gifts were exempt transfers under s 11. The Special Commissioner held that the reasonableness of the provisions had to be considered in the light of the circumstances as they were reasonably believed to be at the time of the gift and not as they later turned out to be. However, the transferor's view of what was reasonable was not the standard by which the gift was to be judged. An objective standard had to be applied. The Commissioner in deciding what was reasonably required considered that 'the approach adopted in personal injury cases [was] appropriate'. Using a multiplier of 5.5 being the number of years M would on the evidence have required nursing care and an annual care cost he calculated what he considered to be reasonable. This amount was exempt under s 11 whilst the excess was subject to inheritance tax.

Because the above dispositions (a)–(e) are not transfers of value they are not taken into account even if the donor dies within seven years. It is therefore possible for a terminally ill donor with young children to make substantial transfers from his estate to provide for their maintenance, education or training tax free. This is a rare form of death bed planning.

Where a gift is made on the occasion of a divorce or annulment, 'marriage' includes a former marriage or civil partnership. Thus in the context of a divorce, this exemption covers gifts to a former spouse or civil partner.

Gifts between spouses or civil partners

Inheritance tax

[4.15] Generally, gifts between spouses or civil partners are completely exempt from inheritance tax, but there are exceptions.

Where the transferor spouse or civil partner is domiciled in the UK for inheritance tax purposes but the transferee spouse or civil partner is not, the exemption is limited to a cumulative total of the exemption limit at the time of the transfer, which is £325,000 (IHTA 1984, s 18). It should be noted that currently the transferee spouse will be treated as being deemed domiciled in a country in the UK if he or she has been resident in the UK for 17 out of the previous 20 fiscal years (IHTA 1984, s 267). Therefore, if a husband wishes to make a gift to his wife who has been resident (but not continuously) in the UK for 16 out of the previous 20 years it may be sensible to wait until after 5 April 2017 (when the rules relating to deemed domicile are to change) depending upon the value of the gift. This does not, however, preclude the treatment of such gifts as potentially exempt transfers in appropriate cases. Where the exemption limit applies, gifts are set against it first and never fall out of account, even after seven years. This is in contrast to the potentially exempt transfer regime. Where the exemption limit has been utilised the nil rate band may be available.

From 6 April 2017 an individual will be deemed to be domiciled in a country of the UK if he has been resident in the UK for more than 15 out of the previous 20 tax years. This is discussed in detail in **Chapter 21 UK Residents with Multi-Jurisdictional Affairs**.

Example

Tessa transferred £500,000 on 7 April 2015 to her husband, Tristram, who is non-UK domiciled. The first £325,000 is exempt and the remaining £175,000 is a potentially exempt transfer. Under the terms of Tessa's will, she leaves all her property to Tristram. Tessa dies in 2022 when Tristram is still non-UK domiciled.

Although Tessa made a gift more than seven years ago, the exemption limit has been used and is therefore not available. Her nil rate band of £325,000 is available however, as seven years have passed since the gift in 2015.

It is possible for a non-domiciled individual with a UK domiciled spouse to elect to be treated as domiciled in the UK (IHTA 1984, s 267A). This is discussed in more detail in CHAPTER 21 UK RESIDENTS WITH MULTI-JURISDICTIONAL AFFAIRS at **21.17–21.23**.

The reservation of benefit provisions may also apply between spouses or civil partners. A gift with reservation is subject to FA 1986, s 102 unless it is an exempt transfer by virtue of s 102(5). The spouse exemption is included, but for a non-domiciled spouse it only extends to the exemption limit. Therefore not only is there a potentially exempt transfer of the excess but there may also be a reservation of benefit in that excess. So one needs to determine whether there is such a reservation of benefit. The Hansard Debates at the time of the introduction of the rules in 1986 made it clear that the original provisions did not automatically treat a gift from which a spouse could benefit as a reservation of benefit. FA 1986, s 102A, by contrast, applies where the donor or his spouse or civil partner enjoys a significant right or interest in land. Care therefore needs to be taken if the donor makes a gift of a share in the matrimonial home. Provided the conditions in FA 1986, s 102B are satisfied, no difficulties should arise. If a gift other than of land is made, care needs to be taken to ensure that a benefit is not reserved. Therefore, when a transfer is being made to a non-domiciled spouse or civil partner, care should be taken to ensure that a benefit is not being reserved by the donor.

The spouse exemption is not available for lifetime gifts into a trust of which the settlor's spouse or civil partner is the life tenant.

The spouse exemption is available to couples who are separated and living apart. This is in contrast to capital gains tax and income tax where spouses or civil partners have to be living together to benefit from any spousal benefits. The spouse exemption is not available for cohabitees. In *Holland (Holland's Executor) v IRC* [2003] STC (SCD) 43 (SpC 350) it was held that the spouse exemption applied only to persons legally married and did not apply to a person who had lived with another person as husband and wife.

There have been attempts to extend the spouse exemption by relying on the Human Rights Act 1998. In *Burden v United Kingdom* (Application 13378/05) (2008) 47 EHRR 857, [2008] STC 1305 two sisters living together claimed that their rights under the European Convention on Human Rights had been violated by the United Kingdom's restriction of the spouse exemption. The majority of the Grand Chamber held that the applicants as cohabiting sisters could not be compared to that of a married couple or civil partners and so their case failed.

The spouse exemption was extremely important in the past in its use in equalising estates to ensure that each spouse utilised their nil rate band on death. Now, of course, unused nil rate bands can be transferred between the estates of spouses or civil partners (IHTA 1984, s 8A). The effect of this is that when the surviving spouse or civil partner dies, the nil rate band available at their death will be increased by the proportion of the nil rate band that was not used on the death of their spouse or civil partner. This is discussed in **CHAPTER 18 MAKING A WILL**.

Uses

[4.16] The rebalancing of estates should be seen as part of an overall lifetime strategy designed to enable both spouses and civil partners to have sufficient assets which they can each use to make potentially exempt transfers and gifts within the annual exemption. Spouses and civil partners should consider the balance of their estates both when acquiring new assets and when deciding out of which estate an intended gift should be made. Where one spouse or civil partner has a significantly greater life expectancy than the other, then there is much to be said for keeping the bulk of their assets in the estate of the first spouse or civil partner to allow potentially exempt transfers to be made. On the other hand, any assets showing large unrealised gains should perhaps be kept in the estate of the other spouse or civil partner to get the benefit of the capital gains tax free base uplift on his or her death.

In addition, the rebalancing of assets between the spouses or civil partners may also result in capital gains tax savings. This may also confer income tax advantages but one needs to take account of the possibility that legislation might be introduced which negates any income tax savings (see **4.18**).

Another use of the spouse or civil partner exemption is to enable assets to be given by one spouse or civil partner to the other so that the other spouse or civil partner may then give away the assets and thereby use his or her annual exemption or make potentially exempt transfers (on the basis that he or she may be the more likely of the two to survive for the necessary seven-year period). The danger of this type of 'channelling' exercise is that HMRC may attempt to apply the 'associated operations' provisions contained in IHTA 1984, s 268 and tax the gift as if it had been made directly to the ultimate transferee by the first spouse or civil partner. HMRC has indicated, however, that it would not regard the provisions as applicable unless in such circumstances it was a condition that the second gift was made (Revenue Press Release dated 8 April 1975), a practice which is still adopted. Care should be taken over the timing of the gifts and the evidencing of them. Where, however, the transfer between spouses or civil partners is part of a more complex series of transactions whereby one of them makes a disposition to a third party, HMRC may consider the application of the associated operation rules. (HMRC Inheritance Tax Manual, para 14833). One also needs to consider the application of the General Anti-Abuse Rule to such transactions (see **CHAPTER 2 THE GAAR**).

Capital gains tax

[4.17] A husband and wife and civil partners are connected persons for capital gains tax purposes (TCGA 1992, s 286) and so a disposal of assets between them would be deemed to be a disposal for a consideration equal to the market value of the assets at the date of the disposal (TCGA 1992, s 17). However, where they are living together the consideration is deemed to be for such consideration as gives rise neither to a gain nor a loss (TCGA 1992, s 58). This effectively means that the donee inherits the donor's base cost of the asset.

Income tax

Settlements legislation

[4.18] The settlements legislation found in ITTOIA 2005, ss 624–628 provides that where during the life of a settlor any property subject to a settlement, or any derived property, can become payable to, or applicable for the benefit of, the settlor, or spouse or civil partner of the settlor in any circumstances whatsoever, the income of the settlement is treated as the settlor's income for all income tax purposes. This is a very broad definition. It covers both payment or use of money and the provision of non-cash benefits. It is important where there are joint owners of a bank account, where one party has provided the funds, to ensure that the beneficial interest in the account is transferred and not retained by the provider of the funds. That was the position in *Bingham v Revenue & Customs Comrs* [2013] UKFTT 110 (TC), [2013] SFTD 689 where the court held that the settlement provisions applied and the entire income was assessable on the settlor.

There are a number of exemptions to the settlement provisions including a spouse exemption (ITTOIA 2005, ss 625–626).

For the spouse exemption to apply there must be an outright gift. Section 626(4) provides that a gift is not an outright gift if it is conditional or there are any circumstances in which the property or related property is:

(i)   payable to the giver;
(ii)   applicable for the benefit of the giver; or
(iii)   will, or may become, so payable or applicable.

(ii) and (iii) are not defined.

Therefore, if school fees are paid by one spouse using money arising under a settlement where both parents are liable to pay, then property will be being applied for the benefit of the settlor spouse and the gift is not an outright gift. It is therefore important that evidence is kept as to the application of the funds in the event that HMRC raise an enquiry. Although a full discussion of this subject is beyond the scope of this work, set out below are the main considerations which should be borne in mind when considering the transfer of assets between spouses.

HMRC's interest in applying the settlement provisions was prompted by what it perceived as the use of small companies and partnerships to divert income earned by one spouse to the other. In *Jones v Garnett (Inspector of Taxes)* [2007] UKHL 35, [2007] 4 All ER 857, [2007] 1 WLR 2030, the House of

Lords held that the arrangement entered into by Mr and Mrs Jones constituted a statutory settlement within the meaning of ITTOIA 2005, s 620 and therefore Mr Jones was subject to charge under s 625. However, it was held that Mr Jones's transfer to his wife was an outright gift and the spouse exemption in ITTOIA 2005, s 626 applied. Mr Jones was therefore not assessable on the dividends received by his wife under the arrangement. In *Patmore v Revenue & Customs Comrs* [2010] UKFTT 334 (TC), [2010] SFTD 1124 Mr and Mrs Patmore purchased company shares funded by a mortgage on a jointly owned property. New shares were created so that Mr Patmore held 98% of the 'A' shares and his wife held 2%. Subsequently, 'B' shares were issued to Mrs Patmore on which dividends were paid. The dividend income was used to repay the loans. HMRC argued that the settlement provisions applied. Interestingly, the judge raised a point which had not been advanced by the parties in argument and on which the case was finally decided. The judge held there was no element of bounty by Mr Patmore or any intention on Mrs Patmore's part to make a gift to her husband of her fair share of the company. The judge found that Mrs Patmore had not received sufficient shares for her 50% shareholding and that there was a constructive trust in favour of Mrs Patmore. Although this decision has been criticised by commentators, it does reinforce the view expressed by the House of Lords in *Jones v Garnett*.

To avoid the ambit of ITTOIA 2005, s 624 as explained by the House of Lords in *Jones v Garnett*, it is essential that either the lower-income spouse acquired their shares by way of subscription from their own resources or acquired the shares by an 'outright gift' from their spouse. ITTOIA 2005, s 626(4)(b) defines when a gift is not an outright gift.

In *Jones v Garnett*, although the dividends were paid into a joint bank account, no evidence was put before the Special Commissioners as to whether the property or any derived property was applied for the benefit of Mr Jones. The result may have been different if such evidence had been presented. The problem is being able to show, within a typical marriage, that moneys received by each spouse are applied for the personal benefit of that spouse. There is some evidence that HMRC is enquiring into the application of the funds received: are the moneys received applied for the personal benefit of that spouse. Within a marriage it may be difficult to provide such evidence when a joint bank account is used. Taxpayers should, therefore, be careful to retain evidence of the application of funds.

Waiver of dividends

[4.19] The waiver of dividends can fall within the settlement provisions as illustrated by the case of *Buck v Revenue & Customs Comrs* [2009] STC (SCD) 6. Mr Buck held all but one share in his company, with his wife holding the remaining share. Mr Buck waived his entitlement to the declared dividends, with the effect that Mrs Buck received all the dividends. It was held by the Special Commissioner that the settlement provisions applied and there was no outright gift in the broad sense of that word suggested by the House of Lords in *Jones v Garnett*. There was merely a one-off dividend waiver.

HMRC in its Trusts, Settlements and Estates Manual at para 4225 outlines the factors that it will consider when determining whether the settlement provisions apply as was illustrated in *Donovan and McLaren v Revenue and Customs Comrs* (TC/2013/00400) [2014] UKFTT 048 (TC). Dividend waivers cannot fall within the spouse exemption under ITTOIA 2005, s 626. That is because one of the conditions that must be satisfied for the exception to apply is that the property is not wholly or substantially a right to income and a waiver is a right to income. Although the application of the settlements legislation is of primary importance for income tax planning between members of married couples, it should be borne in mind that transfers of interests in small family companies as between spouses, for the purposes of capital tax planning, may bring these provisions into effect.

Income splitting is still worth exploring where there is a spouse with little significant income of his or her own, particularly where one spouse is paying the 45% additional rate of income tax. Careful planning is, however, a pre-requisite taking into consideration the application of the GAAR.

Pre-owned assets charge

[4.20] For the purposes of the charge to income tax by reference to enjoyment of property previously owned (also referred to as tax on pre-owned assets), gifts between spouses or civil partners are excluded transactions (FA 2004, Sch 15, para 10(1)(b)). This is an important exemption as spouses or civil partners may continue to make gifts to one another without triggering an income tax charge under these provisions. This charge to income tax is discussed in greater detail at **4.35**.

Gifts to charities

[4.21] The making of gifts to charities may perhaps not be regarded as an aspect of estate planning by some, although such gifts will clearly reduce the amount of inheritance tax payable on a person's death. As many wealthy individuals feel a moral obligation to pass some of the benefit of their good fortune and hard work to those less favoured than themselves, the subject is properly within the scope of this book. Immediate, unconditional and indefeasible gifts to charities are completely free of inheritance tax (IHTA 1984, s 23). In addition, a reduced rate of inheritance tax (36%) will apply to those estates where a charitable legacy of 10% or more of an individual's estate is made. Income tax relief is available for single gifts made by individuals to charities. As charities may realise chargeable gains free of tax (TCGA 1992, s 256), a transferor proposing to give a capital sum to a charity should consider transferring investments or property which show large unrealised gains rather than cash. The gift of the investments or the property will not give rise to a charge to capital gains tax (TCGA 1992, s 257). The value of listed shares, securities, certain collective investments and qualifying interests in land given to charities will be deductible from the transferor's income for income tax purposes (ITA 2007, ss 431–446). These reliefs, with some further restrictions, also apply to gifts to Community Amateur Sports Clubs.

Charities generally and Community Amateur Sports Clubs are dealt with in more detail in CHAPTER 15 GIFTS TO CHARITIES AND OTHER NON-PROFIT ORGANISATIONS.

Gifts of 'excluded property'

[4.22] For the purposes of inheritance tax no account is taken of 'excluded property' which ceases to form part of a person's estate (IHTA 1984, s 3(2)). Thus, gifts of excluded property may be made completely free of inheritance tax.

Excluded property appears mainly in two situations. The first is in connection with property owned by, or settled in trust by, a person who is neither domiciled in the UK nor treated as being so domiciled for inheritance tax purposes at the time the settlement was made (IHTA 1984, ss 6 and 48(3)). This situation is considered further in Chapter 21 UK Residents With Multi-Jurisdictional Affairs and Chapter 22 The Overseas Client.

The other situation is that of settlements and settled property where there is a reversionary interest. Broadly, a 'reversionary interest' is excluded property unless:

(i)   it has been acquired for a consideration in money or money's worth;

(ii)   it is one to which the settlor of the settlement or his spouse or civil partner is or has been beneficially entitled; or

(iii) it satisfies certain conditions of IHTA 1984, s 74A(1), is a reversionary interest and the individual has or is able to acquire another interest in the settled property (IHTA 1984, s 48(1)(d)).

Example

> Matilda is 87 years of age. The Baxter Settlement provides that she is entitled to the income of the settlement for her lifetime with the remainder to be divided between her two children Milly and Molly who have children of their own. Milly and Molly's interests are reversionary interests. As they are both financially secure they consider assigning their interests in remainder to their children. During Matilda's lifetime they are able to assign or re-settle their interests for the benefit of their children without incurring any inheritance tax charge.

This is considered in more detail in Chapter 7 Existing Settlements.

The type of settlement under which there is a life tenant with one or more remaindermen often arises under wills drawn up in estate duty days when an exemption applied on the death of a surviving spouse, where that spouse had been left a life interest in the estate of the deceased. In the case of property settled in this way by a person dying before 13 November 1974, the exemption continues to apply on the death of the surviving spouse or on any prior termination of the life interest (IHTA 1984, Sch 6, para 2).

This type of settlement can also arise from former intestacy rules where the deceased died intestate leaving a spouse or civil partner and children: in such cases the spouse or civil partner would take absolutely the deceased's personal chattels, a statutory legacy and a life interest in one half of the residue of the deceased's estate with the children taking the interests in remainder on the statutory trusts (Administration of Estates Act 1925, s 46). Since 1 October 2014, no such settlements arise because from that date the surviving spouse or civil partner receives half of the residue absolutely.

Gifts with reservation

General

[4.23] Having looked at the most important exemptions and quasi-exemptions from inheritance tax, and before dealing with some of the practical aspects of giving, consideration must first be given to the gifts with reservation rules contained in FA 1986, ss 102–102C and Sch 20. These rules are designed to prevent an individual giving away an asset whilst continuing to enjoy the benefit from it.

The legislation provides that a gift of property subject to a reservation is treated, so far as the donor is concerned, as a partial nullity for inheritance tax purposes. This is achieved by deeming the relevant property still to form part of the donor's estate on death. The rules apply where either:

(a)   possession and enjoyment of the property is not *bona fide* assumed by the donee at least seven years before the donor's death; or

(b)   the property is not enjoyed to the entire exclusion, or virtually to the entire exclusion, of the donor and of any benefit to him by contract or otherwise (or by virtue of any associated operations within the meaning of IHTA 1984, s 268) at any time within seven years of the donor's death.

In essence, this means that a gift of property may fall foul of these provisions if the donor receives, or is capable of receiving, any direct or indirect benefit whatsoever which is in some way referable to the gift. The benefit does not have to be provided out of the donated property (*A-G v Worrall* [1895] 1 QB 99), nor does it have to be provided by the donee. The benefit may be financial, such as an annuity (*A-G v Worrall*), a rent charge (*Grey (Earl) v A-G* [1900] AC 124, [1900–1903] All ER Rep 268), or a right to remuneration (*Oakes v Comr of Stamp Duties of New South Wales* [1954] AC 57, [1953] 2 All ER 1563, PC). Equally, it may well be the right to use or occupy (even as a bare licensee), or the ability to use or occupy, the donated property (*Chick v Stamp Duties Comr of New South Wales* [1958] AC 435, [1958] All ER 623, PC). Not every benefit to the donor, however, results in a gift being caught by FA 1986, s 102(1)(b). The Court of Appeal in *Buzzoni v Revenue & Customs Comrs* [2013] EWCA Civ 1684, [2014] 1 WLR 3040, [2014] WTLR 421, held that a benefit had to impair the donee's enjoyment of the gift. This decision may be contrasted with the First-tier Tribunal's decision in *Viscount Hood (Executor of the Estate of Lady Hood) v HMRC* [2016] TC 04858, which was distinguished because the terms on which Lady Hood (as the sub-lessor) granted the sub-lease to her sons required positive covenants to be given by her sons to her rather than direct covenants being given to the head lessor, hence the benefit of the positive covenants was derived from the donated property.

There is a wealth of complicated and contradictory case law on the meaning of the original provisions contained in the estate duty legislation. Whilst the current provisions are closely based on earlier estate duty sections, it should be remembered that inheritance tax is fundamentally different from estate duty so that old cases should be considered with a degree of circumspection. In the case of *Melville v IRC* [2000] STC 628, 74 TC 372 (Ch D) Lightman J in the High Court said at page 636:

' . . . I do not think that authorities on the estate duty legislation are helpful on the quite different legislation which replaced it.'

Although that may be true of the relationship of estate duty and inheritance tax generally, it does not indicate that one cannot refer to estate duty cases on reservation of benefit where the old and new legislation have substantially similar wording.

It is beyond the scope of this book to provide a detailed analysis of the complexities of the current provisions and of the old case law. The following comments are, however, offered as a guide. It is paradoxical really that over 30 years after the introduction of inheritance tax, including the reservation of benefit provisions, very few cases have considered these provisions. Interestingly, in those cases, it has been the taxpayer who has been successful and not HMRC.

Property given away

[4.24] In determining whether there has been any reservation of benefit, it is essential to first identify the property which has been given away by the donor (see for example, *Munro v Stamp Duties Comr of New South Wales* [1934] AC 61 (PC) and *St Aubyn v A-G (No 2)* [1952] AC 15, [1951] 2 All ER 473 (HL)). It is this property which the donor has to continue to either possess or enjoy. Property in which the donor retains no interest and does not possess or enjoy will not be subject to a reservation. A gift made to a spouse or civil partner after 19 June 2003 will be a gift with reservation where:

- the property becomes settled property by virtue of the gift;
- the trusts of the settlement give an interest in possession to the donor's spouse or civil partner (who is defined as the 'relevant beneficiary'), so that the gift is exempt from inheritance tax by reason of the spouse or civil partner exemption and the rule which treats an interest in possession as equivalent to outright ownership (IHTA 1984, s 49(1));
- between the date of the gift and the donor's death the interest in possession comes to an end; and
- when that interest in possession comes to an end, the donor's spouse or civil partner does not become beneficially entitled to the settled property or to another interest in possession in it (FA 1986, s 102(5A)).

In applying s 102 in such circumstances, the original disposal by way of gift will be treated, where relevant, as having been made immediately after the beneficiary's interest in possession ends, so that the circumstances before that time will not be considered in determining whether the property given away is 'property subject to a reservation' for inheritance tax purposes. This followed the Court of Appeal's decision in *IRC v Eversden (exors of Greenstock, dec'd)* [2003] EWCA Civ 668, [2003] STC 822, 75 TC 340. These provisions are likely to be relevant only to trusts established before 22 March 2006 because for trusts made on or after that date the spouse or civil partner exemption is unlikely to be available because s 49 only applies to a very limited range of interest in possessions created *inter vivos*.

This concept of first carving out a separate proprietary interest from an asset to be given away and then giving away the remaining interest (often called 'shearing') was accepted practice in estate duty days and HMRC appears to accept its efficacy under the inheritance tax regime, subject to certain important qualifications.

A particular application of the shearing principle was the lease carve out scheme. This was commonly used by estate planners in relation to the family home. The House of Lords considered the scheme and found in favour of the taxpayer in Ingram v IRC [2000] 1 AC 293, [1999] 1 All ER 297, HL. It was that case that led to the reservation of benefit provisions being extended to certain gifts of interests in land where the donor continues to occupy, or enjoy some right in, the land after the gift (FA 1986, ss 102A, 102C). This is examined in more detail in CHAPTER 11 THE FAMILY HOME AND OTHER RESIDENTIAL PROPERTY at **11.49–11.51**.

The shearing technique is of wider application than the family home and remains important in relation to estate planning.

The reservation

[4.25] The provisions only catch benefits reserved to the donor and not those reserved to his or her spouse or civil partner whereas the estate duty provisions caught both. Whilst this does give some scope for flexibility in estate planning – for example, the donor's spouse or civil partner could be a discretionary beneficiary of a trust while the donor may not be – great care must be taken to ensure that any benefit reserved to a spouse or civil partner cannot be treated as a benefit to the donor including a benefit obtained by virtue of any associated operations (FA 1986, Sch 20, para 6(1)(c)). Thus, for example, a wife who receives a distribution of capital from a discretionary trust of which her husband was the settlor should not pay the money into a joint bank account or one on which her husband has drawing facilities. Nor should she use the money to maintain him or to discharge any liabilities which would normally be regarded as his responsibility. It should also be borne in mind that the inclusion of the settlor's spouse or civil partner as a beneficiary under a trust can have adverse income tax and capital gains tax consequences for the settlor.

Possession and enjoyment

[4.26] Where possession and enjoyment is not bona fide assumed by the donee at or before the beginning of a relevant period or at any time in the relevant period the property is not enjoyed to the entire exclusion or virtually to the entire exclusion of the donor and of any benefit to him by contract or otherwise, a benefit will have been reserved.

The gifts with reservation provisions do not apply where the donor and donee occupy the land and the donor does not receive any benefit, other than a negligible one, which is provided by or at the expense of the donee for some reason connected with the gift (FA 1986, s 102B(4)). The donee must not pay more than his or her share of the outgoings. There is not, however, a requirement for the proportionate sharing of expenses. It would cover the situation where elderly parents make unconditional gifts of a share in their house to their children and the property is occupied by the parents and their children each bearing his or her pro rata share of the running costs. This is not a gift with reservation because the children have taken up occupation and the parents' occupation is referrable to their joint ownership and not the gift. (HMRC Inheritance Tax Manual, para 14332). The scope for this type of arrangement is fairly limited and problems may arise if one or more of the children leave home but retain their interest.

It is unwise to assume, relying on the authority of *A-G v Seccombe* [1911] 2 KB 688, that the words 'by contract or otherwise' in FA 1986, s 102 will be construed in accordance with the *'ejusdem generis'* rule. It was categorically stated by the government spokesman in the Standing Committee G debates on the 1986 Finance Bill that the non-enforceable enjoyment or benefit of property is sufficient to bring the gifts with reservation provisions into play.

Continuation of reasonable commercial arrangements

[4.27] A director or employee of a company who wishes to give away some or all of his shares in the company should beware of reserving a benefit. The continuation of reasonable commercial arrangements in the form of remuneration or other benefits for the donor's services in the company entered into before the gift will not be considered by HMRC to be a reservation of benefit provided the benefits were in no way linked to or affected by the gift (HMRC Inheritance Tax Manual, paras 14337 and 14395). What is reasonable will depend upon all the facts. Generally speaking, it will be determined by what might be reasonably expected under arm's length arrangements between unconnected persons (HMRC Inheritance Tax Manual, para 14337). However, if the donor attempts to entrench his position and benefits, eg by way of a fixed term service contract, or if following the gift he receives remuneration or other benefits in excess of normal commercial rates, he will be running the risk of reserving a benefit.

If the donor is the sole trustee, or one of the trustees, of the donated property, his interest as trustee will not amount to a reservation of a benefit. This was the position under the estate duty legislation (*Comr of Stamp Duties of New South Wales v Perpetual Trustee Co Ltd* [1943] AC 425 (PC)). HMRC has confirmed that in its view, the donor or his spouse or civil partner being a trustee of a settlement does not of itself give rise to a reservation of benefit (HMRC Inheritance Tax Manual, para 14394). The position is the same even if the donor and spouse are entitled to payment for their services as trustees provided the remuneration is not excessive. This is despite the decision in the *Oakes* case.

Simply because a settlor is a trustee of a settlement established in favour of his or her minor children should not itself cause a reservation to arise. Yet where such settled funds are subsequently applied to meet a contractual liability of the parent which was incurred to maintain his children, a reservation would then arise.

The position is more complex in the case of a settlor who acts as trustee of shares in a company of which he or she is a director. Specific relieving provisions are generally required in the trust instrument if the trustee is to retain the remuneration received from that company, unless a timely application is made to the court for relief (*Re Keeler's Settlement Trust, Keeler v Gledhill* [1981] 1 Ch 156, [1981] 1 All ER 888). In this type of situation, HMRC accepts that the continuation of reasonable commercial arrangements governing remuneration and benefits entered into prior to the gift would not, by itself, amount to a reservation (HMRC Inheritance Tax Manual, para 14395). This assumes that the remuneration package was not linked to, or affected by, the gift. However, it is suggested by some commentators that the donor should enter into a legally binding long-term service agreement prior to settling the shares, whilst having due regard to company law considerations; the idea being for the donor to 'carve out' rights in his favour, excluding those from the property gifted. Doubts have been expressed concerning this suggestion. The argument being that the associated operations provisions contained in FA 1986, Sch 20, para 6(1)(c) might be applied to link the contractual arrangements with the subsequent gift of shares.

As a result it may be generally prudent to dissuade an executive director from being a trustee when settling shares in his or her private company. As such settlors are often reluctant to relinquish control in this way it will be necessary to arrange matters within the published parameters. A further precaution might be for the donor to enter into a suitable long-term service agreement prior to giving the shares away, albeit that doubts may exist over the degree of protection this will afford.

Exclusion or virtual exclusion

[4.28] HMRC accepts that the word 'virtually' in FA 1986, s 102(1)(b) is not defined but considers that it means 'to all intents' or 'as good as'. It interprets 'virtually to the entire exclusion' as covering cases in which 'the benefit obtained by the donor is insignificant in relation to the gifted property' (HMRC Inheritance Tax Manual, para 14333).

HMRC outlines a number of situations where limited benefits could arise to a donor without causing the reservation of benefit rules to come into play (HMRC Inheritance Tax Manual, para 14333). These are set out below:

(a)   A house which becomes the donee's residence but where the donor subsequently stays, in the absence of the donee, for not more than 2 weeks each year, or stays with the donee for less than one month a year.

(b)   Social visits, excluding overnight stays made by a donor as a guest of the donee, to a house which he had given away. The extent of the social visits should be no greater than the visits which the donor might be expected to make to the donee's house in the absence of any gift by the donor.

(c)   A temporary stay for some short-term purpose in a house the donor had previously given away; for example, while the donor convalesces after medical treatment or looks after a donee convalescing after medical treatment or while the donor's own home is being redecorated.

(d)   Visits to a house for domestic reasons; for example, baby-sitting by the donor for the donee's children.

(e)   A house together with a library of books which the donor visits less than 5 times in any year to consult or borrow a book.

(f)   A motor car which the donee uses to give occasional (ie less than 3 times a month) lifts to the donor.

(g)   Land which the donor uses to walk his dogs or for horseriding provided this does not restrict the donee's use of the land.

The following are suggested by HMRC as representing cases where the reservation rules are likely to apply:

(i)   A house in which the donor stays most weekends, or for a month or more each year.

(ii)   A second home or holiday home which both the donor and the donee use on an occasional basis.

(iii) A house with a library in which the donor continues to keep his own books, or which the donor uses on a regular basis; for example, because it is necessary for his work.

(iv)   A motor car which the donee uses every day to take the donor to work (HMRC Inheritance Tax Manual, para 14333).

Gift exemption

[4.29] Gifts which qualify for certain inheritance tax exemptions – in particular the exemption for gifts in consideration of marriage or civil partnership – cannot constitute a gift with reservation (FA 1986, s 102(5)). Gifts to charities or registered clubs are also outside their scope but this is not surprising as the charity/registered clubs exemption contains its own reservation of benefit provisions in IHTA 1984, s 23(4). Potentially exempt transfers and gifts within the annual exemption or normal expenditure out of income can, however, be caught by the provisions.

Full consideration exemption

[4.30] The underlying principle is that the reservation rules will not apply where an interest is given away and the donor pays full consideration for the future use of the property.

Where a donor gives full consideration, the retention or assumption by him of the actual occupation or enjoyment of land, or of a right over land, or the actual possession of a chattel, is to be disregarded in determining whether the property is enjoyed to his exclusion or virtual exclusion and of any benefit to him by contract or otherwise. What constitutes full consideration has always been of concern for those involved in estate planning because, taken literally, the failure to satisfy this requirement by however small a margin would be fatal. HMRC's interpretation of full consideration in this context is given in the Revenue Interpretation 55:

'While we take the view that such full consideration is required throughout the relevant period – and therefore consider that the rent paid should be reviewed at appropriate intervals to reflect market changes – we do recognise that there is no single value at which consideration can be fixed as 'full'. Rather, we accept that what constitutes full consideration in any case lies within a range of values reflecting normal valuation tolerances, and that any amount within that range, can be accepted as satisfying the para 6(1)(a) test.'

A difficulty arises in relation to establishing a rental value for assets where there is no meaningful rental market. It was HMRC's view that 'it is unlikely that any . . . arrangement could be overturned if the taxpayer [could] demonstrate that it resulted from a bargain negotiated at arms' length by parties who were independently advised and which followed the normal commercial criteria in force at the time it was negotiated' (HMRC Inheritance Tax Manual, para 14341). As of 10 November 2014 this has been removed from the Manual. In relation to items such as country house chattels or valuable works of art where there may be no meaningful rental market HMRC's accepted norm is 1% of capital value. It admits that this rate 'has no robust basis but is regularly accepted by HMRC on a without prejudice basis' (Chattels Valuations Fiscal Forum – see STEP Journal April 2007). HMRC has warned that where purely nominal rental rates are used taxpayers 'can expect them to be vigorously challenged'. With regard to chattels, the procedure in the Bills of Sale Acts should be followed.

Infirm relative exemption

[4.31] There is an exemption of limited application which, broadly speaking, will cover the case where a donor gives a house to a relative whose circumstances have changed since the original gift and who has become unable to maintain himself for reasons of old age or infirmity. This only applies if the donee is a relative of the donor or of the donor's spouse or civil partner.

Interest in possession trusts

[4.32] FA 1986, s 102ZA subjects the exercise of the trustees' discretion to terminate an interest in possession to the reservation of benefit rules. Where the section applies, an individual is treated as having disposed of, by way of gift, property in which his interest in possession has come to an end. The section applies where an individual became beneficially entitled to the interest in possession before 22 March 2006 or did so after that date where the interest is an immediate post-death interest, a disabled person's trust, a transitional serial interest or a IHTA 1984, Sch 5(IB) interest and the interest in possession comes to an end during the individual's lifetime. This section seems to have been introduced to prevent the re-organisation of trust interests resulting in passing interests to children without incurring tax charges, although HMRC claims it was to 'align the treatment of cases involving trust property formerly subject to an interest in possession . . . with the treatment of similar facts where the property was formerly owned outright'.

Tracing

[4.33] FA 1986, Sch 20 contains various provisions enabling the property subject to the reservation to be 'traced' into other property. These provisions are necessary in order to ascertain the value and nature of the property which is to be treated as forming part of the donor's estate immediately before his death. Where the original gift, however, is one of cash (and the gift is not to a settlement), it is arguable that the tracing provisions do not apply. This will effectively freeze the value of the property subject to the reservation, but in addition it raises the interesting argument, that if by the time of the death of the donor, the cash has ceased to exist, then there will be nothing on which FA 1986, s 102 can bite. Thus, for example, if a donor gives his son a cash gift and the son subsequently uses the money to buy a property which the donor occupies until his death, it might be thought that there is a reservation of benefit by associated operations to the donor (by virtue of his occupation of the property provided by his son). HMRC considers this to be the case. One argument, however, is that as the cash ceases to exist as from the date of the purchase of the property, and because there are no provisions tracing the cash into the property, it is difficult to see how there can be any property subject to a reservation at the donor's death. The contrary argument is that by being expended the cash does not cease to exist but merely becomes the property of another (and so on *ad infinitum*) so that the property subject to the reservation continues to exist (although not in the hands of the donee) until the donor's death. Until such time as this matter is tested in the courts the uncertainty will remain. In any event, this kind of arrangement will be subject to an income tax charge on pre-owned assets which is discussed in greater detail in **4.35**.

Effect of rules

[4.34] The effects of the gift with reservation provisions are far reaching. In the event of these provisions being of relevance when advising a client, one should consider whether the client is making a gift of the right property. One has to consider the wasted time and costs of not only implementing the transaction but any subsequent correspondence with HMRC together with the uncertainty for the client as to whether he has a potential inheritance tax charge. If the reservation of benefit provisions are found to apply, the donor will have to pay the inheritance tax on his death as if he still owned the property but that property will not benefit from any capital gains tax market value uplift on death.

The pre-owned assets charge

General

[4.35] The pre-owned asset charge ('POA charge') is not a charge to inheritance tax but a charge to income tax.

A charge is imposed where assets have, broadly speaking, been given away by an individual but under such circumstances that the individual has retained the right to use or enjoy the assets given away while circumventing the inheritance tax gift with reservation rules (see **4.23**). Much capital tax planning has been designed to create situations which do not fall within the gifts with reservation rules. In the examples used in this section, for the sake of simplicity, it is assumed that the gifts with reservation rules have been circumvented unless otherwise stated.

The pre-owned assets provisions may be very unfortunate for those individuals who have owned assets which have been disposed of, in whole or in part, since 18 March 1986. Although an election to opt out of the pre-owned asset provisions is possible (see **4.47**), such an election still does not put an individual who has undertaken tax planning in the same position as he would have been if the planning had never been implemented. It may be expensive to unwind the structures already put in place. In some cases, it may not be possible to do so at all or to do so only by incurring a further tax charge.

The legislation relating to the POA charge is found in FA 2004, s 84 and Sch 15. Guidance published by HMRC is found at para 44000 onwards of its Inheritance Tax Manual.

There are three separate charges under the POA charge as the legislation differentiates between land, chattels and intangible property in a settlor-interested settlement.

Land

[**4.36**] Under FA 2004, Sch 15, para 3, an income tax charge will arise where an individual (the chargeable person) occupies land (referred to as the 'relevant land'), whether alone or with other persons, and the 'disposal condition' or the 'contribution condition' is satisfied in relation to the land.

An 'interest in land' has the same meaning as that found in IHTA 1984, Pt VI, Ch IV where it is defined by IHTA 1984, s 190 as not including any estate, interest or right by way of mortgage or other security.

Occupation

[**4.37**] Occupation is not defined in the legislation and so one would apply its normal meaning, that of 'taking possession'. HMRC states that 'the meaning . . . should be taken quite widely' (HMRC Inheritance Tax Manual, para 44003). HMRC distinguishes occupation from residence as residence 'implies a greater level of permanence so a lower threshold is required to satisfy the occupation condition'. HMRC states that a visitor may not be in occupation but someone who has a key who can freely enter and leave premises 'is more likely to be in occupation; even if they are absent for significant periods'. A person storing possessions in a property may be regarded by HMRC as occupying a property but only if the person had a right of access to use the property as he wished, or was the only person with the means of access. Storing possessions on its own is not occupation but it may be evidence of occupation.

HMRC does not regard a person as occupying a property from which he receives rent from the actual occupier (HMRC Inheritance Tax Manual, para 44003). This is significant in considering the scope of the exemption in FA 1986, s 102B(3)(a) from the reservation of benefit charge. HMRC says that, where occupation or use is limited in nature or duration, it may not fall within FA 2004, Sch 15, para 3; each case will depend on its own facts. There is no provision providing exemption from charge where the taxpayer's occupation is limited. What HMRC probably means is that limited periods of physical presence or limited usage will not amount to occupation. HMRC will apply its interpretation of occupation found in RI 55 (in the context of the gifts with reservation) to the pre-owned assets regime. Be that as it may, HMRC gives a number of examples of what it calls limited occupation which will not fall within FA 2004, Sch 15, para 3. One such example is a house which is the owner's residence but where the chargeable person, subsequently to the gift, stays in the house with the other person for less than 1 month each year or, in their absence, stays for not more than 2 weeks each year. (HMRC Inheritance Tax Manual, paras 14333 and 44003).

Further examples have been provided by the professional bodies on which HMRC has commented. It has, for example, confirmed that where an individual has a right to the property throughout the year but does not in fact use it 'it is unlikely that there would be a Schedule 15 charge'. HMRC has declined to confirm that no charge would arise where there is a right to use the property throughout the year and the chargeable person uses the property but it falls within the *de minimis* limit set out in the guidance notes that there would be no charge. Where there is a right to use the property throughout the year and an individual uses the property, for example, for 3 months of the year, the charge will be based on the whole year, even where others have a right to use the property during that period. This is of particular relevance in relation to holiday homes.

Due to the lack of definition of occupation it will be necessary to judge each situation on its facts which will inevitably lead to some uncertainty for the taxpayer.

The question of 'what is occupation' was considered in the VAT case of *Principal and Fellows of Newnham College in the University of Cambridge v Revenue & Customs Comrs* [2008] UKHL 23, [2008] 2 All ER 863, [2008] 1 WLR 888. The House of Lords held that mere physical presence on land was not enough to constitute occupation. For a person to be in occupation they should have the right to occupy the property as if they are the owner and to exclude any other person from enjoyment of such a right in addition to physical presence. Following this decision, HMRC revised its interpretation of 'occupation' in Revenue & Customs Brief 33/09. Whilst HMRC states that the clarification relates only to the test of occupation in VATA 1994, Sch 10, paras 12–17, it may nonetheless be useful in respect of the pre-owned assets charge.

The 'disposal condition'

[4.38] The 'disposal condition' is satisfied where, at any time after 17 March 1986, a chargeable person has:

- owned an interest in the relevant land (or in other property the disposal proceeds of which were directly or indirectly applied by another person towards the acquisition of an interest in the relevant land); and
- disposed of all or part of his interest in the relevant land or the other property, otherwise than by an excluded transaction (see **4.52**).

These provisions might apply where, for example, a father gives away a property he owns to his son and, sometime later, either the father moves back into the property or the son sells the property and buys a new property which the father later occupies. They can also apply in more complex situations.

Examples

Marjorie gave her shares worth £250,000 to her great granddaughter Jasmine who sold the shares and used the proceeds to purchase a house in which Marjorie now lives.

The disposal condition would be met because Marjorie once owned other property (ie the shares) the proceeds of which were used by Jasmine to acquire the house.

If Jasmine had used the sale proceeds to build a granny annex onto the house in which Marjorie lived, it would appear that the disposal condition would not be met because the sale proceeds of the shares were not used to acquire an interest in land but to improve the land.

The 'contribution condition'

[4.39] The 'contribution condition' is satisfied where, at any time after 17 March 1986, the chargeable person has provided (directly or indirectly), otherwise than by an excluded transaction, any of the consideration given by another person for the acquisition of:

- an interest in the relevant land; or
- an interest in any other property, the disposal proceeds of which were (directly or indirectly) applied by another person towards acquiring the relevant land.

Examples

Andrew gives his son Luke £100,000 towards the purchase of a £200,000 flat. Luke provides the rest of the consideration. Andrew later moves into the flat.

The contribution condition is satisfied and an income tax charge arises.

Gillian gives Maxwell Court to Barbara who exchanges it for Hill House. Gillian moves into Hill House.

The contribution condition is satisfied and an income tax charge arises.

The contribution condition is extremely wide. It has been said, however, that if the chargeable person was only entitled to a share of the proceeds of the other property, then only that share of the proceeds should be regarded as flowing through to the relevant land (Finance Bill Standing Committee, 18 May 2004 col 266). It should be noted that an outright gift of money made at least seven years before the chargeable person occupies the relevant property will be excluded (FA 2004, Sch 15, para 10(2)(c)). HMRC does not consider that the contribution condition is satisfied where a lender resides in property purchased by another with money loaned to him by the lender. It is HMRC's view that 'this is because the outstanding debt will form part of the lender's estate for inheritance tax purposes, and the lender cannot be said to have provided a contribution to the purchase of that property when that money has to be repaid to them, even if the loan was interest free.' (HMRC Inheritance Tax Manual, para 44005). It is clear, however, that the contribution condition is satisfied in these circumstances. This places a taxpayer and his adviser in a difficult position as to whether or not to rely on guidance which is incorrect in law.

A disposition which creates a new interest in land out of an existing interest in land is treated as a part disposal of the existing interest. This is, of course, of relevance to lease carve-out cases.

Excluded transactions

[4.40] There are five excluded transactions in relation to both the disposal condition and the contribution condition (see **4.52**).

The POA charge

[4.41] Where the provisions apply, a taxpayer is deemed to receive an amount of income equal to the chargeable amount on which he will be liable to income tax. The valuation of property follows the rule in IHTA 1984, s 160. It is the price that the property might reasonably be expected to fetch if sold in the open market at that time, without any scope for a reduction on the grounds that the whole property is to be placed on the market at one and the same time (FA 2004, Sch 15, para 15). The chargeable amount is calculated using the formula (set out in FA 2004, Sch 15, para 4) shown below:

$$R \times \frac{DV}{V}$$

where

R is the rental value of the relevant land;

DV is the appropriate proportion of the value of the relevant land at the valuation date. The definition varies according to whether it is the disposal condition or contribution condition that is at issue; and

V is the value of the relevant land at the valuation date.

Broadly speaking, the chargeable amount will be the appropriate rental value of the relevant land less any moneys actually paid to the owners of the relevant land in pursuance of a legal obligation. In respect of the taxpayer's occupation of the land, the intention is that only payments that are taxable in the hands of the recipient should be allowed as a deduction from the POA charge (Finance Bill Standing Committee, 18 May 2004 col 269). So where a person decides to pay a full market rent for occupation of the property in order to eliminate the POA charge, he should put in place a tenancy agreement under which the rent is paid. For a taxpayer who, for example, wishes to benefit his son, such an arrangement has the additional advantage that it passes further value to the son by way of rental payments. The payment must be made during the 'taxable period' which is defined as the year of assessment, or part of the year of assessment, during which a POA charge applies to a chargeable person (FA 2004, Sch 15, para 4(6)). Payments made outside the taxable period are disregarded.

Example

> Robin gives his daughter a property but continues to stay in it when he wishes to do so with no further permission from his daughter. He actually stays at the property 12 weeks per year. Robin enters into a legal agreement to pay his daughter £200 per week for his accommodation whilst he stays with her during the year and so pays £2,400. The appropriate rental value is £5,000 and so he will pay income tax on £2,600.

The rental value is based on an annual value as defined in FA 2004, Sch 15, para 3. The annual value is the rent which might reasonably be expected to be obtained on a letting from year to year if:

- the tenant undertook to pay all taxes, rates and charges usually paid by a tenant; and
- the landlord undertook to bear the costs of the repairs and insurance and the other expenses necessary for maintaining the property in a state to command that rent (FA 2004, Sch 15, para 5).

This is a circular definition because, in order to know the rent which might reasonably be expected, one must know the repairs and other expenses that are necessary to maintain the property in a state to command that rent. In order to know the repairs that are required, one needs to know the rent. The formula could be described as a 'landlord's repairing lease' but the Treasury Notes state that the annual value is the rent which will be paid under a standard tenant's repairing lease. The sources from which the required valuation should be obtained are not specified. HMRC expects the chargeable person to take all reasonable steps to ascertain the valuations, as they would do, for example, if they were looking to let a property in the open market (HMRC Inheritance Tax Manual, para 44010).

Where there has been a disposal of the original property or a cash gift has been used to acquire land, the chargeable person will only be assessed to tax on the portion of the value of the relevant land which can reasonably be attributed to the value of the original property or the cash originally given. HMRC, in its Manual, has referred only to the need to make a reasoned judgement, on the basis of the facts, and of the value of the land disposed of and its ultimate sale price, the consideration provided and the independent financial resources of the recipient (HMRC Inheritance Tax Manual, para 44013). This so-called guidance does not assist a practitioner as it says nothing of use.

Example adapting the Revenue's example

> Marjorie gave land worth £200,000 to her grandson Luke who sold it in 2003 for £500,000. He used the proceeds to buy a house for £300,000 in which his grandmother now lives.

In such a situation, HMRC considers it reasonable to treat the whole value of a new property as attributable to the property originally disposed of. If the value of the new property exceeds the proceeds received from the sale of the original property the proportion of the value reasonably attributable to the original property would be reduced. The value reasonably attributable to the new property cannot exceed the final value of the property originally disposed of.

Sales of land

[4.42] Where there is a sale of an entire interest in a property by the chargeable person for a consideration paid in money (sterling or other currency), other than as an excluded transaction, this is known as a 'non-exempt sale'. An example of a non-exempt sale is an outright sale of a property to a connected person at an undervalue. The legislation attempts to take account of the fact that the proceeds from the sale will be comprised in the value of the chargeable person's estate. In these circumstances the annual rent is reduced by multiplying the annual rent by the 'appropriate proportion' calculated by the following fraction:

$$\frac{MV - P}{MV}$$

where

MV is the value of the interest in land at the time of sale; and

P is the amount paid

Example

> Barbara sold 50 acres of land (worth £2,000,000) to Gillian for £1,600,000. The rental value of the land was £100,000.
>
> The appropriate proportion is
>
> $$\frac{£\,2,000,000 - £\,1,600,000}{£\,2,000,000} = \frac{£\,400,000}{£\,2,000,000} = \frac{1}{5}$$
>
> The rental value is then multiplied by the appropriate proportion
>
> $$\frac{1}{5} \times £\,100,000 = £\,20,000$$

In this way, the amount for the annual rent which is attributable to the sum paid to the chargeable person for his interest is removed from charge.

Chattels

[4.43] A POA charge will arise under FA 2004, Sch 15, para 6 where a chargeable person is in possession of, or has the use of, a chattel, either alone or with others, and the 'disposal condition' or the 'contribution condition' is met.

Use or possession

[4.44] The terms 'use' and 'possession' are not defined in the legislation and will therefore have their normal meaning. The question arises as to whether a mere legal right to have possession of a chattel is enough. It is unlikely that it is; it is necessary for control to be assumed by the individual. HMRC has stated that very limited or occasional use of a chattel will not incur a POA charge. An example is given of a car used to give occasional lifts (less than three times a month) to the chargeable person will not be liable to an income tax charge whereas a lift to work every day will likely incur a POA charge (HMRC Inheritance Tax Manual, paras 14333 and 44006).

The 'disposal condition'

[4.45] The 'disposal condition' is satisfied where, at any time after 17 March 1986, the individual (whether alone or jointly with others)

- owned the chattel or any other property the disposal proceeds of which were (directly or indirectly) applied by another person to acquire the chattel; and
- disposed of all or part of his interest in the chattel or other property otherwise than by an excluded transaction.

Examples

A father gives a valuable painting to his son which hangs in the son's house and later the father resumes possession of the painting by hanging it in his dining room.

A father gives his valuable stamp collection to his son. The son sells the stamp collection and buys a painting. The father later hangs the painting in his dining room.

The 'contribution condition'

[4.46] The 'contribution condition' is satisfied when, at any time after 17 March 1986, the chargeable person has provided (directly or indirectly), otherwise than by an excluded transaction, any of the consideration given by another person for the acquisition of:

- the chattel; or
- any other property the disposal proceeds of which were (directly or indirectly) applied by another person towards acquiring the chattel.

Examples

> A father gives his son the sum of £100,000 towards buying a painting which is worth £200,000 and which the father later hangs in his dining room. The contribution condition is satisfied and an income tax charge arises.
>
> The provisions will also apply to exchanges. For example, a father gives a painting to his son who exchanges it for a stamp collection which the father has at his house. The contribution condition is satisfied and an income tax charge arises.
>
> A father gives his son £250,000 to acquire a painting which he does and then sells it for £300,000. He uses the proceeds to buy a vintage car which his father has at his house. The contribution condition is satisfied and an income tax charge arises.

A disposition which creates a new interest in a chattel out of an existing interest in a chattel is to be taken to be a disposal of part of the existing interest (FA 2004, Sch 15, para 6(4)).

The POA charge

[4.47] Where FA 2004, Sch 15, para 6 applies in respect of the whole or part of a year of assessment, an amount equal to the 'chargeable amount' is treated as income of the individual which is chargeable to income tax.

The chargeable amount is the 'appropriate amount' less any amounts paid to the owner by the chargeable person under a legal obligation in respect of the possession or use of the chattel. The 'appropriate amount' is calculated by using the formula in FA 2004, Sch 15, para 7. The appropriate amount varies according to whether the disposal or contribution condition applies. The formula is similar to that for land except that instead of the appropriate rental value, para 7 refers to the appropriate amount and the formula uses a notional interest rate which is prescribed by regulation (currently 3.25%) which can produce a substantial POA charge.

If a full market rent is paid for the use of chattels then in straightforward circumstances there will be no reservation of benefit because of FA 1986, Sch 20, para 6(1)(a). This will also have the result that the POA charge under FA 2004, Sch 15, para 6 will not apply because of FA 2004, Sch 15, para 11(5)(d). It is very important that there is a regular review of the rent to ensure a full market rent is being paid.

There is no *de minimis* value below which chattels may be disregarded. This means that there is no margin for error in determining a full market rent. As, by definition, chattels are movable it may be difficult to track them.

There are three matters to consider in relation to the formula.

First, the valuation date is prescribed by regulations. It has been set as the 6 April in the relevant tax year or, if later, the first day of the taxable period.

Second, regulations provide that the valuation before the first five-year anniversary is to be made by reference to the first valuation date and thereafter by reference to the valuation at the last five-year anniversary. This regime is compulsory, not optional, and may have an adverse effect in relation to fluctuating chattel values. If there is an interruption in the use or occupation of the property by the taxpayer so that a fifth-year anniversary does not fall in a taxable period, the relevant date in the year when the provisions of Sch 15 next apply will be treated as the next five-year anniversary.

Where the chattel in question is the original gift so satisfying the disposal condition, the appropriate amount is computed by the following fraction:

$$\frac{DV}{V}$$

where

DV is the value at the valuation date of the interest in the chattel that was disposed of by the chargeable person; and

V is the value of the chattel at the valuation date.

Example

Bill grants his son a lease of a painting when the painting was worth £500,000 and the lease £400,000. In 2015/16 the painting is worth £3,000,000 and the lease £1,500,000.

On the assumption that the prescribed rate is 3.25%, the appropriate rental value is:

$$£3,000,000 \times \frac{£1,500,000}{£3,000,000} \times 3.25\% = £48,750$$

Sale of a chattel

[4.48] To take account of the fact that, in cases of sales at an undervalue, the sale proceeds may be relevant property comprised in the estate of the chargeable person, the legislation provides that the sale of a whole interest in a chattel by a chargeable person for a consideration paid in money is a non-exempt sale. A proportion is then not subject to the charge. The appropriate amount is reduced by multiplying it by the following fraction:

$$\frac{\text{Appropriate proportion of the value of the interest on the chattel disposed of}}{\text{Value of the chattel}}$$

The appropriate proportion in such a case would be:

$$\frac{MV - P}{MV}$$

where

MV is the value of the interest in the chattel at the time of sale; and

P is the amount paid

Example

Horatio sells to his son, Augustus, a painting worth £2,000,000 at the date of disposal for £1,600,000. At the valuation date the painting is worth £2,500,000.

The appropriate proportion is:

$$\frac{£\,2,000,000 - £\,1,600,000}{£\,2,000,000} = \frac{1}{5}$$

The appropriate amount is then calculated by the formula in para 7(2):

$$\frac{N \times DV}{V}$$

N is the prescribed interest rate (3.25%) applied to the value of the chattel at the valuation date; in this case 3.25% of £2,500,000 = £81,250.

DV is the appropriate proportion of the value of the interest in the chattel disposed of.

DV is £500,000 = 20% of £2,500,000

V is the value of the chattel at the valuation date.

V is £2,500,000

$$\frac{81,250 \times 500,000}{2,500,000} = £16,250$$

It should be remembered that the non-exempt sale relief is only available in respect of cash sales. Also, the relief is only available if the transferor has disposed of his whole interest in the chattel.

HMRC considers that in relation to the carve-out strategies involving chattels, the provisions of FA 1986, s 102A do not apply (HMRC Inheritance Tax Manual, para 44108).

Settlements

General

[4.49] There are special provisions which apply to settlements. Under FA 2004, Sch 15 para 8, a charge to income tax will arise where:

(a)   there is a settlement under which any income arising from the property would be treated under ITTOIA 2005, s 624 as income of the settlor;

(b)   the income would still be deemed to be the income of the settlor even if ITTOIA 2005, s 625(1) did not include any reference to the spouse or civil partner of the settlor; and

(c)   the property comprised in the settlement includes property which is, or represents, intangible property settled or added to the settlement after 17 March 1986.

The charge under para 8 adopts an entirely different approach to the provisions relating to land and chattels. Under those provisions the taxpayer must have actually benefited. Under para 8 what matters is the possibility of benefiting. In such a case it might be worth considering selling any intangible investments and purchasing tangible assets such as let land or chattels which are not occupied or used or enjoyed by the taxpayer.

Intangible property

[4.50] Intangible property is widely defined and means any property other than chattels or interests in land. This will include cash, shares and insurance policies.

The POA charge

[4.51] The 'chargeable amount' is calculated by applying the prescribed notional rate of interest to the value of the relevant property at the valuation date. The notional rate is prescribed by Regulations and is currently 3.25%. A deduction from the chargeable amount is given for any income tax or capital gains tax payable by the chargeable person under the following specified charging provisions so far as the tax is attributable to the relevant property.

(i)   ITTOIA 2005, s 461 (income tax on chargeable event gains).

(ii)   ITTOIA 2005, s 624 (income tax on income arising in settlor-interested trusts).

(iii)   ITA 2007, ss 720–730 (income tax on income arising on assets transferred abroad).

(iv)   TCGA 1992, s 86 (capital gains tax on gains attributed to settlor of a non-resident trusts).

Unlike under the charge on land and chattels, for a charge to arise there is no need for there to be any benefit arising to the chargeable person nor is there any requirement for there to be any income arising under the settlement.

It should be noticed that the chargeable amount is reduced only by the amount of tax paid under the above provisions, and not for the sums charged to tax. This is a grossly inequitable provision.

Example

Malcolm settled a property on trust of which he is the life tenant. The property was sold for £500,000 and the moneys are held on deposit earning 1% per annum. Malcolm's marginal income tax rate is 45%.

Malcolm is liable to income tax under ITTOIA 2005, s 624 on the income arising of £5,000.

Assuming a notional rate of interest of 3.25%, he is also assessable to income tax on notional income under FA 2004, Sch 15 of £21,250. Against this notional income, he can deduct the tax charged on his actual income of £2,250 (45% of £5,000). Therefore, he only receives credit for the tax paid against notional income and not against the tax charged on notional income assessed on him under ITTOIA 2005, s 624.

His income from the settlement is £5,000 and his POA charge in respect of it is £9,562.50 (£2,250 + ((£21,250 − £2,250) @ 45%)).

Excluded transactions

[4.52] FA 2004, Sch 15, para 10 contains a list of 'excluded transactions' which will not be subject to an income tax charge under the pre-owned assets rules. The HMRC Inheritance Tax Manual at para 44030 states that they 'do not apply to the charge on intangibles' discussed in **4.49–4.51**. That statement is rather misleading as an excluded transaction may involve any kind of property, including intangible property. For example, an excluded transaction could involve intangible property that was later replaced by land or chattels, thus removing the land or chattels in question from the scope of the POA charge. There are different exclusions that apply to the different conditions.

Disposal condition

[4.53] For the 'disposal condition' for land and chattels, the following disposals will be excluded transactions.

(a)   The 'full consideration' exclusion. A disposal by a chargeable person of his whole interest in the property except for any right expressly reserved by him over the property either
    (i)   by a transaction made at arm's length with an unconnected person; or
    (ii)   by a transaction which might be expected to be made at arm's length between unconnected persons.
This would include a third party sale or the sale of land between father and daughter on full commercial terms. If, however, there were any unusual contract terms (of the type a third party would be unlikely to accept) in a sale between connected parties, this is likely to prevent the transaction being an excluded transaction. It should be noted that a disposal of a part interest will not in most circumstances be an excluded transaction with the result that, in the original legislation, equity release schemes were subject to the charge. It has therefore been provided that disposals of part of an interest in any property by a transaction made at arm's length with a person not connected with the chargeable person is specifically exempted from charge (Charge to Income Tax by Reference to Enjoyment of Property Previously Owned Regulations 2005 (SI 2005/724), reg 5). In addition, the exemption is extended to disposals of a part share to anyone provided that they were made on arm's length terms and either took place before 7 March 2005 or took place on or after that date for a consideration not in the form of money or readily convertible assets. It should be noted that equity release transactions

between family members will often be caught by the charge. The definition of a connected person is taken from ITA 2007, s 993 but is extended to include aunt, uncle, nephew and niece (FA 2004, Sch 15, para 2)

(b)   Spouse exemption. A transfer of property to the chargeable person's spouse or civil partner (or to a former spouse or civil partner where the transfer has been ordered by a court). A separation agreement would not be sufficient.

This important exception preserves the ability of married taxpayers or those in civil partnerships to distribute capital assets between them. There is no requirement that the spouse be domiciled in the United Kingdom, so the exemption is wider than the corresponding inheritance tax exemption.

(c)   A disposal by way of gift by virtue of which the property became settled property in which a spouse or civil partner (or former spouse or civil partner if done in accordance with a court order) is beneficially entitled provided such an interest in possession has not come to an end otherwise than on the death of the spouse or former spouse. This exemption mirrors the exemption from the reservation of benefit rules found in IHTA 1984 ss 5 and 5A.

(d)   A disposition for the maintenance of a family within IHTA 1984, s 11. HMRC had thought that this provision would have limited application because it was HMRC's view that IHTA 1984, s 11 applied only to income and not to a gift of capital. In *McKelvey (Personal Representatives of McKelvey, decd) v Revenue & Customs Comrs* [2008] STC (SCD) 944, [2008] SWTI 1752, the Special Commissioners held otherwise. As a result of the decision, HMRC advises in its Inheritance Tax Manual at para 44033, that where the exclusion is claimed the case should be referred to its Technical Department.

(e)   An outright gift to an individual which for inheritance tax purposes is a transfer of value which is wholly exempt because the annual exemption (see **4.5**) or the small gifts exemption (see **4.12**) applies.

Gifts covered by other exemptions (eg gifts in consideration of marriage) are not excluded transactions.

Contribution condition

[4.54] Provision by the chargeable person of consideration for another's acquisition of any property will be an excluded transaction in any of the following circumstances.

(i)   Spouse exemption. Where the other person was the chargeable person's spouse or civil partner (or, where the transfer has been ordered by the court, his former spouse or civil partner).

(ii)   On acquisition, the property became settled property in which his spouse, civil partner or former spouse or civil partner is beneficially entitled to an interest in possession (provided that interest in possession has not come to an end otherwise than on the death of the spouse or civil partner or former spouse or civil partner).

(iii) The consideration provided was an outright gift of money (whether in sterling or foreign currency) by the chargeable person to the other person and was made at least seven years before the earliest date the chargeable person began occupation of the relevant land or obtained possession of the chattel.

This is important as it excludes from the charge all outright gifts of money which were made seven or more years before the earliest date the chargeable person either entered occupation of the relevant land or obtained possession of the chattel. As the earliest date the conditions can be met is 6 April 2005, any provision of consideration by way of an outright gift of cash made before 6 April 1998 will be an excluded transaction. This will mean that taxpayers will only have to look back to the previous seven years when tracing gifts of cash used to acquire land or chattels. A problem may still arise where inadequate records have been kept. There is, however, no seven-year limit for gifts of chattels and land which have subsequently been converted to cash which creates a substantial administrative burden on a taxpayer.

(iv) The provision of consideration falls within the exemption for dispositions for the maintenance of family under IHTA 1984, s 11. Again, HMRC advises in its Inheritance Tax Manual at para 44037 that where this exclusion is claimed, the case should be referred to its Technical Department.

(v) The provision of consideration is an outright gift to an individual which is wholly exempt because the annual exemption (see **4.5**) or the small gifts exemption (see **4.12**) applies.

Example

Rachel and Mark jointly purchased a property in 1995 for £200,000, funding £180,000 of the purchase price by raising a joint mortgage loan. Rachel gave Mark £10,000 which he used to fund his share of the cash funds required. They subsequently married and are still living in the same flat which is now worth £750,000.

The 'contribution condition' is met and Rachel's gift is not an excluded transaction between spouses as they were not married at the time that she made it. Mark will be subject to a POA charge under FA 2004, Sch 15 based on the $1/20$th of the rental value of the property, which is a truly absurd result.

Exemptions from charge

[4.55] There are a number of exemptions from the charges on land, chattels and intangible property which are set out in FA 2004, Sch 15, paras 11–13.

(a) There will be no charge where
  (i) the relevant property, or
  (ii) other property which derives its value from the relevant property and whose value is not substantially less than the relevant property

is either within the chargeable person's estate for inheritance tax purposes or would be treated as such by virtue of the gifts with reservation rules. Property will form part of a person's estate where it is included in their free estate or where the person has a qualifying interest in possession and will include an interest in possession arising before 22 March 2006 or one of the favoured trusts if the interest arose after that date. It is only necessary that the property forms part of the person's estate, not that inheritance tax is paid on the property. Where the taxpayer's estate includes property whose value derives from the relevant property but whose value is substantially less than the value of the relevant property, then there will be a reduced charge to income tax, taking into account the inclusion of part of the value in the taxpayer's estate.

In determining the value of property, a deduction is made for an 'excluded liability' in certain circumstances (FA 2004, Sch 15, para 11(6)). A liability is an excluded liability if the creation of the liability and any transaction by which the person's estate came to include relevant property (or property which derives its value from the relevant property or by which the value of property in his estate came to be derived from the relevant property) were associated operations under IHTA 1984, s 268. It appears that this provision was designed to nullify some forms of the trust of debt strategy (see **11.52**) although its precise effect is unclear.

Additional anti-avoidance provisions apply where the property concerned is subsequently treated as forming part of the original transferor's estate by virtue of his coming to have an interest in possession in the property (see **4.56**).

Relevant property is defined in FA 2004, Sch 15, para 11(9) and is determined by the nature of the property involved and whether the disposal or contribution condition is satisfied.

(b) There is an exemption where the property would be treated as subject to a reservation if it were not an exempt transfer under FA 1986, s 102(5)(d)–(i). This includes gifts to charities, political parties, housing associations, maintenance funds for historic buildings and employee trusts and gifts for national purposes. It does not, however, cover transfers between spouses or civil partners, small gifts and gifts in consideration of marriage.

(c) There is an exemption where the property would be treated as subject to a reservation if it were not a share of an interest in land which the transferor and transferee occupy and where the transferor receives no benefit other than a negligible one under FA 1986, s 102B(4). Where a mother gives her son cash which he uses to buy a house jointly with her in which they both live, sharing expenses equally, there is no reservation of benefit. She is not exempt from a POA charge because her gift of cash was neither a gift subject to a reservation nor a gift of an undivided share in land.

(d)   There is an exemption where the property would be treated as subject to a reservation were it not for FA 1986, s 102C(3) and Sch 20, para 6. This covers the situation where a transferor gives a house to a relative, the transferor's circumstances have changed since the original gift and the transferor has become unable to maintain himself for reasons of old age, infirmity or otherwise.

(e)   There is a *de minimis* exemption where the aggregate of the sums chargeable on an individual in respect of pre-owned assets does not exceed £5,000 in a year of assessment. In such a case, no tax will be payable. If the aggregate exceeds £5,000, it will be fully chargeable. The exemption is applied to the aggregate notional annual values before any amounts paid by the former owner are set off in respect of land and chattels. In practice, this is unlikely to exempt many taxpayers from the charge.
Where the charge applies for only part of the year, the de minimis limit is not apportioned.

Example

Madge made a gift of the house in which she lives to her nephew. The appropriate rental value is £7,000. She pays rent to her nephew of £5,000 under a formal agreement which reduces the amount chargeable to £2,000.

The *de minimis* rule will not apply as the appropriate rental value exceeds £5,000.

(f)   There is no charge on an individual who is not resident in the United Kingdom in a year of assessment. This is considered in more detail in CHAPTER 22 THE OVERSEAS CLIENT.

In determining whether property falls within (b), (c) or (d) above in a case where the contribution condition in **4.36** (land) or **4.46** (chattels) above is met, the exclusion for gifts of money in FA 1986, Sch 20, para 2(2)(b) is to be disregarded (FA 2004, Sch 15, para 11(8)).

Gifts made under deeds of variation or dispositions which are not treated as transfers of value under IHTA 1984, s 17 are disregarded for the purposes of the POA charge (FA 2004, Sch 15, para 16).

Where a person ('A') acts as a guarantor in respect of a loan made to another person ('B') by a third party in connection with the acquisition of any property by B, the guarantee is not regarded as the provision by A of consideration for B's acquisition (FA 2004, Sch 15, para 17).

HMRC has the power by way of regulation to confer further exemptions from income tax.

Reverter to settlor trusts

[4.56] Reverter to settlor trusts have, in the past, been used as tax planning vehicles designed to benefit from the interaction of the gift with reservation rules (FA 1986, s 102) and the pre-owned asset rules (FA 2004, Sch 15). The POA charge did not apply if property given away remained comprised in the estate of the transferor for inheritance tax purposes (FA 2004, Sch 15, para 11(1)). Previously, because of IHTA 1984, s 49(1), an individual entitled to a life interest under a settlement was treated as if he owned the trust property which was charged to inheritance tax on his death. Where, however, on the death of the life tenant the property reverted to the settlor of the trust during the settlor's lifetime, although the life tenant was still treated as owning the trust property, its value was left out of account on his death (IHTA 1984, s 53(3)). Therefore a parent could give property to his child, who then settled the property on trust for his parent's life, subject to which the property reverted to him. Neither the gift with reservation provisions nor the POA charge would apply because of s 49, but on the parent's death the value of the property was left out of account. Legislation was introduced to provide that the POA charge applies where the former owner of an asset (or a person who contributed to its acquisition) enjoys the asset under the terms of a trust which provides that the trust property may revert to the settlor during his lifetime unless he makes an election (see **4.60**) (FA 2004, Sch 15, paras 11(11)–(13). If an election is made, the POA charge will not apply but neither will the revertor to settlor exemption when the interest comes to an end. Of course, s 49 only applies to a limited range of interests in possession so this planning can no longer be implemented but existing arrangements continue to offer advantages.

Due to a drafting error in FA 2006, s 80, FA 2004, Sch 15, paras 11(11)–(13) have a wider application than was intended. The error is that the amendment made by s 80 applies not only to trusts where the life tenant is another beneficiary but also to those where the life tenant is a settlor himself. Following correspondence between the Chartered Institute of Taxation and HMRC, HMRC contends that s 80 does not apply provided the life interest of the settlor has subsisted continuously since the creation of the trust. This therefore means that even in HMRC's view there is still a difficulty where the initial trusts were discretionary or conferred interests in possession on other beneficiaries.

HMRC has said that the effect of s 80 can be avoided by an election being made (see **4.60**) so that revertor to settlor provisions do not apply. Doing so, however may not be straightforward in certain situations such as where land or chattels are held by a non-resident company and the settlor is non-UK domiciled.

Parental gifts

[4.57] One of the more common scenarios that an adviser encounters is the situation where a parent either makes a gift of cash to their child which is used to buy a property in their joint names or makes a gift of property so the property is held jointly by them. There is a crucial distinction between them which is illustrated below.

Example

Cheryl has sold her house and has agreed to buy a house jointly with her daughter, Hollie. Hollie will live with her mother and they will pay all living expenses equally. The tax consequences are as follows.

If Cheryl bought the house in her sole name and then transferred a 50% interest to Hollie so they are joint tenants, there would be a gift of an undivided share of an interest in land. The gift is a PET. Because Cheryl receives no benefit other than a negligible one (she contributes equally to the household expenses) the gift with reservation rules do not apply (FA 1986, s 102B(4)). Nor will a POA charge arise because the disposal satisfies s 102B(4) (FA 2004, Sch 15, para 11(5)(c)).

If Cheryl made a gift of cash (£400,000) to Hollie which is used to buy a house for £800,000, the gift is a PET. Provided the gift was not conditional on Hollie using the money to buy the house there is no gift with reservation. Because it is a gift of money under FA 1986, Sch 20, para 2(2)(b) the tracing rules do not apply. Under FA 1986, Sch 20, para 6(1) one has to consider the associated operations rules under IHTA 1984, s 268. Read literally it is arguable that s 268 applies but many commentators do not consider that the associated operations rule can be used to re-characterise a gift as being of property rather than of cash. However, the comments in the HMRC Inheritance Tax Manual suggest that HMRC may seek to use the s 268 rules in certain circumstances (HMRC Inheritance Tax Manual, para 14372).

In relation to the POA charge, it would seem that under FA 2004, Sch 15, para 11(8) the property acquired with the cash is treated as being comprised in the original gift. Therefore, Cheryl has given Hollie an undivided share in land and so the exemption from the POA charge will apply (see HMRC Inheritance Tax Manual, para 44049).

Valuation

[4.58] Unless otherwise stated, the value of any property will be the price which the property might reasonably be expected to fetch if sold in the open market at that time. There is no assumption that the price be reduced on the grounds that the whole property is to be placed on the market at one and the same time (FA 2004, Sch 15, para 15).

As stated above the valuation is by reference to the first valuation date and this valuation is used for a period of five tax years. When a property has decreased in value over that time the question arises as to what the position is where a property is sold and the taxpayer moves to a smaller property.

Example

Marion gave £700,000 to her son, Martyn, in April 2008. Martyn used the money to purchase 24 Argyll Road. In April 2009 Marion moved to the property. On 6 April 2010 the house was worth £1m on which her income tax charge will be based for the following five tax years. In 2014 Martyn sold the house and bought a small apartment for £500,000 into which Marion moved.

HMRC considers that 'relevant land' is the land currently occupied by the chargeable person (HMRC Inheritance Tax Manual, para 44011). A new valuation should be made when the occupation of that property starts, and it is intended that the new valuation should then be used for the remainder of that 5-year cycle. Therefore, Marion should obtain a valuation of the apartment to reduce her POA charge.

Avoidance of multiple charges

[4.59] It is possible that in any year of assessment there is a POA charge on land or a chattel, and also a charge on intangible property which derives its value in whole or part from the same land or chattel. HMRC uses the example of an individual who has settled shares on a settlor interested trust and the company owns the property which he occupies. In such a situation two charges would arise, one in relation to the shares and one in relation to the land.

To avoid multiple charges on the same property FA 2004, Sch 15, para 18 provides that only the higher amount is chargeable and it is that amount which is taken into account for the *de minimis* provisions. FA 2004, Sch 15, para 19 provides that when a POA charge arises on the same occupation of land or use of any chattel under the pre-owned asset provisions and ITEPA 2003 Pt 3 (benefits from an employer) the income tax charge under ITEPA will take priority with only the excess being subject to a charge under FA 2004, Sch 15.

The Inheritance Tax (Double Charges Relief) Regulations 2005 (SI 2005/3441), gives relief in certain circumstances from a potential double inheritance tax charge which can arise where a taxpayer decides to rearrange his affairs so to avoid a POA charge.

Election to opt out

[4.60] Taxpayers who fall within the pre-owned assets provisions may elect to 'opt out' of the charge in relation to a particular asset. Where an election is made in respect of land or chattels, the property is treated for inheritance tax purposes as a gift with reservation which will continue to apply for so long as the taxpayer enjoys a benefit by occupying the relevant land or retaining possession of the chattel and will be subject to inheritance tax on death (FA 2004, Sch 15, para 21). FA 2004, Sch 15, para 22 gives a right of election in respect of intangible property.

The charge to inheritance tax will be incurred unless the occupation or use ceases permanently (and is not recommended) at least seven years before their death or (in the case of land or chattels) the chargeable person pays full consideration for use of the relevant property. HMRC accepts that where the person is already paying full consideration for use of the land or chattels before making an election and then elects there is no deemed PET at that point (HMRC Inheritance Tax Manual, para 44070). However, if the person ceases to pay full consideration in the seven years prior to death and is still in occupation of the property, the effect of the election is that they will be subject to an inheritance tax charge on their death.

Any election must be made in the prescribed manner (on form IHT 500) no later than the 31 January in the year of assessment immediately following the initial year (the 'relevant filing date') (FA 2004, Sch 15, para 23) or on such later date, as an officer of HMRC may, in a particular case, allow.

The current HMRC guidance states that where a taxpayer can show that an event beyond their control prevented them from sending the election by the relevant filing date, a late election will be accepted. In the HMRC Inheritance Tax Manual at para 44077 examples are given of what HMRC considers to be an event beyond the chargeable person's control which include an election lost or delayed in the post in certain circumstances and serious illness and bereavement. HMRC has stated that it will accept a late election:

'where the chargeable person can show that they were unaware – and could not reasonably have been aware – that they were liable to the POA charge and elected within a reasonable time of becoming so aware.'

Unfortunately 'reasonable time' is not defined. HMRC states that it will only accept a late election provided it is not a result of a chargeable person taking active steps to avoid both a POA charge and an inheritance tax charge under the reservation of benefit provisions or a chargeable person wishing to avoid committing to a POA charge or an election before 31 January in order to have longer to see which will be the most beneficial course of action.

HMRC states that where there has been a change in the law which results in a charge arising from transactions that did not previously give rise to a charge or where there has been a change in HMRC's Guidance which results in a charge arising from transactions that HMRC did not consider previously gave rise to a charge, a late election will be accepted where the chargeable person can show that he elected as soon as practicable after becoming aware of the change.

There is no right of appeal against the refusal to accept a late election.

In the case of a couple who are married or in a civil partnership who jointly own a property and who are both caught by the provisions of FA 2004, Sch 15, if they both wish to have the property treated as property subject to a reservation, they must both make an election. An election by one cannot affect the other.

An election may be amended or withdrawn, during the life of the chargeable person, at any time before the relevant filing date. Otherwise, an election, once made, cannot be revoked.

An election may be held by the holder of a general or enduring power of attorney. It is assumed that the holder of a registered lasting power of attorney is also able to make the election although the explanatory notes (IHT501) makes no reference to a lasting power of attorney.

There is no provision at present for the transferor to notify the transferee of an election, even though the transferee can be made liable for the inheritance tax due on the transferor's death.

The decision whether to opt out will depend upon a number of factors, including the life expectancy of an individual and the type of assets in the estate. An elderly taxpayer who expects the remaining period of his life to be short may decide to incur an income tax liability rather than have his estate incur a 40% inheritance tax charge.

For more detailed discussion in relation to the application of the POA charge on the family home, see CHAPTER 11 THE FAMILY HOME AND OTHER RESIDENTIAL PROPERTY.

Capital gains tax implications of a gift

[4.61] The capital gains tax implications of a gift must be considered. A gift of a chargeable asset is a disposal for capital gains tax purposes. Capital gains tax at a rate of between 10% and 28% (depending upon the nature of the asset and the amount of the donor's income and gains) will be payable on any gain arising on a disposal made by a UK resident (TCGA 1992, s 2). On a 'non-resident CGT disposal' (as defined by TCGA 1992, s 14B), being the disposal of a UK residential property interest by a non-resident (TCGA 1992, s 14D) the rate of capital gains tax is 18% or 28% (depending upon the amount of the gain).

Consideration deemed to be at market value

[4.62] In many situations the consideration for the acquisition or disposal of an asset will be deemed to be the market value of the asset at that time. This will apply where the disposal was otherwise than by way of a bargain made at arm's length (TCGA 1992, s 17) unless:

'(a)   there is no corresponding disposal of it; and
(b)   there is no consideration in money or money's worth or the consideration is of an amount or value lower than the market value of the asset.'

Where the parties are connected (for example, a parent and child and a settlor and the trust he has settled are connected for this purpose), the transaction is deemed not to be at arm's length and therefore to take place at market value (TCGA 1992, s 18).

The result is that most disposals within a family, to companies by controlling shareholders and of assets being settled on trusts will be disposals which are deemed to take place at market value. Charges to capital gains tax, therefore, can and often do arise where there are no actual sale proceeds.

Hold-over relief

[4.63] To modify the harshness of the deemed market value rule, there are two types of hold-over relief. Under TCGA 1992, s 165 and TCGA 1992, s 260, when making a gift it is possible for an election to be made to hold-over certain chargeable gains which would otherwise arise to the transferor. The transferee in effect acquires the gifted property at the transferor's acquisition cost, thus deferring the payment of tax until such time as the transferee disposes of the property in circumstances where it is either not possible to make, or the transferee chooses not to make, a further hold-over election. The general rule is that hold-over relief is not available on disposals to non-resident transferees (TCGA 1992, s 166 and TCGA 1992, s 261), unless the provisions of TCGA 1992, ss 167A and 261ZA apply, where there is a disposal after 5 April 2015 of a UK residential property interest.

Relief is also not available on disposals to settlor-interested settlements (or where arrangements subsist under which the settlor may acquire an interest in the settlement) (TCGA 1992, s 169B). Settlor-interested settlements include trusts for the benefit of a settlor's dependent children. A dependent child is defined as a minor who is unmarried or is not a partner in a civil partnership. There is a clawback period during which the held-over gain may be brought back into charge if the settlor later acquires an interest in the settlement or arrangements subsist under which the settlor will or may acquire such an interest. The clawback period begins immediately following the disposal and ends six years after the end of the year of assessment in which the disposal was made (TCGA 1992, s 169C). There are exceptions for heritage maintenance property and certain settlements for disabled persons (TCGA 1992, s 169D).

Gift of business assets

[4.64] TCGA 1992, s 165 applies to gifts by individuals of the following types of assets.

(a) An asset, or an interest in an asset, used for the purposes of a trade, profession or vocation carried on by:
 (i) the transferor; or
 (ii) his personal company (as defined in TCGA 1992, s 165(8)(a)); or
 (iii) a company which is a member of a trading group of companies (as defined in TCGA 1992, s 165A) of which the holding company is the transferor's personal company.
(b) Shares or securities of a trading company (as defined in TCGA 1992, s 165A) or of the holding company of a trading group where:
 (i) the shares or securities are not listed on a recognised stock exchange; or
 (ii) the trading company or holding company is the transferor's personal company.
 Hold-over relief will not apply to a transfer of shares or securities to a company.
(c) Agricultural property, or an interest in agricultural property, within the meaning of IHTA 1984, Pt V Ch II which is not used for the purposes of a trade carried on as mentioned in (a) above. The claim is not limited to the agricultural value of the asset and applies equally to such assets regardless of the rate of agricultural property relief applicable.

Gifts of UK residential property interests to non-residents

[4.65] As mentioned above the general rule is that hold-over relief under s 165 is not available on gifts made to non-residents. Where, however, a disposal of a UK residential property interest is made after 5 April 2015 to a transferee who is not resident in the UK, relief will be available under s165 (TCGA 1992, s 167A) provided certain conditions are satisfied; the result being that no chargeable gain arises at the time of the disposal. The full amount of the gain that would otherwise have been chargeable may be held-over, although the amount of the gain that would have been chargeable but for the relief is not in this case deducted from the transferee's base cost. Instead, on a subsequent disposal by the transferee the whole or corresponding part of the held-over gain is deemed to accrue at that time, in addition to any gain that actually accrues and is treated as an NRCGT gain chargeable to capital gains tax under TCGA 1992, s 14D. This charge is discussed in more detail in CHAPTER 11 THE FAMILY HOME AND OTHER RESIDENTIAL PROPERTY.

Gifts of assets attracting an inheritance tax charge

[4.66] TCGA 1992, s 260 applies to gifts by individuals and trustees to individuals and trustees which are either

(a) chargeable transfers within the meaning of IHTA 1984 (and transfers which would be chargeable transfers but for IHTA 1984, s 19 (the annual exemption)) and which are not potentially exempt transfers; or

(b) exempt transfers within IHTA 1984, s 24 (transfers to political parties), IHTA 1984, s 27 (transfers to maintenance funds for historic buildings) and IHTA 1984, s 30 (transfers of designated property);

(c) transfers of settled property to be held on maintenance funds;

(d) vesting of property held on A&M trusts by virtue of IHTA 1984, s 71(4);

(e) certain transfers of property on which no inheritance tax is charged by virtue of IHTA 1984, ss 71B(2), 71E(2); namely, a transfer from a TBM either to the bereaved minor on his 18th birthday, becoming absolutely entitled before then or on his death before his 18th birthday or a transfer from an 18–25 trust either to the relevant beneficiary before his 18th birthday or on his death before the age of 18;

(f) transfers of property leaving and entering maintenance funds for heritage property.

In the past, relief under TCGA 1992, s 260 was used mainly in respect of gifts to discretionary trusts, whether or not its value fell within the 'nil rate' band, and on gifts covered by the annual exemption. Since 22 March 2006 relief under s 260 is available for gifts to most types of trust except privileged interest trusts.

The rationale behind the existing statutory rules seems reasonably clear. Where the gift is a potentially exempt transfer and comprises readily realisable assets (eg stock exchange investments) capital gains tax is chargeable on the gift. In the case of most types of illiquid assets (eg land, unquoted shares) either hold-over relief will apply or the tax arising may be paid by equal instalments over ten years under TCGA 1992, s 281.

Where the gift is subject to inheritance tax or eats into the transferor's 'nil rate' band (which will affect subsequent chargeable transfers), the relief under TCGA 1992, s 260 will be available to avoid any double charge to tax. In cases where both reliefs might otherwise be applicable, TCGA 1992, s 260 relief takes priority over TCGA 1992, s 165 relief (TCGA 1992, s 165(3)(d)).

Gifts of UK residential property interests to non-residents

[**4.67**] As with section 165 hold-over relief on a disposal of a UK residential property interest made after 5 April 2015 to a transferee who is not resident in the UK, relief will be available under s 260 (TCGA 1992, s 261ZA) provided certain conditions are satisfied. On a subsequent disposal by the transferee, the whole or corresponding part of the held-over gain is deemed to accrue at that time, in addition to any gain that actually accrues and is treated as an NRCGT gain accruing on a non-resident CGT disposal.

Making an election

[**4.68**] A claim for hold-over relief under TCGA 1992, ss 165 or 260 must be made in the prescribed form (found at the end of Help Sheet HS295) by both the transferor and transferee (except where the transferee is a trustee). For gifts made in 2016/17, a claim must be made within four years. In principle it is necessary to agree the amount of the held-over gain. In practice, however, a computation of the gain and formal valuation is in many cases not required (Statement of Practice SP8/92). Both the transferor and transferee need to make the application, provide full details of the asset transferred and confirm that a gain would occur.

Both reliefs operate so that any chargeable gain which would otherwise arise on the gift (called the 'held-over gain') is reduced to zero whilst the transferee's acquisition cost of the donated property is reduced by a like amount so that in effect the transferee takes over the transferor's acquisition cost (TCGA 1992, s 165(4) and TCGA 1992, s 260(3)). The reliefs effectively defer any chargeable gain arising on the gift until the transferee sells the donated property or otherwise disposes of it in circumstances where it is not possible to make a further hold-over election.

Where the transferor acquired the asset on or before 31 March 1982, his acquisition cost for the purposes of calculating the held-over gain will be the asset's value on 31 March 1982 (TCGA 1992, s 35(2)) except in the circumstances specified in s 35(3), unless an election is made under s 35(5).

Where the disposal of an asset giving rise to a potential capital gains tax charge also gives rise to an inheritance tax charge (either immediately or as a result of the death of the transferor within seven years) and a claim for hold-over relief is made under either section, the inheritance tax paid may be deducted from the chargeable gain when calculating the capital gains tax due on a subsequent disposal of the asset by the transferee (TCGA 1992, s 165(10) and TCGA 1992, s 260(7)). Alternatively, IHTA 1984, s 165 allows the capital gains tax arising on the gift, provided it is paid by the transferee, to be deducted when calculating the value transferred for inheritance tax purposes. Special rules apply where there is a gift of a UK residential property interest to a non-resident.

Example

A transfers her shares in X Ltd to her son B who is 25 years of age and a higher rate taxpayer. The value of the shareholding is £750,000 but has a base cost of £125,000. A has already used her nil rate band. B sells the shares shortly after the gift. Less than a year after the gift A dies. Should A's executors claim hold-over relief allowing B to deduct the inheritance tax chargeable on the gift on his subsequent disposal of the shares or should the capital gains tax be borne on the gift so that it will be deductible in calculating the inheritance tax on the gift?

Claim for hold-over relief

	£	£
Inheritance tax on gift (£750,000 @ 40%)		300,000
Capital gains tax on subsequent disposal		
Proceeds	750,000	
Deduct: Base cost	125,000	
Deduct: inheritance tax	300,000	
	325,000	
	325,000 @ 20%	65,000
		£365,000
No claim for hold-over relief		
Proceeds	750,000	
Deduct: Base cost	125,000	
	625,000	
	625,000 @ 20%	125,000
Value of shares on gift	750,000	
Deduct: capital gains tax	125,000	
	625,000 @ 40%	250,000
		£375,000

It can be seen that it is marginally beneficial for the executors to claim hold-over relief rather than pay the capital gains tax.

Triggering the held-over gain

[4.69] As mentioned above, the gain will be held-over until the transferee disposes of the asset although, if the transferee in turn makes a gift of the asset, a further hold-over claim may be made. Where the individual transferee dies still owning the asset, the whole of the gain is extinguished by the tax-free uplift on death. Where a gain has been held-over into a trust which is or becomes an interest in possession, the held-over gain crystallises on the death of the life tenant (TCGA 1992, s 74(2)).

Where an election is made for hold-over relief under TCGA 1992, s 165 or TCGA 1992, s 260 (or has been made prior to 14 March 1989 under FA 1980, s 79), at a time when the transferee was UK resident, the held-over gain will come into charge if the transferee becomes non-UK resident within six years after the end of the year of assessment in which the relevant disposal took place and the asset has not been disposed of (TCGA 1992, 168(7), (8)). The tax liability is primarily that of the transferee. Where, however, the tax is still outstanding twelve months after the due date, HMRC can assess and charge the transferor (but in the name of, and at the rate and charge applicable to, the transferee).

To protect the transferor against any contingent liability, the following methods may be adopted:

(a)   the retention by him of an amount of the donated property equal to the held-over gain as bare trustee for the transferee for the 6-year period; and

(b)   the taking of indemnities from relatives of the transferee who are not likely to go abroad,

Both of these, however, may represent 'reserved benefits' thereby possibly tainting the gift for inheritance tax purposes.

Special rules apply where the asset is a UK residential property interest, the disposal of which would give rise to an NRCGT gain if the person making the disposal was not UK resident. An election can be made under TCGA 1992, s 168A, which has the effect that the held-over gain does not come into charge on emigration but is deemed to accrue on a subsequent disposal of the UK residential property interest.

Anti-avoidance provisions

Clawback on trust becoming settlor interested

[4.70] Hold-over relief may be clawed back under provisions in TCGA 1992, s 169C. If, during the clawback period, either of the following two conditions is met, then the relief is withdrawn and the capital gains tax which would have been payable but for the relief will be clawed back:

•   during the clawback period, the settlement becomes settlor-interested or an arrangement subsists under which a settlor will or may acquire an interest;

•   in computing the chargeable gain which would (assuming that the transfer had not been eligible for hold-over relief) accrue to the transferor on the disposal, the allowable expenditure would fall to be reduced as a consequence, either directly or indirectly, of a claim under TCGA 1992, s 165 or s 260 in respect of an earlier disposal made by an individual (whether or not to the transferor) and at any time during the clawback period the individual has an interest in the settlement or an arrangement subsists under which such interest will or may be acquired by him.

The clawback period is the period beginning immediately after the making of the relevant disposal and ending six years after the end of the year of assessment in which that disposal was made. Where the clawback provisions apply, a chargeable gain equal to the amount of the held-over gain on the relevant disposal is treated, for the purposes of tax in respect of chargeable gains, as accruing to the transferor at the time either of the two conditions above is fulfilled.

Example

A transfers her shares in X Ltd to her son B who is 25 years of age. The value of the shareholding is £750,000. The shares have a base cost of £125,000. A year later, the market value of the shares has risen to £850,000. B makes a gift of the shares into a settlement from which he and his wife are excluded from benefitting. Once again, an election is made to hold-over the gain. The trust contains a power for the trustees, at the behest of the settlor (B) to add beneficiaries to the settlement. The power cannot be exercised in favour of the settlor, his spouse or civil partner. Five years after making the transfer to the trustees, B enters an agreement with the trustees under which, should B die before his mother, A, the trustees will add A to the settlement as a life tenant of a portion of the trust fund.

A charge will not arise under TCGA 1992, s 169C by reason of the arrangement. B has not acquired an interest in the settlement. A has done so but, in the absence of any sort of arrangements between A and B as to the making of the settlement, she is not a settlor of the settlement.

There is an exemption from the clawback provisions in relation to a disposal to the trustees of a settlement which is a heritage maintenance settlement or is a settlement for disabled persons, provided certain criteria in TCGA 1992, s 169D are fulfilled.

Paying the tax by instalments

[4.71] Under TCGA 1992, s 281, the instalment option applies to the following assets:

(a)   land or an estate or interest in land;
(b)   shares or securities giving control of a company;
(c)   shares or securities not listed on a recognised stock exchange.

Interest on the unpaid tax will run from the due date and not from the date on which each instalment is due. This detracts from the attraction of the facility.

Capital gains tax considerations in making a gift

[4.72] Taking account of capital gains tax is an essential element of lifetime estate planning. Both the nature of assets to be given away and the identity of the transferee need to be carefully considered, as will the funding of any tax charge arising. The following points should be borne in mind when considering any planning strategy.

(1)   Where a gift is being made solely to save inheritance tax at 40%, an immediate charge to capital gains tax at a rate of between 10% and 28% depending on the nature of the assets and whether the transferor is a higher rate taxpayer, may be worth incurring for the potential inheritance tax saving. There is an obvious cash flow advantage in

deferring any tax charges for as long as possible (ie until death when there will also be the benefit of the capital gains tax free base uplift) although the risk in such a strategy is that the rates of inheritance tax may change for the worse or a less favourable form of taxation may come into force. Another relevant factor is the extent to which the current value of the asset reflects an accrued chargeable gain — the charge to capital gains tax is only on the amount of the gain whereas the charge to inheritance tax will be on the asset's full value, including any increase in the value of the asset as time goes on. Where an asset is expected to increase significantly in value, an immediate gift of it (even if subject to an immediate capital gains tax charge) will save inheritance tax both on its present value and on the 'growth' element.

(2)   Gifts of non-chargeable assets (eg cash, gilts, qualifying corporate bonds, life policies and chattels under £6,000 in value) will not give rise to a capital gains tax charge.

(3)   Chargeable assets showing the lowest gain should be identified and given away.

(4)   The capital gains tax arising on a gift may be reduced if the transferor also realises capital losses (eg by sales or by gifts to the same transferee) in the same tax year. Although one needs to consider the provisions of FA 2007, s 27 which disallow losses arising under arrangements, one of the main purposes of which is to obtain a tax advantage.

(5)   Where possible, advantage should be taken of the option to pay the capital gains tax by instalments.

(6)   Gifts of chargeable assets should be made by whichever spouse has an available annual exemption or available capital losses. To allow this to be done, it may be necessary for one spouse to first give the asset to the other. This is, of course, subject to a possible challenge under the provisions of FA 2007, s 27 which disallows losses arising under arrangements, one of the main purposes of which is to obtain a tax advantage. In addition, the application of the GAAR to such arrangements should also be considered.

(7)   Because moving assets around a family may create a capital gains tax charge, it is very important that chargeable assets are acquired by the right person (whether an individual or a family trust) at the outset.

Stamp duty and stamp duty land tax

[4.73] Stamp duty is not chargeable on an instrument giving effect to a gift of shares.

For the transfer of land by way of gift, no stamp duty land tax will be payable.

Advice should be sought where the transferee is assuming a liability, for example, a mortgage, as the assumption of any debt will constitute chargeable consideration (FA 2003, Sch 4, para 87) with the result that stamp duty or stamp duty land tax may be payable.

Which assets to give away?

[4.74] Given that there are a number of ways in which an individual may make immediate gifts without incurring an immediate charge to inheritance tax or capital gains tax, the next aspect to consider is whether in fact he has any assets which he can afford to give away. This can be a very difficult matter. On the one hand, the individual may be concerned about the amount of tax that will be payable on his death, or on the death of his wife, but on the other he may be very reluctant to jeopardise his or his wife's present and future standard of living and financial security. He should only be encouraged to give away those assets which are clearly surplus to his present and estimated future living requirements. In theory, the more wealthy a person is, the more surplus assets he will have. In practice, however, it is often the case that the more wealthy a person is, the more he will want to retain to cushion and secure his, usually high, standard of living. The inheritance tax 'gifts with reservation' provisions, as we have seen, can make it extremely difficult for a person to give away an asset whilst retaining the ability to get it back in times of hardship. In addition, the income tax charge levied on pre-owned assets will act as a deterrent. There are various insurance products which allow individuals to make large transfers out of their estates whilst retaining a right to 'income' during their lifetime. These products have been designed to avoid the reservation of benefit rules. For a more detailed consideration see CHAPTER 9 INSURANCE. It should be emphasised that most effective estate planning has to be conducted on the basis that once an asset is given away, it is gone for good. Whilst every case is different and must be judged on its own merit, the following are the types of assets which are usually the most suitable subjects of gifts.

Non- or low-income-producing assets

[4.75] Many people tend to live off their income (whether earned or unearned), regarding their capital primarily as a source of income and secondly as a reserve which can be called upon in times of hardship. Any assets which produce little or no income may be suitable for giving away, although it is important not to forget the psychological importance of the mere existence of the reserve.

Unfortunately, in many cases, the major non-income producing asset - indeed the major asset itself - will be the home and the gifts with reservation provisions have rendered ineffective most methods of giving away the entire home whilst retaining the ability to live there. There may be more scope for estate planning with regard to a second home, but again the possible implications of these provisions must be fully explored. These aspects are dealt with in greater detail in CHAPTER 11 THE FAMILY HOME AND OTHER RESIDENTIAL PROPERTY.

On the other hand, valuable paintings, books or similar chattels are clearly suitable candidates, provided that both ownership and (to avoid any reservation of benefit) possession are ceded. Woodlands, another non-income-producing asset, is a possible candidate.

Assets likely to grow in value or suffering a temporary reduction in value

[4.76] These types of assets, such as shares in private companies or let property, are obvious candidates because of the advantage in taking the future growth out of the transferor's estate.

In making gifts of assets which are pregnant with gain or in respect of which significant gains are anticipated, it is important to bear in mind that whilst the asset will on the transferor's death escape the charge to inheritance tax, the ability of the transferor's heirs to acquire, for capital gains tax purposes, the asset at its market value at the death of the transferor under TCGA 1992, s 62(1), thereby wiping out any chargeable gain then latent in the value of the asset, will be lost. This may be a significant factor if it is anticipated that the assets will one day be sold by the transferee.

Because the rates of capital gains tax are now between 10% and 28%, depending upon the type of assets disposed of and whether the transferor is a higher rate taxpayer, it may be attractive for an individual to make a gift of an asset and pay capital gains tax on any capital gain rather than to hold the asset until death when inheritance tax at 40% would be payable.

Where a transferor has property which is capable of qualifying for inheritance tax business property relief or agricultural property relief and that asset is both pregnant with gain and likely to be sold by the intended transferee it may, for tax purposes, be beneficial to allow the property to pass to the intended transferee on the transferor's death. This would allow advantage to be taken of the capital gains tax-free uplift to base cost. This would be preferable to removing the property from the transferor's estate only to permit the transferee then to suffer a capital gains tax charge on a gain arising on the sale. Obviously, much will depend on how much of the value of the asset reflects a potentially chargeable gain and the level of inheritance tax relief available.

The other factor which now has to be considered is whether, on the gift, any capital gain already latent in the value of the asset can be 'held-over' to the transferee. This will depend upon the nature of the asset and the type of gift – see **4.63**. In the case of shares in private companies, hold-over relief may be available; but in relation to other assets where the relief is not available, an immediate charge to capital gains tax may be a small price to pay to take the expected increase in value out of the transferor's estate.

Creating surplus assets to give away

[4.77] It is sometimes possible to create surplus assets where none appear to exist. For example, an investment portfolio worth £100,000 and yielding (say) 2%, could be split into two. One half is then invested in higher yielding fixed interest investments to produce (say) a 4% yield and the other half is then free to be given away. This releases assets for a gift whilst maintaining the current income. Two points should, however, be borne in mind. First, the re-investment may create a significant capital gains tax charge. Secondly, the investment in fixed interest securities is unlikely to have any potential for significant capital growth in the future.

Encouraging an individual to live off capital itself rather than the income produced by that capital is another way of creating a surplus. Consider, for example, an elderly person who expects to live for another ten years and who has an investment portfolio worth £1,000,000 which produces an annual income of £30,000. He could retain £500,000, giving away the balance of £500,000. The individual could then fund a part of his annual expenditure from capital.

Another method which is sometimes suggested for freeing assets, otherwise required to produce income, is for an individual to borrow (usually on the security of his home) in order to buy an annuity, the income of which is intended (after tax) to cover the mortgage payments and provide a suitable level of maintenance. However, the annuity rates are unlikely to be attractive (they are usually below the life office's normal rates) and the net return after the interest payments have been made is often poor. The loss caused if the individual dies prematurely can wipe out the benefit of any saving in inheritance tax as the individual is exposed to the risk of fluctuating property prices and interest rates.

The grant of a tenancy can be used to reduce the value of land to facilitate a gift of the land. The grant of any tenancy which confers statutory security of tenure on the tenant, or which confers a significant term of years on the tenant, will effect an immediate reduction in the value of the property over which the tenancy is granted. In the case of a rack rent agricultural tenancy this can be by a substantial amount. The grant may have inheritance tax, capital gains tax and income tax implications all of which will need to be considered. The main use in estate planning of the granting of a tenancy specifically to reduce value is to enable a subsequent transfer of the freehold reversion to be made to the tenant at a significantly lower value than if the unencumbered freehold had been transferred. Again, this technique is subject to the application of FA 1986, s 102A and the GAAR. It is also considered in more detail in CHAPTER 13 THE FAMILY FARM.

Cash gifts

[4.78] Gifts of cash and investments are both equally effective for inheritance tax purposes. There are, however, two points worth considering.

(1)   If an individual is contemplating giving his son a cash sum in order for him to buy, say, a car, it is often said that it is better for the individual to buy the car himself and then give it to his son. The second-hand value of the car is likely to be less than the amount of the cash gift. Clearly, this device will only work in relation to assets which depreciate on resale (unlike land) and, in practice, is only worth doing in respect of assets which are of substantial value and exempt from capital gains tax. Furthermore, the purchase and the gift are so clearly associated operations within IHTA 1984, s 268 that the transferor will be chargeable on the total loss to his estate resulting from the purchase and the gift if one is made in contemplation of the other.

(2)   Gifts of investments may give rise to a capital gains tax charge where these are chargeable assets which cannot be 'held over' under either TCGA 1992, s 165 or s 260.

The transferee

[4.79] An individual who has decided that he wants to give assets away and has identified those assets which are surplus to his requirements must also consider the recipient of the gift and the manner in which the gift should be made.

Where the individual is considering a gift to his children, and there are also grandchildren in existence, some thought should be given to skipping the first generation and passing the assets over to the second. This is a course which usually only commends itself to children who consider themselves already adequately provided for, but any property passed to the second generation may, if held in trust, be used to maintain the grandchildren and to meet the cost of their education in an income tax efficient manner (see below). Such an approach can thus indirectly benefit their parents as well.

A gift may be in the form of an outright gift to an individual or may be a gift into trust. Gifts to individuals or to disabled trusts are potentially exempt transfers. Whereas, gifts to discretionary trusts, accumulation and maintenance trusts, and most interest in possession trusts, are not potentially exempt transfers. Discretionary trusts are now most likely to be used as vehicles to receive regular gifts within the inheritance tax annual or 'normal expenditure out of income' exemptions or gifts within a person's nil rate tax band, particularly in view of their flexibility.

Each type of trust has its own uses and limitations and these are dealt with in more detail in CHAPTER 6 CREATING SETTLEMENTS.

It should be remembered that an outright gift to a trust for the benefit of a minor child of the transferor does not provide any income tax advantage. Any income arising on the property given away is taxed as part of the transferor's total income under ITTOIA 2005, s 629 whilst the child is a relevant child (that is, an unmarried minor child not in a civil partnership), subject to the £100 limit for small amounts of income. Gains arising to a trust under which the settlor's dependent children could benefit are not assessable on the settlor.

An individual pays capital gains tax at a rate between 10% and 28% depending upon the nature of the assets disposed of and whether he is a basic or higher rate taxpayer. The method of calculating whether or not an individual is a higher rate taxpayer is complicated. Gains must be added to income to determine whether the higher rate threshold has been met (£43,100 for 2016/17). If and to the extent that the gains fall below the individual's higher rate threshold, the rate is either 10% or 18% depending upon the nature of the asset disposed of. Gains above the threshold are subject to a rate of either 20% or 28%, depending upon the nature of the asset disposed of. For trustees, there is a flat rate of capital gains tax at either 20% or 28%, depending upon the nature of the asset disposed of.

Making a gift

[4.80] A gift of property may be effected in two ways, namely by the appropriate transfer of ownership or by a declaration of trust by the owner. A gift by way of declaration of trust will take effect on the date of the declaration. A gift by transfer of ownership will take effect on the date of the transfer. A gratuitous disposition of heritable subjects in Scotland takes place when it is delivered to the transferee and not when it is recorded in the Register of Sasines (*Marquess of Linlithgow v Revenue & Customs Commissioners* [2010] CSIH 19, [2010] STC 1563).

In the case of gifts to trustees there are further requirements; there must be an effective transfer of property on trusts that are certain and are administratively workable. In reality, there should be little difficulty in establishing that the trust property has been given in a manner complying with the appropriate legal formalities, and some of these rules are set out below. In practice, if difficulties are going to arise it is far more likely that this will be because the gift has not been perfected. As a general rule, if the transferor does not complete all the formalities associated with the gift, then it will fail (*Fry, Re, Chase National Executors and Trustees Corpn Ltd v Fry* [1946] Ch 312, [1946] 2 All ER 106); if the transferor (including his agents) has accomplished all that can reasonably be undertaken, but an independent third party delays the legal formalities, the gift is valid (*Rose, Re, Rose v IRC* [1952] Ch 499, [1952] 1 All ER 1217). (See also the decision in *Pennington v Waine* [2002] EWCA Civ 227, [2002] 4 All ER 215, [2002] 1 WLR 2075.)

Transfers of some types of property (eg registered stocks and shares, land, life assurance policies) can only be effected by an instrument of transfer.

A transfer of chattels can be effected by delivery. Where possession remains with the transferor, a gift of chattels should be effected by a bill of sale, duly attested and registered under the Bills of Sale Act 1878 if it is not to become void as against the transferor's trustee in bankruptcy and creditors. The registration process is not straightforward and it should be remembered that the register is a public document. For many clients, the lack of confidentiality if there are conditions attached to the gift is particularly off-putting.

Delivery is effected by change of possession. Where the chattel is in the possession of a third party, the transferor must indicate to the third party that he is to look to the transferee as the owner of the chattel. Where the chattel is already in the possession of the transferee, the transfer may be effected simply by words (oral or written) indicating an intention to transfer ownership (*Stoneham, Re, Stoneham v Stoneham* [1919] 1 Ch 149). Gifts of money in the form of bank notes or an irrevocable banker's draft are made by delivery. Gifts by way of cheque are not effective until the transferee's account is credited (*Owen, Re, Owen v IRC* [1949] 1 All ER 901, [1949] TR 189). This principle was applied in *Curnock (Personal Representative of Curnock (dec'd)) v IRC* [2003] STC (SCD) 283, (SpC 365)).

HMRC may challenge whether a gift has been made as it did in the case of *M Scott v HMRC* [2015] UKFTT 266 (TC).

Evidencing the gift

[4.81] It is important to retain evidence of a gift or to make clear whether the transaction is a gift or a loan. The case of *Silber (personal representative of the* *estate of Lerner, deceased) v Revenue & Customs Comrs* (TC 2369) [2012] UKFTT 700 (TC), [2013] SWTI 326 concerned whether a payment was a loan or a gift. HMRC successfully argued there was no evidence that the transaction had been a gift and indeed it was shown in the company accounts as an amount due to the deceased as a creditor. It is important that evidence is retained as to the nature of a payment and that accounts and similar documentation adequately reflect the nature of the transaction. It is primarily the responsibility of a personal representative to make an accurate return to HMRC under FA 2007, Sch 24, para 1 and so enquiries should be made to ascertain whether the deceased made any gifts within seven years of death. There is also an obligation on the recipient of the gift to report it (FA 2007, Sch 24, para 1A). Where the transferee has failed to inform the personal representative of any such gifts, that failure to report the gift will be considered by HMRC as deliberate behaviour. The minimum penalty in such circumstances is 50% of the tax undeclared and could be up to 100% of the undeclared tax. The penalty in such cases is payable by the transferee and not the personal representative. The approach of HMRC was upheld in the case of *CRC v Hutchings* [2015] UKFTT 9 (TC).

Setting aside of gifts

[4.82] Gifts can be made between living persons, in contemplation of death (*mortis causa*) or by will. Their validity is dependent on different sets of rules. When making a gift it is essential that care is taken to avoid a gift being set aside. A gift can be set aside for example under the Insolvency Act 1986 or under the Matrimonial Causes Act 1973 (MCA 1973), which are discussed below. In addition, a court can set aside a gift on the grounds that it was an unconscionable transaction following the decision in *Evans v Lloyd* [2013] EWHC 1725 (Ch), [2013] 2 P & CR D57, [2013] All ER (D) 264 (Jun). In that case the High Court refused to follow the case of *Langton v Langton* [1995] 3 FCR 521, [1995] 2 FLR 890 and held that the equitable doctrine of unconscionable transactions could apply to gifts because 'to exclude this from the doctrine would make its application turn on form over substance'.

Bankruptcy

[4.83] Any gift, transaction in consideration of marriage or civil partnership, or sale at an undervalue where the price paid is significantly less than the value of the assets sold in money or moneys' worth will amount to a transaction at an undervalue within the terms of the Insolvency Act 1986 (IA 1986). The court can set aside such transactions in the following situations:

(i)   Where an application leading to bankruptcy is made within two years. It is not necessary to prove that the transaction was intended to prejudice creditors or to establish the financial status of the donor at the time of the transaction (IA 1986, s 341).

(ii)   Where it pre-dates the making of the bankruptcy application as a result of which or (as the case may be) the presentation of the bankruptcy petition on which the individual is made bankrupt by more than two, but less than five years. The donor must either have been insolvent at the time that the transaction was undertaken or have become insolvent as a result of the transaction. For these purposes a donor is deemed to be insolvent if he cannot pay his debts as they fall due or if the value of his liabilities exceed the value of his assets after taking into account contingent and prospective liabilities. Where the transaction is with an associate of the donor, the burden of proof is on the donor (IA 1986, s 341(2)). The trustee of a family trust will be an associate of the donor where the trust beneficiaries include, or the terms of the trust confer a power that may be exercised for the benefit of, the donor or his associate (IA 1986, s 435(5)).

(iii)   Where it can be proved to the court's satisfaction that the transaction at an undervalue was undertaken by the donor in order to put his assets beyond the reach of his existing or future creditors or of otherwise prejudicing the interests of his existing or future creditors (IA 1986, s 423). In the case of *IRC v Hashmi* [2002] EWCA Civ 981, [2002] 2 BCLC 489, [2002] BCC 943 the issue arose as to whether it was necessary for an applicant under s 423(3) to show that the statutory purpose had been the dominant purpose behind the transaction, or whether it was sufficient that the statutory purpose was a substantial purpose. The Court of Appeal held that the statutory purpose did not have to be the sole or predominant purpose.

The result of the transactions being set aside is that they will be void *ab initio* – that is, they will be treated as not having taken place.

Divorce

[4.84]   On a divorce, a trust will not necessarily prevent a division of property between the parties (see also CHAPTER 17 RELATIONSHIP BREAKDOWN).

First, the court has jurisdiction under the MCA 1973, s 24 to make one or more property adjustment orders and can exercise its power as it thinks fit.

Second, it might be tempting for a spouse to give away family wealth so as to exclude the current spouse from benefiting on divorce. Under MCA 1973, s 37, a disposition may be set aside if it is made with the intention of preventing financial relief being granted to a party to the marriage or to that person for the benefit of a child of the family. Where an application is made to the court within three years of the settlement there is a rebuttable presumption that the settlement was made with the intention to defeat a claim for financial relief (MCA 1973, s 37(5), see *Whittingham v Whittingham* [1979] Fam 9, [1978] 3 All ER 805).

The court can also have regard to the availability of other trust funds, to be taken into account in dividing the family assets on divorce. In *Browne v Browne* (1988) Times, 25 November, the Court of Appeal held that assets held outside the jurisdiction on discretionary trusts in favour of one spouse were financial resources to be taken into account in considering the other spouse's application in matrimonial proceedings for financial relief. Where a spouse has an interest in a settlement, the court will ask what the beneficiary may reasonably expect to receive from the settlement: see *J v J (C intervening)*

[1989] Fam 29, [1989] 1 All ER 1121. The cases of *Thomas v Thomas* [1996] 2 FCR 544, [1995] 2 FLR 668, *Charman v Charman* [2007] EWCA Civ 503, 9 ITELR 913 and *Whaley v Whaley* [2011] EWCA Civ 617, 14 ITELR 1, [2011] 2 FCR 323 have reformed the court's approach in undertaking this exercise.

Order of gifts

[4.85] When making a number of gifts, care should be taken to ensure that they are made in the most tax efficient order. Where a number of gifts are to be made which are all potentially exempt transfers, the order is important if the transferor survives the gifts by three years but dies within seven years of them. Where the transferor survives the potentially exempt transfer by seven years, then the order is immaterial. It is also usually immaterial if the transferor dies within three years of the gifts because then they will all be chargeable at death rates. There is some merit in all the gifts being made on the same day so that the gifts will be treated as made in the order which results in the lowest chargeable value and any inheritance tax payable as a result of the gifts (whether immediately payable or payable as a result of the transferor's death within seven years) is charged on each gift on a pro-rata basis. This is the effect of IHTA 1984, s 266 and avoids the later gifts bearing the tax charge due to the earlier gifts using up the nil rate band and any exemptions.

Where, however, the proposed gifts include both a chargeable transfer (such as a transfer to a relevant property settlement) and potentially exempt transfers, the chargeable transfer should be made before the potentially exempt transfers and on a different day. This is because if the potentially exempt transfer becomes chargeable it will not be necessary to recalculate the tax on the chargeable transfer. In addition, currently any nil rate band would be used by the discretionary trust which would have an impact in reducing future rates of charge on the trust.

It is also important that, where tax is paid on a lifetime chargeable transfer, it is impossible to obtain a refund of any of the tax paid in the event of the recomputation of the tax on death producing a lower liability as a result of taper relief (IHTA 1984, s 7(5)). In the converse position, additional tax would be due. This means that the order of making gifts can be very important where potentially exempt transfers and chargeable transfers together exceed the transferor's nil rate band. The following example, ignoring annual exemptions, illustrates the point.

Example

Horace wished to make two gifts, one of £325,000 to his daughter, Rebecca and one of £340,000 to a discretionary trust for the benefit of his grandchildren.

The gift to Rebecca would be a potentially exempt transfer whereas the gift to the discretionary trust would be a lifetime chargeable transfer.

Horace made the gift to Rebecca on the day before he made the settlement. Horace died six years later and so taper relief was available.

The effect of the potentially exempt transfer being made first:

		Tax
		£
Day 1:	Gift to Rebecca of £325,000	Nil
Day 2:	Gift to the discretionary trustees of £340,000	
	The trustees pay the tax	
	(340,000 – 325,000) @ 40% × 50%	3,000

Further tax due on Horace's death:
No tax is due on the PET because it falls within the nil rate
band of £325,000

		Nil
Tax on chargeable transfer allowing for taper relief:		
340,000 @ 40% × 20%	27,200	
Deduct: Tax previously paid by the trustees	3,000	
		24,200
Total tax		£27,200

If, however, Horace had made the gift to the trustees before the gift to Rebecca the situation would have been different.

		£
Day 1:	Gift to the discretionary trustees	
	Trustees pay the tax	
	(340,000 – 325,000) @ 40% × 50%	3,000
Day 2:	Gift to Rebecca of £325,000	Nil

Further tax due on Horace's death:

Tax on chargeable transfer:		
(340,000 – 325,000) @ 40% × 20%	1,200	
Deduct: Tax paid	3,000	
		Nil
Tax paid on potentially exempt transfer:		
325,000 @ 40% × 20%		26,000
		£29,000

Who should pay the inheritance tax on lifetime gifts?

[**4.86**] It is always important for the transferor to decide whether he or the transferee should pay the inheritance tax on a gift.

With immediately chargeable lifetime transfers such as those made to non-privileged trusts the transferor is primarily liable to pay the tax (IHTA 1984, s 199). The gross value of the gift will therefore need to be calculated to reflect the loss to the transferor's estate which will include the inheritance tax liability arising by reason of the transfer. Alternatively the transferee, namely the trustees, could pay the tax from the value transferred, therefore avoiding the need to gross up.

For potentially exempt transfers, inheritance tax will only be due if the transferor fails to survive for the necessary seven-year period. If he fails to do so and tax becomes payable, there is no question of grossing-up as the transferor himself has no liability to pay the tax so that the provisions which allow the liabilities to be taken into account in determining the value of a transferor's estate immediately after the transfer do not apply (IHTA 1984, s 5(4)).

The tax liability on a potentially exempt transfer which becomes chargeable falls primarily on the transferee. If, however, the tax is not paid within 12 months after the end of the month in which the transferor died, the transferor's personal representatives also become liable (IHTA 1984, s 204(8)). To avoid any question as between the transferee and the transferor's personal representatives as to who should pay the tax, the matter should be settled at the outset. If the transferee is to pay the tax – and in many cases this is the preferable course especially if the interest-free instalment option is likely to be available - the transferee should enter into a binding commitment to do so. It is difficult to see that such a commitment could amount to a 'reserved benefit' for the transferor as it does no more than reflect where the primary statutory liability for the tax falls. HMRC is understood to take the same view. If, however, the transferor wishes the tax to be borne by his estate, then a specific provision to this effect should be put in his will. This would amount to a legacy in favour of the transferee for inheritance tax purposes, and if the will includes gifts of residue which in whole or in part qualify for exemption, then the legacy may have to be grossed-up when calculating the inheritance tax payable on the transferor's death (IHTA 1984, s 38).

There are two distinct advantages in ensuring that the burden of the tax falls on the transferee.

(1)   In the case of a chargeable transfer, there will be no 'grossing-up' (ie when calculating the inheritance tax payable no account will be taken of the tax itself in determining the reduction in the transferor's estate).

(2)   Where the donated property is land, shares or securities in a company which gave the deceased control of that company or certain non-controlling holdings of shares or securities there may, where applicable, be the option of paying any inheritance tax by ten equal annual interest-free instalments. The payment of the tax may then be funded by the transferor by his making further gifts to the transferee within his annual exemption or regular gifts within the 'normal expenditure out of income' exemption. In the case of the inheritance tax payable in respect of a potentially exempt transfer, the interest-free instalment option (if available) may depend on the transferee retaining the donated property until the death of the transferor or until his own death if he predeceases the transferor.

Term assurance

[4.87] Regardless of whether the inheritance tax is to be borne by the transferee or by the transferor's personal representatives, consideration should be given to term assurance being effected on the life of the transferor. The term should be for seven years but the policy should ideally have an option to extend the term to cater for any legislative changes. Where the liability to tax is to be borne by the transferee, the policy may be taken out either by the transferee, as he has an insurable interest in the life of the transferor, or by the transferor himself and then assigned to the transferee. Where the liability is to be borne by the transferor's personal representatives, the transferor should take out the policy and ensure that the policy proceeds do not form part of his estate on death by holding the policy on separate trusts, either similar in terms to those in his will concerning his residuary estate or (where appropriate) wide discretionary trusts for the benefit of his family. The premiums on the policy may continue to be paid by the transferor and if met out of income may be exempt from inheritance tax within the 'normal expenditure out of income' exemption. Otherwise, the premiums may be covered by the annual exemption. In the case of a policy taken out by or for the transferee, decreasing term assurance may be appropriate as the tax charge decreases as time elapses. In the case of a policy taken out by the transferor, however, decreasing term assurance may well be inappropriate since although the tax payable on the potentially exempt transfer will decrease, the amount of the potentially exempt transfer will be aggregated with the transferor's estate on death and may therefore operate to increase the overall rate at which his estate is taxed. Indeed, it may be worth considering additional insurance cover to meet this potential increased liability.

Who should pay the capital gains tax?

[4.88] If the gift gives rise to a chargeable gain which cannot be held-over, then the primary liability for the tax falls on the transferor. However, under TCGA 1992, s 282, if the tax is not paid by the transferor within 12 months from the date when it becomes payable, the transferee may be assessed and charged (in the name of the transferor) to the tax.

The advantage of the transferee bearing the burden of the tax is that if the gift is, or becomes (by reason of the death of the transferor), a chargeable transfer for inheritance tax purposes, the amount of capital gains tax borne by the transferee is treated as reducing the value transferred by the chargeable transfer (IHTA 1984, s 165).

It is possible that any agreement between the transferor and the transferee that the transferee should be responsible for the capital gains tax might amount to a 'gift with reservation' for inheritance tax purposes. However, even if this were to be the case, the reservation of benefit should cease on the tax being paid by the transferee, with the result that a second potentially exempt transfer would be made by the transferor at that time (FA 1986, s 102(4)).

The option of paying capital gains tax by instalments conferred in certain circumstances by TCGA 1992, s 281 applies whether the tax is paid by the transferor or the transferee.

Chapter 5

Introduction to Trusts

Introduction

[5.1] In spite of the substantial changes to the taxation of trusts in 2006, trusts are still commonly created as an integral part of estate planning strategies. The aim of this chapter is to outline some of the key concepts involved and highlight potential problem areas. In addition, at the end of the chapter there is a more detailed examination of three areas: powers of maintenance, powers of advancement and protective trusts.

What is a trust?

[5.2] Probably one of the most useful definitions was provided by Sir Arthur Underhill and approved in *Re Marshall's Will Trusts* [1945] Ch 217 at 219, [1945] 1 All ER 550, who described a trust as:

> 'An equitable obligation binding a person (who is called a trustee) to deal with property over which he has control (which is called trust property) for the benefit of persons (who are called beneficiaries or *cestuis que trust*) of whom he may himself be one and any one of whom may enforce the obligation.'

This definition highlights three important areas: first, the duties imposed on trustees are equitable in nature. Secondly, the trustees' ownership of the property does not in itself allow them to benefit from it; they hold it for the benefit of the beneficiaries who own the equitable interest in the property subject to the terms of the trust. The trustees own the legal interest. Thirdly, the equitable rules binding the trustees can be enforced in the courts, primarily by the beneficiaries themselves.

Settlors

[5.3] As a general rule, if a person can give property away, he has sufficient legal capacity to settle the property. If a settlor subsequently becomes incapacitated, that does not invalidate any prior settlement he may have made. The settlor must understand the nature of his actions in settling the property. In *Bhatt v Bhatt* [2009] EWHC 734 (Ch), [2009] STC 1540 the court granted rescission of a trust deed entered into on the basis of a fundamental misunderstanding of its effects.

A settlor can establish a trust under which he is the principal beneficiary whilst also being the sole trustee. Legally he is regarded as acting in a number of different capacities. However, if the demarcation lines are not observed, the court may determine that no settlement was created.

Trustees

[5.4] Trustees are a continuing body of persons who hold the trust property in a fiduciary capacity on behalf of beneficiaries. Any person can be a trustee provided he or she possesses sufficient legal capacity. There is no requirement for trustees to be individuals and therefore companies can also act as trustees.

Legally, there are few restrictions on the number of persons who may be trustees, although, in practice, there should always be at least two. This is because there has to be a minimum of two trustees to give a valid receipt for capital received on the sale of land, unless the trustee is a trust corporation. It is rarely sensible for there to be more than four trustees. This is because trustees must act unanimously and if there are too many trustees it may be difficult to achieve unanimity and administratively difficult to obtain the necessary signatures on documents. Four is the conventional maximum because there cannot be more than four trustees holding a legal estate in land (Trustee Act 1925, s 34(2)).

Beneficiaries

[5.5] A beneficiary does not have to be legally competent to benefit under a trust. However, a lack of legal capacity may have other ramifications. For example, where a beneficiary has a deputy appointed by the Court of Protection because he cannot manage his affairs, it does not mean that the trustees cannot exercise their discretion in his favour. It means that they cannot give him the money or property direct, as he is unable to give a valid receipt. Accordingly, the trustees would have to transfer the trust property to his deputy, appointed by the Court, who could then apply the property received for his benefit.

Creating a trust

[5.6] In order for a valid trust to be created there must be an effective transfer of property by means of a complete gift on trusts, which are certain and not illegal. It is essential not only that the correct legal procedures are observed but that the donor completes the gift so that the gift is effective. Where the donor is entirely responsible for the delay, the gift will fail. However, as a general rule, if the donor has done all that he can in order to complete the gift but the delay is as a result of the inaction of a third party, the gift will be valid following *Re Rose, Rose v IRC* [1952] Ch 499, [1952] 1 All ER 1217, *T Choithram International SA v Pagarani* [2001] 2 All ER 492, 3 ITELR 254 and *Pennington v Waine sub nom Pennington v Crampton* [2002] EWCA Civ 227, [2002] 4 All ER 215, [2002] 1 WLR 2075.

Whilst no particular form of wording is required to establish a trust, its terms must be certain. In *Knight v Knight* (1840) 3 Beav 148, Lord Longdale identified three certainties that had to be present before a valid trust could exist namely, certainty of intention, of subject matter and of the persons or objects intended to benefit under the terms of the deed.

No illegality

[5.7] Over the centuries, case law has evolved indicating that in certain circumstances trusts may be held to be invalid where the object of the trust is clearly illegal, or where recognising their full effect would not be in the public interest.

Perpetuities

[5.8] Under English law, property must vest in a beneficiary within the perpetuity period otherwise the trust is void. At common law, property must vest within a life or lives in being plus 21 years and a possible period of gestation thereafter for instruments taking effect after 15 July 1964. The Perpetuities and Accumulations Act 1964 (the 'Old Regime'), applies to such instruments. For instruments taking effect after 5 April 2010, the Perpetuities and Accumulations Act 2009 (the 'New Regime') will apply. A will executed prior to 6 April 2010 is subject to the Old Regime, even where the testator's death occurs after 5 April 2010. Under the Old Regime the maximum duration of a trust established after 1964 could be the period of the lifetimes of one or more persons living when the trust was created plus 21 years (the 'Common Law Period') or a fixed period of up to 80 years. The fixed period only applied if specified in the trust. Where an existing will or trust has a Common Law Period and the trustees believe that it is 'difficult or not reasonably practicable for them to ascertain whether the perpetuity period has ended' they may, by deed, irrevocably elect for a perpetuity period of 100 years to apply (Perpetuities and Accumulations Act 2009, s 12). The perpetuity period can also be extended by an application under the Variation of Trusts Act 1958. In *Allfrey v Allfrey* [2015] EWHC 1717 (Ch), [2015] WTLR 1117, [2015] 2 P & CR D43 the perpetuity period of a trust created before the 2009 Act was extended to 125 years. In that case HMRC was not a party to the proceedings but had agreed that if the court approved the proposed arrangements it would not argue that the variation was a resettlement with the result that no capital gain tax disposal would arise.

Lifetime trusts made after 5 April 2010 will be subject to the New Regime. Will Trusts will only be subject to the New Regime if the will was executed after 5 April 2010. Under the New Regime the perpetuity period of trusts is 125 years. This period applies irrespective of any period specified in the trust deed (Perpetuities and Accumulations Act 2009, s 5(1)).

Charitable trusts have no perpetuity period limitations.

Accumulations

[5.9] The rule on accumulations of income was introduced to avoid the excessive build-up of wealth in trusts. For settlements created before 6 April 2010 the Perpetuities and Accumulations Act 1964 and Law of Property Act 1925 provided that the permitted accumulation periods were as follows:

(i)   The life of the settlor in relation to lifetime settlements where no other period is specified;

(ii)   21 years from the date of death of the settlor or the testator (in the case of will trusts this period will apply where no other period is specified);

(iii)   The minority or minorities of any person benefiting under the terms of the trust who was alive at the time the trust is made;

(iv)   The minority or minorities of any person who would for the time being, if of full age, be entitled to the income directed to be accumulated;

(v)   21 years from the date of making the disposition;

(vi)   The minority or minorities of the persons living or *en ventre sa mere* at the death of the settlor.

Where there was a direction to accumulate for a period in excess of the statutory periods specified above, the entire gift was void if that period was also longer than the perpetuity period. However, where the accumulation period does not exceed the perpetuity period, the direction to accumulate was only invalid as to the excess over the statutory period.

For settlements created after 5 April 2010, the restrictions listed above do not apply. They have been removed by the Perpetuities and Accumulations Act 2009. For settlements created after 5 April 2010 the trustees may retain income within the trust without having to distribute it to the beneficiaries for the entire lifetime of the trust. Trustees of charitable trusts may accumulate income for a period of 21 years only or during the life of the settlor or one of the settlors (Perpetuities and Accumulations Act 2009, s 14).

Bankruptcy

[5.10] A court can set aside transactions made at an undervalue (including gifts to a settlement) within certain time limits of a bankruptcy. The result of which is that the transaction will be void *ab initio*; that is, it will be treated as not having taken place. This is discussed in more detail in Chapter 4 Lifetime Planning: Making Gifts.

Divorce

[5.11] On a divorce, a trust will not, by itself, avoid a division of property between the parties. That is because the Matrimonial Causes Act 1973, s 24 gives a court the power to make property adjustment orders. In addition, a court may take into account the availability of trust funds. This is discussed in more detail in Chapter 17 Relationship Breakdown.

Inheritance laws

[5.12] Unlike most civil law jurisdictions, English law does not impose forced heirship or reserved property rights. For example, a Frenchman is required under the Code Napoleon to leave a very substantial portion of his estate to his surviving lineal descendants where he is survived by his issue.

By way of contrast, under English common law a testator's spouse and children have no legal right to inherit a fixed proportion of his estate. However, when a person dies domiciled in England and Wales, the Inheritance (Provision for Family and Dependants) Act 1975 provides that the court has power after death to make provision out of the deceased's net estate for certain defined persons.

A claim can be made irrespective of whether the deceased left a will or died intestate.

Applications under the Act must be made within six months of the date on which a grant of probate or letters of administration of the deceased's estate were first taken out. The court has an unfettered discretion to extend this time limit in appropriate cases (I(PFD)A 1975, s 10). Where gifts predate the date of death by at least six years, they fall outside the ambit of the court's review. It would be unwise to rely on this, however, as it is at least arguable that such a transfer could be challenged.

Trustees' powers and duties

[5.13] A considerable body of case law has evolved over the years clarifying trustees' powers and duties. In addition, relevant legislation including the Trustee Act 1925, Trustee Investments Act 1961, the Trusts of Land and Appointment of Trustees Act 1996, the Trustee Act 2000 and the Trusts (Capital and Income) Act 2013 has to be considered. These powers and duties are discussed in outline in this chapter. Where lay trustees are involved, the court judges the actions of the trustees by reference to the standard of behaviour that would be expected of an ordinary and sensible businessman. However, a higher standard of care and skill is expected of professional trustees.

When accepting the position of trustee, there are three key areas which require immediate action. First, the trustee should ensure that he understands the trusts involved. In the event of any ambiguity the trustee is under an obligation to clarify matters as soon as possible. It is also essential for the trustee physically to examine the trust instrument. This may reveal, for example, a notice of assignment by a beneficiary of a beneficial interest. If the trustee was unaware of this he might distribute trust property to the wrong claimant.

Secondly, all property should be placed in the joint names of the trustees or in proper custodial care. Where a new trustee is appointed to a continuing trust, or where he replaces an existing trustee, certain categories of trust property will automatically vest in the trustees as a result of Trustee Act 1925, s 40 where the appointments are by deed and the relevant declaration is made. The category of assets where automatic vesting occurs is restricted but includes freehold land and bank accounts. It does not extend, for example, to land conveyed by way of mortgage for securing money subject to the trust, certain leases of land, life assurance policies or stocks and shares.

Thirdly, where the trustee appointed succeeds another he may, in the absence of unduly suspicious circumstances, safely assume that the previous trustees have acted properly in discharging their duties. However, where there are suspicious circumstances suggesting earlier previous breaches of trust, he is under a duty to investigate these matters.

Trust law distinguishes between:

(a) *Trust duties.* These are obligatory, in that there is a direct legal requirement for the trustees to exercise them. This obligation arises from the intention of the settlor, and the courts will enforce the exercise of these duties if the trustees do not exercise them.

(b) *Trust powers.* These impose an obligation on the trustees to consider whether the power should be exercised, but they are under no obligation to exercise it. The trustees need only consider exercising the power where it would be appropriate to do so.

There is also a class of intermediate powers which are somewhere betwixt and between these two categories.

In the case of a trust duty, the trustees have to make a decision within a reasonable length of time. However, in the case of a trust power the trustees simply have to consider periodically whether or not to exercise the power, and, if they think it is proper, to exercise it within a reasonable period of time.

The length of time the trustees can delay in taking a decision is unclear. In the case of a trust power, they will lose the ability to exercise it after a reasonable period of time unless there are special circumstances. By way of contrast, a trust duty continues to be exercisable albeit only in favour of those beneficiaries who would have been eligible to benefit had the power been exercised promptly. Where the trustees fail to execute a trust duty, the court itself will, if necessary, exercise it or procure its execution. In a case of a trust power the court is extremely reluctant to interfere unless it is clear that the trustees are acting improperly, or simply not addressing their minds to the issue at all.

Investment of trust funds

[5.14] Trustees are under a duty to invest trust funds, maintaining an even balance between beneficiaries where they have differing interests in relation to income and capital. Lord Lindley, Master of the Rolls, stated in *Whiteley (Re)* [1886] 33 ChD 347 that the duty of care expected of a trustee is:

> 'to take such care as an ordinary prudent man would take if he were minded to make an investment for the benefit of other people for whom he felt morally bound to provide.'

A leading case on trustees' investment duties is *Cowan v Scargill* [1985] Ch 270, [1984] 2 All ER 750. The Vice-Chancellor Sir Robert Megarry's comments summarise the position of trustees as regards investment duties in general:

'[The] trustees [have] to exercise their powers in the best interests of the present and future beneficiaries of the trust, holding the scales impartially between different classes of beneficiaries . . . When the purpose of the trust is to provide financial benefits for the beneficiaries, as is usually the case, the best interests of the beneficiaries are normally their best financial interests. In the case of a power of investment . . . the power must be exercised so as to yield the best return for the beneficiaries, judged in relation to the risks of the investment in question; and the prospects of the yield of income and capital appreciation both have to be considered in judging the return from investment . . . .'

Older case law continues to give valuable guidance on the application of general principles to various situations.

The trustees may only invest trust funds in investments authorised by the trust instrument or permitted by legislation.

The powers of trustees of land are governed by the Trusts of Land and Appointment of Trustees Act 1996 (TLATA). 'Trusts of land' are trusts that include land whether or not there are also other assets subject to the trust (TLATA, s 1(1)(a)). Trustees of land have all the powers of an absolute owner and are given an express power to purchase land for investment (TLATA, s 6). The trustees must exercise these powers according to the statutory duty of care under the Trustee Act 2000 (see below).

With regard to other investments, trustees have a 'general power' of investment. This general power permits a trustee to make any kind of investment he could make if he were absolutely entitled to the assets of the trust (Trustee Act 2000, s 3(1)). This general power does not, however, permit a trustee to make an investment in land other than in loans secured on land (Trustee Act 2000, s 3(3)). However, a specific power is given by the Trustee Act 2000, s 8 in relation to land.

In exercising any power of investment, a trustee must have regard to the standard investment criteria which are:

(a)   the suitability to the trust of investments of the same kind as any particular investment proposed to be made or retained and of that particular investment as an investment of that kind; and

(b)   the need for diversification of investments of the trust in so far as is appropriate to the circumstances of the trust (Trustee Act 2000, s 4).

The only exception to applying the standard investment criteria is in relation to social investments made by charity trustees after 30 July 2016. The trustee is also required to review the investments of the trust from time to time and consider whether, having regard to the standard investment criteria, they should be varied (Trustee Act 2000, s 4(2)).

The general power of investment is in addition to powers otherwise conferred on trustees but is subject to any restriction or exclusion imposed by the trust deed.

'Suitability' includes consideration as to the size and risk of the investment and the need to produce an appropriate balance between income and capital growth to meet the needs of the trust. It also includes any relevant ethical considerations as to the kind of investment which it is appropriate for the trust to make.

Before exercising any power of investment, a trustee must obtain and consider proper advice about the way in which, having regard to the standard investment criteria, the power should be exercised. However, a trustee need not obtain such advice if he reasonably concludes that in all the circumstances it is unnecessary or inappropriate to do so (Trustee Act 2000, s 5(1), (3)). The only exception to applying the standard investment criteria is in relation to social investments made by charity trustees after 30 July 2016.

The Trustee Act 2000, s 8 details the specific powers of trustees in relation to land. A trustee may acquire freehold or leasehold land in the UK for investment, for occupation by a beneficiary or for any other reason. This power is subject to any restriction or exclusion imposed by the trust deed. These provisions apply to all trustees and not just to trustees of land. However, the provisions do not apply to a trust which consists of, or includes, settled land.

The provisions of the Trustee Act 2000 apply to a trust whether or not it was created before, or on or after, 1 February 2001. It has been suggested that it is uncertain whether the Act applies to trusts which are not in writing (such as constructive or resulting trusts). The better view appears to be that it does. Rather surprisingly, the Act does not widen the definition of investment derived from case law. Many assets popularly regarded as investments, such as life insurance policies and financial futures contracts are not investments within this definition.

Accounts

[5.15] Trustees are under a duty to maintain accounts, and produce them to the beneficiaries on request. Whilst the trustees are not obliged to provide beneficiaries with free copies of the accounts, this has become normal practice. Beneficiaries with interests in the capital of the trust are entitled to see capital accounts, whereas income beneficiaries may see full accounts.

Under Trustee Act 1925, s 22, trustees may arrange for their accounts to be audited once every three years, unless good cause exists to increase the regularity. The audit fees will be payable by the trust. It is unusual for trust deeds to require trusts to be audited. Audit investigations can be instigated by either trustees or beneficiaries, by agreement or by the Public Trustee.

Distributing trust assets

[5.16] Trustees are under a positive duty to distribute trust assets to the correct beneficiaries. Where there is an overpayment of income or capital or payments are payable in instalments, adjustments can usually be made to later payments. The trustees can recover trust property where the payment is made to the wrong person, due to a mistake arising from an issue of fact rather than one of law. An aggrieved beneficiary, as well as having recourse against the trustees, can seek to trace the property given to the wrong person by the beneficiaries. This right extends to the proceeds of sale of the property concerned. However, it does not extend to the property itself where a *bona fide* purchaser for value has acquired it, without notice of the breach of trust.

Where trustees have acted honestly and responsibly, they may claim relief against liability for breach of trust in distributing property incorrectly under Trustee Act 1925, s 61. In any event it is good practice for the trustees to seek an indemnity from beneficiaries upon the trustees presenting their final accounts on termination of a trust. However, the trustees do not have an absolute right to such an indemnity or other discharge.

Duty not to profit

[5.17] Owing to the strict fiduciary nature of trusteeship, there is no entitlement to fees or remuneration other than those authorised in the trust deed itself, by a court or by statute. Trustees must not place themselves in a position of conflict as regards their fiduciary duties. They cannot purchase trust property, or derive any benefit from it, unless expressly permitted to do so by the trust instrument.

The Trustee Act 2000, s 29(1) provides that, where no express provision as to trustee remuneration is made in the trust deed, a trustee which is a trust corporation is entitled to reasonable remuneration out of the trust fund except that this does not apply to trustees of charitable trusts. Section 29(2) provides that professional trustees not being a sole trustee (or a trust corporation) may also receive reasonable remuneration in the absence of express provisions in the trust deed, if the other trustees each agree in writing. Again, this does not apply to trustees of charitable trusts. Section 31(1) provides that a trustee is entitled to be reimbursed out of the trust fund for any expenses properly incurred by him when acting on behalf of the trust.

Trustees' decisions

[5.18] Trustees can only exercise powers which are available to them either under the terms of the general law including any statutory provisions, or under the express wording of the trust deed itself. Even where sufficient powers do exist, an effective decision will only be made where the trustees have directed their minds to the issues. Trustees have to consider all the circumstances of the case, and especially the legal consequences of any proposed course of action.

Trustees' decisions must be unanimous unless the trust deed directs otherwise.

There are wider obligations placed upon trustees of land to consult beneficiaries and give effect to their wishes so far as is consistent with the general interest of the trust (Trusts of Land and Appointment of Trustees Act 1996, s 11).

Trustees must make their own decisions, unless they are authorised to delegate them. A failure to make their own decisions will result in a purported disposition of trust property being a nullity (see, for example, *Turner v Turner* [1984] Ch 100, [1983] 2 All ER 745).

Delegation

General

[5.19] The general principle that trustees should exercise judgement and perform their duties personally has been substantially changed by case law and statute. Trustees have very wide powers to delegate and appoint agents, nominees and custodians. An individual trustee can in the absence of a contrary intention expressed in the trust deed or a contrary rule of law or equity delegate the exercise of all trusts, powers and discretions vested in them as trustee for a period of up to one year (Trustee Act 1925, s 25).

Delegation to a Beneficiary

[5.20] The Trusts of Land and Appointment of Trustees Act 1996, s 9 allows trustees of a trust of land to delegate 'any of their functions as trustees which relate to the land' to a beneficiary of full age who is entitled to an interest in possession in land.

Delegation to an Agent

[5.21] The Trustee Act 2000, s 11 provides that trustees may authorise any person to exercise any or all of their delegable functions as their agent. A distinction is made between charitable and non-charitable trusts. This chapter will deal only with non-charitable trusts.

The trustees' delegable functions consist of any function other than

(a) any function relating to whether or in what way any assets of the trust should be distributed;
(b) any power to decide whether any fees or other payment due to be made out of the trust funds should be made out of income or capital;
(c) any power to appoint a person to be a trustee of the trust; or
(d) any power conferred by any other enactment or the trust instrument which permits the trustees to delegate any of their functions or to appoint a person to act as a nominee or custodian.

The persons whom the trustees may authorise to exercise functions as their agent include one or more of their number, and a person who is also appointed to act as their nominee or custodian (Trustee Act 2000, s 12). A beneficiary cannot be authorised by the trustees to exercise any function as their agent, even if the beneficiary is also a trustee (Trustee Act 2000, s 12(3)). In addition, two or more persons can only be authorised to exercise the same function if they are to exercise the function jointly.

The statutory duty of care is limited to trustees only. It does not apply to an agent in the performance of his agency, although he will owe a separate duty of care to the trust under the general law of agency. Where a person is authorised under these provisions to exercise a function, whatever the terms of the agency, he is subject to any specific duties or restrictions attached to the function. A person who is authorised to exercise a power subject to a requirement to obtain advice is not subject to that requirement if he is the kind of person from whom it would have been proper for the trustees, in compliance with the requirement, to obtain advice, for example, a reputable independent financial adviser.

Where the trustees have a duty to consult beneficiaries and to give effect to their wishes, the trustees may not authorise a person to exercise any of their functions on terms that prevent them from complying with that duty. The duty is not delegable.

The trustees are able to authorise a person as their agent on such terms as to remuneration and other matters as they may determine (Trustee Act 2000, s 14). The trustees may not authorise a person to exercise functions as their agent on the following terms unless it is reasonably necessary for them to do so:

(i)   A term permitting the agent to appoint a substitute;
(ii)   A term restricting the liability of the agent or his substitute to the trustees or any beneficiary;
(iii)   A term permitting the agent to act in circumstances capable of giving rise to a conflict of interest.

Where asset management functions are delegated by the trustees, a person may not be authorised by the trustees to exercise any of their asset management functions as their agent except by an agreement which is in writing or evidenced in writing (Trustee Act 2000, s 15). In addition, the trustees must first prepare a policy statement which gives guidance as to how the functions should be exercised in the best interests of the trust. This must be in, or evidenced in, writing. The agreement under which the agent is to act must include a term to the effect that the agent will secure compliance with the policy statement or, if the policy statement is revised or replaced, the revised or replacement policy statement.

The restriction that certain functions cannot be delegated and the restrictions relating to the delegation to beneficiaries only apply to the statutory power of delegation. These restrictions do not apply if the trust confers its own power of delegation (as is the case in the STEP standard form). It is reasonably clear that the same applies to the restriction relating to joint delegation and the matters which can only be delegated if reasonably necessary. It is arguable that the same applies in relation to the restrictions on asset management functions made by the Trustee Act 2000, s 15.

Delegation to a nominee or custodian

[5.22] Under the Trustee Act 2000, s 16, trustees may appoint a person to act as their nominee in relation to such of the assets of the trust as they determine (other than settled land), and may take the necessary steps to secure that those assets are vested in a person so appointed. Similarly, trustees may appoint a person to act as a custodian in relation to certain assets of the trust (Trustee Act 2000, s 17). In both cases, the appointment must be in writing or evidenced in writing. These provisions do not apply to any trust having a custodian trustee.

The appointment of a nominee or custodian is subject to certain restrictions. Section 19 provides that a person may not be appointed as a nominee or custodian unless one of the following conditions is satisfied.

(1)   The person carries on a business which consists of or includes acting as a nominee or custodian.

(2)   The person is a body corporate which is controlled by the trustees.

(3)   The person is a body corporate recognised under s 9 of the Administration of Justice Act 1985.

The trustees may appoint one of their number as a nominee or custodian, if a trust corporation, or two or more of their number, if they are to act as joint nominees or joint custodians. The person appointed as nominee or custodian may also be appointed as custodian or nominee, as the case may be, or be authorised to exercise functions as the trustees' agent.

Generally, the trustees may determine the terms on which a person is appointed to act as a nominee or custodian as they so wish. They may not, however, appoint a person to act as a nominee or custodian on any of the following terms unless it is reasonably necessary for them to do so:

(i)   A term permitting the nominee or custodian to appoint a substitute;

(ii)   A term restricting the liability of the nominee or custodian or his substitute to the trustees or any beneficiary;

(iii)   A term permitting the nominee or custodian to act in circumstances capable of giving rise to a conflict of interest (Trustee Act 2000, s 20).

The Trustee Act 2000 again imposes restrictions on the statutory powers contained in ss 16–20. These can, however, be overridden by suitable wording contained in the trust deed.

There are statutory provisions relating to the review of, and liability for, agents, nominees and custodians. These apply whether they were authorised or appointed under the Trustee Act, or under the trust instrument or by any enactment or any provision of subordinate legislation.

Whilst the agent, nominee or custodian continues to act for the trust:

(a)   the trustees must keep under review the arrangements under which the agent, nominee or custodian acts, and how those arrangements are being put into effect;

(b)   if circumstances make it appropriate to do so, the trustees must consider whether there is a need to exercise any power of intervention that they have; and

(c)   if the trustees consider that there is a need to exercise such a power, they must do so (Trustee Act 2000, s 22).

An agent authorised to exercise asset management functions has a duty of review which includes, in particular:

(i)   a duty to consider whether there is any need to revise or replace the policy statement;

(ii)   if the trustees consider that there is a need to revise or replace the policy statement, a duty to do so; and

(iii)   a duty to assess whether the policy statement (as it has effect for the time being) is being complied with.

A trustee is not liable for any act or default of an agent, nominee or custodian unless he has failed to comply with the duty of care applicable to him either when entering into the arrangements under which the person acts as agent, nominee or custodian or when carrying out his duty of review (Trustee Act 2000, s 23).

Where a trustee has agreed a term under which the agent, nominee or custodian is permitted to appoint a substitute, the trustee is not liable for any act or default of the substitute unless he has failed to comply with the duty of care applicable to him when agreeing that term or when carrying out his duty of review insofar as it relates to the use of the substitute.

Unanimity

[5.23] The general rule is that trustees must make collective decisions. All decisions must be unanimous. Where a difference of opinion arises, a trustee can quite validly endorse the views of the other trustees where he is relying on their greater experience or simply to avoid deadlock. The general rule will be overridden where the trust deed itself provides for majority decisions. Often in such cases the minority will have the right to record the fact that they dissented. It is unusual for any trusts, other than pension trusts, to include majority voting provisions.

Common powers over income

[5.24] Trustees will usually have duties or powers or a combination of both to apply income in favour of beneficiaries. There are three main areas to consider.

(i) *Fixed entitlements.* Under many trusts, beneficiaries will have a definable and fixed interest in the trust's income. For example, X might be entitled to receive the income from the trust for his life with the remainder going to Y absolutely thereafter. Accordingly, the trustees have no discretion over the beneficiary's current entitlement, although they might have powers under the trust deed which permit them to redirect the flow of income.

(ii) *Powers of appointment.* In cases not within (i) above, principally involving discretionary trusts, trustees will have a power of appointment in respect of income. This will often enable them at their discretion, to allocate trust income amongst a wide class of potential beneficiaries. Usually the balance of any income retained is to be accumulated provided the accumulation period has not expired. Accumulation has the effect of transforming 'income' into trust capital. Where the accumulation period has expired, trustees cannot retain income and it has to be distributed amongst the income beneficiaries. However, trustees will usually retain an element of discretion as to who receives the income within this class.

(iii) *Powers of maintenance.* In the case of infant beneficiaries, it is quite common for express or implied trust powers to enable the trustees to apply income in their favour. The statutory rules introduced by Trustee Act 1925, s 31 enable trustees to maintain infant beneficiaries. The

121

rules can be expressly or impliedly excluded, so care is required in examining a trust deed in order to establish the trustees' powers. This aspect is considered in more detail below.

Common powers over capital

[5.25] There are four common types of powers that trustees may exercise over capital in favour of beneficiaries.

(i)   *Powers of appointment.* These are usually exercisable in favour of a limited class of persons or objects. Limitations created following their exercise are treated as written into the original trust instrument which created them; they do not normally create a new trust. Lord Romer explained in *Muir (Williams) v Muir* [1943] AC 468, 112 LJPC 39, HL, it 'is as though the settlor had left a blank in the settlement which [the donee of the special power of appointment] . . . fills up for him if and when the power . . . is exercised'. In some cases a special power of appointment can expressly or by necessary implication authorise trustees to remove assets from the original settlement, by making them subject to the trusts of a separate settlement.

(ii)   *Transfers between settlements.* It is common practice to include wide powers of appointment or expressly authorise transfers between settlements. Some older trust deeds contain narrow powers of appointment which will not enable trust assets to be transferred to another settlement.

(iii)   *Powers of allocation.* Such powers enable trustees a discretion to allocate assets amongst the various interests of the beneficiaries within the overall framework of the existing trusts without enabling the trustees to establish fresh or overriding trusts.

(iv)   *Powers of advancement.* Advances of assets from the settlement, whether under an express power or under statutory rules, are not solely limited to outright payments or transfers to beneficiaries. They can include settled advances, altering or varying the trusts created by the settlement from which it was derived. This aspect is considered in more detail below.

Beneficiaries' rights

[5.26] Beneficiaries do not have an automatic right to interfere with the administration of a trust when its affairs are being properly run. However, where the trust administration is not being carried out correctly, the beneficiary can take steps to ensure proper administration and preserve his interests under the trust. This will almost invariably involve the assistance of the court. When a beneficiary considers that a trust is not being properly administered he can apply to the court either as regards specific issues, or generally. Similarly, a beneficiary can apply to the court where the trustees fail to take steps to preserve the trust assets. The right of application to the court has been considerably widened in respect of beneficiaries with an interest in property subject to a trust of land (Trusts of Land and Appointment of Trustees Act

1996, s 14). A beneficiary also has the right to see 'trust documents' and this is a proprietary right which exists independently of whether a court action has been commenced. Minutes recording the reasons for trustees exercising their discretion are generally private to the trustees (*Re Londonderry Settlement* [1965] Ch 918, [1964] 3 All ER 855, CA).

The courts will not support attempts by the beneficiaries to limit or fetter the exercise of the trustees' discretion. In *Brockbank, Re, Ward v Bates* [1948] Ch 206, [1948] 1 All ER 287 (Ch D) the beneficiaries were ascertainable and legally competent. Due to a disagreement with the existing trustee they wanted to appoint a new trustee. The court held that the power of appointing a new trustee was exercisable by the existing trustees, and that the beneficiaries could not usurp this discretion. Under the Trusts of Land and Appointment of Trustees Act 1996, s 19, beneficiaries under a trust who are of full age and capacity and together absolutely entitled to the trust property, in the absence of any person nominated to appoint new trustees in the trust deed, may give a written direction that a trustee retire from the trust or that a specified person be appointed as a new trustee. Where all the beneficiaries are known and of full age and capacity, they can bring a trust to an end. In the event that some of the beneficiaries have insufficient legal capacity, or where there is a prospect of as yet unascertained or unknown beneficiaries benefiting under the trust, the necessary consent for terminating or varying the trust will have to be given by the court.

Power of maintenance

[5.27] The Trustee Act 1925, s 31(1) provides trustees with an implied statutory power of maintenance where trust property is held for an infant beneficiary. This enables the trustees to distribute so much of the income as they think fit to the child's parents or guardian or otherwise apply it for their education, maintenance or benefit. It is at the trustees' discretion and so the decision must be taken in good faith after due consideration of the circumstances. Any income which is not paid or applied in this manner has to be accumulated (s 31(2)). The trustees however, are able to apply such accumulations, or any part of them, as if they were income arising in the current year. This power is particularly interesting as it represents one of the limited number of ways of converting capital into income for tax purposes (*Stevenson (Inspector of Taxes) v Wishart* [1987] 2 All ER 428, [1987] 1 WLR 1204, CA).

Income at majority

[5.28] Another key feature of the statutory power of maintenance for minors is that Trustee Act 1925, s 31(1)(ii) provides that where a beneficiary has not already attained a vested interest in the trust income by the age of 18, the trustees must immediately pay to him the income of that property and any accumulations until either he attains a vested interest in income, he dies or his interest fails.

Excluding Trustee Act 1925, s 31

[5.29] Trustee Act 1925, s 31 cannot apply in any event where the trust predates 1926. It can be expressly or impliedly excluded by the trust instrument itself (*Turner's Will Trusts, Re, District Bank Ltd v Turner* [1937] Ch 15, [1936] 2 All ER 1435, CA) which makes the provision hard to 'pin down' so as to establish with any degree of certainty whether or not it does apply to a particular trust. In *Delamere's Settlement Trusts, Re* [1984] 1 All ER 584, [1984] 1 WLR 813 (CA), Lord Justice Slade said:

> 'The present case well illustrates that the existence of section 31 . . . for all its obvious advantages and uses, could in one sense, be said to present a potential trap . . . In many cases the draftsmen may well be advised out of caution either expressly to provide that the section is to apply with or without stated modifications, or expressly to exclude its application altogether.'

This power cannot apply where another beneficiary has a prior entitlement to receive the trust income; similarly an express direction to accumulate the whole of the trust's income would have the effect of excluding the statutory power. In addition, the provision has no application where income is distributable amongst a discretionary class of beneficiaries.

Unlike the statutory power of advancement considered below, the statutory power of maintenance will apply irrespective of the type of assets held by the trust. However, like the statutory power of advancement it is quite common for the draftsman to 'tinker' with the terms of the statutory power of maintenance in the instrument itself.

Entitlement to accumulations

[5.30] A beneficiary's entitlement to undistributed income accumulations will be primarily governed by the trust instrument. Where there is no such direction, a beneficiary with a vested income entitlement will become entitled to the undistributed income on attaining 18 or marrying or forming a civil partnership under that age. Similarly, he or she will become entitled to accumulations of income on attaining 18, or marrying or forming a civil partnership under that age, if as a result he or she thereby becomes entitled to the trust's capital.

Power of advancement

[5.31] The statutory power of advancement contained in Trustee Act 1925, s 32 enables trustees to pay or apply trust capital to or for the advancement or benefit of those entitled to the trust capital. In this context it does not matter whether the right to participate in trust capital is to some or all of the property or that the interest itself is absolute or simply contingent upon some occurrence. Although the power has a number of important limitations, its great value is its flexibility – particularly in the case of settled advances.

Advancement and benefit have special meanings.

Advancement

[5.32] Viscount Radcliffe in *Pilkington v IRC* [1964] AC 612, [1962] 3 All ER 622, perhaps best summarised the meaning of advancement:

> '[the] word "advancement" itself meant in this context the establishment in life of the beneficiary who was the object of the power, or at any rate some step that would contribute to the furtherance of his establishment.'

He cited typical instances of such expenditure in the nineteenth century as being 'an apprenticeship or the purchase of a commission in the army or an interest in business. In the case of a girl, there could be an advancement on marriage'. However, the word does also have a slightly restrictive inference. Viscount Radcliffe commented that advancement had to some extent a limited range of meaning since it was thought to convey the idea of some step in life of permanent significance. There was a suggestion in another case that advancement would only really be appropriate where the recipient was starting to make his way in life (*Kershaw's Trust (Re)* 1868 LR 6 Eq 322). It is not clear how relevant these cases are in the modern context, and in any event the question is largely redundant because of the width given to the meaning of the word 'benefit'.

Benefit

[5.33] The actual scope of the term 'benefit' is immense being 'the widest possible word one could have' (*Moxon's Will Trusts, Re, Downey v Moxon* [1958] 1 All ER 386, [1958] 1 WLR 165). It includes outright applications to the beneficiary direct as well as trustees settling funds on new trusts for a beneficiary (*Pilkington v IRC* [1964] AC 612, [1962] 3 All ER 622) even where the objective was to save tax (*Re Moxon's Will Trust* above). Also, in order to mitigate the charge to tax, an advancement can still be for the benefit of a beneficiary despite his not taking any direct financial interest in the property advanced (*Clore's Settlement Trusts, Re, Sainer v Clore* [1966] 2 All ER 272, [1966] 1 WLR 955). Indeed, 'benefit' need not meet a 'need'. As a result, an advance of funds to establish a new trust for a beneficiary is perfectly proper irrespective of whether the beneficiary actually requires access to those funds.

When does Trustee Act 1925, s 32 apply?

[5.34] Unless excluded, s 32 applies to:

(i)   minor beneficiaries who have contingent interests or default interests under trusts for bereaved minors;

(ii)   minor beneficiaries who have interests under bare trusts;

(iii) minor beneficiaries who have contingent interests under the intestacy rules;

(iv)   beneficiaries under the age of 25 who have contingent interests or minor beneficiaries who have default interests under 18-to-25 trusts;

(v)   beneficiaries of any age who have remainder interests under interest in possession trusts.

Section 32 does not apply (unless the trust instrument provides otherwise) to:

(i)   potential beneficiaries of powers of appointment in discretionary trusts;
(ii)   life tenants of interest in possession trusts who have no separate interest in capital.

The provision of Trustee Act 1925, s 32 can be expressly or impliedly excluded by the provisions of the trust instrument. For example, an express power of advancement contained in the trust deed which does not refer to 'benefit' has been held to exclude the wider statutory provision (*Evans' Settlement, Re, Watkins v Whitworth-Jones* [1967] 3 All ER 343, [1967] 1 WLR 1294) whilst in *IRC v Bernstein* [1961] Ch 399, [1961] 1 All ER 320, CA, a provision for accumulation was held to have the same effect.

The scope of the statutory power is also quite narrow. It only applies to trusts created or effective after the enactment of the Trustee Act 1925. It will not apply to capital money arising under the Settled Land Act 1925. However, it will apply to trusts of land. In a well-drafted trust deed it is quite common for the statutory power to be widened. Usually this relates to the requirement for consent by a beneficiary with a prior interest, and to enable the trustees to advance up to the entire expectant interest concerned. Both of these aspects are considered below.

Statutory limits

[5.35] Trustee Act 1925, s 32 cannot be exercised without the written consent of a beneficiary entitled to a prior interest who is of full age and legal capacity and who would be prejudiced by the advancement. Following the case of *Forster's Settlement (Re)* [1942] Ch 199, [1942] 1 All ER 180 a power will be improperly exercised where there has been a failure to obtain the consent of a beneficiary who is incapable of being contacted, the court having no jurisdiction to provide the consent required.

For trusts or will trusts created or arising after 30 September 2014 the trustees are able to exercise their discretion to advance up to the whole of the capital of a beneficiary's share in the trust fund. For trusts or will trusts created or arising before that date, the statutory power can only be validly exercised if no more than half of a beneficiary's vested or presumptive share is advanced. The value of the trust fund taken into account is the value at the time of the actual advance itself. As a result, if the value of the fund subsequently increases but a beneficiary has already received his maximum entitlement under the statutory power, no more can be advanced. Similarly, if the value of the trust assets decreases after a beneficiary has received his maximum entitlement – so that retrospectively it appears that he or she has received far too much – the other beneficiaries would not be able to challenge the prior advancement on these grounds.

Another limiting factor is the requirement that any advance (albeit of cash or non-cash assets) must be brought into account as part of the share. However, if a beneficiary never becomes absolutely entitled, for example, because his interest ultimately fails, there is no liability to repay the amount advanced or bring it into account.

Settled advances

[5.36] Trustees exercising a power for advancement are normally able to advance funds on new trusts for the benefit of an individual beneficiary. There are, however, two limitations that have to be considered, namely the range of the powers possessed by the new trustees and the perpetuity period.

The trustees must take into account all of the terms of the new trusts, not only those under which the new trustees are likely to act in practice. Viscount Radcliffe outlined the starting point in *Pilkington v IRC* [1964] AC 612, [1962] 3 All ER 622:

> 'The law is not that trustees cannot delegate: it is that trustees cannot delegate unless they have authority to do so. If the power of advancement which they possess is so read as to allow them to raise money for the purpose of having it settled, then they do have the necessary authority to let the money pass out of the old settlement into the new trusts.'

It is therefore necessary to look at the power being used to determine if trust assets can be passed to new trustees who also possess particularly wide dispositive powers.

Protective trusts

[5.37] A protective trust is a particular form of interest in possession trust. Trustees are directed to pay income to the life tenant but if he should sell his right to trust income or becomes insolvent, then his interest ceases and the income becomes held on discretionary trusts for him and his family. The Trustee Act 1925, s 33 provides the statutory mechanism for creating protective trusts. By simply referring to the term 'protective trusts' a draftsman can incorporate the trust provisions set out in s 33. The effect of the Insolvency Act 1986 must, however, be considered.

Protective or spendthrift trusts are particularly useful where a settlor has concerns over the financial stability or maturity of a beneficiary.

The statutory provisions in s 33 state that where income (including an annuity) is held on protective trusts for the benefit of a person (called 'the principal beneficiary') for a period of his life or a lesser period of time ('the trust period') then the income will be held on the following trusts.

(a)   Upon trust for the principal beneficiary during the trust period or until some event occurs whereby that beneficiary would lose the right to receive the income concerned. (This would extend, for example, to situations where the principal beneficiary purports to sell his interest or where he becomes bankrupt.)

(b)   If the trust fails or determines during the trust period, then the income is to be held on trust for the remaining period for the maintenance and support of:

(i)   the principal beneficiary and his or her immediate family; or

(ii)   the principal beneficiary and the persons who would be entitled to the trust property and income if he were dead, provided that the principal beneficiary is not married and has no issue in existence.

The statutory wording can be modified by the trust instrument. In practice, a great deal of care has to be taken when dealing with such trusts not to inadvertently trigger the protective discretionary element. For example, in *Dennis's Settlement Trusts, Re, Dennis v Dennis* [1942] Ch 283, [1942] 1 All ER 520 the execution by a principal beneficiary of a deed varying the terms of a protective trust caused the protective discretionary trusts to come into play. However, s 33(1)(i) expressly provides that advances under any express or statutory power will not bring the discretionary trusts into operation.

Because of the risk of a discretionary trust arising automatically if a beneficiary tries to dispose of his interest, it may be sensible to provide in the trust deed that the beneficiary's interest is terminable at the trustees' discretion.

The Hastings-Bass rule

Background

[5.38] The *Hastings-Bass* rule is an exception to the general rule that a court will not interfere in a decision reached following the exercise of a trustee power or discretion. This rule was radically revised by the Court of Appeal in the joined cases of *Futter v Futter* [2011] EWCA Civ 197, [2012] Ch 132, [2011] 2 All ER 450; *Pitt v Holt* [2011] EWCA Civ 197, [2012] Ch 132, [2011] 2 All ER 450 which greatly restricted its scope. In the Supreme Court the decision was unanimous and largely confirmed the Court of Appeal's decision with Lord Walker giving the only substantial judgment and the other six Law Lords simply agreeing with it (*Futter v Revenue & Customs Comrs; Pitt v Revenue & Customs Comrs* [2013] UKSC 26, [2013] 3 All ER 429, [2013] 2 WLR 1200).

Before the Court of Appeal's decision, the *Hastings-Bass* rule was thought to be based on the statement by Buckley LJ in *Hastings-Bass v IRC* [1975] Ch 25, [1974] 2 All ER 193, [1974] STC 211 where he said:

' . . . where by the terms of a trust . . . a trustee is given the discretion as to some matter under which he acts in good faith, the Court should not interfere with his action notwithstanding that it does not have the full effect which he intended, unless:

(1)   what he has achieved is unauthorised by the power conferred on him; or
(2)   it is clear that he would not have acted as he did:
(a)   had he not taken into account considerations which he should not have taken into account; or
(b)   had he not failed to take into account considerations which he ought to have taken into account.'

This was essentially a statement of an exception to the negative rule that a disposition would not be set aside merely because the trustees had misunderstood its true effect.

In *Mettoy Pension Trustees Ltd v Evans* [1991] 2 All ER 513, [1990] 1 WLR 1587 at 1621H Warner J gave what became known as the rule in *Hastings-Bass* a positive form as follows:

' . . . Where a trustee acts under a discretion given to him under the terms of the trust, the court will interfere with his action if it is clear that he would not have acted as he did had he not failed to take into account considerations which he ought to have taken into account or taken into account considerations which he ought not to have taken into account.'

It is this positive version of the rule that was applied by courts at first instance in a number of cases (see *Green v Cobham* [2002] STC 820, 4 ITELR 784; *Abacus Trust Co (Isle of Man) Ltd v NSPCC* [2001] STC 1344, 3 ITELR 846; *Burrell v Burrell* [2005] EWHC 245 (Ch), [2005] STC 569, 7 ITELR 622; *Sieff v Fox* [2005] EWHC 1312 (Ch), [2005] 3 All ER 693, [2005] 1 WLR 3811; and *Jiggens v Low* [2010] EWHC 1566 (Ch), [2010] STC 1899).

In other cases the courts have said by way of obiter dicta that they would have applied the rule in the alternative to granting some other remedy (see *Amp (UK) plc v Barker* (2000) 3 ITELR 414; and *Gallaher Ltd v Gallaher Pensions Ltd* [2005] EWHC 42 (Ch), [2005] OPLR 57).

Lord Justice Lloyd in *Sieff v Fox* [2005] EWHC 1312 (Ch), [2005] 3 All ER 693, [2005] 1 WLR 3811 summarised what he called 'the *Mettoy* formulation' of the *Hastings-Bass* rule as follows:

'Where a trustee acts under a discretion given to him under the terms of the trust, but the effects of the exercise is different from that which he intended, the court will interfere with his action if it is clear that he would not have acted as he did had he not failed to take into account considerations which he ought to have taken into account, or taken into account considerations which he ought not to have taken into account.'

This rule has proved useful in a number of cases where trustees have entered into transactions without understanding the taxation consequences of them in allowing them to escape from those consequences.

The rule, however, was always acknowledged to have its limits. In *Breadner v Granville-Grossman* [2001] Ch 523, [2000] 4 All ER 705, Park J refused to treat a power of appointment, exercised by trustees one day after the time limit, for its exercise had expired, as having been exercised before its expiration. Park J held that to do so would have been an unwarranted extension of the rule transforming a power for the court to regard a transaction as void into a power to substitute a different transaction. Park J said that:

'It cannot be right that whenever trustees do something which they later regret and think that they ought not to have done, they can say that they never did it in the first place.'

The rule was subject to extra-judicial criticism by Lord Walker and Lord Neuberger and in previous editions of this book we warned:

' . . . it is to be expected that the Courts will take an opportunity in the future to limit the rule'.

That opportunity was given by two cases, both decided in favour of the appellant in the High Court, which were heard together by the Court of Appeal and the Supreme Court.

Historically, HMRC had declined to be named as a party to proceedings where the *Hastings-Bass* rule had been in issue. In June 2006, however, HMRC announced 'their concern . . . that the principle as currently formulated is too wide in its scope'. Where large amounts of tax were at stake and/or where it was felt that it could make a useful contribution to the elucidation and development of the principle, HMRC would, it announced, consider intervening. It would be particularly ready to intervene in cases where there would otherwise be no party in whose interest it would be to argue against the application of the principle (Revenue Interpretation 278). HMRC stated that in the future it was likely that HMRC would take a more active role in resisting the extension of the rule. Interestingly, it was felt by some commentators that in certain trust proceedings there was a strong case for denying HMRC standing because it did not have sufficient interest in the proceedings, only in their outcome. HMRC first chose to take part in the Guernsey case of *Gresh v RBC Trust Company (Guernsey) Ltd* 2009–10 GLR 216. In the Jersey case of *Re Seaton Trustees Limited* [2009] JRC 050, HMRC at first instance was denied *locus* to intervene but that was reversed by the Jersey Court of Appeal. The Jersey Court of Appeal held that HMRC was not attempting indirectly to secure the court's action in enforcing a foreign tax but to resolve an issue which might have been important in enforcing foreign revenue legislation in its own country.

Pitt v Holt; Futter v Futter

[5.39] *Futter v Futter* [2011] EWCA Civ 197, [2012] Ch 132, [2011] 2 All ER 450; *Pitt v Holt* [2011] EWCA Civ 197, [2012] Ch 132, [2011] 2 All ER 450 were the first cases concerning the *Hastings-Bass* rule in which HMRC was joined as a party in an English court.

Futter v Futter concerned an application to have capital appointments made to the settlor and his children from an offshore trust set aside because although Mr Futter and his advisers correctly understood that capital gains would be attributed to the recipients of the advances under TCGA 1992, s 87, they incorrectly believed that those gains could be offset against allowable losses arising to the recipient beneficiaries. They sought to have the capital appointments declared void on the basis of the *Hastings-Bass* rule.

Pitt v Holt concerned a terribly sad series of events. The husband of the claimant suffered serious brain damage in a road accident in 1994 and his wife, Mrs Pitt, was appointed receiver under the Mental Health Act 1983. A damages claim was compromised and Mrs Pitt received, on behalf of Mr Pitt, a lump sum and a right to an index-linked annuity. Mrs Pitt's advisers were a firm of solicitors and a financial advisory company. She was advised to settle both the cash and the right to the annuity on discretionary trusts for herself, her husband and their children as beneficiaries. Permission for the settlement to be made was given by the Court of Protection. Unfortunately, no consideration was given to the inheritance tax consequences of the settlement. There was an immediate liability to inheritance tax on its creation which would have been avoided if the trust had provided that at least one half of the settled property was applied for Mr Pitt's benefit during his lifetime so that it met the conditions of IHTA 1984, s 89. Other than the money received in the settlement, the couple had only modest financial resources, and by the time of Mr Pitt's death in 2007 only £6,000 remained in the settlement. So it appears that HMRC sought to impose a ruinous tax liability on a widow who had suffered the most terrible misfortune in order to establish a novel restriction of this well-established legal principle. The irony was that HMRC did not need to appeal against the High Court's decision in Mrs Pitt's favour because the appeal in the linked case of *Futter v Futter* was sufficient to allow the higher courts to review the *Hastings-Bass* rule. Ultimately HMRC was unsuccessful in *Pitt v Holt* on another ground, as we shall see, and Mr Pitt's settlement was voided.

The grounds of the application in *Pitt v Holt* were based on the *Hastings-Bass* rule and on the doctrine of mistake. HMRC had argued in the High Court that the *Hastings-Bass* rule applied only to the actions of trustees. The court rejected this contention holding that there was no material distinction between a trustee exercising a power for the benefit of a beneficiary ' . . . and a receiver exercising a power for the benefit of a patient pursuant to the Mental Health Act 1983 . . . ' and HMRC did not challenge this part of the decision on appeal.

In both *Futter* and *Pitt*, the taxpayers won in the High Court. The Court of Appeal allowed HMRC's appeal, holding that the *Hastings-Bass* rule in either case did not apply and dismissed the claim of Mr Pitt's executors based on mistake. An appeal was made to the Supreme Court.

The Supreme Court had to consider whether in the exercise of a discretionary power by a fiduciary, a mistake as to the tax consequences of their actions would fall within the *Hastings-Bass* rule. Lord Walker identified three defects that a disposition might contain:

- Excessive execution – the fiduciary had no power to make the disposition which was not the case in either *Pitt* or *Futter.*
- Fraudulent appointment – the disposition was within the fiduciary's powers but was effected for an improper purpose which again was not the case in *Pitt* or *Futter.*
- Inadequate deliberation – the fiduciary had the power to make the disposition and was exercising the power for a proper purpose but failed to give adequate consideration to all relevant factors.

The Supreme Court, agreeing with the Court of Appeal, held that the *Hastings-Bass* rule was concerned with inadequate deliberation. That enabled the court to decide that where the principle applied, the transactions concerned were voidable at the discretion of the court rather than, as had been previously thought, being automatically void. The court also held that it was not sufficient that the trustees or the fiduciary should have failed either to take account of something of which they should have taken account or had taken account of something of which they should not have taken account. That failure must amount to a breach of fiduciary duty. In both cases the application failed because the court held that the trustees/fiduciary had not committed a breach because they had taken professional advice on which they could properly rely even though that advice turned out to be wrong.

In *Pitt v Holt*, Mrs Pitt had also argued that the settlement should be set aside on the ground of mistake. In *Futter v Futter* the trustees had not pleaded mistake. There had been some uncertainty whether a mistake as to the consequences, and in particular the tax consequences, of transactions as opposed to their legal effects could found a claim in mistake. The mistake must be of a sufficiently serious nature, which will normally require that it will be as to the legal character or nature of the transaction, or as to some matter of fact or law which is basic to the transaction and it must, on an objective assessment, be unconscionable for the donee to retain the property in the light of the mistake. There is no general rule that a mistake relating to tax cannot attract equitable relief. Tax consequences relate to the seriousness of the mistake regardless of whether they are basic to the transaction. It was accepted by the Supreme Court that Mrs Pitt held an incorrect conscious belief that the disposition would have no adverse tax consequences and this was sufficiently serious to merit equity's intervention. Her appeal was allowed, therefore, on the grounds of mistake. The trust was set aside because the trust she was intending to create 'was precisely the sort of trust to which Parliament intended to grant relief by s 89'.

Lord Walker went on to consider briefly whether the doctrine of mistake can apply to persons attempting to engage in tax avoidance. He said:

'In some cases of artificial tax avoidance the Court might think it right to refuse relief, either on the ground that such claimants, acting on supposedly expert advice, must be taken to have accepted the risk that the scheme would prove ineffective, or on the ground that discretionary relief should be refused on ground of public policy. Since the seminal decision of the House of Lords in *WT Ramsay Ltd v IRC* there has been an increasingly strong and general recognition that artificial tax avoidance is a social evil which puts an unfair burden on the shoulders of those who do not adopt such measures. But it is unnecessary to consider that further on these appeals.'

The view that tax avoidance is a social evil is startling as it is indeed the comment that discretionary relief should be refused on grounds of public policy which would seem to be contrary to the general principle that the judiciary is not entitled to impose tax. However, in the Guernsey case of *BiGDug Limited Remuneration Trust*, the Royal Court of Guernsey did not refuse an order where there was a clear tax avoidance motive. The Royal Court of Jersey in *IFM Corporate Trustees Ltd v Helliwell & Mountain* [2015] JRC 160, 18 ITELR 662 commented that if the scheme (involving an employee benefit trust) had been aggressive tax avoidance, that might have been a relevant factor in the exercise of its discretion, which might have led to a refusal to exercise its discretion in favour of the trustee. This case signals a change in judicial attitude which suggests that such a consideration might be relevant in future.

Other jurisdictions

[5.40] It is not only the English Courts, however, that have applied the *Hastings-Bass* rule in its wider form. It has also been applied in Jersey, Guernsey and the Cayman Islands.

Jersey

[5.41] The Trusts (Amendment No 6) (Jersey) Law 2013 allows the Royal Court to remedy the adverse effects of the consequences of mistakes, where the acts or omissions are made by settlors, trustees and others. The legislation identifies four different situations where the court has the power to declare that the transfer of property to a trust, or the exercise of a power, as the case may be, is voidable and is to have such effect that the court determines, or is to be of no effect from the time of its exercise. These situations, the first two relating to a transfer into a trust and the second two relating to the exercise of powers by an existing trust, are as follows:

(1) Where a transfer or other disposition (together referred to as a 'transfer') of property to a trust has been made by a settlor or through another person exercising a power on behalf of a settlor, the settlor or other person made a mistake in relation to the transfer and would not have made the transfer but for the mistake and the mistake is so serious that it is just for the court to make a declaration.

(2) Where a transfer of property to a trust has been made by a settlor through a person exercising a power on behalf of a settlor, that person owing a fiduciary duty in relation to the exercise of that power, the person failed to take into account any relevant considerations or took into account irrelevant considerations and he would not have exercised the power as he did, but for such failure. This situation reflects the *Hastings-Bass* rule.

(3) Where a power has been exercised by a trustee or by another person in relation to a trust or trust property, the trustee or other person made a mistake in relation to the exercise of the power, and he would not have exercised the power at all, or in the way in which it was exercised, but for the mistake and the mistake is so serious that it is just for the court to make a declaration.

(4) Where a power has been exercised by a trustee or by another person in relation to a trust or trust property (where that person owes a fiduciary duty to a beneficiary in relation to the exercise of the power), the trustee or other person failed to take into account any relevant considerations or took into account irrelevant considerations and he would not have exercised the power at all, or in the way in which it was exercised, but for that failure. This situation reflects the *Hastings-Bass* rule.

In relation to (2) and (4) above, there is no requirement to establish fault by the person exercising the powers or by his advisers.

Guernsey

[5.42] In the unreported case of *HCS Trustees Ltd v Camperio Legal &*
Fiduciary Services plc, the Guernsey Royal Court held that the *Hastings-Bass*
rule now formed part of Guernsey law.

Cayman Islands

[5.43] The Cayman Islands' Chief Justice has indicated that the Cayman Courts will continue to permit trustees to rectify their mistakes under the
Hastings-Bass rule.

The doctrine of mistake

[5.44] Because of the restriction of the *Hastings-Bass* rule, trustees will be
relying on the law of mistake to correct errors made. For a decision on the
grounds of mistake there must be a causative mistake of sufficient gravity. This
will normally be satisfied where there is a mistake either as to the legal
character or nature of the transaction or as to some matter of fact or law which
is basic to the transaction. The consequences (including tax consequences) are
relevant to the gravity of the mistake.

Where a trust deed does not express the settlor's intentions it can be rectified
to reflect his true intention. Such a claim can be made by the settlor, a
beneficiary or by the trustees in certain circumstances. In *Fine v Fine* [2012]
EWHC 1811 (Ch), [2012] All ER (D) 286 (Jul), the High Court ordered
rectification to create new interest in possession trusts out of discretionary
trusts. The ultimate reason for their execution was to avoid a decennial charge.
The mistake arose in a misunderstanding of the effects of the trust deeds and
not their fiscal consequences.

In *Kennedy v Kennedy* [2014] EWHC 4219 the doctrine of mistake was used
to set aside a clause in a deed of appointment, the effect of which resulted in
a substantial capital gains tax liability. It has also been used in *Freedman v
Freedman* [2015] EWHC 1457 (Ch), (2015) Times, 23 June, [2015] WTLR
1187 where the establishment of a trust resulted in an unexpected inheritance
tax charge. In the case of *Van Der Merwe v Goldman and HMRC* [2016]
EWHC 926 (Ch), the claimant transferred the matrimonial home from his sole
name into the joint names of himself and his wife, as trustees of a settlement
in which they both had life interests. Unknown to the claimant, the effect of the
Budget announcement made on 22 March 2006 resulted in a substantial
inheritance tax charge. The High Court held that the claimant had made a
mistake. His ignorance of the effect of the Budget announcement together with
the advice he had taken in November 2005 led him to believe that no
inheritance tax charge would arise. The Court held that the transaction should
be set aside.

In *Bainbridge v Bainbridge* [2016] EWHC 898 (Ch), [2016] WTLR 943, a
father and son, on the advice of their solicitor, transferred various parcels of
farmland to a discretionary trust. They had been advised (wrongly) that no
capital gains tax charge would arise. Subsequently, the trustees sold two
parcels of land and used the proceeds to acquire new farmland, and to pay

various tax and partnership liabilities, including the SDLT on the purchase of the new farmland. It was at that stage they discovered the transfer of land had created a capital gains tax liability in excess of £200,000. The Court considered that the mistake was fundamental and it would be unconscionable or unjust to allow the discretionary trustees to keep the land. As some of the land had been sold, the Court applied a tracing process so the new land represented the old land. The father and son were to be treated as having elected to ratify the subsequent transactions entered into by the trustees. The Court took an innovative approach by rescinding the transfers whilst adopting the trustees' later sales so that the new land was restored to the father and son in place of their original holdings. The case illustrates that rescission on the grounds of mistake may be ordered even in the situation where damages could be sought from the professional advisers.

Chapter 6

Creating Settlements

Introduction

Devolution by will

[6.1] The simplest way of passing one's wealth to succeeding generations is to leave it by will. Most parents, however, wish to provide for their children during their lifetime. That may be simply from an impulse of generosity or because the circumstances of their children's lives require help immediately rather than later. One's children, for example, may need an income to support them at university or to supplement their earnings in the early years of their career or they may need a house in which to live on leaving home. What is more, if one's estate does not pass before one's death its whole value will be brought into charge to inheritance tax. Of course, it is not only parents who wish to help members of a younger generation; grandparents, aunts, uncles, godparents and many others may also want to do so.

Outright gifts

[6.2] For these reasons many people make transfers of wealth during their lifetimes. The simplest way of doing that is by way of an outright gift which is discussed in CHAPTER 4 LIFETIME PLANNING: MAKING GIFTS.

Often, however, outright gifts will not be the appropriate way of providing for the next generation. The donee may be too young to have the responsibility of dealing with investment assets or the freedom to spend substantial amounts of cash. A parent, or grandparent, needs to balance his desire to provide for those he loves and to establish their independence against the possibility that the possession of wealth at a young age may undermine their self-reliance and provide a temptation to indolence. The need to provide for a surviving spouse, particularly if that spouse is significantly younger than the other or there has been a previous marriage, may require one to divide rights over property over time. Certain sorts of assets are likely to be difficult to administer if their ownership is divided amongst a group of people wishing to take different approaches to their management. These problems are particularly acute in relation to share holdings in family companies and to farmland and commercial property.

Settlements

[6.3] All of these considerations may require one to separate the control of assets from their benefit and to divide interests in assets between individuals either concurrently or over time. It is for these reasons that settlements have been an important element in estate planning. Their flexibility and adaptability are now valued throughout the world and are, as much as physical inventions, a major achievement of the British genius.

Unfortunately, in recent years successive governments have regarded settlements as mere tax avoidance devices the use of which should be discouraged. From the introduction of capital transfer tax in 1974 until 2006, that tax and its successor, inheritance tax, had dealt with settlements in a conceptually consistent way. Where a person had a right to the income from settled property as it arose (an interest in possession) he was treated as if he were the beneficial owner of the property in which his interest subsisted. Where that was not the case (that is, where the settlement was discretionary) the settlement was treated as an independent entity suffering periodic charges at decennial intervals and a further charge on the settled property ceasing to be held on discretionary trusts. Various particular forms of favoured settlements were then given additional reliefs. The underlying concept was to approximate the taxation of settled property to the taxation of property held absolutely. This rational system of taxation has been replaced by a system designed to penalise the creation of settlements in order to discourage their use. The current Government has repeatedly refused to reinstate a rational scheme of inheritance taxation of settlements.

What is a settlement for tax purposes? — General principles

Definitions

[6.4] A settlement is defined for inheritance tax purposes as:

' . . . any disposition or dispositions of property, whether effected by instrument, by parol or by operation of law, or partly in one way and partly in another, whereby the property is for the time being:

(a)   held in trust for persons in succession or for any person subject to a contingency; or

(b)   held by trustees on trust to accumulate the whole or part of any income of the property or with power to make payments out of that income at the discretion of the trustees or some other person, with or without power to accumulate surplus income; or

(c)   charged or burdened (otherwise than for full consideration in money or money's worth paid for his own use or benefit to the person making the disposition) with the payment of any annuity or other periodical payment payable for a life or any other limited or terminable period,

or would be so held or charged or burdened if the disposition or dispositions were regulated by the law of any part of the United Kingdom; or whereby, under the law of any other country, the administration of the property is for the time being governed by provisions equivalent in effect to those which would apply if the property were so held, charged or burdened.'

(IHTA 1984, s 43(2)).

A lease of property granted for life or lives or for a period ascertainable only by reference to a death will also be treated as a settlement unless full consideration is paid (IHTA 1984, s 43(3)).

Both for capital gains tax and income tax purposes settled property is any property held on trust other than property held as nominee or for any person absolutely entitled as against the trustee or held for any person who would be so entitled but for being a minor or under a disability (or for two or more persons who are or would be jointly so entitled) (ITA 2007, s 466 and TCGA 1992, ss 60, 68). There is no generally applicable definition of a settlement for either income tax or capital gains tax purposes although the anti-avoidance legislation found in ITTOIA 2005 Pt 5, Ch 5 contains a definition of a settlement for the purposes of that legislation only.

It can be seen from the above that property held on bare trusts (ie property in which all the beneficiaries have absolute interests) does not fall within the definition of settled property for either inheritance tax, capital gains tax or income tax purposes.

Preliminary considerations

Duties of trustees and the terms of the settlement

[6.5] In creating a settlement the settlor settles assets on trustees to be held upon stated terms for the benefit of chosen beneficiaries. Although the donor (and his spouse) may be a trustee (or trustees) of a settlement, thereby retaining a measure of control over the assets given away, their actions must be governed by the terms of the settlement and their powers must be exercised and their duties carried out solely for the benefit of the beneficiaries. The donor must consider the possibility of conflicts arising between his interests and those of the beneficiaries. While a settlement of quoted shares is unlikely to give rise to such problems, settlements of unquoted shares frequently do.

The introduction of new shareholders to a family company may make its management more difficult, particularly if one or more of the beneficiaries for whom those shares are held (and who may, in due course, become the outright owners of those shares) are not, and have no intention of becoming, active participants in the affairs of the company. In these circumstances, a trustee of a trust who is also the trust's settlor must, like any other trustee, have regard to his duties as a trustee in exercising the powers and discretions conferred by the settlement rather than letting outside considerations (for example, those he has as 'founder' of the business) influence his decisions. The trustees cannot merely act upon the settlor's instructions.

If the settlor wishes to retain a power to exclude those beneficiaries who show no interest in the business from benefit and to concentrate the shares of the company into the hands of those who are active participants, it may be advisable for him not to act as a trustee of the settlement. He may then exercise this power, conferred upon him other than in a fiduciary capacity, without regard to any duty to the beneficiaries which he would have as a trustee.

Whilst it may be possible to 'unwind' a settlement which does not achieve the settlor's aims, the terms upon which the trust property is held may make the undoing complex and expensive because of taxation and professional fees. The unscrambling may place property in the hands of the 'wrong' beneficiary. Further, any provision enabling the settlement to be undone in favour of the donor may, as a result of the reservation of benefit rules, negate the intended estate planning benefits. The settlor must, therefore, be sure that the terms of the trust achieve his aims and that they are (within the limits imposed by taxation rules) as flexible as possible in order to enable the trust to be adapted as circumstances require.

Reservation of benefit rules

[6.6] On the creation of a settlement, one must consider the inheritance tax 'reservation of benefit' rules in FA 1986, s 102. Generally the settlor will be treated for inheritance tax purposes on death as beneficially entitled to the trust property unless he is excluded from benefit. If the settlor's spouse is a beneficiary this will not in itself bring the reservation of benefit provisions into effect (FA 1986, s 102(2), (5)). Property distributed from the trust, however, and used for the benefit of both the settlor and his spouse will not be property enjoyed to the settlor's entire exclusion and will therefore be property subject to a reservation. What is more, the value for inheritance tax purposes of the gift is not frozen at the date on which it is made. The current value of the property in which the benefit was reserved will be taken into account in calculating the inheritance tax charge. This charge may arise on death or, if the settlor is subsequently excluded from benefit but dies within seven years of the exclusion, on a deemed potentially exempt transfer which as a result of his death becomes chargeable (subject to the provisions relating to double charges in such circumstances under the Inheritance Tax (Double Charges Relief) Regulations 1987 (SI 1987/1130)). The provisions of FA 1986, Sch 20, para 5 ensure that the value of any property representing or deriving from the original property will be taken into account in calculating the charge to inheritance tax in such circumstances.

To ensure that the trust property is enjoyed to the exclusion of any benefit to the settlor the terms of the settlement require careful scrutiny. It should be noted that a settlor as trustee of his settlement may be remunerated for his service without giving rise to a reservation of benefit provided the remuneration is not excessive.

Further, the possibility of a benefit being reserved to the settlor as a result of the nature of the property given away must not be forgotten. For example, a service contract with unusually favourable terms as to remuneration or duration entered into between the settlor and his family company may, in the light of the gift, fail to satisfy the requirement that the property must be enjoyed to the entire exclusion of the donor and of any benefit to him by contract or otherwise. Similarly, land given away which continues to be farmed by a partnership in which the donor is a partner may not be enjoyed to the exclusion of the donor unless a full rent is paid.

Pre-owned assets charge

[6.7] When considering creating a settlement, one must also consider the income tax charge on pre-owned assets. Intangible property which a UK resident and domiciled settlor transfers into a trust and any land or chattels from which the settlor continues to enjoy a benefit, either immediately following the settlement or at a later date, may give rise to an income tax charge. This is discussed in more detail in CHAPTER 4 LIFETIME PLANNING: MAKING GIFTS.

This is particularly important because, once in place, many trust structures are expensive or difficult to unwind, leaving the settlor with a choice of either doing nothing (and being liable to the income tax charge) or making the election to bring the assets back into his estate (to be treated as though they were subject to a reservation of benefit).

A specific exception provides that where the settlor has reserved a benefit in the settled property, no income tax charge will arise under the pre-owned assets rules.

Example

In 2003/04, Mr Lawson created a settlement with a life interest for his son, Matthew. Mr and Mrs Lawson were not excluded from benefiting under the trust. Mr Lawson added a Constable painting to this trust. The painting was delivered to Matthew who hung it in his dining room.

Mr and Mrs Lawson are within the class of beneficiaries of the trust and are, therefore, treated as having reserved a benefit in it.

In 2014/15, Matthew asks his parents to look after the painting for him while he goes abroad and it is hung in their dining room.

Under the pre-owned assets rules, Mr Lawson enjoys possession of a chattel which he had previously owned and given away. A charge to income tax would have arisen were it not for the fact that Mr Lawson had reserved a benefit in the painting.

Categories of settlements

[6.8] Settlements can be broadly divided between those which are trusts of relevant property governed by IHTA 1984, Pt III, Ch III and those which are not.

Trusts which are not relevant property trusts include the following and are discussed later in this Chapter:

(a)   trusts which either confer or are deemed to confer an interest in possession falling within IHTA 1984, s 49(1A). In this book we refer to such trusts as 'privileged interest trusts';

(b)   young person's trusts being trusts for bereaved minors falling within IHTA 1984, s 71A and age 18–25 trusts falling within IHTA 1984, s 71D;

(c)   specially relieved trusts being various categories of trust receiving a special treatment.

Relevant property trusts

Inheritance tax

Settling assets

[6.9] The settlement of any property will be a settlement of relevant property unless the settlement falls within one of the categories listed in **6.8** above. Most settlements made after 21 March 2006 are relevant property trusts. The settlement of relevant property is a chargeable transfer and cannot be a potentially exempt transfer ('PET'). The settlement will therefore trigger a charge to inheritance tax unless it is covered by an exemption or relief or by the unused portion of the transferor's nil rate band. The exemptions or reliefs which might normally apply are:

(a)   the annual exemption;
(b)   the exemption for normal expenditure out of income;
(c)   the exemption for gifts in consideration of marriage;
(d)   the relief for business property;
(e)   the relief for agricultural property.

Caution should be exercised when creating a relevant property settlement if other gifts are to be made at or about the same time. A potentially exempt transfer made before a chargeable transfer to a relevant property settlement, which subsequently becomes chargeable, will affect not only the amount of charge on the transfer to the settlement but also the decennial and exit charges on the settlement for as long as it continues.

Decennial charges under IHTA 1984, s 64 (see **6.13** below) are calculated in part by reference to the settlor's chargeable transfers in the seven years before the settlor made the settlement. An exit charge under IHTA 1984, s 65 (see **6.17** below) similarly takes into account such chargeable transfers either directly, in the case of occasions of charge before the first decennial of the settlement (under IHTA 1984, s 68), or indirectly because the computation incorporates the computation made on the preceding decennial. If the settlor were to die in the first seven years after the creation of the settlement, the potentially exempt transfers which they had made in the seven years before their death would become chargeable. If those chargeable transfers were made before the creation of the settlement they will affect future decennial charges (under IHTA 1984, s 64) and exit charges (under IHTA 1984, s 65). So in deciding whether to make advances from a settlement in the period which ends before the earlier of the settlor's death and seven years after the settlement is made, the trustees will not know the rate at which tax will be charged under IHTA 1984, s 65. In many cases it will be possible for the trustees to retain sufficient assets as a reserve to guard against this risk or to make some sort of indemnity arrangement but in order to avoid such problems it will usually be prudent to ensure that transfers to such relevant property settlements pre-date any potentially exempt transfers.

The amounts which can be settled without triggering an immediate charge to inheritance tax may be increased significantly if business or agricultural property is used. Business and agricultural property relief may be available at either 50% or 100% depending upon the nature of the property.

Where business or agricultural property would qualify for relief at 100% there is no inheritance tax advantage to be gained from transferring it out of a taxpayer's estate unless it is going to be converted, for example by a sale, into an asset which does not receive the full relief.

So, for example, if one holds shares in a family trading company which one expects to sell within the next two or three years for cash, one might settle those shares immediately so as to place them in trust with the benefit of the relief. There is, however, a potential trap here. As we shall see (see **6.17** below), on a distribution of property from a relevant property trust prior to the first decennial charge, the exit charge is calculated at a rate derived by reference to the value of property comprised in the settlement immediately after it became so comprised. For the purpose of this hypothetical charge, therefore, the property will not be able to satisfy the minimum ownership periods which are part of the conditions of these reliefs. That will not matter if the property continues to qualify for 100% relief but, if it does not, one could be in the position of either suffering an exit charge on advancing the property out of the settlement or suffering a decennial charge (see **6.13** below). What is more, settling such property will have the result that on the settlor's death its base cost for capital gains tax purposes will not be adjusted to its then market value as it would have been had it not been settled.

Of course, there will often be good commercial and other non-fiscal reasons for settling business or agricultural property. Unfortunately, in most circumstances there will be a tax penalty in doing so.

Taxation of the trustees

[6.10] In deciding whether to make a relevant property settlement one obviously needs to consider how the trust will be taxed over its life.

There are two occasions of charge. The settlement will be subject to a decennial charge on each tenth anniversary of its being made and an exit charge whenever property which is relevant property ceases to be so.

Same-day additions

[6.11] The Finance (No 2) Act 2015 (F(No 2)A 2015) amended IHTA 1984 in respect of what are referred to as 'same-day additions' to most forms of settlement for the purpose of calculating decennial and exit charges and also made certain simplifications to such calculations so that, for example, it is no longer necessary to take account of property that has never been relevant property. These amendments apply to tax charges arising after 17 November 2017, the date on which the Royal Assent was given to the F(No 2)A 2015. For these purposes, IHTA 1984, s 62A provides that:

' . . . there is a "same-day addition", in relation to a settlement ("settlement A"), if–

(a)   there is a transfer of value by a person as a result of which the value immediately afterwards of the property comprised in settlement A is greater than the value immediately before,

(b)   as a result of the same transfer of value, or as a result of another transfer of value made by that person on the same day, the value immediately afterwards of the property comprised in another settlement ("settlement B") is greater than the value immediately before,

(c)   that person is the settlor of settlement A and settlement B,

(d)   at any point in the relevant period, all or any part of the property comprised in settlement A was relevant property, and

(e)   at that point, or at any other point in the relevant period, all or any part of the property comprised in settlement B was relevant property.

    . . .

(2)   Where there is a same-day addition, references . . . to its value are to the difference between the two values mentioned in subsection (1)(b).

(3)   "The relevant period" means–

(a)   in the case of settlement A, the period beginning with the commencement of settlement A and ending immediately after the transfer of value mentioned in subsection (1)(a), and

(b)   in the case of settlement B, the period beginning with the commencement of settlement B and ending immediately after the transfer of value mentioned in subsection (1)(b)).

(4)   The transfer or transfers of value mentioned in subsection (1) include a transfer or transfers of value as a result of which property first becomes comprised in settlement A or settlement B; but not if settlements A and B are related settlements.

(5)   For the purposes of subsection (1) above, it is immaterial whether the amount of the property comprised in settlement A or settlement B (or neither) was increased as a result of the transfer or transfers of value mentioned in that subsection.'

IHTA 1984, s 62B(1) then makes certain exceptions to this definition of same-day additions:

'(1)   There is not a same-day addition for the purposes of this Chapter if any of the following conditions is met–

(a)   immediately   after   the   transfer   of   value   mentioned   in section 62A(1)(a) all the property comprised in settlement A was held for charitable purposes only without limit of time (defined by a date or otherwise),

(b)   immediately   after   the   transfer   of   value   mentioned   in section 62A(1)(b) all the property comprised in settlement B was so held,

(c)   either or each of settlement A and settlement B is a protected settlement (see section 62C), and

(d)   the transfer of value, or either or each of the transfers of value, mentioned in section 62A(1)(a) and (b)–

(i)   results from the payment of a premium under a contract of life insurance the terms of which provide for premiums to be due at regular intervals of one year or less throughout the contract term, or

(ii)   is made to fund such a payment.

(2)   If the transfer of value, or each of the transfers of value, mentioned in section 62A(1) is not the transfer of value under section 4 on the settlor's death, there is a same-day addition for the purposes of this Chapter only if conditions A and B are met.

(3)   Condition A is that—

(a)   the difference between the two values mentioned in section 62A(1)(a) exceeds £5,000, or

(b)   in a case where there has been more than one transfer of value within section 62A(1)(a) on the same day, the difference between—
(i)   the value of the property comprised in settlement A immediately before the first of those transfers, and
(ii)   the value of the property comprised in settlement A immediately after the last of those transfers,
exceeds £5,000.

(4)   Condition B is that—

(a)   the difference between the two values mentioned in section 62A(1)(b) exceeds £5,000, or

(b)   in a case where there has been more than one transfer of value within section 62A(1)(b), the difference between—
(i)   the value of the property comprised in settlement B immediately before the first of those transfers, and
(ii)   the value of the property comprised in settlement B immediately after the last of those transfers,
exceeds £5,000.'

It can be seen, therefore, that the exemptions relate, expressing the matter loosely, to transfers to charities and small additions of £5,000 or less.

Protected settlements

[6.12] IHTA 1984, s 62C provides that a settlement is a protected settlement for this purpose if:

'(1)   . . . it commenced before 10 December 2014 and either condition A or condition B is met.

(2)   Condition A is met if there have been no transfers of value by the settlor on or after 10 December 2014 as a result of which the value of the property comprised in the settlement was increased.

(3)   Condition B is met if—

(a)   there has been a transfer of value by the settlor on or after 10 December 2014 as a result of which the value of the property comprised in the settlement was increased, and

(b)   that transfer of value was the transfer of value under section 4 on the settlor's death before 6 April 2017 and it had the result mentioned by reason of a protected testamentary disposition.

(4)   In subsection (3)(b) "protected testamentary disposition" means a disposition effected by provisions of the settlor's will that at the settlor's death are, in substance, the same as they were immediately before 10 December 2014.'

In the paragraphs that follow we first describe the rules as amended by the F(No 2)A 2015 which apply to settlements that are not protected settlements.

The decennial charge

[6.13] At each decennial of a settlement in which relevant property is comprised, inheritance tax is charged on the value of the relevant property on that date (IHTA 1984, s 64). The rate at which tax is charged is three tenths of the rate (called the 'effective rate') at which tax would be charged on a hypothetical chargeable transfer of a description specified in IHTA 1984, s 66(3).

IHTA 1984, s 66(4) provides that the hypothetical chargeable transfer is of an amount equal to the aggregate of:

'(a)   the value on which tax is charged under section 64 [that is, the value of the relevant property in the settlement at the decennial];

(b)   . . .

(c)   the value, immediately after a related settlement commenced, of the relevant property then comprised in it;

(d)   the value of any same-day addition; and

(e)   where–

    (i)   an increase in the value of the property comprised in another settlement is represented by the value of a same-day addition aggregated under paragraph (d) above, and

    (ii)   that other settlement is not a related settlement,

    the value immediately after that other settlement commenced of the relevant property then comprised in that other settlement;'.

This is subject to IHTA 1984, s 66(6), which contains provisions that apply to settlements that commenced before the introduction of capital transfer tax (as inheritance tax was originally called) on 27 March 1974.

IHTA 1984, s 66(5) provides that the hypothetical chargeable transfer is to be treated as if it had been made immediately before the decennial by a transferor who has, in the preceding seven years, made chargeable transfers of value equal to the aggregate of:

'(a)   the values transferred by any chargeable transfers made by the settlor in the period of seven years ending with the day on which the settlement commenced, disregarding transfers made on that day or before 27 March 1974, and

(b)   the amounts on which any charges to tax were imposed under section 65 [exit charges] above in respect of the settlement in the ten years before the anniversary concerned;'.

This is subject to ss 66(6) and 67 (which makes provision in respect of property which is added to a settlement after it commences).

Income of a settlement arising directly or indirectly from relevant property in the settlement immediately before the decennial at a time when no person was beneficially entitled to an interest in possession in the underlying property, is treated as relevant property for the purposes of the decennial charge under IHTA 1984, s 64(1A) if the income arose before the start of the five years ending immediately before the decennial. There are a number of exclusions to this deeming rule, which takes effect in relation to tax charges under IHTA 1984, s 64 arising after 5 April 2014.

Other settlements made on the same day by the same settlor are 'related settlements' unless the property is held for charitable purposes only (IHTA 1984, s 62).

Before the coming into force of the provisions of F(No 2)A 2015 relating to same-day additions, two principal techniques existed involving the use of multiple settlements with the purpose of reducing future decennial and exit charges where the settled property was expected to increase in value. We consider below these formerly common tax planning techniques and the extent to which, in respect of settlements which are protected settlements and those which are not, they continue to confer inheritance tax advantages.

The Pilot Settlements Strategy

[6.14] It was in order to negate the advantages of the Pilot Settlements Strategy that HMRC proposed the enactment of the same-day additions rules. The strategy involved making two or more settlements on different days followed by making large additions to the settlements on the same day.

Not a single settlement?

[6.15] The Revenue (as it then was) had claimed that techniques such as these, in which settlements are created successively, create single settlements by associated operations at the time that the final settlement is made.

The case of *Rysaffe Trustee Co (CI) Ltd v IRC* [2003] EWCA Civ 356, [2003] STC 536, 5 ITELR 706, concerned two brothers who each made five discretionary settlements by separate trust instruments. Each settlement was in exactly the same form, except for the date, which was inserted by the settlors' solicitors after the execution of the deeds. The trust fund of each settlement was £10 paid by each settlor. Shares were later settled on each of the settlements, apparently simultaneously. The Revenue contended that, in respect of each settlor, the creation of the five settlements and the transfer of the shares to the trustee were all associated operations. Therefore, there was a single settlement within the meaning of IHTA 1984, s 43 and, for the purposes of the decennial charge, tax should have been charged under IHTA 1984, s 64 at the rate applicable to the total value in all five settlements. In the alternative, it considered that the five settlements were five 'dispositions of property' within the meaning of IHTA 1984, s 43, which resulted in one settlement.

The Court of Appeal held that it was not relevant that the five settlements were nearly identical. There were separate documents with separate dates and the settlor had intended to create five different settlements. The five settlements could not be artificially amalgamated merely because their terms were similar. The associated operations provisions did not apply and it was not appropriate to regard the five settlements as created by associated operations.

In its GAAR guidance at Example D26, published in a revised form on 30 January 2015 (and therefore before the enactment of F(No 2)A 2015), HMRC gives an example of an individual creating seven trusts over seven days settling £100 on each trust. Under his will he leaves £250,000 to each trust. The guidance says that the 'practice was litigated in the case of *Rysaffe Trustee v IRC* [2003] STC 536. HMRC lost the case and having chosen not to change the legislation, must be taken to have accepted the practice . . . the arrangements accord with established practice accepted by HMRC and are accordingly not regarded as abusive.' In spite of this, the Government has chosen to enact the same-day additions rules designed to counteract this longstanding estate planning technique which even HMRC acknowledged in its guidance not to be abusive. As we shall see, however, the same-day additions rules seem only to reduce the advantages of the strategy and not to negate them entirely.

We illustrate the Pilot Settlements Strategy in the following examples starting with an example of a simple settlement to give a point of comparison.

Pilot Settlements Strategy – Example I: single unprotected settlement

Mr A made a chargeable transfer of £20,000 on 31 December 2010. On 31 December 2014, he settled £305,000 on trusts (the 'A Settlement') from which he was excluded from benefitting but of which his children and grandchildren were beneficial objects. On 30 December 2024, the settled property had a market value of £1,305,000. Mr A had made no other settlements or chargeable transfers and no exit charges had arisen on the settlement under IHTA 1984, s 65. Rates and allowances are assumed to be unchanged in all relevant periods.

The first decennial charge arose on the 31 December 2024 (actually it is arguable that it arises on 30 December 2024 but most commentators and HMRC seem to assume that a charge arises on the decennial, although by reference to the value of the relevant property, immediately before the decennial (see HMRC Inheritance Tax Manual para 42081). The calculation of the tax chargeable was as follows:

	£	£
Hypothetical Chargeable Transfer under IHTA 1984, s 66(4)		
Amount on which tax is chargeable under IHTA 1984, s 64	1,305,000	
Value immediately after it commenced of relevant property in a related settlement	0	
Value of any same-day additions	0	
Value of relevant property in certain other settlements immediately after the settlement concerned commenced (IHTA 1984, s 66(4)(e))	0	
		1,305,000
By Transferor who has made chargeable transfers in the last seven years of the following aggregate value		
Chargeable transfers made by settlor in seven years ending with day on which the settlement commenced disregarding transfers on that day	20,000	
Amounts on which exit charges in last ten years were imposed	0	

	20,000
	1,325,000
Nil Rate Band	325,000
	1,000,000
Tax thereon @20%	200,000
Effective Rate (Tax calculated above/ Hypothetical chargeable transfer)	15.32567%
Rate at which tax is chargeable (30% of Effective Rate)	4.59770%
Tax charged (Rate at which tax is chargeable x amount on which tax is chargeable under IHTA 1984, s 64)	60,000

Pilot Settlements Strategy – Example II: two protected settlements

If Mr A had made his settlement before 10 December 2014, the date from which the rules in respect of same-day additions had effect, he would probably have been advised to make two or more settlements in a pattern such as the following:

- 30 November 2014 settles £1,000 on Trust I.
- 1 December 2014 settles £1,000 on Trust II.
- 9 December 2014 adds £151,500 to each of Trust I and Trust II.

These settlements are not related settlements because they are not made on the same day and they are protected settlements. Therefore, the first decennial charges on the settlements (on the 30 November and 1 December 2024) would have been calculated as follows:

	Trust I		Trust II	
	£	£	£	£
Hypothetical Chargeable Transfer under IHTA 1984, s 66(4)				
Amount on which tax is chargeable under IHTA 1984, s 64	652,500		652,500	
Value immediately after it commenced of relevant property in a related settlement	0		0	
Value of any same-day additions	0		0	
Value of relevant property in certain other settlements immediately after the settlement concerned commenced (IHTA 1984, s 66(4)(e))	0		0	
		652,500		652,500

	Trust I		Trust II	
	£	£	£	£
By Transferor who has made chargeable transfers in the last seven years of the following aggregate value				
Chargeable transfers made by settlor in seven years ending with day on which the settlement commenced disregarding transfers on that day	20,000		21,000	
Amounts on which exit charges in last ten years were imposed	0		0	
		20,000		21,000
		672,500		673,500
Nil Rate Band		325,000		325,000
		347,500		348,500
Tax thereon @20%		69,500		69,700
Effective Rate (tax calculated above/hypothetical chargeable transfer)		10.65134%		10.68199%
Rate at which tax is chargeable (30% of Effective Rate)		3.19540%		3.20460%
Tax charged (rate at which tax is chargeable × amount on which tax is chargeable under IHTA 1984, s 64)		20,850		20,910

So by making two settlements and doing so a month earlier, Mr A would have saved his trustees' inheritance tax of £18,240 (£60,000 – (£20,850 + £20,910)).

Pilot Settlements Strategy – Example III: two unprotected settlements with additions

What would have happened if Mr A had adopted the same two-settlement strategy after the 10 December 2014 so that the two settlements were not protected settlements?

	Trust I		Trust II	
	£	£	£	£
Hypothetical Chargeable Transfer under IHTA 1984, s 66(4)				
Amount on which tax is chargeable under IHTA 1984, s 64	652,500		652,500	
Value immediately after it commenced of relevant property in a related settlement	0		0	

	Trust I		Trust II	
	£	£	£	£
Value of any same-day additions	151,500		151,500	
Value of relevant property in certain other settlements immediately after the settlement concerned commenced (IHTA 1984, s 66(4)(e))	1,000		1,000	
		805,000		805,000
By Transferor who has made chargeable transfers in the last seven years of the following aggregate value				
Chargeable transfers made by settlor in seven years ending with day on which the settlement commenced disregarding transfers on that day	20,000		21,000	
Amounts on which exit charges in last ten years were imposed	0		0	
		20,000		21,000
		825,000		826,000
Nil Rate Band		325,000		325,000
		500,000		501,000
Tax thereon @20%		100,000		100,200
Effective Rate (tax calculated above/hypothetical chargeable transfer)		12.42236%		12.44720%
Rate at which tax is chargeable (30% of Effective Rate)		3.72671%		3.73416%
Tax charged (rate at which tax is chargeable × amount on which tax is chargeable under IHTA 1984, s 64)		24,317		24,365

It can be seen that the property initially settled in Trust I is taken into account twice in the computation for it is included in the total in respect of IHTA 1984, s 66(4)(e) as part of the hypothetical chargeable transfer and it is included as part of the hypothetical prior transfers under IHTA 1984, s 66(5)(a). Even so, if Mr A had adopted the strategy of settling two settlements and subsequently making same-day additions to them, even though the settlements would have been unprotected settlements, he would still have saved inheritance tax for his trustees, albeit of a lesser amount (being £11,318 (£60,000 – (£24,317 + £24,365)) than would have been saved had the settlements been protected settlements. Surprisingly, the introduction of the same-day additions rules has only reduced and not entirely eliminated the advantages which making multiple settlements can offer. It may be, however, that the administrative burden of multiplying settlements now outweighs the rather modest tax benefits which they confer.

Pilot Settlements Strategy – Example IV: two unprotected settlements without additions

This pattern of making two settlements on successive days followed by same-day additions may be contrasted with the charge which would have arisen had Mr A simply made two settlements of £162,500 on successive days without making subsequent additions:

	Trust I		Trust II	
	£	£	£	£
Hypothetical Chargeable Transfer under IHTA 1984, s 66(4)				
Amount on which tax is chargeable under IHTA 1984, s 64	652,500		652,500	
Value immediately after it commenced of relevant property in a related settlement	0		0	
Value of any same-day additions	0		0	
Value of relevant property in certain other settlements immediately after the settlement concerned commenced (IHTA 1984, s 66(4)(e))	0		0	
		652,500		652,500
By Transferor who has made chargeable transfers in the last seven years of the following aggregate value				
Chargeable transfers made by settlor in seven years ending with day on which the settlement commenced disregarding transfers on that day	20,000		182,500	
Amounts on which exit charges in last ten years were imposed	0		0	
		20,000		182,500
		672,500		835,000
Nil Rate Band		325,000		325,000
		347,500		510,000
Tax thereon @20%		69,500		102,000
Effective Rate of Tax (tax calculated above/hypothetical chargeable transfer)		10.65134%		15.63218%
Rate at which tax is chargeable (30% of Effective Rate)		3.19540%		4.68966%
Tax charged (Rate at which tax is chargeable x amount on which tax is chargeable under IHTA 1984, s 64)		20,850		30,600

It will be seen that the total tax charged is higher than where the majority of the property is settled by way of same-day additions but is still less than if only a single settlement were made.

The 'cascade' strategy

[6.16] Under this strategy a series of pilot relevant property settlements are established at intervals over a period of time by a settlor with no history of chargeable transfers (and, ideally, no potentially exempt transfers) made within the last seven years. For example, the establishment of ten successive settlements of £32,500 would have the result that the first settlement of £32,500 would itself have to reach £325,000 in value at its decennial for a decennial charge to arise. However, the 'clock' of each subsequent settlement would take into account the earlier settled gifts, with the scope for future inheritance tax-free growth in the later trusts being reduced accordingly.

Example

Discretionary Trust No	Initial value	Available 'margin' for future growth
	£	£
1	32,500	292,500
2	32,500	260,000
3	32,500	227,500
4	32,500	195,000
5	32,500	162,500
6	32,500	130,000
7	32,500	97,500
8	32,500	65,000
9	32,500	32,500
10	32,500	Nil
	£325,000	£1,462,500

This strategy is unaffected by the introduction of the same-day addition rules. A disadvantage of the strategy is that the number of trusts involved may be unwieldy and might be difficult to co-ordinate. Although this is undoubtedly a practical disadvantage of the strategy the keen-eyed reader will have seen that the example, 'the Pilot Strategy – Example IV' is a version of the cascade strategy involving just two settlements and that it results in a tax liability which is 15% less than the inheritance tax which would have been charged on the first decennial if just one settlement were made. Determining the optimum number of settlements to be made in implementing this strategy is a matter of balancing the inheritance tax savings from having more settlements against the additional administration costs of doing so.

Exit charges

[6.17] There is a charge to inheritance tax under IHTA 1984, s 65:

'(1)   . . .

   (a)   where the property comprised in a settlement or any part of that property ceases to be relevant property (whether because it ceases to be comprised in the settlement or otherwise); and

   (b)   in a case in which paragraph (a) above does not apply, where the trustees of the settlement make a disposition as a result of which the value of relevant property comprised in the settlement is less than it would be but for the disposition.'

On an occasion of charge under IHTA 1984, s 65, the tax chargeable is found by applying the appropriate fraction of the effective rate charged at the previous decennial to:

'(2)   . . .

   (a)   the amount by which the value of relevant property comprised in the settlement is less immediately after the event in question than it would be but for the event, or

   (b)   where the tax payable is paid out of relevant property comprised in the settlement immediately after the event, the amount which, after deducting the tax, is equal to the amount on which tax would be charged by virtue of paragraph (a) above.'

If a distribution is made prior to the first decennial the rate to which the appropriate fraction is applied is found by applying a special computational basis (IHTA 1984, s 68).

The appropriate fraction is 1/40th for each complete quarter in the period from the last decennial (or the creation of the settlement) to the day before the date of distribution (IHTA 1984, s 69) multiplied by 30%.

The special computational basis, set out in s 68, for determining the rate applying to exit charges before the first decennial is as follows.

The rate of tax is calculated as though an individual with the cumulative total of the settlor immediately prior to the creation of the settlement had made a transfer of value equal to the total of:

'(5)   . . .

   (a)   the value, immediately after the settlement commenced, of the relevant property then comprised in it;

   (b)   the value, immediately after a related settlement commenced, of the relevant property then comprised in it;

   (c)   the value, immediately after it became comprised in the settlement, of property which–
      (i)   became comprised in the settlement after the settlement commenced and before the occasion of the charge under section 65 above, and
      (ii)   was relevant property immediately after it became so comprised,
      whether or not the property has remained relevant property comprised in the settlement;

   (d)   the value, at the time it became (or last became) relevant property, of property which–

(i) was comprised in the settlement immediately after the settlement commenced and was not then relevant property but became relevant property before the occasion of the charge under section 65 above, or

(ii) became comprised in the settlement after the settlement commenced and before the occasion of the charge under section 65 above, and was not relevant property immediately after it became comprised in the settlement, but became relevant property before the occasion of the charge under that section,

whether or not the property has remained relevant property comprised in the settlement;

(e) the value of any same-day addition; and

(f) where–

(i) an increase in the value of the property comprised in another settlement is represented by the value of a same-day addition aggregated under paragraph (e) above, and

(ii) that other settlement is not a related settlement,

the value immediately after that other settlement commenced of the relevant property then comprised in that other settlement.'

Payments received by a beneficiary from trustees of a discretionary settlement which is his income for income tax purposes do not suffer an inheritance tax charge on their distribution to him (IHTA 1984, s 65(5)(b)).

As a result of this method of charging inheritance tax, where the settlor, immediately prior to the creation of a relevant property settlement, has made no chargeable transfers in the previous seven years and the value of the relevant property comprised in the settlement immediately after it commenced, together with the value of later additions, did not exceed the maximum amount that can (at the time of distribution) be transferred without incurring a charge to inheritance tax (£325,000 for 2016/17), distributions from a relevant property settlement before the first decennial will not bear inheritance tax. This is because the rate of tax for distributions before that date is under these circumstances fixed at nil. Where, however, the property settled qualifies for agricultural or business property relief, such relief is not taken into account when determining the applicable rate under IHTA 1984, s 65. So unless the economic value of the property settled falls below the nil rate band, only appointments of property which qualify for 100% agricultural or business property relief can be made after the first decennial without incurring an actual inheritance tax charge (see the further discussion at para **6.19** below).

Added property

[6.18] Care must be taken if at any time property is to be added to an existing relevant property settlement. If the settlor has made any chargeable transfers since creating the settlement, his cumulative total prior to the date of any addition, if greater, may be substituted for his pre-settlement cumulative total for the purposes of calculating the rate of inheritance tax on the subsequent decennial (IHTA 1984, s 67). In calculating the settlor's cumulative transfers prior to the date of addition, one ignores transfers which were themselves additions to the settlement.

These special rules, which apply where there have been additions to a settlement, only apply where the additions were chargeable transfers. The annual exemption may, for example, be used to top up relevant property settlements without adverse effect as may transfers falling within the normal expenditure out of income exemption (which is discussed in CHAPTER 4 LIFETIME PLANNING: MAKING GIFTS). Additions may also be made before the first decennial without affecting the rate at that time if the settlor's nil rate band (including any uplift since the creation of the settlement) has not been fully utilised.

Business and agricultural property relief

[6.19] On any distribution of property from a relevant property settlement prior to the first decennial, no account is taken of the fact that the property (when it became comprised in the settlement) may have been of a type eligible for business or agricultural property relief. This is because one of the steps in calculating the inheritance tax on such a distribution involves calculating the tax that would be due on a hypothetical transfer of property. Under IHTA 1984, s 68(5) the value transferred by that hypothetical transfer is the aggregate of six amounts including 'the value, immediately after the settlement commenced, of the relevant property then comprised in it'. That will include the value of agricultural property and business property but the value of that property will not be reduced by business or agricultural property relief because immediately after the settlement commenced the trustees will not have held the property for the minimum ownership period.

Where the settled property will not qualify for agricultural or business property relief on ceasing to be relevant property, because, for example, the property has been replaced by property of another type, the tax charge may be reduced by forward planning, as the following example illustrates.

Example

Mr A intends to settle, for non-fiscal reasons, property qualifying for 100% business property relief with a value of £650,000. The settled property will be relevant property. He has made no prior transfers and anticipates that the business property will be sold for cash within one year. In five years' time it is likely that the trustees will decide to distribute the settled property, in the form of money, to the beneficiaries when its value is expected to be £1,000,000.

There would be no charge on making the settlement because the property would be wholly relieved by business property relief. On the distribution to the beneficiaries the tax charge would be calculated by reference to a deemed transfer when the settlement was created which did not qualify for business property relief as follows:

Exit charge before first decennial: single settlement

	£	£
Hypothetical Chargeable Transfer under IHTA 1984, s 68(5)		
(a) The value, immediately after the settlement commenced, of the relevant property then comprised in it.	650,000	

	£	£

(b) The value, immediately after a related settlement commenced, of the relevant property then comprised in it. — 0

(c) The value, immediately after it became comprised in the settlement, of property which (i) became comprised in the settlement after the settlement commenced and before the occasion of the charge under s 65, and (ii) was relevant property immediately after it became so comprised. — 0

(d) The value, at the time it became (or last became) relevant property, of property which (i) was comprised in the settlement immediately after the settlement commenced and was not then relevant property but became relevant property before the occasion of the charge under s 65, or (ii) became comprised in the settlement after the settlement commenced and before the occasion of the charge under s 65, and was not relevant property immediately after it became comprised in the settlement, but became relevant property before the occasion of the charge under that section. — 0

(e) The value of any same-day addition. — 0

(f) Where (i) an increase in the value of the property comprised in another settlement is represented by the value of a same-day addition aggregated under para (e) above, and (ii) that other settlement is not a related settlement, the value immediately after that other settlement commenced of the relevant property then comprised in that other settlement. — 0

650,000

By Transferor who has made chargeable transfers in the last seven years of the following aggregate value

Chargeable transfers made by settlor in seven years ending with day on which the settlement commenced disregarding transfers on that day — 0

		0
		650,000
Nil Rate Band		325,000
		325,000
Tax thereon @20%		65,000
Effective Rate (tax calculated above/hypothetical chargeable transfer)		10.00%
Rate at which tax is chargeable (30% of Effective Rate × 20/40)		1.50%

	£	£
Tax charged (rate at which tax is chargeable × amount on which tax is chargeable under IHTA 1984, s 65(2), being £1,000,000)		15,000

As an alternative Mr A considers the following course of action.

Mr A makes two relevant property settlements (Trusts I and II) on succeeding days settling business property with a value of £325,000 on each. The beneficial class of each settlement is to consist of his children and grandchildren. One year later, the settled property will be sold. On the fifth anniversaries of the settlements, the trustees will advance the whole of the capital of each trust, then being £500,000 each, to one or more beneficiaries of the settlement concerned.

Exit charge before first decennial: relieved property strategy

	Trust I		Trust II	
	£	£	£	£
Hypothetical Chargeable Transfer under IHTA 1984, s 68(5)				
(a) The value, immediately after the settlement commenced, of the relevant property then comprised in it.	325,000		325,000	
(b) The value, immediately after a related settlement commenced, of the relevant property then comprised in it.	0		0	
(c) The value, immediately after it became comprised in the settlement, of property which (i) became comprised in the settlement after the settlement commenced and before the occasion of the charge under s 65, and (ii) was relevant property immediately after it became so comprised.	0		0	
(d) The value, at the time it became (or last became) relevant property, of property which (i) was comprised in the settlement immediately after the settlement commenced and was not then relevant property but became relevant property before the occasion of the charge under s 65, or (ii) became comprised in the settlement after the settlement commenced and before the occasion of the charge under s 65, and was not relevant property immediately after it became comprised in the settlement, but became relevant property before the occasion of the charge under that section.	0		0	
(e) The value of any same-day addition.	0		0	

	Trust I		Trust II	
	£	£	£	£
(f) Where (i) an increase in the value of the property comprised in another settlement is represented by the value of a same-day addition aggregated under para (e) above, and (ii) that other settlement is not a related settlement, the value immediately after that other settlement commenced of the relevant property then comprised in that other settlement.	0		0	
		325,000		325,000
By Transferor who has made chargeable transfers in the last seven years of the following aggregate value				
Chargeable transfers made by settlor in seven years ending with day on which the settlement commenced disregarding transfers on that day	0		0	
		0		0
		325,000		325,000
Nil Rate Band		325,000		325,000
		0		0
Tax thereon @ 20%		0		0
Effective Rate (tax calculated above/ hypothetical chargeable transfer)		0.00%		0.00%
Rate at which tax is chargeable (30% of Effective Rate × 20/40)		0.00%		0.00%
Tax charged (rate at which tax is chargeable × amount on which tax is chargeable under IHTA 1984, s 65(2), being £500,000 per settlement)		0		0

Mr A will make no chargeable transfer on his settlement of Trust I because the property he settles qualifies for business property relief. So, although business property relief does not reduce the hypothetical chargeable transfer in respect of which the effective rate is calculated, it does reduce the prior chargeable transfers of the hypothetical transferor which is also brought into the calculation of the effective rate. It is this which accounts for the reduction of the exit charge when comparing the result of making a single settlement with the result of the alternative course of action.

Valuation of relevant property

[6.20] One of the interesting consequences of the extension of the decennial and exit charges to most interest in possession trusts is in relation to the valuation of property. If property is held in a trust to which IHTA 1984, s 49 applies — namely, a privileged interest trust — it will be valued as if it were owned by the holder of the interest in possession and therefore in conjunction with the property actually owned by that beneficiary. If an interest in possession trust is a relevant property settlement however, the property in the settlement will be valued in isolation. Consider the following example.

Example

The valuations of shareholdings in an investment company, InvCo, reflect the greater control conferred by a majority holding so that the shareholdings have the following values:

An 80% holding = £1,000,000

A 40% holding = £250,000

Mr A owns a 40% holding in InvCo as do the trustees of a trust in which he has an interest in possession. Because the trust was established after 22 March 2006 it is a relevant property trust to which IHTA 1984, s 49 does not apply. Therefore Mr A's shareholding and that of the trust are both valued at £250,000. Had s 49 applied to the trust, Mr A would have been treated as owning an 80% shareholding worth £1,000,000 (although a specific valuation rule would have applied had his interest in possession come to an end during his lifetime).

Capital gains tax

The settling of assets

[6.21] The settling of assets will be a disposal of those assets deemed to take place at their market value (TCGA 1992, s 17(1)(a)). Hold-over relief under TCGA 1992, s 260 (gifts on which inheritance tax is chargeable etc) will be available on a transfer to a relevant property trust unless the trust is a non-resident trust or the settlor has an interest in the settlement. If the property qualifies as a business asset within TCGA 1992, s 165 hold-over relief for gifts of business assets would be available as an alternative, subject to the same exceptions.

Gains realised by the trustees

[6.22] Trustees of settlements are treated as if they were a single body of persons (distinct from the persons who are trustees of the settlement from time to time) and are therefore subject to capital gains tax on their disposals. The trustees have their own capital gains tax allowance which is normally one half of the personal allowance so that in 2016/17 it is £5,550. However, this exemption is divided by the number of qualifying settlements created after 6 June 1978 by one settlor. Essentially, a qualifying settlement is one which is not either a non-resident settlement, a charity or a retirement benefit scheme. The annual allowance cannot be reduced to less than one fifth of the normal trustee allowance under this provision and so, in 2016/17, cannot be less than £2,220.

Gains realised on disposals made by trustees are chargeable at 20% except that gains on residential property are charged at 28%.

Gains arising on disposals of assets to beneficiaries by the trustees of a relevant property settlement may also be held over under s 260, regardless of whether the disposal gives rise to an inheritance tax liability. Section 260 applies, *inter alia*, only where a chargeable transfer occurs, even if it is one chargeable at a nil rate of tax.

Relief for gifts of business assets under TCGA 1992, s 165 may also be available.

Income tax

[6.23] The general rule is that trustees are subject to income tax at the basic rate (20% in 2016/17) on all the income arising from assets held by the trustees. A beneficiary entitled to the income receives a credit for the tax paid by the trustees. There are, of course, exceptions to this general rule. Income tax at the trust rate or dividend trust rate (45% and 38.1% respectively in 2016/17) will be payable where the income arising to the trustees is income which is to be accumulated or which is payable at the discretion of any other person and which is not, before being distributed:

(a)   the income of any person; or
(b)   charitable income; or
(c)   income arising, loosely, to a retirement benefit scheme (ITA 2007, ss 479 and 480).

Such income is referred to as 'discretionary trust income' in this Book. Other income arising to the trustees not falling within the three exceptions given above is referred to in this Book as 'IIP income'.

Discretionary trust income

[6.24] Discretionary trust income will be subject to tax at the trust rate of 45% in 2016/17 unless it is dividend income in which case it will be taxed at the dividend trust rate of 38.1%. This is subject to the following exceptions.

The first £1,000 of income ('the standard rate band') is chargeable at 7.5% in respect of dividend type income and 20% for all other income (ITA 2007, s 491). Over £1,000 the rate is 38.1% for dividend type income and 45% for all other income. Similar provisions to those applying to the capital gains tax annual allowance reduce the standard rate band where a single settlor makes several settlements. The standard rate band cannot be less than £200.

A discretionary beneficiary has no right to income. Any payments that he receives are chargeable as his income and he receives a credit for the tax paid in respect of that income by the trustees. The £5,000 tax free dividend allowance applies only to individuals and not, therefore, to trustees.

In relation to discretionary trusts, until this fiscal year, the fact that the dividend tax credit was not repayable represented a considerable tax penalty on the use of trusts. The abolition of the dividend tax credit has removed that penalty but the fact that the trust rate and dividend trust rates are set at the same rate as the additional, and additional dividend, rates for individuals which apply only to taxable income over £150,000 means that where discretionary trust income is distributed to a beneficiary whose income bears tax at a marginal rate lower than the additional rates there may be a cash flow disadvantage when that situation is compared to the income arising to the beneficiary directly. This is always the case where the income is distributed in a fiscal year after the year in which it arises.

Where trustees have the power to accumulate, it is advisable that they should also have power to distribute accumulated income as though it were income of the year in which it is so distributed. That is so that accumulated funds may subsequently be distributed as income rather than as capital if a consideration of the beneficiary's rates of income tax and the rate of inheritance tax charged if a capital payment is made suggest that this would be advantageous. It should be noted, however, that HMRC says in its Trust Manual that 'accumulated income becomes capital in the hands of the trustees. They may be able to pay it as if it were income but it remains capital.'

If the trust is a trust for a vulnerable beneficiary (see **6.41** below) and an election has been made, the trustees can in effect be taxed on trust income as if it were income of the vulnerable beneficiary taking into account the beneficiary's personal allowances, starting and basic rate tax bands.

IIP income

[6.25] The trustees of an interest in possession trust do not pay tax at the trust rate except on certain amounts which are capital for trust law purposes but are subject to income tax. They are:

(a)   payments made by a company by way of qualifying distribution on the redemption, repayment or purchase of its own shares or on the purchase of a right to acquire its own shares (in this case the dividend rate of 38.1% will apply);
(b)   deemed income receipts under the accrued income scheme;
(c)   offshore income gains;
(d)   chargeable events in relation to employee share ownership trusts;
(e)   profits of a property business in relation to lease premiums;
(f)   profits on the disposal of deeply discounted securities where the trustees are resident in the UK;
(g)   gains on contracts for life assurance;
(h)   profits on the disposal of deposit rights;
(i)   profits on the disposal of a future or option contract;
(j)   proceeds of sale of a foreign dividend coupon;
(k)   gains on the disposal of land where the gain is brought within the charge to income tax by the anti-avoidance provisions (ITA 2007, ss 481 and 482).

On other income the trustees pay tax at the basic or dividend ordinary rate according to the type of income concerned. Income mandated to be paid directly to the life tenant will not form part of the trustees' assessable income and therefore is not included on the trustees' tax return (HMRC Trusts,

Settlements and Estates Manual, para 3040). The life tenant will be assessable to income tax on an amount equal to the income arising from the trust in the year in which it arises regardless of whether it has been distributed to him after deduction of trust management expenses deductible from income under general trust principles. He will receive credit for the tax paid on the income by the trustees.

Settlor interested trusts

[6.26] Under ITTOIA 2005, Pt 5 Ch 5, where the settlor or his spouse can benefit under a settlement in any circumstances or where income is paid to, or for the benefit of, an unmarried minor child of the settlor who is not a party to a civil partnership, the income is deemed to be that of the settlor (ITTOIA 2005, s 619(1)). This is subject to the following three exceptions:

(a)   where there has been an outright gift between spouses or civil partners (ITTOIA 2005, s 626);
(b)   in respect of certain types of income which are listed in ITTOIA 2005, s 627;
(c)   where there has been a gift to a charity (ITTOIA 2005, s 628).

The First-tier Tax Tribunal held in *Rogge v Revenue & Customs Comrs* [2012] UKFTT 49 (TC), [2012] SWTI 1206 that the settlor of a settlor-interested trust is liable to income tax on all trust income, even where that income had been generated from payments made by him to the trust. The Tribunal was bound by two High Court decisions, both of which had showed that it was possible for a settlor to be subject to tax on a payment he had himself made.

Where a settlor receives a tax repayment in relation to trust income that arose after 5 April 2010 (because he was liable to income tax at a lower rate than the trustees) he must pay such repayments to the trustees. Prior to 6 April 2010 a repayment was only required if it was in respect of an 'allowance or relief' which the settlor would not have obtained if the trust income was not deemed to have been his (ITTOIA 2005, s 646). There is an example of this in HMRC's Trusts, Settlements and Estates Manual at para 4550.

Stamp duty and stamp duty land tax

[6.27] Stamp duty is generally only chargeable under FA 1999, Sch 13 on instruments relating to stock or marketable securities where the amount of the consideration is £1,000 or less and the instrument is certified at £1,000.

Stamp duty is not chargeable on an instrument giving effect to a gift of shares.

For the transfer of land by way of gift, no stamp duty land tax will be payable (FA 2003, Sch 3, para 1). Care does need to be taken if assets are transferred which are subject to a mortgage which the transferee assumes. The amount of the mortgage constitutes consideration on which stamp duty or stamp duty land tax may be payable depending on the amount.

Privileged interest trusts

[6.28] As mentioned above, where trusts are created over property, the property will be relevant property for inheritance tax purposes unless a qualifying interest in possession exists in it or it is subject to trusts which fall into various defined categories (including trusts for bereaved minors and age 18 to 25 trusts). The qualifying interests that can be created are discussed below. In this work these interests are known as privileged interests.

Inheritance tax

General

[6.29] An interest in possession will be a privileged interest where the person beneficially entitled to the interest became so entitled after 21 March 2006 and the interest is:

(a)   an immediate post-death interest (an 'IPDI') An IPDI can only be created by will or on an intestacy; or

(b)   a disabled person's interest (a 'DPI'). A DPI can be created either during the settlor's lifetime or under his will.

A person beneficially entitled to a privileged interest is treated for the purposes of inheritance tax under IHTA 1984, s 49, as beneficially entitled to the property in which his interest subsists. Property which is the subject of a privileged interest is not relevant property and therefore will not be subject to decennial and exit charges under IHTA 1984, Ch 3, Pt 3.

Immediate post-death interests

[6.30] An interest in possession to which a person ('L') is entitled is an IPDI if:

(a)   the settlement of the property in which the interest subsists was effected by will or under the law relating to intestacy;

(b)   L became beneficially entitled to the interest in possession on the death of the testator or intestate deceased;

(c)   the property in which the interest subsists is not held on a trust for bereaved minors ('TBM') within IHTA 1984, s 71A;

(d)   the interest is not a disabled person's interest ('DPI') (IHTA 1984, s 49A).

Conditions (c) and (d) must have been satisfied at all times since L became beneficially entitled to the interest in possession.

Therefore, most interests in possession arising on death will be IPDI's and outside the relevant property regime.

Example

David leaves property on a life interest trust for his wife, Catherine, with a further interest in possession for his daughter, Lucinda. On Catherine's death, the interest in possession in favour of Lucinda is not an IPDI because she did not become beneficially entitled to the interest on the death of David. If David had left a life interest to Catherine together with a general power of appointment exercisable by will then Catherine, in her will, could have exercised the power to appoint a life interest to Lucinda which would have been an IPDI as Lucinda would have become beneficially entitled to the interest on the death of the testator under whose will it arose.

The ability to create an IPDI is often important in situations where the testator is survived both by his spouse and by his children by a former spouse.

Example

Stewart is survived by Lucy and Jane, his daughters by his former spouse from whom he was divorced and by Sarah, his second wife. He is 75 years old, Sarah is 63 years old and Lucy and Jane are 46 and 44 years old respectively.

He wishes to provide for Sarah after his death but for his capital to pass to his children thereafter. He therefore leaves his residuary estate on life interest trusts for Sarah with absolute reversion to Lucy and Jane.

Sarah's life interest is an IPDI. She is therefore treated for inheritance tax purposes as becoming absolutely entitled to the settled property. Because of that, the deemed transfer arising by virtue of Stewart's death will be an inter-spouse transfer and therefore exempt. On Sarah's death her estate will be treated as if it contained the settled property which will therefore bear inheritance tax at the death rate.

If Sarah had renounced her life interest, during her lifetime, she would have made a potentially exempt transfer. That transfer would only have become chargeable if she had died within seven years of making it.

It is possible, therefore, to use IPDI's for tax planning purposes. Consider the following variation to the facts in the above example.

Example

Sarah has her own independent wealth and does not need the income arising from the assets in Stewart's estate. In spite of that, Stewart leaves his assets on interest in possession trusts for Sarah but subject to the trustees' power to defeat those interests. The bequest under Stewart's will is exempt as a transfer to a spouse. The trustees use their powers to defeat Sarah's interest a year after Stewart's death. That is a potentially exempt transfer. Sarah is in good health and at the time the interest is defeated she has a life expectancy of 15 years and in fact survives for that period. She does not die within seven years of her PET and therefore the deemed transfer of value arising from the defeat of her interest is not brought into charge to inheritance tax. Of course, in any tax planning one must consider the risk that the GAAR may apply to it but in the authors' view the risk in respect of this planning is small.

It used to be the case that it was possible to create in this way trust interests from which the surviving spouse could benefit. This is no longer the case because FA 2006 amended the reservation of benefit provisions in FA 1986, with the result that where s 49 applies to treat the holder of an interest in possession as beneficially owning the settled property in which his interest subsists and the interest comes to an end during his lifetime the holder is treated as having made a gift of the property for the purposes of the reservation with benefit provisions.

So, in our example above, if the trustees, after defeating Sarah's interest, continued to have a power to apply capital for her benefit it is arguable that FA 1986, s 102ZA would apply to treat her as having reserved a benefit in the trust property.

Disabled person's interests

[6.31] A DPI is defined in IHTA 1984, s 89B as an interest which falls within (a)–(d) below.

(a) An interest in possession to which a person is treated as being beneficially entitled by virtue of IHTA 1984, s 89(2).
Section 89(2) provides that a trust in which no interest in possession subsist during the life of a disabled person and which secures that, if any of the settled property or income arising from it is applied during the disabled person's life for the benefit of a beneficiary, it is applied for the benefit of the disabled person, that person is treated as beneficially entitled to an interest in possession in the settled property. Different rules apply to property transferred into a settlement before 8 April 2013.

(b) An interest in possession to which a person is treated as beneficially entitled under s 89A(4).
Section 89A applies to settlements under which no interests in possession subsists and which are made by a person, A, and which provide that if any of the settled property or income arising from it is applied to the benefit of a beneficiary it is applied for the benefit of A and that, in the event that the trusts are brought to an end during A's life, either a person will become absolutely entitled to the settled property or a DPI will subsist in the property.
In addition, A must have satisfied HMRC that, when the property was transferred to the settlement, he had a condition that it was at that time reasonable to expect would have such effects on A as to lead to A becoming a disabled person as defined by FA 2005, Sch 1A, para 1.
Where the conditions of s 89A are satisfied, A is treated as beneficially entitled to an interest in possession in the settled property.

(c) An interest in possession in settled property to which a disabled person becomes beneficially entitled on or after 22 March 2006 where the trusts on which the settled property is held secure that, if any of the settled property is applied during the disabled person's life for the benefit of a beneficiary, it is applied for the benefit of a disabled person. Different rules apply to property transferred into a settlement before 8 April 2013.

(d) An interest in possession to which a person, A, is beneficially entitled if:
(i) A is the settlor;

(ii)   A was beneficially entitled to the property immediately before settling it;

(iii)   A satisfies HMRC as to the same matters as are summarised in (*b*) above;

(iv)   the settled property was transferred into settlement on or after 22 March 2006; and

(v)   the trusts on which the settled property is held secure that, if any of the settled property is applied during A's life for the benefit of a beneficiary, it is applied for the benefit of A.

Loosely, therefore, (*a*) covers discretionary trusts for a disabled person who was disabled at the time the settlement was made, (*b*) covers discretionary trusts for a person who expects to become disabled, (*c*) covers interests in possession for a person who is disabled, and (*d*) covers interests in possession for a person who is expected to become disabled. (*b*) and (*d*), however, only cover self-settled property. If a person settles property in anticipation of someone else becoming disabled that settlement cannot create a DPI until the beneficiary is actually disabled.

A trust will not be prevented from being a qualifying trust for the benefit of a disabled person under (c) and (d) above solely because the trustees have certain powers of advancement or a power allowing them to apply capital or income for the benefit of beneficiaries other than a disabled person provided that the total amount that can be applied during any tax year does not exceed the annual limit. The 'annual limit' is the lower of £3,000 or 3% of the maximum value of the settled property. This means that where trustees have powers of advancement the trust can still qualify as a trust for a vulnerable person. This applies to transfers of property into a settlement after 16 June 2013 subject to grandfathering provisions. For the previous rules please see earlier editions of this book.

Meaning of disabled person

[6.32] The definition of a disabled person has been amended often, most recently by FA 2014.

IHTA 1984, s 89(4A) provides that 'disabled person' has the same meaning as that found in FA 2005, Sch 1A. In relation to assets transferred into trust after the 5 April 2014, the definition of a 'disabled person' is:

(a)   a person who by reason of mental disorder within the meaning of the Mental Health Act 1983 is incapable of administering his property or managing his affairs; or

(b)   a person in receipt of attendance allowance; or

(c)   a person in receipt of a disability living allowance by virtue of entitlement to the care component at the highest or middle rate or the mobility component at the higher rate; or

(d)   a person in receipt of personal independence payment;

(e)   a person in receipt of an increased disablement pension;

(f)   a person in receipt of constant attendance allowance; or

(g)   a person in receipt of armed forces independent payment.

(h)   a person who would be entitled to specified benefits but for certain circumstances outlined in FA 2005, Sch 1A, paras 2–7.

Mental disorder for this purpose uses the definition found in the Mental Health Act 1983, s 1 which is 'any disorder or disability of the mind'. To qualify as a disabled beneficiary under this definition the individual has to be very severely disabled. To be eligible for the requisite attendance allowance or disability living allowance, for example, the individual would have to require prolonged or repeated attendance during the day or night, either in connection with his normal bodily functions or to stop the individual being a danger either to himself or others.

The restrictiveness of this definition has been very much criticised. Many people who will not fall within it would still, in most people's estimation, be incapable of managing their finances. For example, individuals suffering from drug addiction, alcoholism, bipolar disorder or schizophrenia in most cases would not be covered.

The creation of the types of trust listed in (a) and (c) in **6.31** above during a person's lifetime in excess of the nil rate band will be a PET. The creation of a trust by the disabled person under (b) and (d) is not a chargeable transfer because the property is treated as remaining in the settlor's estate. On the death of the beneficiary, the underlying property will form part of the beneficiary's estate. There is often a balancing act to be performed between meeting the conditions of being a DPI and providing the trustees with the flexibility appropriate to dealing with property for the benefit of the severely disabled; the difficulty of doing so is illustrated by *Barclays Bank Trust Corpn Ltd as Trustees of the Poppleston Will Trust v Revenue & Customs Comrs* [2011] EWCA Civ 810.

Anti-avoidance provisions

Special rate of charge when settled property affected by potentially exempt transfer

[6.33] Special anti-avoidance provisions exist to limit the inheritance tax planning opportunities of routing property destined for a discretionary trust through an intermediate interest within IHTA 1984, s 49. The point of such planning was that the settling of the trust should be a potentially exempt transfer and the creation of the discretionary settlement should be a chargeable transfer by the holder of the interest in possession who was assumed to have a lower cumulative total than the settlor. To counter such planning IHTA 1984, ss 54A and 54B impose a special charge when the following conditions are satisfied:

(a) an interest in possession comes to an end during the lifetime of the person beneficially entitled to it, or upon his death. Where the termination arises by the death of the life tenant who became beneficially entitled to the interest on or after 22 March 2006 the provisions will apply only if the interest was a DPI or a TSI;

(b) the property in which the interest subsisted became settled property by virtue of a potentially exempt transfer at a time when it was an interest in possession trust;

(c)   the interest in possession ceases and a relevant property settlement arises within seven years of the potentially exempt transfer having been made;

(d)   the settlor is alive at the time the interest in possession comes to an end.

No charge will arise, however, if within 6 months of the interest in possession ceasing, the trust property becomes either:

(i)   held on a trust which is not a relevant property settlement; or
(ii)   owned outright by individual beneficiaries.

Where IHTA 1984, s 54A applies the inheritance tax charge is taken to be the higher of two alternative calculations as defined in IHTA 1984, s 54A(4)–(6). The rules can be extremely complex in their operation.

Transfers between spouses

[6.34] Where, however, a settlor has created an interest in possession for his spouse which is within IHTA 1984, s 49 which is subsequently terminated and the settled property then becomes held on relevant property trusts, ss 54A and 54B will not apply, since the settlor's transfer for the benefit of his spouse was not a potentially exempt transfer but rather an exempt transfer (IHTA 1984, s 18). IHTA 1984, s 80, however, treats the date on which the spouse's interest in possession ceases and the settled property becomes held on relevant property trusts as being the date of commencement of a separate settlement. The spouse's cumulative total immediately prior to that time (rather than that of the settlor before the creation of the interest in possession settlement for his spouse or at the time that the property then becomes held on discretionary trusts) will be taken into account for the purposes of calculating the inheritance tax charges on the property held on relevant property trusts. Where the property first became comprised in the settlement on or after 22 March 2006 s 80 only applies if the interest in possession is either a TSI or a DPI.

Interest in possession for a spouse

[6.35] The spouse exemption will not take priority over the gift with reservation rules where property is settled on an interest in possession trust for a spouse and, before the death of the settlor, the interest in possession comes to an end (FA 1986, s 102(5A)).

Capital gains tax

On settling assets

[6.36] The creation of an IPDI will not constitute a disposal for capital gains tax purposes, because such a settlement must be established under a will or intestacy.

Where a DPI is settled during the lifetime of the settlor there will be a disposal of the assets settled by the settlor deemed to take place at market value. If the property settled is business property within TCGA 1992, s 165 hold-over relief for gifts of business assets will be available on the transfer. Hold-over relief under TCGA 1992, s 260 will not, however, be available, because the transfer into settlement will be a potentially exempt transfer and not an immediately chargeable transfer.

Gains realised by the trustees

[6.37] Gains realised by trustees of settlements in which privileged interests subsist will be subject to capital gains tax in the same way as gains of relevant property settlements as described at **6.22** above except that special provisions apply on the death of the holder of an interest in possession and in relation to trusts for vulnerable beneficiaries.

Beneficiary becoming absolutely entitled

[6.38] TCGA 1992, s 71 provides that where a person becomes absolutely entitled to any settled property as against the trustees of a settlement the assets concerned are treated as having been disposed of by the trustees and immediately acquired by them as bare trustees of the person becoming absolutely entitled. Section 17 then operates to deem the trustees' disposal to have been made for a consideration equal to market value. Section 60 treats the trustees' acquisition as bare trustee as an acquisition by the person becoming absolutely entitled to the settled property and, again, s 17 applies to deem that acquisition to be made at market value. The result of this is that in most circumstances where property passes out of a settlement, a chargeable gain or allowable loss will arise.

The uplift on death

[6.39] Section 73 provides that if the occasion on which s 71 applies is the death of a person entitled to an interest in possession in the settled property, the trustees are deemed to dispose of, and immediately re-acquire, the property in which the deceased's interest subsisted for its market value on the death of the beneficiary concerned. No chargeable gain is to arise on the trustees' disposal. Special provisions are also made for property which reverts to the disponer. Thus, the base cost of the asset is uplifted to its market value at the death and yet no gain becomes chargeable. Effectively, any gain accrued up to the date of the death is taken out of the charge to capital gains tax. A special taxing regime applies where a vulnerable person election has been made and is discussed in **6.41**.

This applies to life tenants and disabled persons with actual interests in possession in qualifying interest in possession trusts and disabled persons who are deemed to have an interest in possession for inheritance tax purposes who die after 4 December 2013, as well as beneficiaries under the age of 18 with an interest in possession in a TBM or age 18–25 trust.

Income tax

[6.40] The income taxation of the trustees and beneficiaries of a privileged trust will be as set out above in relation to relevant property trusts. That is, it is dependent on whether or not the trust confers an interest in possession and whether ITTOIA 2005, Pt 5, Ch 5 applies because the settlor has retained an interest in the settlement or income is paid to an unmarried minor child of the settlor, who is not a party to a civil partnership.

Special income tax and capital gains tax treatment is available where a vulnerable person election is made in relation to the settlement as described below.

Vulnerable person election

[6.41] A vulnerable person election may be made under FA 2005, s 37 when two conditions are satisfied. First, the person in relation to whom the election is made must be a 'vulnerable person'. Secondly, the trust in relation to which the election is made must be a qualifying trust. The election must be made both by the trustees and the vulnerable beneficiary.

A 'vulnerable person' for this purpose is a 'disabled person' or a 'relevant minor' (FA 2005, s 23). The definition of a 'disabled person' is found in FA 2005, s 38 and Sch 1A (see **6.31** above).

The definition of a 'relevant minor' as found in FA 2005, s 39 is a person under the age of 18 at least one of whose parents is dead. It is the same as the definition of a 'bereaved' minor used in defining TBMs for inheritance tax purposes (see **6.42**).

A 'qualifying trust' in relation to a 'disabled person is one where, during the lifetime of the disabled person concerned (or on the termination of the trust if that is earlier):

(a) if any property is applied for the benefit of a beneficiary, it is applied for the benefit of the disabled person; and

(b) either the disabled person is entitled to all of the income of the trust or if such income is applied for the benefit of a beneficiary, it is applied for the benefit of the disabled person. Where trustees have certain powers including a power of advancement under Trustee Act 1925, s 32 or a power to apply either income or capital within the annual limit for the benefit of someone other than the disabled person, it can still be a qualifying trust (FA 2005, s 34). The annual limit is the lower of £3,000 or 3% of the maximum value of the settled property in a tax year.

Thus not all trusts which qualify as trusts for a vulnerable person by reference to a disabled person will be DPIs for inheritance tax purposes. That is because, for example, such a trust is a discretionary trust which may cease during the lifetime of the disabled person. Similarly, a trust in which a DPI subsists may not be a qualifying trust for a vulnerable beneficiary because it is a trust settled in anticipation of the settlor becoming disabled within IHTA 1984, s 89A.

Where property is held on trust for the benefit of a minor, the trust is a 'qualifying trust' if it is held on the statutory trusts for a minor arising under an intestacy (under Administration of Estates Act 1925, ss 46, 47(1)). It is also a qualifying trust where the trusts are established under the will of a deceased parent of the minor or under the Criminal Injuries Compensation Scheme or the victims of Overseas Terrorism Compensation Scheme and the following conditions are met. The conditions are:

(i)   the minor, on attaining 18, will become absolutely entitled to the trust property and any accumulated income;

(ii)   until the minor becomes absolutely entitled to the trust property (or dies), any property which is applied for the benefit of a beneficiary is applied for the minor's benefit;

(iii)   until the minor becomes absolutely entitled to the trust property (or dies), either the minor is entitled to the trust income or if any such income is applied for the benefit of a beneficiary, it is applied for the benefit of the relevant minor (FA 2005, s 35).

Where a vulnerable person election is made, the trustees may make a claim for special income tax and capital gains tax treatment. The relief provided under this treatment is complex but in essence it attempts to ensure that the trustees' liability for tax on the income is reduced to the additional liability which would have arisen on the vulnerable beneficiary if the income had arisen to him directly. If the vulnerable person is UK resident, gains arising to the trustees are deemed to arise to the vulnerable beneficiary. In addition the trustees have an annual exempt amount equal to that of an individual (£11,100 for 2016/17).

If the vulnerable beneficiary is not UK resident, then the calculation of the relief is complex but, in essence, it attempts to ensure that the trustees' liability to tax on capital gains is reduced to the additional liability which would have arisen on the vulnerable beneficiary if the beneficiary had realised the gains.

Trusts for minors and older children

Trusts for bereaved minors ('TBM')

[6.42] The reliefs formerly given to accumulation and maintenance trusts within s 71 were withdrawn by FA 2006. In their place a much more limited relief was given for trusts for bereaved minors ('TBMs') under IHTA 1984, s 71A and 'age 18 to 25 trusts' ('age 18–25 trusts') under IHTA 1984, s 71D.

Section 71A applies to settled property if:

(a)   it is held on statutory trusts for the benefit of a bereaved minor under the provisions of the Administration of Estates Act 1925 relating to succession on intestacy and statutory trusts in favour of the issue of an intestate; or

(b)   it is held on trust for the benefit of a bereaved minor and it is either:
        (i)   established under the will of the deceased parent (a parent includes a step-parent (IHTA 1984, s 71H)) of the bereaved minor; or
        (ii)   established under the Criminal Injuries Compensation Scheme;
        (iii)   established under the Victims of Overseas Terrorism Compensation Scheme;
        and certain conditions are met.

The conditions are that:

(1)   On or before attaining the age of 18, the bereaved minor will become absolutely entitled to:

(a)   the settled property;

(b)   any income arising from the settled property; and

(c)   any income that has arisen from the property which has been accumulated.

(2)   That, for so long as the bereaved minor is living and under the age of 18, if any of the settled property is applied for the benefit of a beneficiary, it is applied for the benefit of the bereaved minor; and

(3)   That, for so long as the bereaved minor is living and under the age of 18, either:

(a)   the bereaved minor is entitled to all of the income (if there is any) arising from any of the settled property; or

(b)   for property transferred into settlement after 7 April 2013, any of the income arising from any of the settled property which is applied for the benefit of a beneficiary, is applied for the benefit of the bereaved minor. For property transferred into settlement before 8 April 2013 no such income may be applied for the benefit of any other person.

A trust will not fail to be a qualifying trust by reason of the trustees having certain powers including a power of advancement under Trustee Act 1925, s 32 or a power to apply either income or capital within the annual limit for the benefit of someone other than a disabled person. The annual limit is the lower of £3,000 or 3% of the maximum value of the settled property in a tax year (IHTA 1984, s 71A(4)).

What is meant by 'will become absolutely entitled' in (1)?

[6.43] If one leaves one's estate to one's daughter contingently on her attaining the age of 18 and to one's niece in the event that she does not, is the section satisfied? Can one say that one's daughter will, on attaining the age of 18, become absolutely entitled to the settled property when it is possible that she will not attain that age and will therefore never become entitled to the property?

A similar question arose in relation to the provisions relating to accumulation and maintenance trusts in IHTA 1984, s 71 in the case of *Inglewood (Lord) v IRC* [1983] 1 WLR 366, [1983] STC 133 (CA). In that case, it was held that the trust did not satisfy the provisions of s 71 because the right of the beneficiaries to take the trust property absolutely at a given age was subject to the trustees' power to revoke the trusts and execute new appointments. The judge went on, however, to consider the wider question of the scope of the provision. Counsel for the taxpayer contended that the word 'will' in the predecessor legislation to IHTA 1984, s 71(1) had to be construed as meaning 'will if no event happens to disentitle the beneficiary'.

The trustees contended that if that was not the case one could not accommodate the provisions of what is now s 71 to the facts that:

(a)   a beneficiary's interest may be lawfully disposed of by the beneficiary after they attain the age of 18 and before it vests in possession;

(b)   their interest may be taken away from them on bankruptcy;

(c)   their interest may be prevented from vesting in them by reason of an order made under Variation of Trusts Act 1958, or under the statutory jurisdiction of the family division on divorce or an order made by the Court of Protection in the event of his incapacity to manage their affairs; or

(d)   they may die before attaining a vested interest.

Lord Justice Fox said:

'As to the last of those, it seems to us that the contingency is inherent in the provisions of the paragraph itself. The paragraph applies where a person will, on or before attaining a specified age not exceeding [a stated maximum] become entitled to an interest in possession in settled property. The paragraph is dealing with contingent interests. A trust cannot be excluded from the operation of the paragraph because of the possible happening of an event inherent in the contingency which brings the trust within the paragraph in the first place . . .

    . . . as to the other matters ((a), (b) and (c)) we think that the answer is this. The paragraph provides that "this paragraph applies to any settlement where . . . ". In our opinion "where" means "whereby". Accordingly we think the paragraph is concerned only with provisions which are contained in the settlement itself. That would include not only the express provisions of the settlement but also any which are incorporated by statutory provision. Some of the matters to which we have referred in (a), (b) and (c) can be so described. Other consequences which cannot be avoided, are the operation of the general law on property interests. They are extraneous to the settlement and are not provisions of the settlement itself . . .

    . . . the result in our opinion is this, the word "will" . . . does import a degree of certainty which is not satisfied if the trust can be revoked and the fund reappointed to some other person of an age exceeding [the stated maximum]. But a power of advancement has been for so long such a normal provision in a settlement for a person contingently on attaining a specified age, and since its sole purpose is to enable the trust property to be applied for that person's benefit before he attains a specified age, it would be artificial to regard the trust as not satisfying the provisions of the paragraph. A trust for A if he attains [the stated maximum age] is within the paragraph. It is impossible to see any rational ground why a trust for A if he attains [the stated maximum age] and with a power of advancement should not satisfy it also, and particularly since the exclusion of the power of advancement in such a case must be rare indeed.

Our conclusion regarding the power of advancement is that while the prima facie meaning [of the relevant legislation] is clear it must be interpreted in the context of the practical application of the law of trusts. The statutory power of advancement is so commonly incorporated in trusts that the relevant legislation must be read so as to accommodate that and not so as to withdraw the benefit of the paragraph from a trust containing such a power. We do not regard the much used extension of the statutory power from a moiety to the whole as being in any different position.'

It is likely, that the courts would adopt a similar approach to the very similar provisions of s 71A. Guidance published jointly by the Society of Trusts and Estate Practitioners and the Chartered Institute of Taxation on 29 June 2007, which was agreed by HMRC, although not completely on the point, provides an indication that HMRC may accept that this is the case. The final point made in the extract quoted from the judgment in *Lord Inglewood* is given statutory form in IHTA 1984, s 71A(4) which provides that trusts are not to be treated as failing to satisfy these conditions simply by virtue of the trustees having the power conferred by the Trustee Act 1925, s 32 or having such a power freed from the, or subject to a less restrictive, limitation than that imposed by s 32 which allows the power of advancement to be exercised only in relation to one half of the prospective share of the beneficiary concerned.

In the guidance published in 2007 it was stated that:

'Both s71A and s71D are drafted by reference to a single beneficiary (in section 71D called "B" and in section 71A called the bereaved minor). However, HMRC consider that it is possible to pluralise B or the bereaved minor to include all beneficiaries within the relevant class provided that they are alive at the date the s71A or s71D trust takes effect and are under the specified age.

Accordingly a will trust in the following terms can qualify as a s71A trust:

"to such of my children alive at my death as attain the age of 18 years and if more than one in such shares as the trustees shall from time to time by deed or deeds revocable or irrevocable appoint and in default of such appointment in equal shares absolutely at 18 provided that no such appointment shall be made and no such appointment shall be revoked so as to either diminish or to increase the share (or the accumulations of income forming part of the share) of or give a new share (or new accumulations of income) to a child who at the date of such appointment or revocation has reached the age of 18 nor to benefit a child who has been excluded from benefit as a result of the exercise of the power."'

This is not an accurate statement of the law and, therefore, HMRC's acceptance of it is concessionary. Statements such as these containing concessionary treatments disguised as statements of the law pose difficult questions as to how far they may be relied upon by taxpayers.

TBMs can only arise on a death, can only be made either on an intestacy, or under a will, of a parent of the bereaved minor's (so that, even grandparents cannot set up TBMs under their wills) and the bereaved minor must become absolutely entitled to trust property at the age of 18. There will be few trusts which are TBMs and the greater number of those that are will be trusts arising on intestacy.

The effect of a trust qualifying as a trust for a bereaved minor is that it will not be a relevant property trust with the result that the decennial and exit charges will not apply to it. There will be no charge to inheritance tax when a bereaved minor becomes absolutely entitled to the trust assets or upon the death of the bereaved minor or on the property being paid or applied for the advancement or benefit of the bereaved minor.

There is a charge on property ceasing to be subject to a TBM in other circumstances. It is difficult to see what those other circumstances might be. A bereaved minor under the age of 18 cannot himself disclaim his interest and once he had reached the age of 18 he would have become absolutely entitled to the trust property so that the settlement would have ceased. If trust property is applied in breach of trust the trust would not come to an end. The trustees would have a duty to recover the trust property from those committing the breach including any trustees who were involved in the breach. The most likely circumstance, therefore, in which a charge would arise under IHTA 1984, s 71B on property ceasing to be subject to a TBM is where the trust is varied by an order of the court.

Age 18–25 trusts

[6.44] It is usually entirely inappropriate to give 18-year olds unfettered control of substantial amounts of money and so an additional class of privileged trusts, age 18–25 trusts, were introduced.

The conditions for an age 18–25 trust are to be found in IHTA 1984, s 71D and are the same as those for a TBM except that the relevant age is 25 years and not 18 years.

Therefore a trust will be an age 18–25 trust if it is created on any date for the benefit of a person (B) under the age of 25 and:

(a)　at least one of B's parents has died;
(b)　the trust was created:
- under the will of a deceased parent (including a step-parent or someone who had parental responsibility for B immediately before their death (IHTA 1984, s 71H));
- under the Criminal Injuries Compensation Scheme; or
- under the Victims of Overseas Terrorism Compensation Scheme;
(c)　it meets the conditions in section 71D(6), which are that:
- B will become entitled to the whole of the trust capital, income and any accumulated income on or before reaching 25;
- while B is living and under 25, any capital applied for the benefit of a beneficiary is applied for B's benefit; and
- while B is living and under 25, either B is entitled to all of the income (if any) or no income may be applied for anyone else's benefit.

A trust is not prevented from qualifying as an 18–25 trust solely because the trustees have the power of advancement in s 32 of the Trustee Act 1925 (or an express power with the same effect), even if the power is extended to apply to the whole of the trust capital (IHTA 1984, s 71D(7)).

Section 71D also applies to existing accumulation and maintenance trusts within IHTA 1984, s 71 (see **CHAPTER 7 EXISTING SETTLEMENTS**) which fell within the s 71D description because capital was to vest at 25.

There is no inheritance tax charge when the beneficiary of an age 18–25 trust becomes absolutely entitled to the trust assets on or before the age of 18, or the trust becomes a TBM while a beneficiary is under 18, a beneficiary dies under 18 or the trustees make an advance of assets for the benefit of a beneficiary on or before the age of 18 (but the assets become relevant property unless they qualify for a different status). An exit charge, however, will arise in all other cases.

The exit charge under IHTA 1984, s 71F is calculated in a similar way to the normal exit charge, except that the charge is for a maximum period of seven years beginning when a beneficiary becomes 18. The maximum rate of charge is 4.2%.

Capital gains tax

[6.45] Unless it is established under the Criminal Injuries Compensation Scheme or Victims of Overseas Terrorism Compensation Scheme, a TBM or age 18–25 trust will arise immediately on a death and therefore the transfer of assets into a settlement will not be a chargeable disposal for capital gains tax purposes.

Such trusts, however, will not always arise immediately on the death of the relevant parent. For example, if A were to leave his property on discretionary trusts for his wife and son to determine on the death of the wife with remainder to the son contingently upon his reaching the age of 18 and the wife were to die during the son's minority the property would be held on a TBM between the wife's death and the son reaching 18. The discretionary trusts would not be a TBM. Once they came to an end, however, the property would be held within a TBM. That is because the son would not be able to give the trustees a good receipt and therefore the trustees would hold the trust property on trust to accumulate the income and with power to make payments out of that income for the son's benefit and would thus fall within IHTA 1984, s 43(2)(b). That settlement would be a TBM because it arose under the will of a deceased parent and provided for the trust capital to be held for the son absolutely and for all income either to be applied for the son's benefit or to be accumulated and passed to the son absolutely on reaching the age of 18.

Because the capital gains tax rules treat a person as being absolutely entitled if he would be so entitled but for being a minor (TCGA 1992, s 62) the TBM will not be a settlement for the purposes of capital gains tax. So when the discretionary trust comes to an end there will be a deemed disposal of the trust property under TCGA 1992, s 71.

If, instead of creating a discretionary trust on his death, the father's will had created an interest in possession for his wife, that interest would have been an IPDI. As such, the coming to an end of the spouse's interest in possession on the death of the spouse would have fallen within TCGA 1992, s 73 (a person becoming absolutely entitled to settled property on the death of a person entitled to a privileged interest). The result would have been that the base cost of the assets would have been uplifted to their market value at the time of death of the spouse but no chargeable gain would have accrued.

Where a TBM is a settlement for inheritance tax purposes but not for capital gains tax purposes because the bereaved minor would be absolutely entitled to the trust assets were he not a minor, capital gains tax applies as if the property were vested in the minor and any acts of the trustees were his acts with the result that the minor would be deemed to make any disposals of assets made by the trustees.

Otherwise, both a TBM and an age 18–25 trust will either be an IIP trust or a discretionary trust with the results set out in relation to relevant property trusts (see **6.9** and **6.20** above) and privileged trusts above (see **6.36–6.39** above).

Income tax

[6.46] The income taxation of TBM and age 18–25 trusts will depend on whether or not an interest in possession subsists in the trust property. If it does, the income tax consequences will be as set out in **6.25** above. If it does not, the income taxation consequences will be as set out in **6.24** above. A TBM will also be a qualifying trust for the purposes of the relief for trusts for vulnerable beneficiaries and therefore a vulnerable person election could be made in relation to it with the consequences set out in **6.41** above.

Specially relieved trusts

[6.47] There are various classes of settlement which receive special reliefs under the inheritance tax legislation. These include:

(a)   Charitable trusts. These are dealt with in CHAPTER 15 GIFTS TO CHARITIES AND OTHER NON-PROFIT ORGANISATIONS.

(b)   Maintenance funds for historic buildings. These are dealt with in CHAPTER 16 HERITAGE PROPERTY.

(c)   Employee trusts. A special relief for trusts for the benefit of employees is conferred by IHTA 1984, s 86.

(d)   Newspaper trusts. A special relief for trusts for newspaper publishing companies is conferred by IHTA 1984, s 87.

(e)   Protective trusts. Protective trusts are designed to protect a beneficiary from the consequences of his own imprudence and fecklessness. The Trustee Act 1925, s 33 sets out the trusts which are to be treated as applying where any income is directed to be held on 'protective trusts'. These standard provisions can be incorporated simply by the use of the term and may be modified by express provisions. Alternatively, a trust deed may set out expressly trusts of a similar, or the same, effect as those arising under s 33. These are also discussed in CHAPTER 5 INTRODUCTION TO TRUSTS.

IHTA 1984, s 88 provides a special treatment for settled property which is held on trusts to the like effect as those specified in s 33(1) of the Trustee Act 1925.

Under s 33 a life tenant's interest in income will divest if he attempts to charge or assign his interest or is declared bankrupt. On the occurrence of such an event, the income becomes held on discretionary trusts for the benefit of the life tenant, his spouse and his children and remoter issue.

Before 22 March 2006, s 88 applied to treat those discretionary trusts as if they conferred an interest in possession on the principal beneficiary with the result that s 49 applied both before and after the triggering event which therefore would not give rise to a transfer of value. Section 88 continues to apply but, without further provisions, it would provide no advantage since 22 March 2006 because most interest in possession trusts are now relevant property trusts. For that reason two special reliefs are given.

First, where settled property became held before 22 March 2006 on protective trusts and the trigger event takes place on or after that date with the result that the principal beneficiary is treated as beneficially entitled to an interest in possession, that interest is treated as if it arose before 22 March 2006. The result of that is that s 49 would apply to the beneficiary's interest who will therefore continue to be treated as beneficially entitled to the trust property. Where a protective trust is established on or after 22 March 2006 and before a triggering event and the interest of the principal beneficiary is a privileged interest that interest is treated as continuing after the triggering event.

Offshore settlements

[6.48] An individual may wish when creating a settlement to do so off-shore, ie by establishing a settlement with all of the trustees resident outside the UK. For a UK resident and domiciled settlor this offers no significant advantage during the lifetime of the settlor if the beneficiaries include the settlor or his immediate family. The taxation of such settlements is discussed in CHAPTER 8 OFFSHORE TRUSTS.

The creation of a settlement with non-resident trustees by a person who is domiciled in the UK gives rise to a duty on any person concerned with the making of the settlement in the course of his trade or profession (other than a barrister) to report to HMRC within 3 months of the making of the settlement the names and addresses of the settlor and the trustees (IHTA 1984, s 218).

Chapter 7

Existing Settlements

Introduction

[7.1] A settlement, like an individual's estate, should be kept under review to determine whether, taking account of the beneficiaries and their circumstances, any steps should be taken in relation to the settled property or the terms upon which it is held.

This overall consideration of the assets of the settlement and the interests and personal circumstances of the beneficiaries may prompt a reorganisation. Often, it will be prompted by a request from one or more of the beneficiaries for capital or by anticipation of an occasion on which the interests of the beneficiaries will alter, such as the death of a life tenant or the vesting of an interest in possession ('IIP') on a contingency being fulfilled.

This chapter considers steps that may be taken in relation to existing settlements. It considers:

(a) the extent to which the familiar techniques of estate planning may be applied to settlements;
(b) means of dealing with the interests of beneficiaries under settlements and the advantages in leaving some older settlements untouched; and
(c) the export of existing settlements.

Except where otherwise indicated it is assumed that all beneficiaries of the types of settlement considered are resident and domiciled in the UK and that the settlors are all UK resident domiciliaries.

Before dealing with these more general matters, we shall first examine the taxation of settlements that were in existence on 22 March 2006 in which subsist:

(a) existing IIPs;
(b) transitional serial interests ('TSIs');
(c) accumulation and maintenance trusts.

Each of these categories is examined below.

Interests in possession (IIPs)

Meaning

[7.2] An 'interest in possession' is not defined in the legislation (except in relation to Scotland: see IHTA 1984, s 46) and so in order to determine whether an interest is an interest in possession one must turn to case law. The decision in *Pearson v IRC* [1981] AC 753, [1980] 2 All ER 479, HL, established that only a beneficiary who has an immediate entitlement to income as it arises, net only of proper income-related trust expenses, has an interest in possession. In *Pearson*, the beneficiaries' right to the income was subject to a prior power of the trustees to accumulate the income. For this reason, at the point when the income arose the beneficiary could not claim the whole or an ascertainable part of it. The provisions considered in *Pearson* may be contrasted with the normal form of modern settlements intended to confer interests in possession where the beneficiaries have a right to the income as it arises, a right which may be defeated as to *future* income by an exercise of a power of the trustees.

Inheritance tax

[7.3] Section 49 deems a person beneficially entitled to an interest in possession in settled property to be beneficially entitled to the property in which his interest subsists. This rule is restricted to the following types of interests:

(a)   an interest in possession in settled property to which the holder became beneficially entitled before 22 March 2006;

(b)   a TSI in settled property to which the holder became beneficially entitled before 22 March 2006;

(c)   an IPDI or DPI to which an individual became entitled after 21 March 2006.

Example

A died on 1 March 2006 leaving property on interest in possession trusts for his son, B, with absolute interest in remainder to his grandson, C. B died in 2040 at which time C was aged 34. All relevant tax law remained unchanged.

When A died, the old rules applied so that B was treated as being beneficially entitled to the trust property immediately on A's death. This treatment continued because B was beneficially entitled to an interest in possession and had become entitled to that interest before 22 March 2006. On B's death, his estate was deemed to include the settled property which was thus brought into charge to inheritance tax. The trust came to an end at that point and C became beneficially entitled to the property and so it formed part of his estate for inheritance tax purposes.

It should be noted that this treatment applies to particular interests in possession and not to settlements. So, if A had settled property before 22 March 2006 on trusts giving a life interest to his son with a succeeding life interest to his daughter and the son had died on say, 31 August 2008, the son's interest would have fallen within s 49 whereas the daughter's would not.

It may be difficult, in some cases, to determine whether an interest in possession is one which has subsisted since before 22 March 2006 or not. Consider the following situations.

Example

Mr A has two sons, B and C. B is 20 years old and C is 10 years old. On 1 March 2006, A settled property on trusts giving B an interest in possession until he was 30 (the 'trigger date'). Contingently on them surviving to the trigger date, B and C were then to take the trust property absolutely in equal shares except that, if either had a child or children living, that one was to take a life interest with absolute interest in remainder to his children. In the event that B or C did not survive to the trigger date and were not survived by issue, the surviving brother was to take the trust property, or an interest in possession in the property if he had children living, to which his brother would have become entitled.

C died eight years later when he was childless and, before he was 30, B had become the father of two children. The result of that was that when the trigger date occurred B continued to have an interest in possession in the whole of the trust property.

So at the trigger date B had an interest in possession in the whole of the trust property and he had had an interest in possession in the whole of the trust property since before 22 March 2006 but was it the same interest? His interest from time to time arose under the same settlement but arose under different provisions of that settlement before and after the trigger date. In the authors' view, where, as here, interests in possession exist in the same property under the same settlement and are held by the same person there is a single interest, even though that interest may be governed at different times by different provisions of the trust instrument.

The Society of Trust and Estate Practitioners and the Chartered Institute of Taxation corresponded with HMRC in relation to various examples on which the question in issue was whether an existing IIP continued or a new interest in possession was created. None of the examples exactly matched these circumstances but some were sufficiently close to provide some indication that HMRC will accept that the original interest continues in such a case as this.

The issue becomes more difficult in the following example.

Example

Mr A settled property conferring an interest in possession on his son, B, before 22 March 2006. On 1 April 2013 the trustees exercised a wide power of appointment to advance the trust assets to a new settlement with identical trust provisions except that the trustee was a company resident in the Isle of Man and the governing law was to be that of the Isle of Man. B had an interest in possession in the trust property throughout but was it a single interest or two successive interests? B continues to have an immediate right to the income arising from the property for his life subject to the same powers of the trustees to defeat that interest but his right arises under a different settlement and is governed by a different country's law. It is HMRC's view that there are two interests in possession. The original interest in possession came to an end when the trustees exercised their power of advancement and a new interest in possession came into being at that point.

Contracts of life insurance

[7.4] It will be seen from **CHAPTER 9 INSURANCE** that it is common to take out life insurance policies on an individual's life so as to provide a fund with which to pay inheritance tax on his death and alternatively, or additionally, as a convenient means of creating an investment fund for the beneficiaries of one's estate. In either case, it is normal to hold such policies on trust so as to ensure that they fall outside one's estate for inheritance tax purposes.

Smaller policies, which are not expected to attain a value in excess of the nil rate band, are commonly held on standard discretionary trusts. Before 22 March 2006, it was usual to hold larger policies on trusts conferring an interest in possession on the person expected to benefit from the life assured's estate on his death, coupled with a broad discretionary power to defeat those interests and to create new interests in capital or income. Such trusts were commonly referred to as 'flexible life interest trusts'.

Such trusts created before 22 March 2006 where the interests in possession have continued are existing IIPs. Because most policies provide for the payment of regular premiums, there was a concern that the interest was not an existing IIP and the property in which it subsisted was relevant property.

As a result, IHTA 1984, s 46A was introduced and applies where:

(a)   a settlement commenced before 22 March 2006;
(b)   a contract of life insurance was entered into before that day;
(c)   a premium payable under the contract is paid on or after that day or an allowed variation is made to the contract on or after that day (an allowed variation is a variation which takes place by operation of, or as a result of, the exercise of rights conferred by provisions forming part of the contract immediately before 22 March 2006);
(d)   immediately before 22 March 2006 and at all subsequent times up to the time concerned there were rights under the contract that:
     (i)   were comprised in the settlement; and
     (ii)   formed part of the settled property in which a transitionally protected interest (an existing IIP or TSI) (whether or not the same such interest throughout that period) subsisted.

Section 46A provides that the rights under the contract of insurance are treated as if they became comprised in the settlement before 22 March 2006 and the person beneficially entitled to the transitionally protected interest is treated as having become beneficially entitled to that interest before that date. If the payment of the premium is a transfer of value, that transfer of value is a potentially exempt transfer.

This relief is generous and its scope is not restricted to rights arising only in consideration of the payment of premiums by the policy holder which he was contractually bound to make before 22 March 2006. Most single premium policies, for example, permit the policy holder to make further premium payments and the benefits under the policies will normally be determined by reference to a notional investment of those premiums. So if one had a small single premium contract held in a flexible life interest trust one could add very large amounts of money to it and still benefit from treating the interest in possession subsisting in the policy as an existing IIP. It should be noted, however, that the relief does not fully deal with the problem of adding further sums to a settlement to allow the trustees to pay insurance premiums. When the sums are added and before they are paid as premiums they will be relevant property. The addition to the settlement will therefore be a chargeable transfer even though s 46A will relieve the trustees from the decennial and exit charges. Of course, the payment of premiums may be relieved under the normal expenditure out of income exemption or may be covered by the annual exemption but as flexible life interest trusts were mainly used to hold large policies these reliefs will often be insufficient to relieve the addition from inheritance tax.

Transitional serial interests ('TSI')

Inheritance tax

[7.5] The intention behind TSIs was to provide a measure of transitional relief when the 2006 changes were introduced.

There are two forms of TSI and once again there are special rules in relation to insurance contracts.

The two categories of TSI are:

(a)   interests to which a person had become entitled during the period 22 March 2006 to 5 October 2008. Of course, these can no longer be created; and
(b)   interests to which a person has become entitled on the death of his spouse or civil partner after 5 October 2008. It is only this type of TSI, and trusts over insurance policies which are treated as TSIs (see **7.8**), that can now come into being.

Interests to which a person had become entitled during the period 22 March 2006 to 5 October 2008

[7.6] An interest in possession (the 'current interest') to which a person ('B') is beneficially entitled is a TSI if:

(a)   the settlement commenced before 22 March 2006 and immediately before that date the property then in the settlement was property in which an interest in possession ('the prior interest') subsisted;
(b)   the prior interest came to an end on or after 22 March 2006 but before 6 October 2008;
(c)   B became beneficially entitled to the current interest at that time;
(d)   a TBM does not subsist in the property and the interest is not a DPI (IHTA 1984, s 49C).

The following example shows how these rules work.

Example

A settled property on his son, B, for life on 1 March 2006 with succeeding life interests to his daughter, C, and then to his granddaughter, D. B died on 30 June 2006 and C died on 30 June 2007.

B's interest in possession was an existing IIP.

C's succeeding interest in possession was a TSI because:

(i) the settlement commenced before 22 March 2006 and immediately before that date an interest in possession (B's life interest) subsisted in the property;

(ii) B's prior interest came to an end on or after 22 March 2006 but before 6 October 2008;

(iii) C became beneficially entitled to the current interest at the time that B's interest ceased;

(iv) the settlement is not a TBM nor is it a DPI.

D's interest, however, is not a TSI. Although an interest in possession subsisted in the property immediately before 22 March 2006 D did not become beneficially entitled to her interest on that prior interest coming to an end. She became beneficially entitled to her interest when C's interest came to an end and that interest did not exist immediately before 22 March 2006.

Interests to which a person becomes entitled on the death of his spouse or civil partner on or after 6 October 2008

[7.7] Where a person ('E') is beneficially entitled to an interest in possession (the 'successor interest') that interest is a TSI if:

(a) the settlement commenced before 22 March 2006 and immediately before that date the property in the settlement was property in which a person ('F') other than E was beneficially entitled (the 'previous interest');

(b) the previous interest came to an end after 5 October 2008 on the death of F;

(c) immediately before F died, F was the spouse or civil partner of E;

(d) E became beneficially entitled to the successor interest on F's death;

(e) the successor interest was not a DPI and the property in which it subsisted was not subject to a TBM (IHTA 1984, s 49D).

Again, an example may help to show how this works.

Example

Before 22 March 2006, A settled property on life interest trusts for his son, B, with a succeeding life interest to his son's wife, C, with absolute interest in remainder to his granddaughter, D. The settlement was subject to an overriding power of appointment exercisable by the trustees.

B died on 31 December 2009. On 31 December 2010 the trustees exercised their power of appointment to defeat C's interest in possession and to advance the trust assets absolutely to D.

B's interest was an existing IIP. His wife's, C's, interest was a TSI. That is because:

(a)   the settlement commenced before 22 March 2006 and immediately before that date an interest in possession subsisted in the property which was held by a person, B, other than the person who was to become the holder of the successor interest, that is C;

(b)   the previous interest for B came to an end on or after 6 October 2008 on the death of B;

(c)   immediately before B died he was the spouse of C;

(d)   C became beneficially entitled to her successor interest on the death of her husband, B;

(e)   C's interest was not a DPI nor, while it subsisted, was the settlement a TBM.

The result was that s 49 applied to both B and C's interests to treat them, whilst those interests subsisted, as beneficially entitled to the property in which their interest subsisted. Therefore on B's death the settled property was treated as forming part of his estate and as passing to his wife, C, and was therefore exempt as an inter-spouse transfer.

When the trustees exercised their power to defeat C's interest s 49 applied to that interest with the result that she was treated as making a transfer of value in favour of an individual, D, which was a potentially exempt transfer.

Contracts of life insurance

[7.8] Section 49E contains complex provisions to treat interests in possession in rights under a contract of life insurance as a TSI in various circumstances where there is a chain of interest in possessions in the rights each of which came to an end on the death of the person entitled to it.

Making additions

[7.9] If property is added to a trust in which an IIP exists, that property is relevant property subject to decennial and exit charges. It would not be an existing IIP because the interest in possession in the added property would not have existed at 22 March 2006.

Capital gains tax

[7.10] On the death of a person entitled to an interest in possession a disposal by the trustees is deemed to take place at market value but no chargeable gain arises (TCGA 1992, ss 72 and 73 (see **6.39**). It may be possible to make a vulnerable person's election in relation to an existing IIP (see **6.41**).

The capital gains taxation consequences for the trustees of an existing IIP will be as set out in **6.22** in relation to interests in possession subsisting in relevant property trusts.

Income tax

[7.11] The income taxation of an existing IIP will be as set out in **6.23** and **6.26** in relation to IIPs subsisting in relevant property trusts.

Accumulation and maintenance trusts

Inheritance tax

[7.12] IHTA 1984, s 71 for many years provided generous reliefs to settlements for beneficiaries, loosely, aged 25 and below.

A form of trust, the accumulation and maintenance trust, was usually chosen as the best method of settling assets for the maintenance and education of grandchildren. The creation of such a trust was a potentially exempt transfer and so no tax was payable provided the donor survived the settlement of the trust by seven years. Although accumulation and maintenance trusts were normally in discretionary form they were not subject to decennial and exit charges under the relevant property regime provided certain conditions contained in s 71 were met. This was all changed by FA 2007. Since 6 April 2008, accumulation and maintenance trusts have been subject to the relevant property regime unless s 71 (in its form before amendment by the FA 2006) applied to it immediately before 22 March 2006 and continued to do so until 5 April 2008, and the following conditions have, since 6 April 2008, been satisfied:

(a) one or more beneficiaries will, on or before attaining a specified age not exceeding 18, become beneficially entitled to the trust property;

(b) no interest in possession subsists in the trust property and the income from the trust property which is not applied for the maintenance, education or benefit of a beneficiary is to be accumulated;

(c) either:
  (i) less than 25 years have elapsed since the time at which the trust property became held upon accumulation and maintenance trusts; or
  (ii) all the persons who are or have been beneficiaries are *either* grandchildren of a common grandparent *or* children, widows or widowers of such grandchildren who were themselves beneficiaries but died before the time when, had they survived, they would have become beneficially entitled.

A trust which is a TBM cannot be an accumulation and maintenance trust under s 71 (IHTA 1984, s 71(1B)).

A settlement created primarily for one person's children or grandchildren may continue for longer than those created primarily for children of different families or children from different generations (although step-children may not actually have a common grandparent — for instance, if both parties to a marriage have children by a previous marriage — they count as their parents' children and therefore the test is satisfied (s 71(8)).

Those accumulation and maintenance trusts which did not meet the conditions of s 71, as amended, after 5 April 2008, became subject to the relevant property regime on 6 April 2008. The charge accrues from that time because the settlement will then have comprised 'settled property'. The first anniversary charge will be at the first decennial from the date when the settlement was first set up falling after 5 April 2008 but inheritance tax will only be levied by reference to the period when the trust was a relevant property settlement.

A trust settled now or in the future cannot fall within s 71 so that individuals wishing to provide for the education of their grandchildren, for example, will now usually create discretionary trusts which provide flexibility but, unfortunately, will be subject to the relevant property regime.

What steps may be taken to deal with the settled property?

General principles

[7.13] The basic principles of estate planning are equally applicable when considering whether any steps should be taken in relation to settled property. This is particularly so when considering the interest of a life tenant of an existing IIP or a privileged trust who, whilst not owning the capital of the trust, will be treated as owning that property in which he has an interest in possession (IHTA 1984, s 49) (special considerations apply to section 5(1B) interests (see **6.20** and **6.29**) to which s 49 applies but which are also charged under the relevant property settlement rules). The steps that may be taken to minimise the inheritance tax charge that will arise on the life tenant's death are similar to those that may be taken by an individual in relation to his own estate. He could, for example, surrender his interest in possession in the settled property in a series of tranches over a number of years in order to make use of his annual exemption of £3,000 per annum.

The principles discussed in CHAPTER 4 LIFETIME PLANNING: MAKING GIFTS of making gifts in order to reduce exposure to inheritance tax at a later date, and implementing a policy of doing so at an early stage, have less application in relation to relevant property settlements. Provided the settlor has not reserved a benefit in the property settled under FA 1986, s 102, no individual will at any time be treated, for inheritance tax purposes, as being beneficially entitled to the trust property. Nevertheless, the approach of a decennial and the rates of inheritance tax applicable to distributions before and after the anniversary may suggest that any distributions proposed should be made sooner rather than later.

Asset conversion

[7.14] Other estate planning steps of a type discussed in CHAPTER 3 LIFETIME PLANNING: AN OVERVIEW may be advantageously taken by the trustees or beneficiaries of a settlement.

Inheritance tax on property in a settlement may be mitigated if the assets held are converted from ones which do not qualify for any form of inheritance tax relief to those which do, such as agricultural property or relevant business property. This will reduce the value on which inheritance tax will be charged on an advance of trust property, the death of a life tenant or on a decennial depending on the nature of the settlement. Any sale of property in order to release funds to acquire property qualifying for relief, however, may give rise to a capital gains tax charge outweighing the inheritance tax benefits. For this reason the most obvious occasions for converting assets may arise in relation to settlements with non-resident trustees which are outside the provisions of TCGA 1992, s 86 and Sch 5 (see **CHAPTER 8 OFFSHORE TRUSTS**) These settlements will be outside the charge to capital gains tax and any disposal of assets made in order to re-invest the trust fund in other assets will not trigger a capital gains tax charge for the trustees (although beneficiaries resident in the UK will suffer a capital gains tax charge in respect of the gains realised by the trustees if they receive a distribution or other benefit from the settlement). Important exceptions to this general rule are where such trustees own, directly or indirectly, residential property in the UK or directly owned assets used in connection with a trade, profession or vocation undertaken in the UK through a branch or agency.

Property settled by a settlor domiciled in the UK remains liable to inheritance tax even though the life tenant is domiciled and resident abroad. In such circumstances, if the settled property is disposed of and the proceeds invested in exempt gilts and certain conditions are met, no inheritance tax will be chargeable on the life tenant's death or on a lifetime surrender or assignment by him of his interest in the exempt gilts (IHTA 1984, s 48(4)). The conditions are that either the settled property falls within IHTA 1984, s 49 and the holder of the interest in possession is neither resident nor domiciled in a country of the UK, or all of the beneficiaries who could benefit from the settlement were neither so resident nor so domiciled. In addition, no capital gains tax will be suffered as a result of the change of investments provided the settlement is outside the provisions of TCGA 1992, s 86 and Sch 5.

Similarly, where a settlement with non-resident trustees was created by a settlor domiciled outside the UK for inheritance tax purposes but holds property situated in the UK, that property will not be excluded property within IHTA 1984, s 48 and inheritance tax will be chargeable upon the value of that property. In the case of a settlement within IHTA 1984, s 49, by selling the UK situated property to a company incorporated outside the UK, the property held by the trustees becomes the foreign situated shares in the foreign company and is therefore excluded property and outside the charge to inheritance tax. At the time of the Chancellor's Budget Speech on 8 July 2015, however, the Government announced that it intended to bring all UK residential property held directly or indirectly by foreign domiciled persons into charge to inheritance tax. On 18 August 2016, the Government published a consultation document entitled '*Reforms to the taxation of non-domiciles: further consultation*'. It stated that these proposals will take effect from 6 April 2017 and will be enacted in the Finance Act 2017. Draft legislation to effect the proposals was published with the consultation document. These changes are considered in more detail in **CHAPTER 11 THE FAMILY HOME AND OTHER RESIDENTIAL PROPERTY**.

In respect of relevant property settlements, an inheritance tax charge will arise where 'relevant property' ceases to be held. For these purposes excluded property is not relevant property (IHTA 1984, s 58(1)(f)). It is arguable that, where the trustees dispose of relevant property and acquire excluded property, an exit charge under IHTA 1984, s 65 could arise. There is, therefore, a specific exemption preventing a tax charge arising when relevant property ceases to be situated in the UK, thereby becoming excluded property (IHTA 1984, s 65(7)).

Some commentators have suggested that this is a narrow relief and applies only where the situation of particular property in a settlement changes; for example where a chattel is shipped to another country. Under this view it does not apply where a UK situated asset is replaced with a foreign asset; for example, where UK shares are sold and foreign shares are bought. The better view is that where s 65(7) refers to 'property comprised in a settlement', it refers to aggregate property just as the reference in s 65(2) to 'relevant property comprised in the settlement' must, in the context, refer to aggregate relevant property. If this construction is correct, s 65(7) will have the effect of relieving from charge any reduction in the value of relevant property which is due to UK situated property being replaced by property which is not situated in the UK.

Where a trust held UK land, often that land was transferred to an overseas company to change its situs and, therefore, take it outside the scope of UK tax. The difficulty with this now is that there are a number of tax charges that arise where UK residential property is owned by a non-natural person.

First, there is a 15% rate of SDLT payable on the purchase of interests in single dwellings over £500,000 where the purchaser is a company or a collective investment scheme or the acquisition is made by or on behalf of a partnership one or more of the members of which is a company (FA 2003, Sch 4A). If a 15% rate is not payable, a rate of 3% may be paid in addition to the relevant rate payable.

Secondly, there is an annual charge (an ATED charge) imposed where residential properties worth over a certain amount on the valuation date are owned by non-natural persons. The charges depend upon the value of the property. For 2016/17, they apply where the value is £500,000 or more.

Thirdly, capital gains tax is chargeable on ATED-related gains, that is, certain gains realised on disposals of UK residential property by non-resident non-natural persons, including companies but not trustees.

Fourthly, capital gains tax is also now charged on disposals of UK residential property by non-resident individuals and trustees. These capital gains tax charges are discussed in more detail CHAPTER 11 THE FAMILY HOME AND OTHER RESIDENTIAL PROPERTY.

Fifthly, if the proposals, referred to above, to remove indirect interests in UK residential land from the category of excluded property are enacted, as it is to be expected that they will be, the planning will become ineffectual.

Value freezing

[7.15] Techniques of estate planning involving freezing the value of assets held in a settlement are useful in relation to settled property as they are in relation to an individual's free estate. The general duty of trustees, however, to consider the interests of all beneficiaries and their specific duties in relation to the exercise of investment powers may mean that the steps they are able to take are more limited than are those of an individual so that, normally, they should not, as a matter of trust law, participate in the reduction or freezing of the value of their trust property. Such exercises, however, may be permissible if the persons benefited by them hold the interests the values of which are frozen. It may, therefore, be appropriate to create a 'parallel' settlement with similar beneficiaries and to arrange for assets with a frozen or gradually depreciating value to remain in one settlement with increasingly valuable assets being held in the 'parallel' settlement.

One possible route is for an existing IIP settlement holding shares in a family company to create a new class of shares in the company with little value at the time of their creation but which will participate in the future growth in value of the company or at a future date become of greater value. The original shares would remain in the settlement in which the interest in possession subsists and, provided that the trustees have power to do so, the new (deferred) shares could be advanced to a new settlement for the benefit only of the remaindermen of the original settlement. Provided the new shares advanced are of little or no value at the time of the advance, no inheritance tax should become chargeable as a result of the advance. On the death of the life tenant it would be hoped that the original shares would have lost a substantial part of their value or, at the very least, would not have increased in value from the date at which the new class was created and that this value or the growth in value since that date would have accrued to the new settlement for the benefit of the remaindermen of the original settlement. (Clearly a sufficiently large holding of shares carrying the necessary degree of control must be held in the first settlement or the other shareholders must agree to the issue for such an arrangement to be implemented.) If the mechanism by which this is achieved is for the deferred shares subsequently to rank equally, or become merged with, shares of another class, in HMRC's view IHTA 1984, s 98(1)(b) will apply because there will have been an alteration of rights (Law Society Gazette, 11 September 1991). If the second settlement is a relevant property settlement and the deferred shares rise in value above the nil rate band decennial and exit charges may arise. This problem would not arise if a bare trust were used to hold the deferred shares.

In private trading companies, the necessity of carrying out such value freezing exercises has been reduced because of the availability of 100% business property relief.

Another estate planning opportunity to consider is for the trustees of an existing IIP to make a loan at a low rate of interest, with the life tenant's consent, to a new settlement for the benefit of the remaindermen of the original settlement. The difference between the return obtained (in the form of both income and capital appreciation) by the trustees of the new settlement from the use of the money and the interest being paid to the original settlement would accumulate in the new settlement. The capital value of the loan in the original settlement would have been frozen. Since interest on the loan would be charged it should not be possible for HMRC to argue that the life tenant's interest in possession had terminated in favour of the beneficiaries of the second settlement; a dubious argument in any case. Where, however, those beneficiaries are the minor and unmarried children of the life tenant, care should be taken to ensure that the income of the new settlement cannot be taxed as the income of the life tenant under ITTOIA 2005, s 629 since the life tenant's consent to the arrangement would almost undoubtedly make him a 'settlor' within those provisions.

Creation of 'surplus assets'

[7.16] One estate planning measure discussed in CHAPTER 3 LIFETIME PLANNING: AN OVERVIEW which should also be considered in relation to settlements is that of creating 'surplus assets'.

Surplus assets may be created by investing the trust fund in higher income yielding assets. The principal beneficiary may consider giving away income-producing assets from his free estate in the knowledge that his total income will be undiminished by the arrangement because his income from the settlement has increased. For inheritance tax purposes this gift will be a potentially exempt transfer provided that the relevant conditions are fulfilled. An element of 'value freezing' will also be achieved since high income yielding investments are unlikely also to grow substantially in capital value. The value of the fund will not therefore increase as substantially as it might otherwise have done. Therefore, the potential charge to inheritance tax on the settled property will have been reduced and so too will the inheritance tax on his free estate.

Where an interest in possession was conferred upon a surviving spouse under the will or intestacy of an individual who died before 13 November 1974, the value of the capital to which the surviving spouse is treated as being beneficially entitled will be left out of account in calculating the inheritance tax payable on his or her death (IHTA 1984, s 273 and Sch 6, para 2). By increasing the amount of income arising to the surviving spouse from such a trust it may be possible to place him in a position to give away assets which do not benefit from this exemption during his lifetime by way of potentially exempt transfers, thereby enabling the bulk of his estate to pass free of tax. The capital gains tax implications of restructuring the investment portfolio, as well as that relating to any gift, must always be taken into account.

Dealing with the interests of the beneficiaries

[7.17] The circumstances in which a reorganisation of interests under a settlement or the distribution of capital from a settlement may be appropriate and the most efficient methods of achieving the desired result (together with other means of dealing with settled property to achieve similar ends) are considered later in this chapter. First, it is necessary to consider, briefly, the means by which the interests of beneficiaries may be altered either by the exercise of powers incorporated in a settlement or otherwise and some of the advantages of allowing existing settlements to continue.

How can the interests of beneficiaries be altered?

[7.18] The terms of older settlements are often more rigid than those of more recently drafted ones. More recent settlements usually include wide and flexible powers of appointment exercisable in favour of a wide class of beneficiaries or powers to revoke the existing trusts and declare completely new trusts which may be exercised (by the settlor, the trustees or others) to rearrange the interests of the beneficiaries, whereas older settlements may only incorporate powers to pay over capital to beneficiaries.

It may still be possible to vary older settlements (and will trusts) without such internal powers to alter beneficial interests. Where all of the beneficiaries are of full age and capacity, the rule in *Saunders v Vautier* (1841) 4 Beav 115 allows them to require the trustees to advance the settled property to them absolutely. The beneficiaries, however, can only modify the existing trusts with the consent of the trustees (*Brockbank, Re, Ward v Bates* [1948] Ch 206, [1948] 1 All ER 287). In most circumstances, however, this will result in the creation of a new settlement rather than the variation of an existing one. In any event, where there are minor, unborn or unascertained beneficiaries, an application to the court to sanction a variation under the Variation of Trusts Act 1958 will be necessary. Occasionally, an alteration of interests may arise from a compromise following a dispute between beneficiaries as to their rights and interests under a settlement and where minor or unborn beneficiaries are interested the court has power to sanction the compromise on their behalf. However, the court will not exercise its jurisdiction to sanction a compromise where it believes that there is no real dispute or point of uncertainty as to the interests of the beneficiaries (*Chapman v Chapman* [1954] AC 429, [1954] 1 All ER 978, HL). In such circumstances an application under the Variation of Trusts Act 1958 is appropriate; it was as a direct result of the decision in *Chapman v Chapman* that this statute was enacted. A successful application was made in *Ridgeway v Ridgeway* [2007] EWHC 2666 (ChD) for the surviving spouse of the life tenant to be given a life interest on his death and that the trustees' power of appointment be exercisable during the life of the life tenant and his spouse. Although this may have postponed the children's interests, the trustees had a power of appointment to enable potentially exempt transfers to be made which would save inheritance tax. The judge noted that prior to March 2006, one possibility would have been to make advancements on accumulation and maintenance trusts under which the children took at 25.

Alternatively, one beneficiary of an interest in possession settlement may 'sell' his interest to another or he may surrender or assign his interest to another by way of gift. The surrender of an interest by the life tenant, however, will not be sufficient to place capital in the hands of the remaindermen if the interests in remainder are held for a class of beneficiaries living at the death of the life tenant and, therefore, as yet undefined. If the interests of the remaindermen are contingent upon their surviving the life tenant and their interests do not expressly carry the intermediate income, undesirable inheritance tax consequences may follow if as a result of the surrender the income of the trust fund becomes held upon a resulting trust for the settlor.

When a beneficiary wishes to sell his interest he must consider the tax consequences to the trustees of doing so as well as to himself. A capital gains tax charge will arise on the trustees in certain circumstances where a beneficiary of a trust sells his or her interest in it to someone else. Generally, this will affect UK resident settlements (TCGA 1992, Sch 4A, para 5) in which the settlor (who was resident in the UK in the year of assessment or any of the previous five years of assessment (TCGA 1992, Sch 4A, para 6)) has an interest or where any of the trust property is derived from a trust which was a settlor-interested trust at any time in the previous two tax years (TCGA 1992, s 76A and Sch 4A, para 7). The effect of the provisions is to treat the underlying assets to which the interest relates as though they are disposed of by the trustees and immediately reacquired by them at market value (TCGA 1992, s 76A and Sch 4A, para 4).

The inheritance tax implications for the purchaser also need to be considered where a beneficiary becomes beneficially entitled to an interest in possession after 8 October 2009 as a result of a commercial transaction to which s 10 applies, as his interest will form part of his estate for inheritance tax purposes under IHTA 1984, s 49.

It may be possible to exercise statutory or other powers of advancement to place some or all of the trust fund in the hands of one or more of the beneficiaries. In respect of settlements made before the 1 October 2014, however, the statutory power of advancement in Trustee Act 1925, s 32 is restricted to one half of the presumptive share of the beneficiary concerned and in some older settlements there may be no express powers to advance capital to a life tenant and no powers (as became common later) to extend the statutory power of advancement.

Similarly, if property is held on protective trusts, any attempt by the life tenant to assign or surrender his interest will trigger the discretionary trusts which in such trusts follow a protected life interest. It will be impossible to vary such trusts, whether before or after a forfeiture, without the consent of the court since minor and unborn beneficiaries (and future spouses) will be included in the class of beneficiaries who would or may benefit in the event of the life interest divesting from the protected life tenant. However, under the terms of the statutory protective trusts set out in Trustee Act 1925, s 33, the life tenant may consent to the statutory power of advancement, or an express power of advancement may be exercisable without giving rise to a forfeiture, and similar provisions may have been incorporated in express protective trusts; such powers may therefore be used to achieve some alteration of the interests.

Discretionary trusts, being by their nature more flexible, do not, generally, give rise to these problems. The capital and income may be appointed to beneficiaries absolutely or upon new trusts.

Not only may the beneficial trust provisions of older settlements be less flexible than those of their modern counterparts but other dispositive powers may be more limited. Dispositive powers, incorporated in a settlement, such as that to permit beneficiaries to occupy properties owned by the trust or to lend trust money free of interest to the beneficiaries, may be exercised to confer benefits on individual beneficiaries other than by the outright appointment of capital to them or for their benefit.

When should existing settlements be left alone?

[7.19] Existing settlements are not always burdensome and will often confer advantages. On the death of the life tenant of an existing IIP there will be an uplift in the base value of all of the settled property to its market value at the date of his death free of capital gains tax. If the settlement had been broken before the life tenant's death and assets passed absolutely to the remaindermen (eg by way of potentially exempt transfer in the hope of avoiding an inheritance tax charge on the trust assets on the death of the life tenant) any unrealised gains which had been held-over into the hands of the remaindermen would still be potentially chargeable to capital gains tax.

If assets incorporating gains have been transferred to an existing IIP or a TSI and a hold-over election under TCGA 1992, s 165 has been made, the death of the life tenant will trigger a claw-back charge on the gains held over if the assets subject to the election are still held in the settlement at the life tenant's death (TCGA 1992, s 74). It may be possible to make a further election for hold-over relief at the life tenant's death to avoid this charge or it may be more advantageous to advance the assets to the life tenant absolutely and elect to hold over the gain realised provided the terms of the settlement permit this and the relevant assets still fall within the scope of TCGA 1992, s 165. If the assets fall within his estate at death they will benefit from the tax-free uplift to their market value at the date of the life tenant's death. No claw-back provisions operate in relation to held-over gains crystallising on the death of an outright owner of assets. This technique will operate most successfully where the life tenant is likely to be survived by his UK-domiciled spouse, so that no inheritance tax charge will arise on the beneficiary's death where the spouse inherits the property concerned. An election for hold-over relief on the death of the life tenant will not be possible where the trust is settlor-interested or an arrangement subsists under which the settlor might acquire an interest (TCGA 1992, s 169B).

Accordingly, careful consideration will be required in each case to determine whether the capital gains tax advantages of leaving assets in an existing IIP, a TSI or an IPDI until the death of the life tenant outweigh the inheritance tax and other advantages of breaking or altering the settlement before it has run its course (whether by advance to the life tenant or by some other means). Much will depend on whether the assets are ever likely to be sold. The decision as to whether or not to break the settlement and if so, in whose favour, used to be finely balanced when the maximum rates of capital gains tax and inheritance tax were both 40%. Now of course, whereas the rate of inheritance tax is unchanged at 40%, the rates of capital gains tax are 28%, 20%, 18% and 10%. Where 100% business property relief is available on the settled assets and no hold-over relief has been claimed in respect of gains arising on the transfer of the assets to the settlement, there may be advantages in leaving the assets settled until the death of the life tenant. This will clearly be the case if a substantial part of the value of the assets represents unrealised gains potentially chargeable at 20% which will fall out of charge to capital gains tax on the life tenant's death, whilst the availability of 100% business property relief will relieve the property from all inheritance tax on death provided the settled assets remain unsold.

It may be that some settlements still exist which benefit from the estate duty surviving spouse exemption which, by virtue of IHTA 1984, Sch 6, para 2, continues where the surviving spouse is still living. This exemption provides that property subject to this provision is not taken into account in calculating for inheritance tax purposes the value of the surviving spouse's estate on death, although the property can be taken into account for certain valuation purposes. Such settlements should, ideally, be left untouched to ensure that this protection remains on the death of the surviving spouse. Although the termination of the surviving spouse's interest in possession in such a trust, whether by a lifetime surrender or assignment or on death, would not give rise to a charge to inheritance tax, it is preferable for the surviving spouse not to make a lifetime gift of her interest but to retain the benefit of the complete inheritance tax exemption for the funds in which her interest subsists until her death and to give away, by means of potentially exempt transfers, other assets which fall within the inheritance tax charge. Unless there is a need for income, the assets of such a settlement should be invested for capital growth since the gains will pass free of inheritance tax. An interesting attempt to take advantage of the relief was made in *P J Davies (Mrs) and A D Rippon (Mrs) (R J Goodman's (Mrs) Executrices) v Revenue and Customs Comrs* [2009] UKFTT 138 (TC) but floundered on the inability of the appellants to prove that the surviving spouse had had a life interest, rather than an absolute interest, in the assets concerned.

Discretionary settlements created before 18 March 1986 under which the settlor is included as a beneficiary do not fall within the gifts with reservation provisions since FA 1986, s 102 requires a gift to have been made after 17 March 1986. Such settlements are, therefore, likely to be best left alone. No property should now be added by any interested beneficiary (including the settlor) since the provisions of s 102 would apply to treat the donor beneficiary as beneficially entitled to that property (and property deriving from it) which is held in the settlement at his death. This would necessitate keeping the property separate from the other property in the settlement for identification purposes which would be administratively inconvenient. If the settlor of a post-17 March 1986 settlement is excluded from benefit he would be treated as having made a disposition of the donated property (and property deriving from it) at that time by way of a potentially exempt transfer (FA 1986, s 102(4)). This also applies where additions have been made after 17 March 1986 to a pre-18 March 1986 settlement and the settlor is later excluded. As a result of the income tax settlement rules, the settlor will be assessed on the income received by the trustees. The settlor has a statutory right of recovery against the trustees for any income tax so assessed on him. The settlor may also be subject to an annual income tax charge on any benefit retained under the pre-owned assets charge. This is considered in detail in CHAPTER 4 LIFETIME PLANNING: MAKING GIFTS.

A reversionary interest which is defined as including any future interest under a settlement whether vested or contingent (IHTA 1984, s 47) is excluded property for inheritance tax purposes subject to four exceptions (IHTA 1984, s 48). The assignment of a reversionary interest will not usually give rise to a charge to inheritance tax and this is a useful method by which individuals may pass assets to others. Not only does no inheritance tax charge arise immediately on the gift but also there will be no further charge if the donor dies within seven years of the gift. Further, even if the assignment could not be a potentially exempt transfer (because it was made to a relevant property settlement), no inheritance tax will be payable and the donor's cumulative total will be unaffected. Since a reversionary interest is necessarily a future interest in settled property the donor is less likely to count on receipt of benefits from the interest or to include it in his present assets when considering the resources available to him. He may be more prepared to give away something which he has not yet considered to be his (or at least part of it). For this reason it may be preferable to leave an existing settlement unbroken and for estate planning steps to be taken instead in relation to the reversionary interests existing under it.

Inheritance Tax Act 1984, s 81A contains two anti-avoidance provisions in relation to reversionary interests in relevant property which are either owned by persons who acquired their interests for a consideration in money or money's worth or are owned by the settlor, the settlor's spouse or civil partner. The first provision is that the falling in of the reversion in circumstances in which the person entitled to it becomes entitled to an interest in possession is treated as a disposition by that person of the reversionary interest. The second is that a transfer of value of such a reversionary interest is not a potentially exempt transfer. The legislation appears to be intended to have the result that when the settlor's interest in possession arises he will make a transfer of value equal to the value of the reversion and that transfer will be immediately chargeable. It is not altogether clear, however, that s 81A has the effect that HMRC intended it to have.

Business and agricultural property relief

[7.20] If business property relief or agricultural property relief would be available on settled assets should a chargeable occasion arise, then care should be taken to ensure that the relief is not lost when the interests of beneficiaries under a settlement are rearranged.

Where an existing IIP or a privileged interest subsists in a settlement the life tenant will be treated as owning the settled property for the purposes of determining whether the period of ownership qualifications are satisfied. If the life tenant's interest terminates (by whatever means) the succeeding 'owners' will have to own the settled assets (whether by being absolutely entitled to them or by holding a privileged interest in the assets) for the relevant period before that relief will be available. Careless reorganisations may cause business property relief or agricultural property relief to be unavailable at the crucial moment.

Further, if a life tenant's interest in settled property qualifying for business property relief or agricultural property relief is terminated in favour of others and the termination, because of the nature of the interests, is a potentially exempt transfer, the requirement that the transferees must continue to 'own' that property, or its qualifying replacement, should not be forgotten.

Capital gains tax issues

[7.21] Modern trusts should be sufficiently flexible to permit their internal reorganisation without precipitating a capital gains tax charge especially where hold-over relief would not be available.

When reorganising older, less flexible, settlements, it is often important that the reorganisation should not create a new settlement for capital gains tax purposes. In such an instance there would be a deemed disposal and reacquisition of the property held giving rise to a charge under TCGA 1992, s 71. The fact that the same persons were trustees of the old and the new settlement would not prevent the charge arising.

Such reorganisations can be used to make what are, in effect, gifts to members of a family by enhancing their interests under a settlement, again without incurring any immediate capital gains tax liability.

Key considerations

[7.22] If steps are to be taken to alter the status of a trust, whether for income tax, capital gains tax or inheritance tax mitigation purposes, one needs to identify those situations where a deemed disposal and reacquisition might arise. There are three key considerations to bear in mind:

(a)   the nature of the power effecting the reorganisation;
(b)   the extent to which that power is being used;
(c)   in cases of doubt, the nature of the external evidence that exists indicating that a new settlement has been created.

Under the terms of the trust instrument, the trustees will be subject to a number of binding obligations which regulate the manner in which they hold the settled property on behalf of the beneficiaries and they will also have a range of powers. These powers will divide into those of a purely administrative nature and those of a dispositive nature, the latter enabling the trustees to apply the trust property for the beneficiaries' benefit.

In order to achieve a trust reorganisation, the trustees will rely primarily upon dispositive powers. Such powers come in a variety of forms, each having its own distinct characteristics. Some are more powerful tools than others. Accordingly, the basic approach adopted by the courts has been to identify both the nature of the power that the trustees are exercising and the nature of the trustees' intention in exercising it, in order to establish whether a new settlement has arisen. There are four leading cases in this area.

In *Roome v Edwards* (1981) 54 TC 359, [1981] STC 96, [1981] 1 All ER 736 (HL), a settlement was established in 1944. In 1955 further deeds were executed with the net effect of appointing some of the assets to be held primarily for two beneficiaries absolutely, contingent upon their attaining the age of 25 (the appointed fund). After this date the 1944 settlement (the parent trust), and the appointed fund were administered separately, but there continued to be common trustees of both funds. In 1972 non-resident trustees were appointed in respect of the parent trust, whilst the appointed fund continued to have UK resident trustees. The non-resident trustees realised a significant capital gain and the Revenue sought to assess the UK trustees of the appointed fund. It argued that both trusts together constituted one settlement for capital gains tax purposes, with the result that the resident trustees of the appointed fund were liable in respect of the capital gains made by the non-resident trustees. The House of Lords found in favour of the Revenue, and its reasoning is of key importance in determining whether an internal trust reorganisation will trigger a charge under TCGA 1992, s 71.

Lord Wilberforce, delivering the leading speech, said that the existence of separate trusts, separate trustees and separate and defined trust property would not necessarily be decisive. He said that a practical and commonsense approach should be adopted, in deciding whether a new trust had been created, after taking into account established legal doctrine. He also sought to distinguish between situations where different types of powers had been exercised by the trustees.

The illustrative comments he made were in the particular context of special powers of appointment and these should be read in the light of the later gloss added by Vinelott J in *Ewart v Taylor* (see below). Taking this into account, where a special power of appointment is exercised it would not be correct to say that 'a separate settlement had been created . . . if it were found that provisions of the original settlement continued to apply to the appointed fund, or that the appointed fund were liable in certain events, to fall back into the rest of the settled property'.

Lord Wilberforce contrasted such an exercise with a power to appoint and appropriate a part or portion of the trust property to beneficiaries and to settle it for their benefit:

> 'If such a power is exercised, the natural conclusion might be that a separate settlement was created, all the more so if a complete new set of trusts were declared as to the appropriated property, and if it could be said that the trusts of the original settlement ceased to apply to it. There can be many variations on these cases each of which will have to be judged on its facts.'

The facts in *Ewart v Taylor (Inspector of Taxes)* [1983] STC 721, 57 TC 401 were complex, but a subsidiary issue depended on whether a separate settlement (Angela's fund) had been created for a beneficiary following the exercise by the trustees of a power of appointment. Following Lord Wilberforce's observations in *Roome v Edwards*, the fact that a power of appointment, albeit of a wide nature, had been used suggested that no new settlement had arisen. Against this, the appointment was exhaustive in that it represented a complete severance from the beneficiaries' interest under the main trust, it had its own key management powers and new trustees could be appointed without reference to the original trust provisions.

A consideration of the intention of the parties in separating Angela's interests from the rest of the original trust and of how the trustees' accountants had treated the reorganisation resulted in the court holding that a new trust had been established. The accountants had prepared separate accounts, and the notes to these accounts clearly suggested that they considered that a separate settlement had arisen.

In *Bond (Inspector of Taxes) v Pickford* [1983] STC 517, 57 TC 301, CA, property was transferred to trustees on discretionary trusts for the benefit of a settlor's child and grandchildren in 1961. In 1972, the trustees executed two deeds allocating part of the settled property to the settlor's grandchildren absolutely, contingent upon their attaining 22. The provisions in the 1961 settlement dealing with investments, the execution of trusts and powers, and the appointment and remuneration of trustees still applied to the allocated property and the 1961 settlement trustees continued to act. However, the new trusts exhausted the beneficial interests. The Revenue, relying on this, argued that a new settlement had been created. This, it argued, was supported by the wording of the power of allocation which suggested that the allocated funds were to be governed by their own separate administrative powers. The trustees contended that as the allocated property continued to be held by the same trustees and subject to the same administrative powers as the remainder of the settled property, no separate settlement had arisen. The Court of Appeal found for the trustees.

Lord Justice Slade explained that:

> 'there is . . . a crucial distinction to be drawn between (*a*) powers to alter the present operative trusts of a settlement which expressly or by necessary implication authorise the trustees to remove assets altogether from the original settlement (without rendering any person absolutely beneficially entitled to them); and (*b*) powers of this nature which do not confer on the trustees such authority.'

He felt that the former represented 'powers in the wider form' and the latter 'powers in the narrower form'.

In *Swires (Inspector of Taxes) v Renton* [1991] STC 490, 64 TC 315 (Ch D) the trustees of a settlement executed a deed of appointment by which the trust fund was divided into two parts. One part was appointed to Isabelle, the settlor's daughter, absolutely. The second was placed on trust, and the income paid to Isabelle for life. It was agreed that the absolute appointment gave rise to a charge to capital gains tax under TCGA 1992, s 71(1). However, the Revenue argued that a deemed disposal and reacquisition also took place in connection with the second appointment on the basis that a new and separate settlement had been created.

Here a widely drawn special power of appointment was exercised, albeit that the trustees of the original settlement continued to act in connection with the newly appointed settled fund. The new trusts affecting the settled fund were exhaustive in that no part of the original trusts were still subsisting, and there was no possibility of them reviving to govern the future disposition of the trust assets. The administrative powers and provisions, however, continued to govern the trust assets, under the terms of the deed of appointment, which was expressed to be supplemental to the original trust deed.

Despite the fact that the power exercised was found to be in the 'wider form', Hoffmann J found that no new settlement had been created using the approach set down by Lord Wilberforce in *Roome v Edwards* (*above*). Accordingly, the case is a useful authority demonstrating that the exercise of a power of appointment in a wider form will not always create a new settlement. Rather, it is necessary to establish the intent behind the exercise of the power itself. Hoffmann J also observed that where a power in the wider form is exercised which expressly purports to vary the beneficial trusts in some relatively minor way, it would be somewhat artificial for this to be 'construed as the creation of a new settlement to be read with all the provisions of the old one together with the variation' (at 500g).

The position of three commonly encountered powers is discussed below.

Special powers of appointment

[7.23] Special powers are generally exercisable by the trustees under the terms of the trust instrument. They are exercisable in favour of a limited class of persons or objects. The person who exercises the power is seen as fulfilling the original intention of the settlor. Generally, the limitations which arise as a result of such powers being exercised are treated as if they had been written into the original trust instrument which created them. As such they do not usually create a new trust. For example, if a special power of appointment is exercised to alter the vesting age of a beneficiary who has to satisfy some contingency, it is unlikely that any deemed disposal will arise under TCGA 1992, s 71. This is provided that the balance of the trust provisions remains otherwise unaltered.

This does not mean, however, that special powers of appointment cannot be exercised either expressly or implicitly to authorise trustees to remove assets from the original settlement, and make them subject to trusts of a new settlement. In such circumstances a chargeable disposal and reacquisition of the trust assets would arise for capital gains tax purposes within TCGA 1992, s 71. *Swires v Renton* [1991] STC 490, 64 TC 315 (Ch D) is an example of a case where the court held that the exercise of a power of appointment did not operate to resettle an appointed fund and precipitate a capital gains tax disposal.

Powers of advancement

[7.24] Advancement involves expenditure towards establishing a beneficiary in life. Irrespective of whether such advances are made under an express provision in the trust deed or under the statutory power of advancement in Trustee Act 1925, s 32, they need not be limited to straightforward payments or transfers of assets to beneficiaries. They can include settled advances which effectively alter or vary the trusts created by the settlement from which it was derived. As a result, powers of advancement are generally within the wider category of powers capable of removing assets from one settlement and subjecting them to the provisions of another. Not every exercise of a power of advancement, however, will create a new settlement.

Power of allocation

[7.25] A power of allocation is a power to allocate assets to particular interests within a settlement. It does not empower the trustees to create fresh or overriding trusts. This type of power was considered in *Bond v Pickford* [1983] STC 517. Accordingly, such powers fall within the 'narrower form' and no charge under TCGA 1992, s 71 will arise as a result of their exercise. This is the case even if administrative provisions that had previously applied under the original trust instrument cease to be applicable as a result of the exercise of the power of allocation.

Revenue guidelines

[7.26] Following the Court of Appeal's decision in *Bond (Inspector of Taxes) v Pickford* [1983] STC 517, 57 TC 301, the Revenue issued a Statement of Practice (SP7/84) (see Capital Gains Manual para CG37841) which stated:

' . . . the Commissioners for Her Majesty's Revenue and Customs considers that a deemed disposal will not arise when . . . [powers in the wider form, which may be powers of advancement or certain powers of appointment, are] . . . exercised and trusts are declared in circumstances such that:

(a)   the appointment is revocable, or

(b)   the trusts declared of the advanced or appointed funds are not exhaustive so that there exists a possibility at the time when the advancement or appointment is made that the funds covered by it will on the occasion of some event cease to be held upon such trusts and once again come to be held upon the original trusts of the settlement.

Further, when such a power is exercised the Commissioners for Her Majesty's Revenue and Customs considers it unlikely that a deemed disposal will arise when trusts are declared if duties in regard to the appointed assets still fall to the trustees of the original settlement in their capacity as trustees of that settlement . . . Finally, the Commissioners for Her Majesty's Revenue and Customs accept that a Power of Appointment or Advancement can be exercised over only part of the settled property and that the above consequences would apply to that part.'

Settlements within IHTA 1984, s 49

[7.27] The treatment for inheritance tax, capital gains tax and income tax purposes of privileged interest trusts which continue to fall within IHTA 1984, s 49 is discussed in detail in **CHAPTER 6 CREATING SETTLEMENTS**. The tax treatment of existing IIP trusts, TSIs and section 5(1B) interests is discussed in this Chapter.

Interests in possession for inheritance tax purposes and the consequences of termination

[7.28] For the purposes of the discussion below the expressions 'life interest' and 'interest in possession' are treated as synonymous and it is assumed that the terms of the settlements considered confer on the life tenant an interest in possession for his life.

For inheritance tax purposes where IHTA 1984, s 49 applies to the settled property, a life tenant is treated as being beneficially entitled to the trust property in which his interest subsists. Any termination of an existing IIP, a privileged interest or a section 5(1B) interest will be treated as though it were a transfer of value made by the life tenant (IHTA 1984, s 52) of a value equal to the value of the property in which the interest subsisted. A disposal of such an interest to which s 49 applies is treated as not being itself a transfer of value. Rather the interest which is the subject of the disposal will be treated as coming to an end (IHTA 1984, s 51) with the result that s 52 will apply to treat the beneficiary as if he had made a transfer of value equal to the value of the property in which the interest subsisted.

The fact that the termination of an interest within s 49 is not an actual transfer of value but is merely treated as being such has some important inheritance tax consequences which must be considered on the termination of a life tenant's interest in possession.

(a)   *Life tenant becoming absolutely entitled to the settled property.* If, as a result of a deemed transfer of value, the life tenant becomes absolutely entitled to the property in which his interest has terminated, no inheritance tax will be chargeable (IHTA 1984, s 53(2)).

(b)   *Potentially exempt transfers.* If, as a result of the termination (in whole or part) of a life tenant's privileged interest (or an interest within IHTA 1984, s 5(1B)), the property in which his interest subsisted becomes:
(i)   comprised in the estate of another; or
(ii)   held upon a DPI within IHTA 1984, s 89, or
(iii) held on a bereaved minor's trust on the coming to an end of an IPDI,
the life tenant will be treated as having made a potentially exempt transfer. Provided he survives for a period of seven years after this, it will not become chargeable (IHTA 1984, ss 3A, 51, 52).

(c)   *Other exemptions.* IHTA 1984, s 3(4) provides that references in the Act to a transfer of value made by any person include references to events on the happening of which tax is chargeable 'as if' a transfer of value had been made by that person and that 'transferor' is to be construed accordingly. The operation of this sub-section, however, is specifically excluded by IHTA 1984, ss 19–22 which contain the annual exemption, and the exemptions for small gifts, normal expenditure out of income and gifts in consideration of marriage. IHTA 1984, s 57, however, provides that a life tenant may give notice to the trustees that the whole or part of his annual exemption or his exemption for gifts in consideration of marriage is unused. The exemption can then be set against the deemed transfer of value made on the termination of his interest. Even where the deemed transfer of value is not chargeable but is potentially exempt at the time it is made the life tenant should, if appropriate, give notice to the trustees of the availability of these exemptions under s 57. Otherwise, if he dies within seven years of the deemed transfer of value, the exemptions will not be available to the trustees to set against the potentially exempt transfer which has now become chargeable. A claim must be made within six months of the termination in the prescribed form (IHTA 1984, s 57(4)).

(d)   *Reliefs for certain dispositions.* Since there is no actual transfer of value on the termination of a life interest, the reliefs relating to dispositions which would be transfers of value (ie dispositions not intended to confer gratuitous benefit (IHTA 1984, s 10), dispositions for family maintenance (IHTA 1984, s 11) and dispositions allowable for income tax (IHTA 1984, s 12)) do not apply. However, IHTA 1984, s 51(2) provides that if the assignment or surrender by the life tenant satisfies the conditions in IHTA 1984, s 11, the assignment or surrender will not be treated as the coming to an end of his interest and, accordingly, no inheritance tax will be chargeable on this occasion.

Value on which inheritance tax is charged

[7.29] There is a further difference between the charge to inheritance tax made when an interest in possession which is an existing IIP, a privileged interest or a section 5(1B) interest is terminated during the life of the life tenant and that which would be made if he were to give away part of his free estate. IHTA 1984, s 52(1) provides that on the termination of an interest in possession by whatever means, the life tenant will be treated as having made a transfer of value equal to the value of the property in which his interest subsisted. This value must be distinguished from the value which he would be treated as having transferred if, instead, he had made a lifetime gift of the same property from his free estate. In that case inheritance tax would be chargeable on the amount by which his estate was diminished as a result of the transfer. This amount might be greater than the value of the property which is the subject of the transfers. For example, where a majority shareholding in a private company is held in an interest in possession settlement, if the life tenant surrenders or assigns his interest in a part of the fund representing a minority shareholding in the company and, after the assignment, has an interest in possession only in a minority shareholding, the charge to inheritance tax will be calculated on the value of the minority holding in which he has released his interest. Had the majority holding of shares been part of his own free estate, the charge to inheritance tax under similar circumstances would have been calculated, not by reference to the value of the minority holding given away, but by reference to the difference between the value of the majority shareholding held before the transfer and the value of the minority shareholding he retained.

This means that the order in which gifts are made may be important.

Example

Mr A owns 46% of the issued share capital of an investment company, Investment Company Limited ('ICL') and has an existing IIP in a trust the only asset of which is a 6% shareholding in ICL. He wishes his two daughters to receive shareholdings of 6% each in ICL. He considers the following alternatives:

(a) Transferring 6% shareholdings to each of his daughters simultaneously.
(b) Transferring a 6% shareholding to one of his daughters and the trustees of the trust then exercising their power of appointment to appoint the trust's shareholding to the other daughter absolutely.
(c) The trustees of the trust using their power of appointment to appoint the trust's shareholding to one daughter absolutely and thereafter Mr A transferring a 6% shareholding to his other daughter.

The value of shareholdings in the company do not vary proportionately to their size but rather reflect the fact that at key points significant degrees of control are acquired; for example a 51% shareholding allows the holder to ensure that an ordinary resolution of the members is passed. The value of the various sizes of shareholdings in the company are as follows:

	£
Value of 52% shareholding	5,200,000
Value of 46% shareholding	2,300,000

Value of 40% shareholding	2,000,000
Value of 6% shareholding	180,000

Because he has an existing IIP in the shares held by the trust, Mr A is treated as the beneficial owner of the shares in which his interest subsists. On the coming to the end of his interest in the trust property the value on which tax would be charged under s 52 would not be the loss to his estate from the termination of his deemed beneficial interest in the property but rather the value of the property in which the interest subsisted. The values on which tax would be charged therefore, under each of the three alternatives are as follows:

(a)   The value charged is the fall in value of Mr A's estate resulting from the gift and so his transfer of value is £3,200,000 (£5,200,000 – £2,000,000). Thus the total value charged is £3,200,000.

(b)   The value charged on Mr A's gift is the fall in value of his estate resulting from his gift; that is £2,900,000 (£5,200,000 – £2,300,000). By reason of the advance Mr A is treated as making a transfer of value equal to the value of the property in which his interest subsisted; that is £180,000. Thus the total value charged is £3,080,000 (£2,900,000 + £180,000).

(c)   By reason of the advance Mr A is treated as making a transfer of value equal to the value of the property in which his interest subsisted; that is £180,000. The value charged on Mr A's gift is the fall in value of his estate resulting from the gift; that is £300,000 (£2,300,000 – £2,000,000). The total value charged is £480,000 (£180,000 + £300,000).

So the value charged under option (c) is £480,000 compared with £3,080,000 under option (b) and £3,200,000 under option (a). The significant difference is that under option (c) the combined holding drops from a majority to a minority holding on the appointment by the trustees to which the loss to the donor method of measuring the value transferred does not apply.

Life interest for capital gains tax purposes and the consequences of termination

[7.30] Where settled property within IHTA 1984, s 49 includes assets in respect of which there are held-over gains which will suffer a claw-back charge on the death of the life tenant the trustees might advance their assets to the life tenant provided the settlement terms allow them to do so and s 165 hold-over relief is available. The trustees and the life tenant will have to make an election for hold-over relief. On the life tenant's death, the held-over gains will fall out of charge to capital gains tax. These considerations will only be relevant if assets which were the subject of a hold-over election when transferred to a settlement have not been, and are not to be, disposed of prior to the life tenant's death since the actual sale of these assets would in any event trigger the capital gains tax charge on held-over gains.

The lifetime termination of a life interest will not give rise to a charge to capital gains tax unless as a result some person becomes absolutely entitled to the settled property. No occasion of charge will arise on the change of interests provided that the property remains within the same settlement after the termination of the interest. Where a person does become absolutely entitled to the trust property (either the life tenant who has had the settled property transferred to him or a beneficiary with a succeeding interest who, as a result of the termination of the life tenant's interest, becomes absolutely entitled to the trust property) the trustees will be treated as having disposed of the trust property at market value at the date of termination of the life interest and as having reacquired it at that date as nominees for the individual who has become absolutely entitled (TCGA 1992, s 71). A capital gains tax charge will arise if the market value of the assets at the date of termination is greater than their acquisition cost. Depending upon the nature of the trust assets, it may be possible to hold-over the gain under TCGA 1992, s 165 by the trustees and the individual who has become absolutely entitled to the trust property making an election.

In making a decision whether to terminate a life interest settlement in favour of the life tenant or the remaindermen or to accelerate the interests of the remaindermen or assign the life tenant's interest to others (outright or into some other form of settlement) capital gains tax will be a significant factor. The differing profiles for capital gains of the trustees and the beneficiaries need to be taken into account — for example either the beneficiaries or the trustees may have current year or brought forward losses or may be able to realise losses on assets which have fallen in value.

Reasons for breaking a settlement within IHTA 1984, s 49

[7.31] The reasons for breaking a settlement within IHTA 1984, s 49 may be many. It may simply be that the settlement is thought to be too expensive to continue, the administration charges being disproportionately high in comparison to the value of the trust fund. The life tenant or the remaindermen may decide to assign or surrender their interests to each other and thus terminate the settlement or they may partition the fund, each taking part of the capital.

A partition might be proposed for a variety of reasons. For example it would enable a life tenant to invest the capital he receives on the partition in the acquisition of assets expected to increase in capital value rather than to yield a large income. He will also be free to give away that capital as and when and to whom he chooses. Another option is for the life tenant to apply capital received on the partition of the trust property in acquiring an annuity the capital element of which would not suffer income tax in his hands. Since the annuity will have no value at his death, his estate will have been reduced because there will no longer be capital owned by him nor settled property to which he will be treated as being entitled by virtue of his interest in possession.

The property in which the interest in possession subsists will be aggregated with the life tenant's estate for the purposes of calculating the rates of inheritance tax applicable to the settled property on his death. Both the life tenant and the remaindermen may wish to mitigate this potential charge. This can be achieved either by the life tenant surrendering his interest to the remaindermen, by the partition of the trust property between the life tenant and the remaindermen or by the purchase by the remaindermen of the life tenant's interest. One needs to consider, however, the capital gains tax charge that may arise on the trustees under TCGA 1992, Sch 4A. In accordance with the general principle that capital should be passed on down the generations in order to mitigate inheritance tax, the most sensible course for the life tenant to adopt (if he has sufficient other assets available for his needs) would be to surrender his interest in favour of the remaindermen. However, if the remaindermen are not the people whom he wishes to benefit from his estate, a partition of the fund or the sale by the life tenant or the remaindermen of their interests might be appropriate. The life tenant would then secure some free capital with which he would be able to make gifts to those whom he wished to benefit.

The remaindermen, whose remainder interest confers no immediate benefit, may need capital to start a business or to invest in other ways and may, therefore, prefer to receive capital now rather than to await the death of the life tenant and to suffer an inheritance tax charge on that occasion. They may prefer to take immediate estate planning steps in respect of the capital they receive rather than to risk receiving it when efficient measures may no longer be taken. For this reason they may propose a partition of the trust property, a purchase of the life tenant's interest or a sale to the life tenant of their interests.

Where, on a trust reorganisation, one or more of the beneficiaries becomes absolutely entitled to some of the trust assets, any capital gains arising may be held-over if the trust assets are business assets within TCGA 1992, s 165. Even if this relief is not available, it will be possible to pay any capital gains tax due on disposals of land or of certain holdings of shares and securities by ten equal annual instalments (TCGA 1992, s 281). The outstanding balance, however, will bear interest. Whether the charge to capital gains tax outweighs the advantages of the reorganisation will have to be considered in respect of the particular situation and this will entail considering not only the nature of the assets of the trust but also the extent to which their values reflect unrealised gains.

Means of dealing with the interests under a life interest trust within IHTA 1984, s 49

[7.32] The trusts upon which property will be held following a termination of the life tenant's interest may dictate what steps, if any, a life tenant and the remaindermen and/or the trustees may wish to take in relation to the beneficiaries' interests.

The methods which we set out below for dealing with an interest in possession will only apply to an interest which is an existing IIPs or a privileged interest so that IHTA 1984, s 49 applies to treat the holder of the interest as beneficially entitled to the assets in which his interest subsists.

There are two basic methods available to a life tenant of dealing with an interest in possession: assignment or surrender of the interest. In practice, similar results may be achieved by the exercise of powers conferred upon the trustees (such as powers of appointment or revocation). The essential difference between an assignment and a surrender is considered here together with other means of dealing with the interests of the beneficiaries in order that further consideration can then be given to particular situations.

Assignment of a life interest

[7.33] An assignment by the life tenant of his interest is effected by a written document of assignment (in order to comply with the requirements of Law of Property Act 1925, s 53(1)(c)). The assignment may be made by the life tenant in favour of other beneficiaries of the settlement or to complete strangers to the settlement. In either case the assignee steps, or the assignees step, into the life tenant's shoes and becomes or become entitled to the income arising from the trust property in which the assignor's interest subsists during his lifetime. The life tenant may assign his life interest either outright to one or more individuals or to trustees of a new settlement. In the former case the assignee may deal with the income to which he is now entitled as he chooses and in the latter case the trustees must deal with the income which they are entitled to receive in accordance with the provisions of the trusts imposed upon them.

It is possible that a similar result may be achieved by the exercise of powers conferred upon the trustees of the settlement under which the life tenant's interest exists. For example, the trustees may have power to revoke the life interest and to declare that in future the income will be paid to some other beneficiary of the settlement during his life. In this case there will not have been the assignment of an asset; the first life tenant's asset (his life interest) will have ceased to exist and his interest under the settlement will have been replaced by that of another. That interest may be a TSI or it may be an interest in a relevant property settlement. Where the trustees exercise their powers in this way they may (provided the terms of the settlement permit them to do so) confer a capital interest upon the beneficiary for whose benefit they create the new interest. They may, for example, declare that in future they will pay the income of the trust property to X during his life or until he attains 35 at which time they may specify that they will transfer the capital to him. (Provision will also be made for the eventuality that X dies before attaining 35.)

The life tenant himself will have no power to declare such new interests in the trust property unless the power is expressly reserved to him by the terms of the settlement. So unless the trustees can and are willing to exercise their powers he can only attempt to achieve the same result by assigning or surrendering his interest. It will be necessary for a life tenant to assign his interest in income where the individuals upon whom the life tenant wishes to confer a benefit are not beneficiaries of the settlement. Those to whom he assigns his interest will become entitled to his income interest and can have no greater entitlement to capital than he had. If, under the terms of the settlement the life tenant will become entitled to capital if he attains, for example, the age of 35, he may assign this contingent interest to those he wishes to benefit in addition to assigning his income interest. Provided he does not die before his 35th birthday, his assignees will take his share of capital. However, if, under the terms of the settlement, the life tenant is entitled to income only, he can only confer this benefit on others by assignment.

Surrender of a life interest

[7.34] The alternative means by which a life tenant may deal with his interest is to surrender it in favour of those whose interests succeed his. They may either take capital absolutely as a result of his surrender or if their interests are only life interests following that of a life tenant then those interests will be accelerated. The interests under the settlement following the life interest then fall into possession. There may be a temporary gap in the beneficial interests giving rise to a resulting trust for the settlor where there are no interests ready to fall into possession. A surrender by a life tenant may not therefore operate to vest capital in the hands of succeeding beneficiaries and, indeed, their income interests may not even be accelerated. In these circumstances it may be advisable for the life tenant to assign his interest to them rather than to surrender it.

A similar effect to the surrender of the life tenant's interest may be achieved instead by the exercise of express or statutory powers vested in the trustees or others to appoint interests in favour of those whose interests follow the life interest, to extinguish the life interest or to advance assets to remaindermen. Such powers are particularly useful where a surrender by the life tenant will not accelerate the interests of the remaindermen or where the life interest is a protective life interest and an attempted surrender by him would give rise to a forfeiture. There may be income tax, capital gains tax and inheritance tax advantages if the trustees can exercise powers to achieve an end which, otherwise, the life tenant would achieve by assigning or surrendering his interest. In the case of an assignment or surrender if, for example, his minor, unmarried children benefit from the surrender or assignment, then for income tax purposes he would be treated as having made a settlement for the benefit of his children. He would be treated as continuing to be entitled to the income arising to his children unless the income was accumulated for so long as his children remained under 18 and were unmarried (ITTOIA 2005, s 629).

Similarly, if the life tenant (or his spouse or civil partner) is capable of benefiting from the interest he assigns (for example, by being a beneficiary of a settlement to which he has assigned his interest), the income may continue to be taxed as his, under the provisions of ITTOIA 2005, s 624 regardless of whether or not he receives it, subject to limited exceptions.

Where an interest in possession, to which s 49 applies, comes to end in the holder's lifetime, the holder is treated as having made a transfer of value equal to the value of the property in which the interest subsisted. This may be a potentially exempt transfer.

If the life tenant continues to enjoy a benefit in some way from the property in which his interest formerly subsisted by the exercise of the trustees' powers, he will be treated as having reserved a benefit and the property in which his interest has ceased will be treated as being part of his estate on death. The pre-owned assets charge contains no equivalent rule.

Assignment by the remaindermen of their interests

[7.35] For inheritance tax purposes an interest in remainder being a future interest under a settlement is a 'reversionary interest'. As reversionary interests are generally excluded property for inheritance tax purposes (IHTA 1984, s 48(1)) interests in remainder may be dealt with by way of gift either to other beneficiaries of the settlement under which it exists or to strangers to the settlement without giving rise to any inheritance tax consequences in certain circumstances.

It is for this reason that assignments of their interests by remaindermen to their children are particularly efficient for inheritance tax purposes.

Normally, the gift will not give rise to any inheritance tax charges and as a result does not require the assignor to survive seven years; nor can his cumulative total be in any way affected by the gift. Yet when the prior interests terminate, the children will receive the whole benefit of the fund or that part of it in respect of which the reversionary interest was assigned. Although a charge to inheritance tax is likely to arise on the cessation of the prior interests this charge would have arisen even if the assignor had retained his interest. The potential inheritance tax charge avoided is that which might have arisen (either on the death of the assignor or on his making a gift of the assets in which his reversionary interest had previously subsisted) after the reversionary interest had fallen in.

If the remaindermen are all ascertained and of full age and between them will take the entire trust fund on the death of the life tenant, they may assign their interests to the life tenant and he will as a result of the merger of the interests in his hands become entitled to the capital of the trust fund, although as a result a capital gains tax charge under TCGA 1992, s 71 might arise. Although the assignments by the remaindermen of their interests will not have any inheritance tax consequences, if IHTA 1984, s 49 applies to the life tenant's interest it is likely that the life tenant will be older than the remaindermen and, if that is the case, generally it would be unwise to place the capital in his hands where it would be chargeable to inheritance tax as part of his estate on his death. Ordinarily, it would be preferable for the life tenant to assign or surrender his interest to the remaindermen thereby passing capital on to future generations.

If the life tenant is not old and intends to deal with the capital to which he becomes entitled, by making gifts of that capital, for example, by way of potentially exempt transfers, the assignment by the remaindermen of their interests to the life tenant may present advantages. More frequently, however, it will be advantageous for inheritance tax purposes for remaindermen to assign their interests, which may be vested or contingent, to younger generations.

Where a reversionary interest is given away after 8 December 2009, and the person taking the actual interest either purchased the reversionary interest or is the settlor, spouse or civil partner of the settlor, there will be a lifetime chargeable transfer (IHTA 1984, s 81A).

Example

Prior to March 2006 Augustus settled £10m on the following trusts:

* on interest in possession trusts for the benefit of his daughters Abigail and Peggotty until 30 September 2012 to provide for their university education; and then
* on interest in possession trusts for his son Horatio until he reached age 25; and then
* on interest in possession trusts for his wife Livia.
  Subject thereto on wide discretionary trusts for his issue.

Horatio's 25th birthday was on 31 March 2013. Abigail's and Peggotty's interests were existing IIPs but Horatio's interest was in a relevant property trust. Livia's reversionary interest was a reversionary interest in relevant property and she is the spouse of the settlor. Therefore, when her reversionary interest came to an end on her becoming entitled to an interest in possession, she was treated as having made a disposition of the reversionary interest which was not a potentially exempt transfer. She made a chargeable transfer equal to the value of her reversionary interest immediately before it fell into possession.

A reversionary interest will not be excluded property when the conditions in IHTA 1984, s 74A(1) are met and the individual has or is able to acquire another interest in the relevant settled property. Therefore, such an interest will only be excluded property where it is the only interest in the settled property to which the individual is beneficially entitled.

Section 74A will apply where:

(a)   one or more persons enter into arrangements after 19 June 2012;
(b)   in the course of the arrangements:
        (i)   a UK domiciled individual acquires or is able to acquire an interest in property in a settlement; and
        (ii)   consideration in money or moneys worth is given by one or more of the persons who had entered into arrangements whether or not in connection with the acquisition of the interest or the individual becoming entitled to it;
(c)   there is a relevant reduction in the value of the person's estate;
(d)   Condition A or B is satisfied.

Condition A is that the settlor was not UK domiciled at the time the settlement was made and the relevant settled property is situated outside the UK at any time during the course of the arrangements.

Condition B is that the settlor was not an individual or close company at the time the settlement was made and condition A is not met.

When conditions (a) to (d) are first satisfied, the settled property is not treated as excluded property. The individual is deemed to have made a transfer of value at that time of an amount defined by the legislation. The transfer of value cannot be a potentially exempt transfer.

HMRC claim that this legislation is designed to frustrate arrangements exploiting the excluded property rules by converting UK assets to ones that are excluded from a charge to inheritance tax and do not create a transfer of value when the conversion arises.

Sale of the interests of life tenant or remaindermen

[7.36] Any assignment or surrender by the life tenant or remainderman of their interests may be made by way of sale.

In general trustees may not exercise their powers to alter interests under settlements for consideration (although in certain commercial situations they may do so).

The life tenant or the remaindermen may be prepared, and have the resources available, to buy the other's interest so as to become entitled to the capital of the trust fund. If the sale is an arm's length transaction between unrelated parties the cash price paid will relate to the value of the interest to be acquired. That will often be assessed by an independent actuary.

If the parties are related and the sale price does not reflect the value of the interest acquired, the inheritance tax consequences may be severe.

Whether undertaken strictly on an arm's length basis or not, the benefits arising from a sale of interests for each party will be that each takes a sum of money or assets absolutely with which they can deal as they please.

If neither the remainderman nor the life tenant has sufficient resources to acquire the interest of the other, either may sell his interest to a third party. The life tenant would thereby obtain a capital sum in place of his income interest. The remainderman would replace his future interests with an immediate capital sum.

As will be seen, sales of interests present both inheritance tax and capital gains tax pitfalls.

Partition of the trust fund

[7.37] One of the more usual forms of reorganisation of interests under a settlement is where a life tenant surrenders his life interest in part of the trust fund to the remaindermen (who following the termination of his interest will become absolutely entitled to the capital of that part of the fund in which the life tenant has surrendered his interest). In return the remaindermen assign their interests in remainder in the balance of the fund to the life tenant. In each part of the fund the interests in possession and in remainder merge. The life tenant takes the capital of that part of the fund in which he has not surrendered his interest and the remaindermen take the capital of the rest. This arrangement places capital in the hands of each which they may then deal with as they independently determine. Neither has to find a capital sum in order to acquire the interest of the other so this route may be preferable to the sale of interests discussed above.

A partition of the trust property such as is described in the preceding paragraph will frequently be undertaken on an arm's length basis. An actuarial valuation of the life tenant's interest having regard to their prospective lifespan will be obtained. The funds to which the life tenant and the remaindermen become absolutely entitled as a result of the partition will be determined according to the values placed upon each of the respective interests.

The transaction is sometimes analysed as one under which each is taking what he is entitled to from the trust fund, assessed according to the value of his interest. The better view is that each of the life tenant and the remaindermen surrender their interests in part of the fund in order to acquire the other's interest in the remainder so the partition is therefore akin to a sale by each of them of part of their interests.

Such a partition might also be appropriate where one or more of the life tenant and the remaindermen wish to confer a gratuitous benefit on the other or others of them in part of the fund and the amounts of capital to pass to each may be determined by estate planning motives and without regard to the actuarial values of their respective interests.

Exercise of a power of appointment in favour of the life tenant

[7.38] Another means of placing capital in the hands of the life tenant which he can then give to others is the exercise of a power of appointment. It is arguable, however, that trustees should not exercise their power of appointment to confer a capital benefit on a life tenant whom they know intends to use that capital for the benefit of persons who are not beneficiaries under the settlement. This would be the main instance in which consideration might be given for the exercise of a power of appointment to place a life tenant in funds to make potentially exempt transfers. There may be less risk of a claim for breach of trust if the trustees' exercise of their power of appointment is to enable the life tenant to make gifts of capital to the remaindermen.

Taxation consequences

Assignment or surrender by the holder of an interest in possession within IHTA 1984, s 49 by way of gift or sale

Inheritance tax

[7.39] An assignment or surrender by way of gift of their interest by the life tenant will be a deemed transfer of value which may be potentially exempt if the relevant conditions are fulfilled.

The surrender by a life tenant of his interest may not be sufficient to vest capital outright in the remaindermen if they comprise a class of beneficiaries which has not closed. In this case, the remaindermen then living will become entitled to interests in possession in the settled property. Although this will not enable them to deal with the underlying capital the deemed transfer by the life tenant will still be a chargeable transfer assuming that his interest fell within IHTA 1984, s 49. If it did not there will be no chargeable transfer because the settled property will remain relevant property. Until the class closes the settlement will be a relevant property settlement subject to decennial and exit charges. When the class closes the remaindermen then living would become entitled to the capital of the fund. There would be an exit charge as a result of their becoming so entitled.

In some cases, a surrender by the life tenant may not accelerate the interests of the remaindermen: for example, where their interests are contingent upon their surviving the life tenant. As mentioned in **7.34**, in such a case, the attempted surrender might cause a gap in the beneficial interest if the interest does not carry the intermediate income (Trustee Act 1925, s 31(3)) and a resulting trust of the income to the settlor (or his estate) may arise. This is unlikely to have been the parties' intention and the settlement, unless it qualifies as a TSI, will become a relevant property settlement and a reservation of benefit will arise in the settled property.

If the life tenant, holding an interest within IHTA 1984, s 49(1), sells his interest for a consideration equal to the market value of the interest, either by assigning it or by surrendering it, inheritance tax will be chargeable as if the value transferred (ie the value of the property in which his interest subsisted) was reduced by the amount of the consideration (IHTA 1984, s 52(2)). It is important to note that because the charge under s 52 is imposed on a hypothetical transfer even if the life tenant were to sell his interest to a complete stranger on a negotiated basis at its market value (which would, of course, be less than the value of the underlying capital), the provisions of IHTA 1984, s 10 (dispositions not intended to confer gratuitous benefit) could not apply.

The purchaser of a life tenant's interest may also make a transfer of value of part of the amount of the consideration. This is determined by reference to the actual value of the life interest sold without regard to whether or not the life tenant is treated for inheritance tax purposes as owning the capital of the fund in which his interest subsists (IHTA 1984, s 49(2)). Thus, if a purchaser pays to the life tenant an amount in excess of the capitalised value of the life tenant's interest that excess will be a transfer of value by the purchaser (since his estate will have been reduced by that excess) unless it is a disposition not intended to confer a gratuitous benefit within IHTA 1984, s 10. Any transfer of value made by a purchaser of a life interest may, however, be a potentially exempt transfer. If s 10 does apply to the acquisition, the acquired interest will be a section 5(1B) interest.

A section 5(1B) interest exists where a UK domiciled individual has become beneficially entitled to an interest in possession after 8 December 2009 by virtue of a disposition falling within IHTA 1984, s 10 (dispositions not intended to confer a gratuitous benefit). Such an interest is treated for most purposes in the same way as a privileged interest.

Capital gains tax

[7.40] The assignment by the life tenant of his interest (whether to the remaindermen or to strangers to the settlement) or the surrender by him of his interest will only have capital gains tax consequences for the trustees or the life tenant if:

(a)   as a result one or more people become absolutely entitled to the trust property. The trustees will be deemed to have disposed of the trust property in which the life tenant's interest has ceased (TCGA 1992, s 71) and to have reacquired it at market value as nominees for those who become absolutely entitled. Depending upon the nature of the trust assets, the trustees and the beneficiaries may be able to elect under TCGA 1992, s 165 to hold-over some or all of any gain arising and thereby avoid an immediate charge to capital gains tax;

(b)   the life tenant acquired his interest for a consideration in money or money's worth or the settlement has been at any time resident outside the UK. A capital gains tax charge will arise to the life tenant on the difference between the market value of his interest at the date of his disposal or the actual sale price (if made to an 'unconnected' person) and his acquisition cost taking into account the wasting asset rules in TCGA 1992, ss 44 and 46; or

(c)   the beneficiary sells his interest to another. The underlying assets to which the interest relates are deemed to be disposed of by the trustees and immediately reacquired by them if the body of trustees and the settlor are UK resident and the settlor has an interest in the settlement (TCGA 1992, s 76A and Sch 4A).

Income tax

[7.41] Subject to the points made below, if the life tenant has assigned or surrendered his interest but the property remains settled, the income arising to the assignee or those whose interests are accelerated by the surrender will be chargeable at his or their personal rates of income tax. Where one or more individuals have become entitled to the income, basic rate income tax will be collected by assessment upon the trustees and an assessment will be made on the assignee or remaindermen for any higher rate or additional rate income tax due.

Where a life tenant has assigned his interest to a discretionary trust or, following a surrender of his interest, the settled property becomes subject to such trusts, the trustees (of the new settlement in the case of an assignment) will be liable at the trust rate (ITA 2007, s 479). Where the income is applied to or for the benefit of the beneficiaries it will be treated as having been received by them net of the trust rate and the sum of tax which is treated as having been deducted from the distribution received will be treated as income tax paid by the recipient beneficiary (ITA 2007, s 494).

Where the minor and unmarried children of the life tenant are the outright assignees or receive absolute interests following the surrender or if the income or capital is distributed to them from the continuing settlements, the life tenant will suffer income tax on the income which arises to his children (ITTOIA 2005, s 629).

Stamp duty and stamp duty land tax

[7.42] An assignment or surrender by way of sale may suffer either *ad valorem* stamp duty or stamp duty land tax (depending on the type of asset). As a general rule, stamp duty is payable in relation to stock and marketable securities whereas stamp duty land tax is payable in relation to land. Stamp duty is not chargeable on an assignment or surrender by the life tenant of his interest by way of gift. Where the underlying assets are UK land, no stamp duty land tax will be payable.

Revocation of the life tenant's interest by the trustees or the exercise of a power of appointment by them to terminate the life tenant's interest and confer benefits on others

[7.43] The taxation consequences of the termination of a life tenant's interest by these means are very similar to those discussed in relation to the assignment or surrender by way of gift by a life tenant of his interest. There are, however, some important differences. The first of these is the possible avoidance of the charge to income tax under ITTOIA 2005, s 629 where the trustees exercise their powers to terminate the life tenant's interest rather than the life tenant surrendering or assigning his interest to achieve the same result.

The second is the avoidance of the capital gains tax provisions in TCGA 1992, s 86, even if the life tenant can benefit from the settled property or its income following the revocation of his interest or the appointment away from him.

The third is that the termination will not be a disposal for the purposes of the pre-owned-assets charge.

Assignment of interests in remainder by way of gift or sale

Inheritance tax

[7.44] No account is to be taken of the value of excluded property in determining whether there is, and the amount of, a transfer of value (IHTA 1984, s 3(2)). An interest in remainder, being a reversionary interest, is usually excluded property for inheritance tax purposes. The principal exceptions are where the interest was acquired for a consideration in money or money's worth, is one to which the settlor or his spouse or civil partner is (or has been) beneficially entitled or where certain conditions of IHTA 1984, s 74A are satisfied and an individual is beneficially entitled who has or is able to acquire another interest in the relevant settled property.

A sale of a reversionary interest will not give rise to an inheritance tax charge for the assignor and assignee unless a sale is made to the life tenant or between connected persons and is not a bargain at arm's length. If the sale is to the life tenant of the fund in which the reversionary interest subsists the consideration paid by the life tenant will be a transfer of value since his estate will be reduced by payment of the consideration but will not be increased by the value of the reversionary interest (IHTA 1984, s 55). Moreover, the payment will not qualify as a transaction not intended to confer gratuitous benefit as the operation of IHTA 1984, s 10 is excluded for transactions to which IHTA 1984, s 55(1) applies.

In response to the decision in *Melville v IRC* [2001] EWCA Civ 1247, [2002] 1 WLR 407, [2001] STC 1271, IHTA 1984, s 272 was amended to provide that a settlement power is not property for the purposes of inheritance tax. A settlement power for this purpose is ' . . . any power over, or exercisable (whether directly or indirectly) in relation to settled property or a settlement'. Because of this change, IHTA 1984, s 55A was inserted to make similar provisions in relation to settlement powers as those applying to reversionary interests under IHTA 1984, s 48. Where a person makes a disposition by which he acquires a settlement power for consideration in money or money's worth:

(a)   the exemption for dispositions not intended to confer a gratuitous benefit under IHTA 1984, s 10 does not apply;
(b)   the person is treated as making a transfer of value;
(c)   the value transferred is determined without taking account of any value acquired by the disposition; and
(d)   the exemptions for transfers to spouses or civil partners, charities, political parties, housing associations, maintenance funds for historic buildings, etc and for national purposes do not apply to the transfer.

Capital gains tax

[7.45] Where the reversionary interest is sold for actual consideration, the trustees will be treated as having disposed of the underlying trust assets to which the interest relates and as having immediately reacquired them at market value (TCGA 1992, s 76A and Sch 4A). Any gain will not be eligible for hold-over relief under TCGA 1992, s 165 as the deemed disposal is a disposal under a bargain at arm's length (TCGA 1992, Sch 4A, para 9(1)). If the reversionary interest was acquired for a consideration in money or money's worth or if the trustees of the settlement have been at any time resident outside the UK, a charge to capital gains tax will arise on any gain realised on the disposal of the reversionary interest (TCGA 1992, ss 76 and 85). If as a result of the assignment someone becomes absolutely entitled to the settled property, the trustees will be treated, under TCGA 1992, s 71, as disposing of the settled property to which that person has become absolutely entitled and reacquiring it at market value as the nominee of that individual. Depending upon the nature of the trust assets it may be possible for some or all of the gain arising to be held-over under TCGA 1992, s 165 by the trustees.

Income tax

[7.46] There will be no income tax consequences as the reversionary interest is a future interest which produces no income. However, if the interest is assigned to the minor children of the remainderman who are unmarried or not in a civil partnership, or to trusts for their benefit, and falls in whilst those children remain unmarried minors, the income arising may be treated as the income of the assignor (ITTOIA 2005, s 629).

Stamp duty and stamp duty land tax

[7.47] No charge to stamp duty or stamp duty land tax will arise on the assignment unless made by way of sale.

Partition of a life interest settlement between life tenant and remaindermen

Inheritance tax

[7.48] Under a partition between a life tenant who holds an interest within s 49 and the remaindermen, the life tenant who surrenders part of his interest to the remaindermen will be treated as having made a transfer of value under IHTA 1984, s 52 equal to the value of the property in which his interest has ceased. No account is taken of the value of the reversionary interest assigned to him by the remainderman in the part of the fund which the life tenant takes absolutely (IHTA 1984, s 52(2)). This transfer of value will be treated as being potentially exempt. As we have seen, s 55(2) excludes IHTA 1984, s 10 so that the life tenant's surrender will not be prevented by that section from being a transfer of value.

The remainderman will not make a transfer of value by assigning his reversionary interest in that part of the fund to the life tenant since his interest is excluded property (IHTA 1984, ss 3(2) and 48(1)). The transfer of a section 5(1B) interest will, however, be a lifetime chargeable transfer.

If the interest of the life tenant is a section 5(1B) interest there will also be an exit charge under IHTA 1984, s 65.

Capital gains tax

[7.49] Neither the life tenant nor remainderman will suffer a charge to capital gains tax as a result of the disposal by each of part of his interest provided that neither acquired their interests for a consideration in money or money's worth (TCGA 1992, s 76(1)) and the trustees have always been resident in the UK or that no actual consideration is given for the disposal of the interest.

Under TCGA 1992, s 71, however, the trustees will be treated as having disposed of the entire settled property to which the life tenant and the remainderman become absolutely entitled as a result of the partition and as having reacquired it at market value as nominees for the life tenant and the remainderman. They may, therefore, realise a gain although in some cases an election for hold-over relief under TCGA 1992, s 165 or s 260 may be made.

Income tax

[7.50] The life tenant and each of the remaindermen will become absolutely entitled to part of the trust fund and will subsequently suffer income tax at their own personal rates in respect of future income. It is unlikely in these circumstances that ITTOIA 2005, s 629 will apply to the life tenant, because, unless the partition of the trust fund is undertaken with court approval, a partition will not be possible where the remaindermen are not of full age and capacity. Accordingly, it is unlikely that the remaindermen will be the unmarried minor children of the life tenant, income applied for whose benefit may be treated as being the income of the life tenant under s 629.

Exercise of a power of appointment in favour of life tenant holding an interest within IHTA 1984, s 49

Inheritance tax

[7.51] This will not give rise to an inheritance tax charge by virtue of IHTA 1984, s 53(2).

Capital gains tax

[7.52] The life tenant will become absolutely entitled to the settled property and as a result gains may be chargeable on the trustees under TCGA 1992, s 71 subject to the possible availability of hold-over relief under TCGA 1992, s 165 or s 260.

Future gains will be taxable in the hands of the life tenant.

Income tax

[7.53] There will be no change in the income tax position.

Stamp duty and stamp duty land tax

[7.54] The instrument effecting the exercise of the power will not be stampable. Any instrument transferring legal title to settled property consisting of shares to the life tenant will be exempt from stamp duty. Where the underlying assets are UK land, no stamp duty land tax will be payable.

Relevant property settlements

[7.55] Since relevant property settlements generally incorporate wide powers which may be exercised to alter the trusts upon which the trust property is held, little needs to be said about the precise mechanics of any changes in the beneficial interests under such settlements. The inheritance tax charge that may arise on relevant property leaving such a settlement or ceasing to be relevant property should be considered carefully in the light of the proposed timing of any distribution.

Inheritance tax

[7.56] As the rates of inheritance tax on distributions from relevant property settlements are calculated by reference to the value of the trust fund at the preceding decennial or, if a decennial has not passed, at the time of commencement of the settlement, one needs to consider whether the distribution should be made before or after the next decennial.

Example

A relevant property settlement was created by a settlor who had made no previous transfers of value and whose cumulative total at the time of creation of the settlement was, therefore, nil. The property was then worth £100,000 but is now worth £1,000,000. This property can be distributed prior to the first decennial without incurring any charge to inheritance tax whereas, if it were kept in the settlement, at the decennial inheritance tax would be charged on the present value of the fund and future charges would be made at rates calculated by reference to the value of the fund at that date.

In two particular circumstances consideration should be given to postponing a distribution from a relevant property settlement beyond a decennial namely:

(a) If the business property or agricultural property relief available is less than 100% in respect of the trust fund or part of it, it may be worth postponing distributions from the settlement until after the first decennial. This is because on any distribution prior to the first decennial the rate of tax applicable will be calculated by reference to the value of the property in the settlement immediately after it commenced. This value is not reduced by business or agricultural property relief as the trustees would not have then owned the settled property for the requisite period of time. Accordingly, the value of the trust assets, unrelieved by business or agricultural property relief, has to be taken into account in calculating the rate of tax to be applied on any exit charge prior to the first decennial. That does not mean that business property relief or agricultural property relief is to be ignored. Such relief would reduce the value of the trust property (the subject of the exit charge) provided that the trustees had held the assets concerned for the requisite period of time at the time the exit charge arose. By way of contrast, on the first decennial (and subsequent ones) inheritance tax is charged on the trust fund as if there had been a transfer of value of the trust fund at that time. Accordingly, business property relief and agricultural property relief may operate to reduce the value of the trust property and will set the applicable rate of tax for the next decennial until the next decennial charge. As a result, the operation of the rules can make it very difficult to decide whether relieved assets should be appointed from a relevant property trust before, or after, the first decennial. A great deal will depend on the expected growth in value of the property concerned, as well as the level of the nil rate band at the relevant time. Of course, in the case of assets which fully qualify for 100% business property relief or agricultural property relief, these particular considerations are not present and it may well be advantageous to retain the assets within the trust in any event.

(b)   Where a distribution (whether outright or on new trusts) is being considered a few years prior to the occasion of a decennial charge to inheritance tax, it may be worth postponing the distribution beyond that anniversary if, in the intervening time, it is likely that the amount of the nil rate band will increase more substantially than the value of the trust property. The nil rate band, however, has been fixed at £325,000 until 2020/2021.

Example

A distribution of property from a settlement is under consideration in the current tax year. The decennial of the settlement will fall in the following year. The settled property had a value, when the settlement commenced, in excess of the nil rate band at that time and the settlor had made no chargeable transfers in the seven years prior to the creation of the settlement.

The postponement of the distribution until after the decennial would remove the settled property from charge to inheritance tax on distributions during the ten years following the decennial if the settled property is worth less than the applicable nil rate band at that decennial.

The rate of tax which applies at any decennial after the first (which in turn determines the rate applicable on subsequent exit charges under s 65) is calculated by reference to a hypothetical transfer by a transferor who has made chargeable transfers in the previous seven years equal to the transfers made by the settlor in the seven years before the commencement of the settlement and the amounts on which exit charges under s 65 have been imposed in the last ten years. Therefore, property which is advanced out of the settlement can continue to affect the inheritance tax charged on the trustees until the second decennial following the advance.

As has been mentioned, discretionary settlements created prior to 18 March 1986 and under which the settlor is a discretionary beneficiary should, if possible, be left alone. The settlor will not be treated as having reserved a benefit in such settlements since FA 1986, s 102 only operates in relation to gifts made after that time. The settlor, therefore, remains able to benefit from such a settlement but the property in it remains entirely outside his estate. Certainly the settlor should not now add any further funds to this type of settlement (unless by will) since to do so would cause the gifts with reservation provisions to apply to the added property.

Generally, the decision whether or not to break a relevant property settlement depends to a large extent on the prevailing rates of inheritance tax applicable to distributions and to the charge on each 10-year anniversary. Where these rates are low (the maximum rate is 6% as it has been for many years), there is every incentive to keep the settlement intact because of the flexibility it offers. The tax charges can often be serviced out of accumulated income.

Capital gains tax

[7.57] When a beneficiary becomes absolutely entitled to an asset as against the trustees (on the occasion of a distribution to him) they will be deemed to dispose of the asset and reacquire it at that time as the nominees of the beneficiary. It will usually be possible to hold-over any chargeable gain arising under TCGA 1992, s 260. Any other form of reorganisation of the interests under a discretionary settlement will not give rise to any charges to capital gains tax.

Income tax

[7.58] If, on a reorganisation of interests under a relevant property settlement, any person becomes entitled to receive the income from a part or the whole of the settled property the trustees will suffer income tax at the basic rate on such income but will cease to suffer the rate applicable to trusts. Instead, the beneficiary entitled to the income will suffer income tax at his marginal rates on the income to which he is entitled but will receive a credit for the tax suffered by the trustees.

Chapter 8

Offshore Trusts

Introduction

[8.1] The aim of this chapter is to examine briefly the main issues arising from the rules relating to non-resident settlements. A comprehensive review of the subject is outside the scope of this book. This chapter is only concerned with non-UK resident trusts established by UK resident domiciliaries. The position of UK resident but non-UK domiciled settlors is considered in CHAPTER 21 UK RESIDENTS WITH MULTI-JURISDICTIONAL AFFAIRS.

Background

[8.2] Tax legislation contains a number of measures to discourage individuals who are both resident and domiciled in the UK from seeking to avoid or defer their capital gains tax or income tax liabilities through the use of offshore trusts.

In respect of capital gains tax there is, firstly, a capital gains tax charge on the trustees at the time they become non-resident, calculated on the basis that they dispose of all the settled property at the time they change their residence and immediately reacquire it at market value ('the emigration charge') (TCGA 1992, s 80). The First-tier Tribunal has referred a case to the ECJ for a preliminary hearing on whether the emigration charge is compatible with the freedom of establishment, freedom to provide services and free movement of capital. Secondly, the gains of a non-resident settlement are attributed to its settlor if he is both domiciled and resident in the UK and (broadly) the settlor, his spouse or civil partner, any children and grandchildren of the settlor or of the settlor's spouse or civil partner, the spouse or civil partner of any such child or grandchildren or any companies controlled by any of them, are capable of benefiting from the income or capital of the settlement ('the offshore settlor charge') (TCGA 1992, s 86 and Sch 5). Thirdly, a charge to capital gains tax is calculated by matching the trustees' gains with capital payments made to, or benefits conferred on, beneficiaries ('the capital payments charge') (TCGA 1992, s 87). Fourthly, the amount assessable under the capital payments charge is increased by what is, in effect, an interest charge ('the supplementary charge') (TCGA 1992, s 91). A capital gains tax charge will also arise in certain circumstances where there is a disposal of an interest in settled property for consideration or where trustees make a transfer of value to another person and the transfer is treated as linked with trustee borrowing (TCGA 1992, ss 76A and 76B and Schs 4A and 4B).

In general, during the lifetime of the settlor, offshore trusts will not offer any advantage where the settlor and the beneficiaries are resident and domiciled in the UK. After the settlor's death, there may be some advantages to beneficiaries, although the sums settled must be sufficiently large for the taxation savings to outweigh the costs of the structure.

In respect of income tax, first, where a settlor makes a settlement from which he or his spouse can benefit, income tax will be charged on him on the settlement income as it arises (ITTOIA 2005, s 625). Secondly, an income tax charge can arise on a transferor who has the power to enjoy the income of a person abroad (including trust income) as a result of relevant transactions (ITA 2007, s 720). Thirdly, where a non-transferor receives a benefit as a result of a relevant transaction, an income tax charge will arise under ITA 2007, s 731.

Residence

[8.3] The rules determining the residence of a body of trustees are the same for capital gains tax and income tax purposes (ITA 2007, s 475 and TCGA 1992, s 69(2)).

The trustees of a settlement are treated as a single body of persons distinct from the persons who are trustees of the settlement from time to time.

A trust is treated as resident in the UK if either Condition 1 or Condition 2 is satisfied:

(a)   Condition 1 is that all the trustees are resident in the UK; or
(b)   Condition 2 is that:
    (i)   at least one trustee is resident in the UK; and
    (ii)   at least one trustee is not resident in the UK; and
    (iii)   a settlor of the settlement was resident or domiciled in the UK when the settlement was made (if the settlement arose on death, that is immediately before the settlor died).

For these purposes, a trustee who is not resident in the UK is treated as if he was resident here at any time when he acts as trustee in the course of a business which he carries on in the UK through a branch, agency or permanent establishment (TCGA 1992, s 69(2D)) (the 'professional trustee deemed residence rule'). 'Permanent establishment' is a phrase of very wide meaning and imprecise scope and the risk that purchasers of ancillary services might inadvertently create a permanent establishment has driven trustees to engage investment management, accountancy, banking and other business services from overseas suppliers which would otherwise have been engaged from UK suppliers. HMRC has issued guidance entitled 'HMRC Trustee Residence Guidance' found in Appendix 1 to the Trusts, Settlements & Estates Manual which sets out their understanding of the principles which govern the application of the professional trustee deemed residence rule and examples of its application. The Tax Faculty, the CIOT and the STEP have published a joint Technical Release (TAXGUIDE 02/15 (TECH 03/15 TAX) Trustee Residence), the text of which has been agreed by HMRC.

An individual trustee who is resident in the UK for a year will be resident for every day in that year, including those days that fall within the overseas part of a split year for that individual. Where the individual is a trustee of a settlement only in the overseas part of a split year then he or she is treated as not resident for that year in applying the residence rules to that settlement. This exception is overridden if the trustee is acting as such in the course of a UK business.

Exporting a trust

Capital gains tax

[8.4] Under TCGA 1992, s 80 where a UK resident trust becomes resident outside the UK, the trustees will be deemed to have disposed of the 'defined' assets and immediately reacquired them at their current market value, and will be assessed to tax on the amount due. 'Defined assets' are all trust assets, other than those which would in any event remain within the UK tax charge because they are used for the purposes of a trade carried on in the UK by the trustees or those exempt from capital gains tax under a double tax agreement (TCGA 1992, ss 80(3),(4),(5)). Anti-avoidance rules apply to UK trusts which fall to be treated as non-resident under the terms of an applicable double taxation agreement (TCGA 1992, s 83). A number of ancillary provisions restrict roll-over relief, and prevent a double charge to tax arising by reference to disposals of interests under trusts. Further provisions limit the charge to tax where there is an inadvertent change in residence resulting from the death of a trustee, and the former residence status is resumed within 6 months. Finally, there are provisions governing the liability for tax of past trustees, where a UK trust becomes non-resident and an export charge remains unpaid.

Example

In 1985, Mr Arnold, a UK resident domiciliary settled his 25% stake in Widget Enterprises, a UK trading company, on a UK resident interest in possession trust in his favour. The shares were then valued at £30,000 on a minority basis and had an original base cost on purchase in 1984 of £10,000. The gain was held-over. In July 2013, the trustees were replaced by non-resident trustees, and the body of trustees ceased to be resident in the UK, immediately prior to the sale of the shares for £2m as part of a takeover. If there was no material difference between the market value of the shares when the body of trustees ceased to be resident in the UK and the amount for which they were subsequently sold, the trustees were deemed to realise a chargeable gain of £1,990,000 (£2,000,000 – £10,000) immediately before the change of residence.

The net effect of these provisions in practice normally confines the export of settlements to cases where

(a)   either the settlement is holding non-chargeable assets, such as cash, or the gain which will arise on the export of the trust is considered to be a price worth paying for the ability to defer the capital gains tax charge on gains realised by the trustees once non-resident; *and*

(b)   either the beneficiaries of the settlement do not include the settlor or members of his immediate family or the settlor is dead; and

(c)   there is likely to be a significant gap between the making of the gain and the distribution of the proceeds to the beneficiaries.

Considerations

[8.5] There are several points to consider where an export of a settlement is proposed.

First, whether the settlement is one in which the settlor has an interest (as defined in TCGA 1992, Sch 5, para 2) on which the offshore settlor charge will arise. This broadly is where either the settlor or his spouse or civil partner, any of their children and their spouses or civil partners, any grandchild of the settlor or his spouse or civil partner, or any companies controlled by any of them (or any companies associated with any companies so controlled) benefit or are capable of benefiting from the income or capital of the settlement. Where these conditions are satisfied, the settlor will be taxable on any gains realised by the trustees, unless he is:

(i)   domiciled outside the UK in the relevant tax year; or
(ii)   not resident in the UK for the year; or
(iii)   dead at the end of the relevant tax year.

This offshore settlor charge arises in the year following the export of the settlement.

In a family context, therefore, the scope for deferring the payment of capital gains tax by the export of a settlement, the settlor of which is domiciled and resident in the UK, will normally only arise where the beneficiaries of the settlement are the great-grandchildren or remoter issue of the settlor or the unmarried 'cohabitee' of the settlor who is not the settlor's civil partner.

Secondly, on the trustees of the settlement becoming non-UK resident, the trustees will be deemed to have disposed of the settled property and to have immediately reacquired it at its market value. Any chargeable gain arising as a result will be taxable in the hands of the retiring trustees. If it is not paid by them within six months from the time when it becomes payable, however, HMRC can recover the tax from any other person who was a trustee of the settlement within 12 months of the date of export, unless he retired before the end of the 12-month period and can show that when he retired there was no proposal that the settlement be exported (TCGA 1992, s 82). It is advisable, therefore, for a retiring trustee to make the relevant enquiries immediately before his retirement and retain documentary evidence of this.

For some settlements this potential capital gains tax charge may outweigh the advantages of the settlement becoming non-resident. There may be cases, however, where the prospect of deferring capital gains tax on an anticipated future increase in the value of an asset will outweigh the disadvantage of triggering an immediate charge to capital gains tax.

Thirdly, there must be no time in the fiscal year when the trustees are resident in the UK. If there is, subject to any applicable double tax treaty, they will be subject to capital gains tax in respect of disposals taking place at any time in the fiscal year. Therefore, the trustees will not be outside the UK capital gains tax net until the start of the tax year immediately following that in which the settlement is 'exported'. The retiring trustees should also be aware that they will remain liable to capital gains tax in respect of gains realised on disposals of trust assets made by the new non-resident trustees up to the end of the tax year in which the new appointment is affected. It is preferable, therefore, for UK resident trustees to retire towards the end of a tax year in order to minimise their exposure to charges which they will have no assets to meet.

Fourthly, save as to a limited class of assets used in a UK trade and to certain disposals of residential property, non-resident trustees will not usually themselves have any capital gains tax liability in respect of gains realised by them, even in the case of settlements within TCGA 1992, s 86 and Sch 5. A further charge ('the capital payments charge') under TCGA 1992, s 87, however, treats gains as arising to beneficiaries who receive 'capital payments' from the settlement in which those gains were realised.

Fifthly, difficulties may also arise where funds held on separate trusts derive from one settlement. TCGA 1992, s 69 provides that trustees are to be treated as a single and continuing body of persons being resident in the UK if there is at least one UK resident trustee. The export of one fund of a settlement leaving another with trustees resident in the UK may leave the trustees of the UK fund bearing the capital gains tax liability for gains made by the offshore trustees of the fund exported as happened in *Roome v Edwards (Inspector of Taxes)* [1982] AC 279, [1981] 1 All ER 736, HL, and *Bond (Inspector of Taxes) v Pickford* [1983] STC 517, 57 TC 301, CA. It may be difficult to determine on the face of the trust documents whether the funds are separate funds of the same settlement or two different settlements relating to those funds (and by which they were created). HMRC's practice set out in Statement of Practice SP 7/84 may be of assistance. It will be helpful to know whether any charge to capital gains tax was incurred or held-over under TCGA 1992, s 165 or s 260 when the two funds separated (as it should have been if separate settlements were created since the trustees of the newly created settlement would then have become absolutely entitled to the settled property over which the power of appointment was exercised) and whether each fund claims its own share of the annual exemption available to trustees. If there is any doubt as to whether or not separate settlements exist, for safety's sake both should be exported.

Inheritance tax

[8.6] The export of an existing settlement by the appointment of non-resident trustees will have no inheritance tax consequences. If, at the time of creating the settlement, the settlor was domiciled in the UK (whether as a matter of general law or under the deemed domicile provisions in IHTA 1984, s 267) all of the settled property will remain subject to UK inheritance tax even if the trustees become non-UK resident and whether or not the settlor and all beneficiaries are now domiciled and resident outside the UK.

Income tax

[8.7] Trustees resident outside the UK for income tax purposes are not liable to UK income tax except on income arising in the UK.

Income arising in the UK is usually either not charged on non-residents or tax will have been deducted at source and so UK income tax may not be of great concern to non-resident trustees, although it may have an effect on cash flow. Income arising under an interest in possession the holder of which is resident and domiciled in the UK and which is paid directly to the holder of the interest, whether arising to the non-resident trustees from a UK source or not, will be taxable on the beneficiary at his personal rates of income tax. Non-resident trustees of settlements under which income may be accumulated or paid out at the discretion of the trustees are liable to income tax at the trust rate under ITA 2007, s 479 on some UK source income. Encouragement is given to the trustees to discharge their liability by Revenue Extra-Statutory Concession B18 which is discussed below. In practice, non-resident trustees will often not be liable to income tax because of ITA 2007, ss 810–814 which limits the UK source income that is chargeable on non-residents.

Beneficiaries who receive distributions of income from a non-resident discretionary settlement will not be entitled to the double tax reliefs to which they would have been entitled had they received the income direct from its original source. Nor will that income be within ITA 2007, s 494 and, therefore, treated as being a net payment from which income tax at the trust rate has been deducted. If income is to be distributed on a regular basis to beneficiaries, it may be advantageous for the non-resident trustees to submit tax returns to HMRC and pay any tax due on UK source income since under the provisions of Revenue Extra-Statutory Concession B18, HMRC will then allow the beneficiaries to claim relief for any foreign and UK tax charged on, or withheld from, the trust income.

If the settlor (and his spouse) are not entirely excluded from benefit under the settlement, the settlor may be charged to income tax on income arising to the trustees whilst he remains resident and domiciled in the UK even though he does not actually receive that income (ITTOIA 2005, s 624). Even if he is excluded from benefit but is able to direct how income from the settlement is distributed or has in some other way 'power to enjoy' that income within ITA 2007, Part 13, Chapter 2 (transfer of assets abroad) the income will be treated as arising directly to the transferor (normally the settlor) who will be charged to income tax on that income (ITA 2007, ss 720 and 721) unless the transferor can establish that he satisfies the 'no tax avoidance motive defence' (ITA 2007, ss 736–742). Chapter 2 has effect not only where the settlor has power to enjoy *income* but also where he may receive *capital* from the settlement (ITA 2007, s 728).

If income is accumulated in an accumulation and maintenance settlement, a trust for a bereaved minor or an age 18–25 settlement for the benefit of the settlor's children and no capital sums are paid out to or for their benefit until they attain 18, subsequently each child may suffer a charge to income tax under ITA 2007, s 732 on the income which arose to the trustees (before or after they attained 18) and was accumulated and which could, when it arose, have been (directly or indirectly) used to provide a benefit for them. This charge will arise to the extent that they subsequently do receive a benefit from the trustees if, when they receive that benefit, they are resident and domiciled in the UK. Benefit is widely defined and does not include only benefits of an income nature.

ITA 2007, s 732 will also operate to impose an income tax liability on a beneficiary (other than the settlor) of a discretionary settlement who receives benefits (from the settlement) to the extent that income has arisen, or arises, to the trustees which may be used to provide a benefit to the beneficiary in the future, and has been or is accumulated.

It will be seen that provided the settlor and his spouse are excluded from benefit and cannot direct how the income of the settlement should be applied, a measure of income tax deferral may be achieved by the creation of an offshore discretionary settlement since income will only be charged to UK income tax when beneficiaries resident here receive income or benefits from the settlement. For so long as the income is rolled up offshore no charge will arise.

Actual tax cost of export

[8.8] One of the results of the export charge is that many old settlor retained interest trusts will remain UK resident for the indefinite future. There may, however, still be UK resident trusts which were established by settlors who are now dead, or for individuals outside the settlor's immediate family circle which it may be advantageous to 'export' (that is, for the body of trustees to become non UK resident).

Legal issues

[8.9] Before a trust can be exported, the following legal issues are relevant, in addition to the tax implications of the export.

When may non-resident trustees be appointed?

[8.10] In the past it has been argued on the basis of Sir John Pennycuick's *dicta* in *Whitehead's Will Trusts, Re, Burke v Burke* [1971] 2 All ER 1334, [1971] 1 WLR 833 and by analogy to the principle applied in *Weston's Settlements, Re, Weston v Weston* [1969] 1 Ch 223, [1968] 1 All ER 720, CA, that the appointment of non-resident trustees would normally be 'improper.'

In *Richard v Mackay* (1990) 1 Offshore Tax Planning Review 1 Millett J said:

> ' . . . I doubt that the language of Sir John Pennycuick is really in tune with the times. In my judgment where the trustees retain their discretion . . . the court should need to be satisfied only that the proposed transaction is not so inappropriate that no reasonable trustee could entertain it.'

So the appointment of non-resident trustees under an express or statutory power is unlikely of itself to be 'improper'. It is true that, in *Richard v Mackay*, Millet J commented as *obiter* that the court was unlikely to appoint non-resident trustees 'where the scheme is nothing more than a scheme to avoid tax and has no advantages of any kind'. He drew a distinction, however, between the court's approach when it exercised a discretion of its own from its approach when asked to authorise the trustees' exercise of their own discretion.

'Where the Court is invited to exercise an original discretion of its own . . .
the Court will require to be satisfied that the discretion should be exercised in the
manner proposed . . . Where, however, the transaction is to be proposed to be
carried out by the trustees in exercise of their own discretion, entirely out of court,
. . . then in my judgment the question the Court asks itself is quite different. It is
concerned to ensure that the proposed exercise of the trustees' power is lawful and
within the power and that it does not infringe the trustees' duty to act as ordinary,
reasonable and prudent trustees might act, but it requires only to be satisfied that the
trustees can properly form the view that the proposed transaction is for the benefit
of the beneficiaries or the trust estate.'

If the appointment of offshore trustees is 'improper', however, what is its
effect?

It appears from *Re Whitehead* that it is unlikely to mean that the exercise of
the power is invalid. If it is invalid then the original trustee will not have been
validly discharged from the trusts. If that were the case, the result could be that
the settlement concerned will have remained resident in the UK after the
purported change of trustees and remained within the charge to capital gains
tax.

It is more likely, however, that the retirements and appointments would be
valid though improper at the time they were made and therefore the court
would be called upon to exercise its jurisdiction to avoid the retirements and
appointments on an application of the beneficiaries under, for example, the
Trustee Act 1925, s 41. The result of such a decision is that the appointments
and retirements would be reversed from the time that the court's judgment was
made.

As has been said, in all but the most exceptional circumstances, it is unlikely
that the court would interfere with the appointment of non-resident trustees
under a statutory, or an express, power of appointment. This must particularly
be so where the trust deed expressly authorises the appointment of non-
resident trustees.

It is common practice, however, for trustees to protect themselves against
whatever residual risk there may be by seeking the agreement of, and an
indemnity from, the adult beneficiaries of the settlement.

Other trust points to be watched

[8.11] There are two particular provisions of the Trustee Act 1925 which
must be considered with care when a settlement is to be exported.

(1)   Trustee Act 1925, s 37(1)(c) provides that a trustee shall not be
        discharged from his trust unless there will be either a trust corporation
        or at least two persons to act as trustees to perform the trust. The
        exception to this is where a sole trustee was originally appointed and a
        sole trustee will be able to give a good receipt for all capital money
        because the settlement only permits the trustees to hold property which
        is personalty. It is not clear that s 37(1)(c) can be expressly excluded
        under the terms of the settlement.
        If the settlement provides powers for the trustees to buy and sell land,
        as most will, a sole trustee (other than a trust corporation) should not
        be appointed even if only one trustee was originally appointed. The

Trustee Act 1925, s 68(18) contains a narrow definition of a trust corporation which does not include a foreign incorporated company. It is doubtful that this provision is compatible with EU law. Prudence dictates that a foreign incorporated company, therefore, should not be appointed as a sole trustee on the export of a settlement. Where a foreign incorporated company is appointed to be the trustee of a settlement which is to be exported, an additional trustee should be appointed to ensure that the retiring trustee or trustees are discharged from their trusts. If the UK resident retiring trustees are not properly discharged as required by s 37(1)(c) they will remain trustees. In that case the result may be that the settlement remains resident in the UK and therefore that the UK resident trustees remain liable to capital gains tax in respect of gains realised on disposals of the settled property.

In the case of *Jasmine Trustees Ltd v Wells & Hind (a firm)* [2007] EWHC 38 (Ch), [2008] Ch 194, [2007] 1 All ER 1142 a husband and wife purported to retire as trustees of the settlement in favour of a single company which was not a trust corporation. Because their retirement was invalid, all subsequent attempted appointments of trustees were held also to be invalid on the grounds that the couple, although not aware of that fact, had continued as trustees and had not consented to the appointments.

(2)   Trustee Act 1925, s 40 provides that, on the appointment by deed of a new trustee, the settled property will, save in the circumstances mentioned below, vest automatically in the new trustee or trustees whether or not the deed contains an express declaration that it should do so. However, certain types of assets are expressly excluded from vesting automatically (s 40(4)). Therefore, on the appointment of a new trustee or trustees the transfer into the names of the new trustees must be effected by the usual means for transferring such assets. These assets include land conveyed by way of mortgage, land held under a lease and any shares or securities or property which is only transferable in books kept by a company or in a manner directed by Act of Parliament.

If the settlor is either resident or domiciled in the UK at the time a settlement is made, an appointment of non-resident trustees will only result in the body of trustees being non-UK resident if all of them are resident outside the UK. All assets held in the settlement should be transferred to the new trustees before the beginning of the tax year for which it is desired to ensure that the trustees are non-resident. Care should be taken to ensure that, so far as possible, all formalities have been completed. Although it should be sufficient if all that remains is for the non-resident trustees to arrange the registration of themselves as shareholders in the various companies.

Doubts have been raised as to whether s 40 is effective to transfer from retiring trustees to new trustees equitable interests (such as reversionary interests) held by trustees or whether, as a result of the provisions of Law of Property Act 1925, s 53(1)(c), these fall within one of the exceptions in s 40(4) as being property the transfer of which must be carried out as prescribed by Act of Parliament. The safest course is to ensure that any equitable interest which is to pass to the new trustees is assigned in writing (this can be incorporated into the deed of appointment of new trustees). Again, this avoids any argument that the administration of the settlement has not been transferred outside the UK.

It used to be the case that the place where a trust was administered was directly relevant to determining the residence of its body of trustees. This is no longer so, but the place where individual trustees carry on their trustee duties may be of relevance to determining their individual residence and therefore, indirectly, be relevant to determining the residence of the body of trustees. This is so particularly where one is dealing with companies carrying on a trust management business. As explained at **8.1** above, there is a special rule that if a trustee of a settlement acts as trustee in the course of business which the trustee carries on in the UK through a branch, agency or permanent establishment, then in determining the residence of a settlement, that trustee is to be treated as if he were UK resident. The nature of a 'permanent establishment' has been much considered in relation to double tax treaty provisions applying to companies. A very low level of activity in a country can be enough for there to be a permanent establishment in that country. The best rule of thumb, therefore, is that all activities in relation to a trust should be carried on outside the UK.

Since most civil law jurisdictions do not have a trust concept and do not recognise the division of ownership of assets into legal and equitable ownership, it is preferable, when exporting a settlement, to appoint trustees resident in a common law jurisdiction where the courts will enforce the duties and responsibilities of the trustees. Usually, trustees resident in a tax haven are appointed in order to ensure that the jurisdiction in which the new trustees are resident will not impose charges on realised gains similar to the UK capital gains tax they seek to avoid.

Protectors

[8.12] It is not unusual, before certain trustee powers can be exercised, for the consent to be required of someone upon whom the settlor feels he can rely who is resident outside the UK. That person is often called the 'protector'. The protector's role is to act as a watchdog over the trust's affairs, sometimes on behalf of the settlor and sometimes in order to protect the interests of all or some of the beneficiaries. Sometimes this function is delegated to an Advisory Committee or Board. The exact status and powers of the protector will depend on the terms of the trust, although prima facie the powers are fiduciary in nature (*IRC v Schroder* [1983] STC 480, 57 TC 94).

Whilst this would not be an issue where a protector simply acts as a sounding board, the position is uncertain where they have important powers. Where a protector in effect possesses a power of veto over the exercise of certain trustee powers, there may be reasonable grounds for arguing that the powers are not of a fiduciary nature. However, where positive powers are involved (such as the power to replace trustees), there is a higher likelihood that those powers are fiduciary.

The risk in this is that a protector's possession of fiduciary powers may result in his being a type of trustee, and his residence in the UK may affect the residence of the trust for tax purposes. It is prudent to ensure that where protectors are appointed, they are resident outside the UK. Naturally, it will be important to confirm that there are no local tax difficulties for a person accepting the position. Alternatively, if the settlor insists on the appointment of a UK protector it will be prudent to ensure that the protector only holds powers of veto.

Generally, the role of a protector is to provide an extra comfort to clients who are not otherwise entirely comfortable with giving up both the legal ownership and a part of the beneficial ownership of their assets to trustees of whom their knowledge may be small. In practice, the solution to such concerns may be relatively straightforward: it is to identify professional offshore trustees which have been established for a long time and have a reputation for integrity and efficiency.

'Flee clauses'

[8.13] In some trust documents a flee clause or resettlement clause can be found providing that on the occurrence of certain events the trustees will automatically be removed from office and other trustees resident in another jurisdiction appointed. The efficacy of such clauses (which is largely untested) may depend on whether they are triggered before or after the happening of the event the effect of which they are seeking to avoid. If a particular event occurs before the new trustees are automatically appointed it may be impossible to transfer assets out of the names of the old trustees and into those of the new trustees. Even if the automatic appointment of new trustees is triggered before the measures sought to be avoided are introduced there may still be difficulty in transferring assets out of the names of the old trustees. The flee clause may provide that assets will, from the date of the automatic appointment, be held by the old trustees merely as nominees for the new trustees but the success of this provision will depend upon the nature of the measures introduced.

Taxing the settlor – the offshore settlor charge

[8.14] Under the offshore settlor charge (TCGA 1992, s 86) gains realised by non-UK resident trustees are attributed to a UK resident and domiciled settlor where the settlor can benefit from the settlement. The settlor is entitled to recover the tax so paid from the trustees. Gains arising on assets disposed of, during a temporary period of non-residence (see **CHAPTER 21 UK RESIDENTS WITH MULTI-JURISDICTIONAL AFFAIRS**) which is less than five years, which the trustees had acquired before the period of non-residence will be assessable in the settlor's year of return (TCGA 1992, ss 10A and 86A).

This charge applies irrespective of the time the settlement was made. In general terms, a settlor has an interest in a settlement for the purposes of the offshore settlor charge where he or his immediate family can benefit under the settlement, unless the benefit can only arise as a result of certain specified events outside the settlor's control. The charging provisions do not apply if the settlor dies in the relevant year, or if the beneficiary, by virtue of whom the settlor has an interest, dies.

The five linking factors

[8.15] The substantive provisions are contained in TCGA 1992, s 86 and Sch 5. There have to be five linking factors present before the rules can apply in any year of assessment.

(a) There must be a qualifying settlement.
(b) The trustees must be non-UK resident, or dually resident.
(c) The settlor must be domiciled and resident in the UK (subject to TCGA 1992, s 86A).
(d) The settlor must have a retained interest.
(e) Applying the fiction that the trust was UK resident during the year of assessment, there must be a gain arising in respect of a disposal of settled property originating from the settlor.

Qualifying settlements

[8.16] Since 6 April 1999 all settlements have been qualifying settlements.

Non-resident trusts

[8.17] The trusts caught under these provisions are those which are non-UK resident throughout the year of assessment, or the trustees of which are UK resident in the year but, whenever they are UK resident, are treated under a double taxation relief arrangement as resident outside the UK (TCGA 1992, s 86(2)).

The settlor

[8.18] For a settlor to be within these provisions he must be UK domiciled, and resident at some time in the year of assessment concerned. A person is treated as a settlor where the settlement concerned contains property treated as originating from him (TCGA 1992, Sch 5, para 7). This will largely be where he provided the property himself or, in certain circumstances, where the trust property represents assets which he originally provided (TCGA 1992, Sch 5, para 8). Also caught is property added by companies, in which case the shareholders are treated as settlors (TCGA 1992, Sch 5, para 8(4)). Property added as a result of reciprocal arrangements with others is also caught. Property is to be taken as being added if it is provided directly or indirectly by a person (TCGA 1992, Sch 5, para 8(7)).

In *Coombes v Revenue & Customs Comrs* [2007] EWHC 3160 (Ch), [2008] STC 2984, a beneficiary of an offshore settlement who was not otherwise a settlor gave money to an offshore company owned by the settlement. The company used the money to buy land which the trustees later sold at a gain. HMRC assessed the beneficiary on a gain arising under TCGA 1992, s 86 on the basis that he was a settlor of the settlement. It was held that the relevant definition of a settlor was that in TCGA 1992, Sch 5, para 7 and that the beneficiary was not a settlor of the trust within that definition because none of the property of the settlement consisted of, or included, property originating from the beneficiary.

In the case of *Thomas v HMRC* [2016] UKFTT 133 (TC), the First-tier Tribunal held that although it was for HMRC to show a prima facie case that the taxpayers were settlors of an offshore trust, it was for the taxpayers in that case to show that they were not settlors, even if that involved proving a negative.

Retained interests caught

[8.19] In broad terms a settlor is treated as having an interest under a settlement if income or property originating from him can or does become available for the benefit of any one or more of the following ('defined') persons, namely:

(a) the settlor;
(b) the settlor's spouse or civil partner;
(c) any child of the settlor or of the settlor's spouse or civil partner;
(d) the spouse or civil partner of any such child;
(e) any grandchild of the settlor or of the settlor's spouse or civil partner;
(f) any spouse or civil partner of any such grandchild;
(g) a company controlled by any of the above; or
(h) a company associated with a controlled company (TCGA 1992, Sch 5, para 2(3)).

There are a number of limited exclusions found in TCGA 1992, Sch 5, para 2(4) which reduce the possibility of a person inadvertently being treated as a settlor as a result of circumstances beyond his control which are similar to the exceptions in ITTOIA 2005, s 625(2).

A chargeable gain must arise

[8.20] The final condition is that, as a result of the disposal of any settled property originating from the settlor (which has a wide definition), there is an amount on which the trustees would be chargeable to tax if they were UK resident, disregarding the terms of any applicable double taxation treaty.

In quantifying the chargeable gains involved, no account is to be taken of the annual exemption. Full deduction is available for past and current losses made by the trustees in quantifying the amount of gain. In the past HMRC has taken the view that losses arising at a time before the new rules applied to the settlement could not be set against gains arising at a time when the rules did apply. HMRC now accepts that the set-off is possible. The trust gains taxable on the settlor can be increased where the trustees hold shares in a non-UK resident company and, had the trust been UK resident, gains would have been apportioned to it under TCGA 1992, s 13. Special provisions apply where a trust holds assets protected under a double taxation treaty (TCGA 1992, s 86(2)(b) and Sch 5, para 1(4)).

Where the conditions listed above are satisfied, an amount of chargeable gains equal to the aggregate gains of the trustees is treated as arising to the settlor in the year of assessment in which the trustees' gains arose. The apportioned gains are treated as forming the highest slice of the settlor's chargeable gains for that year.

Exceptions to charge

[8.21] The charging provisions do not apply where the settlor dies during the year of assessment (TCGA 1992, Sch 5, para 3). Similarly, the provisions do not apply in a fiscal year where the only reason the settlor is caught is because someone other than the settlor has or may benefit under the trust and that person dies during that fiscal year (TCGA 1992, Sch 5, para 4). Where the settlor is excluded from benefit, but is caught because two or more persons have or may benefit under the trust, the provisions will not apply if both or all of those persons die in the fiscal year concerned (TCGA 1992, Sch 5, para 5).

Link with TCGA 1992, s 87

[8.22] Where a gain is charged on a settlor under the offshore settlor charge, it is set against the amount of any trust gains for the purposes of the capital payments charge (TCGA 1992, s 87(4)).

Losses

[8.23] In the past there was a further disadvantage in holding one's assets in an offshore trust because personal losses could not be set against gains allocated to an individual under the capital payments and offshore settlor charges. A settlor can now set personal losses first against personal gains and then against gains attributed under the offshore settlor charge. He cannot, however, offset personal losses against gains treated as accruing to him under the capital payments charge.

Income tax charge on pre-owned assets

[8.24] UK resident domiciliaries must also have regard to the income tax charge on pre-owned assets in relation to their tax planning using offshore structures. This subject is discussed further in CHAPTER 4 LIFETIME PLANNING: MAKING GIFTS.

Taxing the beneficiary – the capital payments charge

The charge

[8.25] TCGA 1992, s 87 applies where there is no time in the tax year when the trustees of a settlement are resident in the UK. Gains realised in a year (on actual and deemed disposals) by the non-resident trustees which had the trustees been UK resident would have been chargeable to capital gains tax (the s 2(2) amount for the year), will be apportioned to a beneficiary to the extent that they are matched with a capital payment received by him. Where the gains realised by the non-resident trustees exceed the value of the capital payment received by the beneficiary, the excess may be apportioned to any beneficiary who receives a capital payment in subsequent years. Where a beneficiary receives a capital payment from non-resident trustees in a year before any trust gains have arisen, gains realised by the trustees in subsequent tax years may be apportioned to the beneficiary. The capital payments charge is a significant factor in deciding whether a trust should be exported. A beneficiary will be chargeable if he is resident in the UK when the gain is deemed to accrue to him. The beneficiaries may suffer a higher capital gains tax rate in respect of gains realised by the non-resident trustees (depending upon the length of time that gains have been 'stockpiled') whereas a lower rate might have been applicable had the settlement not been exported.

The capital payments charge can, however, operate in an advantageous manner because, until a capital payment is received by a UK resident and domiciled beneficiary, no capital gains tax will be payable as a result of a disposal by the trustees. If the beneficiaries do not need the proceeds of asset sales, they can be reinvested by the trustees and funds that would have been used to pay capital gains tax can earn profits for the benefit of the beneficiaries. This 'deferral' aspect of s 87 is only partially blocked by the supplementary charge.

What is a capital payment?

[8.26] A capital payment is defined, in TCGA 1992, s 97, as meaning any payment which is not chargeable to income tax on the beneficiary or, if the beneficiary is not resident in the UK, any payment received otherwise than as income. The meaning of "payment" for this purpose is extended to include any transfer of assets or the conferring of any benefit. Where a capital payment is made by way of a loan to a beneficiary, the value of the capital payment is taken to be equal to the value of the benefit conferred by the loan (TCGA 1992, s 97(4)).

Most informed opinion considered that capital payments would accrue over time where trustees allowed a life tenant the use of a trust asset on favourable terms, subject to the trustee's right to require the return of the asset at will. An example of this would be where trustees permitted a life tenant to occupy a property without charge but subject to a condition that he must quit the property on being given notice by the trustees. In *Edwards (Inspector of Taxes) v Fisher; Billingham (Inspector of Taxes) v Cooper* [2001] EWCA Civ 1041, [2001] STC 1177, 74 TC 139, the Court of Appeal held that where the trustees of a non-resident settlement lent trust moneys interest-free and repayable on demand to a life tenant, a capital payment arose.

The capital payments charge applies to any settlement irrespective of the domicile of the settlor.

A non-resident beneficiary may be deemed to realise capital gains under TCGA 1992, s 87 and yet be outside the charge to capital gains tax by reason of his non-residence. Therefore, an export of a settlement will be particularly advantageous if all beneficiaries are resident outside the UK or if it is anticipated that the beneficiaries who will receive capital payments will become non-resident so that capital payments may be made to beneficiaries who are not within the charge to capital gains tax. Where some beneficiaries are resident in the UK and it is intended that they will receive capital payments, it may be advantageous to make payments to non-resident beneficiaries in an earlier tax year than that in which payments are to be made to UK resident beneficiaries. The gains realised by the non-resident trustees before the payments are made would be matched first with the payments to the non-resident beneficiaries who will suffer no capital gains tax in respect of them. This course of action is subject to the application of the GAAR. HMRC's guidance gives an example of an offshore trust organising its capital payments so as to pay non-resident beneficiaries before resident beneficiaries so as to wash out the trust gains. The guidance says that such arrangements are not subject to the GAAR (HMRC GAAR Guidance, paras 20.2.1–20.7). In addition, care will need to be taken to ensure that the attribution rules which apply where there is a transfer of value to which TCGA 1992, Sch 4B applies (trustee-linked borrowing) are not applicable. This is because payments made to non-chargeable beneficiaries are ignored when calculating the amounts taxable on a UK beneficiary under Sch 4B.

The charge on temporary non-residents under TCGA 1992, s 10A provides that gains allocated to non-residents whose temporary period of non-residence is five years or less will become chargeable when they resume UK residence. Care therefore needs to be taken if an individual has received a capital payment which has not yet been matched in full to trust gains as otherwise capital gains may be allocated to a beneficiary under the capital payments charge in a later year when the trust realises a gain. If he proves to have been temporarily non-resident in that fiscal year that gain will be treated as accruing to the beneficiary in his period of return.

Where the beneficiary is taxable on the remittance basis under ITA 2007, ss 809B, 809D or 809E (which will only apply to individuals who are not domiciled in a country of the UK), any gains treated under the capital payments charge as accruing to the individual will be foreign chargeable gains and therefore taxable only if remitted to the UK.

As already mentioned, where a capital payment to a beneficiary precedes the realisation of gains by non-resident trustees, the capital payments charge operates to attribute the trustees' subsequent gains to the beneficiary if they were resident outside the UK when he received his capital payment. A capital payment made to a beneficiary prior to the export of a settlement may also cause gains realised by the trustees once they have become non-resident to be attributed to him. However, TCGA 1992, s 89 gives protection from the capital payments charge if the capital payment received by the beneficiary was not made in anticipation of a disposal made by the trustees in a non-resident period.

Supplementary charge

[8.27] The supplementary charge applies where beneficiaries receive capital payments which are subject to the capital payments charge. It is important to appreciate that the offshore settlor charge considered earlier on the one hand and the capital payments and supplementary charges on the other are not mutually exclusive. In some circumstances it is possible for charges to arise under both sets of provisions in respect of the same settlement.

The idea behind the supplementary charge is to discourage the long-term retention of gains within an offshore trust. In essence, the longer trust gains remain undistributed (within the first six year period), the greater the potential tax charge when the beneficiary receives a capital payment.

The supplementary charge is calculated by applying a notional rate of interest (currently 10% a year for a maximum of 6 years) to the amount of tax payable under the capital payments charge where the beneficiary receives a capital payment (TCGA 1992, s 91). The amount of the capital payment is allocated to past gains previously made by the trustees, and operates to increase the amount of tax due on the capital payments received by the beneficiary. Hence, if the beneficiary receives a capital payment of, say, £100,000 on which he has to pay capital gains tax of £20,000, he could be faced with an additional tax liability of as much as £12,000 (ie £20,000 × 60%) if the maximum supplementary charge were to apply.

Three additional points are worth noting.

(a)   The supplementary charge cannot operate unless a capital payment is made after 5 April 1992. This may still be relevant where a later trust gain is being matched with an earlier capital payment although, of course, such circumstances, are now likely to be very rare.

(b)   The supplementary charge applies regardless of when the trust was established.

(c)   The supplementary charge can only apply where the capital payment charge applies.

Operation of the rules

[8.28] A supplementary charge will be imposed where there is at least one tax year between the tax year in which the gain is realised and the tax year in which the capital payment is made. Although the overall effect of these provisions is reasonably straightforward, they are in themselves extremely complicated. Broadly, they operate by matching capital payments made with the gains accruing to the trustees in each tax year. The capital payments are matched with the gains of each year on a 'last in, first out' basis (TCGA 1992, s 87A(2)). Where a number of capital payments are made in the same tax year, they are only matched to the extent that the capital payment results in a trust gain accruing to a beneficiary under TCGA 1992, s 87(4).

Where a capital payment is made which is matched with a gain (the section 2(2) amount) made by the trust in a previous tax year and there is at least one year between the capital payment and the end of the tax year in which the gain was made, the capital gains tax paid by the beneficiary under s 87 as a result of the capital payment is increased by the deemed interest charge of 10% per annum. This is limited to a six-year period and therefore the time covered by the charge begins on the later of:

(a)   1 December in the tax year following the year in which the disposal occurred; and

(b)   1 December six years before 1 December in the year of assessment following that in which the capital payment was made;

and ends on 30 November in the tax year following that in which the capital payment is made (TCGA 1992, s 91).

Where only part of a capital payment is matched with a particular section 2(2) amount, or where a capital payment is matched with more than one section 2(2) amount, then the capital gains tax charge to which the capital payment gives rise has to be apportioned, to enable the interest charge to be calculated on the appropriate proportion of the capital gains tax and by reference to the appropriate number of years (TCGA 1992, ss 87A–87C).

An example may help to show how the provisions work in practice.

Example

Captain Broad, now deceased, had settled property (the 'Captain Broad Settlement') on non-resident trustees. Having made no previous capital gains the trustees made the following capital gains and capital payments to the primary beneficiaries of the Captain Broad Settlement, Samantha Duffin and Honoria Tremlett. In all relevant periods Samantha was UK resident. Honoria was not resident in the UK. Neither beneficiary made any other chargeable gains in any of the years concerned.

Fiscal year	Section 2(2) amount	Capital payment	
		Samantha Duffin	Honoria Tremlett
	£'000	£'000	£'000
2013/2014	500	0	0
2014/2015	0	0	0
2015/2016	250	0	250
2016/2017	500	0	600
2017/2018	0	0	0
2018/2019	0	0	0
2019/2020	0	0	0
2020/2021	0	850	0
Totals	**1250**	**850**	**850**

Tax rates, allowances and rules are assumed to remain unchanged from those ruling in 2016/2017.

Applying the method of calculation set out in TCGA 1992, s 87(4) to the capital gains and capital payments of the Captain Broad Settlement it is apparent that until the tax year 2015/2016 the s 2(2) amounts are not matched with any capital payments. We shall begin by applying s 87A(2)–(4) to 2015/2016.

2015/2016

Step 1   Section 2(2) amount = £250,000.

Step 2   Capital payments in year = £250,000.

Step 3   Capital payments of 2015/2016 of £250,000 matched with s 2(2) amount of that year under subpara (a).

Step 4   Section 2(2) amount and capital payments of 2015/2016 reduced to nil.

Step 5	Because subsection 3 applies by virtue of sub-subsection 3(a) no further steps can be applied.

Gains equal to the s 2(2) amount for 2015/2016 of £250,000 are deemed to have accrued to Honoria in that year under s 87(2). Because she is not resident in the UK in the year she is not chargeable to capital gains tax on those gains.

2016/2017

Step 1	The s 2(2) amount is £500,000.
Step 2	Capital payments in year are £600,000.
Step 3	As paragraph (b) applies, the s 2(2) amount for the year is matched with 5/6 of the capital payments for that year.
Step 4	As paragraph (b) of Step 3 applies, the s 2(2) amount for 2016/2017 is reduced to nil and the capital payments for the year are reduced to £100,000 (£600,000 − (£600,000 × 5/6)).
Step 5	Because subsection (3) does not apply, one starts again at Step 1.
Step 1	2013/2014 is the latest previous year in which the s 2(2) amount was not nil. That amount was £500,000.
Step 2	The total amount of the capital payments for 2016/2017 reduced under Step 4 above is £100,000.
Step 3	As paragraph (a) applies £100,000 of the 2013/2014 s 2(2) amount is matched with the capital payment to Honoria made in 2015/2016.
Step 4	As paragraph (a) of Step 3 applies, the s 2(2) amount for 2013/2014 is reduced by £100,000 to £400,000.
Step 5	Because subsection (3) applies by virtue of subsubsection (3)(a), no further steps are applied.

Total gains of £600,000 (£500,000 + £100,000) are deemed to accrue to Honoria in 2016/2017. Because she is not resident in the UK in the year, she is not chargeable to capital gains tax on these gains.

2020/2021

Step 1	The s 2(2) amount for 2020/2021 is 0.
Step 2	The total amount of capital payments in 2020/2021 is £850,000.
Step 3	As subparagraph (b) applies, the capital payment made in the year is reduced by the relevant proportion. The relevant proportion is 0 (£0 / £850,000).
Step 4	As paragraph (b) of Step 3 applies, the s 2(2) amount for 2020/2021 is nil and the capital payments for the year are £850,000 (£850,000 − (£850,000 × 0/850,000)).
Step 5	As subsection 3 does not apply, start again at Step 1.
Step 1	2013/2014 is the latest previous year in which the s 2(2) amount is not nil. After reduction by the capital payments made in 2016/2017 that amount had become £400,000.
Step 2	The total amounts of capital payments in the year were £850,000.
Step 3	As paragraph (b) applies the s 2(2) amount for 2013/2014 is matched with the capital payment to Samantha.

Step 4   As paragraph (b) of Step 3 applies the s 2(2) amount for 2013/2014 is reduced to nil and the capital payment made to Samantha in 2020/2021 is reduced to £450,000 (£850,000 – £400,000).

Step 5   Because subsection (3) applies by virtue of subsubsection (b), no further steps are applied.

Gains of £400,000 are deemed to accrue to Samantha. She is assessable in the following way.

	£	£
Gains charged under s 87	400,000	
Less: annual exemption	(11,100)	
	388,900	
CGT thereon at 20%		77,780
Supplementary charge under s 91:		
Chargeable period: 1 December 2014 – 30 November 2020 (restricted to 6 years)		
£77,780 × (6 × 10%) =		46,668
Capital Gains Tax chargeable		124,448

There are unmatched capital payments in respect of 2020/2021 of £450,000. These may be matched with gains accruing to the trustees in the future.

Notice that the trustees have distributed £1,700,000 (£850,000 + £850,000) and have realised gains of £1,250,000 but only £400,000 of gains have been brought into charge and these have suffered tax of £124,448.

In the light of the provisions of TCGA 1992, ss 87 and 97 it is prudent to assume that, where all involved are resident and domiciled in the UK, gains realised by the trustees will eventually give rise to capital gains tax charges equal to (or possibly greater than) those that would have been suffered had a UK trust been established. Thus, if it is anticipated that on the disposal of an asset incorporating large gains the proceeds will be distributed almost immediately to UK resident and domiciled beneficiaries, the appointment of non-resident trustees will not achieve any postponement of the capital gains tax liability and the costs of the exercise will be wasted.

Even where the interval between the realisation of the gain and any distribution from the settlement is likely to be less than 6 years (the maximum period over which the interest charge may be calculated), the appointment of non-resident trustees will only be advantageous if the funds which would otherwise have been paid over to HMRC in capital gains tax can earn profits for the beneficiaries in excess of 10% per annum.

Minimising the charge to tax

[8.29] As the supplementary charge is based upon the amount of capital gains tax levied on a capital payment, reducing the tax on a capital payment under s 87 will also reduce the supplementary charge under s 91. There are a number of techniques which, if properly implemented, will avoid or minimise the capital gains tax charge which would otherwise arise on providing a benefit to the beneficiaries. These include:

(a)   the offshore trustees providing free use of assets to a beneficiary rather than providing him or her with the funds to acquire the property concerned; and

(b)   the offshore trustees investing for income rather than capital gains in cases outside ITA 2007, ss 720–730 and the income tax rules relating to settlor retained interest settlements. The supplementary charge will only apply in respect of capital gains and not income 'gains'.

Transfer of assets abroad

Background

[8.30] Income Tax Act 2007, ss 714–751 are extremely widely drawn anti-avoidance provisions which seek to prevent the avoidance of income tax by individuals who are resident in the UK and who establish offshore structures to shelter income. These provisions have a long legislative history, and were rewritten under the Rewrite Project. It was held in the case of *Fisher v Revenue & Customs Comr* [2014] UKFTT 804 (TC) that the provisions, in the form that they were in the periods relevant to the case, were incompatible with EU law. In an attempt to make them so compatible they were amended by FA 2013, s 26 and Sch 10, although it is doubtful that the amendments were sufficient to remove the incompatibility.

In the following discussion, where a case has been decided in relation to a statutory provision, we refer to the actual provision considered in that case. Elsewhere the references are to ITA 2007 unless otherwise stated. In general terms, the net effect of the provisions is to 'look through' any offshore arrangement, deeming the income received to be that of the settlor/beneficiary. The *quantum* of the assessable income is, in general, the gross income received by the trustees.

The scope of what was then charged under ICTA 1988, s 739, but which has been rewritten in ITA 2007, s 720, came under detailed scrutiny by the House of Lords in the case of *IRC v Willoughby* [1997] 4 All ER 65, [1997] 1 WLR 1071 which concerned the tax treatment of offshore personal portfolio bonds (see **CHAPTER 9 INSURANCE** under **9.16**). It was held that in order for the provision to apply, it was essential that the transfer of assets should be made by an individual who was UK ordinarily resident at that time (see also the House of Lord's decision in *Vestey v IRC (No 2)* [1980] AC 1148, [1979] 3 All ER 976). With the abolition in FA 2013, Sch 46 of the status of ordinary residence, amendments were made to define the assessable individuals by reference to residence in the UK (ITA 2007, ss 720 and 728 as amended by FA 2013, s 219, Sch 46, paras 54, 60 and 63).

In *R v Allen; R v Dimsey* [2001] UKHL 45, [2002] 1 AC 509, [2001] 4 All ER 768 it was argued unsuccessfully that, because the transfer of income abroad provisions deem the income of a transferee company to be the transferor's, it was therefore also deemed not to be the transferee company's income. The House of Lords held that on the true construction of ICTA 1988, s 739(2) a foreign transferee of assets was not relieved of a liability to tax on income.

Conditions

[8.31] Where an individual makes a relevant transfer of assets and as a result of the transfer or of associated operations, income becomes payable to a person abroad and the transferor has either power to enjoy that income (ITA 2007, s 720) or to receive a capital sum (ITA 2007, s 727), the income of the person abroad is treated as that of the transferor. There must be a relevant transfer of assets by an individual. This means a transfer of property or rights of any kind and includes shares in or obligations of any company to which assets have been transferred or obligations of any other person to whom assets have been transferred (ITA 2007, ss 716 and 717). Second, as a result of the transfer, either alone or together with associated operations, income must become payable to a person abroad (ITA 2007, s 716). A person abroad is defined as a person who is resident or domiciled outside the UK (ITA 2007, s 718). Trustees treated as non-resident under ITA 2007, s 475(3) and personal representatives treated as non-resident under ITA 2007, s 834(4) are treated as being non-resident for the purposes of the transfer of asset abroad rules (ITA 2007, s 718). A UK resident company which is incorporated overseas is not treated as being non-resident.

An associated operation is widely defined in ITA 2007, s 719.

Power to enjoy

[8.32] An individual has the power to enjoy income if one of the enjoyment conditions in ITA 2007, s 723 is satisfied. Those provisions use the term 'benefit'; a term which is not defined in the legislation. It will include benefits in kind, such as the interest foregone on an interest-free loan, as well as straightforward distributions of capital. HMRC considers that the free use of property is a 'benefit'. In *Edwards (Inspector of Taxes) v Fisher; Billingham (Inspector of Taxes) v Cooper* [2001] EWCA Civ 1041, [2001] STC 1177, 74 TC 139, the Court of Appeal held that, for the purposes of the capital payments charge under TCGA 1992, s 87, an interest-free loan to the life tenant repayable on demand was a benefit and, by conferring such a benefit, a capital payment had been made under TCGA 1992, s 97. (The Special Commissioners had held that the benefit of such a loan was nil.) HMRC accept that the appointment of a life interest is not a benefit within the meaning of the section because it is not 'provided out of assets' as required by the provisions (Law Society: agreed note of meeting with the Board of Inland Revenue 1981). Income tax is charged on the 'amount of income treated as arising in the tax year'.

Chargeable income

[8.33] In calculating the income which is chargeable under ITA 2007, ss 720 and 727, the transferor is treated as if the individual had actually received the amount by reference to which the income treated as arising under s 721 or s 728 is determined (ITA 2007, s 746). Trust management expenses are generally not deductible. Relief for foreign taxes is allowable only to the extent that such taxes would have been paid had the individual actually received the amount by reference to which the income treated as arising to him is determined (ITA 2007, s 746).

The remittance basis for non-UK domiciliaries who are taxable under s 720 is preserved by ITA 2007, ss 726 and 735. Section 726 provides that the remittance basis applies to foreign income which, if it were the individual's, would be relevant foreign income. Section 735 contains similar provisions and s 735A provides how the amount should be calculated.

ITA 2007, s 727 applies where, in connection with a transfer of assets abroad, an individual receives or is entitled to receive any capital sum whether before or after the relevant transfer. A capital sum is defined as a sum paid or payable by way of loan or repayment of a loan or any other sum (not being income) which is paid or payable otherwise than for full consideration in money or money's worth (ITA 2007, s 729(3)).

Defences

[8.34] There are three defences to these anti-avoidance provisions found in ITA 2007, ss 737–742A. The application of some of the exemptions depend upon when the relevant transactions took place:

All transactions before 5 December 2005

[8.35] Where all relevant transactions took place before 5 December 2005, an individual must satisfy an officer of HMRC that:

(a) the purpose of avoiding tax was not the purpose, or one of the purposes, for which the relevant transactions or any of them were undertaken ('Condition A'); or

(b) the transfer and any associated operations were genuine commercial transactions and were not designed for the purpose of avoiding tax ('Condition B') (ITA 2007, s 739).

Willoughby concerned the operation of the defence available under what was then ICTA 1988, s 741(1)(a). The House of Lords held that as the offshore policies or bonds held by Professor Willoughby were themselves subject to a separate statutory charging regime, the transfers had not been effected with a view to avoiding income tax. Accordingly, it was held that Professor Willoughby could avail himself of the defence in ICTA 1988, s 741(1)(a), as the transaction itself was entirely commercial.

The Special Commissioners case of *Burns v Revenue & Customs Comrs* [2009] STC (SCD) 165, [2009] SWTI 262 is an example of a case where the motive defence failed.

All transactions after 4 December 2005

[8.36] Where a transfer and any associated operations take place after 4 December 2005, an officer of HMRC must be satisfied that:

(a)   it would not be reasonable to draw the conclusion, from all the circumstances of the case, that the purpose of avoiding liability to tax was the purpose, or one of the purposes, for which the relevant transactions were effected (Condition A); or

(b)   all the relevant transactions were genuine commercial transactions and it would not be reasonable to draw the conclusion from all the circumstances of the case, that any one or more of those transactions was more than incidentally designed for the purpose of avoiding liability (Condition B) (ITA 2007, s 737).

A relevant transaction will only be a commercial transaction if it is effected in the course of a trade or business and for its purpose or with a view to setting up and commencing a trade or business and for its purpose (ITA 2007, s 738). A commercial transaction must not be on terms other than those that would have been made between unconnected parties dealing at arm's length or be a transaction that would not have been entered into between such persons so dealing.

The making and managing of investments is not 'commercial' except to the extent that the persons by whom and for whom the activity is carried on are unconnected persons dealing at arm's length.

In ascertaining whether tax avoidance was a purpose of any arrangements, the intentions of persons who design or effect the relevant transactions or provide advice in relation to the relevant transactions or any of them must be taken into account. This will include a tax adviser.

It should be noted that where there are transactions found in ITA 2007, s 740 some of which were implemented before 5 December 2005 and some after, special rules apply.

Genuine transactions

[8.37] Where a relevant transaction takes place after 5 April 2012 and Conditions A and B are satisfied, income will be left out of account to the extent that the taxpayer satisfies an officer of HMRC that it is attributable to the transaction (ITA 2007, s 742A).

Condition A is that:

(a)   were, if viewed objectively, the transaction to be considered to be a genuine transaction having regard to any arrangements under which it is effected and any other relevant circumstances; and

(b)   were the individual to be liable to tax under the provisions by reference to the transactions;

the individual's tax liability would in the absence of a relevant treaty provision constitute an unjustified and disproportionate restriction on a freedom protected under that relevant treaty provision (as defined in ITA 2007, s 742A(4)).

Condition B is that the individual satisfies an officer of HMRC that viewed objectively the transaction must be considered to be a genuine transaction having regard to any arrangements under which it is effected and any other relevant circumstances (ITA 2007, s 742A(5)).

In order for the transaction to be considered a genuine transaction, the transaction must not be on terms other than those that would have been made between unconnected persons dealing at arm's length or be a transaction that would not have been entered into between such persons having regard to any arrangements under which the transaction is effected and any other relevant circumstances.

Where any asset or income is used for the purposes of, or is received in the course of, activities carried on outside the UK by a person through a business establishment in that country, for a transaction to be considered as a genuine transaction the provision of goods or services by the person must be on a commercial basis and involve the use of staff in numbers and with competence and authority, the use of premises and equipment and the addition of economic value by the person to those to whom the goods or services are provided, commensurate with the size and nature of those activities (ITA 2007, s 742A(8)).

Where the relevant transfer is made by an individual wholly for personal reasons and for the personal benefit of other individuals and no consideration is given or benefit provided for the relevant transfer, it will not be considered to be a genuine transaction.

The Government considers that the proposed definition of 'economically significant activities' is clear and simple and that it will usually be straightforward to determine whether a transaction is for the purposes of such activities. A Consultation Document, however, which was issued on 30 July 2012 at the time that the provisions were under consideration, stated that where this was not straightforward it will be necessary to carry out a function or factual analysis of the business activities, taking into consideration whether there are people genuinely making decisions, managing the economic ownership of assets or assuming risk outside the UK in relation to the provision of goods or services. The document went on to say that the precise nature of the functions that are relevant for this purpose will vary according to the types of activities involved and will need to be carefully analysed where the exemption is claimed.

Where there is a genuine transaction, income will be left out of account only 'so far as' the taxpayer satisfies an officer of HMRC that it is attributable to it. Therefore this exemption may only be a partial exemption. The 2012 Consultation Document proposed that income should be apportioned on a 'just and reasonable' basis where necessary but the legislation does not include any specific rules on attribution.

ITA 2007, s 731 applies where, as a result of a transfer of assets, income becomes payable to a person abroad, and a resident individual receives a benefit provided out of those assets. The provisions apply regardless of the tax status of the settlor, but are only relevant where the UK beneficiary is not otherwise liable to income tax under ITA 2007, ss 720 or 727. As is the case under ss 720 and 727, the rule will only apply where there is a UK tax avoidance motive which leads to the creation of the structure, and taxpayers can therefore rely upon the same defences outlined above. ITA 2007, ss 735 and 735A adopt the remittance basis rules to determine the benefits assessable under s 731.

In essence, the rules apply a remittance basis with UK beneficiaries paying tax when the benefit is received. If the trustees confer a benefit on a beneficiary at a time when they have undistributed income which could be used to benefit him, he is liable to income tax on the value of that benefit to the extent of the undistributed income. Where there is insufficient relevant income to match the value of a benefit, future receipts of relevant income can be set against the unmatched element of any benefit and will result in a liability to income tax arising at that time.

The future for existing offshore trusts

[8.38] As mentioned above, offshore trusts do not offer any significant advantages during the settlor's lifetime where the settlor and beneficiaries are resident and domiciled in the UK. There are, however, many offshore trusts in existence 'set up' by UK domiciled and resident settlors for tax planning purposes which have ceased to have a function.

As many trusts were set up for capital gains tax saving purposes, these trusts will often have substantial realised capital gains. Where a trust was set up before 19 March 1991, such gains will not have been taxed on the settlor if the trust has not been tainted after that date. In such circumstances, capital payments could be made to the beneficiaries who are not UK resident. These payments will have trust gains allocated to them under TCGA 1992, s 87 but the beneficiary will not be chargeable provided two conditions are satisfied. First, the beneficiary is not subject to the temporary non-residence rule in TCGA 1992, s 10A. Otherwise, a capital gains tax charge will arise on their return to the UK. Secondly, there has been no transfer by the trustees linked with a borrowing in the trust resulting in the gain forming part of a Schedule 4 pool. Any distributions made to a UK resident beneficiary should be made in the fiscal year following the one in which distributions are made to a non-resident beneficiary. Alternatively, the trust funds can be divided between two or more settlements. The idea is that funds are transferred to a new settlement leaving some of the stockpiled gains in the original settlement. By virtue of TCGA 1992, s 90, a proportion of the stockpiled gains will be transferred to the new settlement.

Example

The Stevens No 1 Settlement has funds worth £10 million with stockpiled gains of £2 million. It is proposed that a capital distribution is made of £2 million to Jasmine who is UK resident. If such a capital distribution were made it would represent chargeable gains on which she would be assessable.

If instead £8 million were transferred from the Stevens No 1 Settlement to a new settlement, the Stevens No 2 Settlement, the original Stevens No 1 Settlement would hold assets of £2 million. The appointment of £8 million to the Stevens No 2 Settlement would carry 80% of the stockpiled gains by virtue of s 90. Consequently, only £400,000 of gains would remain to be allocated to distributions made from the Stevens No 1 Settlement. The capital distribution to Jasmine from the original Stevens No 1 Settlement must be made in a fiscal year following the advance to the Stevens No 2 Settlement.

Care will need to be taken to ensure that the new offshore settlement receiving funds is not treated as being part of the same arrangement as the existing offshore settlements and consideration should be given to the application of the GAAR.

For some offshore trusts a decision may be taken to bring the trust back onshore by simply appointing UK resident trustees in the place of the offshore trustees. Any stockpiled gains will not disappear but will continue to be attributed to capital payments under TCGA 1992, s 87 in the usual way. The offshore settlor charge will no longer be applicable. The UK resident trustees will instead be liable to capital gains tax.

Chapter 9

Insurance

Introduction

[9.1] Insurance is used widely by private clients and the businesses they own and operate. From a simple way of protecting from catastrophe to a sophisticated cross border savings medium, its uses are varied and diverse.

The insurance industry has a reputation for high costs and clever marketing which many assume disguise the fact that the investment and tax advantages of insurance policies are not worth their cost. In fact, insurance policies can deliver significant tax deferral benefits and are a convenient way of obtaining the benefits of professional administration and investment management and the spread of investment risk in a cost-effective manner. Like any other financial product, however, before one takes out a policy one should ensure that one understands its legal nature and its costs.

The introduction of a 20% capital gains tax rate in 2016/17 has reduced the attraction of insurance as a long term savings vehicle. If, however, the underlying investments held in the policy would not be subject to capital gains tax if held directly, then tax deferral advantages may still remain. One might contrast, for example, insurance policies with non-reporting/non-distributor offshore funds the gains of which are subject to UK income tax on disposal.

Regulatory background

[9.2] The regulation of insurance business is governed by the Financial Services and Markets Act 2000 (FSMA 2000) which established the Financial Services Compensation Scheme (FSCS). For long-term insurance which includes savings related insurance products, the compensation limits are 100% of the first £2,000 and up to 90% of the balance. The cost of the FSCS is funded by a levy on authorised firms.

Under the European Union Consolidated Life Directive, an European Economic Area (EEA) insurance company can transact business in the UK without direct authorisation under the FSMA 2000.

Professional advisers should be aware of the provisions of FSMA 2000 in relation to the giving of investment advice which can constitute investment business. Under s 19 of that Act, it is a criminal offence to carry on investment business without appropriate authorisation. Any contravention is actionable at the suit of a person who suffers loss.

Nature of insurance

[9.3] Before considering in detail the uses that can be made of insurance in the context of estate planning, it is important to understand in general terms the nature and types of insurance available and also the bases on which insurance policies may be held.

The basic contract

[9.4] In general terms, insurance involves a contract (evidenced by a policy) by virtue of which an insurance company (the insurer) undertakes in return for the agreed consideration (the premium) to pay to another person (the insured) a sum of money on the occurrence of a particular and specified event, the happening of which is uncertain. In life assurance, this uncertain event will be the death of a named person (the life insured).

Insurable interest

[9.5] The Life Assurance Act 1774, s 1 requires that a person taking out life insurance must have an insurable interest in the life insured and any policy effected in contravention of this provision is void. The insurable interest must exist when the insurance policy is taken out (*Dalby v India and London Life Assurance Co* (1854) 15 CB 365, but it is not required at the time of loss (for example, on the death of the life assured). Section 3 of the Act provides that, when an insured has an insurable interest, he may recover under the policy in question no more than the amount of the value of his interest.

Thus, it is necessary to establish exactly what constitutes an insurable interest in a life. The person taking out the policy must have a pecuniary interest in the life of the life assured and case law has established that this will be measured by the amount or value of the pecuniary loss which the person for whose benefit the insurance is effected is likely to sustain by reason of the death of the life assured.

An individual taking out a policy on his own life, or on the life of his spouse for his own benefit, is presumed to have an insurable interest of an unlimited extent in the policy regardless of the amount insured. In all other circumstances there must be an actual pecuniary interest so that the insured must show that he would suffer financially by the loss of a right enforceable in law on the death of the life insured. Apart from the case of a spouse (and the special case of industrial life assurance), an insurable interest cannot be presumed merely from a family relationship. In the family context, therefore, a relative must have a claim for support enforceable by law, or some other pecuniary interest enforceable by law. Thus, generally speaking, parents will not have an insurable interest in the lives of their children. A child who is a minor would probably have an insurable interest in the lives of his parents who will usually have a legally enforceable duty to support the child who would suffer financially by the loss of that right on their death, although it might be argued that a liability of support only crystallises when a maintenance order is made by the court. Certainly, an adult child would be unlikely to have an insurable interest in their parent's life.

In practice, insurance companies are often prepared to take a relaxed view as to the presence or not of an insurable interest. To do otherwise in respect of a policy on which premiums have been duly paid and received would create bad publicity. Strictly, however, if a policy is void, any premiums paid to the insurance company would be held by the insurance company on resulting trust for the payer or for his or her personal representatives and, thus, are capable of falling back into the estate of that person.

The requirement for an insurable interest does not exist in many offshore jurisdictions. It is therefore easier to insure multiple lives – for example, parents and children – in such jurisdictions.

Uses of insurance

Protection

[9.6] Life assurance was originally designed and developed to provide protection and financial stability for dependants from adverse financial consequences in the event of a person's premature death. This function continues to be important. In many cases, such protection is the main reason for effecting appropriate cover. Life assurance is also important in business. 'Keyman' life policies, for example, are specifically designed to protect businesses against the losses arising from the death or extended incapacity of key executives and to provide appropriate financial compensation. In the context of partnerships, it is common for each partner in a firm to effect a policy on his own life, written in trust for the benefit of his surviving partners, or to effect policies on a life of another basis on the other partners, including where appropriate 'cross-option' agreements.

Home ownership

[9.7] Life assurance is also important in respect of home ownership. Lending institutions prefer borrowers to take out life assurance to ensure that a repayment mortgage is discharged on their premature death. This will be a form of term assurance and will either secure a decreasing capital sum, designed to match the capital liability under a repayment mortgage, or a fixed capital sum, designed to match the capital liability under an interest only mortgage. Endowment mortgages which were once very common are also insurance based. The proceeds of a related endowment policy (which is charged to the lender as additional security) are used to repay the loan, with the policy maturing at the end of the mortgage term or earlier on the death of the life assured. Some insurance companies now attach critical illness cover to endowment policies so that the mortgage is paid off on diagnosis of one of a number of pre-defined diseases.

Funding tax liabilities

[9.8] Life assurance is important in funding tax liabilities arising on the death of an individual. Seven year gift 'inter vivos' term assurance on the life of a donor is commonly used to cover the inheritance tax liability which would arise were the donor to die within seven years of making such a transfer. The lump sum payable is reduced in line with the potential inheritance tax liability tapering over seven years. Also, appropriate insurance (if written in trust) can provide the family and dependants of the life insured with funds shortly after death to settle any inheritance tax due, without the need to wait for the administration of his estate to be completed. To this end, insurance companies will provide model trust-wordings. Independent advice should be taken to ensure that the model wordings are suitable to an individual's circumstances. The impact of the relevant property provisions of IHTA 1984, Part III, Chapter III when writing policies on trust needs to be considered.

Investment

[9.9] Lump sum insurance policies (known as single premium bonds) are an important form of investment permitting tax on the investment yield to be deferred until withdrawals are made. Tax liability is deferred until the occurrence of a 'chargeable event' and in this way the investor benefits from a tax deferral which over a long period of time can deliver a significant benefit. Investments that can be held in single premium bonds are now mainly restricted to collectives.

Such policies, however, also carry a tax disadvantage as gains on an equity based fund, which would be taxable at 20%, if held directly are converted into taxable income suffering tax at up to 45% if they are held in a single premium bond.

Regular premium policies (mainly endowments) have become less popular as a savings medium in recent years.

Life policy taxation

[9.10] For income tax purposes policies are divided between qualifying and non-qualifying policies.

The proceeds of qualifying policies are not normally subject to income tax in the hands of the policyholder unless the policy is surrendered or otherwise realised prematurely, whereas on the surrender of a non-qualifying policy any gain will be subject to income tax. Although it is not appropriate to set out in detail here the precise basis on which policies are classified, a general understanding of the rules and their taxation consequences is important.

Generally speaking, most policies issued by UK companies apart from single premium policies will be qualifying policies.

The following is a summary of the more important conditions applying to the main types of assurance policy described above if they are to be qualifying policies. The legislation is contained in ITA 2007, s 989 and ICTA 1988, s 267 and Sch 15.

(a)   Where *term assurance* is taken out for ten years or less, the policy must secure a capital sum on death and the surrender value (if any) must not exceed the total premiums paid. A term assurance policy for less than one year, however, cannot be a qualifying policy.

(b)   The premiums payable in respect of *whole life assurance* must be payable at yearly or shorter intervals until the death of the life assured or for a minimum period of ten years. The sum of the premiums payable in one year must not exceed more than twice the total premiums payable in any other year. The sum assured on death must not be less than 75% of the total premiums that would have been paid if death occurred at the age of 75. Where, however, two lives are insured by means of a single policy, for the purposes of calculating the minimum sum assured, the relevant age is assumed to be that of the older life if the sum assured is payable on the first death or that of the younger life if the sum assured is payable on the second death.

(c)   The term of an *endowment assurance* policy must not be less than ten years and premiums must be payable at yearly or shorter intervals for a minimum of ten years. The sum assured on death must not be less than 75% of the total premiums payable, if the age of the policyholder when the policy is taken out is under 55. If, however, the age of the policyholder when the policy is taken out exceeds 55, the 75% figure is reduced by 2% for each year of the excess over 55. Where an endowment policy is for more than ten years, premiums must be payable at yearly or shorter intervals until the death of the life assured or for a minimum period of ten years or three-quarters of the policy term (whichever is the shorter period).

(d)   Since 6 April 2013 the maximum premium that an individual can pay into a qualifying policy is capped at £3,600 per annum (ICTA 1988, Sch 15, para A3(1)). Gains attributable to premiums in excess of this amount will be taxable. The method for calculating gains is given in ITTOIA 2005, ss 463A–463E. Policies issued before 21 March 2012 are treated as 'protected policies' and are not affected by these rules unless certain events occur (ICTA 1988, Sch 15, para A4).

(e)   Pure protection policies are also not affected (ICTA 1988, Sch 15, para A2(4)(a)). A pure protection policy is defined in ICTA 1988, Sch 15, para A6(1)(c) and is a policy that has no surrender value.

One important consequence of these conditions is that a *single premium* whole life or endowment policy cannot be a qualifying policy.

Consequences

[9.11] The main consequence of a policy being qualifying rather than non-qualifying is that, if a chargeable event gain arises, no further tax charge will usually arise on the policyholder (ITTOIA 2005, s 485). Generally speaking, if a policy has been maintained for a minimum period before realisation, the proceeds on realisation will be free of income tax although the investments within the insurance companies' funds will already have suffered tax at approximately 20%. The minimum periods in question are ten years from the making of the policy or, if sooner, three-quarters of the term of the policy. A realisation in the context of a life assurance policy is likely to be either its total or partial surrender in return for a capital sum on its maturity (ie when it reaches the date on which it is set to mature) or the death of the life assured.

If a qualifying policy is surrendered (and sometimes when there is a partial surrender, such as a withdrawal of capital) or assigned for value before the expiry of ten years from the making of the policy or, if sooner, three-quarters of the term of the policy, a higher rate income tax charge will be made on any gain arising on such a chargeable event. A charge may also arise on any gain arising on a surrender, on an assignment for value, on the death of the insured or on the maturity of a policy if the policy has been converted into a paid-up policy within the same period (ITTOIA 2005, ss 484, 485). A policy becomes 'paid up' when the policyholder agrees with the life office to stop paying premiums under the policy but not to surrender the policy, so that it still continues in being. In such a case the life office may reduce the sum assured payable under the policy. Thus, neither the death of the insured nor the maturity of a qualifying policy will give rise to an income tax charge unless the policy has been paid up within the specified period.

The amount to be treated as the gain in respect of a policy depends on the chargeable event in question. If the event is an assignment for value, the amount will be the excess of the amount of the consideration received over the total premiums previously paid under the policy. If the event is the maturity of the policy, the surrender of rights under it or the death of the insured, the amount is the excess of the value of the sums then payable over the total premiums previously paid under the policy and any chargeable event gains which have previously arisen in respect of the policy (ITTOIA 2005, ss 491–497).

Such a gain will be treated as part of the total income of the individual policyholder for the year of assessment in which the event occurs if he is UK resident in that year, but the tax charged will be the excess of the individual's marginal rate of income tax over the basic rate. Where immediately before the chargeable event giving rise to the charge to income tax, the policy in question is held on trusts created by an individual or is held as security for a debt owed by him, the tax liability in respect of the gain will fall on that individual and any chargeable event gains previously charged in respect of the policy (ITTOIA 2005, s 465).

An individual who is chargeable to tax in respect of amounts being included in his total income for a year of assessment may claim a form of 'top slicing' relief (ITTOIA 2005, ss 535–537). The effect is that the whole gain will (subject to certain rules) be effectively charged to income tax at the rate which would be applicable if only an 'appropriate fraction' (broadly, the gain divided by the number of years for which the policy ran) was included in his total income.

There will be no capital gains tax liability on the disposal or surrender of a life policy unless it has been acquired at any time for consideration other than the payment of premiums under the policy. Where a policy has been acquired in the second-hand market, the price paid for the policy and future premiums paid are set against the proceeds of disposal to determine the gain. There is a thriving market in 'second-hand' endowment policies. Policies traded in this way are known as Traded Endowment Policies ('TEPs'). Where a person acquires an existing policy for consideration, a chargeable event gain may arise on its subsequent disposal. In the case of non-qualifying policies, a chargeable event gain arises if the maturity value and benefits paid exceed the premiums paid over the entire life of the contract. If any rights in a qualifying policy are assigned on or after 6 April 2013, the policy will be a non-qualifying policy after the assignment (ICTA 1988, Sch 15 para A2(1)). Therefore, any TEPs, traded on or after that date will be non-qualifying policies. The gain is charged to income tax. Any chargeable capital gains arising on the maturity of the policy will be computed subject to TCGA 1992, ss 37 and 39 which provide relief for amounts charged to income tax (see *Drummond v Revenue & Customs Comrs* [2009] EWCA Civ 608, [2009] STC 2206).

Non-qualifying policies

Disadvantages

[9.12] The main disadvantage of a non-qualifying policy is that income tax will be due on the occurrence of a chargeable event. (But see below regarding partial surrenders).

A chargeable event will occur on (ITTOIA 2005, s 484):

- a surrender of the policy;
- an assignment for money or money's worth;
- the death of the last life assured;
- the maturity of the policy;
- a loan being made under the policy.

If the policy is owned beneficially by an individual, the gain will normally be deemed to form part of his total income in the year of assessment in which the chargeable event in question occurs (ITTOIA 2005, s 465). If, however, the policy has been transferred into trust and the individual who assigned the policy is still alive or his death gave rise to the gain, or if the policy is held as security for a debt owed by an individual, it will be deemed to form part of that individual's total income for the year of assessment in which the chargeable event in question occurred (ITTOIA 2005, s 465). Again, top slicing relief may be available to the individual on making a claim to HMRC (ITTOIA 2005, ss 535–537).

Where a non-qualifying life assurance policy is held on a bare trust for a minor, HMRC will assess any gains on the minor (Insurance Policyholder Taxation Manual, para IPTM35250). In respect of chargeable event gains arising before 2007/08, the same paragraph of HMRC's manuals states:

' . . . settlors remain liable for income tax on chargeable event gains arising for years up to and including 2006/07 . . . '

Where, however, either of the child's parents is the settlor of the bare trust HMRC claims that they will still be assessable under ITTOIA 2005, s 629.

HMRC says that this is because income for this purpose includes amounts deemed to be income for tax purposes such as chargeable event gains. This view is incorrect, however, because ITTOIA 2005, s 629 catches 'income arising' under a settlement, and the chargeable events legislation, whilst it imposes an income tax charge, does not deem the chargeable event gains to be income.

Partial surrenders

[9.13] A partial surrender of a non-qualifying policy of an amount not exceeding 5% of the premiums paid may be made each year without giving rise to a tax liability at that time (ITTOIA 2005, s 507(5)). Any unused part of the 5% may be carried forward to subsequent years. Thus, such surrenders can be used to provide the policyholder with a regular (annual) amount of money (often marketed as 'income') which can be utilised as the policyholder thinks fit. Indeed, regular 5% annual withdrawals can be made for up to 20 years without a tax charge. However, when the policy is finally surrendered or matures, the gain subjected to higher rate income tax at that stage is the surrender or maturity value together with the amount or value of any previous partial surrenders, less the original premiums paid (ITTOIA 2005, s 491).

It is important that the tax consequences are considered before a partial surrender takes place. This is because the rules can produce costly and surprising results as the case of *Lobler v Revenue & Customs Comrs* 2015 UKUT 152 TCC demonstrated although, in that case, the Upper Tribunal found that Mr Lobler's surrenders, which were actually partial surrenders of all his policies, could be treated as having been total surrenders of only some of his policies on the grounds of mistake.

At Budget 2016, the government announced its intention to change the tax rules relating to partial surrenders with the aim of ensuring that disproportionate gains can no longer arise on part surrenders. On 20 April 2016, HMRC published a consultation document entitled 'Part surrenders and part assignments of life insurance policies' setting a closing date for comments of 13 July 2016.

The consultation identified three possible methods of taxing part surrender gains:

(1)   Taxing the economic gain; the current 5% allowance would be retained and any surrender in excess of 5% would be taxed according to part surrender rules using a formula of A/(A+B), where A = the amount withdrawn and B = the policy value immediately after the withdrawal.

(2)   The 100% allowance; no gain would arise until all of the premiums had been withdrawn.

(3)   Deferral of excessive gains; this option would maintain the current method for calculating gains but if the gain exceeded a pre-determined amount of the premium (the document suggests 3% pa cumulative) the excess would be rolled over until the next part surrender or part assignment, tested again at that point and if excessive, rolled over again up to maturity or full surrender.

Onshore and offshore policies

[9.14] Life policies may be issued onshore (ie by companies resident in the UK) or offshore (ie by companies not so resident).

Offshore policies cannot be qualifying policies unless issued by either:

(a)   a company resident outside the UK which is lawfully carrying on life assurance business in the UK through a branch where the policy premiums are payable to that branch and form part of the company's business receipts arising from that branch, or

(b)   a company resident outside the UK where a portion of the company's life fund income is subject to corporation tax.

Offshore single premium bonds allow for gross roll-up of investment income and capital gains subject to withholding tax and imputed tax deducted in the country of origin. Over time this tax deferral can present the investor with a substantial benefit. Furthermore, a UK or overseas based portfolio can be held within an offshore insurance bond and still provide gross roll-up of income and exemption from capital gains tax on any sales made within the bond.

The law which governs a policy issued by a non-UK insurance company may not contain a requirement for there to be an insurable interest. For this reason, by including lives assured on the policy who are far younger than the policyholder (eg their children or grandchildren) the death of the last life assured and hence the chargeable event can be delayed for many years.

On the occurrence of a chargeable event on an offshore policy, tax will be due on any gain at the investor's marginal income tax rate. For an onshore policy the chargeable event gain will be taxed at the difference between the policyholder's highest marginal rate and the basic rate, reflecting the fact that tax has been suffered at source in the insurance company's internal life fund. So a person whose general income bears income tax at a marginal rate of 45% will bear income tax on a chargeable event gain on an offshore policy at 45% and on an onshore policy at 25% (45% – 20%).

In computing a gain in respect of both offshore and onshore policies, a reduction may be made to take account of periods of residence which the individual liable to Income Tax on the policy has spent outside the UK (ITTOIA 2005, s 528). Special rules apply to personal representatives and trustees of a trust created by a deceased person (ITTOIA 2005, s 528A).

Capital redemption bonds

[9.15] Capital redemption policies (CRPs) are contracts 'made in the course of a capital redemption business' (ITTOIA 2005, s 473(1)). ICTA 1988, s 431(2ZF) provides that:

> 'In this Chapter [ITTOIA 2005, Part 4 Chapter 9] "capital redemption business" means any business of a company carrying on insurance business in so far as it consists of the effecting on the basis of actuarial calculations, and the carrying out, of contracts under which, in return for one or more fixed payments, a sum or series of sums of a specified amount become payable at a future time or over a period.'

CRPs are very similar in nature to offshore single premium bonds but there is no life assured. For this reason CRPs can continue for many years without a chargeable event arising for income tax purposes. In the case of offshore single premium bonds similar long-term income tax deferral can be achieved by having multiple lives assured.

The relevant legislation for taxing the emerging benefits from a capital redemption bond is contained in ITTOIA 2005, Part IV, Ch 9, ss 461–546.

Personal portfolio bonds

[9.16] The legislation relating to personal portfolio bonds (PPBs) is contained in ITTOIA 2005, ss 515–546.

Where a bond is of a highly personalised nature, HMRC used to assert that ITA 2007, s 721 (previously ICTA 1988, s 739) applied to deem the investment income by reference to which the bond's benefits were calculated to be the policyholder's. Section 721 does not apply to capital gains. In the case of *IRC v Willoughby* [1997] 4 All ER 65, [1997] STC 995, the House of Lords held that whether the benefits arising on insurance bonds were linked to the issuer's funds or to an individual portfolio was of no significance in determining whether ICTA 1988, s 739 applied and that it did not in fact apply to the highly personalised bonds which were the subject of the case.

In response to this decision, legislation now found in ITTOIA 2005, s 526 was enacted to confer a wide power on the Treasury to make regulations to tax personal portfolio bonds (PPBs). A PPB is defined in ITTOIA 2005, s 516 and is essentially a policy which allows the policyholder, or anyone connected to the policyholder or acting on his or her behalf, to choose the property held in the policy. The regulations are very wide ranging and designed to catch policies in respect of quoted and unquoted shares, family company shares and exotic assets such as fine wines, vintage cars, paintings and racehorses.

There is, however, an exemption under ITTOIA 2005, s 517(2) for property listed in s 520 which includes:

- internal life funds offered by the insurance company;
- units in authorised unit trusts, shares in investment trusts and OEICs;
- cash (excluding cash acquired for speculative purposes);
- interests in collective investment schemes constituted by non-UK residents including offshore unit trusts and any other arrangements which create rights in the nature of co-ownership under the law of a country outside the UK.

In addition to falling within s 520, the property held in the bond must also meet one or both of:

(a) the general selection condition of ITTOIA 2005, s 521(2) – this is satisfied if the property is available for selection by all policy holders of the insurance company;

(b) the class selection condition of s 521(3) which is satisfied if the opportunity to select the property falls to a particular class of policyholders not limited to connected persons.

For bonds that are personalised, a taxable gain is deemed to arise in each policy year. This is calculated as 15% of the sum of the total amount of premiums paid under the bond and the aggregate total of similarly calculated 15% amounts for earlier years since the bond was first taken out. Tax is charged at the individual's marginal rate on the gains each year.

PPBs taken out before 17 March 1998 can also continue to hold stocks, shares, warrants and options listed on a recognised stock exchange, AIM and the Unlisted Securities Market. Pre-17 March 1998 PPBs must, however, not be enhanced.

The government announced that it would review the property categories at ITTOIA 2005, s 520 and it has issued a consultation document 'Personal Portfolio Bonds – Reviewing the Property Categories'.

The consultation considers extending the exempted property listed above to include:

–   real estate investment trusts (both UK and foreign equivalents);
–   overseas equivalents of UK approved investment trusts; and
–   UK authorised contractual schemes; a type of investment fund which is authorised and regulated by the Financial Conduct Authority and may take the form of a limited partnership or co-ownership contractual arrangement.

Income tax and policies held on trust

[9.17] ITTOIA 2005, ss 467 and 468 charge tax on trustees and beneficiaries where the settlor has died.

Gains arising on bonds held within a trust can be taxed on the settlor of the trust, the trustees or even the beneficiaries. Furthermore, bonds can be assigned out of the trust without creating an immediate tax charge, hence transferring the liability to the recipients of the bonds.

These rules, therefore, provide much scope for tax planning with a variety of different tax rates to select from. For example, if a bond is surrendered within a trust while the settlor of the trust is still alive, then the tax charge will fall on the settlor at his marginal rate. If the bond is surrendered after the settlor's death, then the trustees will be liable to tax at 45% with an allowance for basic rate tax in the case of a UK policy. If the trustees assign the bond to beneficiaries who then surrender it, the beneficiaries will pay tax at their marginal rates. If they are non-UK resident, they may escape tax altogether.

Estate planning with insurance

[9.18] The use of insurance for estate planning falls into two categories.

(1)   Funding for an inheritance tax liability by using a term or whole of life policy;
(2)   Mitigating exposure to inheritance tax by using a lump sum invested in a single premium bond.

Funding an inheritance tax liability

Term policies

[9.19] Term policies provide for a capital sum to be paid in the event of the death of the life or lives assured within a specified period or before a specified age. No payment will be made, however, if the insured survives to the end of the period or attains the specified age, hence these are one of the cheapest forms of life assurance available.

Basic term policies lack flexibility. Due to this most life offices market a convertible term assurance where, at the end of the term, there is a right to convert the policy (usually without further medical evidence) to an endowment or whole life policy (or, sometimes, to renew the existing policy for another term). The value of this right is that it preserves insurability in cases where the policyholder in question becomes otherwise uninsurable during the original term of the policy or insurable only at a higher than normal premium, because, for example, they develop a serious illness.

Term policies are not investment vehicles as they do not usually acquire a surrender value. Their main use in estate planning, apart from preserving insurability, has been as a comparatively inexpensive way of providing 'disaster' cover. For example, a young newly-married man may have few resources to maintain his young family if he dies. He might therefore take out life cover by term assurance as a temporary measure for which the premium per annum would be less than for whole life cover of a similar amount. (Whole life cover is dealt with in **9.20** below.)

The insurance industry has responded to the increased market for term policies. Some insurance companies offer policies which enable cover to be increased or decreased if circumstances change or if the period of cover needs to be extended.

When the purpose of taking out the policy is to fund an inheritance tax liability which will arise on the death of the life assured, the policy can be taken out by the person on whose death the liability will arise (the 'donor') and then assigned to, or into trust for the benefit of, the person who will bear the economic burden of the liability (whom we shall call the 'donee'). Alternatively, the donee could take out the policy for his own benefit but on the life of the donor, since he will have a sufficient insurable interest in the donor's life. In either case, the donor may require the donee to enter into a legally binding commitment with the donor to be responsible for the inheritance tax liability in exoneration of the donor's personal representatives (who have a secondary liability to pay the tax if the donee fails to pay within 12 months of the end of the month in which the donor died (IHTA 1984, ss 199(2) and 204(8)).

Although the inheritance tax liability if the donor dies within the seven-year period will be determined by using the death rates prevailing at the time of the death where they have altered for the better (IHTA 1984, Sch 2, para 1A), the level of cover will usually be fixed by reference to the rates in force at the time of the gift. Decreasing term assurance may also be appropriate because the rate at which inheritance tax is charged will be tapered where the donor dies more than three years after making the gift. However, to provide adequate protection for the donee, it will be necessary to insure the full amount of inheritance tax potentially payable for the first three years after the gift was made by the donor.

In assessing the likely tax liability (and therefore in effecting the appropriate level of term cover), other factors may need to be taken into account. For example, where a potentially exempt transfer may prove to be a chargeable transfer, and thus become subject to inheritance tax, and business property or agricultural property relief may then be in point, additional requirements relating to the donee must be satisfied. That is to say, in the case of relevant business property (for example), if such relief is to be available in full, the donated property must have been retained in the ownership of the donee from the date of the gift until the death of the donor or the earlier death of the donee or the conditions relating to replacement property must be satisfied (see IHTA 1984, ss 113A, 113B). Any term assurance effected should therefore take account of the possibility that the relief in question may not be available. In other words, when planning for inheritance tax one may wish to consider the worst possible case to prevent an unwelcome shortfall in the insurance cover which is to meet the tax liability.

Term cover may also be considered where a donor makes an actual chargeable transfer as death within the seven-year period following the transfer will result in the death rates of inheritance tax (subject to tapering relief applying to the transfer) rather than the lifetime rates. The position may be further worsened where the chargeable transfer is made after a potentially exempt transfer. The death of a donor, who has made both potentially exempt transfers and subsequent chargeable transfers in the seven years before his death, will necessitate the re-calculation of the inheritance tax payable on the chargeable transfers. The inheritance tax on the chargeable transfers will originally have been calculated on the basis that the potentially exempt transfers were exempt. This will have to be corrected since the potentially exempt transfers will come into cumulation as prior chargeable transfers if made within the previous seven years. The personal representatives will also need to calculate the liability to inheritance tax in respect of the potentially exempt transfers themselves and the amount of tax will also be determined by reference to the cumulative total of chargeable transfers (if any) in the previous seven years prior to the date of the potentially exempt transfers in question.

The existence of chargeable transfers in the seven years prior to the donor's death (whether original chargeable transfers or potentially exempt transfers which have been brought into charge by reason of the death) may also affect the amount of tax payable on the donor's estate because the earlier transfers will be brought into cumulation. Therefore, consideration should be given to taking out seven-year *level* term assurance to cover the increased amount of tax payable by the personal representatives and putting the policy in trust for the donor's residuary beneficiaries under his will who can then use the proceeds to help fund the tax. As there is currently a single rate of inheritance tax above the nil rate, the increase is effectively limited to 40% of the value of the nil rate band (currently £325,000).

Another use for term policies is as a means of providing the funds to pay inheritance tax where an individual emigrates from the UK. Under IHTA 1984, s 267 a person cannot shed his UK domicile for inheritance tax purposes until he has ceased to be resident in the UK for at least three complete tax years. Currently, for inheritance tax purposes, an individual is deemed to be domiciled in the UK if he has been resident in the UK for 17 out of the last 20 years. The risk of the emigrant dying within this period and incurring an inheritance tax charge in respect of his world-wide estate can be insured against, with the policy proceeds being settled outside his estate.

Term assurance, when used in inheritance tax planning, is normally limited to terms of seven years. However, longer terms, extending well beyond the likely date of the life assured's death, might be used as a way of funding for an eventual liability, similar to a whole of life contract.

Whole life policies

[9.20] Whole life policies provide for a capital sum to be paid on the death of the insured, whenever it occurs, or on earlier surrender.

All whole life policies are now either unit-linked or guaranteed. In the past there were also 'with profits' policies. Unit-linked policies rely on a certain level of investment return to sustain the level of cover at the amount set at outset. If the required return is not achieved then the level of cover may be reduced or the premiums increased generally after a review once the policy has been in place for ten years and thereafter at more regular intervals.

Guaranteed policies provide a set level of cover but have no investment content and therefore are not subject to review. As there is no investment content guaranteed policies do not have a surrender value.

Other unit-linked policies are established on one of the following bases.

- Maximum cover. These policies provide for maximum insurance and minimum investment. Therefore, they are generally the cheapest form of whole life cover available, but are unlikely to have much of a value if surrendered early. Furthermore, in the past, in calculating the premiums necessary to maintain the original level of cover and premiums throughout the policy's life, many life offices assumed that underlying investment growth on premiums would be in the region of 6–7% per annum net of charges. In practice, returns in recent years have been lower than this and consequently many policies have been reviewed and increased and/or the cover they confer has been reduced.
- Balanced cover. These policies provide a balance between investment and insurance. Therefore, premiums are normally higher than maximum cover policies.

Whole life policies are often employed to fund the likely inheritance tax payable on death, in respect of an individual's estate, regardless of when the death occurs.

Where one is advising a married couple, the basic question to be decided is which of the two lives should be insured:

(a)   the first to die (whether husband or wife); or
(b)   the survivor.

The answer will depend on when the main (or only) inheritance tax charge will fall. Whole life policies can be applicable in either situation. The appropriate policy under (b) is a joint life last survivor policy.

Whole life cover is the best way of establishing a fund which will grow over the years and will be available to fund the anticipated inheritance tax charge on death, but the provision of such cover (particularly full cover) is usually expensive, except when the life assured is young. Also, whilst the level of cover is likely to be fixed by reference to the inheritance tax payable should the life assured die immediately after the policy is taken out, regard should be had to the likely increases in the assured's estate through income accumulation, capital growth and inflation and augmentation by gifts or legacies. A level of cover which seemed appropriate originally may, after a number of years, become inadequate. The amount of cover should always be kept under review.

Term and whole of life policies held in trust

[9.21] When used for estate planning purposes policies will generally be written in trust so as to ensure that the sum assured falls outside the life assured's estate. An appropriate trust can allow the person taking out the policy a greater degree of control over the destination of the proceeds than an outright assignment of the policy so that he can ensure the proceeds are applied for the purpose he intends.

The form of trust most often used to hold a life policy is a flexible power of appointment trust (a type of life interest trust). Prior to FA 2006 for inheritance tax purposes there were no initial, decennial or exit charges on such a trust. For policies issued on or after 22 March 2006, it is necessary to consider whether or not the value of the policy is in excess of the nil rate band. If it is, then an immediate charge to inheritance tax will arise at 20% of the excess over the nil rate band.

At the decennial or when there is a distribution of assets, whether or not a policy is held on interest in possession or discretionary trusts, it is necessary to calculate whether a decennial or exit charge arises. In some cases, where the life assured dies soon after a decennial charge HMRC might claim that the policy had a higher value than the aggregate premiums paid at the ten-year point, reflecting the poor health of the life assured.

The impact of FA 2006 is only felt on policies either issued on or after 22 March 2006 or placed in trust on or after that date unless the terms of an existing trust are altered.

Mechanism

[9.22] Procedures for creating an effective trust from the outset vary from life office to life office, but the usual way of doing so is for the individual concerned (as proposer) to complete a trust form declaring that the policy is to be held under trust and requesting that the office issue it to him as sole trustee. This ensures that the trust is completely constituted and thus enforceable from the moment the life office goes on risk. Most life offices will have standard forms available to effect such a trust which can be completed by the individual before payment of the first premium. The policy itself will be effective once the proposal has been accepted by the life office which will usually go on risk once the first premium has been paid.

The sole trustee should always appoint additional trustees of the policy to act jointly with him, so that on his death when the policy proceeds become payable (assuming of course that the proposer is also the life assured, which will often be the case) they can be paid immediately to the continuing trustees on production of the deceased's death certificate without any need to obtain a grant of representation to the deceased's estate.

The payment of the first premium will prima facie be a transfer of value but may fall within the individual's annual exemption or normal expenditure out of income exemption. Subsequent premium payments may also have inheritance tax implications. Because of the declaration of trust beneficial ownership of the policy will have vested immediately in the named beneficiaries.

The main taxation benefit of the overall arrangement is that the policy (and thus its proceeds) will fall outside the estate of the individual for the purposes of inheritance tax on his or her death.

Married Women's Property Act 1882 policies

[9.23] It will not, however, be necessary to create an express trust where a policy falls within the ambit of the Married Women's Property Act 1882. The effect of s 11 of that Act is to create in the appropriate circumstances, a trust of a life policy where no express declaration of trust is made. When a policy is effected by a man (or a woman) on their own life and expressed to be for the benefit of their spouse, civil partner and/or children s 11 will then create a trust in favour of the beneficiaries named in the policy. There is no need to use words expressly declaring a trust or even to refer to the Act in the policy (although it is preferable to do the latter so as to ensure there is no doubt that the policy is intended to create a trust under the Act).

The Act only applies where policies are effected for the benefit of a spouse, civil partner or children. An express trust remains necessary where a policy is effected for the benefit of remoter issue (such as grandchildren) or other relatives. The Act applies to all forms of life policies but only to those with a single life assured. It does not extend to policies on joint lives. A joint life policy for the benefit of a spouse, civil partner or children therefore needs to be written in trust expressly.

A trustee (or trustees) of the policy can be appointed by the assured in the policy itself or by any memorandum under his hand and legal title to the policy will vest in the trustees so appointed without there being an express assignment of the policy into their names. If he makes no appointment (or until he does so), he himself will be the sole trustee and, if he dies, his personal representatives will become the trustees.

Notwithstanding the ease with which the Act enables a trust of an appropriate policy to arise, it is prudent to specify the precise terms of the trust expressly so as to tailor the trust to the circumstances of the beneficiaries. The provisions prescribed by the Married Women's Property Act 1882, s 11 might not be appropriate to those circumstances. For example, under that section, a policy for the benefit of a named spouse, civil partner or child will give that person a vested interest in the whole policy whereas it will often be sensible for children to have interests which are contingent on reaching a specified age or on surviving the life assured.

Existing policies

[9.24] Where a policy is already in existence, its removal from the beneficial ownership of the insured will normally involve the insured assigning the policy either outright to another person or to trustees (who may include the insured) to be held by them for specified beneficiaries. If such an assignment is effective, the policy (and its proceeds) will no longer form part of the assignor's estate for inheritance tax purposes.

Assignments

[9.25] An assignment of a life policy must comply with the Policies of Assurance Act 1867. The Act provides for the legal assignment of life policies, giving an assignee the right to sue an insurer in his own name, if three conditions are satisfied.

(a)   There must be an effective equitable assignment of the policy, indicating that its object is to transfer the benefit of the policy to the transferee (s 1). The assignment must be sufficient to transfer the property in the policy itself (ie beneficial ownership).

(b)   The assignment must be in writing, either by endorsement on the policy itself or by a separate instrument, in the words or to the effect set out in the Act. Stamp duty is generally not payable on assignments of policies.

(c)   Written notice of the date and purport of the assignment must be given to the insurers before the assignee can sue on the policy.

Initial transfer

[9.26] The assignment itself may or may not lead to an immediate inheritance tax charge. If the policy is transferred by way of outright gift to an individual or into a bare trust for one or more persons, absolutely entitled, it will constitute a potentially exempt transfer for the purposes of inheritance tax. It will therefore occasion no immediate charge to inheritance tax, and no charge at all provided the transferor survives the required seven-year period. A transfer into a relevant property settlement will trigger an immediate charge to inheritance tax on any value above the nil rate band. The donor must not be capable of benefiting under the trust or the gift will be rendered ineffective by the gifts with reservation provisions, the application of which is examined in greater detail below.

The value transferred will be the price that the policy might reasonably be expected to fetch if sold on the open market at the time of transfer, subject (except in the case of most forms of term policy) to a minimum value equal to the total cost incurred in providing the policy (ie the premiums or other consideration paid) at that time less any sum which has been paid under the policy or contract in question (IHTA 1984, s 167).

A transferor in these circumstances, however, should be able to take advantage of his nil rate band and any other relevant exemptions (such as the annual exemption) to restrict his liability to inheritance tax on the initial transfer into settlement. The tax liability (if any) will also be affected by the type of policy to be transferred. Most types of life policy will have a low initial surrender value if they have one at all. For example, a term assurance policy will, on the basis mentioned above, have little if any value, having no surrender value in any circumstances, and its transfer into settlement should not therefore occasion a significant transfer of value.

The assignment into trust will not give rise to any charge to capital gains tax (TCGA 1992, s 210).

Type of trust

[9.27] As to which form of trust should be used, again much will depend on the circumstances of the case (in particular, the type of policy involved) and on the basic tax treatment afforded the trust in question. As mentioned above, the transfer of the policy itself to the trust should occasion only a minimal charge to inheritance tax. Provided that the initial value of the policy when first settled and when aggregated with any chargeable transfers made by the settlor in the seven years preceding the creation of the trust do not exceed the inheritance tax nil rate band, there should be no exit charge (IHTA 1984, s 65) provided the proceeds are distributed before the first 10-year anniversary of the creation of the trust. It would, however, be necessary to check the settlor's history of chargeable transfers of value at the time the settlement is to be created before transferring the policy. In addition, account would have to be taken at that time of any increase in the aggregate value of the property in the settlement due to chargeable transfers as this will affect the computation of any exit charge.

It may also be unwise for the settlor to pay further premiums in respect of the policy after it has been settled if such payments would be chargeable transfers, as HMRC would then have an alternative seven-year history of the settlor's chargeable transfers (ie those within seven years of the payment of the premium in question) for determining the rate of an exit charge (IHTA 1984, s 67). The settlor should always, however, consider whether any of the inheritance tax exemptions would be applicable, as these could enable premiums to be paid without being chargeable transfers. In particular, the annual exemption and the exemption for normal expenditure out of income could be applicable.

Type of policy

[9.28] The most appropriate type of trust under which to hold the policy will depend upon the purpose for which the policy was made.

If, for example, a whole life policy taken out to fund inheritance tax on death is to be held on trust, in most cases the trust should mirror the interests of the residuary beneficiaries under the insured's will, who can then use the proceeds to fund the tax.

It is of course always possible that the beneficiaries under the will may be changed. It may therefore be necessary to ensure that the trust employed is sufficiently flexible to cater for this and that some form of discretionary (or power of appointment) trust would be appropriate.

If a seven-year term assurance is taken out to cover a potential liability to inheritance tax and the policy is effected by the donor, it should be held on trust for, or assigned to, the donee of the gift in question so as not to be payable to the donor's estate on his death and be available to the donee to pay the tax.

Where some form of insurance-based savings scheme is entered into to provide a lump sum (when the policy matures) during the lifetime of the person taking out the policy, the capital sum in question can be accumulated outside the estate of that person by ensuring the policy is held on trust. For example, an individual could take out an endowment policy on his own life, but held on trust for the benefit of his children. When the policy matures, the proceeds will pass to the trust and then to his children free of any inheritance tax liability falling on him. If, however, the individual himself wishes to benefit from the policy, then a trust will be inappropriate.

Payment of premiums

[9.29] Once the basic estate planning structure has been established and the policy in question has become held on trust, the question of who then should continue to pay the premiums under the policy must be decided. The settlor will probably have paid the first premium to ensure the life office assumes risk. If the settlor is to continue to pay them, they are capable of being transfers of value for inheritance tax purposes. However, if the policy in question is beneficially owned by an individual or held in a privileged interest trust or an existing IIP, the payment of premiums by an individual can be structured so as to constitute potentially exempt transfers. The individual could make gifts of cash to the individual donee or trustees in question who could then use the cash to fund payment of the premiums. Where the policy was issued before 18 March 1986 and is held on trusts under which the settlor is capable of benefiting, it may be more appropriate for the settlor to pay the premium direct to the life office because the inheritance tax gifts with reservation provisions will only not apply to the premiums if they are paid by the settlor 'under the terms of the policy'. It is arguable that they will not meet this condition if they are not paid direct to the life office.

If, however, the settlor does pay the premiums direct to the life office, the payments will only constitute potentially exempt transfers if the policy is beneficially owned by another individual or is held in an existing IIP or a privileged interest trust and only then to the extent that an individual's estate is increased in value (IHTA 1984, s 3A(2)(b)). Thus, to the extent that the amount of the premium is not reflected in the increased value of the policy (which would usually *not* be the case), the payment will not be potentially exempt.

If the payment of premiums can only be made as transfers of value, there are certain inheritance tax exemptions which may be applicable, such as the annual exemption and, if the premiums are funded from income, the normal expenditure out of income exemption. To qualify under this latter exemption, however, there is a need for regularity in the payments made for them to qualify as part of the normal expenditure of the person making the payments (IHTA 1984, s 21(1)).

Where a life policy is held on a trust established on or after 22 March 2006 any initial value on transfer or premiums paid, will constitute chargeable lifetime transfers.

Resident non-domiciled individuals owning UK residential property

[9.30] On 8 July 2015, HMRC published guidance entitled 'Technical briefing on foreign domiciled persons/Inheritance tax residential property changes'. The proposals were further refined in a consultation document issued on 19 August 2016 entitled 'Reforms to the taxation of non-domiciles: further consultation'. The government intends to bring all UK residential property held directly or indirectly through an offshore company or partnership, into charge to inheritance tax.

It is likely that life assurance will have an increasing role to play in helping resident non-domiciled individuals and the trustees of offshore settlements holding UK properties fund an eventual inheritance tax liability that will no longer be easily avoided through careful structuring. The sum assured will typically be set at approximately 40% of the property value and the policy will be written under a suitable trust to ensure no inheritance tax liability arises on the policy proceeds on the policyholder's death.

As the resident non-domicile is likely to leave the UK at some future point and to sell their UK home, a term policy for an appropriate number of years may be appropriate. If, however, the individual is likely to maintain a UK property even after leaving the UK then a guaranteed whole of life policy may be more appropriate conferring a right to pre-determined payment whenever death occurs.

Whatever policy is selected the individual must give consideration to how the premiums can be funded. Many resident non-domiciliaries although rich in capital assets do not have sufficient UK income to pay the substantial premiums that are often required by policies effected for these purposes and bringing income or mixed capital to the UK will often trigger a charge on the remittances of income or gains.

Non-UK policies suitable for providing insurance cover in such circumstances are offered by some foreign insurers. At least one offshore provider markets a form of maximum cover whole of life policy.

One or two international providers of Universal Life assurance are now offering significant levels of cover for UK inheritance tax liabilities with the policies held through a suitable offshore trust structure. 'Jumbo' life, as it is often known, involves the payment of a lump sum premium (rather than a number of regular premiums) which secures a much higher level of life assurance but with a surrender value available throughout the lifetime of the policy.

However, a resident non-domiciliary taking such cover should be aware of the potential income tax charge that will arise on their death by which the time the policy may well have a significant surrender value. The remittance basis is not available for chargeable event gains as these are taxed on an arising basis (ITTOIA 2005, s 461(1)). If the policyholder is a non-UK resident, because, for example, they are the foreign owner of a UK residence, then there would be no UK income tax liability on the maturity of such a foreign policy.

Lump sum plans

[9.31] When considering any of the lump sum inheritance tax plans, careful analysis of the policy terms is required to make sure that any inheritance tax saving is not negated by additional fees and a charge to income tax arising after the settlor's death. This is especially important now that the top rate of income tax is higher than the rate of inheritance tax.

In many cases, the investor might be better advised to invest in low yielding assets potentially chargeable to capital gains tax, where any capital gain is eradicated on death, leaving an inheritance tax charge at 40% rather than a non-qualifying insurance policy held in some form of trust where the beneficiaries may escape inheritance tax at 40% but instead face income tax at 45%.

The sections below consider some of the lump sum plans currently being offered in the UK by leading international insurance companies.

Discounted gift trusts

[9.32] A discounted gift trust generally consists of either a single premium investment into a single premium bond, capital redemption bond, or into a series of non-surrenderable maturing endowment policies subject to either a discretionary trust or a bare trust.

Under a discounted gift trust, an individual (or more than one acting jointly) writes a trust and retains an absolute interest to a series of fixed withdrawals from the underlying fund or maturing policies during his lifetime or until the trust fund is exhausted. It is argued that the retained rights are sufficiently well defined to preclude the gift being a gift with reservation. The value of these withdrawals is determined following an assessment of the life assured's life expectancy using normal underwriting and actuarial principles.

The balance of the fund is held for the beneficiaries of the trust, and the settlor creating the trust is excluded from benefiting from this part of the fund. For joint settlements, the relevant value of each of the funds is independently determined.

An investment into a discounted gift trust constitutes a transfer of value for inheritance tax purposes. The value of the transfer is determined on the loss to the estate principle under IHTA 1984, s 3(1) and represents the difference between the amount invested and the value of the retained rights.

Discounted gift trusts can be seen to fall into two basic types:

(a) A 'trust level carve-out' – this is a scheme whereby regular, normally, annual sums (the 'regular payment rights') are paid to the settlor by the trustees. The trustees are responsible for making the pre-determined regular payments as defined in the trust instrument and must make provision to do this. Under these types of schemes it is normally possible to change the underlying investment and for the trustees to satisfy any appropriate decennial and exit charges by making encashments from the underlying investment vehicle. It should be noted, however, that this could, have tax implications for both trustees and/or the settlor if he is alive.

(b)   A 'policy level carve out' – under this scheme the regular payment rights are paid directly from the underlying policy, eg the investment bond inside the trust. Such a scheme does not depend on the trustees to make an accurate payment of the pre-determined regular payments and will automatically make the payments at the pre-determined date. This releases the trustees from having to make or account for the payments to the settlor.

Calculating the discount

[9.33] HMRC originally issued a Technical Note in May 2007 setting out its practice in arriving at the calculation of the discount. A revised note, Revenue & Customs Brief 22/13, was issued on 6 August 2013 to reflect the decision in *Association belge des Consommateurs Test-Achats ASBL v Conseil des ministres*: C-236/09 [2012] 1 WLR 1933, [2011] 2 CMLR 994, [2012] All ER (EC) 441 (the '*Test-Achats case*') in which the Court of Justice of the European Union held that in order to provide equal treatment between men and women, premiums must not reflect differences in the life expectancies of men and women. Because HMRC's method of valuation of the rights arising under discounted gifts schemes took into account the costs of insurance, HMRC has produced an amended valuation method for discounted gift schemes. Its technical basis for the new treatment is dubious but it represents HMRC's established practice.

HMRC attaches an open market value (OMV) to the rights retained by the settlor, ie the amount that the settlor would obtain for the rights if they were sold in the market. This OMV is determined by a number of factors including the settlor's age and health at the time the gift is made. These factors determine the insurability of the settlor. It is HMRC's view that if the retained rights were sold in the market any purchaser would expect to insure the rights against the early death of the seller otherwise the purchaser is at risk of losing virtually their entire investment. Therefore if the settlor is uninsurable, the OMV of the retained rights is minimal. For this reason HMRC believes that an individual over the age of 90 affecting a discounted gift trust would not merit a discount as it would be very difficult to insure such an individual. In *Revenue & Customs Comrs v Bower (executors of Bower (decd))* [2008] EWHC 3105 (Ch), [2009] STC 510, 79 TC 544 the value of a reserved annuity in respect of a 90-year old woman was considered and the High Court broadly accepted HMRC's view of the issue.

In the case of joint settlors, HMRC takes the view that the rights should be valued in their entirety and then apportioned to each settlor by reference to the OMV of each settlor's retained rights.

How the transfer is treated for inheritance tax depends upon the type of trust used; a discretionary trust or a bare trust.

Type of trust

Discretionary trust

[9.34] A gift into a discounted gift scheme that is subject to a discretionary trust will be treated for inheritance purposes as a chargeable lifetime transfer, which, if it exceeds the nil rate band (£325,000 in 2014/15) when added to any other chargeable lifetime transfers made in the previous seven years, will be subject to inheritance tax on the excess amount at the lifetime rate. It is the discounted value of the gift that is relevant in calculating the chargeable lifetime transfer.

It should be noted that whilst the lifetime rate is 20% this assumes the trustees pay the tax from the settled capital in the trust. During the lifetime of the settlor it is not normally possible for capital to be applied for this purpose and so, normally, the settlor will pay the inheritance tax at the grossed up rate of 25% (20% (100% ÷ 80%)). Also, if at each decennial, the settlor is still alive, he will usually pay the decennial charge as the trustees will normally be unable to access capital for this purpose. This does, however, depend upon the nature of the discounted gift scheme.

Provided the settlor survives for more than seven years, the chargeable lifetime transfer will fall out of account for inheritance tax purposes.

Bare trust

[9.35] The gift will be treated as a potentially exempt transfer which, provided the settlor survives for more than seven years, will not be chargeable.

The beneficiaries are absolutely entitled to their share of the trust fund and this interest is included in the beneficiaries' estates for inheritance tax. Following death, provided a beneficiary is *sui juris*, he can request the trustees to pay him his benefits. A person is *sui juris* when they are aged at least 18, are mentally capable and are not an undischarged bankrupt.

It should be noted that under both bare and discretionary trusts the value of any investment growth is immediately outside the donor's estate for inheritance tax purposes.

Options after death

[9.36] The trustees normally have the following options after death.

A chargeable event will be created at the point of death of the last life assured. If the policy has been set up with multiple lives assured then there will not be a chargeable event on the death of the settlor, even if he is one of the lives assured, if at that time at least one life assured is still alive. (This will not be a problem with a capital redemption bond as death is not a chargeable event and there are no lives assured in respect of such policies).

It may be possible to consider an assignment of the single premium bond out of the trust at this point as this would not trigger a chargeable event if it is not for money or money's worth (ITTOIA 2005, s 484). The beneficiaries can then surrender their segments of the bond and will be taxed in accordance with their own tax rates.

If a policy utilising maturing endowments has been selected then these policies will generally be structured so that they have no surrender value immediately before death.

Additionally, if the bond is maintained, the selected investment funds can continue to be changed as the need arises.

Tax on 'income' during the lifetime of the settlor/donor – single premium investment bond

[9.37] The tax treatment of the regular payment is the same for both the bare trust and the discretionary trust. For each investment made, a UK resident individual can withdraw up to 5% of the original investment each policy year for 20 years and defer any income tax payable. Where the full 5% entitlement is not taken in any policy year, the unused amount will be carried forward for use in future years. If the withdrawals in any year exceed 5%, the excess will give rise to a chargeable event gain and there may be a liability to income tax. A UK resident individual must include in his UK tax return details of any chargeable event gain arising. It should be noted that any withdrawals in excess of the 5% entitlement may affect the availability of any age-related allowance(s).

Gifts with reservation

[9.38] There are two gift with reservation provisions that need to be considered in relation to discounted gift trusts.

On a strict view FA 1986, s 102 will apply to discounted gift trusts because the settlor retains benefits from the gift made. It is argued, however, that what the settlor actually does is to make a gift of part of the capital and to retain the balance which then funds his income/capital withdrawals. HMRC appears to take the view that there is no gift with reservation apparently on the basis that the retained part is sufficiently well defined. Indeed in the Technical Note issued in May 2007, HMRC stated that 'essentially a DGS (discounted gift scheme) involves a gift of a bond from which a set of rights are retained, typically withdrawals or a set of successively maturing reversions. The retained rights are sufficiently well defined to preclude the gift being regarded as a gift with reservation for inheritance purposes.' It is very doubtful whether that view is correct.

FA 1986, Sch 20, para 7 contains certain provisions, deeming arrangements to be gifts with reservation. It states:

> 'Where arrangements are entered into under which (a) there is a disposal by way of gift which consists of or includes, or is made in connection with, a policy of insurance on the life of the donor or his spouse or civil partner or on their joint lives, and (b) the benefits which will or may accrue to the donee as a result of the gift vary by reference to benefits accruing to the donor or his spouse or civil partner (or both of them) under that policy . . . the property comprised in the gift shall be treated [as being a gift with reservation].'

However in practice discounted gift trusts are designed so that either:

- the policyholder is expressly excluded from benefiting from any of the rights that make up the donated fund and those benefits will not vary by reference to the benefits which will accrue to the policyholder. The beneficiaries will only benefit on the death of the policyholder; or
- the policyholder is not a life assured; or
- para 7 cannot apply as the policy is not a 'policy of insurance' because the policy concerned is a capital redemption bond.

Pre-owned assets and discounted gift trusts

[9.39] In March 2005, HMRC published a technical guide to the income tax charge on pre-owned assets containing comment on the treatment of life policies.

(a) *Discounted gift schemes.* HMRC provided an example where a settlor effects a discounted gift scheme and retains certain rights, represented by a series of single premium policies that revert to the settlor providing he is alive on the relevant maturity date. HMRC stated that where the right to the reversion is held on bare trusts for the settlor, FA 2004, Sch 15, para 8 does not apply because a bare trust is not a settlement for inheritance tax purposes (HMRC Inheritance Tax Manual, para 44112).

Furthermore, where the settlor's rights are held on trust, HMRC said that it would normally be treated as a separate trust of those benefits in which the settlor had an interest in possession and no pre-owned assets tax charge would arise by virtue of FA 2004, Sch 15, para 11(1).

Finally, in any event, where the conditions in FA 2004, Sch 15, para 11 do not provide an exemption from the pre-owned assets charge, the actual charge would be based on the value of rights held on trust for the settlor, not the value of the underlying life policy (HMRC Inheritance Tax Manual, para 44112).

(b) *Loan schemes.* HMRC states that the pre-owned assets charge will not apply to these schemes as there is no reservation of benefit, the settlor is not a beneficiary of the trust receiving the loan and the making of the loan does not constitute a settlement (HMRC Inheritance Tax Manual, para 44113).

Loan trusts

[9.40] A loan trust could be suitable to anyone whose estate will be liable to inheritance tax on their death, but who is unable, or unwilling, to make outright gifts because they require continuing access to their original capital – either on a regular basis to supplement income, or perhaps as a one-off lump sum.

They must, of course, have a lump sum available for investment.

There are many variations of this type of arrangement on offer from life companies. Loan trusts can be established by individuals, married couples or civil partners. Typically the investor (settlor) should be relatively 'young' –

such as someone who is just retired or coming up to retirement and who wishes to take action to mitigate inheritance tax but does not want or is not able to give up access to their capital.

How does a typical loan trust work?

[9.41] The settlor creates a trust and makes an interest-free loan, which is repayable on demand, to the trustees of the loan trust. The money is invested by the trustees, typically into a single premium investment bond. The scheme allows the settlor to take regular repayments of the debt replacing the income which would have arisen on the capital sum had it not been invested in the scheme.

Any growth in the value of the investments belongs to the trust, not the settlor, and is outside the settlor's estate for inheritance tax purposes and goes to the beneficiaries of the trust. Critically, the settlor has access to the original amount of the loan which remains part of the estate for inheritance tax purposes. By taking small, regular repayments of the loan (typically 5% per annum of the original value of the loan), which the insurance company concerned will normally describe in its marketing literature as an 'income', the value of the outstanding loan will reduce over time and the inheritance tax benefit will increase. It is, of course, vital that the settlor expends these loan repayments in order to remove their value from his estate.

Setting up a loan trust

[9.42] In most instances the settlor uses a trust deed to establish a discretionary trust. To be effective for inheritance tax the settlor cannot be a beneficiary. It may be possible to use a bare trust to establish the loan trust. In that case, however, the interests of the beneficiaries cannot be changed.

Lending the trust money

[9.43] Using the loan agreement, the settlor lends the trust a sum of money which is expressed as being interest-free and repayable to the settlor on demand. It is possible to require any amounts to be paid back at any time – up to the value of the original loan.

It is also worth noting that where the settlor requests a repayment of the loan, particularly if the request is made early in the lifetime of the scheme, it is possible that the full value may not be payable due to the performance of the underlying investment.

The tax position of the settlor

[9.44] As the settlor makes an interest-free loan (which is repayable on demand) to the trustees, there is no financial loss to his estate. No immediate inheritance tax liability should therefore arise at inception, regardless of the size of the loan.

When the settlor dies, the amount of any outstanding loan will be a debt due to his or her estate and so will form part of the estate for inheritance tax purposes.

Trust replacement plan

[9.45] One life office markets a scheme that attempts to replicate the benefits of existing interest in possession trusts (see CHAPTER 7 EXISTING SETTLEMENTS). This was introduced in response to the inheritance tax changes introduced by FA 2006.

An investor invests an amount into an offshore single premium bond with general conditions written in a standard format. A special provision is written into the policy schedule providing that:

(a)　the full surrender option is removed for a pre-determined period; and

(b)　there is a similar suppression of the 5% withdrawal facility for the same term.

The investor then assigns the policy by way of an outright gift to, or to bare trustees for, a child, grandchild or other relative.

When the policyholder takes out the policy he makes a transfer of value if the market value of the policy immediately upon its issue is less than the premium which he pays. This transfer of value is not a potentially exempt transfer as it is not made to an individual or to a trust. It is doubtful that the transfer is potentially exempt under IHTA 1984, s 10. Section 10 provides that a disposition is not a transfer of value if it is shown that it was not intended, 'and was not made in a transaction intended, to confer any gratuitous benefit . . . and either that it was made in a transaction at arm's length . . . or that it was such as might be expected to be made in a transaction at arm's length . . . '. Viewed as a composite transaction it is difficult to see how the disposition consisting of making the policy can satisfy the condition that it was ' . . . not made in a transaction intended, to confer any gratuitous benefit on any person . . . '.

Special care should, therefore, be taken when entering into this type of contract so as to ensure that there is not an immediate charge to inheritance tax based on a transfer of value in excess of the nil rate band.

The assignment of the policy on bare trusts is a potentially exempt transfer as it is:

(a)　made by an individual after 21 March 2006;

(b)　would otherwise be a chargeable transfer; and

(c)　constitutes a gift to an individual.

Discounted valuation arrangement

[9.46] One life office markets a product which relies on a discounted value being attached to the policy on death.

The policyholder invests in a policy, with general conditions that is written in a standard format. The policy is written with several lives assured so as to reduce the likelihood of a chargeable event. The policyholder is named as the first life assured. The other lives assured are likely to be much younger than the policyholder.

A special provision is written into the policy schedule to provide that:

(a)   the surrender option is removed; and
(b)   cumulative partial surrenders and regular withdrawals are limited to:
        (i)   10% per annum (of the original premium) while the policy-
                holder is living, then
        (ii)   1% / 2% / 3% per annum beginning in the first calendar year
                after the policyholder's death.

The policyholder has access to a flexible 'income', but there is no requirement for him to take it.

On the policyholder's death the life assurance bond continues because other lives assured survive him. The executors to the deceased's will assent or assign the policy to the beneficiary or beneficiaries entitled.

Access is limited under (b)(ii) above.

The idea is to provide HMRC with actuarial evidence that the value of the policy at death is considerably less than the value of the underlying assets. A leading firm of actuaries has indicated the likely extent of any discount(s) and will also provide an expert valuation for probate purposes.

When the individual enters into the policy, it is likely that the value of his estate is reduced due to the policy's restricted conditions. To prevent this depreciation in the value of the estate being viewed by HMRC as a transfer of value, IHTA 1984, s 10 is relied on. This provides that the transfer will not create a transfer of value providing it was not intended to confer a gratuitous benefit upon any person and it was made at arm's length. It is doubtful that s 10 applies in these circumstances.

IHTA 1984, s 167 substitutes total premiums paid on a policy (less any withdrawals) for the policy value where the policy value is less than the total premiums. This might appear to create a problem for this product but s 167(2)(a) provides an exemption for a transfer of value made on death and in the case of this product, the policyholder owns the policy on death forming part of his estate immediately before that time.

At some point in the future the new legal owner(s) of the policy may ask the insurance company to consider a non-contractual request for a policy surrender, or to access policy benefits via higher withdrawals. The insurance company will consider each request on its merits, subject to such reasonable terms and conditions as it may wish to apply. No consideration will be given to requests made either before probate, or within a reasonable period of time thereafter.

The product is marketed as a flexible alternative to discounted gift trust planning. It is said that higher capital access is coupled with flexibility of income, and there is no reliance on medical underwriting.

Annuities – back-to-back arrangements

[9.47] An elderly taxpayer may wish to increase his net spendable income through a back-to-back insurance and annuity arrangement. First, he would purchase an annuity for the duration of his life. After having done so, in order to replace the capital he has used to purchase the annuity, he may then consider effecting a whole life policy on his own life, which he will write in trust for his heirs, providing that the original capital sum (plus bonuses) will be payable on his death. He has thereby provided himself with a source of income and also effectively removed the capital cost of the annuity from his estate.

Regard must be had to IHTA 1984, s 263 in relation to this type of arrangement. The section applies where the taking out of two policies are associated operations (as defined in IHTA 1984, s 268(1)(b)) and the taxpayer is deemed to have made a transfer of value at the time the life policy became held in trust equal to the lower of the total consideration paid for the annuity and the life policy and the value of the greatest benefit capable of being conferred by the life policy. It seems, however, that in practice policies and annuities taken out in such circumstances will not be regarded by HMRC as associated operations (and thus s 263 will not be applied) provided the life policy was issued on full medical evidence of the assured's health and would have been issued on the same terms if the annuity had not been purchased at the same time (see HMRC Statement of Practice SP E4).

It is also necessary to consider which inheritance tax exemption is being relied on for the payments of the whole of life premiums. If it is the exemption for normal expenditure out of income then it should be remembered that a major part of the annuity will be treated as a return of capital and cannot therefore qualify for this exemption.

Non-domiciled individuals and offshore single premium bonds

[9.48] If the policyholder is resident but not domiciled in the UK, an offshore policy (or any policy issued under seal and held abroad) might be attractive as it would fall outside the ambit of inheritance tax (if any) payable on his death, being property situated outside the UK and thus excluded property for inheritance tax purposes (IHTA 1984, s 6(1)). However, chargeable event gains do not benefit from the remittance basis for income tax and therefore care should be taken in adding sufficient lives assured or in using a capital redemption bond so that any chargeable event can be deferred until the non-domiciled individual has left the UK.

Chapter 10

Pensions

Introduction

[10.1] On 6 April 2006 ('A Day') pension provision in the UK was radically reformed in an attempt to simplify a system which had become unwieldly and complex. The reforms aimed to simplify existing tax rules and limit the tax relief available to the highest earners.

Prior to A Day, tax relief on UK pension contributions was controlled by either:

(a)   placing a cap on the maximum pension that could be funded; or
(b)   stipulating a maximum percentage of earnings that would attract tax relief.

Post-A Day, an annual allowance limits the maximum tax relievable contributions in any tax year and a lifetime limit controls the maximum pension fund that can be accumulated without attracting a tax charge when pension benefits are drawn. A system of 'grandfathering' applies to individuals with pension benefits in excess of, or close to, the lifetime limit at A Day.

From its introduction, however, this rational and straightforward system has been undermined by continual tinkering.

FA 2009 introduced restrictions on tax relief on pension contributions for individuals earning more than £150,000 pa (see below). In the emergency budget on 22 June 2010, the government announced that the whole subject of higher rate tax relief on pension contributions was once more under review. This led to the introduction of a reduced annual allowance of £50,000 from 6 April 2011. Furthermore, F(No 2)A 2010 introduced a temporary two-year extension to the date at which it becomes necessary to annuitise or draw a secured income, from 75 to 77. The age 75 limit was abolished by FA 2011.

Further reductions to the lifetime limit and annual allowance were introduced by FA 2013 and applied from 6 April 2014 but perhaps the biggest changes seen in a generation came with the 'pension freedom reforms' which apply from 6 April 2015 and allow pension holders to remove their entire pension funds with no restrictions. Further changes have been made by FA 2016, ss 19–23, the most important of which are described below.

In most cases, pension structures commonly established before A Day, such as Defined Benefit and Defined Contribution Occupational Schemes, Personal Pension Plans ('PPPs'), Self-Invested Personal Pension Plans ('SIPPS'), Small Self-Administered Schemes ('SSAS') and Retirement Annuity Plans ('RAPs'), continue. The way in which the tax relievable contributions to these schemes are calculated, however, changed at A Day. In this Chapter we consider the treatment of pension provision by employers and individuals, but first, we shall briefly examine the state pension.

State pension

[10.2] The state provides two elements of state pension – basic and earnings related.

Basic state pension

[10.3] Until 5 April 2010 a maximum pension was achieved by making full national insurance contributions for at least 90% of one's working life. The maximum basic pension is now achieved by making full national insurance contributions for at least 30 years.

The retirement age for men is set at 65. The retirement age for women is 60 for those born before 6 April 1950, rising gradually to 65 for those born on or after 6 April 1955. Between 2018 and 2046 the basic state pension age will increase to 68.

The basic state pension for those who reached the state pension age before 6 April 2016 is £119.30 per week for a single person and up to £190.80 per week for a married couple.

For an individual reaching state pension age after 5 April 2016, the maximum state pension is £155.65 per week with the actual amount depending on the individual's national insurance contribution record.

Earnings related state pension

[10.4] The State Earnings Related Pension Scheme ('SERPS') commenced in 1978. It was only relevant for employed individuals (not self-employed). It was replaced in 2002 with the State Second Pension ('S2P').

SERPs provided an earnings related element to the state pension, originally intended to deliver up to 25% of average best year's earnings which was subsequently trimmed to 20% of average lifetime earnings and eventually replaced in April 2002.

Many individuals 'contracted out' of SERPs as a result of their employer's pension schemes taking the decision to contract out. Additionally many individuals chose to 'contract out' of SERPs in return for a national insurance rebate being paid to a personal pension of their own choice.

The replacement in April 2002 of SERPs by the State Second Pension ('S2P') was aimed at delivering more pension than SERPs would deliver for those on low or moderate income. There has been much debate in recent years about whether or not individuals should contract back into the State Second Pension.

From 6 April 2016 the basic and additional state pensions are replaced by a flat-rate state pension worth approximately £155 per week.

Annual allowance (FA 2004, s 228)

[**10.5**] The maximum contribution that can be made to a UK pension plan is now set by the annual allowance. The annual allowance can be set by the Treasury by Order (FA 2004, s 228(2)). For the tax years 2011/12, 2012/13 and 2013/14 the annual allowance was £50,000 and there was no restriction in the relief given to high earners up to the level of the annual allowance. The annual allowance from 6 April 2014 is reduced to £40,000 (FA 2013, s 49).

For 2016/17, the annual allowance is reduced on a tapered basis where the 'adjusted net income' of the individual concerned exceeds £150,000 reducing the allowance to £10,000 when adjusted net income is £210,000 or more (FA 2004, s 228ZA).

The annual allowance measures the total pension inputs which may be made in a pension input period ending in the tax year. This means that contributions made during a pension input period beginning but not ending during a tax year will not count towards the annual allowance of that pension input period (FA 2004, s 238(2)(a)). This may provide scope to make tax relievable pension contributions in excess of the annual allowance in any one tax year. The annual allowance applies to contributions made by or on behalf of an individual and therefore it is now possible to be a member of an occupational scheme and also make significant contributions to a PPP, RAP or SIPP.

Pension contributions by an individual are allowed against annual relevant earnings as mainly defined in ITEPA 2003, s 7(2) and ITTOIA 2005, Pt 2. (It is thought that this definition may include gains on the exercise of share options and share related schemes.) Therefore it is not possible for an individual with relevant earnings of say £40,000 pa to obtain tax relief on a contribution of a higher amount. An individual contribution in excess of relevant earnings, or the annual allowance, is possible but such a contribution will not attract tax relief. Any employer contributions in excess of the annual allowance will be taxable on the employee at up to 45% via self-assessment under FA 2004, s 227.

In most cases it will be easy to measure the pension input. Where a cash contribution is made by an employee or employer to a defined contribution scheme then the pension input is simply the value of the cash contribution. However where benefits accrue in a defined benefit pension scheme then the pension input is equal to the increase in value of the individual's pension rights in the pension input period multiplied by a factor of 16.

It is no longer possible to carry back a contribution to a previous tax year but one can carry forward unused annual allowances from the previous three years (FA 2009, s 228A).

Contributions – occupational schemes

[**10.6**] All individual contributions will normally be made via payroll and tax relief of up to 45% will, therefore, be given automatically. Employer contributions will largely be made in the same way. If employer contributions are made via a salary bonus or sacrifice arrangement then there will also be a saving of employer and employee NIC on the amount that would otherwise have been paid as remuneration.

Contributions – PPPs and RAPs

[10.7] For contributions to personal pension plans (including SIPPS) contributions by employed and self-employed individuals are made net of basic rate tax relief. The additional higher rate relief is claimed through an individual's tax return. Additionally an employer can still contribute to an individual's PPP.

For RAPs, contributions can still be made gross. It was originally anticipated that RAPs would switch to a net of tax relief basis post-A Day, but there were difficulties for RAP providers in adapting long established systems.

Lifetime limit (FA 2004, Part 4)

[10.8] The lifetime limit is the maximum that an individual can hold in pension plans without facing a punitive tax charge when he comes to take pension benefits. The lifetime limit for 2016/17 is £1m.

Some individuals may be entitled to an enhanced lifetime limit if they have had a period of residence overseas and have contributions to a pension on which UK tax relief was not available (see **10.30** below), or in some circumstances if a pension splitting order following divorce is in place (see **10.33** below). Individuals who have elected for either enhanced or primary protection may also have an enhanced lifetime limit (see **10.12**).

An individual's pension or pensions are tested against the lifetime limit on the occurrence of a Benefit Crystallization Event (a 'BCE') (FA 2004, s 216, Sch 32). There are several BCEs when a test must be made and these are:

- BCE 1: where funds are designated to provide a pension member with unsecured pension income (USI);
- BCE 2: where a member becomes entitled to a scheme pension;
- BCE 3: where a scheme pension already in payment is increased beyond a permitted margin;
- BCE 4: where a member becomes entitled to a lifetime annuity under a money purchase arrangement;
- BCE 5: where a member reaches age 75 and still has uncrystallised benefits under a defined benefit scheme;
- BCE 5A: where a member reaches age 75 and is still in USI;
- BCE 5B where a member reaches age 75 with uncrystallised money purchase arrangements;
- BCE 6: where a member becomes entitled to a lump sum;
- BCE 7: where a relevant lump sum is paid on the death of the member
- BCE 8: where a member's pension benefits are transferred to a qualifying recognised overseas pension scheme.

In the simplest case where an individual has only one pension arrangement and takes all of the benefits at the same time then the BCE is calculated by looking at the value of those pension benefits and deducting the lifetime limits. If the benefits are part of money purchase arrangement then it is the cash value of the benefits at the time of the BCE that will determine whether or not there is a lifetime limit charge. Any charge is provided for under FA 2004, s 214.

Example

On the 30 September 2016, Andy who is aged 60 has a SIPP valued at £2m and takes 25% tax free cash and purchases an annuity with the balance. His BCE is calculated as £2m less the prevailing lifetime limit of £1m, giving an excess of £1m.

However, in many cases the calculation will not be so simple. For individuals with a number of different pension arrangements and where these arrangements are vested at different times, it may be necessary to test against the lifetime limit more than once. If for example Andy above had two SIPPs both valued at £800,000 each and one of these vested in September 2008, this would have used 48% of his lifetime limit (£800,000 / the then lifetime limit of £1.65m). If he then vested the other in September 2016 he would have 52% of the then lifetime limit (£1m × 52%) left for this second BCE.

For individuals with defined benefit arrangements or with pensions in payment at A Day the pension is capitalised in order to create a monetary cash value that can be tested against the lifetime limit on the occurrence of a BCE. A factor of 20:1 should be applied for defined benefit arrangements and a factor of 25:1 for pensions in payment at A Day.

Investment growth

[10.9] Although investment growth does not affect the annual allowance in any way, it can affect the lifetime limit. An individual with total pension values below the lifetime limit at A Day could still face a lifetime limit charge if their pension fund investment performance exceeds the increase in the lifetime limit.

Lifetime limit charge (FA 2004, s 214)

[10.10] The charge is levied on a BCE where the benefits exceed the available lifetime limit. The charge is at 55% for any amounts that are drawn as cash and 25% for any amounts that remain within the scheme or are used to purchase an annuity (although of course the income from the annuity will then be taxed at marginal rates).

Example

Andy above has a SIPP valued at £1.4m at A Day which is below the lifetime limit. By September 2016, Andy's SIPP has increased in value to £2m and he then takes full benefits leading to a BCE. In September 2016 the lifetime limit is £1m and therefore Andy has excess benefits over the lifetime limit of £1m. He can draw this as cash and face a one-off tax charge at 55% on £1m or apply it to an income (either an annuity or income drawdown) and pay a one-off charge of 25% on £1m.

Protection

[10.11] There have been five types of protection since A Day. Enhanced protection and primary protection applied from A Day at 6 April 2006 and elections had to be made within three years. Fixed protection applied from April 2012 and elections had to be made by 6 April 2012. Fixed protection 2014 and individual protection apply from 6 April 2014 and fixed protection 2016 and individual protection 2016 apply from 6 April 2016.

Enhanced protection

[10.12] Individuals with pensions in excess of the lifetime limit at A Day (or with pensions below the lifetime limit but who expected their pension benefits to exceed the lifetime limit when they were drawn) could elect to protect the fund from the lifetime allowance charge. In return the individual undertook to make no further contributions to any pension schemes post-A Day including contributions made to a pension scheme to acquire life assurance (eg, pension term assurance). This election had to be made by the 5 April 2009.

Once protected in this manner, on a BCE the pension fund is not referenced against the lifetime limit and there can be no lifetime limit charge. For defined benefit schemes there is a complex calculation which allows for some increase in final pension entitlement.

Death benefits are not similarly protected because they are contingent benefits to which the individual does not have an absolute entitlement. However, death benefits may be paid within the protected limits for pension benefits.

Primary protection

[10.13] Unlike enhanced protection, primary protection only applies where the total pension benefits to which an individual is entitled exceeded £1.5m at A Day. Again the election had to be made by 5 April 2009.

If an election has been made, the individual's pension rights are protected from the lifetime limit charge up to the percentage increase in the lifetime limit between A Day and the relevant BCE.

Example

> George has a SIPP which was valued at £2.25m at A Day. This was equivalent to the lifetime limit at that time multiplied by a factor of 1.5. George elected for primary protection. Many years later when George's SIPP is valued at £2.9m (and the lifetime limit is, say, £2m) he takes all of his pension benefits. The lifetime limit is enhanced by 1.5 and therefore increased to £3m. George's SIPP is below £3m and therefore there is no lifetime limit charge.

At first glance there might appear to be little point in electing for the limited protection afforded by primary protection when enhanced protection protects the entire fund irrespective of any increase in value. However, primary protection permits further contributions to be made in the future if for example a pension fund falls in value due to poor investment performance.

Fixed protection (FA 2011, Sch 18, Part 2)

[10.14] The lifetime limit fell to £1.5m from 6 April 2012. For individuals who expected to have total pension benefits in excess of £1.5m on retirement after 5 April 2012, it was possible to apply for fixed protection under FA 2011, Sch 18, para 15. This meant that such individuals continued to benefit from a lifetime limit of up to £1.8m in return for making no further contributions to pension schemes or receiving any further benefit accrual in the case of defined benefit schemes or employer contributions in the case of defined contribution occupational schemes. The election had to be made by 5 April 2012.

Fixed protection 2014

[10.15] From 6 April 2014 the lifetime limit fell to £1.25m. For individuals who were likely to have pension savings in excess of £1.25m upon retirement it was possible to elect, by April 2014, to protect pension savings from the lifetime limit charge up to £1.5m, the then lifetime limit (FA 2013, Sch 22). No further pension contributions can be made from 6 April 2014 or the election will not apply (FA 2013, Sch 22(1)(3)).

Fixed protection 2016

[10.16] As a result of the reduction in lifetime allowance from £1.25m to £1m from 6 April 2016 individuals with a fund in excess of £1m could elect to protect their existing fund from lifetime allowance charges up to a maximum of £1.25m in return for making no further pension contributions.

Individual protection 2014

[10.17] Individual protection gives a protected lifetime allowance equal to the value of an individual's pension benefits on 5 April 2014 up to a maximum of £1.5m. It is only available for those individuals whose pension funds were valued at over £1.25m on 5 April 2014.

Unlike with fixed protection, under individual protection an individual can make further contributions to pensions after 5 April 2014 but only up to the level of their pension benefits at this date. Individual protection, therefore, opens up the possibility of making future contributions to a pension fund, which has fallen below its 5 April 2014 value.

Individual protection 2016

[10.18] Individual protection gives a protected lifetime allowance equal to the value of an individual's pension benefits on 5 April 2016 up to a maximum of £1.25m. It is only available for those individuals whose pension funds were valued at over £1.25m on 5 April 2016.

Unlike with fixed protection, under individual protection an individual can make further contributions to pensions after 5 April 2016 but only up to the level of their pension benefits at this date. Individual protection, therefore, opens up the possibility of making future contributions to a pension fund, which has fallen below its 5 April 2016 value.

There is no deadline for applications for individual protection 2016. However, individuals will need to apply online for protection before they take their benefits.

Taking benefits

[10.19] There are a number of ways in which pension benefits may be taken on retirement, or indeed, as it is not necessary to retire in order to take pension benefits, before retirement. One may take an annuity, a scheme pension under an occupational defined benefit scheme or a compulsory purchase annuity under an occupational defined contribution scheme but there are also a number of more flexible options which are discussed below.

Under FA 2004, ss 165(1) and 279(1), the normal minimum pension age is 55 and in most cases the lower retirement ages for specialist occupations such as sportspeople was withdrawn with effect from 2010.

Drawdown pension

[10.20] Income drawdown was originally introduced in 1995 to give greater flexibility to the way in which a pension income may be drawn. It was replaced by something called the Unsecured Pension Income (USP), but income drawdown was reinstated from 6 April 2011 by FA 2011, Sch 16. It provides for a pension income to be delivered direct from the pension fund without the need to purchase an annuity. This is known as 'capped drawdown'. Normally the pension holder will also take a 25% lump sum at commencement of the drawdown. Drawdown can now continue throughout life which means that there is no longer an effective compulsion to annuitise at age 75. The new drawdown combines features of the USP and of the Alternatively Secured Pension which was a less attractive form of drawdown that used to come into effect once the pension holder passed the age of 75.

The maximum limit is 150% of a basis amount that is calculated using Government Actuary Department (GAD) tables and the yields on 15-year gilts. It is broadly similar to 150% of the maximum single life annuity rate that could be achieved at that age assuming no escalation and no spouse's pension.

The selected income withdrawal amount must be reviewed every five years although it is possible to move between the minimum and maximum limits.

The minimum limit for drawdown pension taken from the pension fund is zero and hence this opens up the possibility of taking maximum tax free cash, drawing no income and hence leaving the fund to grow tax free (ignoring dividend tax credits).

It should be noted, however, that using a drawdown pension fund to purchase an annuity constitutes a further BCE. This means that a pension fund below the lifetime limit on entry into drawdown pension could be above the limit (and hence subject to a lifetime limit charge) when this second BCE occurs. For this reason consideration should be given to drawing maximum income approaching a further BCE which is taxable at a maximum of 45% rather than face a lifetime limit charge at 55% if the cash option is taken.

Up to 5 April 2015 on death during drawdown the remaining fund is available for:

(a)   a lump sum which is subject to tax at 55%;

(b)   dependant's pensions or annuities;

(c)   dependant's USP with the fund on the death of the dependant also being available as a lump sum, again subject to a 55% tax charge.

The term 'dependant' is defined in FA 2004, Sch 28, Part 2 as:

(i)   a person who was married to, or is a civil partner of, the member at the date of the member's death;

(ii)   a child of the member who is either aged under 23 or dependent on the member due to a physical or mental disability;

(iii) a person who was financially dependent on the member under a relationship of financial mutual dependence, or dependent on the member due to a physical or mental disability.

Flexible drawdown was introduced by FA 2011, Sch 16. This permits individuals who can prove a minimum guaranteed pension income of at least £12,000 pa (defined by FA 2011, Sch 16, Part 20) (it was previously £20,000) to draw down an amount up to the balance of their remaining pension fund. Any amount so drawn is taxable in full as income in the year it is drawn. This creates a planning possibility for individuals who have moved into a lower tax bracket in retirement to draw pension funds out at a lower tax rate than that at which their contributions were originally relieved.

From 6 April 2015 new rules applied. Additional pension flexibility gave all individuals an option to crystallise their entire pension fund as a lump sum. Up to 25% remained free of tax but the balance was to be added to income for the year and taxed at the pension member's marginal rates.

New rules on death benefits during drawdown were introduced by the Taxation of Pensions Act 2014 which amended Chapter 5 of Part 4 of FA 2004 so that from 6 April 2015 on death during drawdown before age 75 the entire fund can be paid as a lump sum free of all taxes.

Post-age 75 all lump sums are taxable at the recipient's marginal tax rate. If paid to trust a 45% tax charge applies.

Example

> John, aged 56, has a pension fund of £400,000. He decides to crystallise the entire pension fund. £100,000 of this will be tax free but £300,000 will be added to his income for 2016/17.

Alternatively Secured Pension (ASP) (FA 2004, s 165 and Sch 28 para 20(2) and (3), FA 2007, Sch 19)

[10.21] The Alternatively Secured Pension ('ASP') was introduced in order to allow schemes to comply with the Sharia making it possible for a pension holder to continue drawing an income from their pension post-age 75 but without taking an annuity. It has now been replaced by drawdown pension which covers drawdown both pre and post age 75.

Death benefits from uncrystallised funds (FA 2004, s 167, Sch 28, Pt 2)

[10.22] Complex rules used to apply to death benefits pre-vesting, that is before any pension had been drawn.

The rules are now simplified and provide that the following benefits can be paid from an uncrystallised money purchase pension on the death of a pension scheme member.

(a) An unsecured pension.
(b) A dependant's annuity.
(c) A lump sum death benefit.

In the case of a defined benefit pension the following may be provided:

(i) A dependant's scheme pension.
(ii) A defined benefits lump sum death benefit.

If lump sum death benefits are not distributed within two years of the member's death a tax charge will arise.

The payment of a lump sum death benefit represents a benefit crystallisation event and the amount will count towards the lifetime limit. If the value of uncrystallised pension rights and lump sum death benefits exceeds the lifetime limit then a lifetime limit charge at 55% will arise. This can be avoided by using the excess to provide a dependant's pension.

Following A Day, pension life cover grew in popularity. Premiums for life cover paid under pension's rules attracted tax relief at 40% for a higher rate taxpayer. Prior to A Day tax relief was also due where premiums for life cover were paid under pensions rules but the limits were far less generous. FA 2007, Sch 18, however, denies tax relief on pension premiums paid on or after 6 April 2007 unless the insurer received the application for the policy before 29 March 2007 and the policy was taken out as part of the pension scheme before 1 August 2007.

Lump sum death benefits and inheritance tax

[10.23] FA 2006, Sch 22 formalised a practice of HMRC dating back to 1992 (Inland Revenue Tax Bulletin 2 February 1992).

An inheritance tax charge arises under IHTA 1984, s 3(3) where a person's omission to exercise a right diminishes the value of that person's estate and the value of another person's estate or of settled property (other than property within IHTA 1984, s 49(1)) is increased. A charge under IHTA 1984, s 3(3) can arise if a pension scheme member does not exercise his right to take pension benefits. The charge applies at the latest time when the right could be exercised; that is, immediately before death. Therefore if a member did not take his pension benefits at his normal retirement date (NRD) as indicated in his pension contract, and subsequently died, an inheritance tax charge could have arisen.

The case of *Fryer (personal representatives of Arnold (deceased)) v Revenue & Customs Comrs* [2010] UKFTT 87 (TC), [2010] SFTD 632 attracted considerable publicity due to the fact that HMRC successfully pursued a claim to inheritance tax on the pension fund of an individual who died within two years of their normal retirement date, having failed to take pension benefits. The facts were as follows:

On 6 November 1955 Mrs Arnold transferred her existing pension rights into an NPI personal pension scheme and declared a trust of the lump sum death benefits of which her children were beneficiaries

The normal retirement date on the NPI policy was 8 September 2002 when Mrs Arnold would be 60 although the plan actually allowed for retirement between ages 50 and 75 as is fairly standard for pension plans.

In April 2002 Mrs Arnold was diagnosed with advanced cancer and she died in July 2003. NPI had written to her in May 2002 asking if she wished to take her retirement benefits and she did not respond to the letter.

Following her death the pension fund was paid into the discretionary trust. HMRC considered that Mrs Arnold had made a transfer of value of part of her estate for the purposes of IHTA 1984, s 3(3). They argued that inheritance tax was due on the grounds that her omission to exercise a right had diminished her estate. The Tribunal dismissed the executors' appeal in a decision which was strongly criticised on technical grounds.

This case was distinguished in *Parry (as personal representative of Stavely, decd) v Revenue & Customs Comrs* (TC03548) [2014 UKFTT 419 (TC), [2014] SWTI 2415, [2014] WTLR 1265. Mrs Staveley, on her divorce, received her share of the pension scheme. She was advised that her only option was to transfer her fund into a FA 1981, s 32 buyout policy. She had the freedom to invest the fund as she chose but any surplus would be returned to her ex-husband's company on her death. Mrs Staveley was unhappy about this arrangement. It was her wish that any surplus should benefit her sons but she was told that she would have to wait ten years before she could transfer the funds to a personal pension plan. Later changes in pension law meant she could make the transfer after six years. When she was terminally ill, she transferred funds to her personal pension plan which meant that the fund would not revert to her ex-husband's company. Under the plan she could draw pension benefits but she did not do so and died some six weeks later. The moneys were paid to her sons. HMRC argued that the transfer to the personal pension plan was a transfer of value and issued a determination. HMRC made a second determination on the basis that Mrs Staveley had not taken any lifetime benefits between the date the personal plan was created and her death. The appellants argued that the transfer was a disposition but not a transfer of value because there was no intention by Mrs Staveley to confer a gratuitous benefit. The Tribunal held that the transfer was a disposition and had been made to ensure that no part of her pension fund reverted to the company. HMRC argued that Mrs Staveley had a dual motive because she wanted to confer a benefit on her sons. The Tribunal disagreed. Her sons were already beneficiaries under her will and would have benefitted from the s 32 policy and, therefore, the transfer could not be said to confer a benefit on them. In relation to the second determination, the Tribunal agreed with HMRC that because Mrs Staveley did not take any lifetime benefits from the plan, she had made a deliberate omission and fell within IHTA 1984, s 3(3).

IHTA 1984, s 12(2ZA) now provides, however, that where a person who is a member of a registered pension scheme or of certain other pension schemes, omits to exercise pension rights under the scheme, IHTA 1984, s 3(3) does not apply to the omission.

There was some concern that inheritance tax could apply to flexi-access drawdown funds where the pension holder failed to draw from a drawdown pension fund during their lifetime so that there were unused funds when they died. Finance Act 2016, s 84 has inserted s 12A into IHTA 1984 introducing an exemption from inheritance tax in these circumstances.

Qualifying investments

Residential property and exotic assets

[10.24] Various punitive tax charges apply where investment regulated pension schemes invest in 'taxable property'. An investment regulated pension scheme is defined as a registered pension scheme where the member or a person related to the member can directly or indirectly influence or advise on the investments. This includes RAPs, SIPPS and SSASs.

Taxable property is defined by FA 2004, Sch 29A, Pt 2 as:

(a)   residential property, which includes buildings used as or suitable to be used as a dwelling and their gardens or grounds. It also includes hotels, similar accommodation and beach huts. For these purposes, residential property excludes homes or institutions providing accommodation for children or the elderly. It also excludes property occupied by an employee who is required to occupy it as a condition of their employment or property used in connection with a business premises e.g. a flat above a shop. However, in both cases the individual occupying the flat must not be a member of the pension scheme or connected to a member of the pension scheme. The phrase 'connected person' is defined in ICTA 1988, s 839; or

(b)   tangible moveable property.

Where the taxable property is held then a number of tax charges may apply. These include:

(i)   an unauthorised payments income tax charge at 40% of the value of the taxable property levied on the recipient of the payment;

(ii)   an unauthorised payments surcharge where the unauthorised payment represents 25% or more of the pension fund value. This is an additional 15% income tax charge, again levied on the recipient of the payment;

(iii)   denial of tax exemption for the pension fund on any income or gains from the property;

(iv)   a scheme sanction income tax charge at 40% levied on the scheme administrator (although offset by any unauthorised payment charge);

(v)   a possible deregistration charge at 40% if the value of the taxable property exceeds 25% of the fund value.

Member connected investments

[10.25] The old rules relating to member connected investments have now mostly disappeared provided any transactions take place on an arm's length basis. If not then the benefit in kind rules will apply. For these purposes assets are valued in accordance with TCGA 1992, s 272 at the price that those assets would reasonably be expected to produce on the open market. Furthermore, there are value shifting rules in FA 2004 to prevent value being extracted from pension schemes and placed in the hands of a member or employer.

Loans to employers

[10.26] Any loans to employers must meet the following conditions:

(a)   be at an interest rate of 1% above the average base rate rounded up to the nearest 0.25%;

(b)   be secured as a first charge on assets;

(c)   last for less than five years;

(d)   be repaid by equal annual instalments;

(e)   not exceed 50% of the value of the pension scheme's assets.

Scheme borrowing

[10.27] Total borrowing is limited to 50% of scheme assets which is considerably less flexible than the pre-A Day position.

Investment in sponsoring employer

[10.28] Pension schemes are now restricted to investing under 5% of pension scheme assets in any one sponsoring employer and under 20% of the value where the shareholdings relate to more than one sponsoring employer. Where the scheme is not sponsored by the employer (eg a SIPP) then higher levels of shareholdings may be possible).

Trustee responsibility in respect of investment

[10.29] A trustee has a general power to make any kind of investment which they could make were they an absolute owner of the trust assets (Trustee Act 2000, s 3(1)). This is subject to specific statutory provisions in respect of investments in land (TLATA 1996, s 6 and Trustee Act 2000, ss 3 and 4). In exercising his investment power, a trustee must have regard to their general duty of care in exercising their trustee powers and to the standard investment criterion (see **5.14** above).

Although pension schemes are able to invest widely, in practice, professional pension trustee companies are reluctant to hold assets that might cause them to breach their general duty of care. Furthermore many unquoted shares now qualify for generous tax reliefs in their own right (including business property relief and enterprise investment scheme relief) so it is often advantageous to hold such assets outside a pension scheme.

The international element

Recognised overseas pension schemes

[10.30] Under FA 2004, ss 221–226, an individual who has been a member of a recognised overseas pension scheme or has been a member of a UK scheme whilst resident abroad may be able to apply to HMRC to have their standard lifetime allowance enhanced.

Where there is a transfer from a recognised overseas pension plan the key point is that the funds in the pension are not UK tax relieved, hence the reason for the enhancement to the lifetime limit. However, there may be an impact on the annual allowance where the transfer is into an occupational scheme.

For a scheme to be a recognised overseas pension scheme it has to meet certain criteria. It must be established in:

(a)   a member state of the European Economic Area;
(b)   a country or territory with which the UK has a double tax agreement providing for exchange of information; or
(c)   any other country or territory if at the time of the transfer the rules are broadly equivalent to UK pension scheme rules.

Where the member is a relevant overseas individual then contributions made to a UK pension plan whilst overseas may not have been relieved for UK taxation purposes, hence the reason for permitting an enhancement to the lifetime limit.

Qualifying recognised overseas pension schemes (QROPS)

[10.31] It is also possible for a UK individual moving abroad to arrange for a transfer from their UK scheme to a qualifying recognised overseas pension scheme (QROPS). A QROPS has to notify HMRC that it is a recognised overseas pension scheme together with providing other information to HMRC regarding its recognised status. It must also confirm its country of establishment. The QROPs can provide greater flexibility both as to the investments that can be held and as to the benefits that may be drawn once the individual has been non UK resident for five complete tax years. After that point, it is arguable that the QROPs provider no longer needs to report crystallisation events in relation to that member to HMRC.

Qualifying non-UK pensions (QNUPs)

[10.32] The rules providing for QNUPs were introduced as part of the Inheritance Tax (Qualifying Non-UK Pensions Schemes) Regulations 2010 (SI 2010/51) in February 2010. The rules were introduced to correct a defect that meant that QROPS could be within the scope of inheritance tax. Therefore an amount transferred from a UK registered pension which is generally inheritance tax free to a QROPS could, prior to February 2010, have come within the inheritance tax net. For the purposes of these regulations a QROPS will always meet the criteria for being a QNUPs and will therefore benefit from the inheritance tax exemption conferred on UK pensions schemes.

However, a QNUPs can be established as a stand-alone pension fund, ie not necessarily via a QROPS, which means that the normal UK pension contribution limits (annual allowance and lifetime limit) do not apply. QNUPs therefore have considerable application as an inheritance tax shelter for UK resident and domiciled individuals.

Divorce

[10.33] Legislation enabling pension splitting came into effect on 1 December 2000. Pension splitting is the court's preferred option for dealing with pensions on divorce as it allows a clean break with the fund of the pension member simply being split according to the divorce agreement. Pension earmarking is still available but this does not provide a clean break as the recipient of the earmarking order has to wait until the pensions scheme member takes their pension.

A pension splitting order may have an impact on the lifetime limit of both the recipient former spouse and the pension scheme member.

If the pension splitting order is post-A Day, then the credit amount will count against the recipient former spouse's lifetime limit, not the pension member's. This means that the pension member may be able to rebuild their pension fund post divorce.

Where the pension came into payment post-A Day, the recipient former spouse can claim an enhancement to their lifetime limit to reflect the fact that the pension will already have been tested against the member's lifetime limit.

Where the pension sharing order was in place pre-A Day, the recipient of the pension credit can claim an enhancement to their lifetime limit. The pension member's lifetime limit excludes any amount paid away as pension credit to a former spouse.

The calculation of the enhancement factor is provided by FA 2004, Sch 36, Pt 2.

Chapter 11

The Family Home and Other Residential Property

Introduction

[11.1] The family home is the principal asset of many people who seek estate planning advice, and as it is often their only significant asset, it merits separate treatment in this book. Although the opportunities for mitigating the charge to inheritance tax on the family home are limited, they are nonetheless the ones which are frequently of most concern to clients.

This chapter is not exclusively concerned with the position of married couples and, where appropriate, will highlight estate planning considerations that are relevant to unmarried couples and others who buy a home jointly, or in their sole name. Except where a planning suggestion depends on creating different interests in land, no distinction will be made between freehold and leasehold ownership. References to a spouse are to be taken to include references to both a party to a same-sex marriage and a civil partner.

Ownership of property

[11.2] In order to set estate planning considerations in context, it is first necessary to outline the two forms of joint ownership recognised by English land law.

English law draws a distinction between legal and beneficial ownership of land. Where legal ownership is held by two or more individuals they will hold it as joint tenants. The legal joint tenants will hold the land on trust for the beneficial owners (who may be, and usually are, themselves) and on the death of one joint owner the legal title vests in the survivor or survivors.

The law recognises two forms of beneficial ownership, namely:

(a)   joint tenancy; and
(b)   tenancy in common.

While in both cases, each beneficial co-owner is as much entitled to possession of any part of the land as the other so that no one joint owner can claim this or that piece of the land as his own, there are two essential differences, which are of fundamental importance for estate planning. First, in the case of a beneficial joint tenancy, each co-owner can only have an equal interest in the land, or in its net proceeds of sale if it is sold, whereas in the case of a tenancy in common, it is possible for one owner to have a greater or lesser share than the other co-owner(s). For this reason, when people contribute to the purchase price of land in unequal shares, the beneficial ownership should normally be in the form of a tenancy in common, unless they are content to accept the equality of interest created by a joint tenancy (which in itself will result in a gift by one of the co-owners to the other with possible inheritance tax consequences). It should be noted that an express declaration of trust is conclusive and overrides any implied, resulting or constructive trusts (*Pankhania v Chandegra* [2012] EWCA Civ 1438, [2013] 1 P & CR 238, [2013] 3 FCR 16). It is therefore essential that such a declaration accurately reflects the parties' intention. Secondly, and more importantly, in the case of a beneficial joint tenancy, when a co-owner dies, his interest passes automatically (and irrespective of any will which he may leave) to the surviving co-owner; whereas, in the case of a tenancy in common, the share of a joint owner passes on death in accordance with his will or, if he leaves no will, the rules of intestacy. For these reasons, of the two forms of beneficial joint ownership, a tenancy in common is usually to be recommended as being the more useful and flexible form of joint ownership for estate planning purposes.

In the case of unmarried couples, if a property is held on a tenancy in common, each co-owner should make a will dealing with the property on their death. This will avoid the property devolving under the intestacy rules in a manner contrary to the deceased's wishes.

Married couples, however, are still frequently recommended to purchase property as beneficial joint tenants on the ground that this is the most convenient and cost effective method of holding property should one of them die. It is true that, in the event of death, no probate or other formalities are required beyond the simple one of placing a certified copy of the death certificate with the title deeds or, in the case of registered land, by submitting an application to the Land Registry together with evidence of the death which would normally be a death certificate. Such advice, however, overlooks the risk of marital breakdown and the lesser risk of both spouses dying at the same time.

In the event of a break-up of the marriage, each party will normally be advised by their respective lawyers to terminate the beneficial joint tenancy in order to ensure that, in the event of premature death before the financial settlement on divorce has been completed, their respective interests do not go to their spouse. Similarly, the risk of both dying at the same time should not be overlooked. The Law of Property Act 1925, s 184 provides that where two people die in circumstances where it is not possible to say which of them died first, the elder will be deemed to have died first.

Whichever form of co-ownership is used, the legal ownership must operate through a trust of land (Law of Property Act 1925, ss 34–36) so that the legal owners hold the property on trust for the beneficial owners who will usually be themselves. Under the Trusts of Land and Appointment of Trustees Act 1996 ('TLATA 1996') trustees are not under a duty to sell the property. Neither party can sell the property without the consent of the co-owner unless an application is made to the court.

Where co-owners cannot agree on a sale, either may apply to the court for an order of sale (TLATA 1996, s 14). In considering whether or not to order a sale, the court, which has complete discretion in the matter, will take into account the intentions of the person who created the trust, the purpose for which the property subject to the trust is held and the welfare of any minor who occupies or might reasonably be expected to occupy any land subject to the trust as his home (TLATA 1996, ss 14, 15).

The legal joint tenants are under a statutory duty to consult beneficiaries and give effect to their wishes insofar as these are consistent with the general interests of the trust (TLATA 1996, ss 5 and 11). Naturally, that is usually only of importance where the legal interests are held by different persons or in different proportions to the beneficial interests.

For the estate planner, the principal advantage of a tenancy in common is that it permits each co-owner to deal with his or her interest during life, or on death, according to their wishes. When compared to this flexibility, the advantages of a beneficial joint tenancy are small in most circumstances. A joint tenancy may be severed at any time by a notice in writing to the other joint tenant (Law of Property Act 1925, s 36(2)). The property will then be held as tenants in common.

In the case of *Grindal v Hooper* [1999] 48 LS Gaz R 41, (2000) Times, 8 February the High Court held that for a severance to be effective, notice had to be served. In that case, the conveyance to the parties specified that any notice of severance should be annexed to the conveyance. This notice whilst served was not attached to the conveyance until after the death of one of the owners. The court held that annexation was not essential to the validity of the notice.

It is important that the original of the severance notice is retained as the case of *Chadda, Nash and Moroney v HMRC* [2014] UKFTT 1061 (TC) illustrates. In that case a joint tenancy had to have been severed in order that a nil rate band discretionary trust came into effect on the first death. The original of the severance notice could not be found but there was evidence that one had been drafted. The Tribunal accepted the joint tenancy had been severed with the result that the nil rate band on the first death was utilised.

A beneficial joint tenancy has an appeal for married couples for whom there is peace of mind in the knowledge that when one of them dies the other automatically becomes entitled to the entire family home, without the need to go to the trouble and expense of obtaining probate. The surviving spouse will take the interest of the first to die subject to any subsisting mortgage debt unless the will provides that another part of the estate will have this burden (Administration of Estates Act 1925, s 35). Repayment of the mortgage debt can be provided for by means of a mortgage protection policy or a low cost insurance policy. Apart from this, the surviving spouse is free to sell or mortgage the property without further formality, as the trust terminates on death and the survivor can give a good receipt for the sale proceeds. Where property is held as tenants in common, the trust of land survives the death of the first co-owner (unless the survivor inherits the share of the deceased co-owner) and the survivor must appoint a co-trustee in order to sell or otherwise deal with the property.

For both inheritance tax and capital gains tax purposes, no distinction is drawn between a beneficial joint tenancy and a beneficial tenancy in common in equal shares. In either case each tenant will be treated as the absolute beneficial owner of his share in the property. In the case of the death of a beneficial joint tenant, this result comes about for inheritance tax purposes because the tax is calculated by reference to the value of the deceased's estate immediately before his death which will include his beneficial interest in the property. An act of severance will not give rise to an inheritance tax, a capital gains tax charge or SDLT liability.

When drafting a will purporting to dispose of a share in jointly owned property, the adviser is under a duty to ensure that the joint tenancy has been or is later severed (*Keckskemeti v Rubens Rabin & Co* (1992) Times, 31 December).

Purchasing the family home

[11.3] The first concern of most married couples is to ensure that, in the event of one of them dying, there will be a secure roof over the head of the survivor. Therefore, it is usual for the family home to be purchased in joint names so that, whoever provides the purchase price or pays the mortgage instalments, each spouse has a beneficial interest in the family home. Although, as has been said in **11.2**, a tenancy in common is generally to be preferred, if the total wealth of the couple does not exceed the inheritance tax nil rate band (£325,000 in 2016/17 to which will be added the residence nil rate amount in 2017/18) the convenience and cost effectiveness of a beneficial joint tenancy may outweigh the advantages of a tenancy in common.

Purchased jointly

[11.4] If the family home is purchased by a couple as tenants in common, then it is important that the spouses either make or review their wills at the same time as completing the purchase. This is of paramount importance if there are children, because in that event the surviving spouse may find that in the absence of a will her entitlement on intestacy may not be sufficient to give her the other half share in the family home.

The entitlement of a surviving spouse or civil partner on intestacy is found in **18.2**. A surviving spouse will have an absolute interest in one half of the residue if there are surviving children. The surviving spouse can elect to take the family home in whole or partial satisfaction of any absolute interest in the deceased's estate (Intestates' Estates Act 1952, s 5, Sch 2). If, as is often the case, the family home consists of the larger part of the value of the estate, the spouse could find herself in a position where part of the family home is held in trust for the children. Moreover, the home is appropriated at its value when the spouse makes her election and not at its probate value, so that increasing property values can have the effect of reducing the value of the statutory legacy, unless an election is made promptly.

Although the rules of intestacy are intended to reflect the wishes of the average person, they should not be relied upon as a substitute for a will. The intestacy rules will not necessarily result in the most appropriate devolution of one's estate; indeed, they may have effects which are entirely out of accord with the deceased's wishes.

In the case of unmarried couples, security and provision for what is to happen on death is just as important as for married couples or those in a civil partnership. Under the current intestacy rules, an unmarried partner has no right to any share of the deceased partner's estate. The Inheritance (Provision for Family and Dependants) Act 1975 provides a partial remedy for surviving unmarried partners in that if the survivor was, immediately before the death of the other partner, being maintained either wholly or partly by him, the survivor can apply to the court for reasonable maintenance out of the deceased partner's estate. This will provide the unmarried partner with provision in the nature of income. Although the court has power to capitalise the sum awarded, it has no power to make capital provision. It may, therefore, be appropriate for both partners to make wills giving their respective interests in the property to their partner.

It should be noted that a Private Member's Bill, the Cohabitation Rights Bill 2016, which at the time of writing has had its first reading in the House of Lords, provides that a 'qualifying cohabitant' will have the same rights as a spouse or civil partner on an intestacy. A person will only be a 'qualifying cohabitant' provided the deceased was not married or in a civil partnership immediately before death.

Valuation of share

[11.5] The general rule of valuation is that the value of property at any time is its open market value (IHTA 1984, s 160) which is the price which the property might reasonably fetch if sold in the open market at that time. That price is not to be reduced on the ground that if the whole property were placed on the market, the price would be less.

The value of a joint tenancy will not be a simple proportion of the market value of the tenancy as a whole. A hypothetical buyer of such an asset will discount the proportion of value by an amount to reflect the fact that his interest is more restricted than an absolute interest. For example, the value of a deceased cohabitee's share must be discounted on the basis that a notional purchaser in the open market would have to share possession with the surviving cohabitee. In the decided cases discounts have been typically 15%.

Where property is held jointly by spouses or civil partners the application of the related property rules in IHTA 1984, s 161 needs to be considered. The First-tier Tribunal considered the related property rules in *Price (executor of Price, dec'd) v Revenue and Customs Comrs* [2010] UKFTT 474 (TC), [2011] SFTD 52. It held that the deceased's spouse's one-half interest as tenant in common in the marital home under consideration in the case, was to be valued for the purposes of section 161 on the basis of the price it would have fetched on the open market if offered for sale in conjunction with the surviving spouse's interest. In addition, it held that whether IHTA 1984, s 161(4) applies to individual shares of land is a matter for the Upper Tribunal (Lands Chamber) (the successor body to the Lands Tribunal).

Purchased in sole name

[11.6] There will of course always be circumstances where the couple wish the house to be bought only in the name of one of them. For example, where one spouse is a partner in a business or a sole trader, they may decide to buy the property in the sole name of the other spouse in the hope of providing some protection against the results of the first spouse becoming bankrupt.

Where property is occupied by an unmarried couple but has been purchased in the sole name of one of the parties, the entire value of the property will normally be subject to inheritance tax on the death of that party. HMRC has argued that even where the surviving cohabitee has made contributions to the cost of the property, this does not reduce the value of property on the death of the deceased cohabitee. It appears that HMRC has taken the view that the beneficial rights of the surviving cohabitee do not exist unless and until a court order is obtained. Whether this view is correct is doubtful as such arrangements create a beneficial tenancy in common either under a constructive trust or by proprietary estoppel which is then enforced by the court after litigation. Therefore, prior to the death of the deceased cohabitee, the surviving cohabitee is already a joint owner in equity of the property. Indeed, in respect of capital gains tax, HMRC seems to accept that a constructive trust creates an interest in property before it is recognised by the court (HMRC Capital Gains Manual CG65422).

The residence nil rate amount

[11.7] For deaths after 5 April 2017, in addition to the nil rate band, there will be a residence nil rate amount (RNRA) which will be available for offset against the value of property that has been occupied as a residence of the deceased. These provisions will apply and are discussed in CHAPTER 18 MAKING A WILL.

Making provision in a will

[11.8] There are various ways in which a tenant in common can deal with his beneficial interest in a property by will. When provision for the surviving spouse is of overriding concern, the will of each spouse should contain an absolute gift of their respective interests in the home to the other. The terms of the gift should not be limited to any particular property they may own at the time, but should be phrased to apply to whatever property is owned at the date of death. This will avoid the need to amend the wills every time the couple move home.

It is also advisable to include in the gift the benefit of any mortgage protection or insurance policy in order to prevent any argument that the surviving spouse must account for the part of the policy which is used to repay the survivor's share of the mortgage debt. It is even more important to cover this point where the house and mortgage are in joint names but the policy is taken out on the life of the principal salary-earner alone. A specific gift of the policy will also mean that any surplus from the policy in excess of the sum needed to repay the loan will pass to the same legatee and will not pass under the gift of residue. If this is not desired, then the will should provide accordingly.

At the same time provision should be made for what should happen in the event that both spouses die at the same time; for example, in a road accident. While the gift to the surviving spouse will be free of inheritance tax, the gift in default may not be, and consideration should be given to whether or not the tax should be borne by the beneficiary who receives the interest in the family home or by the residuary estate. In the absence of express provision, the tax will be treated as a general testamentary expense and paid out of residue (IHTA 1984, s 211). An unmarried couple also need to consider who should bear the tax.

The use of nil rate band discretionary trusts

[11.9] Before the introduction of the transferable nil rate band (see **18.8**) where the family home was the principal family asset, care was needed to ensure that the opportunity to set off the nil rate band of the first spouse to die was not missed. One method was to leave a share of the property equal in value to the deceased's unused part of the nil rate band to the next generation either outright, or on discretionary trusts. In the latter case, the surviving spouse (who might also be a trustee) and their children (and remoter issue) would then be included in the class of beneficial objects of the trust. The will trust would contain a power to enable the trustees to allow the surviving spouse to occupy the property. A problem with this was that if the surviving spouse was given an exclusive or joint right of residence, HMRC argued that an interest in possession had been created (see Revenue Statement of Practice SP10/79). Statement of Practice 10/79 states that where trustees exercise their powers 'with the intention of providing a particular beneficiary with a permanent home HMRC will normally regard the exercise of the power as creating an interest in possession'. In *IRC v Lloyds Private Banking Ltd* [1998] STC 559 (Ch D), [1998] 2 FCR 41 the Court of Appeal held that a life interest was created where a will provided that a surviving tenant in common was to have the right of exclusive occupation of the property concerned for life. Similar decisions were reached in *Woodhall (Woodhall's Personal Representative) v IRC* [2000] STC (SCD) 558, (SpC 261) and *Faulkner (trustee of Adams, dec'd) v IRC* [2001] STC (SCD) 112, (Sp C 278). These decisions provide some support for HMRC's views expressed in SP 10/79 but it should be noted that the cases did not concern the occupation of property at notice by a discretionary beneficiary. The case of *Judge v Revenue & Customs Comrs* [2005] SpC 500 supports the opposing view. The Special Commissioner found that an interest in possession did not exist where a will provided that the trustees were to permit a widow the use and enjoyment of the property 'for such period or periods as they shall in their absolute discretion think fit'. The widow did in fact occupy the property but the will provided that any income from the property was to be held upon the trusts of residue.

The use of the word 'normally' in Statement of Practice 10/79 is unhelpful. In response to correspondence from the STEP and the CIOT, HMRC have said that the circumstances in which it would not regard the exercise of the power by trustees to give an exclusive right of occupation as creating an interest in possession, would be rare. Instances where HMRC said that there might not be an interest in possession were where there was no evidence of an intention by the trustees to provide a particular beneficiary with a permanent home or where significant doubt about the trustees' intentions existed. HMRC also said that where there is evidence that trustees have knowingly exercised their powers so as to give a beneficiary exclusive occupation then an interest in possession will have been created and that the trustees themselves could reasonably form a view on this point if the relevant facts justified that conclusion.

The Debt Strategy, as it was known, was devised to avoid any difficulties where an estate did not have sufficient assets to satisfy a nil rate band legacy apart from the family home. In such a case the nil rate band legacy was satisfied by a debt from the surviving spouse or civil partner where the residuary estate has passed directly to them or was held on trust for them. To avoid the risk of a surviving spouse or civil partner having an interest in possession the debt was expressed to be repayable on demand. The strategy can be rendered ineffective where the estate of the first spouse to die contains assets derived from the surviving spouse. In *Phizackerley (Personal Representatives of Phizackerley deceased) v Revenue & Customs Comrs* [2007] SpC 591 the debt strategy failed because the debt was held not to be deductible under FA 1986, s 103 as the deceased's share in the family home had derived from her surviving husband. Where the surviving spouse has funded the purchase price of a property alone, the deceased's share in the property subject to the debt should be held on trust for a class of beneficial objects which include the surviving spouse. In that case, FA 1986, s 103 should not apply because the debt will not be incurred by the surviving spouse but by the trustees.

As mentioned above, because an unused nil rate band on the first death can be utilised by the surviving spouse on their death, it may seem that nil rate band discretionary trusts no longer need to be used. The freezing of the nil rate band until 2020/2021, however, has tilted the balance of advantage back towards utilising it on the first death. It will often still be appropriate to include in a will a provision to allow the deceased's interest in the family home to be utilised to ensure the nil rate band is fully used on the first death.

Another approach to the problem was to use a discretionary trust of which the surviving spouse was not a beneficial object. He or she would then rely on the right given to him or her by virtue of being a co-owner under a tenancy in common in respect of the remainder of the property in order to occupy the property. Even so, the efficacy of this route is doubtful in light of the decision in *IRC v Eversden (executors of Greenstock (dec'd))* [2003] EWCA Civ 668, [2003] STC 822, for, as Lightman J pointed out, since the enactment of TLATA 1996 a tenant in common no longer has an automatic right of occupation unless the conditions of s 12 of that Act are fulfilled. Furthermore, this strategy can bring other problems. First, it is arguable that the capital gains tax main residence relief will not be available in respect of the proportion of the property held in the discretionary trust (although, in practice, any liability on disposal may be small due to the uplift to market value that will have occurred on death). It is understood, however, that HMRC does not consider that s 12 prevents relief where trustees have the power to allow occupation under the terms of the trust. Secondly, there is the question as to whether the trustees are properly exercising their fiduciary obligations by retaining a proportion of a property which is not producing income and which is occupied by a non-beneficiary. For that reason, there is risk for the surviving spouse unless occupation of the property was secured by some form of tenancy agreement. The trustees may be under a duty to seek to force a sale of the property in order to realise the trust's interest in it by an application to the court under TLATA 1996, s 14 (see **11.2** above).

Often the deceased will prefer to leave his share of the family home directly to the next generation or in trust. It may be felt that the decision as to whether the property should be jointly owned is best left to the surviving spouse as the person directly involved and best placed to judge matters following the death.

The surviving spouse may decide to vary the dispositions of property devolving under the will or passing by survivorship within two years of death (IHTA 1984, s 142). For example, the surviving spouse may decide to give a share of the property equal in value to the deceased's unused part of the nil rate band to the next generation either outright or in trust by means of a deed of variation. Provided the instrument effecting the variation contains a statement that IHTA 1984, s 142 is to apply to it, the gift will be treated as if effected by the deceased. Even if the widow continues to occupy the property, there is no scope for the gift with reservation provisions contained in FA 1986, s 102 and Sch 20 to apply since, if a variation is made, the widow will be treated as not having made a gift within s 102(1). Neither is there scope for a POA charge to arise because by virtue of IHTA 1984, s 17, the disposition is not treated for the purposes of inheritance tax as a transfer of value by the chargeable person (FA 2004, Sch 15, para 16). If the share is subjected to trusts by the variation, however, the same issues arise as to whether an interest in possession is created as are discussed above.

Unmarried couples

[11.10] For unmarried couples, similar considerations apply to will drafting, but special care is needed when considering the payment of inheritance tax. As a spouse exemption is not available to unmarried couples, they must pay particular care as to how the inheritance tax can be paid by the surviving partner. If cash or other assets are not available, life insurance is generally the cheapest solution. However, it is important that the policy proceeds be written in trust for the survivor so that they do not form part of the deceased's estate thereby increasing the inheritance tax payable. In such a situation, care should be taken to ensure that the mortgage is deductible from the deceased's estate (see **3.37**).

There is also a trap for the unwary if the property is mortgaged and there is an endowment or mortgage protection policy. If such a policy is not written in trust the proceeds will form part of the deceased partner's estate for inheritance tax purposes. This may have two unexpected consequences. First more tax than would otherwise be the case may be payable so that the property may have to be sold in order to pay the tax. Secondly, the policy proceeds may fall into residue and pass to the wrong beneficiary either under the will or on intestacy. To ensure that the mortgage is deductible from the deceased's estate, see **3.37**.

Lifetime planning

[**11.11**] Lifetime planning for the family home has always been an area of estate planning fraught with difficulties. On the one hand, an individual wishes to give away all or part of the wealth represented by his home at a low or nil tax cost, and on the other he wishes to continue living in the property. Whilst potentially exempt transfers encourage lifetime planning as no immediate charge to tax arises, at the same time the gift with reservation provisions (FA 1986, s 102 and Sch 20) and the POA charge provisions (FA 2004, Sch 15) make it difficult for an individual to continue to live in the property and to give away some of the wealth represented by his home.

Any gift by an individual, including a gift of his home or an interest in it, is capable of constituting a potentially exempt transfer. No inheritance tax will be chargeable on a potentially exempt transfer unless the donor dies within seven years of making the gift. In the event of a transfer between three and seven years before death taper relief is available.

Capital gains tax will not be an issue in most cases involving the family home because of the availability of main residence relief.

In practice, nearly all lifetime planning for the family home tends to concern a gift to another individual, and only in exceptional circumstances will an individual wish to make a settlement of the family home.

Capital gains tax

[**11.12**] A gift is a disposal for capital gains tax purposes on which a chargeable gain may arise. A gain arising to an individual so far as it is attributable to a disposal of an interest in the whole or part of a dwelling-house which has been the disponer's only or main residence during his ownership period is wholly or partly exempt (TCGA 1992, s 222).

The relief is extended to land which the disponer has for his own occupation and enjoyment with that residence as its garden and grounds up to the amount of the 'permitted area'. The 'permitted area' is the larger of half a hectare and the area required for the reasonable enjoyment of the dwelling-house.

In recent years there has been an increase in the number of cases being heard before the First-tier Tribunal where HMRC has argued that a house was not a residence because its occupation did not have the requisite degree of permanence. In such cases the taxpayer's intention when moving into the property is closely examined by the Court.

For disposals made after 5 April 2015 the dwelling-house or part of a dwelling-house is not treated as being occupied as a residence by an individual at any time in his period of ownership which falls into a 'non-qualifying tax year or non-qualifying partial tax year'. A non-qualifying year is a fiscal year during an individual's period of ownership where neither the individual nor his spouse or civil partner is resident in the tax year in the territory in which the dwelling-house is situated and the individual does not meet the day count test for that year. The day count test is satisfied if the individual or his spouse or civil partner spends at least 90 days in one or more houses in the same territory in which either the individual or his spouse or civil partner has an interest in. A day is counted as spent at the house 'if the individual is present at the house at the end of the day or is present in the house for some period during the day and the next day, has stayed overnight in the house'.

Main residence relief will be available for the final 18-month period of ownership if the property has been the disponer's main residence for any part of his ownership of it. For disposals by disabled persons or long-term residents in care homes (or their spouses) unless an interest is held in another dwelling, the period is 36 months. In addition, certain permitted periods of absence will count as periods of occupation for the purposes of the relief.

Where an individual has two or more residences he can elect which is his main residence (TCGA 1992 s 222(5)). That election can only be made for a fiscal year which is not a non-qualifying tax year. This will mean that any gain attributable to a non-qualifying tax year is chargeable to capital gains tax when the property is sold. A UK resident individual will be charged to capital gains tax in respect of any non-qualifying tax years. A non-UK resident individual will be subject to capital gains tax on his non-resident capital gains tax disposal (see **11.40**).

Inheritance tax: gifts with reservation

[**11.13**] Before considering the planning opportunities available, it is necessary to consider the gifts with reservation provisions in order to understand the restrictions they place on planning in this area. This is discussed in more detail in CHAPTER 4 LIFETIME PLANNING: MAKING GIFTS.

Under FA 1986, s 102, where an individual makes a gift of property and either:

(a)   possession and enjoyment of the property is not bona fide assumed by the donee within seven years of the donor's death; or

(b)   at any time within the seven-year period the property is not enjoyed to the entire exclusion, or virtually to the entire exclusion, of the donor or of any benefit to the donor by contract or otherwise,

the property is said to be subject to a reservation, with the consequence that the property (or its traceable proceeds) will be brought into charge to tax when the donor dies as if he were still beneficially entitled to it at that time.

There are a number of exemptions to the application of this provision set out in s 102(5) but they are of limited relevance to an individual wishing to benefit anyone other than his spouse.

If the property ceases to be subject to a reservation, the donor is treated as making a potentially exempt transfer at the time of the cessation (FA 1986, s 102(4)).

Finance Act 1986, Sch 20, and in particular para 6, provides two further exemptions of importance in the case of gifts of interests in land. First, the donor may retain or assume actual occupation of land or actual possession of a chattel in return for full consideration in money or money's worth. This is a valuable concession which will be considered in **11.17**. Secondly, an exemption may apply where the donor has made a gift of a property to a relative, or to a relative of his spouse or civil partner, in circumstances which did not give rise to a reservation of benefit, but subsequently comes to re-occupy it as a result of an unforeseen and unplanned change in the circumstances of the donor. Provided that at the time concerned the donor has become unable to maintain himself through old age, infirmity or any other reason and his occupation represents reasonable provision by the donee for his care and maintenance, his re-occupation will be disregarded in determining whether the property is subject to a reservation.

Example

> Henry, on retiring to the country, gave a house in London to his son, Charles. Henry subsequently became infirm through ill-health, which resulted in him no longer being able to look after himself. If he had moved back into the house and lived with Henry, provided his re-occupation represented reasonable provision by Henry for the care of his father, no gift with reservation would have arisen. The arrangement will, however, be subject to the POA charge under FA 2004, Sch 15, even though Henry's re-occupation of the house in London was unforeseen and notwithstanding that it represented reasonable provision by Charles for the care of his father. If Henry does nothing, he will be assessed to income tax on an amount equal to the market rent of the property. There are, however, steps he can take to mitigate this income tax liability. These are considered in more detail in **11.14** below.

The gifts with reservation provisions make it very difficult for a person to remove property from his taxable estate whilst continuing to occupy it whether his occupation is long-term under some form of tenancy or other binding arrangement entered into by the donee or merely intermittent under a gratuitous licence of the donee. Clearly, the use of the word 'virtually' in FA 1986, s 102(1)(b) is designed to prevent merely occasional visits by a donor to the donee from tainting the original gift (see HMRC Inheritance Tax Manual, para 14333). HMRC's view on how the word 'virtually' is to be interpreted is discussed in detail in CHAPTER 4 LIFETIME PLANNING: MAKING GIFTS under **4.28**.

Income tax charge on pre-owned assets

[**11.14**] This income tax charge (the 'POA charge') is discussed in detail in CHAPTER 4 LIFETIME PLANNING: MAKING GIFTS, but in relation to tax planning for the family home, there are some specific points which should be made. First, the POA charge will not arise in circumstances in which a reservation of benefit has arisen. If it were not for this provision, arrangements might create an annual income tax charge on the family home as well as an inheritance tax charge on the value of the property following the death of the donor. In order to prevent this double charge, the POA provisions provide an exemption for property which is subject to a reservation (FA 2004, Sch 15, para 11(5)(a)). As is illustrated in **11.13** above, there will be situations in which a gift may have been validly made in the past under which no reservation of benefit has arisen, but which may now (or at some point in the future) be caught by the POA charge.

Broadly, the POA charge will arise in a situation where an individual (the chargeable person) occupies any land (referred to as the 'relevant land'), whether alone or together with other persons, and either the 'disposal condition' or the 'contribution condition' is met in respect of the relevant land.

The 'disposal condition' is met in circumstances in which, at any time after 17 March 1986, the chargeable person

- owned an interest in the relevant land (or in other property the proceeds of which were directly or indirectly applied by another person towards the acquisition of an interest in the relevant land), and
- disposed of all, or part of, his interest in the relevant land or the other property, otherwise than by an excluded transaction.

The 'contribution condition' is met in circumstances in which, at any time after 17 March 1986, the chargeable person has (directly or indirectly) provided, otherwise than by an excluded transaction, any of the consideration given by another person for the acquisition of:

- an interest in the relevant land, or
- an interest in any other property, the proceeds of the disposal of which were (directly or indirectly) applied by another person towards the acquisition of an interest in the relevant land.

In the example given in **11.13** above, the father, having made a gift to his son which is not subject to a reservation of benefit, will, on moving back into the house in London to live with his son, fulfil the disposal condition in relation to that house.

Example

Adopting the facts in the previous example, if, instead of giving the house directly to his son, the donor, Henry, had sold the house and given the proceeds of sale to his son, Charles, then the situation would be slightly different. If Charles had subsequently used the proceeds from the London house and aggregated them with a further sum of his own money to purchase a new property, on Henry moving in with Charles due to illness, the contribution condition would have been met in relation to the new property and a POA charge would have arisen on Henry. Since Henry had given Charles an outright gift of cash, the charge would only arise if Henry had moved in with Charles within seven years of the date of the gift. Provided that the earliest date on which Henry occupied the house was more than seven years after the gift, the disposal would be an excluded transaction for the purposes of the charge.

Advisers need to consider the POA provisions in relation, not just to tax planning steps which their clients may now wish to undertake, but also in relation to tax planning which their clients have undertaken in the past and which has been in place for many years. In the above example, if we suppose that Henry made the gift to Charles in 1988, and moved in with Charles in the year 2000 without suffering any adverse tax consequences, there is a danger that Henry would not realise that he would now be liable to income tax. An adviser should therefore carry out a detailed fact-find going back at least to 17 March 1986 and earlier if possible. Undoubtedly there will be many people who are now subject to a POA charge in relation to gifts they have made in the past, without any tax avoidance motivation, without their being aware of that fact.

The POA charge is based on the appropriate rental value of the relevant land less any payments which, in pursuance of any legal obligation, are made by the chargeable person to the owner of the relevant land in respect of the occupation of the land by the chargeable person. It is important to note that it is only payments under a legal obligation which are deductible from the rental value. This means that any payments made informally will not count. A chargeable person may mitigate his liability to the POA charge by paying a full market rent for the period of occupation under a legal obligation. By so doing, the amount on which the POA charge is assessed is reduced to zero.

Example

Again adopting the facts in the example in 11.13 and assuming that Henry was 44 at the time he made the gift in 1988 and so that he was 61 on 6 April 2005, and, notwithstanding his illness, we shall assume that he was expected to live to the age of 75 and intended to live with Charles for the rest of his life.

If we assume that the house will be worth £2,000,000 at the time of his death and that his available nil rate band is used up by legacies under his will, then, at current rates, the gift of the house to Charles will save him £800,000 in inheritance tax. If the annual rental value of the property is £160,000 and Henry has been and will continue to be a higher rate taxpayer (but not an additional rate taxpayer), he will have paid and will continue to pay £64,000 (£160,000 at 40%) annually in income tax from 6 April 2005. As he is expected to live 14 years after the imposition of the POA charge, he will have paid (assuming that the current rental value does not increase) £448,000 in income tax in order to save £400,000 of inheritance tax.

If, instead of being 61, Henry had been 81 years of age on 6 April 2005, and he had then been expected to live to the age of 86, so he had actually died in 2010, then the income tax he would have paid over the period to his death would have been (£32,000 × 5 = £160,000) in order to save £400,000 of inheritance tax.

If Henry could afford to pay a full market rent to Charles then, provided there is a formal tenancy agreement between them, Henry would have no income tax liability in respect of his occupation of the property, although of course, Charles would be charged to income tax on the rent. This may be an effective way of passing further value out of Henry's estate by reducing it by the amount of the rent paid.

If the chargeable person can neither afford to pay the income tax nor a full market rent, then he may consider making an election under FA 2004, Sch 15, para 21. A chargeable person may make an election which will have the result that the POA provisions will not apply to him but, in return, for as long as the chargeable person continues to occupy the relevant land, he will be treated as having a reservation of benefit in that property. Any such election must be made in the prescribed manner determined by regulations (on Form IHT500) by 31 January in the year of assessment that immediately follows the initial year of assessment (FA 2004, Sch 16, para 23(1)). The 'initial year' is any year of assessment in which, but for the election, a person would be chargeable by reference to his enjoyment of the relevant property, provided that he has not been chargeable under the relevant provision in respect of that property (or any other property for which it has been substituted) in any previous year of assessment (FA 2004, Sch 15, para 21(1)). This means that for people who find themselves subject to the POA charge for the first time in 2016/17, the relevant filing date is 31 January 2018. Where an election is made, the result will be that the relevant land will be deemed to be subject to a reservation of benefit (irrespective of whether or not a reservation of benefit would otherwise arise) and the value of the asset will be brought back within the donor's estate for inheritance tax purposes. However, for capital gains tax purposes and income tax purposes, the relevant land will be treated as belonging to the donee. Once made, an election cannot be withdrawn (unless it is withdrawn before the relevant filing date) and the deemed reservation of benefit will continue for so long as the chargeable person continues to enjoy the land.

Clients who find themselves caught by the POA charge which they cannot or do not wish to pay, may take steps to 'undo' the tax planning undertaken. In many circumstances, this will simply not be possible or, where it is possible, it is likely to be costly.

Another possibility for those clients wishing to avoid the charge is to move out of the property. Finally, the client may attempt to go back to square one.

Example

> In the circumstances outlined in **11.13** above, Charles may consider transferring the land back to his father, Henry. In addition to the transaction costs, Charles will have made a potentially exempt transfer for the purposes of inheritance tax and, should he die within seven years of making the transfer, the value of the property would form part of his estate for inheritance tax purposes. Charles could take out a policy of life assurance to cover this risk.

Strategies

[11.15] Over the years a number of strategies have emerged which were of practical relevance to an individual whose wealth was tied up in his home. They attempted to enable him to unlock some of this wealth whilst continuing to live in the home. Of course, these strategies have been challenged by HMRC and in cases where it was unsuccessful legislation was introduced to nullify their tax effects. In addition, in an attempt to stop people from using them legislation has been introduced which has reduced the benefits of various strategies. Below we deal with a number of arrangements which may still be appropriate for some individuals to adopt.

The four strategies are:

(a)   co-ownership;
(b)   use of the 'full consideration' exemption;
(c)   sale at full value; and
(d)   the use of cash gifts.

Co-ownership

[11.16] This involves the donor making a gift of an undivided share in land so that, after the gift, the donor and the donee share ownership and occupation of the property. A common application of this is where a parent who solely owns their own property transfers an interest in the property to a child or close relative who either takes up occupation or continues occupying the property. Finance Act 1986, s 102B(2) provides that all gifts by an individual of an undivided share of an interest in land are gifts with reservation, subject to two exceptions.

One of these exceptions is found in FA 1986, s 102B(4) which provides that there is no gift with reservation of benefit where the donor and donee occupy the land and the donor does not receive any benefit other than a negligible one which is provided by or at the expense of the donee for some reason connected with the gift. Where there is some collateral arrangement (ie an agreement that the donee should pay more than a proportionate share of the running costs), this will amount to a benefit to the donor 'by contract or otherwise'.

Where the donor and donee so occupy the land within the exception found in FA 1986, s 102B(4), there is no reservation of benefit and the pre-owned assets provisions must be considered. Under FA 2004, Sch 15, para 11(3)(a), there will be a complete exemption from the charge.

Beneficial interests may be conferred by the original owner entering into a declaration of trust specifying in what proportions the beneficial interests are to be shared; and in the case of a sole owner (eg a surviving spouse) one or more other members of the family, or a professional adviser, should be appointed as co-trustee of the legal title to ensure there are at least two (Law of Property Act 1925, s 27(2)) but not more than four trustees of land (Trustee Act 1925, s 34(1)). A gift of the beneficial interest will constitute a 'potentially exempt transfer' for inheritance tax purposes.

The question often arises as to what percentage should be given away. Although it is possible to give away 99% because the remaining 1% will still entitle the donor to occupy the property, it may not be advisable to do so. It used to be the case that HMRC accepted that a property could be held in unequal shares; for example, a mother could retain a 10% interest in a property and give away 45% to each of her two sons. It is understood that HMRC now consider that no greater share can be given than equates to the number of co-owners and will routinely investigate a gift greater than such an equal share (HMRC Inheritance Tax Manual, para 14332). For the reasons explained in CHAPTER 2, the adviser must also be cautious of arousing the irrational hostility of HMRC and of the application of the GAAR to such arrangements.

The donor must bear at least his proportionate share of the maintenance and running costs of the property. A distinction should be drawn between capital expenditure and running costs. Capital expenditure should be borne in proportion to ownership whereas running costs should be borne in proportion to occupation. Where a donor and donee have equal shares, the donor should bear a proportion of the costs at least equal to his percentage interest in the property so that the donor does not receive a benefit from the donee arising out of the gift.

Finance Act 2004, Sch 15, para 11(5)(c) provides that if property would fall to be treated as property which is subject to a reservation but for FA 1986, s 102B(4), the POA charge will not apply. Therefore the POA charge will not apply to co-ownership arrangements exempted from the inheritance tax reservation of benefit rules by s 102B(4).

A problem will arise if and when any one or more of the donees decides to move out of the property. If the donor continues to occupy the entire property, the gifts to the donees who move out will become gifts with reservation and this will largely defeat their original purpose. Where the gifts become subject to a reservation in this way, the donor's occupation of the property will be completely exempt for the purposes of the POA provisions.

Use of the 'full consideration' exemption

[11.17] The second exception is found in FA 1986, s 102B(3) which provides that in the event that one of the joint owners does not occupy the property, there will not be a gift with reservation if the donor pays full consideration for his occupation.

An individual might give away his home entirely and enter into an arrangement with the donee which allows him to continue living there. The arrangement might take the form of either a lease or a licence depending on the circumstances. What is important is that the occupation is for full consideration in money or money's worth (FA 1986, Sch 20, para 6(1)(a)). It is understood that HMRC accepts that if the terms are the result of a bargain negotiated at arm's length with the parties being independently advised and follow the normal commercial criteria in force at the time they are negotiated, the condition of FA 1986, Sch 20, para 6(1)(a) will be satisfied. The provisions of FA 1986, s 102A explained in 11.50–11.51 below contain similar provisions to para 6(1)(a) allowing a donor to occupy property for full consideration (FA 1986, s 102A(3)).

The terms of the agreement and the amount of any rent or licence fee would also be an important commercial consideration. 'Full consideration' implies, in the case of a tenancy, an open market rent. As full consideration is required throughout the period, the rent paid must be periodically reviewed. HMRC does, however, recognise that there is no single value at which consideration can be fixed as 'full' (Revenue Interpretation RI55).

For the purposes of the POA charge, the payment of full consideration (ie the full market rent) is likely to reduce the chargeable amount to nil under FA 2004, Sch 15, para 4, provided that the payments are made in pursuance of a legal obligation. It would therefore be advisable to draw up a tenancy agreement so as to ensure that the amounts paid are deductible.

An alternative to charging an open market rent would be to grant a lease, for example a long lease with a term of at least 21 years at a peppercorn rent but at a market premium. As the lease would normally be for less than 50 years, a part of the premium would attract an income tax charge at a rate of up to 45% depending on the donee's marginal rate of income tax. The lease would be within the terms of the Local Government and Housing Act 1989, Sch 10 which would give the donor, or if he had died in the meantime, his successor, the right to continue in occupation after the lease expired. In addition, the Leasehold Reform Act 1967 might give the donor the right to buy back the freehold on favourable terms.

One would need to consider the matter further if the decrease in the value of the freehold due to the grant of the lease exceeded the market premiums under the lease.

The clear disadvantages of this type of arrangement from the donor's point of view are, first, the payment (out of net income or capital) of the rent or any premium and, secondly, that the lease itself may be a valuable asset in the donor's estate. Whether this is an acceptable price to pay for the ability to divest his estate of a capital asset free of inheritance tax will depend on individual circumstances.

There is a further disadvantage under the POA provisions for an arrangement involving the payment of a premium. The gift of the freehold interest would meet the disposal condition in FA 2004, Sch 15, para 3(2) for so long as the donor continued to occupy under the terms of the lease and the donor would, accordingly, be subject to income tax on the rental value of the property, notwithstanding the payment of the premium. This is because, for each year of assessment in which the POA provisions apply in respect of a property, the only payments which are permitted deductions against the charge to income tax are those made pursuant to a legal obligation in that year of assessment (FA 2004, Sch 15, para 4(1)). Accordingly, in the year the premium is paid, it can be deducted from the appropriate rental value for that period but, in the following periods, no deduction will be permitted.

Sale at full value

[11.18] It may be possible for parents to sell their home for its full value to their children, thus ensuring that any future capital appreciation accrues to the children. The money may be raised by way of a qualifying loan to reduce the purchase price, with the parents paying full rent against which the children's interest liability could be set. This should avoid the gift with reservation of benefit problems because there would be no disposal by way of gift. It should also avoid the POA charge provided that the terms of the sale are such that might be expected to be made at arm's length between persons not connected with each other. If this proviso is met, the disposal will be an excluded transaction for the purposes of the POA provisions and no POA charge will arise (FA 2004, Sch 15, para 10(1)(a)). However, there are problems with security of tenure and there will be stamp duty land tax on the sale by the parents to the children. In addition, main residence relief is unlikely to be available on the ultimate sale by the children.

There is a further difficulty where there is a part disposal of an interest to a connected person; for example, a son buying a 25% interest in his father's property, This is because such a transaction is not an excluded transaction under FA 2004, Sch 15, para 11. In such circumstances there is a charge on the 'benefit' obtained by the father from his continued occupation being a proportion of the market value rent.

Equity release schemes

[11.19] There are two main types of equity release scheme, namely lifetime mortgages and home reversion schemes. With the former, a loan is granted to an individual and the interest accrues until the property is sold or the individual dies. The home reversion scheme involves an individual selling a share or the whole of their property to a provider and a lease for life being granted back to the individual at a nil rent. This type of scheme is only available to people who are aged 65 or older.

When the POA legislation was introduced there was a concern that equity release schemes involving a part disposal would not be excluded transactions under FA 2004, Sch 15, para 10. The Charge to Income Tax by Reference to Enjoyment of Property Previously Owned Regulations 2005 (SI 2005/724), reg 5(1)(a) provides that no POA charge will arise in relation to a disposal of part of an interest in any property if the disposal was by a transaction made at arm's length with a person not connected with him. In addition, a charge will not arise in relation to a disposal of part of an interest in any property if the disposal was by a transaction such as might be expected to be made at arm's length between persons not connected with each other and:

(a) the disposal was for a consideration not in money or in the form of readily convertible assets; or

(b) the disposal was made before 7 March 2005 (SI 2005/724, reg 5(1)(b)).

Evidence will be, as is often the case, crucial in the matter.

The use of cash gifts

[11.20] It seems that the most effective form of planning, for both the reservation of benefit and the POA provisions, will be gifts of cash. Provided that the cash is applied to purchase a property which the donor does not occupy until at least seven years after the gift, there will be no POA charge.

Example

In April 2009, a father gave £250,000 cash to his son. The son used the cash to purchase a house in London. In May 2016, the father moved in with his son in the London house and paid no rent. There was no POA charge.

If the donor wishes to make a gift of cash to enable another person to buy a property, careful consideration should be given to structuring the gift.

Example

> A father gives his daughter £20,000 towards the purchase of a flat worth £270,000. The remainder of the purchase price is met by way of a mortgage. The daughter spends £10,000 on furnishing the flat.
>
> If the father moves into the flat within seven years of making the gift, a POA charge will arise.

If, however, the gift were applied in a different way, the result would be different.

Example

> The daughter purchases the flat using her savings and raising the balance of the purchase price by way of mortgage. Following the purchase, the father gives his daughter £20,000 to spend on furnishing the flat. After six years, the father moves into the property. No POA charge will arise.

In the second example, the gift of cash is not used as any part of the consideration for the purchase of an interest in land. Provided there was no prior arrangement in place that the gift would be made, the gift could not be an indirect contribution towards the consideration for the acquisition of an interest in land.

Other considerations

[11.21] Before embarking on any tax planning affecting the family home, the beneficial ownership of the property should be clarified together with whether there is an outstanding mortgage. A transfer of the ownership of the property subject to a mortgage will require the consent of the mortgagee and may also trigger a charge to stamp duty land tax to the extent of the mortgaged debt if liability is assumed.

Capital gains tax

[11.22] The capital gains tax consequences of any gift of land (or of an interest in land) have to be carefully considered. In relation to the donor's only or main residence there is unlikely to be a problem because any gain arising on the gift is likely to be exempt under TCGA 1992, s 222 as a gain arising on a disposal of a main residence. As the tribunal decisions demonstrate, HMRC is challenging more main residence relief claims. Where the gift relates to a home where main residence relief is not, or is not wholly, applicable, a chargeable gain will arise which can only be held-over if the gift constitutes a chargeable transfer for inheritance tax purposes (TCGA 1992, s 260). Generally, this will only be where the gift is a gift to a relevant property settlement.

If a charge to capital gains tax which cannot be held-over does arise, then the tax may be paid by ten equal annual instalments (TCGA 1992, s 281), although interest on the tax will run from the date the tax is payable (TCGA 1992, s 281(5)).

In relation to a second home, it may be possible depending upon the circumstances to mitigate the capital gains tax charge by electing, under TCGA 1992, s 222(5)(a), for the second home to be treated as the donor's main residence for the 18 months immediately preceding the gift, providing the fiscal year is not a non-qualifying year, although this may result in there being a charge on any later sale or gift of the donor's other property.

Summary and other points

[11.23] In addition to the arrangements discussed in this chapter, the following, rather more obvious but no less effective, options should always be considered in respect of inheritance tax planning and the family home.

(a)   *Move to a smaller home.* Perhaps the most efficient step that can be taken is to sell the property, move to somewhere smaller and thereby realise some of the accumulated capital value. This creates two assets - the new home and a capital gains tax free cash sum that can be given away. This option is likely to be viable only where one's children have reached adulthood and have left home.

(b)   *Reduce the value of the home by mortgage.* If a couple are reluctant to move, but still wish to give away during their lifetime some of the accumulated value of their home, they may be able to do so by borrowing against its value and giving away the proceeds. This is only feasible if there are sufficient funds available from other sources to service the borrowing and it should be borne in mind that the interest payments will not be deductible in computing the borrower's assessable income. On death the outstanding mortgage debt will be deductible for inheritance tax purposes, although, of course, the debt itself will still have to be met by the estate.

(c)   *Equity release scheme.* This is a variation on the theme above and is discussed above. This option is usually expensive.

Where the donors are prepared to give away a property (for example, a second home) and not to occupy it again, then the inheritance tax position is, by comparison, straightforward; but as we have seen the capital gains tax position may be more complicated.

As in all lifetime planning, but especially in the case of the family home, the primary concern will be for the security of the owner or owners — tax saving should always take second place to that. For this reason, lifetime estate planning for the family home is often very limited in scope.

Residential property held by a company

[11.24] Although the majority of individuals will own a family home and other residential property directly, some will, however, own their homes indirectly through a trust or corporate structure. Typically, non-domiciliaries often own UK property through such an arrangement in order that the value of their UK home be outside the charge to UK inheritance tax (see **11.32**). That, of course, will no longer be the case once the proposed legislative changes discussed in **11.32–11.38** are enacted in the Finance Act 2017. Other individuals may own their family home or other residential property through a corporate structure to avoid an SDLT charge, the idea being that instead of purchasing the property, the shares of the company owning the property are purchased, that would either attract a 0.5% rate of stamp duty reserve tax if it was a UK company or no SDRT if it were an overseas company. There are other reasons for using some form of corporate holding structure, namely avoiding UK probate and for reasons connected with other jurisdictions. Some clients may hold residential property through a company because of the phased introduction of restrictions for individuals in deducting the cost of interest payments on dwelling-related loans. Holding residential property through a corporate structure can result in the imposition of various tax charges which are discussed below.

Income tax charge

[11.25] An individual may incur a tax liability under ITEPA 2003, ss 97, 102 as these sections treat the value of any living accommodation provided to an employee (including a director of a company) or a member of his family or household by his employer as earnings.

Living accommodation provided to an employee or director, including a shadow director, is deemed to be provided by reason of his actual or deemed employment (ITEPA 2003, s 97(2)). Under ITEPA 2003, s 67(1) a person in accordance with whose directions or instructions the directors of a company are accustomed to act is deemed to be a director of that company. Such persons are commonly referred to as shadow directors.

In *R v Dimsey; R v Allen* [2001] UKHL 45, [2002] 1 AC 509, [2001] 4 All ER 786, it was argued by the defendant that because a shadow director has no 'actual emoluments' and no 'actual duties', he would not have an employment falling within the earnings from employment provisions with the result that the provision now found in ITEPA 2003, s 67(1) would not apply to him. This argument was rejected. It was held that a shadow director is taxable on the benefit of living accommodation in the same way as a director under ICTA 1988, ss 145 and 154 (now ITEPA 2003, ss 97–113) which provided that the benefit was an emolument of the director's office. It is clear that all earnings from employment provisions apply to shadow directors.

In the non-tax case of *Secretary of State for Trade and Industry v Deverall* [2000] 2 WLR 987, it was suggested that the shadow director test was even wider than had been thought up until then. It was suggested that a person can be a shadow director if he simply made suggestions to the formal board which were followed through even if the suggestions did not cover the whole activities of the company. It would seem, however, that the width of this principle has been restricted by *Ultraframe (UK) Ltd v Fielding* [2005] EWHC 1638 (Ch), [2005] All ER (D) 397 (Jul). In that case it was held that for a person to be classified as a shadow director there must be some substantive course of influence or instruction given or exercised by the individual to the actual board of directors over a period of time regarding substantive matters.

The relief from the employment benefit charge provided in relation to foreign accommodation by ITEPA 2003, ss 100A and 100B only applies to overseas property and not to UK property.

Does that mean that using offshore companies to hold UK property for occupancy by non-UK domiciled but resident individuals will necessarily result in their being assessed on a benefit in kind? No, it does not. *Dimsey* concerned a situation in which it had been found as a fact by the High Court that the defendants had centrally managed and controlled the offshore company in the UK. The defendants were, therefore, clearly shadow directors. There can be no assessment unless an individual resident in the UK is a person in accordance with whose instructions or directions the directors of the company are accustomed to act. Any reputable offshore company management business will ensure that they do not simply accept instructions from shareholders or follow their advice without independent thought or enquiry.

The taxpayer will have added protection on this point if the offshore company is in turn owned by an offshore trust in which he has only a limited interest. Even so, HMRC may still argue that the company's board acts in accordance with the taxpayer's instructions.

Provided the property is held in an excluded property trust, the POA charge cannot arise (see **21.78** for more explanation).

The annual tax on enveloped dwellings (the ATED charge)

[11.26] The Annual Tax on Enveloped Dwellings (ATED) has its own rules found in FA 2013, ss 94–174. Essentially, residential property purchased in excess of £500,000 by a non-natural person (NNP) will be subject to an annual charge. Tax will be charged where loosely a company, partnership with a corporate member or collective investment scheme, has an interest in a single dwelling in the UK with a value in excess of £500,000 as at 1 April 2016 or on acquisition if the property is acquired after that date (FA 2013, s 94). In relation to partnerships, the ATED will apply to the whole value of the property irrespective of the size of the corporate member's interest. It would seem that where a property is held jointly by a company and another person, the ATED applies to the whole interest and not just the company's share. The ATED does not apply to nominee companies or trustees.

A dwelling is defined in FA 2013, s 112, with certain types of property being deemed specifically not to be dwellings (FA 2013, s 112(4)). Where a property consists of a number of self-contained flats, each flat will usually be valued separately. However, where two or more dwellings within a property have internal access between them and are owned by a person or a company connected to the NNP the value of the dwellings will be aggregated. Where different interests in the same property are owned by connected persons, those interests will be aggregated except where the company interest is valued at less than £250,000.

The charge

[11.27] An annual tax charge will arise for a chargeable period where two conditions are satisfied. The first is that a single-dwelling interest in a UK dwelling exists with a taxable value greater than £500,000, and secondly, that a company, partnership or collective investment scheme meets the ownership condition in relation to that interest. A chargeable period begins on 1 April. If the chargeable person is not within the charge on the first day of the chargeable period, because for example a property is acquired during the year, then the charge is the relevant fraction of the annual chargeable amount.

The annual chargeable amount is based on the band into which the taxable value of the interest falls on the relevant day (see below) and is determined in accordance with the table below.

Property value	Annual charge for 2016/17
More than £500,000 but not more than £1 million	£3,500
More than £1 million but not more than £2 million	£7,000
More than £2 million but not more than £5 million	£23,350
More than £5 million but not more than £10 million	£54,450
More than £10 million but not more than £20 million	£109,050
More than £20 million	£218,200

The annual charge will be indexed to the Consumer Price Index (CPI) and updated in April each year based upon the CPI of the previous September subject to an overriding provision in the Finance Bill.

As mentioned above, although the tax is payable for the whole year it is only due for the period during which the property is owned by the NNP. This means that if the property is disposed of during the year a claim for a refund can be made. If a dwelling is acquired during the year, a return and indeed payment must be made within 30 days of the first day on which the NNP is chargeable. Where a new dwelling or dwellings are acquired, the period is 90 days. The tax is payable in advance and is due by 30 April in the year of assessment unless any transitional rules apply.

Exemptions

[11.28] There are some exemptions from the charge, in which case no ATED return needs to be submitted. Charitable companies are exempt providing the property is held by the company for qualifying charitable purposes (FA 2013, s 151). An interest is held for qualifying charitable purposes if it is to be held for use in furtherance of the charitable purposes of the charitable company or of another charity or as an investment from which the profits are (or are to be) applied to the charitable purposes of the charitable company.

A public body (as defined in FA 2003, s 66) and bodies established for national purposes are both regarded as not being companies for the purposes of the ATED (FA 2013, ss 153 and 154). National heritage property satisfying IHTA 1984, ss 30 and 31 is effectively exempt from the ATED because its value is deemed to be zero provided no chargeable event has occurred (FA 2013, s 155).

Reliefs

[11.29] Various reliefs are available which have to be claimed through the submission of a relief declaration return. Relief is available for dwellings falling into the following categories:

(a) property open to the public for at least 28 days per year as a commercial business with a significant proportion of the interior open to the public (FA 2013, s 137);

(b) property let to a third party on a commercial basis and not occupied at any time by a non-qualifying individual, for example, a person connected to the owner (FA 2013, s 133);

(c) property acquired as part of a property developer's trade to develop and sell on and which is not occupied by a non-qualifying individual (FA 2013, s 138);

(d) property which is held as part of a property trading business and which is not occupied by a non-qualifying individual (FA 2013, s 141);

(e) property acquired by a financial institution in the course of lending (FA 2013, s 143);

(f) property used by employees or qualifying partners of the company which owns the property in the course of the company's trade or qualifying property rental business provided the employee does not have an interest in the company of 10% or more (FA 2013, s 145);

(g) a farmhouse occupied by a farm worker for the purposes of the trade or a former long-serving farm worker or their surviving spouse or civil partner (FA 2013, s 148);

(h) property owned by a provider of social housing (FA 2013, s 150);

(i) property held exclusively for the purposes of entering into a regulated home reversion plan (FA 2013, s 144A); or

(j) property where a tenant's management company permits one of the flats in the building to be occupied by a person employed to act as a caretaker of the premises (FA 2013, s 147A).

Relief will be withdrawn where a non-qualifying individual (as defined in FA 2013, s 136) is permitted to occupy the dwelling or in fact occupies it (FA 2013, s 135). Legislation will deem relief to be denied for up to two years retrospectively and up to three years prospectively.

Stamp duty land tax charge

[11.30] The purchase of single residential dwellings for more than £500,000 ('a higher threshold interest') by certain NNPs will be subject to SDLT at the rate of 15% (FA 2003, Sch 4A, para 3). The rate applies where the purchaser is a company or the acquisition is made by or on behalf of members of a partnership, one or more of whose members is a company or the acquisition is made for the purposes of a collective investment scheme (FA 2003, Sch 4A, para 3(3)). This 15% rate does not apply to purchases made by trusts or companies acting in their capacity as a trustee of a settlement (FA 2003, Sch 4A, para 3(4)).

The legislation sets out the rules for determining what counts as a dwelling in FA 2003, Sch 4A, para 7. A building or part of a building is a dwelling if it is used or suitable for use as a single dwelling, and includes the garden, grounds and outbuildings. A 'single dwelling' is not defined but it is HMRC's view that a dwelling has its normal meaning and will comprise a distinct unit of residential property (ATED Technical Guidance para. 19.1). It should be remembered that a building although not used as a dwelling may count as one if it is suitable for use as such.

There are reliefs available which are similar to those which apply to the ATED (see **11.29**) but there are material differences between them. A discussion of these lies outside the scope of this work.

Where the purchase is not subject to the higher SDLT rate of 15%, the purchase by a company may, in any event, be subject to an additional SDLT rate of 3% on what is called a 'higher rate transaction' (FA 2003, Sch 4ZA).

ATED-related capital gains tax charge

[11.31] Capital gains tax at 28% will be payable by any person, who is liable for the ATED who is not an excluded person, on an ATED-related chargeable gain arising on a relevant high value disposal (TCGA 1992, s 2B). It will be payable in respect of a gain realised on the disposal of a high value property held by a NNP (whether or not UK resident), where the property has been within the scope of ATED for one or more days during the period of ownership.

For the purposes of the charge the value of property held at 6 April 2013 is automatically rebased to its market value as at that date.

Gains subject to the special charge on ATED-related chargeable gains are not taken into account in determining chargeable gains accruing under TCGA 1992, ss 13, 86 or 87. Any losses that arise will only be available for set-off against gains arising under TCGA 1992, s 2B.

UK residential property held by non-UK domiciliaries

[11.32] As mentioned above, it has been common for persons domiciled outside the UK (and not deemed domiciled for inheritance tax purposes) to hold UK property (including residential property) through a non-UK resident company which, in turn, was held by a non-UK resident trust. In this way, the trust would hold excluded property (the shares in the company) and would be outside the relevant property regime. Whereas if the trust had held the residential property directly it would have held UK situated property which would not have been excluded property and which would, therefore, be chargeable to inheritance tax. What is more, the gift with reservation of benefit rules would be overridden by the trust's excluded property status and the shares would not form part of the individual's estate on death.

In his Summer 2015 Budget, the then Chancellor announced his intention to 'bring all UK residential property held directly or indirectly by foreign domiciled persons into charge for inheritance tax purposes, even when the property is owned through an indirect structure, such as an offshore company or partnership.'

In the Consultation Document entitled 'Reforms to the Taxation of Non-Domiciles: Further Consultation', published on 18 August 2016 (the 'ConDoc') the Government has, for the first time, consulted on the proposal to charge inheritance tax on UK residential property. Published with the ConDoc was draft legislation on which the following narrative is based. It should be noted that the front page of the draft legislation says that 'the legislation published in this document is not intended to be complete and excludes some issues which will be included in the Finance Bill 2017'.

The Government proposes to achieve its stated purpose by removing UK residential properties owned indirectly through offshore structures from the definition of 'excluded property' found in IHTA 1984, ss 6 and 48. The draft legislation provides that property will not be excluded property 'if, or to the extent that, its value is attributable to a chargeable interest that is exclusively in or over land which consists of a dwelling at that time or consisted of a dwelling at any time in the period of two years ending with that time'. The effect being that shares in offshore close companies and similar entities will no longer be excluded property if, and to the extent that, the value of any interest in the entity derived directly or indirectly from UK residential property. There will be no change to the treatment of companies other than close companies and 'similar entities'. It may be possible, therefore, for investments in UK residential property to be pooled so that a company is not a close company. Where a non-domiciled individual is a member of an overseas partnership which holds UK residential property, that property will no longer be treated as excluded property for the purposes of inheritance tax.

This will also mean that such property held through a trust company structure would be subject to the relevant property regime and exit charges under IHTA 1984, s 65 and the decennial charge under IHTA 1984, s 64 will apply. In addition, the gift with reservation of benefit rules will apply in relation to settlor interested trusts.

Definition of 'UK residential property'

[**11.33**] The Government, fortunately, has chosen not to introduce yet another definition of dwelling for inheritance tax purposes. The ConDoc states that the Government is attracted to using the definition found in the non-resident capital gains tax ('NRCGT') provisions (**11.44**), although 'it has been necessary to make amendments to ensure that the extended IHT charge applies to all UK dwellings as it is intended. This is reflected in the draft legislation published as part of this document.' The published draft legislation, however, actually refers to the ATED definition (**11.26**) and not the NRCGT one. At the time of writing, it is understood that it is likely that the NRCGT definition will be used in the enacted legislation. It is also understood that, for inheritance tax purposes, no relief will be given if the UK residential property is let on a commercial basis.

A property will be within the charge to inheritance tax where it has been a dwelling at any time in the preceding two-year period. Provided the property has wholly or partly met the definition of a dwelling at any time in the previous two years, it will be chargeable to inheritance tax. The liability which arises will be determined by the extent to which the property has a residential use. There is, however, a difficulty with the current definition, as the example illustrates.

Example

Aloysius owned a Jersey company, Flyte Limited, the sole asset of which is Grove House. Flyte Limited purchased Grove House on 23 August 2016, at which time it was a residential property. The following day builders started converting the residential property into small office units which were let out from 1 February 2017. Aloysius died on 29 April 2018. On the basis of the draft legislation, UK inheritance tax will be payable on the shares in Flyte Limited. This is because, in the previous two years, Grove House had been from 29 April 2016 until 23 August 2016 residential property. Even though Grove House had not been used as residential property during Flyte Limited's ownership of it inheritance tax would be chargeable. It is understood that this issue has been raised with HMRC and it is possible that this will be amended.

Chargeable events

[11.34] The proposed legislation will apply to all chargeable events which take place after 5 April 2017. The definition of 'chargeable event' will, according to the ConDoc, include:

- '• the death of an individual holding shares in an overseas close company which owns UK residential property;
- the redistribution of the share capital of an overseas close company which owns residential property;
- the death of a donor making a gift of shares in a close company which owns UK residential property where that gift was made within 7 years of death;
- a gift by a non-domiciled individual of shares in a close company owning UK residential property;
- the death of a donor or settlor who benefits from a gift of UK residential property or of shares in a close company which owned such property, within 7 years of death;
- any ten-year anniversary of a trust holding UK property through an offshore company;
- the death of a life tenant with a pre-March 2006 qualifying interest in possession in a trust from which they have an entitlement to income.'

Valuation

[11.35] Because under the proposed provisions the shares in the offshore company will not be excluded property in part or in whole, it will be the value of those shares (to the extent that that value is attributable to UK property) which will be chargeable. It will, therefore, be necessary to value the shares. The ConDoc says that the valuation will follow the general approach for inheritance tax so that tax will be charged on the open market value of the property at the time of the relevant chargeable event.

The ConDoc gives an example of a non-domiciliary whose only assets are the shares in a wholly owned overseas company which owns a UK residential property. The company has no liabilities. When the individual dies, their estate consists of the shares in the overseas company which have an open market value of £950,000. At the same time, the UK property has an open market value of £1 million. According to the ConDoc, in such a situation the value of the individual's estate is £950,000, which is derived wholly from the UK residential property and inheritance tax would be charged on that amount.

Where the company holds assets other than UK residential property, the calculation will be more complex.

The value of any UK residential property will take into account any relevant debts. For these purposes, relevant debts will be those which relate exclusively to the property; for example, an outstanding mortgage which was taken out to purchase the property. Any debts which are not related to the property, however, will not be taken into account. It is the Government's intention that any loans made between connected parties will be disregarded.

Example

Trustees own UK residential property worth £3.25 million, which was purchased for £3 million using £3 million borrowed from a person connected with the settlor. The trustees have net assets of £250,000 but inheritance tax will be charged on assets of £3.25 million. A difficulty will arise for such trustees if they do not have other assets to fund the tax. If the lender were domiciled in the UK, the loan would be an asset in his estate but it is not deductible in relation to the trustees. The trustees would be liable to inheritance tax on an asset worth £3.25 million, and the lender would also be liable to inheritance tax on an asset worth £3 million. The amount chargeable to inheritance tax is, therefore, more than doubled.

Anti-avoidance

[11.36] The draft legislation includes a targeted anti-avoidance provision which provides that, in determining whether, or the extent to which, property situated outside the UK is excluded property, no regard is to be had to any arrangements the purpose or one of the main purposes of which is to secure a tax advantage by avoiding the effect of the proposed changes discussed in **11.32** and to be found in IHTA 1984, Sch A1.

Liability

[11.37] It is proposed that HMRC should be given an 'expanded power' to impose the inheritance tax charge on indirectly held UK residential property so that the property could not be sold until any outstanding inheritance tax charge is paid. In addition, a liability will be imposed on any person 'who has legal ownership of the property including any directors of the company which holds that property'.

No transitional provisions

[11.38] Despite the suggestion being made by the professional bodies, HMRC does not consider it appropriate to include any transitional provisions in relation to the charge, nor to provide any incentive to encourage individuals to exit from their enveloped structures.

Action to be taken

[11.39] A non-domiciliary holding UK residential property through an offshore structure as outlined in **11.32** should consider the effects of the proposed changes, the options available to him and what action he should take before 6 April 2017. The initial question will be what are the total costs of doing nothing as opposed to the costs of winding up the structure? This will require valuations of the UK residential property which should be obtained as soon as possible.

Where a trust owns the company, a UK resident beneficiary will need to consider whether there will be any matching of capital gains with benefits under TCGA 1992, s 87. Particular care is required where a beneficiary has been living in the property rent-free or at less than the market rent. With regard to inheritance tax, if the trust still owns the company when it is liquidated, the trustees will then have a UK situs asset (the dwelling) on which there may be an exit charge. The trustees could, of course, first distribute the shares in the company to the beneficiaries who could then liquidate the company. The difficulty with this is that any 2008 rebasing election will be lost because such elections only apply to underlying companies whilst they are owned by the trust which made the election. To minimise any SDLT charge, no consideration should be given on the liquidation of the company. Therefore any existing shareholder loans should be capitalised before liquidation and existing bank borrowings repaid.

If a structure is unwound so that UK property is held directly by an individual, any future capital gains arising on the sale of the property will not be taxable if it is the individual's main residence and main residence relief is available.

At the time of writing, the legislation is still in draft and it is clear that amendments are to be made to it. It will be difficult to make recommendations to clients until the draft Finance Bill 2017 is published in December 2016. Nevertheless, in the meantime, a comprehensive comparison and cost benefit of the options of doing nothing or de-enveloping should be undertaken to determine the suitability of the offshore structure. This should be considered together with the client's current situation and his future plans. It may be that the costs of unwinding such a structure will be too great. In such a case life assurance may be used to cover the potential inheritance tax liability.

Capital gains tax on non-residents

Outline of the charge

[11.40] Capital gains tax is charged on gains accruing on a 'non-resident CGT disposal' (NRCGT) made after 5 April 2015. A non-resident CGT disposal is a disposal of a UK residential property interest where condition A or B is met (TCGA 1992, s 14B(1)).

Condition A is met if:

(a)   the person making the disposal is an individual and he is not resident in the UK for the tax year in which the disposal takes place;

(b)   the disposal is made by personal representatives who are not resident in the UK;

(c)   the disposal is made by the trustees who are not resident in the UK during any part of the tax year in which the disposal takes place;.

(d)   In any other case the person is not resident in the UK when the gain accrues, or would accrue if there were a gain.

Whether or not an individual is resident in the UK will be determined by the application of the statutory residence test, which is discussed in detail in **CHAPTER 21 UK RESIDENTS WITH MULTI-JURISDICTIONAL AFFAIRS**.

Condition B applies only where the disposal is made by an individual and any gain accruing on the disposal would accrue in the overseas part of a split tax year.

To prevent double taxation the gain is not chargeable under TCGA 1992, s 14B if it is already chargeable under TCGA 1992, ss 2(1C), 10(1) or 10B (TCGA 1992, s 14B(5)).

These rules take precedence over the temporary non-residence rules in TCGA 1992, s 10A, but s 10A can apply to any part of the gain that is not within the NRCGT rules.

Who is caught?

[11.41] These rules apply to non-resident persons, including non-resident individuals, personal representatives of a non-resident deceased person, trustees, companies and partnerships.

A non-resident company on making a non-resident CGT disposal may be subject to both ATED-related CGT and NRCGT, the ATED-related CGT charge which is taxed at 28% will take precedence (TCGA 1992, Sch 4ZZB).

The legislation provides that an eligible person will not be chargeable on NRCGT gains provided a claim is made under TCGA 1992, s 14F. An eligible person includes a diversely-held company, i.e. any company that is not a 'closely-held company' (TCGA 1992, s 14F(10)), companies carrying on life assurance business and unit trust schemes and open-ended investment companies that satisfy certain conditions. Arrangements entered into to enable a company to be an eligible person in order to avoid a tax charge will be disregarded.

The claim for exemption must be made in the NRCGT return within 30 days of the date the property is conveyed.

UK residential property interest

[11.42] A disposal of an 'interest in UK land' is a 'disposal of a UK residential property interest' provided one of the following conditions is met (TCGA 1992, Sch B1, para 1):

(a)   the land that is disposed of has, at any time from the 'relevant period of ownership', being the period from acquisition or 6 April 2015 (whichever is the later) to the day before the date of disposal, consisted of or included a 'dwelling', or that the interest in UK land subsists for the benefit of land that has consisted of or included a dwelling.

(b)   the interest in UK land subsists under a contract for an off-plan purchase, ie a contract to acquire land consisting of, or including, a building or part of a building that is to be constructed or adapted as a dwelling (TCGA 1992, B1 paras 1(1) & (2)).

Where the owner of the land has acquired more than one interest at different times, the date of acquisition of the first interest is treated as the date on which all the interests were acquired (TCGA 1992, Sch B1, para 1(5)).

Interest in UK land

[11.43] An 'interest in UK land' is very widely defined as an estate, interest, right or power in or over land in the UK, or the benefit of an obligation, restriction or condition affecting the value of any such estate, interest right or power other than an excluded interest (TCGA 1992 Sch B1, para 2(1). An excluded interest is a security right, (being an interest or right held to secure payment of money or performance of any other obligation), a licence to use or occupy land, or a tenancy at will or a manor (TCGA 1992, Sch B1, para 2(2)).

Dwelling

[11.44] A 'dwelling' is defined, for the purposes of NRCGT gains, as a building (including a part of a building) which is used or suitable for use as a dwelling or is in the process of being constructed or adapted for such use (TCGA 1992, Sch B1, para 4). Land (and any building or structure on such land) that is, or is intended to be, occupied or enjoyed with a dwelling as a garden or grounds is taken to be part of the dwelling. There is a similarity with main residence relief except here there is no maximum area. The legislation provides that a building used for certain purposes, such as residential accommodation for school pupils, is excluded from being a dwelling (TCGA 1992, Sch B1, para 4(3)).

A building which is temporarily unsuitable for use as a dwelling is generally disregarded as such except in particular circumstances.

It should be noted that although excluded from the ATED charge, the disposal of let residential property will be subject to the NRCGT, although a disposal of let non-residential property will not. The disposal of shares held in a company holding UK residential property interests will not be subject to NRCGT.

Calculating the gain

[11.45] The calculation of the gain arising on a non-resident CGT disposal is determined by the rules set out in TCGA 1992, Sch 4ZB. A taxpayer can elect for the gain to be calculated by one of three methods. An examination of the methods of calculation is outside the scope of this book.

Tax payable

[11.46] Companies will be charged to capital gains tax (and not corporation tax) on NRCGT gains at a rate of 20%. Individuals will be charged at normal rates of CGT which apply to gains generally. Trustees and personal representatives will be charged at 28%.

It is HMRC's view that where a person will also be charged to tax on the disposal in their country of residence, the UK tax charge still applies and relief for the UK tax paid may be available to set against any tax due in the country of residence (HMRC 'Capital Gains Tax for non-UK residents: sales and disposals of UK residential property' FAQs, Q 22, 18 March 2015).

Capital gains tax is charged on the total amount of the NRCGT gains accruing in the tax year after deduction of any allowable losses on disposals of UK residential property interests (whether or not NRCGT losses) of the same tax year, and any such unused losses brought forward from previous years. Except for an individual's NRCGT losses carried back from the tax year of death no other deductions can be made (TCGA 1992 s 14D(2).

Reporting obligations

[11.47] Where a non-resident disposal is made, an NRCGT return must be made by the appropriate person within 30 days of completion of the disposal. A return must be made except in two specific situations. The first is where a disposal is treated as if neither a gain nor a loss accrues. The second is where an arm's length lease is granted to a person unconnected to the grantor for no premium.

The return must include an advance self-assessment of the 'amount notionally chargeable' and this must be paid within the 30-day period. An advance self-assessment is not required where the appropriate person has been given notice to file a self-assessment return or has delivered an ATED return in the preceding year. In such a case assessment and the payment of the tax due is required by the normal due date for the tax year in which the disposal took place.

Previous inheritance tax strategies

[11.48] As mentioned above a number of well-known strategies have either been nullified by subsequent legislation or have not been completely nullified but on the balance of advantage it would not be prudent to implement them now. Nevertheless, they still need to be understood, in particular because clients may have implemented them in the past and have not taken any action in relation to them.

'Shearing'

[11.49] The gifts with reservation provisions are discussed in CHAPTER 4 LIFETIME PLANNING: MAKING GIFTS, and are, apart from the addition of the words ' . . . or virtually to the entire exclusion' in FA 1986, s 102(1)(b), in identical terms to those which applied under the estate duty regime. Both HMRC and commentators accept that the case law on the estate duty provisions and the principles that these cases establish are still relevant, although comments by Lightman J in the case of *Melville v IRC* [2006] STC 627, 74 TC 372 (Ch D) throw doubt on the extent to which a court will have regard to estate duty principles in relation to inheritance tax. Although the Court of Appeal confirmed the High Court's decision in that case ([2001] EWCA Civ 1247, [2002] 1 WLR 407, [2001] STC 1271 (Spc)) it did not specifically consider this issue.

The case of *Munro v Comr of Stamp Duties of New South Wales* [1934] AC 61 (PC) established the principle that there was no reservation of benefit where the donor retained a benefit referable to a prior right rather than to the property which is the subject of the gift. This led to a strategy being developed under which an individual owning the freehold of his home would grant a lease to a nominee for himself, thereby creating a leasehold interest and a freehold reversion. He then gave away the reversion and continued to occupy the property by virtue of his leasehold interest without, it was hoped, falling foul of the gifts with reservation provisions. The scheme was considered by the House of Lords in *Ingram v IRC* [1999] STC 37 (HL).

The Ingram scheme

[11.50] The House of Lords found this scheme effective in *Ingram*. The scheme involved a two-stage operation. First, the prospective donor granted a lease for a term equal to his life expectancy plus a margin of five or ten years, as appropriate, to a nominee without reserving any rent. As the donor had to create the lease first, he had absolute control over the terms of the lease and there was no necessity to use open market terms.

Secondly, the donor gave the freehold reversion to the donee by way of a potentially exempt transfer.

If the lease still had some time to run at the donor's death, its remaining value would be subject to inheritance tax.

If the lease expired before the donor died, then the donor would have to either move out of the property or pay a rack rent to avoid being in receipt of a 'reserved benefit'.

Legislation was introduced to stop the strategy in the form of FA 1986, ss 102A–102C. For the purpose of these provisions, no account is taken of occupation in circumstances where it would be ignored under FA 1986, Sch 20, para 6(1)(b). This is, broadly, where the donor falls on hard times and the donee makes provision for the donor out of the gift. For the purpose of these provisions, no account is taken of occupation in circumstances where it would be ignored under FA 1986, Sch 20, para 6(1)(b). This is, broadly, where the donor falls on hard times and the donee makes provision for the donor out of the gift.

The *Ingram* scheme clearly falls within the provisions of s 102A. So too will many other arrangements which are not the provisions' ostensible target. For example, the provisions apply in relation to some family farming partnerships.

Under the POA provisions discussed in CHAPTER 4 LIFETIME PLANNING: MAKING GIFTS, any *Ingram* scheme already in existence will be subject to an income tax charge where the donor continues to occupy the property. The gift of the freehold interest will satisfy the disposal condition and a POA charge will arise on the donor. The different options available to the donor for mitigating the POA charge are discussed in **11.14–11.18** above. Which is the most suitable option will depend on the age and financial circumstances of the donor.

The deferred lease strategy

[11.51] This strategy, sometimes known as the reversionary lease scheme, involves the donor making a gift of a long lease, the rights of which are deferred for a period. For example, one might grant a 999-year lease which is not to commence for 20 years. The period of deferral might be longer. The Law of Property Act 1925, s 149(3) provides that a lease granted in consideration of a 'fine limited to take effect more than 21 years from the date of the instrument . . . shall be void'. It is thought that a lease which does not involve the payment of rent (or fine) is outside those provisions.

As the deferred lease is of small value, the value of the potentially exempt transfer is only small. However, the longer the individual survives, the lower the value of the freehold as the period to the beginning of the lease shortens. In effect, the value of the property is transferred to the deferred lease which is outside the estate for inheritance tax purposes. The freehold on the death of the donor will therefore have a much reduced value. HMRC has always indicated that in its view the gifts with reservation provisions applied, but it acknowledged that reversionary interest lease schemes made before 9 March 1999 were effective; however the strategy was ineffective in relation to reversionary leases executed on or after 9 March 1999.

On 29 January 2007, HMRC published a statement (now found in HMRC Inheritance Tax Manual, para 44102) to say that they now considered that 'where the freehold interest was acquired more than 7 years before the gift

. . . the continued occupation by the donor is not a significant right in view of [FA 1986, s 102A(5)], so the reservation of benefit rules cannot apply and a POA charge arises instead'.

In *Buzzoni v Revenue & Customs Comrs* [2013] EWCA Civ 1684, [2014] 1 WLR 3040, [2014] WTLR 421, the owner of a long lease ('the donor') implemented the Deferred Lease Strategy by granting a deferred sub-lease out of a head lease. The sub-lease provided for the tenant to make payments to the head-lessee equal to the rent paid under the head lease to the freeholder and to repair the flat. The Court of Appeal, reversing the previous tribunal decisions, held that the donor had not reserved a benefit in the sub-lease she had given away. That was because the second limb of FA 1986, s 102(1)(b) (whether the donor's enjoyment was exclusive of any benefit to the donor by contract or otherwise) was not satisfied. Both limbs of FA 1986, s 102(1)(b) decided on a narrow point as HMRC had relied only on the second limb of s 102(1)(b). Nevertheless, the decision is helpful as it confirms there is no reservation of benefit if a benefit received by the donor did not affect the donee's enjoyment of the gifted property. It should be noted that the transactions in *Buzzoni* were implemented before the implementation of FA 1986 ss 102A–102C.

In the more recent case of *Viscount Hood (Executor of Lady Diana Hood) v HMRC* [2016] UKFTT 059 (TC), the First-tier Tribunal distinguished *Buzzoni* on the basis that in *Buzzoni* the sub-lessees gave direct covenants to the head lessor whereas in the *Hood* case the covenants were given to the sub-lessor, Lady Hood. The First-tier Tribunal held that the sub-lease was a disposal by way of gift of property subject to a reservation. There are two situations where reversionary leases are not caught by FA 1986 s 102A. First, under s 102A(5) where an individual acquired his right or interest in the property more than seven years before the date of the gift. Secondly, where full consideration in money or money's worth is given for the occupation of the land by the donor.

Where there is a pre-March 2006 interest in possession trust in which the life tenant, who is not the settlor, is elderly and occupies the trust property, the strategy would appear still to offer advantages. The life tenant will not have purchased the property and will usually have had a right or interest in the freehold for more than seven years. In relation to IPDI trusts set up under a will, new arrangements under the strategy may still be advantageous. Finance Act 1986, s 102ZA, which deems that a life tenant makes a gift of the underlying settled property when his interest in possession is terminated, applies for the purposes of FA 1986, s 102 and Sch 20 but not for the purposes of FA 1986, ss 102A–102C. No POA charge should arise because the individual is not making a disposal of an interest in land.

The deferred lease strategy has a number of disadvantages. The base cost of the deferred lease for capital gains tax purposes will be very low because, at the time of acquisition, the deferred lease will not be very valuable but it will increase in value after the acquisition as its commencement date approaches. In addition, the holder of the deferred lease will not receive full main residence relief (see above) and there will be only a small, or no, uplift in value of the freehold on death. There is a further disadvantage under the POA provisions as the disposal of the deferred lease will satisfy the disposal condition and a POA charge will arise on the donor. In most situations, the strategy is now unlikely to be worthwhile.

Trust of debt strategy

[11.52] A strategy for reducing inheritance tax on the family home which was much used before the introduction of the POA charge is the trust of debt strategy. Below is a generic description of the strategy of which there were many variations. Under the strategy, the owner of the home settled a small sum on trusts (the 'residence trust') of which he was the life tenant. He then sold his home to the trustees of the residence trust for an amount which was to be payable upon his death and which was to bear interest which was to be rolled up. He now had a debt due to him which he settled on trusts (the 'debt trust') for those he wished to benefit.

The owner had reserved a benefit in the property which he transferred to the trustees but as he was treated by IHTA 1984, s 49(1) as the beneficial owner of that property, the fact that the property was subject to a reservation did not lead to an increased inheritance tax charge (FA 1986, s 102(3)). The donor had not, however, reserved a benefit in the debt. Although the debt was not repayable until after his death, the property settled was the contractual debt itself including all of its terms. The net effect was that the donor had taken the current value of the debt (which was normally roughly equal to the market value of the property) out of his estate for inheritance tax purposes.

There was no capital gains tax charge on the donor on the assumption that the house had been his main residence throughout the time that he owned it. There was, however, a stamp duty land tax charge on the sale of the home to the residence trust.

If the strategy were now implemented the residence trust would be a relevant property settlement subject to decennial and exit charges. These charges could become significant if the value of the property were to become very much greater than the value of the liability to pay the debt for its purchase price. For schemes implemented before 22 March 2006, however, the interest in possession in the residence trust will be an existing IIP and therefore not a relevant property settlement. If the gift of the debt is made on trusts other than on bare trusts the gift will be an immediately chargeable transfer.

HMRC has developed a litigation strategy and has the view that:

(a)   Finance Act 1986, s 103 applies resulting in the loan not being deductible against the value of the trust fund of the residence trust;

(b)   the transactions are re-characterised under the *Ramsay Principle* so that there was a gift of the house and the continued occupation by the owner is a reservation of benefit;

(c)   where the loan is repayable on demand the loan is a gift with reservation until such time as the trustees call in the loan; and

(d)   where the loan is only repayable after the death of the life tenant, the gift of the loan is a gift with reservation.

This range of arguments may result in different sets of trustees being liable for the inheritance tax on the death of a life tenant. A case has yet to be heard by the Tribunal and so in the absence of a court decision the ICAEW has met with HMRC to determine the basis on which cases may be settled. HMRC has stated that where a liability following death was to be settled, it would not seek more inheritance tax than if the value of the house has remained subject to tax. The estate will be treated as if the value of the house had remained in the estate throughout and no POA charge would have been payable. Where the POA charge has been paid, a notional refund of income tax will be treated as an asset of the estate and a credit for the income tax paid will be given against the inheritance tax. No actual repayment claim will have to be made.

Where a death has occurred but the surviving spouse is still alive, cases are being settled on the basis that a reservation of benefit arises in each half of the house, with the effect that half of the value of the house is taxed on the first death and half on the second death. It should be noted that no joint property discount is applied in either case.

Legislation was introduced by FA 2013 to ensure that no deduction is given for a debt that is not repaid. IHTA 1984, s 175A provides that a liability may only be allowed as a deduction against an estate on death to the extent that the liability is actually discharged on or after death, out of the estate in money or money's worth. Some versions of the trust of debt strategy assume that rolled-up interest on the debt will be waived after the death of the implementer in order to avoid triggering an income tax charge. In order for the debt for accrued interest to be taken into account in reducing the value of an individual's estate there must be a real commercial reason for the liability not to be repaid, the main purpose or one of the main purposes of leaving the liability or part of it undischarged must not be to secure a tax advantage and the liability must not be disallowed under any other provision of IHTA 1984. HMRC states in para 28029 of its HMRC Inheritance Tax Manual that 'it is important to note here that whilst the liability may be part of wider arrangements that are aimed at securing a tax advantage, for example, a home loan or double trust scheme, you should only consider whether it is the non-repayment of the liability [that] gives rise to a tax advantage'.

'Eversden schemes'

[11.53] The case of *IRC v Eversden (executors of Greenstock dec'd)* [2003] EWCA Civ 668, [2003] STC 822 concerned a tax planning strategy. A settlor settled her home ('Beechwood') as to 5% for herself absolutely and as to 95% on trusts giving her husband a life interest subject to a wide power of appointment in favour of a class of beneficiaries which included the settlor. The settlor and her husband occupied Beechwood together until the husband's death. Thereafter, the trustees sold Beechwood and brought another house ('Maitland') again as to 5% for the settlor absolutely and as to 95% subject to what was now a discretionary trust. The settlor continued to occupy Beechwood and then, after its purchase, Maitland until her death. The question for decision was whether the 95% interest held on discretionary trusts was property subject to a reservation in relation to the settlor.

The Court held that, by virtue of the settlor's occupation of the house, the trust fund was not enjoyed to the entire, or virtually to the entire, exclusion of benefit to the settlor. The settled property was not property subject to a reservation, however, because the settlement of the property was an exempt inter-spouse transfer under IHTA 1984, s 18. Finance Act 1986, s 102(5) disapplies the gifts with reservation provisions where the gift is exempt under various provisions which include s 18.

The decision led to the marketing of tax planning strategies branded as 'Eversden Schemes' utilising similar transactions to those which were considered in the case. HMRC's riposte was to amend FA 1986, s 102 to provide that the fact that a transfer receives the spouse exemption will not prevent it from being a gift with reservation where the following conditions apply; property is settled creating an interest in possession for the donor's spouse, at some time after the disposal but before the donor's death the spouse's interest in possession comes to an end and on that occasion the spouse does not become entitled absolutely to, or to a further interest in possession in, the settled property.

Most Eversden Schemes which are in place will now be subject to a POA charge on the donor. Although the initial gift into trust for the donor's spouse is an excluded transaction under FA 2004, Sch 15, para 10(1)(c), where the spouse is entitled to an interest in possession, if that interest has come to an end otherwise than on the death of the spouse, the original disposal into trust ceases to be an excluded transaction (FA 2004, Sch 15, para 10(3)).

Chapter 12

The Family Business

Introduction

[12.1] This chapter deals with estate planning for the person who carries on business either as a sole proprietor, as a partner in a family partnership, as a member of a limited liability partnership ('LLP') or as a shareholder in a family company. Planning for such persons is normally dealt with together under some general heading like 'business property' because of the connection between the financial affairs of the individuals and those of their businesses, stemming from the fact that interests in a business and shares in a trading company may be capable of qualifying for inheritance tax business property relief. Although this chapter follows this practice, it should be borne in mind that the ideas presented here can apply to all types of 'business property' even if not technically capable of qualifying for the relief. Whilst the tax treatment of companies and partnerships can give rise to considerable complexities and, because of their legal nature, can require rather more sophisticated planning techniques, the basic estate planning principles set out in **CHAPTER 1 WHAT IS ESTATE PLANNING?** and **CHAPTER 3 LIFETIME PLANNING: AN OVERVIEW** apply to shares and business interests in the same way as they do to any other item of property.

Inheritance tax

Business property relief

[12.2] Business property relief is a particularly valuable relief which, depending on the type of property, reduces the amount of the value of the business property transferred by either 100% or 50% (IHTA 1984, s 104). The value transferred must be attributable to the net value of the 'relevant business property'. There is no requirement that there must be a transfer of a business. A transfer of business assets will also be eligible for relief (*Revenue & Customs Comrs v Trustees of the Nelson Dance Family* [2009] EWHC 71 (Ch), [2009] STC 802, 79 TC 605).

Relevant business property is:

(a)   property consisting of a business or an interest in a business;
(b)   securities of an unquoted company which, either by themselves or together with other such securities owned by the transferor gave the transferor control of the company. 'Control' for these purposes means voting control on all matters affecting the company as a whole, other

than questions as to the winding up of the company or the varying of class rights (IHTA 1984, s 269(1), (4)). The votes attaching to any shares owned by the transferor's spouse or civil partner, or by a charity (IHTA 1984, s 269(2)), or by a trust in which the transferor has a beneficial interest in possession (IHTA 1984, s 269(3)), will be taken into account in determining whether the transferor has control. No account is taken of the capacity of the shareholder, or of any of the other shareholders, to exercise their votes (*Walding's Executors v IRC* [1996] STC 13);

(c)   any unquoted shares (but not securities) in a company;

(d)   quoted shares which confer control;

(e)   land, building, machinery or plant used wholly or mainly for the purposes of a business carried on by a company controlled by the transferor or by a partnership of which he is a partner;

(f)   land, building, machinery or plant which is settled property in which the transferor has an interest in possession and which is used wholly or mainly for the purposes of a business carried on by him (IHTA 1984, s 105).

For the purposes of business property relief, shares or securities are 'quoted' if they are listed on a recognised stock exchange (IHTA 1984, s 105(1ZA)). Unquoted shares are those shares which are not listed. Shares dealt in on the Alternative Investment Market are regarded as unquoted (HMRC Inheritance Tax Manual, para 18336).It should be noted that if the AIM shares have a secondary listing on another recognised stock exchange, business property relief will not be available.

For land, buildings, machinery or plant used for the purposes of a business carried on by a company under (e) above, to be relevant business property, the relevant company must be controlled by the transferor. Control is defined in IHTA 1984, s 269(1). Essentially, a person has control if they are able to exercise more than 50% of the votes in a general meeting. In determining control, related property under IHTA 1984, s 161 must be included. This means that shares belonging to a spouse or civil partner will be included. Therefore, where two individuals jointly own a company in equal shares and land belonging to one of them is used by the company, the land will not be relevant business property.

IHTA 1984, s 267A provides that property to which an LLP is entitled, occupies or uses is treated as property to which its members are entitled or which they occupy or use as partners and so will be relevant business property.

The value of a business or an interest in a business is taken to be its net value (IHTA 1984, s 110). The net value is the value of the assets used in the business reduced by the aggregate amount of any liabilities incurred for the purpose of the business. It is HMRC's view that a debt for money loaned to an LLP by a member of an LLP is not business property. The assets used in the business have to be identified in order to determine on what relief is available. In the case of *Ninth Marquess of Hertford (executors of Eighth Marquess of Hertford, dec'd) v IRC* (SpC 444) [2005] STC (SCD) 177 the question arose as to whether the whole of the freehold of Ragley Hall or only part was eligible for relief. Ragley Hall was open to the public. The exterior of the Hall was accessible for viewing by the public but only 78% of the interior was open. The Eighth Marquess gave the business to his son within seven years of death. The same parts of the Hall remained in private occupation after the transfer, part of which was let to the Eighth Marquess. It was held that the nature of the business and the part played in it by the physical structure of the Hall meant that the Hall was plainly important as a single structure and the whole building was a vital backdrop to the whole business carried on. The whole interest qualified for relief.

Business or interest in a business

Meaning of business

[**12.3**] A 'business' is not defined except that it is provided that a 'business' includes 'a business carried on in the exercise of a profession or vocation, but does not include a business carried on otherwise than for gain' (IHTA 1984, s 103(3)).

The first question which needs to be determined is whether an activity is a business. HMRC considers that the six indicators of a business identified by Gibson J in the VAT case of *Customs and Excise Comrs v Lord Fisher* [1981] 2 All ER 147, [1981] STC 238 'are equally applicable as a test for IHT purposes' (HMRC Inheritance Tax Manual, para 25152). VAT, however, is concerned with businesses which supply goods and/or services and Mr Justice Gibson's list is to be read in that context. It does not necessarily form a very good checklist for the existence of a business in the context of inheritance tax.

An investment business?

[**12.4**] A business or an interest in a business which consists wholly or mainly of one or more of the following activities cannot be relevant business property, namely making or holding investments or dealing in securities, stocks, shares, land or buildings (other than as a market maker or a discount house); nor can shares and securities in a company whose business wholly or mainly consists of one or more of those activities unless the company is wholly or mainly the holding company of one or more trading companies whose businesses do not consist of one or more of those activities (IHTA 1984, s 105(3),(4)). The HMRC Inheritance Tax Manual states that one should look at 'the main activities of the business, and to its assets and sources of income or gains, over a reasonable period preceding the transfer' (HMRC Inheritance Tax Manual, para 25265).

In the *Trustees of David Zetland Settlement v HMRC* (TC 2690) the Tribunal looked at the activities over a five-year period before the principal charge arose following the method adopted in the case of *Martin (Exors of Martin decd) v IRC* [1995] STC (SCD) 5. The trust fund consisted of a leasehold interest in Zetland House, two ordinary shares in Avidpride Ltd, one share in MainLegion Ltd which owned the freehold of Zetland House and a property portfolio. The trustees offered services such as conference room and gallery hire, porters, 24-hour security, an Internet service, cleaning services, a café, a hair salon and a gym (although these were provided by a third party). They argued that the range and value of services provided at Zetland House meant that their business did not consist merely of making or holding investments. The First-tier Tribunal's judge said that:

> 'The Tribunal must not start with the fact that the business consists entirely of the ownership of land giving rise to investment activity. It must be mindful of the broad spectrum of businesses and the fine distinctions between different businesses. The better approach is for the Tribunal to have an open mind and not to pre-judge the issue at the start.'

In determining the question the Tribunal had to decide whether a quantitative (comparing the income and profits from rent with income and profits from additional services) or qualitative (considering the nature of the services offered) comparison should be made. In *Zetland* it seems to have been agreed by both parties that it was a qualitative rather than a quantitive test. However, the judge said that a 'quantitive assessment is not determinative' and 'qualitatively the business has to be looked at in the round without giving predominance to anyone factor'. The activities carried on by the trustees were far in excess of their obligations under the leases and separate charges were made for those services. From the case it was clear that the amount of income derived from services was important. The Tribunal determined that the income derived from the services was less than 25% of the income. The Tribunal concluded that income from the gym, cafe and hair salon must be regarded as investment income in the hands of the trustees whereas if the activity had been undertaken by the trustees in their own right it would have been viewed as non-investment income. The Tribunal held that relief was not available to the trustees because they were carrying on a business wholly or mainly of the making or holding of investments.

In *Best (executor of Buller, decd) v Revenue & Customs Comrs* [2014] UKFTT 077 (TC), [2014] WTLR 409 a company provided business property letting and management services. The Tribunal held that the business was predominantly one of investment, having asked itself the question of how important any non-investment activities were to the business as a whole.

Because the test is whether the business consists 'wholly and mainly' of the prohibited activities, a taxpayer may conduct, within a single business, two activities one of which is an investment business, but if that activity is not the main part of the business, the entire business can still be relevant business property on which relief is available. It is a question of fact as to whether a mixed business is carried on as a single composite business or as two separate businesses. In determining of what a business consists, one has to look at the question in the round, paying attention to the overall context of the business, the capital employed, the time spent by the proprietors and employees as well as at the turnover and profits.(*Weston (Weston's Executor) v IRC* [2000] STC 1064 (Ch D)).

In *Brander (representative of James (dec'd), Fourth Earl of Balfour) v Revenue & Customs Comrs* [2010] UKUT 300 (TCC), [2010] STC 2666, 80 TC 163, the Earl had the life rent (a right to income of the estate and the power to manage the estate within certain limits). The estate consisted of farms (managed and leased), woodland, shooting and leased cottages. In 2002 the trust was wound up and the Earl became absolutely entitled to the trust property. The estate was put into a farming partnership that he set up with his nephew jointly. The Earl died in 2003. The executors claimed relief on his partnership share relying on the replacement property provisions in IHTA 1984, s 107. It was HMRC's view that the business was an investment business. The Tribunal were asked to determine whether the estate was a single composite business or whether the cottage lettings was a separate business.

If it was a composite business, it had to be decided whether the cottage lettings meant the business was wholly or mainly one of investment on which relief would not be available. The Tribunal held that there was a composite business. In determining whether the business was one of making or holding investments, the Tribunal summarised the case law on the matter. In deciding what the term 'the business of holding investments' means the test is that of an intelligent businessman who would be concerned with the use to which the asset was being put and the way it was being turned to account (*McCall (personal representative of McClean, dec'd) v Revenue and Customs Comrs* [2009] NICA 12, [2009] STC 990, NI CA. The business must be looked at in the round and, in the light of the overall picture, to form a view as to the relative importance to the business as a whole of the investment and non-investment activities in that business; an approach that was emphasised in *IRC v George and Loochin (Executors of Stedman)* [2003] EWCA Civ 1763, [2004] STC 147, 75 TC 735. In doing so, various factors will be taken into consideration such as the overall context of the business, the turnover and profitability of various activities, the activities of employees and other persons engaged to assist the business, the acreage of the land dedicated to each activity and the capital value of that acreage. Not one of these factors was conclusive.

Whilst the relative level of net profit of the different activities will be a factor, it is not the only or principal one, in determining whether or not a business consists wholly or mainly of making or holding investments. In practice, however, with one exception, all of the Special Commissioners' decisions where a business has been held to be predominantly one of investment have been cases where the net profit from the investment activity concerned exceeded 50% of the profit for the whole business. That one exception was Farmer (*(Farmer's Executors) v IRC* [1999] STC (SCD)321).). In that case the deceased had had a single business consisting of farming combined with letting properties on the farm which were surplus to farming requirements. The Special Commissioner held that the relevant factors to consider were the overall context of the business, the capital employed, the time spent by the employees, the turnover and the profit, and that when these had been considered it would then be necessary to stand back and consider whether the business consisted mainly of making or holding investments. The net profit from the lettings consistently exceeded the profits from farming, but it was held that the business consisted mainly of farming because it utilised much more of the land, used more valuable capital assets, had a higher turnover (in most years), and much more management, employee and consultant time was spent on it. The let properties were ones which were formerly used for farming purposes and had become surplus to the requirements of the farm, and were thus in a sense subsidiary to it.

In determining whether letting land to tenants or licensees is wholly or mainly making or holding investments, the basis on which its profits have been charged to income tax is not relevant (*(Powell v IRC)* [1997] STC (SCD)181).).

There have been a number of other cases involving the question of whether relief is available. For example, in Phillips (*(executors of Phillips (dec'd)) v HRMC(SpC 333)* [2006] STC (SCD)639) a company had a business of lending money to related companies. It was held that a loan made to a related investment company was not an investment. The fact that the company to whom the loan was made was controlled by the deceased and his family did not make any difference. Nor did the fact that the loans were not made on commercial terms.

The business of letting furnished flats on assured shorthold tenancies is a business of making and holding investments and is not eligible for relief (see *Burkinyoung (Burkinyoung's Executor) v IRC (SpC 3)* [1995] STC (SCD) 29).

A business consisting mainly of the trade of building and developing can qualify for relief, and housing stocks held as stock in trade are not excepted assets. In *Piercy (executors of, decd) v Revenue & Customs Comrs* [2008] STC (SCD) 858, it was held that a development company's shares qualified for relief notwithstanding the receipt of rent from certain properties. The Special Commissioner held that it was possible for the company to have retained unsold stock and appropriated it as an investment, whilst still conducting a development trade.

In certain circumstances where a company is carrying on a trade but has a number of investment properties, a reorganisation can be done to secure relief on the trading business and remove the investment properties from risk. This can be achieved in a number of ways depending upon the client's circumstances. In giving such advice, all taxes have to be considered.

The *Brander* case is a particularly helpful authority where business property relief is claimed on a business which consists of qualifying and non-qualifying activities. It also illustrates the importance of detailed record-keeping in respect of business property relief questions which are heavily dependent upon actual facts. The taxpayers were able to submit to the Tribunal detailed records which assisted it in assessing the relevant facts.

Some may consider integrating non-qualifying business activities within a qualifying business in order to claim relief on the whole. Care needs to be taken to ensure that such integration does not have the adverse effect of preventing any relief from being available. It should be remembered that in this case it was found that the Earl managed the estate and controlled its running.

Furnished holiday lettings

[12.5] Whilst there are special rules for furnished holiday lettings in relation to both income tax and capital gains tax, there are no such special rules in relation to inheritance tax.

Whether or not relief will be available will depend upon the services that are provided by the owners. In the case of *Pawson v Revenue & Customs Comrs*

[2012] UKFTT 51 (TC) where the services offered were limited, the First-tier Tribunal decided that relief was available by asking the question of whether an intelligent businessman would regard ownership of the holiday letting property as an investment and concluded that such a businessman would consider that it involved too much activity to fall within that category. This decision, however, was overturned by the Upper Tribunal, (*Lockyer v Revenue and Customs Comrs* [2013] UKUT 50 (TCC), [2013] STC 976, [2013] NLJR 291), holding that the First-tier Tribunal were wrong and that the property was an investment and not eligible for relief. Henderson J said:

> 'The owning and holding of land in order to obtain an income from it is generally to be characterised as an investment activity.'

This was his starting point and followed in the case of *Green v HMRC* [2015] UKFTT 0236 (TC). Henderson J went on to say that taking active steps to find tenants, keeping the property in good order and so on were all activities which 'naturally fall on the investment side of the line'. In the case of Green the marketing, pricing, booking accommodation, dealing with complaints and requests, insurance, repairs and maintenance were all held to be investment activities. The additional services offered were relatively minor and ancillary to the provision of the accommodation. In the cases of *Pawson and Green* the services offered were very limited but they demonstrate that in order for furnished holiday lettings not to be an investment, the services provided will have to be very extensive unless the holiday let forms part of a larger trading business such as a farm.

HMRC, in its Inheritance Tax Manual at para 25278, says that its view 'is that furnished holiday lets will in general not qualify for business property relief. The income derived from such businesses will largely consist of rent in return for the occupation of property. There may however be cases where the level of additional services provided is so high that the activity can be considered as non-investment, and each case needs to be treated on its own facts.'

Caravan parks

[**12.6**] A number of cases have examined the boundary between business activities consisting of holding investments and those which do not in relation to caravan parks (see, in particular, *Farmer (Farmer's executors) v IRC* [1999] STC (SCD) 321 (Sp C 216); *Weston (Weston's Executors) v IRC* [2000] STC 1064 (Ch D) and *IRC v George and Loochin (Stedman's Executors)* [2003] EWCA Civ 1763, [2004] STC 147, 75 TC 735). Where a claim for relief is being made in relation to a caravan park, it is to be expected that HMRC will request very detailed information, particularly as to the services offered.

Wholly or mainly

[**12.7**] The legislation does not define 'wholly or mainly' despite the phrase appearing in several places in the inheritance tax legislation. The phrase is also found elsewhere in the tax legislation and has been the subject of a judicial comment in various cases. Nevertheless, this does give rise to some degree of uncertainty.

Partnerships and LLPs

[12.8] Partnerships and LLPs have increasingly been used as the structure through which unquoted shares and business properties are held. It is HMRC's view that partnerships and LLPs are opaque for the purposes of business property relief. This means that if a partner dies, the asset in his estate is not the underlying partnership assets but the chose in action which is his partnership interest. If the partnership business consists of wholly or mainly holding shares in unquoted companies, relief is not available despite the assets being held qualifying themselves for business property relief. Whereas if the assets were held through a company, relief would be available. It is felt by many commentators that this view is incorrect. It is argued that it is necessary to consider whether the value of the partnership interest is attributable to the value of any relevant property and not whether the partnership is transparent. This view is supported by the decision in *HMRC v Nelson Dance*.

Large cash deposits

[12.9] In *Brown's Executors v IRC* [1996] STC (SCD) 277 (SpC 83) a company held the sale proceeds of an asset in a deposit account whilst it searched for suitable new business premises but the shareholder died without new premises having been acquired. HMRC asserted that the company's business had become one of holding investments. It was found that the business continued to consist of the original trading activity and relief was still available. See also **12.12** below.

Ownership requirement

[12.10] To qualify as relevant business property, property must have been owned by the transferor throughout the two years immediately preceding the relevant transfer (IHTA 1984, s 106). It is not a requirement that the property must have been relevant business property throughout that period. The ownership requirement is modified where the property has been acquired to replace other relevant business property or has been acquired by a person on the death of his or her spouse or civil partner (IHTA 1984, ss 107, 108) and where there are successive transfers of business property involving spouses and the later transfer is a deemed transfer on death (s 109).

Changes due to the formation, alteration or dissolution of a partnership are disregarded for the purposes of the restriction of the relief (IHTA 1984, s 107(3)). In *Brander (representative of James (dec'd), Fourth Earl of Balfour) v Revenue & Customs Comrs* [2010] UKUT 300 (TCC), [2010] STC 2666, 80 TC 163 (see **12.4** above) in the two years before the Earl's death, the Earl held first a life rent in an estate. That life rent was released on an application to the court and the Earl became entitled to an absolute interest in the estate. The Earl then entered into a partnership with his nephew to farm the estate. In spite of the changes in the Earl's interest, he was held to have owned the relevant business property for the requisite two years.

A reorganisation of unquoted share capital will not result in a break in the ownership period provided certain conditions are satisfied (IHTA 1984, s 107(4)). There must however, based on the evidence, be a reorganisation. In

Vinton (Executors of Dugan-Chapman (dec'd)) v Revenue & Customs Comrs [2008] STC (SCD) 592, [2008] SWTI 370 the Special Commissioner held that there was a rights issue and not a reorganisation.

In certain situations the successive transfer relief in s 109 can be helpful in mitigating inheritance tax.

Example

Horatio owns a family trading company which qualifies for 100% relief. His wife, Amelia, who owns a half share in their house and share portfolio, is seriously ill and is unlikely to survive for more than a few months. Horatio transfers some of his family company shares to Amelia; there are no inheritance tax or capital gains tax implications because it was an inter-spouse transfer. On Amelia's death, under the terms of her will, the shares passed to a discretionary trust for the benefit of Horatio and his family. Business property relief at 100% was available under s 109 because Amelia's period of ownership was deemed to include Horatio's period of ownership. The shares also benefited from the capital gains tax uplift on death. Horatio can benefit from the trust without the reservation of benefit rules applying. Further, he could now buy back some of the family company shares from the trustees so that he would again hold an asset which, after two years, would qualify for business property relief. One has to consider, however, the application of the GAAR to such a situation (see para D19 of HMRC's GAAR Guidance).

Except where s 109 applies, the principle of aggregation does not apply to inter vivos transfers. Assets given by one spouse or civil partner to the other by way of a lifetime transfer must be retained by the donee for at least two years before the assets will qualify for business property relief.

Replacement property

[12.11] The rule for replacement property provides that where the original property has been sold and replaced by other relevant business property the two-year ownership period is taken to be satisfied provided the original property and the replacement property were owned for a total of at least two years within the preceding five-year period (IHTA 1984, s 107). The question arises as to whether all of the sale proceeds of the original assets must be invested into the replacement business assets. HMRC's Inheritance Tax Manual is silent on the matter. The clawback provisions relating to transfers within the seven-year period before death found in IHTA 1984, s 113A requires the whole of the consideration to be applied in acquiring other property (IHTA 1984, s 113B) **(12.13)**. Section 107 does not contain such a provision and so it would seem that a partial replacement would qualify.

Excepted assets

[12.12] Where part of the value of any relevant business property is attributable to an asset which is not used for the purposes of the business throughout the whole or the last two years of the relevant period or is not required for future use in the business, the value of that asset will not be taken into account when determining the value of the relevant business property (IHTA 1984, s 112). An example of this would be where a company, shares in which qualify for business property relief, owns a house or a yacht which is used solely for the personal benefit of one of the shareholders. HMRC will often argue that a large cash balance held in a trading company is an excepted asset. It is understood that HMRC typically raises this argument where the cash balance exceeds 25% of turnover. Some businesses have been keeping larger cash surpluses than usual to protect themselves in an economic downturn. The professional bodies wrote to HMRC about the effect of holding larger cash sums to which HMRC has replied that 'a business . . . may choose to hold more cash in case of a potential downturn. In trade . . . ' but '[its] guidance remains the same and, . . . the holding of funds as an "excess buffer" to weather the economic climate is not a sufficient reason for it not to be classed as an excepted asset' (ICAEW Tax Guide 1/14).

Where there is cash in a deposit bank account which has not been used for a long period it may be excluded from relief because it cannot be said to be 'required' for future use if it was not in fact used for a long period (*Barclays Bank Trust Co Ltd v IRC* [1998] STC (SCD) 125 (SpC 158)). In that case, however, it does not appear that the taxpayer argued that holding the cash on deposit was itself a business activity. In order to demonstrate that a cash balance is required for future business use, contemporaneous board or partnership minutes etc should be maintained. In some circumstances the receipt of interest can amount to a business activity (*IRC v Dale Steamship Co Ltd* (1924) 12 TC 712), although it will not do so in normal circumstances (*Jowett (Inspector of Taxes v O'Neill and Brennan Construction Ltd* [1998] STC 482, 70 TC 566). In order to apply the excepted assets test one looks at the whole business including activities which, if the business consisted wholly or mainly of those activities, would cause shares or an interest in a business not to be relevant business property by virtue of IHTA 1984, s 105(3).

Where a company has substantial cash balances, the company might consider funding an employee benefit trust for the benefit of all employees of the company. It should be noted that care is required where a close company is funding such a trust.

The relief

[**12.13**] The relief operates to reduce the value of any relevant business property transferred by an actual or deemed transfer of value by 100% in the case of property falling within paragraphs (*a*), (*b*) and (*c*) at **12.2** above. In all other cases, the reduction in value is 50%.

Example

> Carrie has a small company 'Jamboree Ltd' which makes luxurious jams and jellies and is worth £500,000. She owns the freehold premises, worth £2m, from which the business is carried on. The shares in the company will qualify for 100% relief but relief is only available on the premises at 50%. If the company had owned the premises relief at 100% would still have been available on the shares, the value of which would have been increased by the company's ownership of the premises.

The relief applies both to lifetime transfers of value and to the deemed transfer of value arising immediately before a person's death under IHTA 1984, s 4. It can also apply to a potentially exempt transfer which becomes chargeable, and to a lifetime chargeable transfer which becomes chargeable to additional inheritance tax, by reason of the transferor's death within seven years of the transfer. However, in the latter cases, for the relief to apply, certain additional conditions have to be met, otherwise the relief will be clawed back. Broadly speaking, the transferee must continue to own the property until the transferor's death, or until his own death if earlier, and on the assumption that a transfer of value of the property concerned were to take place on the transferor's death, or on the transferee's death if earlier, the property would then satisfy all the conditions necessary for the relief to apply other than the minimum period of ownership requirement. That is, the property must continue to qualify as 'relevant business property' as defined in IHTA 1984, s 105 (IHTA 1984, s 113A). The transferee may dispose of the original property given to him provided, broadly, that he reinvests the proceeds in other 'relevant business property' within three years or such longer period as HMRC allows (IHTA 1984, s 113B).

As much business property is wholly relieved from inheritance tax by business property relief it might be thought that the impact of inheritance tax on business property can safely be ignored. It is, however, important to remember that, even if 100% business property relief is prima facie available in respect of a gift, that relief will be lost if the transferor dies within seven years of making the gift unless the necessary conditions are still satisfied at the time of the transferor's death.

The transferee should therefore be warned, for instance, of the consequences of a sale of the business property within the seven-year period. Less obvious perhaps is the effect of shares which have previously been the subject of a transfer of value becoming quoted on a recognised stock exchange within seven years of the transfer. For instance, where shares were previously unquoted, or dealt in on the Alternative Investment Market and the transferor, prior to the gift, did not have control of the company concerned, a listing of shares on a recognised stock exchange would result in the complete loss of business property relief on the transfer which would otherwise have been available at 100%.

Business property relief may apply to property owned both by individuals and by the trustees of a settlement whether the settlement is one with an interest in possession or not. Where the settlement is one with an interest in possession within IHTA 1984, s 49 the beneficiary with that interest will be the 'transferor' for the purposes of the relief and he will also, by reason of his interest, be treated as the 'owner' of the property comprised in the settlement.

Subject to a binding contract for sale

[12.14] Any property which is subject to a binding contract for sale at the date of the transfer cannot be relevant business property, except where the property is either an unincorporated business, or an interest in one, and the sale is to a company which will carry on that business in exchange for shares or securities of the company, or the sale relates to a reconstruction or amalgamation of shares or securities in a company (IHTA 1984, s 113). Section 113 can sometimes apply in unexpected situations. HMRC states that there is a binding contract for sale where partners or shareholder directors of companies enter into an agreement under which, in the event of the death of one of them, the personal representatives of the partner or director are obliged to sell, and the survivors are obliged to purchase, the interest of the deceased in the business or company. A binding contract similarly arises where such an agreement relates to retirement. See Revenue Statement of Practice SP 12/80. These are commonly known as 'Buy and Sell Agreements'.

There are a number of common arrangements for partnerships in relation to retirement or death, one of which is known as the 'accruer arrangement'. This typically provides that the partnership continues with the share of the former partner accruing to the continuing partners and with the estate entitled to a payment based either on a valuation or on a formula. In such a situation, a deceased's interest does not pass to his personal representatives but it accrues to the surviving partners. At first, when HMRC was asked to confirm whether business property relief would be available in these circumstances, it gave a cautious response, stating that 'the existence of an accruer arrangement does not necessarily prevent business relief from being available'. Since then, HMRC has stated that business property relief will be available where there are such arrangements. This treatment is confirmed in the HMRC Inheritance Tax Manual, para 25292 which states that 'agreements under which the deceased's interest passes to the surviving partners, who are required to pay the personal representatives a particular price . . . do not constitute contracts for sale'.

Section 113 will also not deny relief where there is a provision which confers an option on the continuing partners to buy the share (or indeed cross options which can be exercised to compel such a sale).

Considerations

[12.15] The impact of the 100% rate of business property relief is significant when considering estate planning for sole traders, partners, LLP members and shareholders.

Because business property relief is such a valuable relief it is important that regular reviews are undertaken to ensure that the relief is still available. It is the authors' experience that large cash balances are often held within incorporated and unincorporated businesses and it is therefore necessary to consider both whether the cash is an excepted asset within IHTA 1984, s 112 and whether the business of the company consists wholly or mainly of one of the activities listed in IHTA 1984, s 105(3). Where a large sum of cash is being held for a particular purpose – for example, the purchase of an expensive piece of machinery or land – the purpose should be documented.

It is the authors' experience that although the binding contract for sale rule is well known, there remains a substantial number of old partnership agreements which contain a right for continuing partners to acquire the interest of a deceased or retiring partner. This will prevent relief being available. This can be avoided by restructuring the rights as options.

In the past, HMRC has been reluctant to determine the availability of relief unless there is inheritance tax at stake. HMRC will, however, give business owners and their advisers its view of the application of the tax consequences of significant commercial issues where there is uncertainty regardless of when the relevant legislation was enacted. Applicants must demonstrate the commercial significance of the transaction which is subject to genuine uncertainty and identify which aspects of the law or HMRC practice they consider to be uncertain. HMRC will not accept an application where it considers that the arrangements concerned are primarily to gain a tax advantage.

Interest-free instalment option

[**12.16**] In addition to business property relief, certain types of business property may qualify for the option to pay inheritance tax by ten equal annual instalments. The relevant statutory provisions are to be found in IHTA 1984, ss 227–229 and 234. This option applies to the following types of property.

(a)   Land of any kind.

(b)   A business or an interest in a business.

(c)   Quoted or unquoted shares or securities which confer control (as defined by IHTA 1984, s 269).

(d)   Unquoted shares and securities where the charge arises on death and not less than 20% of the total tax charged at that time is attributable to the value of those shares or securities or to other property which qualifies for the instalment option. For the purposes of ss 227 and 228 'unquoted' in relation to any shares or securities means not listed on a recognised stock exchange.

(e)   Unquoted shares or securities if HMRC is satisfied that the tax attributable to them cannot be paid in one sum without undue hardship. In considering whether undue hardship exists, HMRC looks primarily to whether it is reasonable to expect the tax to be paid immediately in the light of available resources (Hansard Official Report, 22 June 1972, Standing Committee, Cols 1358–1359).

(f)   Unquoted shares (but not securities) if the value transferred exceeds £20,000 and either the nominal value of the shares is not less than 10% of the nominal value of all shares of the company at the time of the transfer or the shares are ordinary shares and their nominal value is not less than 10% of the nominal value of all ordinary shares of the company at that time.

(g)   Woodlands.

If the property concerned is land (except land qualifying for agricultural property relief) or shares in a company the business of which consists wholly or mainly of dealing in securities, stocks or shares, land or buildings or making or holding investments, of being a holding company of such a company or being a market maker or discount house, interest will be chargeable on the normal date calculated by reference to the transfer of value. So, in effect, interest will be charged on the outstanding balance. Where the instalment option applies in other circumstances interest is charged from the date at which the instalment is due (IHTA 1984, ss 233 and 234).

The instalment option applies in the following cases:

(i)   to chargeable transfers on death;
(ii)   to lifetime chargeable transfers, provided the transferee bears the burden of the tax;
(iii)   to charges on trustees of relevant property settlements where the property concerned continues to be comprised in the settlement.

The option only applies to the tax chargeable on a potentially exempt transfer which becomes chargeable, or to the additional tax payable on a lifetime chargeable transfer, because of the death of the transferor within seven years provided certain conditions are satisfied. There is an additional condition in the case of unquoted shares or securities that they must remain unquoted until the death of the transferor or the earlier death of the transferee.

If the property qualifying for the instalment option, or part of it, is sold, then the option ceases to apply to the unpaid tax or, in the case of a sale of part, the relevant proportion of the unpaid tax. For these purposes the payment under a partnership agreement of a sum in satisfaction of the whole or part of a partnership interest will be treated as a sale of that interest.

Capital gains tax

[12.17] Capital gains tax is chargeable at either 10% or 20% on any chargeable gains arising on the disposal of chargeable assets unless the gains qualify for entrepreneurs' relief or investor's relief in which case such gains are subject to tax at 10%.

Entrepreneurs' Relief

Outline

[12.18] Entrepreneurs' relief provides relief from capital gains tax arising on 'qualifying business disposals' (TCGA 1992, s 169H). Gains arising on such qualifying business disposals are charged to capital gains tax at a flat rate of 10% up to a lifetime maximum which is currently £10 million (TCGA 1992, s 169N).

Gains in excess of that amount will be chargeable at 20%.

Example

Cory and Luke jointly owned the entire share capital of 'Boys R Us' which they founded in 2001. They had each invested £100 in the company. In October 2016, they sold the company for £12m. Their individual gains were as follows:

	£
Proceeds	6,000,000
Acquisition cost	100
Gain	5,999,900
Tax at 10%	599,990

Qualifying disposals

[12.19] A qualifying business disposal is defined in the legislation and includes 'a material disposal of business assets', 'a disposal associated with a relevant material disposal' and a disposal of trust business assets (TCGA 1992, s 169H).

There is a 'material disposal of business assets' where an individual makes a disposal of business assets which is a 'material disposal' (TCGA 1992, s 169I(1)).

A disposal of business assets essentially will include:

- all or part of a sole trader's business;
- all or part of an interest in a partnership;
- shares or securities in an individual's personal company;
- certain disposals of business assets used in a business before cessation;
- associated disposals; and
- relevant EMI shares.

Each of these types of disposal of business assets have different conditions which must be satisfied.

A disposal for Entrepreneurs' Relief can either be a sale, a gift or a transfer at an undervalue, a capital sum derived from an asset or a capital distribution received in respect of shares held in a company.

The disposal of certain business assets or shares and securities by trustees may also qualify for relief provided that a qualifying beneficiary has a qualifying interest in the relevant company. However, it should be noted that the limit on gains eligible for relief applies to the trustees and the qualifying beneficiary jointly.

Sole traders and partnerships

[12.20] Entrepreneurs' relief is available for gains arising on the disposal by an individual of the whole or part of a qualifying business. A business means a trade, profession or vocation within the meaning of the Income Tax Acts which is conducted on a commercial basis and with a view to the realisation of profits (TCGA 1992, s 169S(1)). For the purposes of the relief, a trade includes any venture in the nature of a trade (TCGA 1992, s 169S and ITA 2007, s 989). Therefore, a business must be trading in order to qualify for relief.

The disposal of a business will qualify for relief if the following conditions are met on the date of disposal:

(a) the business has been owned by the individual or the individual has been a member of a partnership that owned the business for at least one year; and
(b) the disposal includes at least one relevant business asset (TCGA 1992, s 169L).

There is no requirement that the business has to be disposed of as a going concern and indeed all the assets do not have to be sold to one purchaser. Care needs to be taken regarding timing where assets are to be disposed of to a number of purchasers. Where some assets are sold before a substantial part of the business and a trade continues, gains made on those smaller disposals are unlikely to qualify for relief. This is because they will not qualify as part of a business or as disposals made after a cessation of the business. Difficulties can arise where an asset is disposed of under an unconditional contract. TCGA 1992, s 28 provides that the disposal is deemed to take place at the time the contract is made and not at the time the asset is transferred. The trade may not have ceased at that time. It is understood that HMRC will grant the relief if there is a genuine business disposal linked to a general business cessation.

Relief is also available on the disposal of part of a business. Relief is not available, however, on a disposal of one or more business assets unless the business in which they were used has ceased. In practice, distinguishing between the two may cause difficulties. HMRC often argues that there has not been a disposal of whole or part of a business and, therefore, care needs to be taken. Under retirement relief a number of cases were heard on this point including *McGregor (Inspector of Taxes) v Adcock* [1977] 3 All ER 65, [1977] 1 WLR 864. HMRC acknowledges that the case law concerning the application of retirement relief will not always provide certainty for the taxpayer in respect of Entrepreneurs' Relief (HMRC Capital Gains Manual, para 64015). HMRC's Manual advises that cases of difficulty in applying HMRC's guidance are to be referred to the CGT Technical Team using a defined procedure.

Special rules apply in relation to partnerships. Section 169I(8) provides that:

- where an individual carrying on a business enters into a partnership which is to carry on the business and, on entering into the partnership, he disposes of, or disposes of an interest in, assets used for the purposes of his business, he is treated as disposing of part of a business;
- a disposal by an individual of the whole or part of his interest in the assets of a partnership is treated as a disposal by him of the whole or part of the partnership business;
- at any time when a business is carried on by a partnership, the business is treated as owned by each individual who is at that time a member of the partnership.

Where a qualifying business is not disposed of but simply ceases, relief will be available on gains on assets in use in the business at the time it ceased where the assets are disposed of within three years of the date of cessation.

It should be noted that gains on disposals by sole traders and partners of shares or securities or on assets held as investments will not qualify for relief. There may be circumstances in which relief will be available on the disposal of shares and securities in a trading company and on 'associated disposals'.

Disposal of shares or securities

[12.21] Relief is available on the disposal of shares or securities provided that all of the following conditions are met throughout the one-year period ending with the disposal:

- the company must be the individual's 'personal company'. A personal company is defined as one where an individual holds at least 5% of the ordinary shares of the company and the individual controls at least 5% of the voting rights of the company which are associated with those ordinary shares. In calculating whether a shareholding meets this threshold, shares held by associates or held in another capacity are not included. In the situation where shares are held in the joint names of a husband and wife or civil partners, they are each deemed to have a 50% beneficial interest in the whole shareholding. There is no requirement that all the shares must have been held for at least one year. The condition will be satisfied if the individual has held at least 5% of the shares for one year. Any additional shares acquired within the year before disposal will also qualify for relief. There is no requirement that the shares disposed of must be ordinary shares in order for relief to be available;
- the shareholder must be an employee or an officer of the company or of a company within the same group. Shadow directors are not considered to be officers whereas non-executive directors are (TCGA 1992, s 169S and ITEPA 2003, s 5(3)). An employment is defined in TCGA 1992, s 169S(5) as the meaning found in ITEPA 2003, s 4. The employment does not need to be full-time or indeed for a minimum number of hours. It should be noted that if a director resigns with immediate effect, relief will not be available because at the date of disposal he will be neither an officer nor employee;
- the company must be a trading company or the holding company of a trading group.

There are special rules which apply to EMI shares.

A trading company, trading group and holding company of a trading group are defined in TCGA 1992, ss 165A and 169SA and Sch 7ZA. These definitions apply to disposals made after 17 March 2015.

HMRC has said that relief may be available where the 12-month ownership period includes the holding period of the original shares where there has been a share for share exchange.

Trading company

[12.22] A trading company is one 'carrying on trading activities whose activities do not include, to a substantial extent, activities other than trading activities' (TCGA 1992, s 165A(3)). Trading activities are activities carried on in the course of or for the purposes of the company's trade, but also include activities undertaken for the purposes of acquiring or setting up a proposed new trade, provided that where a new trade is acquired, the company starts to carry on that trade as soon as reasonably practical. 'Trade' is defined as for income tax purposes (ITA 2007, s 989), and includes any venture in the nature of trade. Also included in the definition of trading activities are activities undertaken with a view to acquiring a 'significant interest' in the ordinary share capital of another company which is itself a trading company or the holding company of a trading group and is not already a member of the same group of companies as the company concerned. Again, that acquisition must be made as soon as reasonably practical (TCGA 1992, s 165A(4), (5)). A significant interest for these purposes means either more than 50% or a qualifying interest in a joint venture company but without making the two companies members of the same group (TCGA 1992, s 165A(6)).

HMRC Capital Gains Manual, para 64060 gives HMRC's view as to whether the generation of investment income constitutes a trading or investment activity. Provided that non-trading activities are not carried on to a substantial extent those activities will not prevent a company from being a trading company. It is HMRC's view that 'substantial extent' in this context means more than 20% (HMRC Capital Gains Manual, para 64090). There are a number of factors that HMRC considers when ascertaining a company's trading status. The Manual provides, however, that a HMRC Officer must weigh up the relevance of each factor in the context of the individual's case and judge the matters 'in the round'. Where a company lets property surplus to its current requirements certain activities do not necessarily indicate a non-trading activity (HMRC Capital Gains Manual, para 64085).

There are special rules which apply in relation to partnerships and joint venture companies.

Post-cessation disposals

[12.23] The disposal of certain business assets within three years after the business ceased may be eligible for relief provided certain conditions are satisfied (TCGA 1992, s 169I(4)). An individual does not have to dispose of his business to a third party for a related disposal of assets to qualify for relief. The date at when a business ceases is usually a question of fact (HMRC Capital Gains Manual, para 64105). In *Rice v HMRC* (TC03273) [2014] UKFTT 0133 (TC) HMRC argued that there was no cessation of a trade but a continuance of the trade, albeit at a different location. The Tribunal identified a number of differences between the two trades, including the activities being carried on at the different locations, the type of cars sold and the fact that the stock of cars was greatly reduced, and it was those differences in the way the activities were carried on which meant that there was a cessation of one trade and the commencement of another.

In order for the disposal to qualify for relief the asset must be a relevant business asset of the business, in use at the time that the business ceased and the owner of the asset must have owned the business for at least one year ending with the date of cessation.

A relevant business asset includes any assets (including goodwill provided that the anti-avoidance provisions in s 169LA do not apply) used for the purposes of a business carried on by the sole trader or partnership. It does not include excluded assets which are shares and securities and other assets held as investments (TCGA 1992, s 169L). Therefore any shares or securities held by a sole trader or a partnership will not be eligible for relief even when there is a business reason for holding them.

The asset does not have to be used for any particular length of time before the business ceases, it just needs to be in use at the time that the business ceased.

Assets which have both a mixed business and non-business use also qualify as relevant business assets. The legislation does not impose a requirement that between the date the business ceased and the disposal of that asset, the asset has to be put to a particular use. The owner may let the asset for a commercial rent for that period and still be able to claim relief on its disposal and the period can be as long as three years.

When an individual receives a capital distribution on the liquidation or winding up of a company, he is treated as having disposed of an interest in the shares at that time (TCGA 1992, s 122). Entrepreneurs' Relief may be available if the following conditions are satisfied:

- the company has been the individual's personal company;
- the shareholder has been an employee or officer of the company or of a company in the same group;
- the company has been a trading company or a holding company of a trading group.

These conditions must have applied for a 12-month period ending with either the date that the company ceased to trade or the date that the company left a trading group. The date must also not be more than three years before the date the shares are treated as disposed of.

Where a close company is being wound up the provisions of ITTOIA 2005, s 396B must be considered. These provisions provide that where certain conditions are met, distributions received by a shareholder from the winding up of a close company will be treated as dividends chargeable to income tax.

Associated disposals

[**12.24**] Where an individual qualifies for relief on a material disposal of shares or securities or of a partnership interest, relief may be available on disposals of assets owned by that individual used in the business of a partnership of which he was a member or in his personal company. The relief cannot apply in respect of a sole trader, any such disposal would be within the post cessation rules discussed above.

For there to be an associated disposal, Condition A1, A1A, A2 or A3 must be met together with Conditions B, C and D. These conditions are as follows:

(1) the individual makes a material disposal of the whole or part of their interests in the assets of a partnership, they have disposed of at least a 5% interest in the partnership's assets and there are no 'partnership purchase arrangements' in existence at the date of the disposal (Condition A1); or

(2) the individual makes a material disposal of their whole interest in a partnership which represents an interest of less than 5%, they have held at least a 5% interest in the partnership's assets throughout a continuous period of at least three years in the eight years ending with the disposal and, at the date of the disposal, no partnership purchase arrangements exist (Condition A1A); or

(3) the individual makes a material disposal of business assets which consists of the disposal of shares, all or some of which are ordinary shares, and at the date of disposal, the ordinary shares disposed of,

constitute at least 5% of the company's ordinary share capital and carry at least 5% of the voting rights in the company and there are no 'share purchase arrangements' in existence at the date of disposal (Condition A2). The disposal must not be a capital distribution treated as a disposal under TCGA 1992, s 122 unless it is made in the course of a winding up or dissolution of the company; or

(4)   where the disposal is of securities, they represent at least 5% of the value of the company's securities and there are no 'share purchase arrangements' in existence at the date of disposal (Condition A3); and

(5)   the individual makes the disposal as part of their withdrawal from participation in the business carried on by the partnership or by the company (or a fellow member of a trading group) (Condition B); and

(6)   throughout the one-year period ending with the material disposal, or, if earlier, the date on which the business ceased, the assets which are disposed of, have been in use for the purposes of the business (Condition C) (TCGA 1992, s 169K); and

(7)   if the asset which is the subject of the associated disposal was acquired after 12 June 2016, it must have been owned throughout the period of three years ending with that disposal (Condition D).

In addition, no partnership purchase arrangements or share purchase arrangements must be in existence at the date of the associated disposal.

There are restrictions in certain situations on the amount of gain which is eligible for relief. If the following apply, the gain is reduced on a just and reasonable basis:

*   the asset has only been used by the business for part of the period of the individual's ownership – the gain will reflect the period of business use;
*   only part of the asset has been used for the purposes of the business – the gain will reflect the proportion of the asset used in the business;
*   the individual has only been involved in the business as a partner or officer or employee for part of the time during which the asset was used in the business;
*   any payment of rent was made for the use of the asset by the personal company or partnership.

Qualifying corporate bonds

[12.25] Individuals selling their personal companies often receive qualifying corporate bonds (QCBs) in exchange for their shares. The gains arising on the shares are deferred until the disposal of the QCBs which is often when they are redeemed for cash on maturity. Special rules relating to the relief have been introduced both for QCBs exchanged before 6 April 2008 and for those exchanged after that date (see TCGA 1992, s 169R). The rules are beyond the scope of this book. It should be noted that a taxpayer has the option of not treating the gain as deferred and therefore being able to claim the relief on the disposal of the shares. This will result therefore in an immediate charge to capital gains tax in respect of a disposal which does not give rise to monetary consideration. It will be essential for advisers to advise their clients of this difficulty and arrange (if necessary) for the redemption of sufficient loan notes at the relevant time to meet the liability.

Relevant EMI shares

[12.26] For disposals of shares that were acquired as a result of the exercise of qualifying EMI options, relief will be available provided certain conditions are satisfied (TCGA 1992, s 169I). It should be noted that there is no requirement for the company to be the individual's personal company.

Claim for relief

[12.27] The relief must be claimed by the individual. Where gains have been made by trustees, both the trustees and the qualifying beneficiary must make the claim (TCGA 1992, s 169M). The claim must be made by the 31 January following the tax year in which the gain arose. A claim may be withdrawn within the same period.

Interaction with other reliefs

[12.28] HMRC's view is that hold-over relief under TCGA 1992, ss 165 and 260, roll-over relief on business assets (TCGA 1992, s 152), enterprise investment scheme deferral relief (TCGA 1992, s 169) and incorporation relief (TCGA 1992, s 162) all take priority over Entrepreneurs' Relief. The better view is that Entrepreneurs' Relief takes priority over hold-over relief and incorporation relief.

Investors' Relief

Outline

[12.29] A new relief, known as 'investors' relief' has been introduced for shares issued after 16 March 2016. This relief is intended to provide a financial incentive for unconnected individuals to invest in unlisted trading companies. The relief also applies to particular trustee disposals.

Investors' relief applies where a 'qualifying person' disposes of a holding or part of a holding of shares in a company, some or all of which are 'qualifying shares' and a chargeable gain accrues. If a claim for relief is made, the rate of tax in respect of the 'relevant gain' is 10% (TCGA 1992, s 169VC(1), (2)), subject to an overall cap of £10 million (TCGA 1992, s 169VC(4)). Like Entrepreneurs' Relief, trustees do not have their own separate lifetime limit. Depending upon whether a disposal is made by an individual or by trustees, there are two separate sets of rules that apply in determining the cap on relief.

Relevant gain

[12.30] If, immediately before the disposal, all of the shares in the holding are 'qualifying shares', the 'relevant gain' is the chargeable gain arising on the disposal. If not, the 'relevant gain' is the 'appropriate part' of the chargeable gain (TCGA 1992, s 169VC). A 'holding' of shares means a holding that is treated by TCGA 1992, s 104(1) as a single asset.

The chargeable gain on the disposal (or the appropriate part of that gain) is the chargeable gain (or part) after deduction of allowable losses that fall to be made (TCGA 1992, s 169VC(5)).

Where a disposal of qualifying shares is made by the trustees of a settlement, the 'relevant gain' is the eligible beneficiary's share of the relevant gain or, if there is more than one eligible beneficiary, the aggregate of the relevant beneficiaries' shares of that gain (TCGA 1992, s 169VI(2)).

Qualifying person

[12.31] A 'qualifying person' is an individual or the trustees of a settlement (TCGA 1992, s 169VC(7)).

Where the qualifying person is the trustees of a settlement, there is an additional further requirement that there must be at least one individual who is an 'eligible beneficiary' in respect of the disposal (TCGA 1992, s 169VH(1)).

An individual is an 'eligible beneficiary' where:

• immediately before the disposal, the individual has an interest in possession (which does not include a fixed-term interest) in the settled property that includes or consists of the holding (or interest in the holding, in the situation where the trustees hold the shares jointly with another person) that includes the qualifying shares;

• the individual has had such an interest in possession throughout the three-year period ending with the disposal;

• at no time in that period has the individual been a 'relevant employee' of the company that issued the shares; and

• before the relief is claimed, the individual has elected to be treated as an eligible beneficiary by informing the trustees that he wishes to be so treated. That election may be withdrawn at any time.

Qualifying shares

[12.32] A share is a 'qualifying share' at any time if it satisfied the following conditions found in TCGA 1992, s 169VB:

(a)   it was subscribed for by the person making the disposal ('the investor');

(b)   the investor has held the share continuously from the issue of the share and ending with the relevant time (immediately before the disposal) ('the share-holding period');

(c)   the share was issued after 16 March 2016;

(d)   at the time the share was issued, none of the shares or securities of the company were listed on a recognised stock exchange;

(e)   the share was an ordinary share within the meaning given in ITA 2007, s 989 both when it was issued and immediately before the disposal;

(f)   the company that issued the share was a trading company or holding company of a trading group when the share was issued and has been so throughout the share-holding period;

(g)   at no time in the share-holding period was the investor or a person connected with the investor a 'relevant employee' in respect of that company; and

(h)   the period beginning with the date the share was issued (or 6 April 2016 if later) and ending with the date of disposal is at least three years.

Trading company

[12.33] A 'trading company' and a 'holding company of a trading group' have the same meanings as they do for hold-over relief purposes in TCGA 1992, ss 165A and 169VV(1).

However, for the purposes of this relief only, a company is not to be regarded as ceasing to be either a trading company or holding company of a trading group merely because of anything done in consequence of the company or any of its subsidiaries being in receivership or administration or if a winding up resolution or order has been made in respect of the company or any of its subsidiaries. This will only apply, though, provided that the administration or receivership or winding up order or resolution and anything done as a consequence is for genuine commercial reasons and not part of a scheme or arrangement for the avoidance of tax (TCGA 1992, s 169VV).

Subscribing for shares

[12.34] A person will be treated as having 'subscribed for' shares provided the following conditions are satisfied:

* the person subscribed for the shares;
* the share was issued to the person for consideration wholly in cash;
* the share was fully paid up at the date of issue;
* the share was subscribed for and issued for genuine commercial reasons and not as part of arrangements the main purpose, or one of the main purposes, of which is to secure a tax advantage to any person; and
* the share is subscribed for and issued by way of a bargain at arm's length (TCGA 1992, s 169VU(1)).

'Arrangements' and 'tax advantage' are as defined in TCGA 1992, s 16A.

Where an individual has subscribed for shares and subsequently transfers them (other than on death) to his spouse or civil partner with whom he was then living, the spouse or civil partner is treated for the purposes of investors' relief as having subscribed for the shares and held them continuously for any period for which the individual had held the shares continuously in addition to his or her own holding period (TCGA 1992, s 169VU).

Claim for relief

[12.35] Where the disposal is made by an individual, the individual must make a claim for the relief. In the case of a trustees' disposal, the claim must be made jointly by the trustees and the eligible beneficiary, or all of the eligible beneficiaries if more than one (TCGA 1992, s 169VM).

The claim must be made by the first anniversary of 31 January following the tax year in which the disposal is made (TCGA 1992, s 169VM).

Anti-avoidance provisions

[12.36] Where a qualifying person receives value (other than 'insignificant value') from the company during the 'period of restriction', the shares will be treated for the purposes of investors' relief as excluded shares (TCGA 1992, Sch 7ZB, para 1).

The 'period of restriction' is the period beginning one year before the date that the shares are issued and ending immediately before the third anniversary of the date of issue (TCGA 1992, Sch 7ZB, para 1(4)).

An 'insignificant value' is an amount of value that does not exceed £1,000 (TCGA 1992, Sch 7ZB, para 3(3)). Where, however, the investor receives one or more receipts of insignificant value which, when aggregated, exceed £1,000, he is treated as receiving a receipt of value of that total amount at the time of the receipt that causes the £1,000 limit to be exceeded (TCGA 1992, Sch 7ZB, para 1(3)). For this purpose, a receipt that has previously been aggregated in relation to an issue of shares cannot be counted again in respect of those shares.

If, at any time in the 12 months before the shares are issued there are arrangements entitling the investor (or an associate) to receive value from the company (or person connected with the company) at any time in the period of restriction, no amount of value received is to be treated as a receipt of insignificant value (TCGA 1992, Sch 7ZB, para 3).

Hold-over relief

[12.37] The hold-over relief provisions in TCGA 1992, s 165 and TCGA 1992, s 260 have been considered in CHAPTER 4 LIFETIME PLANNING: MAKING GIFTS and reference should be made to that coverage for a more detailed discussion of these provisions.

The hold-over relief conferred by TCGA 1992, s 165 will apply to most forms of 'business asset' dealt with in this chapter. The relief is capable of applying to disposals made by both individuals and by trustees of settlements. Hold-over relief is not, however, available on disposals to settlor-interested trusts or trusts for which there subsists an arrangement under which the settlor will acquire an interest in the trust. A settlor-interested trust will include any trust from which the settlor's dependent child can enjoy a benefit (TCGA 1992, s 169B). A dependent child is a minor who is unmarried and who is not in a civil partnership (TCGA 1992, s 169F(4)). There is a clawback period during which the held-over gain will become chargeable where the settlor has an interest in the trust or an arrangement subsists for him to acquire such interest. This is dealt with in CHAPTER 4 LIFETIME PLANNING: MAKING GIFTS.

In the case of trustees owning assets used for the purposes of a trade, profession or vocation, the trade, etc may be carried on either by the trustees or by a beneficiary with an interest in possession in the settled property (TCGA 1992, Sch 7, para 2(2)(a)). Where trustees own shares or securities of a trading company or of the holding company of a trading group, the shares or securities must either be not listed on a recognised stock exchange (and for these purposes shares dealt in on the Alternative Investment Market are not listed on a recognised stock exchange) or the trustees must hold at least 25% of the voting rights exercisable by the company's shareholders (TCGA 1992, Sch 7, para 2(2)(b)).

It is interesting to note that s 165 refers to assets 'used for the purposes of a trade, profession or vocation' but not to 'a business or an interest in a business'. At first sight this might seem to preclude any application of the relief to a gift of the whole or part of a business or an interest in a partnership; but since a business is made up of a collection of separate assets used for the purposes of the business (eg stock, plant and equipment, goodwill, etc), there appears to be nothing preventing s 165 applying to each separate asset and thus in effect to the whole business.

Since s 165 applies both to business assets and to 'an interest in' business assets, the same argument should admit the application of s 165 to gifts of interests in a partnership. The business in question must, of course, be a trade, profession or vocation.

If the asset has not been used by the transferor for the purposes of the trade, etc throughout its period of ownership, the amount of the held-over gain will be correspondingly reduced (TCGA 1992, Sch 7, paras 5, 6). On the disposal of shares, if the assets of the relevant company, or where that company is a holding company, any of its subsidiaries, include chargeable assets which are *not* used in the company's trade, profession or vocation, then the held-over gain is reduced to reflect the proportion which the chargeable business assets bear to all the chargeable assets of the company or group (TCGA 1992, Sch 7, para 7).

Hold-over relief is not available on disposals of shares or securities to a company (TCGA 1992, s 165(3)(ba)).

Consideration of the capital gains tax implications of estate planning is extremely important. Where 100% business property relief is likely to be available on death, there is a significant deterrent to making lifetime gifts. For capital gains tax purposes all assets owned by a deceased person immediately prior to his death are deemed to be acquired by his personal representatives at their current market value (TCGA 1992, s 62). This provides a tax-free uplift on death. It should always be remembered that business property relief may be changed or abolished in the future, so that there may be merit in taking advantage of the generous rates of relief whilst they remain.

Incorporation

[12.38] Before considering in detail estate planning in relation to each of the businesses of a sole proprietor, a partnership, a limited liability partnership ('LLP') and a company, a few general points will be made about the advantages and disadvantages of incorporating a business.

A business may be either incorporated or unincorporated. The decision whether or not to start a new business through a company or an LLP or to roll an existing business into a company or LLP will be governed by a number of factors, including the need for limited liability and taxation consequences. Some of these factors are pertinent to estate planning although with 100% business property relief applying to small minority shareholdings in private trading companies, the major tax advantage once associated with a partnership as opposed to a company (ie the availability of 100% relief of any partnership interest irrespective of its size) no longer applies.

There are, of course, more formalities involved in setting up and running a company or LLP than a partnership. There are accounts to be made up and filed, annual returns to be made, annual meetings to be held. In a family context, this extra degree of administration may be an important consideration. On the other hand, shares in a company are, subject to any restrictions or rights of pre-emption contained in the Articles of Association, generally more easily transferable around a family than interests in a partnership or an LLP. Whilst a partnership interest can be assigned without the assignee becoming a partner (Partnership Act 1890, s 31), more usually partnership interests are transferred by inviting the intended donee to join the partnership. It is easier in practice to be a passive shareholder in a company or a passive member of a LLP than a passive partner in a partnership.

A further important tax consideration in comparing a partnership or LLP with a company arises if the vehicle is holding, or is likely to hold, chargeable assets on which a significant capital gain is likely to be realised. A common example is land. On any sale of such an asset by a partnership or LLP, the disposal is treated as made by the partners or the members and is charged to capital gains tax. After deduction of the annual exemption, gains are charged to capital gains tax at either 10% or 20% unless the asset concerned is residential property which does not qualify for main residence relief, or carried interest, in which case it will be charged at either 18% or 28%. The proceeds are then freely distributable to the partners or members without further tax cost. On the other hand, the same sale by a company would result in a corporation tax charge for the company at 20% of the chargeable gain and a further capital gains tax charge for the shareholders if the shares are sold or liquidated. Thus, increases in the value of company assets are potentially subject to a double charge.

From the point of view of flexibility and simplicity there is much to commend the unincorporated business although, for many businesses, the limited liability conferred by incorporation will often be the deciding factor. LLPs offer the advantage of conferring limited liability on the members whilst the income and gains of the LLP are taxed as if they arose to the members directly.

A sole proprietor, partners in a partnership or members of a LLP wishing to transfer their business to a limited company in exchange for shares in that company can do so without any inheritance tax or capital gains tax arising. For inheritance tax purposes, there will be no transfer of value (IHTA 1984, s 10) and for capital gains tax purposes either TCGA 1992, s 162 will apply to 'roll-over' the gain into the shares or s 165 will apply to hold-over any gain against the amount of the assets in the company which would otherwise accrue on the disposal of the business. Section 162 incorporation relief was held to be available on the business property letting in *Ramsay v HMRC* [2013] UKUT 0226 (TCC). In that case the letting of a house which was divided into ten flats was held to be a business and not an investment activity because the activities undertaken by the owner outweighed 'what might normally be expected to be carried out by a new passive investor' and was sufficient to amount to a business. Of course, each situation will depend on its own facts.

Business property relief at 100% is available on small minority holdings in private trading companies. In addition, the replacement property provisions

(IHTA 1984, s 107) ensure that minority holdings received on incorporation will qualify for relief immediately. Where a liability is incurred after 5 April 2013 which is attributable in whole or in part to the financing of the acquisition of property qualifying for relief, the liability will first be deducted against the relevant business property regardless of what assets they are secured against (IHTA 1984, s 162B). This is discussed in more detail in CHAPTER 3 LIFETIME PLANNING: AN OVERVIEW.

One danger on incorporation is if liabilities incurred to acquire the assets which are the subject of the incorporation are re-negotiated creating new liabilities. In that case the liabilities will be deducted from relieved property under IHTA 1984, s 162B.

In addition, the stamp duty and stamp duty land tax implications need to be considered.

In most incorporations a gift of land to a company will be treated as a transfer on sale for a consideration equal to the market value of the property (FA 2003, s 53). A gift of UK land (which is not residential property) to a company is subject to stamp duty land tax at rates of up to 5% and on residential land at rates of up to 15%. Where there are other assets involved such as goodwill, such assets will not attract any stamp duty.

Incorporation may also have income tax consequences (for example, there will be a cessation of the business) which will need to be carefully considered.

Sole proprietor

[12.39] The sole proprietor of a business will usually depend on that business for his livelihood. He is therefore likely to retain it either until his death, when it will be brought into charge to inheritance tax (although 100% business property relief will be available provided the necessary conditions are satisfied) or at least until he retires, when the business may either be sold or passed on to other members of his family who are interested in taking it over. At this stage he may wish to give the business to, for example, his children and again it is possible that 100% business property relief will be available for inheritance tax purposes. Even if it is not because, for example, he does not satisfy the two-year ownership rule, the gift may constitute a potentially exempt transfer (IHTA 1984, s 3A) which will escape the inheritance tax net completely provided he survives for a period of seven years after the gift. Any chargeable gains arising on a gift, provided it is a material disposal within TCGA 1992, s 169I, may be relieved by Entrepreneurs' Relief. If relief is not available, any gains may be held-over under TCGA 1992, s 165. Hold-over relief is not available on disposals made to settlor-interested trusts or trusts for which there subsists an arrangement under which the settlor will acquire an interest in the trust. A settlor-interested trust includes any trust from which the settlor's dependent child enjoys a benefit (TCGA 1992, s 169B). A dependent child is a minor who is neither married nor a party to a civil partnership (TCGA 1992, s 169F(4A)). There is a clawback period during which the held-over gain will become chargeable where the settlor has an interest in the trust or an arrangement subsists for him to acquire such interest. This is dealt with in CHAPTER 4 LIFETIME PLANNING: MAKING GIFTS.

A gift of a business may involve the donee agreeing to indemnify the donor against his liabilities to unpaid creditors. Whilst the commercial reality behind such an agreement is clear and in effect simply means that the donee takes over the net assets of the business, the true legal analysis of the gift is that it involves the sale of the business for a consideration equal to the outstanding liabilities, which will have certain tax consequences. First, stamp duty land tax where land is involved will be payable on the consideration if it is in excess of £150,000 (if it is a non-residential property). Secondly, the ability to hold-over any chargeable gains which would otherwise accrue to the donor on the gift under TCGA 1992, s 165 may be restricted if the consideration exceeds the donor's acquisition cost (TCGA 1992, s s 165(4)). Thirdly, there may arguably be a gift with reservation for inheritance tax purposes under FA 1986, s 102. The argument for the contrary view is that those provisions can only apply to the gift element of the transaction and provided no benefit is reserved to the donor which is referable to the gift element, there can be no reserved benefit. The indemnity from the donee does not, the argument goes on, relate to the gift element. To amount to a gift with reservation there must be a benefit additional to the indemnity.

The sole proprietor of the business may, however, wish to share the running of the business, and its profits, prior to his retirement with other members of his family. In practice, it is most likely that he will do this by bringing them into either a partnership or an LLP with him. For example, he may bring his wife into a partnership or LLP in order to share with her some of the profits of the business which may reduce their overall income tax burden. Provided that his wife takes an active role in the partnership or LLP and her share of the profit is commensurate with this there will be a resulting income tax saving. HMRC attempted unsuccessfully in *Jones v Garnett (Inspector of Taxes)* [2007] UKHL 35, [2007] 4 All ER 857, [2007] STC 1536 to apply the income tax settlement provisions to situations where it considered that a company was being used as a vehicle for diverting income from one spouse to another. This is discussed in more detail in **4.18**.

Before turning to consider the creation of a partnership, however, two further points should be made. The first is in relation to borrowings. This general point is relevant to any property which is capable of qualifying as relevant business property for inheritance tax purposes. In the past where a sole proprietor was wanting to provide additional funds for his business by borrowing, he would have been advised to ensure as far as possible that the borrowings were charged on assets owned by him which did not form part of the business. In this way the charge would be an encumbrance under IHTA 1984, s 162(4) and would have reduced the value of that property which did not qualify for relief on his death rather than reducing the value of property which would in any event qualify for 100% business property relief. Where a liability is incurred after 5 April 2013 which is attributable in whole or in part to the financing of the acquisition of property qualifying for relief, the liability will first be deducted against the relevant business property regardless of against what assets it is secured. Therefore for borrowings in existence on 6 April 2013, their terms should not be renegotiated or changed so as to preserve their deductibility subject to the application of IHTA 1984, s 110. This is discussed in more detail in CHAPTER 3 LIFETIME PLANNING: AN OVERVIEW.

It is important to remember that in the context of a sole proprietor, inheritance tax business property relief only applies where the value transferred is attributable to the value of the whole of a business or to a share in that business and not where it is attributable to the value of an asset used in the business. In *Revenue & Customs Comrs v Trustees of the Nelson Dance Family* [2009] EWHC 71 (Ch), [2009] STC 802, 79 TC 605, it was held that all that is required is that the value transferred should be attributable to the value of relevant business property and, where an asset is transferred which has been part of the assets of a business, this condition is satisfied because the value of the business is reduced by the transfer. It is possible, therefore, to receive 100% relief on the transfer of an asset used in a business but only if that business is a business owned by the transferor.

Partnerships

General

[12.40] Partnerships are extremely flexible vehicles but are subject to considerable complexities and uncertainties in their tax treatment. In particular, it is very difficult to apply the capital gains tax legislation to them largely because of the legal distinction which exists between (on the one hand) partnership property and (on the other) the share or interest of a partner in a partnership. The latter is a chose in action comprising a bundle of contractual rights which one partner has against the other partners and does not necessarily represent a specific quantifiable interest in the underlying partnership assets, although each partner has an interest in those assets and they are jointly owned by the partners. For capital gains tax purposes, the chose in action is largely irrelevant and each partner is treated as owning a specific proportion (whatever that may be) of the underlying assets (see TCGA 1992, s 59) Where the partnership is carrying on a trade, any dealings with the assets of the partnership are treated as dealings by the partners individually.

As a result of the uncertainty which the complex legal nature of partnership rights creates, reliance is placed upon Statements of Practice SP D12, SP1/79 and HMRC Brief 3/2008.

When creating a partnership many factors have to be considered, but foremost from an estate planning point of view are the following.

(a)   The amount of cash or other property to be contributed to the partnership by each partner and the extent to which this is to be reflected in his or her capital account.

(b)   The rights of each partner (or his personal representatives) to extract from the partnership his share of the partnership assets on his death or retirement.

(c)   The proportions in which the partners are to share both the trading profits of the partnership and on a dissolution any surplus assets remaining after all creditors and all capital contributions of the partners have been repaid. (Surplus assets will be shared by the partners in the same proportions as they share in the trading profits, unless the partnership agreement states otherwise.)

An asset surplus on a dissolution will only usually arise as a result of an increase in value in the partnership assets above their original book values (ie ignoring any depreciation and any replacement of assets). Unless there is a revaluation of the partnership assets, with a corresponding increase or decrease in the partners' capital accounts, the original book value of the partnership assets will correspond to the amounts of capital contributed by the partners. Any increase in value therefore will represent a capital profit of the partnership which may be realised or unrealised by the time of dissolution. On a dissolution, the surplus will be distributed between the partners either in stated proportions or, if the partnership agreement is silent on the matter, in the proportions in which the trading profits of the partnership are shared. The partnership agreement may, on the other hand, state that all the capital profits (whether realised or unrealised) arising in respect of a particular asset shall belong to one or more particular partners, and the result of this is that on the dissolution the division of surplus assets will be modified accordingly.

It is important that these matters are detailed in a partnership agreement as the case of *Ham v Ham* [2013] EWCA Civ 1301, [2013] All ER (D) 356 (Oct) illustrates. It is also important for the terms of the agreement to be reviewed regularly to ensure that they are still appropriate.

For capital gains tax purposes, the disposal of a partnership asset is taxed in the hands of the partners in the proportions in which they share the surplus assets of the partnership at the time of the disposal (Statement of Practice D12 para 2). Where an automatic accruer or option provision applies on the death of a partner (see below), he may still be treated for capital gains tax purposes as owning a share in the assets of the partnership during his lifetime and taxed accordingly.

The possible permutations on all the factors mentioned above are enormous and the following are examples of some of the more common types of partnership arrangement.

(1)   A, B, and C agree to introduce capital equally and to share trading profits and any surplus assets on dissolution equally. On the death or retirement of any one of them, he (or his personal representatives) is entitled to take from the partnership the full value of his partnership interest, subject to the continuing partners having the option to buy it for its full market value. Alternatively, if A, B and C contribute capital in unequal shares, they may decide to share the trading profits and surplus assets in the same proportions rather than equally.

(2)   As in (1), except that on the death or retirement of any partner, he (or his personal representatives) is entitled only to take the balance on his capital account and his share of accrued trading profits, with the rest of his partnership interest accruing automatically without payment to the continuing partners.

(3)   A, B and C agree to introduce capital equally and to share trading profits equally, but agree that any surplus assets on a dissolution shall belong only to B and C equally. On the death or retirement of A, he (or his personal representatives) is entitled only to take the balance on his capital account and his share of accrued trading profits (with the rest of his share accruing automatically without payment to B and C); but on the death or retirement of B or C, they (or their respective personal representatives) are entitled to receive the full value of their partnership interests subject only to an option for the continuing partners to buy it at its full market value.

Each arrangement will have differing inheritance tax and capital gains tax consequences for the partners which are discussed in what follows.

Formation of a partnership

Inheritance tax

[12.41] In the case of, for example, a sole proprietor of a business who wishes to bring his son into partnership, it is probable that 100% business property relief will be available so that no actual inheritance tax liability will arise. It is, however, useful to consider how the transaction will be analysed for inheritance tax purposes as there may be occasions where the relief is not fully available, or is subsequently lost because the proprietor dies within seven years of the gift and the necessary conditions are not met at that time (IHTA 1984, s 113A).

The proprietor and his son are connected persons under IHTA 1984, s 270. There will be no transfer of value on the formation of the partnership if the father did not intend to confer any gratuitous benefit on his son (or indeed on any other person) and that the terms of the son's entry into the partnership were such as might be expected to be made in a similar arrangement at arm's length between unconnected persons (IHTA 1984, s 10). In general, for this condition to be satisfied it will be necessary for the son to provide such consideration as would have been required had the transaction been a normal commercial one, but in the context of a family partnership, it is often difficult to identify precisely what would amount to normal commercial terms. Some of the relevant factors are considered below.

Where the formation of the partnership cannot be brought within IHTA 1984, s 10, there will be no transfer of value provided there is no reduction in the value of the father's estate as a result of the formation of the partnership. For example, if the father has the business valued and then introduces it to the partnership with his capital account being credited with the full value of the business then, even if he and his son share the trading profits of the partnership equally, there should be no inheritance tax consequences for the father. This is particularly so if he is able to determine the partnership and recover his capital contribution on demand or within a reasonably short period (say three months).

If the full value of the existing business is not credited to the father's capital account and, for example, the father and son share profits equally, then on the partnership being wound up and the business sold, unless otherwise agreed, the son will share the proceeds of sale equally with his father after the balances on capital account have been repaid. This is the effect of the Partnership Act 1890, s 44, which provides that, in the absence of any express agreement, any surplus assets left after the payment of all debts, advances and capital contributions are shared between the partners in the proportions in which they shared the profits. Partners do not share surplus assets in proportion to their capital contributions unless this is expressly agreed. As a result, the father, on taking his son into partnership on such terms, will clearly have made a gift to him of part of the business unless the partnership agreement was such as might have been made between unconnected persons dealing at arm's length and the father had no gratuitous intent towards either his son or any other person.

One would generally expect that in a normal commercial arrangement the son would have to buy into the partnership and effectively purchase a share of the business from his father. It might be argued that a capital contribution by the son which is credited to his own capital account would not be sufficient. There would have to be some consideration passing to the father – either outside the partnership or perhaps by way of credit to the father's capital account. The case of *A-G v Boden* [1912] 1 KB 539 is often cited as authority for the proposition that consideration may be non-monetary. In that case, it was held that two sons had given full consideration (in the form of an agreement to devote as much time and attention to the business as it required as compared with their father being only required to devote as much time and attention to the business as he thought fit) for a provision that their father's share in the goodwill of the business would automatically accrue to them without payment on his death. It is, however, dangerous to rely on the principles of this case applying to circumstances other than ones very similar to its facts. It may be appropriate to regard a covenant to work full-time in a business as adequate consideration for the deferred acquisition of goodwill on the death of a partner – goodwill being an asset which depends to a great extent on the amount of time and energy put into a business – but it is quite another thing to regard such a covenant as adequate consideration for the acquisition of an immediate interest in a partnership and an interest extending beyond the goodwill to the other assets of the partnership. Undoubtedly, each case will turn on its own facts and there may be circumstances where a similar covenant could make up the difference between partial and full consideration.

Even if 100% business property relief is not fully available, any element of gift inherent in the formation of the partnership may constitute a potentially exempt transfer by the father to his son and will escape inheritance tax provided the father survives for the necessary seven-year period. One can insure against the risk of his death in this period.

Reservation of benefit

[**12.42**] Will the formation of a partnership amount to a gift with reservation for inheritance tax purposes? The provisions of FA 1986, s 102 can apply to a gift where either possession and enjoyment of the property concerned is not *bona fide* assumed by the donee or the property is not enjoyed to the entire exclusion of the donor and of any benefit to him by contract or otherwise. In the context of a partnership, it is often quite difficult to decide whether or not the provisions have any application. Clearly, if the formation of the partnership is on full commercial terms, there is no gift and therefore no question of the provisions applying. Where, however, there is an element of gift, it is essential to first identify the subject matter of the gift. On the formation of the partnership, the subject matter of the gift will not be an interest in the partnership because prior to the gift the partnership will not have existed. Instead, it is the granting of certain contractual rights against the donor in respect of the property which is to become the property of the partnership (the business) coupled with the acquisition of the legal title to and/or a beneficial interest in that property. In almost all cases, possession and enjoyment of the subject matter of the gift will be *bona fide* assumed by the donee; so it is important to establish whether or not the donor is excluded from any benefit from the property given away. It is also necessary to consider the anti-shearing provisions of FA 1986, ss 102A–102C (see CHAPTER 11 THE FAMILY HOME AND OTHER RESIDENTIAL PROPERTY at **11.49–11.53**. It should also be borne in mind that the income tax charge on pre-owned assets may apply where the donor continues to derive benefit from assets he has given away in circumstances in which the reservation of benefit rules do not apply. The charge will only apply in relation to land, chattels or intangible property contained in a settlement in circumstances in which the donor derives a benefit (see CHAPTER 4 LIFETIME PLANNING: MAKING GIFTS). HMRC said in its Appendix to the POA Charge Guidance Notes that there would be no income tax charge in the situation where a father admits his son into a partnership in return for the son's agreement to take on most of the day-to-day running of the partnership, provided that the transaction is one that might be expected to be made at arms' length. This supposes that there is a disposal of the underlying assets (land or chattels) rather than a disposal of the partnership interest. HMRC had also said in its Guidance Notes that 'they do not regard the partnership interest as transparent and the disposal of a share is unlikely to give rise to a Schedule 15 charge in any circumstances'. This has not, however, been reproduced in the Inheritance Tax Manual which has superseded the Guidance Notes.

A father who is already in partnership with one of his sons, may give his partnership share to another son and retire from the partnership but remain as a consultant or employee. Provided the employment is on commercial terms and the remuneration is not excessive, this would not be regarded as a gift with reservation. What is reasonable is to be tested by reference to what might reasonably be expected under an arm's length arrangement between unconnected parties.

If the father were to give his son an interest in a specific percentage of the capital assets of the partnership (eg by way of crediting his capital account), together with an interest in a corresponding percentage of the trading profits, it is unlikely that there will be a problem. However, there may be a problem where the son is given an interest in a particular share of the assets of the partnership but a lesser share of the profits so that the father takes a share of the profits greater than his retained share of the capital assets. This is because the father could be said to have reserved a benefit out of the property given to his son by reason of his receiving a share of the profits in excess of the capital retained by him. In a previous version of the Inheritance Tax Manual HMRC had given the following example of where the reservation of benefit rules will not apply.

HMRC example

'Father and son have been in partnership together since 1980 sharing profits equally. The land is owned by the father and occupied by the partnership rent free without any formal tenancy agreement. In 1989 the father gives the land to the son but the partnership continues to occupy it on the same basis. At the same time the profit sharing ratio is adjusted in favour of the son.

Provided the increase in the son's share of profits represented full consideration in money or money's worth for occupation of the land [FA 1986, Sch 20, para 6(1)(a)] will apply and this will not be a [gift with reservation].

The father is in effect occupying the land through the partnership and this *prima facie* constitutes a reservation. However, we accept that the let-out in para 6(1)(a) may be satisfied by an appropriate upward adjustment (in lieu of rent) reflected in the donee's share of the partnership profits. The circumstances of the case must determine what is "appropriate" having regard to what might be agreed under an arm's length deal between unconnected persons' (HMRC Inheritance Tax Manual, para 14341).

It should be noted that this example has now been changed so that the parties are not father and son.

If, therefore, the father wishes the son to take a greater share of the assets of the partnership but a lesser share of the profits, it is probably safer from the gifts with reservation viewpoint to defer the son's right to share in the assets by means of an option provision to take effect on the father's death or retirement rather than by giving him an immediate interest. However, as we shall see, the introduction of an automatic accruer or option provision gives rise to other inheritance tax problems.

A similar reservation of benefit problem could arise where the father reserves a right to receive the first slice of any profits of the partnership up to a specific amount.

Capital gains tax

[12.43] If the business introduced by the father into the partnership includes any chargeable assets (eg goodwill, land or tangible movables worth more than £6,000 each), then the disposal of these assets may give rise, for capital gains tax purposes, to a capital gains tax charge. As the assets of a partnership are, for capital gains tax purposes, treated as belonging to the partners in the proportions in which they share surplus assets (which in turn will be the proportions in which they share the profits of the partnership unless stated otherwise), for capital gains tax purposes there will be a disposal to the extent of the interest taken by the son. For example, if the father and son simply agree to share profits equally, then there will be a disposal of 50% of the chargeable assets.

It is currently HMRC's view that where an asset is transferred to a partnership by means of a capital contribution, the partner in question is treated as having made a part disposal of the asset concerned equal to the fractional share that passes to the other partners. The market value rule applies if the transfer is between connected persons or is other than by a bargain at arm's length. Otherwise, the consideration for the part disposal is a proportion of the total amount given by the partnership for the asset. That proportion equals the fractional share of the asset passing to the other partners.

If the partnership agreement is subsequently altered so that the son becomes entitled to a proportion of those profits, this alteration will be treated by HMRC as a part disposal for capital gains tax purposes of the father's partnership interest (see Statement of Practice SP D12 para 7) but hold-over relief (under TCGA 1992, s 165) should then be available as no consideration would have been given for the disposal. Where there is a change in the ratios in which surpluses on assets are shared between *unconnected* partners, HMRC treats the disposal as taking place at book value (ie on a no gain/no loss basis), unless there is a direct payment of consideration outside the partnership or there is or has been a revaluation of the partnership assets and a corresponding increase in the partners' capital account (Statement of Practice SP D12 paragraph 4).

A similar capital gains tax problem arises if the father has first taken his wife into partnership with him. At that stage he may well not have had his business valued because of the availability of the spouse exemption (IHTA 1984, s 18) preventing any inheritance tax consequences. However, if their son is taken into partnership having first valued the business and having that value credited to their capital accounts, then on the son receiving a share in the assets of the partnership, HMRC would treat his parents as making a part disposal of the partnership assets (Statement of Practice SP D12).

Options and accruers

[12.44] The terms of the partnership deed should also provide for what is to happen on the death or retirement of one of the partners. It is quite common for an agreement to contain a provision which allows the retiring partner or the personal representatives of the deceased partner to extract his capital contributions and his share of accrued trading profits with the remainder of his partnership interest accruing automatically to the surviving partners or, alternatively, granting the continuing partners an option to acquire the interest for a nominal consideration. Although HMRC does not consider that automatic accruer clauses are contracts for sale, it is advisable for a partnership deed to provide for an option to purchase the share rather than an accruer clause. In such a case, when valuing the interest of the deceased or retiring partner in the partnership, its value should be restricted to the sums due under the partnership agreement and no account should be taken of the then value of the underlying assets of the partnership business. Although the case of *Burdett-Coutts v IRC* [1960] 3 All ER 153, [1960] 1 WLR 1027 is sometimes cited as authority for the proposition that the value of the partnership interest of a deceased partner should be by reference to the underlying assets of the partnership, that case was in fact dealing with the position where the death caused the partnership to dissolve. That is not comparable to a situation which a partnership continues notwithstanding the death of one partner.

In the opinion of HMRC such an automatic accruer or option provision amounts to an exclusion or restriction on the right of the deceased or retiring partner to dispose of his share (HMRC Inheritance Tax Manual, para 25120) and it should only therefore be taken into account when valuing his interest to the extent that consideration was given for it (IHTA 1984, s 163). Whilst HMRC's argument may have some force if the automatic accruer or option provision is added as a term of a partnership *after* its formation, it is more difficult to sustain where the provision is a term of the partnership from the outset. This is because, on introducing any property to the partnership, the partner concerned will exchange his interest in that property for the 'chose in action', comprising his bundle of partnership rights in which the restriction on what he may extract from the partnership on his death or retirement is inherent from the outset. There is no question of the partnership agreement itself placing an exclusion or restriction on his right to dispose of any property which pre-existed the agreement.

If, however, HMRC's argument is correct – and, in practice, it is advisable to order one's affairs on the assumption that it is correct, unless one is prepared to go to considerable time and expense in arguing to the contrary – then on the death of the outgoing partner the existence of the automatic accruer or option provision will only be taken into account in valuing the interest if the continuing partners gave full consideration. This will be a question of fact in each case and will depend on all the circumstances surrounding either the formation of the partnership or, if later, the time when the provision was introduced as a term. In determining this, the precise scope of the accruer or option will have to be taken into account: whether it relates to the entire partnership share, or just to the outgoing partner's interest in surplus assets, or to his share of the goodwill of the partnership. Other factors include the respective amounts of capital contributions; the profit-sharing ratios and the surplus asset-sharing ratios; the time each partner is required to devote to partnership matters; the respective ages of the partners; the duration of the partnership; and the terms on which distributions will be made on the death or retirement of any of the partners. It is understood that if all the partners are of commensurate age, and each partner's share is subject to the same automatic accruer or option provision, then each gives full consideration for its existence because none of them knows which of them is likely to die first. However, the same argument cannot be applied where there is a considerable divergence in the ages and therefore is of little help in a family partnership which includes members of different generations. Possibly, on the strength of *A-G v Boden* [1912] 1 KB 539, a covenant to work full-time in the partnership business by members of the younger generation could count as (or towards) full consideration, if no similar covenant is required of the older generation. In addition, an agreement by the younger partners to provide an annuity to any retiring partner or to the widow of a deceased partner in return for the partnership share could be taken into account as full or partial consideration, although in HMRC's view (see the ICAEW Memorandum TR 557 of 19 September 1984 reproduced in Part 3 of *Tolley's Yellow Tax Handbook 2016/17*) such an automatic accrual of the deceased partner's share to the continuing partners on death in return for a widow's annuity will result in a loss of business property relief.

The HMRC Inheritance Tax Manual, para 25292 states that 'agreements under which the deceased's interest passes to the surviving partners, who are required to pay the personal representatives a particular price . . . do not constitute contracts for sale.' Although the instalment option ceases on sale and the balance of tax falls due at once if the surviving partners pay the purchase price in stages, each part-payment is treated as a part sale of the business (IHTA 1984, s 227(6) and HMRC Inheritance Tax Manual, para 25122).

Unless an automatic accruer or option provision has been incorporated for full consideration, it is unlikely to prevent an inheritance tax charge arising on the death of a partner in respect of the whole of his partnership share subject, of course, to the availability of business property relief. Subject to this, when bringing one or more children into partnership, the father should aim to give to them as large an interest in the partnership as he feels comfortable about giving away in the hope that he will survive the gift by seven years. Due to the impact of the gifts with reservation provisions, the share of trading profits retained by the father should not exceed his interest in the assets of the partnership. An automatic accruer or option provision could also be inserted in an attempt to limit the taxable part of the father's partnership interest to (say) just the balance on his capital account plus his share of any accrued trading profits, but as we have seen this may not be successful.

Alternatively, the partnership agreement could provide that any capital profits, whether realised or unrealised, of the partnership should belong to the next generation. As the passing of the growth element is immediate rather than deferred until death or retirement, IHTA 1984, s 163 should not apply. However, if there is any element of gift in the creation of the partnership the reservation of benefit rules may apply. Another problem with this type of provision is that to insert it in the partnership *ab initio* may well result in a disposal for capital gains tax purposes by the father of the entire business (to the extent it includes any chargeable assets) and (as we have seen) TCGA 1992, s 165 may not be available to hold-over the gains. However, such a provision could subsequently be inserted in a pre-existing agreement and in such circumstances the relief should be available.

Existing partnerships

[**12.45**] Returning to the earlier example, let us assume that the father has now brought his son into partnership with him. The full value of the father's business has been credited to his capital account. The son has introduced a sum of £10,000 into the business which has been credited to his capital account. They share profits equally; but on the death or retirement of either, he, or his personal representatives, are only entitled to extract from the partnership the sum credited to his capital account and his share of accrued trading profits. The balance of the share in the partnership automatically accrues to the survivor without payment. The son has also covenanted to work full-time in the business but there is no corresponding obligation on the father.

As we have seen, this type of arrangement is designed to freeze the value of the father's partnership interest so that any growth in value of the partnership assets will accrue automatically to the son. What further estate planning steps are now available to the father?

In considering the following paragraphs it should be remembered that, in most instances, 100% business property relief will be available whether further steps are taken during the father's lifetime or whether the son inherits under his father's will. In addition, there will be a capital gains tax-free uplift if the father still owns his share in the partnership at the time of his death.

Transfer of capital

[12.46] The father may over a period of time make gifts to his son of his partnership capital, simply by debiting his capital account and crediting his son's. This process can use up the father's annual inheritance tax exemption of £3,000; alternatively, larger sums may be passed over as potentially exempt transfers. HMRC appears to accept that a partner's capital account amounts to an interest in a business, rather than just an asset used in the partnership business (HMRC Inheritance Tax Manual, para 25060). Therefore, if the father were to die within seven years of making a potentially exempt transfer, 100% business property relief will be available (assuming all the other conditions are satisfied) to reduce the value of the gift to nil.

Where sums are left on capital account after a partner's retirement from the partnership, they will not represent an interest in a business and will not, therefore, receive business property relief (*Beckman v IRC* [2000] STC (SCD) 59 (SpC 226)).

Is a gift of part of the capital account a gift with reservation for inheritance tax purposes? As the sum still remains part of the capital of the partnership, it is clearly arguable that the donor continues to benefit from it whilst he remains a partner. However, it will also depend upon whether the proportion given away is also reflected in a reduction in the capital and profit sharing ratios. Where a certain proportion of capital is given away, and there is a corresponding reduction in the profit and capital sharing ratios, it is arguable that there is no reservation of benefit. HMRC gives the following example at HMRC Inheritance Tax Manual, para 14332.

HMRC example

A farmer, on taking his son into partnership, makes a gift to him of a share of all the partnership assets including the land. They then share the profits and losses in the same proportion as they own the partnership assets at commencement. The farmer dies ten years later.

This is not a GWR. The son has taken possession and enjoyment of the partnership share gifted to him in the form of his share of profits. The father's share of profits is referable to his own partnership share, not the share gifted.

The analysis is based on there being no reservation initially rather than on the basis that full consideration was paid to prevent the reservation of benefit rules applying.

Introduction of accruers or options

[**12.47**] Where an existing partnership deed does not contain any automatic accruer or option provision, it would be possible to incorporate one by way of a supplemental agreement. If this gives rise to an immediate reduction in the value of the father's estate but the son gives full consideration, the exemption conferred by IHTA 1984, s 10 should apply. What will amount to full consideration will depend on the precise circumstances and, in particular, the scope of the automatic accruer or option provision itself. If the son does give full consideration, then on the death or retirement of his father full account will be taken of the automatic accruer or option provision and IHTA 1984, s 163 will not be applicable. If, on the other hand, the son does not give full consideration, then any transfer of value by the father will be a potentially exempt transfer for inheritance tax purposes. However, IHTA 1984, s 163 may apply on the subsequent death or retirement of the father to bring the full value of the father's partnership interest into the charge to inheritance tax, subject to the availability of business property relief. Although HMRC accepts that an automatic accruer clause is not a contract for sale, it is advisable for an option clause to be included rather than an accruer clause. It is unlikely that there would be a gift with reservation for inheritance tax purposes, since the property given is a right to all or a part of the donor's partnership interest only on his death or retirement and there is, therefore, no question of the donor ever benefiting from the subject matter of the gift, unless, possibly, the donor becomes entitled to, or receives, an annuity on retirement.

If such a variation in the terms of the partnership is made as part of a bargain of such a kind as would have been reached between parties dealing at arm's length, it is the practice of HMRC not to impose a charge to capital gains tax (see Statement of Practice D12, para 4). Otherwise, the hold-over relief provisions of TCGA 1992, s 165 should be applicable.

Gift of capital profits

[**12.48**] Instead of incorporating an automatic accruer or option provision the father could make an immediate gift of any future growth in the capital assets of the partnership by inserting the type of provision which confers the benefit of any capital profits on his son. Provided this does not involve any immediate reduction in the value of the father's estate, there will be no immediate inheritance tax consequences although it could amount to a gift with reservation unless it can be argued either that there is no disposition of any property within FA 1986, s 102 or that if there is, the father's right to benefit from the property given away (by reason of his continuing to draw the same level of profits) is not referable to the subject matter of the gift but to his pre-existing contractual rights under the partnership. The capital gains tax position is the same as above. The pre-owned assets legislation should be considered to determine whether an income tax charge would arise.

Gift of partnership interest

[**12.49**] Alternatively, the father may simply decide to increase his son's share in the capital assets of the partnership with immediate effect by transferring capital between their capital accounts and by altering their respective surplus asset sharing ratios. This may be done without reducing his share of the trading profits at the same time. The advantage of this over the former course is that it avoids completely any question of the application of IHTA 1984, s 163 on the death or retirement of the father. If full consideration is not given by the son, then the variation will constitute a potentially exempt transfer for inheritance tax purposes. For the same reasons as given above in relation to gifts between capital accounts, it is considered that a gift by way of an increase in the son's share in the assets of the partnership, without a corresponding increase in his profit share, will not amount to a gift with reservation, although HMRC may well not share this view. The pre-owned assets legislation should be considered to determine whether an income tax charge would arise.

So far as capital gains tax is concerned, either the disposal is treated as taking place on a 'no gain/no loss' basis (Statement of Practice SP D12) or hold-over relief under TCGA 1992, s 165 should be available.

Trustee partners

[12.50] Where there are minor children involved, it would be possible to bring into an existing partnership (or into a new partnership) the trustees of a settlement established for their benefit. The trustees will of course have to have the necessary powers in the trust instrument to enable them to become partners and to contribute capital. The trustees should ideally pay full consideration for their partnership interest (eg by contributing the appropriate amount of capital, etc), to avoid any argument that the partnership agreement itself amounts to a 'settlement' within ITTOIA 2005, Pt 5 Ch 5 and that the settlor is taxable on the trustees' share of the trading profits. Further, the trustees should withdraw their share of the profits each year, to avoid any argument that they have made a loan to the settlor or his spouse (by leaving their share in the partnership) and thus fall within ITTOIA 2005, s 633. Section 633 applies where trustees of a settlement make a loan to the settlor and allows HMRC to tax the settlor on any undistributed income of the settlement. With such an arrangement, ITTOIA 2005, s 850C, which reallocates distributed profits of mixed partnerships, will need to be considered.

Retirement

[12.51] If on the retirement of a partner, his share automatically accrues to the continuing partners or is subject to an option to acquire at nominal value, this should not result in any chargeable transfer if his share has been subject to this provision at all times. This is because the reduction in the value of his share by reason of his retirement will always have been inherent in it and consequently any reduction in the value at the date of his retirement should be minimal. However, HMRC may not accept this view. The position would undoubtedly be different if the provisions had been introduced as a result of a later agreement (as in the case, for example, of *A-G v Ralli* (1936) 15 ATC 523 (KB)) since IHTA 1984, s 163 will be applicable and the automatic accruer or option provision will only be taken into account if it was granted for full consideration. This may or may not have been the case. If not, then any reduction in value on retirement should amount to a potentially exempt transfer for inheritance tax purposes, and in any event 100% business property relief is likely to be available provided all the relevant conditions are fulfilled.

The capital gains tax position is more complicated. Either para 4 of the Statement of Practice SP D12 will apply to deem the disposal to take place on a 'no gain/no loss' basis or hold-over relief under TCGA 1992, s 165 may be available.

If, on retirement, the continuing partners are obliged to pay to the outgoing partner an annuity, the payments by them will not give rise to any inheritance tax charge if the annuities form part of an arm's length transaction between them. Otherwise, the payment of the annuities should fall within the normal expenditure out of income exemption.

Death

[**12.52**] The position on death is similar to retirement, except for the fact that no capital gains tax will be payable; and any chargeable transfer arising by reason of the death cannot constitute a potentially exempt transfer and will therefore give rise to an immediate tax charge, subject to the availability of 100% business property relief and the interest-free instalment option (if necessary). There will be no question of any subsequent loss of the business property relief.

Insurance

[**12.53**] The death or retirement of a partner is likely to necessitate the continuing partners (if the partnership continues) finding the cash either to repay to the partner (or their personal representatives) the sums due on their capital account or to purchase their interest in the partnership. To provide for this eventuality, and in particular where the partnership includes members from different generations, the elder partners might consider taking out whole life policies on their lives and holding them on trust for the other partners subject to an overriding power of appointment exercisable in favour of a class consisting of the life assured's spouse or civil partner and his or her issue and his or her parents. Ideally, there should also be power to add other persons (other than the settlor) to the members of this class. Many life offices have standard 'flexible trust' wordings along these lines. Property held on such trusts will be 'relevant' property and subject to the settlement charges under IHTA 1984, Pt III, Ch III.

On the death of the life assured, the policy will provide the continuing partners with cash which they can use to fund any payments due to the deceased's personal representatives. In the event that the life assured retires from the partnership the policy may be surrendered and the proceeds similarly used. If the partnership is dissolved the policy can be appointed away from the continuing partners to members of the life assured's family.

If new partners enter the partnership, they may be included in the class of objects of the overriding power and this power may then be exercised in their favour so as to allow them to benefit from the policy along with the existing partners.

The settlor is usually excluded from the trusts to ensure that the inheritance tax gifts with reservation provisions cannot apply. However, the provisions may still apply where all the partners make similar reciprocal arrangements since the settlor, by reason of his being a beneficiary under the other trusts, could be said to have reserved a benefit by associated operations (FA 1986, s 102(1)(b), Sch 20 para 6(1)(c)). Where such reciprocal arrangements are entered into as part of a commercial agreement between the partners, they may lack the element of bounty necessary to bring s 102 into play at all; but it is understood that HMRC takes the view that if beneficiaries other than just the other partners are capable of benefiting under the trusts then the arrangements will not be regarded as 'commercial'.

In relation to the income tax charge arising under the pre-owned asset regime, HMRC has confirmed that, provided a partner is not a potential beneficiary of his own policy, then an income tax charge will not arise. Where, however, the partner retains the benefit for himself – for example, where he can cash in the policy during his lifetime for his own benefit – then, even if the arrangement is on commercial terms so that it is not a gift with reservation, the trust is a settlement for inheritance tax purposes and a charge to tax under para 8 will arise (HMRC Inheritance Tax Manual, para 44115).

Assets held outside the partnership

[12.54] It is necessary to consider carefully whether assets should be held within or outside the partnership. Assets, such as the premises from which the business is run, held within the partnership as part of the partnership assets qualify for 100% business property relief, whilst those held outside but used for the partnership business qualify for 50% relief only.

From a taxation viewpoint therefore there is considerable merit in transferring the asset, whether by way of gift or sale, into the partnership, subject to any stamp duty land tax charge. However, other factors must be taken into consideration, and the tax consequences of the transfer into the partnership must not be forgotten. The simplest transaction would involve the creation of a new class of partnership capital to which the transferor is entitled. Any transfer which benefits other members of the partnership will need careful consideration where the partners are other than an individual and his spouse or civil partner.

Liabilities

[12.55] One other important factor to consider is the nature of the assets upon which any debt is secured.

Where a partner has taken a loan before 6 April 2013 secured against personal assets in order to contribute additional partnership capital, rather than against assets qualifying for business property relief, the debt will reduce the value of the personal assets. This will result in the assets qualifying for relief receiving the benefit of that relief and the value of the personal assets on which tax is chargeable being reduced. Where loans were taken out after 5 April 2013 the rules are different. A loan taken out after 5 April 2013 to finance the acquisition, maintenance or enhancement of relevant business property will be deducted from the value of the relevant business property. Care should, therefore, be taken where a loan taken out before 6 April 2013 is varied in case the variation jeopardises the relief available.

ITA 2007, s 384 provides that no income tax relief is available for interest paid on an overdraft. Income tax relief should be available under ITA 2007, ss 383 and 398 subject to ss 384A and 385. Section 384A provides that tax relief will not be available on a loan which is entered into to provide capital to a partnership where the loan is made as part of arrangements which 'appear very likely to produce a post-tax advantage and the arrangements seem to have been designed to reduce any income tax or capital gains tax to which the borrower . . . would be liable apart from the arrangements'.

Limited liability partnerships

[**12.56**] The Limited Liability Partnership Act 2000 ('LLPA 2000') permits the creation of partnerships where, in contrast to limited partnerships, members may participate in the management of the business of the LLP whilst having limited liability.

LLPA 2000, s 1(2) provides that such a partnership is a body corporate with a legal personality separate from that of its members.

For tax purposes, an LLP is, except in limited circumstances, transparent, that is to say that the tax is levied on its members rather than on the corporate body itself. Each member is treated as being self-employed. Anti-avoidance provisions have been introduced, under which certain salaried members of an LLP are treated as employees for tax purposes, rather than as partners. Apart from tax, there are other factors which affect the choice of an LLP as an appropriate business structure, the chief one being the protection of limited liability which is offered to its members. This advantage is also afforded by incorporation as a company, but that may also produce for its members, a liability to pay-as-you-earn tax and Class 1 and 1A National Insurance contributions.

An LLP is formed by being incorporated under LLPA 2000. Its members are those persons who subscribe their names to the incorporation document and any other persons becoming members by and in accordance with an agreement with the existing members. A person may cease to be a member by death or by dissolution of the LLP, by agreement with the other members or by giving reasonable notice to the other members. The mutual rights and duties of members are governed by agreement between the members or between the LLP and its members.

ITTOIA 2005, s 863 provides that where an LLP carries on a trade, profession or other business with a view to profit, all its activities are treated as carried on in the LLP by its members and not by the LLP itself. Anything done by, to, or in relation to the LLP for the purposes of, or in connection with, any of its activities is treated as done by, to, or in relation to the members as partners. The property of the LLP is treated as held by the members as partnership property.

An LLP carrying on a trade, profession or other business with a view to profit is treated as a partnership for the purposes of capital gains tax (TCGA 1992, s 59A). The assets of the LLP are treated as belonging to the members who are directly taxable on their share of any chargeable gains arising on disposal of those assets. If there is a temporary cessation of trade, the tax status of the LLP continues. This is also the case in a winding up, provided that the process is not unnecessarily prolonged and that the purpose of the winding up is not the avoidance of tax.

On the liquidation of an LLP, however, the LLP ceases to be treated in this way from the earlier of the appointment of a liquidator or a court order for winding up. The normal capital gains rules then cease to apply and the LLP is taxed through the liquidator as a company on any chargeable gains arising on disposals of its assets. The only asset then held by the members is their capital interest in the LLP; there will be a disposal of the whole or part when capital distributions are made by the liquidator. The acquisition dates and costs of these capital interests will depend on their actual acquisition by the member concerned.

The commencement and cessation of a partnership's status as an LLP does not of itself give rise to a charge to capital gains tax on its members. TCGA 1992, s 169A, however, provides that any gain held over under TCGA 1992, s 165 when the LLP status no longer applies does not fall out of charge. Where a member holds an asset acquired from a disposal to him, any gain which has been held over under TCGA 1992, s 165 or s 260, immediately becomes chargeable.

As an LLP has the same tax transparency as a normal partnership except where the anti-avoidance provisions in FA 2014 apply, similar considerations in relation to estate planning will apply, as discussed above.

Family limited partnerships

[12.57] In recent years limited partnerships have generated a great deal of interest. Because of the changes made to the taxation of trusts in FA 2006, such partnerships are considered as an alternative to trusts. A family limited partnership (FLP) is a limited partnership which holds assets on behalf of a family in accordance with the terms of a partnership agreement. A limited partnership is a partnership registered in accordance with the Limited Partnerships Act 1907. It must be formed between two or more persons and must carry on a business in common with a view to profit (Limited Partnerships Act 1907, s 7). A limited partnership has two categories of partner: general partner – who has responsibility for managing the business and has unlimited liability for the partnership's debts and obligations, and limited partners who invest capital but do not take an active role in the operation of the partnership and will have limited liability. The attraction of a limited partnership is the ability to separate the economic benefits (held by the limited partners) from control (which is held by the general partner). Typically, the general partner will be a limited company with nominal share capital and will hold 1% of the capital of the FLP. The shareholders of the company will usually be the partners. The partnership should be operated as a business with a view to profit but it can hold a range of investments provided they are actively managed.

For tax purposes a limited partnership is transparent in the same way as a general partnership or an LLP. In some jurisdictions, though, a limited partnership is treated as a separate legal entity. An FLP can provide asset protection on a divorce because the courts do not usually have the power to vary a partnership agreement.

As you would expect, there are some drawbacks to an FLP. First, in the UK, FLPs operate as collective investment schemes and are therefore subject to regulation by the Financial Conduct Authority ('FCA'). This is because the limited partners do not have day-to-day management control over the property. Therefore an FCA authorised investment manager must be appointed which will increase costs. This can be avoided if the FLP is located in another jurisdiction, for example, Jersey or the Isle of Man. It may be that the Financial Services and Markets Act 2000 can be avoided but non-compliance can result in criminal sanctions. Secondly, problems can arise in relation to the transfer of partnership interests. Although the partnership agreement can be drafted to restrict limited partners from selling their shares, the validity of such provisions has yet to be tested in the courts. Thirdly, there are complications where there are minors. There is a risk that on reaching the age of 18 a person will repudiate the partnership agreement thereby dissolving the FLP. Nevertheless, FLPs are useful entities in the appropriate situation. Where the value of assets are below the nil rate band or business or agricultural property relief is available, a trust may be more appropriate.

Family company

Gifts of shares

[**12.58**] The majority shareholder in a trading company may find himself in something of a dilemma. His shareholding, by virtue of its ability to control the company, will carry most of the company's value. Under present legislation, business property relief at 100% is available provided various conditions are fulfilled (see **12.2** above).

There may be some merit in his giving away some or all of his shares now to take advantage of this relief, which may not still be available at the time of his death. On the other hand, a lifetime gift will mean the loss of the tax free uplift on death for capital gains tax purposes under TCGA 1992, s 62 since hold-over relief under TCGA 1992, s 165 merely postpones the liability to tax. In addition, there may be claw-back of the business property relief if the donor dies within seven years (see above).

In addition, for the donor to reduce his holding below 50% will deprive him of control over a business on which his livelihood depends.

Before making any gift of shares, the prospective donor and his advisers should consider the following questions.

(a) Does the donor rely on his director's fees or other emoluments for his livelihood? If so, should any steps be taken to secure these prior to the gift?

(b)   Does the donor rely on any dividend income from the shares? Again, can any steps be taken to compensate him for this loss if he gives away his shares?

(c)   Is there likely to be a sale or a stock exchange quotation of the shares of the company in the foreseeable future? If so, this may have an impact on any decision whether or not, and if so, to whom, the shares should be given.

(d)   Are there any pension arrangements in place for the donor and his wife which may be prejudiced by the gift?

(e)   Are there any surplus profits in the company which the donor would like to extract prior to the gift (although any distribution of these by way of dividend may result in an income tax charge)?

(f)   Will the intended donees of the shares be involved in running the company or be merely passive shareholders? Is there likely to be any friction between them if more than one person is involved?

In many cases where 100% relief is available, lifetime gifts may now be positively disadvantageous because the capital gains tax uplift on death will be lost. There are a number of circumstances, however, where lifetime gifts may still be worthwhile or necessary. In particular:

(i)   where it is likely that the company will be sold prior to the death of the shareholder but probably not in the next seven years;

(ii)   where 'excepted assets' within IHTA 1984, s 112 are held in the company and business property relief will therefore be severely restricted; and

(iii)   where family circumstances require the next generation to be given an interest.

In these circumstances it may be sensible for the majority shareholder to consider reducing his holding to the minimum 51% by making regular use of his annual inheritance tax exemption or by making a potentially exempt transfer and insuring against the risk of his death within the seven-year period.

Where 100% business property relief is not available it is sensible for any shareholder who wishes to divest himself of control simply to make the gift (which will be a potentially exempt transfer) and insure his life.

What can be done to protect the shareholder from his loss of control? Any attempt by him to entrench his right to remuneration as, for example, an executive director, by giving himself a long-term service contract, or even a contract for any length which allows him remuneration beyond that commensurate with his duties, may be treated as a gift with reservation within FA 1986, s 102, as would any attempt to secure favourable pre-emption rights over the shares given away. On the other hand, there should be no difficulty in his continuing to draw a reasonable commercial remuneration under a pre-existing service contract or renewing that contract on similar terms (provided they are still appropriate and reasonable) when it expires. Similarly, it is considered that he may still benefit from any pre-emption rights contained in the Articles of Association of the company prior to the gift.

One way of providing a degree of control for the donor would be for him to give the shares to a discretionary trust of which he is the first named trustee.

Because this will be a chargeable transfer for inheritance tax purposes, an inheritance tax charge is likely to arise unless the value of the shares are within the nil rate band or are fully relieved business property. The case of *Comr of Stamp Duties of New South Wales v Way* [1952] AC 95, [1952] 1 All ER 198 (PC) provides authority for the proposition that powers exercisable by a person in a fiduciary capacity do not amount to a reservation of benefit for estate duty purposes and HMRC seems to accept that this is the case for inheritance tax purposes (HMRC Inheritance Tax Manual, para 14394). In addition, the donor's spouse or civil partner can be a trustee. However, the settlor as a trustee, must exercise his powers in the best interests of the beneficiaries under the trust and not in his own interests. Failure to do so may make him susceptible to an action for breach of trust by an aggrieved beneficiary; it may also allow HMRC to claim that there has in fact been a gift with reservation. The settlor should also bear in mind that although as first named shareholder he is the one who is able, so far as the company is concerned, to exercise the votes (the company having no notice of the trust), he should only exercise them as all the trustees agree, as trustees have to be unanimous in exercising their powers unless the settlement itself says otherwise. Any provision in the settlement attempting to give the settlor sole control over the votes might cast doubt on his exercising them in a fiduciary capacity and hence the gift with reservation provisions might apply.

Where the settlor-trustee is also a director of the company, if the settlement contains any provisions relieving him of his duty to account to the trust for any profits made through using, or failing to use, the trust votes to secure his position, the gift may amount to a gift with reservation. HMRC, however, has indicated that such relieving provisions will not in its view prejudice a gift where they permit the retention of reasonable commercial remuneration (HMRC Inheritance Tax Manual, para 14395).

When structuring the capital of a company, it is important to consider the precise wording of the definition of 'relevant business property'. For example, if a shareholder has sufficient shares to give him control of the company and also owns non-voting securities, the shares will be relevant business property but the securities will not. This is because the securities do not give the shareholder control of the company together with the unquoted shares. The shares give control in their own right. It should be remembered that for inheritance tax purposes there is a distinction between shares and securities.

Minority holdings

[12.59] All sizes of minority shareholdings in unquoted trading companies may be eligible for business property relief at 100%. As for controlling holdings, it may be sensible to retain the shares until death and obtain the capital gains tax uplift. However, it may be, for the same reasons as are set out above in respect of controlling holdings, that lifetime gifts are appropriate.

The minority shareholder may, however, have fewer non-tax-related problems in deciding whether to make a lifetime gift. If he considers his interest in the company purely as an investment and does not rely on it to help secure a remunerated office, his only loss in giving away the shares will be any dividend income (which in the case of many unquoted companies is negligible) and any loss in capital appreciation.

To enable shareholders to reduce their taxable estate whilst retaining some of their dividend rights, a device involving the issue of fixed dividend preference shares by way of bonus to existing shareholders can be implemented. The preference shares are non-voting and on the winding-up of the company carry the right only to repayment at par. The idea is that the bonus issue frees the ordinary shares (which, depending on the income and net asset value of the company, may well carry the bulk of the value of the company), for gifts, whilst allowing the donor to retain the benefit of the income from the preference shares. This type of scheme may be attractive both to minority shareholders who rely on regular dividends to secure their standard of living and to controlling shareholders nearing the age of retirement who wish to pass control of the family company on to the next generation but at the same time need the security of an income flow to support them in their retirement.

Quoted shares

[12.60] If shares become quoted, that is, listed on a recognised Stock Exchange, they will cease to qualify for any inheritance tax business property relief unless they are part of a controlling holding owned by the transferor (IHTA 1984, s 105(1)(b)). The loss of relief can be a significant disadvantage especially where there are a number of elderly shareholders. Where minority shareholdings are concerned, the effect may be to move the holding from a non-tax paying position (because 100% business property relief was available whilst unquoted) to a position where it is fully taxable at 40%. Additionally, its value may considerably increase.

If a flotation is considered necessary in order to give the company access to the public as a new source of funds, rather than simply to unlock the value inherent in the shares, a solution would be for the company to create and issue a new class of shares for the purposes of the public sale leaving the existing shareholders with their original shares which would continue to be unquoted and therefore capable of qualifying for business property relief. The new class of shares issued should rank *pari passu* with the existing shares in all material respects. To enable the existing shareholders to realise their shares, they could be made convertible into the quoted class at the option of the holder.

A similar problem exists where unquoted shares have been the subject matter of a potentially exempt transfer but have become quoted before the seven-year period has expired. In such a case, the shares would not attract business property relief if the transferor dies within the period (IHTA 1984, s 113A(3)). Again, a new class of shares could be created especially for the purposes of the flotation.

Where there are two or more shareholders who between them control a quoted company, by transferring their shares to a newly formed 'holding' company which they own jointly they can in effect convert shares which will not qualify for business property relief (ie the quoted shares) into shares which do (ie the unquoted shares in the holding company). Although the only business of the new company is the holding of investments, this does not prevent the shares of the company from being relevant business property (IHTA 1984, s 105(4)(b)).

Once shares or securities have become quoted they also cease to be assets capable of qualifying for hold-over relief under TCGA 1992, s 165 unless in the case of an individual the company concerned is the transferor's personal company (as defined in TCGA 1992, s 165(8) or in the case of trustees, they are able to exercise 25% of the voting rights exercisable by the company's shareholders in general meeting (TCGA 1992, Sch 7, para 2). However, in the appropriate circumstances, hold-over relief under TCGA 1992, s 260 may still be available.

Other devices

[12.61] Two other strategies involving companies must be mentioned: the 'deferred share' proposal and the 'value freezing' proposal. Both are designed to pass the value inherent in a company to other members of a family, the first by creating a new class of shares to which deferred rights are attached but which automatically convert into ordinary shares after a specified period of time; the second by creating a new class of shares which from the outset carry any increase in the value of the company over its value at the date of issue. Although strategies of this nature are of less relevance because of the availability of 100% business property relief it is still worthwhile including them in this chapter as they are of relevance where 100% business relief is not available.

Deferred share strategy

[12.62] A bonus issue of deferred shares is made to the existing ordinary shareholder or shareholders of the company. For a fixed period these deferred shares carry minimal (or no) voting rights, dividend rights or rights to receive distributions on a winding-up. At the end of the period the deferred shares automatically rank *pari passu* with the existing ordinary shares, or assume all the rights previously attached to the ordinary shares, with the ordinary shares correspondingly losing their rights (and becoming valueless).

The idea is to create a new class of shares which are initially of low value (and an important factor in determining this value is the length of the fixed period) and can therefore be given at little or no inheritance tax cost, but which then grow in value over a period of time and at the end of the period assume virtually the full value of the company if at that time the rights attaching to the ordinary shares cease.

It is debatable whether the expiry of the fixed period will result in a disposition by the ordinary shareholders in the company (assuming of course that the company is 'close' for tax purposes) under IHTA 1984, s 98. However, HMRC is of the view that an alteration of rights within the meaning of IHTA 1984, s 98(1)(b) occurs when deferred shares come to rank equally with another class of shares (Shares and Assets Valuation Manual, para 108280). Even if HMRC's view is correct, it is difficult to see how an inheritance tax charge can arise because the reduction in value (if any) of the shareholders' estates due to the disposition is minimal. This is because the value of the ordinary shares will discount the coming to an end of the fixed period when the deferred shares will rank *pari passu* in all respects with the other shares, and will therefore gradually decrease in value over the years as the value of the deferred shares increases, so that immediately before the disposition the ordinary shares are likely to have virtually the same value as after the disposition.

In a press release dated 11 September 1991, HMRC stated that inheritance tax would not be chargeable when deferred shares subsequently came to rank *pari passu* with another class of shares provided the deferred shares were issued before 5 August 1991. The CIOT, in correspondence with HMRC, raised the situation of deferred shares having been issued before 5 August 1991 with a long deferral period where subsequently there is a reconstruction of the company for commercial reasons. HMRC confirmed that where new deferred shares are issued as part of a sale or reconstruction post-1991, the shares mirror the rights of the pre-1991 deferred shares and there is no transfer of value or change in the deferral period, no inheritance tax charge should arise when the shares come to rank equally with another class of shares (CIOT press release dated 4 October 2012).

To counter the argument that prior to the end of the fixed period the failure of the ordinary shareholders to cancel the deferred shares or to liquidate the company results in a transfer of value under IHTA 1984, s 3(3), it is important that the rights of the deferred shareholders are entrenched by giving them the ability to block any resolution to alter the rights attaching to their shares or to wind up the company or to create any new share capital. For the same reason it is also important that the ordinary shareholders ensure that as much of the profits of the company as are not required commercially for its operations are paid out by way of dividend. This is to ensure that value is not left in the company which the ordinary shareholders fail to extract. This 'enforced' payment of dividends may make the scheme unattractive to some shareholders.

To allow as much time as possible for the relevant period to expire (and therefore for the ordinary shares to lose their value) before an event which gives rise to an inheritance tax charge occurs, the ordinary shareholders should leave their ordinary shares to their respective spouses on their deaths.

So far as capital gains tax is concerned, the value shifting provisions contained in TCGA 1992, ss 29 and 30 should not be in point. Section 29 does not apply because the deferred shares are initially issued to the ordinary shareholders and consequently there is no transaction for which any consideration could have been obtained. Section 30 also does not apply because although the gift of the deferred shares would be a disposal for the purposes of the section, there has been no scheme or arrangement whereby the value of the deferred shares has been materially reduced.

As gifts of unlimited amounts may be made without inheritance tax implications, provided the donor survives for the necessary seven-year period, and with business property relief at 100% being available, the use of the deferred share scheme has diminished. A straightforward gift of shares must be far less provocative to HMRC than what is undeniably a very artificial arrangement involving a number of complicated – and potentially contentious – tax points.

The scheme also involves the creation of a complex share structure for the company which of necessity must last for a number of years. Having said that, however, the scheme still has its place in estate planning. An owner of a company who expects to retire in 10 years in favour of his sons, may find it attractive to enter into a scheme now which can secure the passing of control on his retirement without the need to make an immediate outright gift of his shares and without the worry as to whether the present favourable inheritance tax regime will still remain in a decade's time.

The deferred share strategy is less apposite for investment companies. This is because shares in investment companies tend to be valued on a net asset basis and in this regard the most crucial right attaching to the shares is the ability to wind up the company. As mentioned above, the deferred shares must carry the same voting rights on a winding up as the ordinary shares and although for the duration of the fixed period the ordinary shares carry the right to the bulk of the distributions on a winding up, the ordinary shares will not carry the ability to wind up the company. This may therefore limit the discount attaching to the value of the deferred shares over the ordinary shares (to take account of the other deferred rights).

Value freezing strategy

[12.63] Investment companies, for reasons which will be discussed, are more suitable vehicles for the value freezing strategy. This proposal involves a new class of shares being issued to the existing shareholders, again by way of a bonus issue, which carry the right to participate in the winding up of the company only insofar as the net asset value of the company then exceeds its value at the date of issue of the new shares. In this event, the new shares carry the right to participate in all the excess. The new shares may carry dividend and voting rights ranking *pari passu* with the ordinary shares. It is important, for the same reasons as was the case with the deferred share strategy, that the new shares are able to block any resolution to wind up the company or to alter the rights attaching to the shares. These additional voting rights will not prevent the ordinary shares from qualifying for business property relief (assuming it to be otherwise available, which in the case of an investment company will often not be the case), provided they give control on all other matters (IHTA 1984, s 269).

The ordinary shares are retained and the new shares, which will initially be of little value, are given away. It should be remembered that shares in an investment company are not capable of qualifying for hold-over relief under TCGA 1992, s 165, although relief under TCGA 1992, s 260 may be available.

This strategy is best confined to investment companies because the basis of calculating value in respect of their shares is more certain – the net value of the company's assets is taken and then discounted by a percentage depending upon the size of the holding. The value of shares in a trading company is usually calculated on an earnings basis whereby an appropriate multiplier is applied to the earnings per share. This method of valuation is more difficult to apply and determining the initial value of the company is more problematic. This in turn will make it difficult to 'freeze' the value of the company.

As with the deferred share strategy, the existence of the potentially exempt transfer has lessened the importance of this type of arrangement in estate planning. However, its advantages over a straightforward gift of shares is that it enables the donor to retain an interest in both the capital and income of the company, and also in its management (by reason of the votes attaching to the shares) whilst at the same time enabling the future benefit of the company to flow through to the next generation. Clearly, a value freezing exercise such as this is long-term in its operation and effects.

It is considered that under both strategies the gifts of the new shares will not contravene the gifts with reservation provisions because the donor does not benefit in any way from the property which is the subject matter of the gift, nor does he receive any collateral benefit referable to the gift. Any benefits he continues to receive are from the company and flow from pre-existing property retained in his estate, namely the original shares.

Dividend waivers

[12.64] A shareholder paying higher or additional rate income tax might consider waiving his rights to dividends in order to divert the income to taxpayers paying lesser rates of tax, eg a basic rate taxpayer. With the top rate of income tax on dividends now at 38.1%, the saving has increased. Basic rate taxpayers are liable to pay tax at 7.5% on their dividend income over £5,000. Trusts currently pay 45% on their general income over £1,000 and 38.1% on dividend income.

Provided the waiver is made within 12 months before any right to the dividend accrues, it will not be a transfer of value for inheritance tax purposes (IHTA 1984, s 15).

Subject to the articles of association of the company, in the case of an interim dividend, the right accrues from the date of payment; and in the case of a final dividend, it accrues from the date it is declared unless the dividend is expressed to be payable at a future date, when the right accrues at that date (see *Potel v IRC* [1971] 2 All ER 504 at 511, 512).

A dividend waiver should be by deed. For the purposes of ITTOIA 2005, Pt 5 Ch 5 HMRC treats most dividend waivers as 'settlements'. However, not all dividend waivers will be treated as such (see HMRC Trusts Manual, para 4225). Any waiver which results in a greater dividend being paid to minor unmarried children or a spouse or civil partner of the settlor will result in the dividends continuing to be taxed as part of the total income of the settlor. Although this will clearly destroy any income tax benefit of the waiver, the inheritance tax advantage of reducing the settlor's estate by the after-tax amount of the dividend still remains. For a more detailed discussion, see para **4.19**.

Assets held outside the company

[12.65] As with partnerships, there is a significant inheritance tax disadvantage in holding assets outside a company. This is because such assets can only qualify for 50% business property relief where the owner of the asset is the controlling shareholder of the company. Where he is only a minority shareholder there will be no relief at all, even though the asset may be used exclusively for the company's purposes.

For instance, if two or more individuals (not being husband and wife) own an unquoted company equally, their shareholdings in the company will qualify for business property relief at 100%. On the other hand, a property also owned by them equally and let to the company for the purposes of its trade will not qualify for business property relief.

The solution as with a partnership (see above) may be to transfer the asset such as land into the company with the owner(s) either giving the asset to the company or selling it for its capital gains tax base cost. In either case to avoid an actual capital gains tax liability a hold-over election under TCGA 1992, s 165 would be required.

A gift to a company is not a potentially exempt transfer for inheritance tax purposes (IHTA 1984, s 3A) so care needs to be taken where the company is owned other than by the individual transferor or that individual and his spouse. Even where the property and the shares in the company are owned in the same proportions, there may be an element of loss to the transferor's estate because of the discount applied to minority holdings and so a valuation will have to be carried out.

It may be possible to issue shares to the transferor(s) in exchange for the asset so as to avoid any element of gift for inheritance tax purposes. As this will prevent an election for hold-over relief for capital gains tax purposes under TCGA 1992, s 165, any unrealised gain on the asset will be brought into charge. In addition, where land is being transferred to a connected company a stamp duty land tax charge based on market value will arise.

The capital gains tax liabilities on the ultimate disposal of an asset should also be considered. If the asset is held by the individual, capital gains tax at either 10% or 20% will be payable, unless the asset concerned is residential property not qualifying for main residence relief or carried interest, in which case it will be charged at 18% or 28%. If the asset is held by a company, corporation tax at 20% will be payable.

Each case will need to be carefully considered depending on all the circumstances.

Death

[**12.66**] Historically, unquoted shares have always caused problems on death. These problems, however, are much alleviated by the availability of business property relief at 100%. The main problem, namely of an inheritance tax charge arising on an asset which is not readily realisable, will now only apply:

(a)   where there are 'excepted assets';
(b)   where the company is not a trading company; or
(c)   where the shares are not eligible for relief because of some other reason.

Where an actual liability to tax is likely to arise, whole of life insurance should always be considered as a means of funding the tax. This can either be on a single life basis, if a charge is likely to arise on the death of the shareholder, or on a joint life last survivor basis if the shareholder proposes to leave the shares to his surviving spouse or civil partner, when the inheritance tax charge will arise on the second death. However, particularly where business property relief is available at 100%, leaving shares to the surviving spouse or civil partner should be avoided unless done for purely practical reasons. It is preferable to leave assets qualifying for 100% business property relief to children or grandchildren (or in trust for them) compensating the spouse or civil partner with other assets not qualifying for relief.

Another way of funding the inheritance tax on the death of a shareholder is for the company, assuming it has power to do so in its articles of association, to buy some or all of the deceased's shares. The payment made by the company will not amount to a distribution of income for corporation tax purposes provided the company is an unquoted trading company or the unquoted holding company of a trading group and the whole or substantially the whole of the payment is used (apart from paying any capital gains tax) to discharge an inheritance tax liability within two years of the death (CTA 2010, s 1033). This relieving provision does not apply where the tax could be paid in some other way without undue hardship.

Where the company has surplus funds sufficient to discharge the inheritance tax liability on the death of a controlling shareholder, HMRC takes the view that there is no hardship since the liability can be met by dividend payments (Hansard 17-3-88).

Enterprise Investment Scheme (EIS)

[12.67] EIS relief is a multi-faceted relief which essentially comprises a capital gains tax deferral, an income tax relief and a capital gains tax exemption. A detailed analysis of the rules surrounding the relief is outside the scope of this book but the following describes the relief in broad terms and goes on to consider how the relief might usefully be employed in an estate planning context.

Capital gains tax deferral

[12.68] The relief allows the deferral of capital gains tax arising on the disposal of any assets if the gain is reinvested in newly issued ordinary shares of a qualifying unquoted trading company within certain time limits. The effect is to defer the tax liability until the EIS shares are sold and even then the charge may be further deferred by reinvesting the gain in different qualifying EIS shares.

The asset disposed of can be virtually any asset except that, on the disposal of shares or securities, the investment cannot be in the same company or group of companies (TCGA 1992, Sch 5B, para 10).

For this element of the relief there is no connected persons rule beyond substitution of market value in certain cases. It is possible for an individual to invest in a company which he already owns or controls.

The qualifying investment must be made within a period commencing one year before and ending three years after the disposal of the original asset (TCGA 1992, Sch 5B, para 1(3)(a)). This period can be extended at HMRC's discretion. (TCGA 1992, Sch 5B, para 1(3)(b)).

A qualifying investment is an acquisition for cash of newly issued eligible shares in a qualifying company. Eligible shares are defined as fully paid up ordinary shares which for a period of three years, do not carry present or future preferential rights to dividends or assets or any present or future right to be redeemed (TCGA 1992, Sch 5B, para 19). Any preferential right, however small, will result in relief not being available (*Flix Innovations Ltd v Revenue and Customs Comrs* [2015] UKFTT 558 (TC), [2016] SFTD 173). Most trades are qualifying trades but amongst those which do not qualify are dealing in land, commodities, futures, shares, other financial instruments, leasing, providing legal or accountancy services, property development, farming, woodlands or market gardening, operating hotels, nursing homes, shipbuilding, producing coal or steel, or residential care homes.

The total amount of relevant investments made in the company in the previous year must not exceed £5m (TCGA 1992, Sch 5B, para 1(2)(da)). The gross assets of the investee company must not exceed £15m immediately before the investment or £16m immediately after. The company must have no more employees than the permitted limit. The permitted limit is 250 full-time employees at the time that the relevant shares are issued, or 500 for knowledge intensive companies.

The investment must be made by subscribing in cash for 'eligible shares'. The amount of EIS relief is limited to the amount claimed by the taxpayer, which allows him to first make use of capital losses, annual exemptions and hold-over relief. There is no minimum holding period for the shares in which the gain is reinvested. However, relief will be clawed back if there is a disposal of the shares otherwise than to a spouse or if the conditions on which the relief was granted cease to be fully met at any time within three years after the investment.

Relief can also be denied or clawed back under complex anti-avoidance provisions. These counteract any return of value within three years after reinvestment. This concept is widely defined, catching, for example, instances where there are advance arrangements for a return of value at any time (eg guaranteed exit route).

Any clawback charge can itself be deferred by further investment, subject to satisfying the normal conditions.

Income tax relief and capital gains tax exemption

[12.69] To obtain income tax relief of up to 30% on qualifying investments of up to £1,000,000 in any fiscal year the following additional conditions must be satisfied:

(a)   the taxpayer must be liable to UK tax;

(b)   the taxpayer must not be connected with the company at any time during the period beginning two years before the issue of the shares and three years after the share issue in question;

(c)   the taxpayer must not receive value from the company (or have breached any of the other anti-avoidance provisions) during the defined period.

The taxpayer will be connected with the company where he, and his associates, own (as widely defined) more than 30% of the company.

Provided that the EIS shares are held for at least three years and EIS income tax relief has not been withdrawn, any capital gains arising on the disposal of the shares (excluding the held-over gains) will be exempt from capital gains tax.

Relief in estate planning context

[12.70] Whilst the relief affords considerable scope for deferring capital gains tax, there are significant commercial risks involved in making any qualifying investment. This point is reinforced by the fact that specific anti-avoidance legislation ensures that relief is denied where there is a guaranteed exit route at the outset. The financial services industry is becoming more adept at developing products which minimise the risks whilst still qualifying for the relief but EIS investments are not low risk investments. The main role of the relief in an estate planning context is in the sphere of the private company proprietor. He will understand the risks involved and, in the case of many disposals, will have a ready made vehicle in which he may invest.

If the investor and his associates own more than 30% of the investee company they will receive capital gains tax deferral relief but not income tax relief or a capital gains tax exemption on a later sale of the shares.

Take, for example, a private company proprietor, Mr A, who makes a substantial gain on a disposal of quoted investments when aged 55. The gain will be charged to capital gains tax at either 10% or 20%. To defer this liability he might, however, subscribe for new shares in his existing private company. Providing he subscribes for 'eligible shares' and the company is a 'qualifying company', EIS capital gains tax deferral relief will, in principle, be available. It will be necessary for the company to retain its qualifying status for the next three years but there is no reason why this should not be achieved providing the cash is wholly employed for permissible purposes. Care must be taken to ensure that there is no return of value (as widely defined) which would result in a clawback of relief but this does not preclude the payment of reasonable remuneration and dividends.

If instead of being a company proprietor, Mr A was in business as a sole trader or in partnership with his wife, he might still be able to take advantage of EIS relief. For example, he could form a company and give to it the assets of the existing business, any gain arising being held-over under TCGA 1992, s 165 (although it is likely that a stamp duty land tax charge would arise on the transfer of any land to the company). He could then subscribe for capital in the newly-formed company to the extent of the gain made on his investment disposal. EIS relief should be available provided the necessary criteria are met as regards the new company. It would, of course, be necessary to consider all the other tax and non-tax implications of incorporation if this route were to be pursued.

Business property relief may be available on the shares on death. It is interesting to note the differing results where an individual having invested in EIS shares on which he had received income tax relief which had not been clawed back makes a lifetime gift to his wife of his shares or he leaves them to her under his will.

Example

Norman had invested £100,000 in Fluffy Feet Ltd on which he claimed income tax relief. In 2016, Norman died. His wife, Mildred, inherited the shares at a probate value of £200,000. In 2019 she sells those shares for £6,000,000. The capital gains are as follows:

	£	
Proceeds	6,000,000	
Less: Probate value	200,000	
	5,800,000	on which she will be subject to capital gains tax

If Norman had made a gift of the shares to Mildred before his death, the same gain would arise but it would be exempt under TCGA 1992, s 150A(2).

The Seed Enterprise Investment Scheme

[12.71] The Seed Enterprise Investment Scheme (SEIS) applies to shares issued after 6 April 2012 and its rules mirror those applying to the EIS. The shares must be 'ordinary shares' which do not carry any present or future preferential rights as outlined in ITA 2007, s 257CA. The company must itself satisfy a number of requirements for relief to be available.

Income tax relief of 50% of the cost of the shares on a maximum annual investment of £100,000 is given (ITA 2007, s 257AB). For 2016/17, gains of up to £100,000 can be rolled over against the cost of the SEIS shares. After three years there will be no clawback of the income tax relief on a disposal of the shares and any gain will be free of capital gains tax.

The generosity of the tax reliefs reflects the high-risk nature of the investment required in very small, unquoted trading companies. Such SEIS investments are unlikely to form a very significant part of an individual's estate planning.

Venture capital trusts (VCT)

[12.72] As with EIS investments, investments in VCTs qualify for a special form of capital gains tax deferral. In addition, it is possible to claim income tax relief of 30% on investments in VCTs of up to £200,000 in a fiscal year (ITA 2007, ss 262 and 263). VCTs are quoted investment trusts which invest in certain qualifying unquoted trading companies. Restrictive rules govern the types of investment which may be acquired, the activities of the investee companies and the size and diversity of the VCTs investments.

It should be remembered that an investment in a VCT will not qualify for business property relief because its shares are quoted.

Chapter 13

The Family Farm

Introduction

[13.1] The farmer has very particular problems in relation to estate planning. He owns a valuable capital asset that is absolutely vital to his business which, in many cases, is carried on by the same family for several generations. If inheritance tax were imposed on such an asset, it might have to be sold and the accumulated farming skills of generations might then be lost. It is for this reason that agricultural property relief is given, which is at a rate of 100% on untenanted land and on let land where the tenancy began after 31 August 1995. It is very important, therefore, to ensure that the criteria for the application of the relief are met and that the best possible use is made of it. Inheritance tax is still payable on tenanted land let prior to 1 September 1995 as only 50% relief is available.

Over the years, agriculture has changed in many ways. Farming structures have changed as more farmers have engaged farming contractors for many farming tasks. Planning is often also complicated by the fact that the farmer may want only one or some of his children to succeed to the farming business.

As the farmer is primarily a man of business much of **CHAPTER 12 THE FAMILY BUSINESS** will also be relevant to the family farm and reference should be made to it. There will be a number of matters in this chapter which will repeat topics covered there and accordingly they will not be dealt with in such detail here.

The farmer may be the sole proprietor of a farming business, a partner in a partnership, a member of an LLP or a director/shareholder of a family company. In the case of a partnership, an LLP or a family company, the farmland may either be owned by the partnership, the LLP or the company, or it may be owned by one of the partners, members, or one of the shareholders of the company. In the latter case, the partnership, the LLP or company may have an agricultural tenancy of the land or it may simply occupy it under a gratuitous licence. Each one of these possibilities has different estate planning ramifications and they will be considered below. First, however, the inheritance tax and capital gains tax provisions having most impact on farmers will be considered.

Inheritance tax

Agricultural property relief

[13.2] The relief for agricultural property is given by IHTA 1984, ss 115–124C, which reduces the 'agricultural value' of any 'agricultural property' by a stated percentage.

The 'agricultural value' is the value of the property on the assumption that it is subject to a perpetual covenant (or such other equivalent) prohibiting its use otherwise than as agricultural property (IHTA 1984, s 115(3)). Any development or hope value or value attributable to minerals, therefore, is not relieved. It may, however, be relieved by business property relief.

The relief only applies to agricultural property in the UK, the Channel Islands, the Isle of Man or a state which is an EEA state (IHTA 1984, s 115(5)). Where a UK domiciled individual owns farmland outside the EEA, no agricultural property relief will be available. However, there is no such territorial limit in respect of business property relief and so business property relief may be available on such farmland. Business property relief may not be available on the farmhouse.

Agricultural property

[13.3] The definition of 'agricultural property' has three limbs:

(1) agricultural land or pasture;
(2) woodland and any building used in connection with the intensive rearing of livestock or fish if the woodland or building is occupied with agricultural land or pasture and the occupation is ancillary to that of the agricultural land or pasture;
(3) such cottages, farm buildings and farmhouses, together with the land occupied with them, as are of a character appropriate to the property (IHTA 1984, s 115(2)).

The meaning of 'agriculture'

[13.4] 'Agriculture' is not defined for the purposes of inheritance tax and so one should look to its normal meaning which, according to the *Shorter Oxford English Dictionary*, is 'the science or practice of cultivating the soil and rearing animals; farming; occas. spec. tillage'. In considering the meaning, the Court has referred to definitions used in other statutes. For example, the Court in *Dixon v IRC* [2002] STC (SCD) 53 referred to the definition found in the Agricultural Tenancies Act 1995, s 38(1) which includes ' . . . horticulture, fruit growing, seed growing, dairy farming and livestock breeding and keeping, the use of land as grazing land, meadow land, osier land, market gardens and nursery grounds.'

Property used for the breeding and rearing of horses on a stud farm and the grazing of horses in connection with those activities qualifies as agriculture (IHTA 1984, s 115(4)). There is no definition in the legislation as to what constitutes a stud farm. It is HMRC's view that relief will only be available where the normal requirements for commerciality apply and not for a hobby which is not carried on for gain. HMRC often make enquiries as to proof of commercial motive and usually a business plan will be requested.

In determining whether there is a stud farm HMRC consider a number of factors which are listed in HMRC Inheritance Tax Manual, para 24068. A field which was let for the grazing of horses used for leisure was held not to be 'occupied for the purposes of agriculture' (*Wheatley's Executors v IRC* [1998] STC (SCD) 60 (SpC 149))). The decision focused on the nature of the animals grazing rather than on the main purpose of the occupation of the land. This decision highlights the difficulty where landowners or their tenants diversify into horse and paddock activities.

The relief also applies to farmland dedicated to wildlife habitats (IHTA 1984, s 124C).

In the case of *Dixon v IRC* [2002] STC (SCD) 53 (SpC 297) it was held that although fruit growing and the use of land as grazing land could be agriculture, whether or not these activities were agriculture was a matter of fact and degree to be determined in the light of the purposes of the Act.

In its Inheritance Tax Manual, HMRC gives illustrations of what land it accepts as being for agricultural purposes (HMRC Inheritance Tax Manual, para 24061).

Under a farm business tenancy, it is the activities of the tenant that are relevant to determining occupation. It is therefore essential that the tenant covenants that the land will only be occupied for agricultural purposes.

Agricultural land or pasture (Limb 1)

[13.5] Limb 1 of the above definition is restricted to bare land and pasture used for agriculture and does not include buildings (*Starke (Brown Executors) v IRC* [1996] 1 All ER 622, [1995] STC 689 (CA)) (HMRC Inheritance Tax Manual, para 24031).

Where a farmer gives away the bulk of his farm, which was the situation in *Starke*, whilst retaining only the farmhouse and a small amount of land, such retained property will rarely qualify for relief. This problem may be avoided if the farmer continues to be a partner with perhaps a relatively small partnership share.

Occupation (Limb 2)

[13.6] For relief to be available under Limb 2 any woodlands must be occupied with the agricultural land or pasture and the occupation must be ancillary to that of the agricultural land or pasture. Any building must be used in connection with the intensive rearing of livestock or fish, be occupied with the agricultural land or pasture and the occupation must be ancillary to that of the agricultural land or pasture.

In *Williams v Revenue & Customs Comrs* [2005] STC (SCD) 782 (SpC 500), the issue arose as to the nature of the link required, for example, whether occupation or ownership between a property (in this case broiler houses) and the agricultural land or pasture to which the occupation of that property must be ancillary. It was held that the broiler houses would qualify only if they were occupied as an 'add on' to or as a subsidiary part of the purposes of a larger agricultural enterprise carried out on other land with which they were occupied.

Farmhouse, cottage or farm building (Limb 3)

[13.7] A farmhouse, cottage or farm building will only qualify as 'agricultural property' under IHTA 1984, s 115(2) if it is 'of a character appropriate' to the bare land or pasture owned and occupied with them. It is this limb that has caused the most difficulty particularly in relation to farmhouses. There is essentially a dual purpose test. First, the property must be a farmhouse and, secondly, it must be of a 'character appropriate' to the property.

A farmhouse

[13.8] There is no statutory definition of a farmhouse in the inheritance tax legislation. It is therefore not surprising that over the years there have been a number of cases relating to the availability of relief in respect of farmhouses. In *Lindsay v IRC* (1953) 34 TC 289 it was described as 'a building used by the person running the farm'. In the later case of *IRC v John M Whiteford & Sons* (1962) 40 TC 379 the Court of Session accepted the Revenue's contention that *Lindsay* defined a farmhouse as a building used by the person running the farm. In *IRC v Korner* [1969] 1 All ER 679, [1969] 1 WLR 554, HL, (an income tax case), Lord UpJohn stated *obiter* that the question should be judged in accordance with 'ordinary ideas of what is appropriate in size, content and layout, taken in conjunction with the farm buildings and the particular area of farmland being farmed and not part of a rich man's considerable residence'. There have been a number of cases relating to farmhouses which are discussed below. We have only included a very brief summary of the facts of the cases discussed.

In *Higginsons Executors v IRC* (Spc 299) [2002] STC (SCD) 483 there was little evidence of any agricultural use having been made of the house, the Lodge, the status of which was at issue in the case. It was held that the Lodge was not a farmhouse but an attractive residential property surrounded by an estate. The 'single most significant fact' that went against the taxpayer in that case was the high price for which the estate was sold shortly after the death indicating that the house had a value which was unrelated to its agricultural function.

In *Rosser v IRC* [2003] STC (SCD) 311 the Special Commissioner concluded 'the ordinary and natural meaning that [he] would attach to the word "farmhouse" in s 115(2) is that it must be a dwelling for the farmer from which the farm is managed'. The house was not a farmhouse because 'the prime function of the house [was] as a retirement home'.

In *Antrobus No 2*, the Lands Tribunal adopted a narrow construction of what may constitute a farmhouse. It said that 'a farmhouse . . . is the house of the person who lives in it in order to farm the land comprised in the farm and who farms the land on a day to day basis'. Although the Lands Tribunal's function is to value land rather than to determine taxation concepts, so that it is arguable that it exceeded its competence in this case, the Lands Tribunal's definition was according to the Special Commissioner in *Arnander (executors of McKenna, dec'd) v Revenue and Customs Comrs* [2006] STC (SCD) 800, [2007] RVR 208 'a helpful principle'.

It is HMRC's view that:

> 'the occupant of a "farmhouse" must be a farmer. In other words, the person farming the land on a day to day basis. Whether a person is actually a "farmer of the land" will depend on all the facts of a particular case. So, a person with overall control of an agricultural business is not necessarily a "farmer". The key factor is to identify if the occupant of the house has a significant role in the management, or actual operations, of the farming activity being carried out on the land involved. Conversely, it is not necessarily the case that a "farmer" of land is a person whose principal occupation consists of farming the land.

> The test is therefore essentially a functional one. As the Special Commissioner in *Arnander (Executors of McKenna (dec'd)) v Revenue & Customs Comrs* [2006] STC (SCD) 800 pointed out, "the proper criterion is the purpose of the occupation". Since in that case the day to day farming was undertaken solely by contractors and a land agent was responsible for the management of the land, the deceased's residence was not a "farmhouse".

> So you will need to investigate in detail exactly what the occupier of the residence was doing in the way of agricultural activity in the relevant period before the deceased's death, to be able to determine whether their residence could properly be called a "farmhouse". You should be particularly careful in cases where the farmer had retired and let their land on grazing agreements'.

> (HMRC Inheritance Tax Manual, para 24036)

Where the executors claim agricultural property relief, IHT Form 400 requires a considerable amount of information in respect of the day to day farming activities carried out on the farmland and of its use by the deceased.

What is clear from the above is that claims for relief made on the basis that management is conducted from the farmhouse, will be subject to close examination. It is therefore important that records of all meetings, activities and decisions that are made at the farmhouse are kept to provide evidence of the operations if required.

Character appropriate test

[13.9] To fall within the definition of 'agricultural property', farmhouses, cottages and outbuildings must be 'of a character appropriate to the property'. 'The property' to which reference is made is not expressly stated in the legislation. The use of the definite article indicates that it should be property to which reference has been made previously in the subsection but the only previous use of the word 'property' is in the phrase 'agricultural property', which is the subject of the definition and which cannot therefore be the property referred to. On the basis of decided cases it can be said that the property must be agricultural land or pasture. There must be a nexus between the land and the farmhouse (or cottages or farm buildings) on which relief is claimed, but what must that nexus be? It is HMRC's view based on *Rosser v IRC* [2003] STC (SCD) 311 that the nexus required is one of ownership. In the case of *Hanson (trustee of the William Hanson 1957 Settlement) v Revenue & Customs Comrs* [2013] UKUT 224 (TTC), [2013] STC 2394, however, the Upper Tribunal upheld the FtT decision which departed from the principle adopted by the Special Commissioner in *Rosser*, which, as a decision of a body of equal status to the Tribunal, was not binding upon it, in holding that the nexus was common occupation and that common ownership was not required. The Upper Tribunal concluded that:

'on the facts of the . . . case, the common occupation of the entire land holding . . . and the house (the house being occupied by the respondent as a farmhouse in the sense in which we have described that word so that there is a functional connection between the house and the farmland) provides the nexus between Limb [1] and Limb [3] by which the "character appropriate" test is to be assessed . . . We consider that this reading in s 115(2) is entirely consistent with the scheme of the legislation and, indeed, reflects a more natural construction of that section than HMRC's reading. Our reading does not, we consider, undermine the scheme of the legislation or produce difficulties or uncertainties such as to lead us to a different conclusion. HMRC's reading has the unsatisfactory consequences which we have identified . . . We would only add that we do not decide that common occupation would always and necessarily constitute a sufficient nexus. It may be right that there can be situations in which, although there is common occupation of agricultural land and a cottage, farm building or farmhouse, there is not a sufficient nexus. We have not thought of an example where this would be so, but do not rule out the possibility. In any case, it is unlikely that such an issue would ever arise since the "character appropriate" test might itself not be fulfilled in such a case.'

The property to which the farmhouse must be appropriate is the farmland and will not, for example, include land subject to fishing rights, industrial units or a farm shop selling brought-in produce (*Starke (Brown's Executors) v IRC* [1995] STC 689).

The question of whether a farmhouse is of a character appropriate to the agricultural land is one of fact and degree and any factor could be relevant. There has been a number of Special Commissioner's decisions which have applied various principles to determine whether a farmhouse is of an appropriate character. Whilst an extensive analysis of these cases is beyond the scope of this book, a brief narrative of the relevant cases follows.

The case of *Dixon v IRC* [2002] STC (SCD) 53 (SpC 297) concerned a cottage standing in 0.6 acres of ground comprised of a garden and an orchard. The case turned primarily on the question of whether the orchard and garden were agricultural land or pasture. The Commissioner found on the facts that it was not but went on to consider the question of whether '[i]f the land was agricultural the cottage was of a character appropriate to it'. The Commissioner quoted with approval the ninth supplement of McCutcheon on Inheritance Tax, para 14.72 as follows:

'The present position is that the "character test" is considered against three main tests:

(1)   the elephant test:
        although you cannot describe a farmhouse which satisfies the character test you will know one when you see it!
        [This can hardly be said to be a principle at all – rather it is just a power of arbitrary decision.]

(2)   man on the (rural) Clapham Omnibus:
         would the educated rural layman regard the property as a house with land
         or a farm?
         [Again this can hardly be said to be a principle at all.]
(3)   Historical dimension:
         how long has the house in question been associated with the agricultural
         property and is there a history of agricultural production?'

In *Lloyds TSB (Personal representatives of Rosemary Antrobus dec'd) v IRC* [2002] STC (SCD) 468, Miss Antrobus had occupied and farmed Cookhill Priory for 59 years as a tenant and grazing licensee. The farmhouse was in a very poor state of repair. The land and buildings were agreed to be agricultural property with the exception of the Priory and two let properties. The Revenue (as it then was) argued that the Priory was not 'of a character appropriate' to the land owned by Miss Antrobus. In finding for the taxpayer, the Special Commissioners summarised the relevant principles for deciding the s 115(2) test as follows:

•   Is the house appropriate, by reference to its size, content and layout, to the farm buildings and the particular area of farmland being farmed? In applying this principle two factors were relevant, namely the history of the property and comparison with other properties in the area.
•   Is the house proportionate in size and nature to the requirements of the farming activities conducted on the agricultural land or pasture in question?

The relevant facts were the history of Miss Antrobus' personal involvement in the business (although it was not financially successful in her later years), together with the evidence that most farmers were making less profit than previously and financial information in respect of comparable farms.

•   Although one cannot describe a farmhouse which satisfies the 'character appropriate' test, one knows one when one sees it.
•   Would an educated rural layman regard the property as a house with land or as a farm?
•   How long has the house in question been associated with the agricultural property? Was there a history of agricultural production?

In *Rosser v IRC* [2003] STC (SCD) 311, there was a farming partnership between the deceased and her husband, the assets of which included 41 acres of land, a house and a barn. In 1989, they gave 39 acres to their daughter, Mrs Rosser, who farmed the land. In 1990 she also farmed the two acres retained by the farming partnership. The partnership was dissolved in 1996 and the agricultural activities carried out in the house were the provision of refreshments to the farm workers and the storage of pesticides and tools. The barn was used for agricultural purposes in respect of the two acres. HMRC argued that neither the house nor the barn were 'of a character appropriate' to the agricultural land. It was held that relief was available in respect of the barn but not the house. The house was not considered to be a farmhouse but rather a retirement home for the deceased and her husband.

The case of *Arnander (Executors of McKenna, dec'd) v Revenue & Customs Comrs* [2006] STC (SCD) 800, [2007] RVR 208, involved a Cornish estate consisting of a house with 6 acres of garden and domestic outbuildings ('the house') and land of 187 acres, the majority of which was farmland. It was purchased in 1945. The house was not associated with the farming activities from 1908 to 1984 when a tenant farmer surrendered his tenancy. At that time, Mr and Mrs McKenna entered into arrangements for an arable farming contract. A land agent was responsible for managing the land and dealing with the contractors. Meetings were held with Mr McKenna who prepared and maintained detailed records of the arrangements. After a period of ill health Mr and Mrs McKenna died within a short period of each other. The Special Commissioner said that the principles derived from the authorities were that a farmhouse was a dwelling for the farmer by whom the farm was managed. The farmer was the person who farmed it on a day-to-day basis and not the person who had overall control of the agricultural business. The purpose of the occupation of the property had to be considered. It was held that the house was not the main dwelling from which the agricultural operations over the land were conducted and managed. Although it was held that the house was not a farmhouse, the Special Commissioner did address the character appropriate issue on the hypothesis that the house was indeed a farmhouse. The Commissioner stated:

> 'In my view it is not appropriate to compile an exclusive list of relevant factors which are to be considered in deciding whether a farmhouse is of a character appropriate to the agricultural land. The question is one of fact and degree and any factor could be relevant. No one factor is determinative but relevant factors in this appeal are: the historical associations; the size, content and layout of the house; the farm outbuildings; the area being farmed and whether the house is proportionate to the land being farmed; the view of the educated rural layman; and the relationship between the value of the house and the profitability of the land.'

It would seem that the class of relevant factors is not closed and only some may be material in particular cases. It is of interest that the Special Commissioner accepted that profitability and the value of the house are both relevant. Of more concern was the fact that the Special Commissioner concluded that even if the house had been a farmhouse and of a character appropriate to the agricultural land or pasture, because the deceased was unable to engage in farming matters in the two years before his death because of ill health it could not have been a farmhouse immediately before the deceased's death.

HMRC states that a temporary cessation of activity due to ill health will not in itself prevent a residence being a farmhouse provided it 'can properly be considered as functionally remaining attached to the farm' (Inheritance Tax Manual, para 24036). It is difficult to ascribe any clear meaning to this.

In *Golding v Revenue & Customs Comrs* [2011] UKFTT 351 (TC) the FtT held that a farmhouse with 16 acres was a farmhouse of a character appropriate despite the lack of extensive agricultural activity on the land in the years before Mr Golding's death. The case involved an elderly smallholder who had farmed the land intensively but before his death he had mainly grown food for his own consumption and sold a few eggs to a small number of customers making a small profit. The farmhouse was in a poor condition. The Tribunal did not accept that the lack of substantial profit precluded the dwelling from being a farmhouse. It recognised that as farmers grow older and there is a decline in their work rate, reduced business turnover and profitability do not of themselves mean that relief will not be available. Interestingly, there was no direct reference to day-to-day farming being required for a house to be a farmhouse. It would seem that profitability is not required. HMRC, however, despite losing the case, has said that 'the decision is not of binding precedent' (see **13.10** below). The case is important in the common situation where a farmer's activities decline as he advances into old age. The case also demonstrates a trend in farmhouse cases which seems to suggest that the worse the condition of the house, the more likely it is to be viewed as a farmhouse. The Tribunal commented that a working farm is not expected to be furnished to the standards of a domestic residence.

In *Revenue & Customs Comrs v Atkinson* [2011] UKUT 506 (TCC), [2012] STC 289, Mr Atkinson's estate included farmland let on an agricultural tenancy to a family farming partnership of which Mr Atkinson was a partner. The farmland included a bungalow in which Mr Atkinson lived until he became ill in 2002 when, after a spell in hospital, he went into a care home. The other partners, his grandson and daughter-in-law attended the bungalow two to three days a week to collect post and deal with frost and to access the water supply. Mr Atkinson continued to be a partner until his death, he took part in partnership discussions concerning the farm and returned to the bungalow occasionally which continued to house his possessions.

The FtT found for the taxpayer but the Upper Tribunal allowed HMRC's appeal, commenting that:

' . . . the Tribunal failed to apply the correct approach and to ask the correct questions. The correct approach is to identify what does and what does not amount to a sufficient connection between the use and occupation of the property in question (the Bungalow in the present case) and the agricultural activities being carried on on the agricultural property (the Farm in the present case); and to ask whether the facts give rise to a sufficient connection. If the Tribunal had adopted that approach it could, in our judgment, have come to only one conclusion, namely that the Bungalow was not immediately before Mr Atkinson's death, occupied for the purposes of agriculture and had not been so occupied since, at latest, it had become apparent that he would never be able to return there to live. In particular, neither the occasional attendance of [his partners] at the Bungalow to deal with post or frost, nor the fact that some of Mr Atkinson's belongings and furniture remained at the Bungalow, can be said to constitute occupation for the purposes of agriculture throughout the seven years prior to Mr Atkinson's death.

On their primary findings of fact and in the light of the applicable law, only one conclusion was open to the Tribunal, namely that the Bungalow was not occupied for the purposes of agriculture for the entirety of the period required.'

HMRC's view

[13.10] HMRC has produced, in HMRC Inheritance Tax Manual, para 24051, a list of the main factors which in its view should be considered when determining whether a farmhouse is of a 'character appropriate'. These are:

- 'Is the farmhouse appropriate by reference to its size, layout and content with the farm buildings and the particular area of farmland being farmed?
- Is the farmhouse proportionate in size and nature to the requirements of the agricultural activities conducted on the agricultural land? You should bear

in mind that different types of agricultural operation require different amounts of land. This is an aspect on which the VOA will be able to give advice.

- Within the agricultural land does the land predominate so that the farmhouse is ancillary to the land?
- Would a reasonable and informed person regard the property simply as a house with land or as a farmhouse?
- Applying the "elephant test", would you recognise this as a farmhouse if you saw it? Although this test involves some subjectivity it can be useful in ruling out extremes at either end of the scale.
- How long has the farmhouse and agricultural property been associated and is there a history of agricultural production? The matter has to be decided on the facts that existed as at the date of death or transfer but evidence of the farmhouse having previously been occupied with a larger area of land may be relevant evidence.
- Considering the relationship between the value of the house and the profitability of the land, would the house attract demand from a commercial farmer who has to earn a living from the land, or is its value significantly out of proportion to the profitability of the land? If business accounts have been supplied, copies should be forwarded to the VOA. Business accounts can give a useful indication of the extent of the agricultural activity being carried on, although a loss making enterprise is not on its own considered to be a determinative factor.
- Considering all other relevant factors, including whether any land is let out and on what terms, is the scale of the agricultural operations in context?
- There must be some connection or nexus between "such cottages, farm buildings and farmhouses, together with the land occupied with them" and the property to which they must be of a character appropriate. The argument that the nexus must be derived from common ownership rather than common occupation was accepted by the Special Commissioner in *Rosser v Inland Revenue Commissioners* [2003] STC (SCD) 311.'

The Manual goes on to say:

'For the purposes of IHTA84/S115 (2) you should in particular note that property can include:

- the deceased's/transferor's interest in an agricultural tenancy or farm business tenancy, even though the tenancy may be treated as of negligible value as an asset in the deceased's estate, and
- agricultural land or pasture owned by a company controlled by the deceased/transferor, or owned by a partnership of which the deceased/transferor was a partner.

You should be aware that for character appropriate (IHTM24050) purposes land leased by the deceased may increase the likelihood of any farmhouse being within IHTA48/S115 (2) [sic]. But, it may work in the opposite direction regarding the occupation of the farmhouse for the purposes of agriculture (IHTM24060) if the farming operations and management were being conducted by others from elsewhere.'

As can be seen from the above, HMRC's views on the significance of profitability are at odds with the relevant case law. HMRC's Guidance in their Inheritance Tax Manual at para 24052 outlines to its caseworker the investigation to be carried out in certain circumstances. It says that 'it is important that each case must be judged on its own facts'. As mentioned at **13.9** above, the case of *Golding* was lost by HMRC and it is advising that 'as the decision is not of binding precedent the decisions in the cases of *Rosser, Higginson, Dixon, Antrobus I* and *2* and *McKenna* are still relevant' (HMRC Inheritance Tax Manual, para 24053). HMRC also says that it was 'prevented by order of the Tribunal from arguing that the house was not a farmhouse'. That argument did not arise, however, because as the Tribunal reported, it had been agreed by both parties as a result of the correspondence that the house 'was a farmhouse' and the appeal was dealt with on that basis. HMRC advises its officers that if a taxpayer wishes to rely on *Golding* to argue that a residence should qualify as a farmhouse, they should be referred to HMRC's Guidance at para 24036 which contains a different explanation. It is implicit that despite the FtT's decision (and now the decision of the Upper Tax Tribunal), HMRC's view should be preferred. The Inheritance Tax Manual states that:

> 'The tribunal found that the lack of profit was not detrimental to a decision that the farmhouse was of a character appropriate to the land and highlighted the deceased was making a profit, though relatively small.
>
> In the High Court decision of *Starke* (see **13.9**) the character appropriate test was defined as:
>
> > "proportionate in size and nature to the requirements of the farming activities conducted on the agricultural land or pasture in question." So, in assessing whether or not property is proportionate to the farming activities undertaken on the land it remains HMRC's view that the income or profit of a farmer is a useful indicator of the activities undertaken, particularly in extreme cases.'

HMRC's comments here indicate that it is not going to take any notice of the decision relating to profitability and that its view remains the same. It indicates HMRC's willingness to refer to cases in which it was successful and with which it agrees and its unwillingness to do so with cases with which it disagrees.

HMRC is now challenging more modest properties to deny relief. The HMRC Inheritance Tax Manual, para 24255 outlines the information required to be submitted in form IHT414 to support a claim. It is therefore essential that consideration is given to possible enquiry by HMRC and to have these answers already prepared.

Contract farmers

[**13.11**] Many landowners enter into contract farming agreements. HMRC, relying on the decision in *Arnander*, takes the view that the farmhouse must be occupied by a working farmer with the result that it will attempt to deny relief in respect of a house owned by a landowner who has entered into a contract farming agreement. The distinction between a person conducting the day to day operations of the farm and one who merely has overall control of the farm is not always an easy one to draw. In the context of the deemed transfer on death, HMRC states in its Inheritance Tax Manual at para 24082 that, where the question at issue is whether a property was a farmhouse immediately before a person's death and that person employed contractors to farm the relevant land it is:

> 'a question of fact and degree to be decided in each case and may involve consideration of aspects such as:
> * the degree of financial risk for the deceased

- the deceased's involvement in the day to day agricultural activity including the regularity and scope of any meetings with the share/contract farmer
- the deceased's involvement in decisions relating to the selection of crops, sowing, harvesting, sales, and so on.

. . . These cases can be difficult to decide and if [the HMRC official is] uncertain as to whether the extent of the deceased's involvement in the agricultural activity of the farm was sufficient [he] should seek advice from [its Technical Department].'

It is important for individuals with such arrangements to keep contemporaneous records of meetings, telephone conversations and decisions to provide evidence to support a relief claim.

Grazing licences

[13.12] A grazing licence over relevant agricultural land may have a number of tax implications which will not only include the availability of agricultural property relief. The first matter to consider is how the income from the grazing activity is to be disclosed in the individual's self-assessment return. Is the owner carrying on a trade of farming the land? For income tax purposes, farming in the UK is treated as the carrying on of a trade, whether or not the land is managed on a commercial basis and with a view to the realisation of profits (ITTOIA 2005, s 9). Farming is defined as ' the occupation of land, wholly or mainly for the purposes of husbandry' (ITA 2007, s 996(1)). So there are two tests which must be satisfied, first, the person must be in occupation of the land and secondly, the purpose of the occupation must be wholly or mainly for husbandry. It is HMRC's view that husbandry should be given 'a common-sense interpretation to include activities normally recognisable as farming such as growing crops and the raising of farm livestock (see *Lowe v JW Ashmore Limited* [1970] 46 TC 597)'. There have been a number of cases concerning grazing licences and whether an owner is farming the land or not. The owner, rather than the grazier, should be responsible for growing the crop of grass and be responsible for the seeding, fertilising and weeding of the grass and these responsibilities should be reflected in the agreement between the parties. Acts of maintenance alone (such as the maintenance of hedges, fences and gates) are unlikely to amount to husbandry because they do not relate to the growing of a crop of grass. It is also important because this may have an impact on the relief available on the farmhouse. It is HMRC's view that:

'It is unlikely that a landowner who has allowed most or all of the agricultural land to be occupied on a grazing licence agreement where he or she does nothing but collect the rent and maintain boundaries, will be considered to be in agricultural occupation of that land. Consequently, as there is no farming activity actually being carried out, any associated house cannot be considered to be a farmhouse, so it would not be eligible for agricultural relief.' (Inheritance Tax Manual para 24074)

In addition, it is important that the agreement is not a farm business tenancy for grazing because such a tenancy will confer exclusive possession on the grazier and not the owner.

If an owner is carrying on a farming activity he may also be eligible for entrepreneurs' relief thus reducing the rate of capital gains tax to 10% on a disposal of the land and roll-over relief on replacement of business assets.

It is also necessary to consider whether business property relief is available which is discussed in **13.19**.

Farm cottages

[13.13] A farm cottage is eligible for relief if it satisfies the following conditions:

(i)   it is occupied for the purposes of agriculture; and
(ii) it is of a character appropriate to the agricultural land.

In *Revenue and Customs Commissioners v Atkinson* [2011] UKUT 506 (TCC), [2012] STC 289 the Tribunal said that 'the search is for some sort of connection between the residential use of the cottage and an agricultural purpose sufficient to make the use occupation for the purpose of agriculture'. When occupied by an agricultural worker 'the agricultural worker uses the cottage as a home because that is what he is and because he works on the farm. There is a sufficient connection between that use and the agricultural activities on the agricultural land for his occupation to be seen as being for the purposes of agriculture.'

Cottages occupied by retired farm workers (who have worked on the agricultural property concerned) or their widowed spouses or surviving civil partners can be eligible for relief (Extra-Statutory Concession F16) provided certain conditions are satisfied. The HMRC Inheritance Tax Manual at para 24034 states that the term 'retired' means someone who has ceased full-time work and is in receipt of a pension. It does not include a person who has simply left one job to work elsewhere.

Relief at 100% is available for farm cottages where:

(a)   the agricultural worker's occupation of the cottage was protected and the benefit of the 'transitional provisions' in IHTA 1984, s 116(2)(b) and s 116(3) are available to the transferor;
(b)   the agricultural worker occupied the cottage under an unprotected service tenancy or assured shorthold tenancy;
(c)   the worker's occupation arose under a tenancy which began after 31 August 1995;
(d)   when suitable alternative accommodation is available for the tenant, irrespective of whether the tenant was in default of the terms of their occupation.

In all other cases, HMRC takes the view that the rate of relief will only be 50% (HMRC Inheritance Tax Manual, para 24034).

In *Atkinson* the Tribunal used an example of a cottage temporarily let for one year to a person unconnected to agriculture and concluded that the cottage would not be occupied for agricultural purposes. HMRC in its Inheritance Tax Manual at para 24083 states: 'This does not mean that a property will be automatically disqualified from relief if the agricultural occupier is absent for a year, as each case will need to be judged on its own facts.' It goes on to say that 'after a year of non-occupation, it may be difficult to demonstrate that the requisite occupation for agricultural purposes has not been broken'.

Ownership and occupation

[13.14] No relief is given unless either the agricultural property was:

(a)   occupied by the transferor for the purposes of agriculture throughout the period of two years ending with the date of the transfer; or

(b)   owned by the transferor throughout the period of seven years ending with that date and was throughout that period occupied (by him or another) for the purposes of agriculture (IHTA 1984, s 117).

Agricultural property relief will also be available on agricultural property owned by trustees, whether or not an interest in possession subsists in the settled property. Where an interest in possession subsists in the settled property and is a privileged interest, the holder of the interest will be regarded as the 'transferor' of the property and also as the 'owner' of the property and if the trustee's interests carries the right of vacant possession, as having that right. In the case of a trust without a qualifying interest in possession, the trustees are the 'transferor' and the 'owner' of the property.

Occupation by a company which is controlled by the transferor is treated as occupation by the transferor; and occupation of any property by a Scottish partnership is treated as occupation of it by the partners (IHTA 1984, s 119). 'Control' of a company is defined in IHTA 1984, s 269 and means control of powers of voting on all questions affecting the company as a whole which, if exercised, would yield a majority of the votes capable of being exercised on them. When determining if a person has control, the votes attaching to any shares or securities which are 'related property' within the meaning of IHTA 1984, s 161 (broadly, property comprised in the estate of the transfer-or's spouse or civil partner or which is or has been owned by a charity or charitable trust because of a transfer made by the transferor's spouse or civil partner) are taken into account. The votes attaching to any shares or securities owned by the trustees of a settlement in which the transferor has a beneficial interest in possession will also be taken into account (IHTA 1984, s 269(2), (3)).

For the purposes of agricultural property relief it is possible for a person to inherit the periods of occupation or ownership of a deceased spouse or civil partner. If, for example, farmland passes to a farmer's widow, she can add to her period of occupation or ownership that of her husband's (IHTA 1984, s 120(1)(b)). In addition, where farmland is sold and replaced by other farmland, the successive periods of occupation or ownership of the two areas of land may, in certain circumstances, be treated as one to ascertain whether the minimum periods of occupation or ownership are satisfied (IHTA 1984, s 118).

Where there are two successive transfers of agricultural property, and the first transfer was eligible for the relief, or would have been so eligible if the relief had been available at the time, then the relief will be available in respect of the second transfer even if the transferor has not at the time satisfied the minimum ownership or occupation requirements provided:

(i)   the transferor in relation to the second transfer (or his spouse or civil partner) acquired the property as a result of the first transfer;

(ii)   at the time of the second transfer the property is occupied for the purposes of agriculture either by the second transferor (or his spouse or civil partner) or by the personal representatives of the transferor in relation to the earlier transfer; and

(iii)   either the first transfer or the second transfer was made on the death of the transferor (IHTA 1984, s 121).

It should be remembered that the property must be occupied for agricultural purposes. The test of occupation is factual. HMRC has listed the situations in which it considers that a property is occupied (HMRC Inheritance Tax Manual, para 24072). As we have seen, this can lead to difficulties where a farmer has fallen ill and has either left the property or somebody else is running the business. It would seem that HMRC accepts that relief may still be available in such circumstances but that such cases may be 'contentious and difficult to decide'. As we have seen, *Atkinson v Revenue & Customs Comrs* [2011] UKUT 506 (TCC), [2012] STC 289 concerned a bungalow on a farm lived in by Mr Atkinson who was a partner in a farming partnership but who moved to a care home four years before his death. Mr Atkinson continued to go to the bungalow from time to time, as did the other partners. Throughout Mr Atkinson's illness and until his death no-one lived in the bungalow. The bungalow was exempt from council tax on the basis that Mr Atkinson was resident elsewhere. Mr Atkinson had taken part in discussions related to the farm at least once a week, occasionally returning to the bungalow, which remained furnished and contained his belongings. He remained a partner until his death in 2006. The Tribunal held that the occupation by the partners did not amount to occupation for the purposes of agriculture immediately before Mr Atkinson's death.

One asset or many?

[13.15] When dealing with land, an issue which often arises is whether there is one asset or many. In the business property relief case, *Ninth Marquess of Hertford (Executors of Eighth Marquess of Hertford Deceased) v IRC* (SpC 444) [2005] STC (SCD) 177 (see **11.2**), it was held that the land concerned was a single asset and, therefore, that business property relief was available on the whole asset although only 78% of its area was used for business purposes.

Unquoted shares

[13.16] In addition to agricultural property, relief is also given in respect of shares of a company the assets of which include agricultural property where the value of the company's shares can be attributed to the agricultural value of that property (IHTA 1984, s 122(1)). However, the relief only applies if the transferor has control of the company immediately before the relevant transfer (IHTA 1984, s 122(2)). In order for the shares to qualify for the relief, the company must also fulfil the same ownership and occupation requirements of the land as an individual and, in addition, the transferor must have owned the shares for whichever of the two or seven-year minimum periods is appropriate (IHTA 1984, s 123(1)).

Rates of relief

[13.17] Agricultural property relief operates to reduce the whole or part of the value transferred by a transfer of value which is attributable to the agricultural value of agricultural property. The reduction is either 100% or 50%. Relief at 100% is available where:

(a)   The interest of the transferor in the property immediately before the transfer carried the right to vacant possession or the right to obtain it within the next 12 months. Extra statutory concession F17 extends the relief where the transferor's interest in the property immediately before the transfer either carried the right to vacant possession within 24 months of the date of the transfer because an unchallenged notice to quit had been served prior to the date of transfer and where the transferor and the tenant are so closely connected that in practice the open market value of the property is broadly equivalent to its vacant possession value.

(b)   The interest does not carry such a right to vacant possession because the property is let on a tenancy which began after 31 August 1995. Where a transfer of value occurs following the death of a tenant after 31 August 1995 but before a new tenancy has been formally granted to a successor who takes under a statutory provision, relief will be available. In addition, where a tenant has, prior to the transferor's death, given notice of his intention to retire in favour of a new tenant and the actual retirement takes place after the death but within 30 months after the notice was given, relief will also be available.

Relief at 100% relief is also available where the transferor has been beneficially entitled to his interest since before 10 March 1981 and:

(1)   if the transferor had disposed of his interest by a transfer of value immediately before that date and had duly made a claim under the earlier agricultural property relief provisions contained in FA 1975, Sch 8, the value transferred would have been relieved in accordance with those provisions and would not have been limited by the restrictions then applying on transfers exceeding £250,000 in value or 1,000 acres; and

(2)   the transferor's interest did not at any time during the period beginning with 10 March 1981 and ending with the date of the transfer carry a right to vacant possession or the right to obtain it within the next 12 months and did not fail to carry this right by reason of any act or deliberate omission of the transferor during that period (IHTA 1984, s 116(2)(b), (3)).

Broadly, the old 'working farmer' relief applied where the transferor was in at least five of the seven tax years preceding the year of the transfer wholly or mainly engaged in the UK in farming (either as a sole trader, a partner, an employee, a director of a farming company or a person undergoing full-time education) and the property was occupied by him for agricultural purposes and was so occupied throughout the two years immediately preceding the transfer (FA 1975, Sch 8, para 3).

There are three important points to make about the continuing availability of transitional relief. The first is that it is vital to ensure that any tenancies in existence at 10 March 1981 are continued, to ensure that there is no question of the transferor's interest ever carrying the right to vacant possession, or the right to obtain it within 12 months. Secondly, apart from the case where the land passes on death to a surviving spouse or civil partner when the survivor may step into the deceased's shoes and preserve the relief (IHTA 1984, s 120(2)), the transitional relief will apply only to the first transfer of the relevant land after 9 March 1981. It is important, therefore, not to waste the relief by, for example, an inter vivos transfer of the land to a spouse or civil partner, when the transfer would be exempt in any event. Thirdly, the relief no longer applies once the cumulative transfers of agricultural property qualifying for the old relief, or in relation to post-9 March 1981 transfers qualifying for the transitional relief, exceed £250,000 in value or 1,000 acres.

In all other cases the rate of relief is 50%.

As relief at 50% will only be available for pre-1 September 1995 tenancies one might consider granting a new tenancy to the existing tenant of the whole or substantially the whole of the existing holding whilst protecting the tenant's security or varying the terms of the existing tenancy under the Regulatory Reform (Agricultural Tenancies) (England and Wales) Order 2006 (SI 2006/2805) (HMRC Inheritance Tax Manual at paras 24143 and 24241). The provisions of the legislation must be strictly adhered to, so as to ensure that a new tenancy is granted to the existing tenant. Particular care is required where the parties are connected. One must also consider the CGT and SDLT implications of such a transaction.

Where land is owned by one or more joint tenants or tenants in common, if the interests of all of them together carry that right each interest is taken to carry a right to vacant possession (IHTA 1984, s 116(6)). Accordingly, where land is owned by a farming partnership, the relief will apply to the value transferred by any transfer of a partnership interest so far as its value is attributable to the agricultural property. Where land is owned outside the farming partnership but occupied by the partnership on licence but with no partnership agreement or other documentation detailing the terms of occupation, it is understood that HMRC takes the view that 100% relief may not be available to the landowner. As such a partnership can usually only be terminated on the next accounting date following notice being given, this may take in excess of the 12-month period. HMRC argues that, until the partnership can be determined, the landowner does not have vacant possession. A counter argument to this is that, subject to any agreement to the contrary among the parties, under the Partnership Act 1890, s 26 retirement can be effected simply by notice. The partnership will be dissolved as soon as the notice is communicated to all the parties or, if later, on the date specified in the notice. In such cases, therefore, a document should be entered into confirming that the partnership can be dissolved and the landowner can recover his land within a period of less than 12 months. It is advisable in any event that the partnership agreement contains a clause entitling the owner partner to vacant possession within the 12-month period.

Where a farmer owns a farmhouse and, in partnership with his children, farms the land occupied with the farmhouse, the amount of land which will be taken into account for the purposes of the character appropriate test in IHTA 1984, s 115(2) will depend on the provisions in the partnership deed. If the farmer is only entitled to 20% of income and capital profits, it is understood that HMRC's view is that the farmer will only be entitled to agricultural property relief on 20% of the land occupied with the farmhouse, ie the amount of land which is commensurate with the farmer's partnership share. This issue has not been considered by the courts but HMRC's view is probably incorrect.

Where the relief is to be applied to the value of shares in a farming company which owns agricultural property, then the rate of relief will depend on the interest of the company itself (IHTA 1984, s 122(3)).

Binding contract for sale

[13.18] Agricultural property relief will be lost if the transferor has entered into a binding contract for sale prior to the transfer unless the sale is made for the purposes of reconstruction or amalgamation (IHTA 1984, s 124). This is discussed in detail in CHAPTER 12 THE FAMILY BUSINESS.

Business property relief

[13.19] In cases where both agricultural property relief and business property relief might be available, agricultural property relief takes precedence over business property relief (IHTA 1984, s 114(1)). Thus, for example, where there is a transfer of an interest in a partnership which owns agricultural property, the value of that partnership interest which is attributable to agricultural property will qualify for 100% agricultural property relief assuming the relevant conditions are met. The remaining value of the partnership interest will qualify for business property relief.

In a farming context, there will be some cases where business property relief is available where agricultural property relief is not. For example, where the agricultural land is situated outside the UK, the Channel Islands, the Isle of Man or a state which is an EEA state; or where the value of agricultural property exceeds its 'agricultural value' because it has some development or hope value or where part of the farm has been used for diversification projects. In such cases, business property relief may apply to the excess value. Business property relief may also be available in relation to assets of a farming business apart from the land, for example, farm machinery and stock. In *Farmer (Farmer's Executors) v IRC* [1999] STC (SCD) 321 (SpC 216) a farming partnership had separated some buildings and land which had been let from its farming operations. In deciding whether or not business property relief was available, the Special Commissioners decided that the matter must be looked at in the round. Regard must be had not just to the issue of profitability but also the turnover of the respective sides of the business, the market values of the underlying assets used in the trading and investment sides of the business, and the time spent on each side of the business. It was held that there was a single business and the let property was not excluded from relief.

It may be advantageous, therefore, to keep a single set of accounts for the whole business, including the farm, and to exercise unified management over the whole business. In *Brander (representative of James (dec'd), Fourth Earl of Balfour) v Revenue & Customs Comrs* [2010] UKUT 300 (TCC), [2010] STC 2666, 80 TC 163 relief was given despite separate business accounts and VAT registrations being kept. It should be noted that Lord Balfour's active role and involvement in the management of the estate was hugely influential in establishing that it was a single composite business.

It should be remembered that where land is held as a partnership property it will quality for 100% relief whereas when it is held by individual partners outside the partnership, relief at only 50% will be available. It is often the case that very little documentary evidence exists of partnership arrangements and whilst the HMRC Inheritance Tax Manual, para 25104 says that the presence of land and buildings on a partnership balance sheet 'almost certainly means that it is property which belongs to the partnership', that should not be relied upon. It is essential in all relevant cases that there is clear evidence in the form of the partnership deed to show that any agricultural land is held as partnership property.

As discussed in CHAPTER 12 THE FAMILY BUSINESS, business property relief is not available if the business is wholly or mainly one of dealing in land or buildings or making or holding investments. In *McCall (personal representative of McClean, dec'd) v Revenue & Customs Comrs* [2009] NICA 12, [2009] STC 990, land was let under both conacre and agistment agreements. A letting in conacre is a temporary easement creating a licence to use the land. Agistment by contrast is a letting of land for grazing. The Northern Ireland Court of Appeal held that the business was one which consisted wholly or mainly of making investments. The activities carried on on behalf of the deceased, such as inspecting and repairing fences, weed control and finding tenants were all activities related to making the land available and related to the business of holding an investment. Care needs to be taken when advising on grazing agreements as discussed in **13.12**. Where possible, one should provide that some of the agricultural operations are carried out on the farm by the owner. In the case of grassland it may be sensible to have grazed livestock on the land before the agreement commences or for the owner to graze some of his own stock on the land in addition to the grazier's stock.

It is understood that HMRC consider that a DIY livery business is a lettings business (following *Lockyer v Revenue and Customs Comrs* [2013] UKUT 50 (TCC), [2013] STC 976, [2013] NLJR 291) and so falls 'on the investment side of the line' unless substantial services are offered. It will often be the case that the owner of the yard provides a number of services, such as being on call 24 hours a day, overseeing the horses, organising the paddocks, pasture management, providing hay and foodstuffs, general management of the yard and dealing with the horse owners. It is therefore important to have evidence of these services to refute HMRC's claim.

The conditions governing the availability of business property relief are considered in detail in CHAPTER 12 THE FAMILY BUSINESS at **12.2**.

Instalment option

[13.20] Where an inheritance tax liability payable by the donee, on death or in respect of a lifetime transfer, is attributable to property which qualifies for agricultural property relief, the tax can be paid by ten annual equal interest-free instalments (IHTA 1984, ss 227 and 234). The interest-free instalment option also applies to controlling shareholdings in a family farming company and in certain circumstances (considered in CHAPTER 12 THE FAMILY BUSINESS at **12.15**) to specific minority shareholdings in unquoted companies.

Lifetime exemptions

[13.21] A potentially exempt transfer is a transfer of any amount or value either to an individual or to certain types of settlement. A transfer will escape inheritance tax completely provided the donor survives the gift by a period of seven years (IHTA 1984, s 3A). If the transferor of a potentially exempt transfer dies within the seven-year period, inheritance tax may be payable. Where the tax is attributable to the value of agricultural property, agricultural property relief may be available to reduce the value transferred, provided certain conditions are met. These are:

(a)   that the agricultural property is owned by the transferee throughout the period beginning with the date of the potentially exempt transfer and ending with the death of the transferor (or if earlier the death of the transferee). The property must not at the date of death be subject to a binding contract for sale;

(b)   that the property has been occupied (by the transferee or another) for the purposes of agriculture throughout this period; and

(c)   where the agricultural property consists of shares in or securities of a company, throughout the relevant period the land was owned by the company and occupied (by the company or another) for the purposes of agriculture (IHTA 1984, s 124A).

There are provisions extending the availability of the relief, subject to certain conditions, where the original agricultural property is transferred by the transferee to a company in return for an issue of shares in that company (IHTA 1984, s 124A(6)(b)), although there is some doubt as to whether s 124A(6)(b) is effective to achieve its purpose. Where the transferee sells the property and replaces it with other agricultural property which is occupied for agricultural purposes throughout the relevant period (IHTA 1984, s 124B) the relief will be extended. It appears, however, that the replacement property provisions contained in s 124B will only operate where the transferee sells land and buys more land (HMRC Inheritance Tax Manual, para 24181). They will not apply where the transferee either sells land and instead buys shares in a land-owning company; or sells shares in a land-owning company and buys land; or sells shares in a land-owning company and buys further shares (IHTA 1984, s 124A(6)).

There is an even more extraordinary quirk in ss 124A and 124B where, for example, a transferor transfers farmland into a discretionary trust and the property ceases to be relevant property before the settlor dies. If, for example, the trustees advance the farmland to the settlor's son absolutely and the settlor later dies, then s 124A cannot apply in any circumstances because, on the son acquiring an absolute interest, the trustees of the settlement (who will be the 'transferees' for the purposes of the section) will cease to 'own' the original property and therefore the condition contained in (a) above cannot be satisfied. This should be borne in mind when considering the amount of any insurance cover on the life of the settlor.

Gifts with reservation

[13.22] The gifts with reservation provisions contained in FA 1986, ss 102–102C and FA 1986, Sch 20 operate where either the donee does not *bona fide* assume possession and enjoyment of the property given away or at any time within the seven years preceding the donor's death the property is not enjoyed to the entire exclusion, or virtually to the entire exclusion, of the donor and of any benefit to him by contract or otherwise. For a more detailed discussion see CHAPTER 4 LIFETIME PLANNING: MAKING GIFTS. They are designed to nullify the inheritance tax effects of a gift of property where the donor continues to enjoy or benefit from the donated property or receives any other form of collateral benefit which is in some way referable to the original gift. For example, the provisions would nullify the effect of a gift by a farmer of his farm to his son if the donor continues to occupy the property or enjoy any benefits from it. In addition, an income tax charge may arise on the donor of a gift of property where he has retained a right to use or enjoy the asset given away and which is not subject to the gifts with reservation rules. The income tax charge affects past arrangements as well as those made after the introduction of the POA charge. These provisions are considered further in CHAPTER 4 LIFETIME PLANNING: MAKING GIFTS. The provisions also have a considerable impact in relation to farming partnerships and this is considered in some detail in CHAPTER 12 THE FAMILY BUSINESS at 12.33.

Currently, occupation by the donor of land which he has given away is disregarded for the purposes of the reservation of benefit provisions if he provides full consideration in money or money's worth (for example, if he pays a rack rent under a tenancy (FA 1986, Sch 20, para 6(1)(a)). This exemption also applies where a donor gives away an undivided share in land which is then occupied jointly by the donor, provided the donor does not receive any benefit, other than a negligible one, which is provided by or at the expense of the donee for some reason connected with the gift (FA 1986, s 102B(4)). Such arrangements should be reviewed in the light of the income tax charge on pre-owned assets. Provided that, in the above example, the donor of the land pays a full market rent for the property, in accordance with the provisions set out in FA 2004, Sch 15, para 4, there should be no benefit on which the income tax charge will arise.

Agricultural property relief at 100% will often protect against the effects of the gifts with reservation provisions as is illustrated by the example given in HMRC Inheritance Tax Manual, para 24205.

HMRC's Example

In 1980 A purchases a farm and occupies it. In May 1990 he gives it to his son B. But A continues in occupation rent-free until his death in December 1992 (without infringing B's right to vacant possession).

This is a GWR. The farm qualifies for relief at the date of gift. Although B has neither owned the property for seven years nor occupied it for agricultural purposes for two years ending with the date of the notional transfer by B on A's death, relief is available at the higher rate (100%) because B can count A's occupation as his own.

A farmer can now make the ultimate reservation of benefit (ie retaining the property until death rather than giving it away) and still have the property wholly exempt from tax. Nevertheless, the provisions must still be considered in planning for tenanted land let pre-1 September 1995 and other situations where a gift should be made for reasons which are not concerned with taxation.

Grant of tenancies of agricultural property

[13.23] The grant of a tenancy of agricultural property in the UK, the Channel Islands or the Isle of Man for agricultural purposes is not a transfer of value for inheritance tax purposes by the grantor if he makes the grant for full consideration in money or money's worth (IHTA 1984, s 16). This provision is, however, applied strictly.

To ensure in a family context that any grant of an agricultural tenancy is for full consideration in money or money's worth, the initial rent for the tenancy should be that which would be obtainable on a grant of the tenancy in the open market. To ensure that such a value is achieved between the parties, independent valuers should act both for the grantor and the grantee.

In determining whether there is full consideration, one needs to take account of all the surrounding circumstances, such as the terms of the tenancy and the personal circumstances of the tenant. It is assumed that full consideration requires the rent payable under the tenancy to be the 'open market rent', ie the rent which would be expected to be achieved on the grant by a willing grantor to a willing grantee of the tenancy in the open market (on its particular terms) of the land in question. In determining the open market rent, one would place greater weight on evidence of 'tender rents' in the area (ie the rent which would be expected to be achieved by an owner inviting tenders for the grant of a new tenancy) rather than local 'arbitration rents' (ie the new rent determined on a three-yearly rent review of an existing tenancy).

Capital gains tax

[13.24] Where a farm has been in a family for generations and is likely to remain the only or main source of livelihood for succeeding generations, capital gains tax is likely to have minimal impact because the land is unlikely to be sold.

A gift of farmland or a farming business will be subject to capital gains tax at 10% or 20% on any chargeable gains arising. The rate of 20% may be reduced to 10% if entrepreneurs' relief is available. Of course, there has to be the disposal of the whole or part of a business. The disposal of 'part of a business' is not the mere sale of farmland (*McGregor (Inspector of Taxes) v Adcock* [1977] 3 All ER 65, [1977] STC 206). See also *Russell v HMRC* (2012) TC 2299. The gain arising on a gift to a family member may be held-over under TCGA 1992, s 165 or 260. Hold-over relief will defer the chargeable gain until a subsequent disposal by the donee. Hold-over relief is not available on disposals to settlor-interested trusts or trusts for which there subsists an arrangement under which the settlor will acquire an interest in the trust. There is a clawback period during which the held-over gain will become chargeable if the settlor acquires an interest in the trust or a later arrangement subsists for him to acquire such interest. This is dealt with in CHAPTER 4 LIFETIME PLANNING: MAKING GIFTS.

The farmer who wishes to raise funds by making some small sales from his holding can elect that the transfer should not be treated as a disposal for capital gains tax purposes (TCGA 1992, s 242). TCGA 1992, s 242 provides that an election can be made where there is a disposal of land forming part only of a holding, and the consideration for the sale does not exceed the lower of £20,000 and one-fifth of the market value of the holding prior to the sale. The consideration received will be taken into account on a subsequent disposal of the holding.

Where land has been purchased and subsequently part is resold, the gain arising on the disposal cannot be rolled over into the acquisition cost of the property still retained by the taxpayer (*Watton (Insp of Taxes) v Tippett* [1997] STC 893, 69 TC 491, CA).

In considering possible lifetime gifts of farmland where there is a likelihood that the land will one day be sold (eg following the death of the present owner/occupier), the loss of the capital gains tax free base uplift available on death (TCGA 1992, s 62) should not be overlooked and should be weighed against the potential inheritance tax saving on the death. This is of even greater importance if agricultural property relief is available. Where the land will qualify for 100% inheritance tax agricultural property relief on the death, any liability to capital gains tax will amount to an additional charge to tax as the property could have been retained until death at no inheritance tax cost and the capital gains tax free base uplift obtained. The impact and interaction of these provisions is considered in more detail in CHAPTER 4 LIFETIME PLANNING: MAKING GIFTS at **4.61–4.64**.

Reference should also be made to CHAPTER 12 THE FAMILY BUSINESS at **12.28** for a more detailed discussion of the workings of TCGA 1992, s 165.

Structure of the business

[13.25] The comparative advantages and disadvantages of an incorporated and an unincorporated business have been considered in CHAPTER 12 THE FAMILY BUSINESS. In the context of a farming business, the corporate advantage of limited liability is less likely to be a significant consideration and, in any event, may now be obtained through a limited liability partnership. One must, however, consider the rate of corporation tax payable by a company and the rate of income tax payable by an individual, either as a sole trader or through a partnership. In the average farming family, the ability to spread the farming assets around the family by transfers of small blocks of shares is probably of more theoretical than practical benefit. The principal disadvantage of a company, however, namely the potential double liability to a capital gains charge, will not be a significant consideration if the land a company owns is unlikely ever to be sold. As always, it is important when structuring a business to aim for as flexible a structure as possible, which will enable lifetime gifts to be made, but which will also minimise the tax payable on death.

In relation to companies and partnerships, the most difficult question to resolve is exactly what to do about the land. Should it be owned by the partnership or the company; or should it be retained outside the farming vehicles? If so, should it be tenanted or not? With the sole proprietor of an unincorporated business, these questions do not arise.

Tenanted or untenanted?

[13.26] Agricultural property relief is available at 100% in respect of vacant possession land, land let on a tenancy commencing after 31 August 1995 and certain succession tenancies providing all the normal criteria are met. This effectively removes inheritance tax from the decision making process where new structures are being contemplated.

However, a tenancy has other implications which can be disadvantageous. One (which is alleviated to some degree by the Agricultural Tenancies Act 1995) is its lack of flexibility, but the principal one is the fact that it will give rise to rental payments. The payment of a rack rent may cause cash flow problems for the company or partnership paying it. The payment of rent under a tenancy will convert earned income into unearned income which will be significant in respect of pension planning.

Rental income can always be waived by a deed before its due date for payment. However, to avoid the application of the associated operations rules in IHTA 1984, s 268, the waiver should not be made within three years of the grant of the tenancy. Such waivers can themselves constitute transfers of value, but if done on a regular basis, it is possible to argue that the normal expenditure out of income exemption applies to avoid any liability to inheritance tax. There is no equivalent to the provisions in IHTA 1984, s 15 which provides that waivers of dividends do not by reason of the waiver constitute a transfer of value.

It should be remembered that an agricultural tenancy may have a capital value which is important in valuing an interest in a partnership, an LLP, or shares in a company, which owns a tenancy. To date, the question has been considered in relation to tenancies protected under the Agricultural Holdings Act 1986 and the following discussion relates specifically to such tenancies. With regard to farm business tenancies under the Agricultural Tenancies Act 1995, the position will depend on the degree of security of tenure given to the tenant under the terms of the lease and its length although it seems likely that, in practice, it will be difficult to ascribe any significant capital value to most tenancies dealt with under the 1995 Act.

At one end of the spectrum it has been suggested that an agricultural tenancy has no value and at the other that a tenancy may have a value somewhere in the region of one half of the difference between the vacant possession value and the tenanted value of the land (on the basis that this is what a landlord might be prepared to pay to obtain vacant possession of his farm). The truth probably lies somewhere between these two extremes. Even if an agricultural tenancy may be expressly non-assignable, this does not prevent a hypothetical sale of the tenancy being assumed for valuation purposes, although in valuing the tenancy account must be taken of the fact that the hypothetical purchaser would be in the same position as the hypothetical vendor and accordingly unable to assign the tenancy (*IRC v Crossman* [1939] AC 26, [1936] 1 All ER 762). This factor may mean that the tenancy in question has a very low value because no tenant is likely to pay much in the way of a capital sum for an asset which he himself cannot realise and which commits him to paying a rack rent.

Two general approaches have developed to the valuation of these tenancies. *Baird's Executors v IRC* [1991] 1 EGLR 201, [1991] 09 EG 129 puts the emphasis on the vacant possession premium. If land subject to a tenancy is worth less than if it were vacant, that difference in value could be unlocked by the merging of the two interests. The valuation would be based on the division of the vacant possession premium reflecting the balance between the two parties which is often assumed to be equal. The Baird approach would apply where it is shown that there is a special purchaser for the tenancy.

In the case of *Walton (Walton's Executor) v IRC* [1996] STC 68, [1996] 1 EGLR 159, CA, it was held that a tenancy will not automatically be valued on the basis of a percentage of the freehold value on the assumption that the freeholder will always be a special purchaser. The sale has to take place 'in the real world' and the actual persons in addition to the actual property need to be taken into consideration. The value of the tenancy will be determined by comparison with other tenancies of its kind. It will be based on an appraisal of profit rent which compares the current rent, the rent potentially due at the next review and a rent where the land is newly let. The case of *Greenbank v Pickles* (2000) 81 P & CR D28, [2000] NPC 107 appears to confirm the *Walton* basis in the absence of a special purchaser of the tenancy.

It is therefore essential to determine whether there are or were any special purchasers at the date of valuation. The most likely person to be a special purchaser is the landlord.

Where the current rental under the tenancy is less than the open market rent and the next review date is in a couple of years, this may give some value to the tenancy. Another factor to be taken into account is the event which requires the value of the tenancy to be calculated. Under the 'hypothetical sale' procedure, the hypothetical purchaser is placed in exactly the same position as that occupied by the vendor. If the time of valuation is the death of the vendor, the hypothetical purchaser would pay nothing for the tenancy on the basis that the landlord would be in a position to serve an incontestable notice to quit on the deceased tenant's personal representatives (Agricultural Holdings Act 1986, Sch 3 Pt I Case G). On the other hand, where the tenancy is not vested solely in the deceased, for example, where it is owned by a partnership, or LLP, the tenancy could have a value as it could continue until the death of the last of the joint owners.

Farming business carried on by a company

[13.27] If the farmland is owned by a company, then its shares will qualify for 100% agricultural property relief to the extent that their value is attributable to the farmland, provided the transferor of the shares controls the company. The remaining value of the shares should qualify for business property relief if the farmland is not let. A minority holding will qualify for 100% business property relief but not agricultural property relief because the transferor will not control the company. On the valuation of a minority holding a significant discount will, of course, be achievable on the net asset value of the company.

If farmland is let to a company under a tenancy, then the freehold reversion will qualify for 50% agricultural property relief if the tenancy was entered into before 1 September 1995 and 100% relief if entered into or succeeded to after 31 August 1995. Where the company is wholly owned by the landowner, or is at least controlled by him, HMRC argues that the 100% or controlling shareholding together with the freehold reversion to the land will have an aggregate value approaching the land's vacant possession value. An open market purchaser would be prepared to pay such a sum, so the argument goes, because of his ability either to liquidate the company and merge the tenancy with the reversion (this assumes a 100% holding), or to compel the company to surrender the tenancy, thereby securing vacant possession.

The argument has some force, but whether an open market purchaser would be prepared to pay a price near to the vacant possession value will depend upon the particular facts in each case. So if, in arriving at a value, one assumes that the land owner will exercise his control of the company to procure a surrender of the tenancy before the sale and the purchaser would pay a price recognising that he could do so after the sale, one would also have to take into account the tax charge which might arise on the hypothetical surrender which is likely to be a distribution. Where the shareholding is less than 100%, one would take into account the fact that, to avoid prejudicing the minority interests, the landlord would have to purchase the tenancy from the company at its full surrender value with all the taxation and other costs that that would entail.

Even if HMRC's argument is correct, where the land was let prior to 1 September 1995 the land will nevertheless only qualify for the 50% relief because of the existence of the tenancy (subject of course to ESC F17 discussed at **13.16** above).

In the case of a company owning a tenancy of agricultural property which it farms, the shares will qualify for business property relief at 100%. As we have seen, the tenancy itself may have some value within the company, and probably the shares themselves, if a majority holding, will have an even greater value than that reflected by the value of the tenancy alone, since the company has perpetual existence and since the tenancy, even if non-assignable, becomes *de facto* assignable through a transfer of the shares which are not so restricted.

It can be seen that the letting of farmland to a company with the owner retaining the freehold reversion will give rise to an unnecessary exposure to inheritance tax where the land is let on a tenancy which commenced prior to 1 September 1995 and where no succession has occurred since that date. The question arises as to whether such tenancies should be terminated with a new agreement being entered into which will enable the let land to benefit from the 100% relief.

Problems can arise in relation to a farmhouse being held by a company for a number of reasons including the fact that main residence relief will not be available in respect of the farmhouse. In addition, the ATED charge may apply although there is relief for farmhouses. Where a person carries on a trade of farming commercially and with a profit seeking motive and owns a dwelling ('farmhouse') on the same land, relief may be available to reduce the ATED charge to nil (FA 2013, ss 148, 149). A number of conditions must be satisfied for the relief to apply including that a 'qualifying farm worker' must occupy the property and that the farmer or farm worker has a substantial involvement in the day-to-day work of the trade or the direction and control of the conduct of the trade. This is important particularly where a farmer is considering reducing his hours or retiring. The benefit in kind charge could also arise although there is the argument that occupation by the farmer is necessary or it is customary in order to perform his work. The difficulty is that the exemption does not apply if occupation is by a director who has a material interest in the company. It is therefore advisable that farmhouses are not held by the farming company. The farmhouse should still qualify for relief provided that it is occupied for agricultural purposes. The decision in *Hanson v HMRC* held that agricultural land and the farmhouse need not be in the common ownership; what is required is that it is in common occupation. HMRC Inheritance Tax Manual at para 24051 acknowledges that land owned by a company and controlled by the person residing in the farmhouse can be taken into account for the purposes of the 'character appropriate' test. Although if there is no control, this does rather suggest that relief will be denied in such circumstances.

The creation of a new farming company is likely to be an unattractive structure unless there are commercial reasons for creating a company. There are two situations where a company structure may be sensible. The first is where there is a large unrealised gain on a possible disposal of development land. The whole business, including the land, could be transferred to a company in consideration of shares. Under TCGA 1992, s 162 the gain would be rolled over into the shares of the company. Therefore, the company would acquire the assets at market value at the date of the transfer. The company could then sell the land soon after, thus realising an insignificant gain. Like everything, there are disadvantages. The first being that the gain rolled over crystallises when the shares are sold although, if the shares are held until death, there will be the free capital gains tax uplift on death. In addition, an SDLT charge would arise on the transfer of non-residential property to a connected company at a rate of up to 5%. The rates will be higher if residential property is transferred.

A company may also be used to take advantage of the larger tax deduction for contributions made to an approved company pension scheme for directors and employees.

Farming business carried on by partnership

[13.28] As in the case of a company, a partnership or limited liability partnership carrying on the farming business may either own the land on which that business is carried on or occupy it either under an agricultural tenancy or under a gratuitous licence.

Where the partnership owns the land, the partners' interests in the partnership, to the extent that their value is attributable to the value of the land, will qualify for 100% agricultural property relief, with the balance of the value qualifying for 100% business property relief.

Where the partnership occupies the farmland under a tenancy, 50% agricultural property relief will be available, in most cases, if the tenancy was entered into before 1 September 1995 and 100% relief will be available, in most cases, where it was entered into or succeeded to after 31 August 1995. Business property relief at 100% will be available in respect of the partnership interests of the partners and depending upon the terms of the partnership the value (if any) of the tenancy may be taken into account.

Where the land is let to a partnership and the freeholder is himself a major partner, the freehold reversion and partnership share is treated as a single unit of property for the purposes of valuation (see *IRC v Gray (Executor of Lady Fox)* [1994] STC 360, [1994] RVR 129, CA). The effect is to remove the majority of the discount normally applicable to tenanted land. In *Walton (Walton's Executor) v IRC* [1996] STC 68, [1996] 1 EGLR 159, CA, no allowance or discount was made in calculating the deceased partner's interest. This basis appears to have been confirmed in *Greenbank v Pickles* [2001] 1 EGLR 1.

Where a farmer owns a farmhouse and, in partnership with his children, farms the land occupied with the farmhouse, the amount of land which will be taken into account for the purposes of the character appropriate test in IHTA 1984, s 115(2) will depend on the provisions in the partnership deed. If the farmer is only entitled to 30% of income and capital profits, HMRC's view is that the farmer will only be entitled to agricultural property relief on 30% of the land occupied with the farmhouse, ie the amount of land which is commensurate with the farmer's partnership share. This matter has yet to be considered by the courts.

Where an Agricultural Holdings Act 1986 protected tenancy is already in existence, see the comments above in relation to a farming business carried on by a company with regard to the termination of the existing arrangements and the making of new ones.

The Basic Payments Scheme

[**13.29**] Currently, under the Basic Payment Scheme ('BPS'), direct payments are made to farmers based on the area and historical entitlement of the land. To qualify for the BPS a claimant must be an 'active farmer', which is defined using a negative list of business types that do not qualify. The entitlement to payment can be traded in the same way as entitlement was traded under the predecessor scheme, the Single Farm Payment Scheme. Although HMRC has not given any guidance on the tax treatment of entitlements to BPS, it is assumed that the tax treatment is the same as for the Single Farm Payment Scheme.

Capital gains tax

[**13.30**] An entitlement is a chargeable asset for capital gains tax purposes. Any gains arising from transactions in entitlements will be chargeable to capital gains tax following the normal capital gains tax rules. An entitlement is not linked to a particular parcel of land and therefore does not form part of the land for capital gains tax purposes. As it is a separate asset that was not derived from any pre-existing asset, its base cost is nil in relation to an originating statutory claimant. Whether an entitlement is a business asset for capital gains tax purposes will depend on the facts of each case. Broadly, if the income from the BPS is charged to income tax as the profits of a trade under ITTOIA 2005, ss 9 or 10 then the entitlement is likely to be a business asset for capital gains tax purposes.

Inheritance tax

[**13.31**] Transfers of entitlement are liable to inheritance tax like the transfer of any other asset.

As an entitlement is an asset separate from the land in relation to which it is granted, it cannot qualify for agricultural property relief. It may however, qualify for business property relief provided it is an asset of a trading business which satisfies the normal conditions for the relief. HMRC Tax Bulletin June 2005 stated in relation to payment entitlement under the Single Farm Payment Scheme that 'the transfer of PE by someone who is not carrying on a trading business will not qualify for business property relief'. Similarly, the transfer of a PE as an individual asset, rather than the transfer of a business or an interest in the business one of the assets of which is a PE, will not qualify for business property relief.

A claim for a BPS payment can only be made by an active farmer who owns a farm business registered with the Rural Payments Agency so it is important that one does not bequeath the entitlement to a person who will not be the owner of a registered farm business.

Example

Giles has two children, Sam and Katie. Sam helps his father with the day-to-day running of the farm whilst Katie is a civil servant. Under the terms of his will Giles leaves the farm to Sam and the residue to Katie. Sam will receive the farm and the PE will pass to Katie as part of the residue but she will be unable to claim it as she has no registered farm business.

Giles should therefore change his will to ensure the PE passes with the land to Sam.

Strategies for the farmer

[**13.32**] We examine below a selection of estate planning strategies for the farmer and his family. No single strategy is necessarily the best one. Each case must be considered separately taking into account the circumstances of the family, the nature of the farming business and the personalities involved.

Doing nothing

[13.33] Doing nothing is a strategy that has appealed to many farmers over the years because they are often by nature conservative. Due to agricultural property relief being available at 100% for untenanted land and for land let on tenancies commencing after 31 August 1995, the vast majority of working farmers can now retain their land until death and obtain complete exemption from inheritance tax on its value. Any unrealised capital gain inherent in the value of the land will also be washed out on death, thus achieving the optimum result in respect of both taxes.

Whilst a policy of doing nothing will now be the most effective policy for most farmers, that will not be the case for all. For example, practical circumstances may require the property to be passed down to the next generation prior to death or there may be a pre-1 September 1995 tenancy which does not qualify for 100% relief.

Where action is required by a working farmer, it will fall into one of two categories: action on retirement and action before retirement.

Action before retirement

[13.34] Where a farmer has one or more children who wish to come into the business, then he should consider bringing them into a traditional partnership or an LLP. Farmers have in the past brought their wives into partnership or made them shareholders of a family company in order to transfer taxable income to their wives. HMRC tried unsuccessfully to apply the settlement provisions to husband and wife partnerships and company arrangements in circumstances in which it considered that the assets transferred were being used as a vehicle for diverting income from one spouse to the other (see *Jones v Garnett*). If the provisions had applied, they would have deemed the partnership or company concerned to be a settlement and the settlement income to be that of the 'settlor'; the settlor for these purposes being the spouse (normally the husband) who was the original farmer of the land.

If the land is to be brought into the partnership it would normally be done by transferring it into the joint names of the partners. The farmer may decide to credit his capital account in the partnership with the full value of the land brought in by him, and in this case he may also wish to perform a 'value freezing' exercise by incorporating automatic accruer provisions in the partnership, under which any surplus value in the land will pass to his children on his death or retirement from the partnership, or by providing that any realised or unrealised capital profits attributable to the land shall belong only to them. Alternatively, he may decide to share the land immediately with his children either by crediting both his and their capital accounts equally with the full value of the land or by specifying in the partnership deed how the land is to be beneficially owned. The gifts with reservation rules will not apply if the profits are shared in the proportions in which the partners own the partnership assets at commencement (HMRC Inheritance Tax Manual para 14332). It is often the case that older family partners transfer assets into a partnership on the understanding that the younger partners will devote more time to the business. It is argued that such transfers are not intended to confer a gratuitous benefit and are such as might be expected to be made in a transaction at arm's length between persons not connected with each other and are therefore not a transfer of value by virtue of IHTA 1984, s 10. It would seem that, if a transfer satisfies the second arm of the s 10 test, the income tax settlement provisions will also not apply. However, if the donor receives profits from the partnership in excess of his share of the land, the gift with reservation rules will apply. No income tax charge on pre-owned assets will arise in this situation because of the application of the gift with reservation rules.

Even if the untenanted land is brought back into the estate of the donor, it may still qualify for 100% relief on death. It is dangerous, however, to rely on this as it is necessary for certain criteria to be met at that stage. To avoid a gift with reservation, the children might enter into the partnership on full commercial terms in order to ensure that there is no element of gift — although, in a family context this is often impractical.

As is considered in more detail in **CHAPTER 12 THE FAMILY BUSINESS** under **12.34**, the introduction of land into a partnership may give rise to a capital gains tax charge which cannot be held-over under TCGA 1992, s 165 to the extent that the landowner receives a credit for the land in his capital account.

Borrowings

[13.35] It used to be the case that farmers were advised to secure any borrowings of a farming business on property which did not qualify for any form of relief. That was because if borrowings were secured against assets, those borrowings would be deducted from the value of the assets. Where borrowings were secured against property qualifying for relief, they would be taken into account when valuing the relevant property before the application of the relief — the effect being that the deduction of the borrowing would be wasted because the borrowings would reduce the value which would otherwise be reduced by agricultural property relief. Legislation was introduced in FA 2013 to provide that any loans attributable in whole or part to finance the acquisition of agricultural property or the maintenance or enhancement of its agricultural value will first reduce the value attributable to the agricultural value of the agricultural property (IHTA 1984, s 162B). Loans which were taken out prior to 6 April 2013 to finance the acquisition, maintenance or enhancement of agricultural property that are secured against non-agricultural property will still be deductible. It is therefore advisable that such loans remain as they are. This is discussed in more detail in **CHAPTER 4 LIFETIME PLANNING: AN OVERVIEW**.

Action on retirement

[13.36] On his retirement, the retiring farmer may be prepared to give away his farming business, including his land, to those of his children who wish to continue the business. They may, in fact, already be farming in partnership with their father and the land may either be an asset of the partnership or may still be owned by the father, with the partnership occupying under a tenancy or a gratuitous licence. Such a gift of the farming business and the land should be structured as a potentially exempt transfer, with the father's life being insured for the seven-year period to the extent that the gift does not qualify for 100% relief.

Entrepreneurs' Relief may be available to reduce the capital gains tax payable on any gift provided certain conditions are satisfied (see **12.17**). Elections may be made under TCGA 1992, s 165 to hold-over the chargeable gains arising on the gift. Where a substantial gain will arise, the gift should be considered very carefully as retention by the donor until death will result in the gain being washed out as described above.

A gift 'on retirement' should ideally be made just before retirement to ensure that the farmer will have occupied the property for the purposes of agriculture for the two years prior to the gift. Otherwise, agricultural property relief may be lost unless the seven-year ownership test can be satisfied.

Whilst the retiring farmer may be prepared to give up the farmland and his share of the business to the next generation, he may be reluctant to move out of the farmhouse in which he may well have lived for almost all his life. If the farmhouse remains in the ownership of the farmer, then on his death HMRC is likely to refuse agricultural property relief on it, on the grounds that it was no longer occupied for agricultural purposes (*Starke (Brown's Executors) v IRC* [1995] STC 689, [1996] 1 All ER 622; *Atkinson v Revenue & Customs Commissioners* [2012] UKUT 506 (TCC)).

HMRC has indicated that, where a farmer falls ill and is unable to continue to farm so that he has a period when he is not physically present in the property concerned, IHTA 1984, s 117 may be satisfied but the stated intentions of the owner need to be tested against the evidence (HMRC Inheritance Tax Manual, para 24083).

A farmer may not have any family members who are interested in taking on the farming business. In such a case a farmer could enter into a number of different arrangements with a third party agreeing to share occupation for specified agricultural purposes. Although it is advisable that such agreements are in writing, it is the practices adopted that will determine whether relief is available. It is therefore essential that factors such as the period of the agreement, the interest (if any) granted, the responsibility for the maintenance of the land, the activities undertaken by the farmer in practice in relation to growing the crop of grass etc, the impact on a farmer's responsibilities under the Basic Payment Scheme, the responsibility of any livestock placed on the land and the degree of control that the farmer has over the livestock owned by another person and the sharing of any commercial risks and rewards, are considered when making such an agreement.

HMRC may also challenge the availability of business property relief in relation to the agricultural land on the basis that the land is not occupied by the farmer and not being used for a business.

Where the retiring farmer wishes to exercise sporting rights over the land he should ensure that he pays a full commercial rent for doing so, so as to bring himself within the exemption provided by FA 1986, Sch 20, para 6(1)(a).

The 'two sons' problem

[13.37] It is a common problem that, although a farmer wishes all of his children to benefit equally from his estate, only one or some of them wish to be involved in farming the family farm. For example, consider a farmer who has two sons, one of whom wishes to take over the business (and the land) and the other of whom does not, as he wishes to pursue his own career. To carry on the business, however, the farming son may require all of the land. In many cases this will mean that the bulk of the inheritance will have to pass to the farming son. How may the other son be compensated?

Sadly, there is no general solution to the problem. Possibly, the two sons could inherit the freehold of the land, with the farming son taking a rack rent tenancy. This would enable the non-farming son to derive an income from the land and would at the same time give him a share in the capital asset. The payment of rent, however, may place an intolerable burden on the business of the farming son.

Alternatively, the two sons could inherit the land jointly and farm it together in partnership. The non-farming son could be a sleeping or limited partner with a small profit share, to give him an income from the property. This may be a more satisfactory solution than a tenancy, but does make the farming son vulnerable to an attempt by the non-farming son to use his rights as co-owner to force a sale of the land and, in effect, put an end to the farming business. Under the Trusts of Land and Appointment of Trustees Act 1996, s 12, a tenant in common does not have an automatic right to enforce a sale but he can apply to the court which has a discretionary power to do so.

Another possibility would be for the parents to leave the non-farming son a legacy charged on the farmland which is to be paid only on the death of the other son or on a sale of the land, if earlier. In practice, such a legacy may be of limited value to the non-farming son because of its deferred payment, although it does enable him to benefit from the land if it is ever sold.

In recent years landowners have been diversifying particularly in relation to renewable energy. In such a situation a farmer might leave those assets and their income stream to the non-farming son.

Perhaps, ultimately, farming parents who find themselves in this position should grasp the nettle and ensure that the farming son alone inherits the farming business and the land (including the entitlement to the Basic Payment Scheme (see **13.29** above)). At the same time, they should endeavour to compensate the non-farming son on their deaths out of their other property and concentrate on building up funds for the benefit of the non-farming son during their lifetimes. These funds could either be left to him on their death or made over to him from time to time during their lifetimes by the appropriate use of the lifetime exemptions. The taking out of a regular premium with profits or unit-linked whole life policy settled in trust for the non-farming son would be one way of achieving this objective.

Death

[13.38] Where a farmer dies leaving to his widow his farming business or land which is occupied at his death by either a farming partnership or LLP (which may include his widow and one or more of his children) or by a company (the shareholders of which may include his widow and children), the widow has a number of options. She may:

(a)   retain the land and business in her estate with a view to it passing on her death to the next generation — in many circumstances agricultural property relief at 100% will be available on her death;

(b)   decide to redirect the property to one or more of her children by way of a deed of variation effected within two years of the death — in this case the property would again pass reduced by agricultural property relief normally at 100%; or

(c)   where relief at 100% is not available, decide to give the property to one or more of her children by way of a potentially exempt transfer in the hope that she will survive the seven-year period so that the gift will escape tax completely.

The right option will depend on the precise family circumstances in each case, and, of course, the availability of agricultural property relief.

Where an inheritance tax liability is anticipated on the death of the farmer or his widow, consideration should always be given to funding the tax by a whole life insurance policy written either on a single life or a joint life last survivor basis held in trust for the next generation.

Chapter 14

Woodlands

Woodlands are afforded special tax treatment presumably because of the time needed for trees to mature and to avoid deforestation. This Chapter outlines not only the inheritance tax treatment of woodlands but the income tax and capital gains tax treatment as well.

Income tax

[14.1] The commercial occupation of woodlands in the UK is not a trade or part of a trade. Income derived from the occupation of commercially managed woodlands in the UK is, therefore, outside the scope of income tax (ITTOIA 2005, s 11) and corporation tax (CTA 2009, s 980). This means that the occupation of commercial woodlands does not give rise to a trading profit or allowable loss (ITTOIA 2005, s 11 and CTA 2009, s 37). The occupation of woodlands is commercial if the woodlands are managed on a commercial basis and with a view to the realisation of profits. The nature of the business should be clear from the business' accounts.

Since trees on commercially managed woodland are also outside the scope of capital gains tax (TCGA 1992, s 250(1)), any profit arising from the sale of such trees is completely outside the scope of any charge to tax. As a corollary, the expenses of planting and managing such trees cannot create a deduction for income tax purposes.

However, income from the grant of an easement of, for example, shooting rights, may be assessable as profits of a property business. In addition, the profits of a separate trade carried on in conjunction with the occupation of the woodlands (for example, the production of finished timber goods) which goes beyond such basic activities as felling and sawing which are necessary to render raw timber marketable may be assessable as trading profits (*Christie v Davies* [1945] 1 All ER 370, (1945) 26 TC 398).

Short rotation coppice is treated for all tax purposes as farming rather than forestry, so that land under such cultivation is farm or agricultural land and not woodlands (ITA 2007, s 996(3), (4)) and is therefore assessable to income tax. Short rotation coppice is a perennial crop of tree species planted at high density, the stems of which are harvested above ground level at intervals of less than ten years. In *Jaggers (t/a Shide Trees) v Ellis* [1997] STC 1417 (ChD), 71 TC 164 it was held that the income from land planted with coniferous trees, intended to be sold as Christmas trees, were not within the exemption provided by ITTOIA 2005, s 11 since the land was not woodland as it was covered by trees resembling bushes rather than timber trees.

Capital gains tax

[14.2] TCGA 1992, s 250(1) provides that in the case of woodlands managed by the occupier on a commercial basis and with a view to the realisation of profits, the consideration for the disposal of trees from the woodlands is excluded from the capital gains tax computation on a disposal by the occupier. This exemption applies whether the trees are standing, felled or cut. Similarly, sums derived from an insurance policy effected in respect of the destruction of, or damage or injury to, the trees are also excluded if the person making the disposal is the occupier. Section 250(3) provides that in this respect the provisions of s 22(1) dealing with disposals arising on the receipt of a capital sum are overridden. Section 250(4) and (5) stipulates that in computing the cost and the gain on the disposal of woodland, the cost or consideration, as the case may be, which is attributable to trees (which by virtue of s 250(6) includes saleable underwood) growing on the land is to be left out of account (HMRC Capital Gains Manual CG73200).

If the woodland has been commercially managed then any consideration for the disposal of the trees alone (whether felled or standing) is excluded in computing any gain on the disposal provided the person making the disposal is the occupier. In any other case, each felled tree is treated as a single chattel and a chargeable gain will only arise if each tree has a value in excess of £6,000 (TCGA 1992, s 262). The provisions of TCGA 1992, s 262(4) regarding 'sets' do not apply to trees (HMRC Capital Gains Manual CG73200).

Trees growing on woodland may be disposed of by the owner granting to another person the right to enter the woodland and fell the trees. If the trees are growing on commercial woodland, the exemption in TCGA 1992, s 250(1) will apply. If the trees are not growing on a commercial woodland, HMRC takes the view that the capital gains tax consequences will depend on the precise nature of the right which is granted. If the person to whom the right is granted is not entitled to benefit from the future growth of the trees, that is if he must fell the trees within a short time, the owner of the woodlands is treated as disposing of the trees as individual chattels. If the person to whom the right is granted is entitled to benefit from the future growth of the trees, that is if he is granted the right to fell trees over a long period, then the owner is treated as having made a part disposal of his land (HMRC Capital Gains Manual CG73200).

Woodland managed on a commercial basis is an asset used for the purposes of a trade within TCGA 1992, s 165 and therefore a gift of woodlands is capable of qualifying for hold-over relief under that section and for roll-over relief under TCGA 1992, s 158(1)(b).

Inheritance tax

[14.3] Woodlands managed on a commercial basis may be eligible for business property relief at 100% provided the conditions in s 105 are satisfied. There does not seem to be any reason why a commercial forestry business should not qualify for business property relief as a business in its own right.

This is supported by the case of *Brander (representative of James (dec'd), Fourth Earl of Balfour) v Revenue and Customs Comrs* [2010] UKUT 300 (TCC), [2010] STC 2666 (see **12.9**) where the Upper Tribunal stated that the in-hand farming and woodlands were to be regarded as non-investment activities. Non-commercial woodlands would not qualify for relief as no business is being carried on. Where woodlands are let, this will be treated as an investment and will only qualify for business property relief if the let woodland is part of a larger estate that qualifies for business property relief under the principles established in the *Farmer* and *Balfour* cases. However, where the woodlands do not represent a business or an interest in a business in the hands of the transferor or do not qualify for another reason (eg they have been held for less than two years) the treatment for inheritance tax purposes will vary depending on whether the woodlands form part of an estate on death or are the subject matter of a lifetime gift.

Relief on death

[**14.4**] It is possible to elect for relief on death with the effect that the value of such trees or underwood are excluded in determining the value of the estate on death for inheritance tax purposes (IHTA 1984, s 125). The tax is deferred until the trees are actually disposed of. If there is no disposal, tax is charged on the next death in the usual way, unless, of course, another election is made.

Conditions for the relief

[**14.5**] IHTA 1984, s 125 provides for a specific relief on the transfer of woodlands on death. Relief will be available where two conditions are satisfied. First where part of the value of a person's estate immediately before his death is attributable to the value of land in the UK or another state which is an EEA state on which trees or underwood (which do not represent agricultural property) are growing

Secondly, the deceased must either have been beneficially entitled to the land throughout the five years immediately preceding his death or have become beneficially entitled to the land otherwise than for a consideration in money or money's worth (ie by gift or devise). This is to prevent exploitation of the relief by death-bed purchasers of woodlands. It should be noted that there is no requirement for the woodlands to be managed on a commercial basis with a view to profit.

The election

[**14.6**] In order for the relief to apply, an election must be made. The election is made by the deceased's personal representatives or any other person who would otherwise be liable to pay the inheritance tax on the deceased's estate. The election must be made within two years of the death or such longer period as HMRC may allow (IHTA 1984, s 125(3)), although any election submitted after the two-year period will be referred to Technical Guidance (HMRC Inheritance Tax Manual, para 4375). Where the woodlands can be divided into clearly distinct geographical areas, HMRC accepts that elections may be made in relation to one or more of the areas (HMRC Inheritance Tax Manual, para 4375). It is possible for an election to be withdrawn. HMRC state that where the parties wish to withdraw the election within two years of a death 'they should normally be allowed to do so'. Where a request is made more than two years after death for the election to be withdrawn, and there are special circumstances, the HMRC Inheritance Tax Manual, para 4375 states that 'the case should be given sympathetic consideration but enquiry should be made whether the timber has been or is about to be sold'.

The inheritance tax charged as a result of the subsequent disposal is payable by the person entitled to the sale proceeds or who would be so entitled if the disposal were a sale (IHTA 1984, s 208). The tax is due six months after the end of the month in which the disposal took place (IHTA 1984, s 226(4)).

This last provision could produce some strange results. Suppose, for example, that the deceased has made a specific devise of the woodlands to a beneficiary and, because of a direction in the will, the tax in respect of this devise is to be borne out of residue. The deceased's personal representative (who is 'the person liable for the whole or part of the tax') elects for relief under s 125. The value of the trees and underwood on the woodlands is then left out of the calculation of the tax due on death (to the benefit of the residuary beneficiary). However, if the timber is sold a few years later it is the specific legatee of the woodlands who has to pay the inheritance tax charge arising. Not only is the amount of tax on the timber (almost certainly) more than it would have been had the election not been made, but also the specific legatee is liable to pay that tax despite the direction that the tax should be borne by residue. It is unclear whether the specific legatee could claim to be indemnified by the residuary legatee and/or the personal representative as IHTA 1984 does not provide him with a specific right of recovery. Equally unclear is whether the specific legatee could apply, as one of the persons liable for the tax on the timber (under IHTA 1984, s 200), to have the personal representative's election under s 125 disallowed.

Effect of claim

[14.7] The effect of a claim under IHTA 1984, s 125 is to reduce the overall inheritance tax bill on the estate. The value of the trees or underwood (but not of the underlying land) is left out of account in determining the value transferred by the deceased on death. However, the election acts only to give a deferral of the tax that would otherwise have been charged rather than a total exemption.

The deferred inheritance tax will become chargeable on the first disposal of the trees or underwood in respect of which relief has been claimed (excepting a disposal to the transferor's spouse or civil partner (IHTA 1984, s 126)), provided the disposal occurs before the land on which the trees or underwood stood again passes on someone's death. Thus, if the recipient of woodlands on another's death makes a gift of the trees or underwood or sells it during his lifetime, the inheritance tax charge deferred from the deceased's death will become chargeable. If, however, the recipient dies with the trees or underwood still forming part of his estate the inheritance tax charge deferred from the first deceased owner's death will fall out of charge, although the trees or underwood will form part of the second deceased owner's estate. Relief may again be claimed under s 125 in relation to the inheritance tax chargeable on his estate.

The inheritance tax charge which arises on the subsequent disposal depends on whether the disposal is a sale for full consideration in money or money's worth. If it is, the amount on which tax is calculated is the net proceeds of sale whether the disposal is of the trees and underwood or of an interest therein. If the disposal is not such a sale, the amount on which tax is calculated is the net value at the time of disposal of the trees or underwood (IHTA 1984, s 127). The amount on which tax is charged is then added to the deceased's cumulative total, which for these purposes includes all the property in respect of which inheritance tax was chargeable on his death, and tax is charged at the highest marginal rate. The lower rate of tax, ie 36%, will not be charged even if the 10% test was satisfied originally. Where there has been a subsequent reduction in the rates (ie a raising of the thresholds for each rate band or a change in the rates themselves), the tax chargeable on the disposal is calculated on the rates in force at the date of disposal (IHTA 1984, Sch 2, para 4).

Should an election be made?

[**14.8**] This question will only really be of relevance where it is not clear if business property relief will be available. If trees are relatively mature at the date of death and little or no further appreciation in value is expected, an election may be beneficial. Alternatively, if the trees are immature and a significant increase in value is expected, an election may not be beneficial. In addition, the age of the recipient also needs to be considered.

Where business property relief is available at 100%, there will be no reason to make the election. In fact, because of an apparent quirk in the drafting of IHTA 1984, s 127(2), it would seem positively disadvantageous to do so as relief would then only be available at 50%.

Where 100% business property relief is not available, the decision as to whether or not the s 125 election should be made is not always an easy one. There is a definite cashflow advantage in making the election. In addition, the rate of tax charged on a subsequent disposal of the timber will be reduced if there has been a reduction in the rates since the date of death. However, this must be set against the fact that the tax is charged on the net disposal proceeds or market value of the timber at the date of disposal and not the value at the date of the deceased's death. Also, consideration should be given to who will bear the tax if an election is not made.

Subject to the above comments, the wisdom of making an election will probably depend on the maturity of the trees. If they are very young and the present owner intends to hold the woodlands as part of his estate for some time, it will probably make sense not to make the election. Alternatively, if he intends to give away the timber or the woodlands quite soon, he might consider making the election (particularly if he would be bearing the tax if no election were to be made) if only because the amount of tax charged as a result of the disposal in relation to the deceased previous owner's death can be deducted from the value transferred by his subsequent lifetime transfer.

However, if the subsequent lifetime transfer is to be made at a time when the woodlands have become eligible for 100% business property relief, this deduction will be of no relevance. Where he wishes to transfer the woodland within two years of the previous owner's death, he would be well advised to consider making the transfer by means of a variation and election under IHTA 1984, s 142.

Meaning of 'woodlands'

[14.9] There is no statutory definition of woodlands in IHTA 1984. The *Shorter Oxford English Dictionary* defines woodland as 'land covered with trees; a wooded region or piece of ground'. In the income tax case of *Jaggers (t/a Snide Trees) v Ellis* [1997] STC 1417, 71 TC 164 mentioned above, Lightman J considered that 'the term "woodland" connotes a wood, a sizable area of land to a significant extent covered by growing trees of some maturity, height and size'. He went on to say that 'there is something to be said for the rule of thumb that their wood should be capable of being used as timber for woodlands are frequently used and cultivated for timber production . . . '. There is a concern therefore that although the case related to income tax and TA 1988, s 53(4) has different wording to IHTA 1984, s 125, claims for woodland relief may be challenged in respect of wooded areas of land that are cultivated for the purpose of timber production.

It should also be noted that short rotation coppice will be treated as being agricultural property so woodlands relief cannot be claimed in respect of the land on which the trees or underwood stand.

Agricultural or business property relief

[14.10] Agricultural property relief will be available on ancillary woodland if the woodlands are occupied and the occupation is ancillary to that of the agricultural land or pasture (IHTA 1984, s 115(2)). For example, it may be available on amenity woodland, shelter belts, coppices and coverts but not on substantial areas of land.

As mentioned above, woodlands run as a business on a commercial basis may constitute 'relevant business property' for the purposes of business property relief. Business property relief is available to relieve the land on which the trees or underwood stand where a s 125 election is made and will also be available when the deferred inheritance tax charge becomes chargeable on the subsequent disposal of the timber provided that business property relief would have been available on the previous owner's death if a s 125 election had not been made (IHTA 1984, s 127(2)). This is only of academic interest in most cases as 100% relief will be available rendering an election under s 125 unnecessary. Evidence may need to be given to demonstrate the commercial basis of the woodland if business property relief is claimed.

Payment by instalments

[14.11] For land on which the timber stands, there is no relief for the tax chargeable in respect of its value, apart from business property relief. The tax can, however, be paid in ten equal annual instalments provided a written election is made (IHTA 1984, s 229). The balance outstanding will become payable if the land is subsequently sold and interest at normal rates will run on the balance outstanding after the date when the first instalment is due (ie six months after the end of the month in which death occurred). Where the land itself qualifies for business property relief then the instalments are only subject to interest if they are not paid on the due date.

Relief for lifetime gifts

[**14.12**] There is generally no specific relief for a lifetime gift (chargeable transfer or potentially exempt transfer) of woodlands unless business property relief is available.

There is an exception where the lifetime gift is a disposal which revives an inheritance tax charge deferred from the previous owner's death in which case two forms of relief are available. The first is that the amount of tax charged on the transferor by reference to the deceased previous owner's estate and cumulative total can be deducted from the value transferred by him on his subsequent gift (IHTA 1984, s 129). (This is a relief of tax against the taxable amount, not tax against tax). The second is that the tax charged in respect of the subsequent gift can be paid by ten equal annual, interest-free, instalments if an election is made. It is available regardless of whether the donee or the donor is paying the tax. The first instalment is due when the tax as a whole would have been due but for the election to pay by instalments.

For land on which timber stands there is no relief for the tax chargeable in respect of its value, unless business property relief is available. The instalment option will, however, be available.

Purchasing woodlands

[**14.13**] Clearly, the financial returns to the investor in woodlands must be scrutinised as closely as the tax benefits. In recent years, investment in woodlands has increased for a variety of reasons. It should be remembered that investing in woodlands will require substantial expenditure on the purchase of land and planting of trees. Depending on the rate of growth of the trees chosen, there will be no income generated by the investment for several years (ten or more).

The incentive to invest in woodlands has over the years been reduced. Apart from the favourable inheritance tax treatment of 100% business property relief available to woodlands managed on a commercial basis, their tax treatment is akin to more conventional forms of investment, with no tax deduction on investment but the advantage of a tax-free profit. It will be a considerable length of time, however, before any profit accrues. A gift of immature woodlands into a trust has the attraction that it is a gift of an asset producing no income but considerable capital growth in the longer term.

If an individual considers woodlands attractive as a long-term investment for the benefit of his minor children, he might, for example, buy the woodlands, plant them with trees predicted to mature in 15 to 20 years' time. After two years the woodlands could be settled on discretionary trusts for his children. Provided 100% business property relief was available the gift would be free of inheritance tax. When the timber matures and is sold, any profits arising can be passed to the children free of tax.

The deduction of liabilities

[14.14] IHTA 1984, s 162B provides that where a liability has been incurred to acquire assets on which business property relief, agricultural property relief or woodlands relief is available, that liability will reduce the value of those assets which qualify for relief. These provisions take effect in relation to any liabilities incurred after 5 April 2013.

IHTA 1984, s 164B is discussed in more detail in CHAPTER 3 LIFETIME PLANNING: AN OVERVIEW.

Chapter 15

Gifts to Charities and Other Non-Profit Organisations

Introduction

[15.1] No book on estate planning would be complete without some mention of charities and how best to structure gifts to them and benefit from the tax reliefs available. This chapter details the tax reliefs and exemptions for making gifts to charities and the anti-avoidance provisions to be aware of. When advising a client wishing to make a substantial gift to a charity or charities under his will, an adviser should discuss the possibility of leaving assets on discretionary trusts, guiding the trustees by means of a letter of wishes to consider making appropriate advances to the testator's chosen charities. This is becoming more common due to some charities being more aggressive than others in their pursuit of bequests and devises.

What is a charity?

General law

[15.2] A charity is defined by the Charities Act 2011 ('CA 2011') as 'an institution which is established for charitable purposes only and falls to be subject to the control of the High Court in the exercise of its jurisdiction with respect to charities'. A charitable purpose is a purpose which falls within the purposes listed below and is for the public benefit (CA 2011, s 2). Charitable purposes include:

- the prevention or relief of poverty;
- the advancement of education;
- the advancement of religion;
- the advancement of health or the saving of lives;
- the advancement of citizenship or community development;
- the advancement of the arts, culture, heritage or science;
- the advancement of amateur sport;
- the advancement of human rights, conflict resolution or reconciliation or the promotion of religious or racial harmony or equality and diversity;
- the advancement of environmental protection or improvement;
- the relief of those in need by reason of youth, age, ill-health, disability, financial hardship or other disadvantage;
- the advancement of animal welfare;

- the promotion of the efficiency of the armed forces of the Crown, the police, fire and rescue services or ambulance services; and
- a 'sweep up' category for charitable purposes not listed in the other categories, plus any purposes analogous to recognised charitable purposes.

Under CA 2011, s 4 a charity will have to demonstrate that its activities are for the public benefit. The Act removes the presumption of public benefit but it does preserve the definition that has developed through case law. The Charity Commission has produced its own guidance on what it considers the public benefit requirement means, which can be found on their website.

Revenue law

[15.3] It was the case that a lifetime gift or legacy to a foreign charity would not qualify for an inheritance tax exemption because it was not subject to the jurisdiction of the UK courts. However, following the European Court's decision in *Persche v Finanzamt Ludenscheid*: C-318/07 [2009] ECR I-359, [2009] All ER (EC) 673, [2009] 2 CMLR 819 legislation was introduced in FA 2010 to extend various tax reliefs to certain organisations and Community Amateur Sports Clubs in the EU, Norway, Iceland and, with effect from 31 July 2014, Liechtenstein, and to align the definition of charity for all charitable reliefs and exemptions.

Under FA 2010, Sch 6 a charity is defined as a body of persons or trust that:

(a) is established for charitable purposes only. The definition is the same as that found in CA 2011, s 2;
(b) meets the Jurisdiction Condition;
(c) meets the Registration Condition; and
(d) meets the Management Condition (FA 2010, Sch 6, para 1).

The Jurisdiction Condition will be satisfied where the body of persons or trust is within the authority of the High Court, Court of Session, High Court in Northern Ireland or any other court of a corresponding jurisdiction under the law of another EU Member State or Territory to be specified in regulations, currently Iceland, Norway and, since 31 July 2014, Liechtenstein (FA 2010, Sch 6, para 2).

The Registration Condition is satisfied where a body of persons or a trust is a charity within the meaning of the Charities Act 2011, s 10, has complied with any requirement to be registered in the Register of Charities kept under s 29 of that Act or where a body of persons or trust has complied with the law of a territory outside of England and Wales to be registered in a similar register (FA 2010, Sch 6, para 3). HMRC Charities is responsible for deciding whether a charity meets the definition and is a qualifying charity, and will also determine which countries are specified for this purpose. HMRC Charities administers a non-statutory approvals process so that charities can obtain certainty in advance of receiving a donation. All new charities must register with HMRC to claim the tax reliefs even if they are already registered with the Charity Commission. HMRC's Inheritance Tax Manual at para 11112 states that charities receiving UK tax reliefs at 1 April 2010 automatically qualify for exemption.

If a charity meets all the conditions it may qualify for the exemption without having formal approval from HMRC Charities. In general, transfers made to a charity in England and Wales that has been registered with the Charity Commission can be accepted as exempt without enquiry. Similarly, transfers to charities that have been approved by HMRC Charities can be accepted as exempt without enquiry unless there are indications that the status of the charity has changed since the approval was given.

The Management Condition is satisfied by a body of persons or trust if its managers are 'fit and proper persons to be managers of the body or trust' (FA 2010, Sch 6, para 4). Managers are the persons having the general control and management of the administration of the body or trust. The condition will be satisfied throughout the period if HMRC consider that any failure to meet it has not prejudiced the charitable purposes of the charity or it is just and reasonable in all the circumstances for the condition to be treated as met (FA 2010, Sch 6 para 5). There is no statutory definition of a 'fit and proper person' although needless to say guidance has been issued by HMRC which can be found at www.gov.uk/governmentpublications. According to this guidance, which of course does not have the force of law, the 'fit and proper persons' test is concerned with ensuring that charities are not 'managed or controlled by individuals who present a risk to the charity's tax position.'

The guidance identifies some factors that:

'may lead to HMRC deciding that a manager isn't a fit and proper person include, . . . where individuals:

- have been involved in tax fraud . . . or other fraudulent behaviour including misrepresentation and/or identity theft
- are known by HMRC to have involvement in attacks against, or abuse of, tax repayment systems
- have used a tax avoidance scheme featuring charitable reliefs or using a charity to facilitate the avoidance
- have been involved in designing and /or promoting tax avoidance schemes
- have been barred from acting as a charity trustee by a charity regulator or Court, or being disqualified from acting as a company director.'

When this guidance was revised in November 2014, the professional bodies protested against the penultimate factor which resulted in HMRC announcing that it would clarify the situations at which the guidance was directed but at the time of writing, nothing has been published.

It is advisable for charities to ask all of their managers to sign the Model Declaration for Fit and Proper Persons which can be found on the gov.uk website.

The Charities (Protection and Social Investment) Act 2016, which received Royal Assent on 16 March 2016 and which comes into force at various stages, gives the Charity Commission new powers to disqualify individuals from acting as trustees where certain conditions are satisfied (Charities (Protection and Social Investment) Act 2016, s 10 which comes into effect on 1 October 2016). One such condition is where the person has been found by HMRC 'not to be a fit and proper person to be a manager of a body or trust, for the purposes of [FA 2010, Sch 6, para 4] and the finding has not been overturned' (Charities (Protection and Social Investment) Act 2016, s 10(7)).

Exemptions and reliefs on gifts to charities

Inheritance tax

Exemption on gifts

[15.4] A charitable donation made by an individual is a transfer of value which is generally exempt from inheritance tax (IHTA 1984, s 23) to the extent that the value transferred by it is attributable to the donated property. Where the value transferred exceeds the value of the gift in the hands of a charity, HMRC takes the view that the exemption extends to the value transferred (Statement of Practice SP E13).

Example

> Cory holds 60% of the shares in a company. The shareholding is worth £200,000. A 30% shareholding is worth only £50,000, since it is only a minority shareholding. Cory gives half of his 60% shareholding to a charitable trust. The loss to his estate (because the property in the trust is 'related property' under IHTA 1984, s 161(2)(b)(i)) is £100,000 ($^1/_2 \times$ £200,000). The value of the gift in the hands of the charity is £50,000.

In the above example, the value transferred by the transfer of value is £100,000, but is it wholly or only partly 'attributable to property' given to the charitable trust? HMRC has stated that in such a case the transfer would be wholly exempt (Statement of Practice SP E13). (The phrase 'attributable to property' is also used in IHTA 1984, s 3A in the definition of potentially exempt transfer. It is understood that HMRC applies the same interpretation.)

Section 23(1) refers to 'property which is given to charities'. The terms 'give', 'given', 'gift' are rarely to be found in the inheritance tax legislation, and nowhere are the words 'give' and 'gift' actually defined. However, s 23(6) provides that ' . . . property is given to charities if it becomes the property of charities or is held on trust for charitable purposes only . . . '. Therefore, to qualify for exemption a gift (*inter vivos* or by will) need not be to a recognised charitable body provided it is applicable only for charitable purposes. This is an important planning point, for it enables the testator of a will to leave a legacy, or a share of residue, for charitable purposes and at the same time express a wish that the money be applied by his executors to particular named charities or to charities of a certain type or class.

A charity must acquire an interest on the death of a testator. In the case of *Bailhache Labesse Trustees Ltd v Revenue & Customs Comrs* [2008] STC (SCD) 869, it was held that appointments made by trustees within 12 months of death to charities were transfers of value and not exempt transfers under IHTA 1984, s 23 with effect from the date of death.

In order for a trust for charitable purposes set up under a will to be exempt the trust must be for charitable purposes under UK law and the trust itself must be subject to the jurisdiction of the UK Courts. In *Routier v Revenue and*

Customs Comrs [2016] EWCA Civ 938 a trust was governed by Jersey law. The Court of Appeal considered that the second limb of IHTA 1984, s 23 must be seen in the context of the whole provision. The exemption under IHTA 1984, s 23(6) was not available. It is important to inform a donor of this restriction when he is choosing the charities that he wishes to benefit.

Anti-avoidance provisions

[15.5] IHTA 1984, s 23 contains provisions (in subsections (2) to (5)) to prevent the avoidance of tax by use of the general exemption for property given to charities in subsection (1).

Since it is only individuals who can make chargeable transfers, there are no charging provisions dealing with the situation where a charitable company or the trustees of a charitable trust make a transfer of value. It might be thought that by giving a limited interest to a charity a transfer could be made by an individual which would be entirely free from inheritance tax.

Example

> Luke wishes to create a discretionary trust. If he transfers property to trustees on discretionary trusts there would be an immediate charge to inheritance tax on him. However, if Luke were to make the transfer to a trust in which a charity had an initial interest in possession (say for one year) with the remainder on discretionary trusts, he might hope that the transfer would be exempt and that there would be no charge on the termination of the charity's interest in possession.

Quite apart from the vulnerability to an attack under the associated operations rules (IHTA 1984, s 268) and the tendency of the courts to depart from the literal construction of legislation where transactions are undertaken for the purposes of tax planning, s 23(3)(b) provides that there is no exemption available where the property transferred to the charity is given to it for a limited period.

If, instead of creating an interest for a limited period, it is decided to create a defeasible interest (ie one liable to be terminated on the happening of a specified event), the exemption will also not be available by virtue of s 23(2)(c). For these purposes any disposition which has not been defeated within 12 months of the transfer and is not defeasible after that time is treated as not being defeasible (whether or not it was capable of being defeated before that time).

Similarly, where the property transferred consists of an interest in other property, then if the transferee charity's interest is less than the transferor's interest, no exemption will be available (IHTA 1984, s 23(3)(a)). Thus, where the holder of a freehold estate in land grants a lease of that land to a charity (with the probable aim of transferring the freehold estate in reversion at a greatly reduced value) no exemption will be available.

If a postponed interest, or an interest subject to a condition precedent which is not satisfied within the following 12 months, is created, no exemption will be available (IHTA 1984, s 23(2)(a) and (b)).

Section 23(4) contains special 'reservation of benefit' provisions applying to gifts to charities. FA 1986, s 102(5)(d) disapplies the general reservation of benefit provisions in s 102 to transfers where the s 23 exemption is available. Section 23(4)(a) disallows the exemption where the transferor transfers land or a building to a charity subject to the right for him, his spouse, civil partner or a connected person to possess or occupy the property transferred rent-free or other than on arm's length terms. Section 23(4)(b) applies where the property transferred is not land or a building. The exemption is disallowed where there is an interest reserved to or created by the transferor other than one for full consideration or which does not substantially affect the enjoyment of the property by the transferee charity.

Finally, s 23(5) provides that where the whole or any part of the property given may be applied for purposes other than charitable purposes no exemption will be available in respect of any part of the gift.

As a result of these anti-avoidance provisions there is no economic advantage to an individual in making a lifetime gift to charity. While such gifts may be exempt from inheritance tax and other taxes, an individual cannot usually bestow a greater benefit on himself or someone else (a non-charity) by making a gift of property to charity than if he retained the property or gave it to that other person.

Reduced rate of inheritance tax on death

[15.6] For deaths after 5 April 2012, estates that include charitable legacies of at least 10% of a testator's net estate are subject to inheritance tax at a rate of 36% rather than 40%. Although the concept of the relief seems simple, in practice it is anything but. In order for the lower rate to apply, the charitable giving condition must be satisfied (IHTA 1984, Sch 1A, para 2(1)). This condition is met if for one or more components of the estate (taking each component separately) the donated amount is at least 10% of the baseline amount. The legislation defines these terms and sets out the rules by which a calculation is to be made to determine whether the 36% rate of tax applies to the estate.

For these purposes, a deceased's estate is split into three component parts which are:

(a)   The survivorship component – essentially all the jointly held property in which the deceased had an interest and which passes by survivorship or under a special destination in Scotland. It also includes overseas property that passes under the law of the country in which it is situated that corresponds to survivorship or special destination.

(b)   The settled property component – property in which the deceased was beneficially entitled immediately before death and in respect of which a charge arose under IHTA 1984, s 49(1). This will include all pre-March 2006 interests in possession, immediate post-death interests and disabled person interests where the deceased is treated as being entitled to an interest in possession.

(c)   The general component – essentially this will include the deceased's free estate and any joint property owned as a tenant in common. Any property subject to a reservation is expressly excluded. This is intended to ensure that such property does not benefit from the lower rate, although such property may be eligible for the reduced rate if an election to merge two or more components is made (see **15.8** below).

Calculating the baseline amount

[**15.7**] The legislation sets out three steps in order to calculate the baseline amount (IHTA 1984, Sch 1A, para 5). The baseline amount must be determined for each component separately unless an election to merge the components has been made (see **15.8** below).

Step 1

Determine the value transferred by the chargeable transfer attributable to property in that component.

Step 2

Deduct from this the appropriate proportion of the available nil-rate band. The available nil-rate band is the nil-rate band maximum that applies on death plus any transferable nil-rate band less any amount used up by any lifetime transfers in the previous seven years. The appropriate proportion is defined as the proportion equal to 'the proportion that the amount determined under *Step 1* bears to the value transferred by the chargeable transfer as a whole.' This effectively is the amount of the nil-rate band apportioned to the component concerned in relation to the whole chargeable transfer on death.

Step 3

Add the amount of the charitable legacy that was deducted at *Step 1* to the amount calculated under *Step 2*. This will be the baseline amount for that component. It should be noted that the normal rules for grossing up and interaction are varied for the purpose of establishing whether or not the charitable giving condition is met (IHTA 1984, Sch 1A, para 6). Where there are two or more components to the estate, the calculation becomes more complex as is illustrated below.

Example

Horatio died in May 2014 leaving an estate valued at £1,500,000 and also a flat which he held with his daughter, Charlotte, as beneficial joint tenants, his share being £500,000. Under the terms of his will, he had left £200,000 to a named charity. The flat passed by survivorship to Charlotte. His estate contained two components:

- the survivorship component;
- the general component.

No reduced rate is available on the survivorship component because there is no 10% share passing to charity.

The baseline amount for the general component is calculated as follows:

Step 1 (Determine value of component)

	£
Estate on death	1,500,000
Legacy to charity (donated amount)	– 200,000
Chargeable transfer	1,300,000

Step 2 (Deduct appropriate proportion)

Appropriate portion of the nil-rate band is:

$$\frac{1,300,000}{1,300,000+500,000} \times 325,000 \qquad = \qquad £234,722$$

	1,300,000
–	234,722
	1,065,278

Step 3 (Add back charitable legacy)

	1,065,278
+	200,000
Baseline amount	1,265,278

The legacy of £200,000 exceeds 10% of £1,265,278 so the general component qualifies for the lower rate.

Total Tax Liability

General component	=		383,500
1,065,278 × 36%			
Survivorship component			
Chargeable transfer	=	500,000	
Less: proportion of nil rate band		(90,278)	
		409,722	
409,722 × 40%			163,889
			547,389

A tax liability of £547,389 arose rather than a tax liability of £590,000.

Of course, where the amount qualifying for charity exemption in one component exceeds the 10%, consideration could be given to making an election to merge the components under IHTA 1984, Sch 1A, para 7 as discussed below.

Making an election to merge

[15.8] IHTA 1984, Sch 1A, para 7 provides that an election may be made to merge two or more components and apply the 10% test as if there were a single component. For an election to be made, an estate must consist of more than one component, and the donated amount of one of the components must be at least 10% of its baseline amount. Where the donated amount for the merged components is at least 10% of the baseline amount for that merged component, each of the individual components will qualify for the lower rate. This will be of most relevance where the beneficiaries of the different components of the estate are the same.

For the purposes of the merger only, property in which a reservation of benefit exists may be merged with another component and qualify for the lower rate where the 10% test is met (IHTA 1984, Sch 1A, para 7(5)).

The election must be made by all those who are appropriate persons in respect of the qualifying component and each of the eligible parts to be treated as a single component. Appropriate persons are defined in IHTA 1984, Sch 1A, para 7(7) as:

(a) for the survivorship component, all those to whom the property in the survivorship component passes on death;

(b) for the settled property component, the trustees of all the settled property in the settled property component;

(c) for the general component, all the personal representatives of the deceased or, if there are none, those who are liable for the tax attributable to the property in the general component; and

(d) all those in whom the property which is the subject of a gift with reservation is vested when the election is made.

The election must be made by notice in writing to HMRC within two years of the deceased's death (IHTA 1984, Sch 1A, para 9). It is possible for the election to be withdrawn by written notice given to HMRC by all of those who would be entitled to make such an election within two years and one month of the deceased's death. An officer of HMRC has the discretion to extend this time period. HMRC's Inheritance Tax Manual at para 45044 provides that the circumstances in which a late claim may be made are the same as those in respect of a late claim being allowed for the transfer of the nil-rate band and the guidance found in HMRC's Inheritance Tax Manual, para 43009 should be followed.

Example

Taking the example above, Charlotte and the personal representatives of Horatio's estate have been advised to consider whether an election should be made to merge the survivorship and general components.

Merged estate	2,000,000
Legacy to charity	200,000
Chargeable transfer	1,800,000
Less: nil rate band	325,000

	1,475,000
Add back charitable legacy	200,000
	1,675,000

The baseline amount for the merged component is £167,500 and the legacy is £200,000 and so the lower rate applies to both components.

The total tax liability would be £531,000 (£1,475,000 × 36%) thus saving £16,389).

In order for the lower rate of 36% to apply, a legacy must be of property to which IHTA 1984, s 23(1) applies; namely, a gift of property to a charity or a registered club. It should be noted that the lower rate does not apply to gifts of property made to a museum or gallery under IHTA 1984, s 25. The Chartered Institute of Taxation wrote to HMRC who explained that the exemptions under ss 23 and 25 were for different purposes. It was pointed out, however, that many of the bodies named in Sch 3 are in fact treated as charities under the new definition of charity.

Grossing Up

[15.9] When grossing up is necessary because, for example, the residue of the estate passes to a surviving spouse or civil partner or to a charity and there are legacies free of tax, the baseline amount will increase. This may result in the 10% test not being met where the charitable legacy is of a fixed amount or is a share of the residue. Therefore for the purposes of determining whether the charitable giving condition is met, the grossing up calculation uses the reduced rate of 36%. If the 10% test is not met, the estate will be subject to tax at 40%. The grossing up calculations will have to be done again at the full rate. Where the legacy is, however, formulated to be an amount necessary to obtain the relief, the 10% test will not need to be done.

Election to opt out

[15.10] It is possible for an election to be made by the appropriate persons for the estate component concerned to be treated as if the donated amount for the component is less than 10% of the baseline amount, whether or not it actually is. Where such an election is made, the component concerned is subject to tax at 40% (IHTA 1984, Sch 1A, para 8). This election may be appropriate in such circumstances where the administrative costs of valuing the assets outweigh the benefit of the lower rate of tax.

Again, an election must be made within two years of the deceased's death in writing by the appropriate persons which are the same as those mentioned above in relation to a merger election.

Deeds of variation

[15.11] In certain circumstances, the beneficiaries of an estate may consider executing a deed of variation to take advantage of the lower rate of tax. This may be done by leaving or increasing a legacy to charity. The variation will only be treated as having been made by the deceased under IHTA 1984, s 142 provided that it can be shown that the appropriate person has been notified of the existence of the deed of variation (IHTA 1984, s 142(3A)), being the charity or registered club to which the property is given or the trustees of the charitable trust or registered club. There is no requirement for a charity or the trustees of the charitable trust to be a party to the deed of variation. Evidence of the awareness by the charity or trustees that property is to be redirected to them is what is required. Copies of correspondence between the parties showing that the charity or trustees are aware of the arrangements will be sufficient (HMRC Trusts & Estates Newsletter April 2012). It should be noted that there is no similar requirement for IHTA 1984, s 144.

Duty of an adviser

[**15.12**] The question arises as to whether representatives of an estate are under a duty to advise the intended beneficiaries on the maximisation of the lower rate of tax. On the basis of the decision in *Cancer Research Campaign v Ernest Brown & Co (a firm)* [1997] STC 1425, [1998] PNLR 592 it is arguable that there is no such duty.

Draft clause

[**15.13**] Where a client wishes to ensure that the lower rate will apply to his estate, careful drafting of the relevant clause is important. Merely providing that a certain sum will be left to charity may result in that legacy being insufficient because other assets in the estate have increased or alternatively the value of other assets have fallen resulting in a much larger proportion being left to a charity then the testator intended. The answer, therefore, is to include a clause which provides that a sum equal to 10% of the baseline amount is left to charity. HMRC has included in its Guidance a draft clause which it considers will satisfy IHTA 1984, Sch 1A although it includes an upper limit of the legacy which will apply even if the result takes the estate outside the 10% test. STEP has also produced a draft clause which HMRC has approved and can be found at www.step.org/step-model-clause-iht.

Care does need to be taken when using such a precedent as a formula may not be appropriate in all cases. Where an estate holds property qualifying for Agricultural Property Relief or Business Property Relief, the operation of the attribution rules may cause unexpected results. In such situations, it may be preferable to use a discretionary will trust. Where the formula includes the survivorship component and the estate contains survivorship property, a legacy under this formula may amount to the entire free estate. It is therefore advisable not to use the survivorship component in a formula. Where an individual holds joint property and wishes to obtain the lower rate, they should consider severing their joint tenancy.

HMRC has produced a calculator which calculates whether the reduced rate is available. It will also calculate the amount which should be left to charity for the relief to apply. Where a person intends to leave 4% of his net estate to charity, he can in fact increase that to 10% without the chargeable beneficiaries suffering any reduction in the value of the benefits they receive, as the table below illustrates.

Percentage of estate received by a charity	3	4	9	10

Rate of IHT	40	40	40	36
Percentage of estate received by beneficiaries	58.2	57.6	54.6	57.6

Income tax

Gift Aid

[15.14] Relief is given for gifts of money which are qualifying donations to charity within ITA 2007, s 414 ('Gift Aid'). To be a qualifying donation, Conditions A to F (below) must be met and a Gift Aid declaration given to the charity by the donor (ITA 2007, s 416).

Conditions A to F are as follows:

- Condition A is that the gift takes the form of a payment of a sum of money;
- Condition B is that the payment is not subject to any condition as to repayment;
- Condition C is that the payment is not a sum falling within ITEPA 2003, s 713(3) (payroll deduction scheme);
- Condition D is that the payment is not deductible in calculating the individual's income from any source;
- Condition E is that the payment is not conditional on, associated with or part of an arrangement involving, the acquisition of property by the charity from the individual or a person connected with the individual;
- Condition EA is that the payment is not by way of and does not amount in substance to waiver by the individual of entitlement to sums due to the individual from the charity in respect of an amount advanced to the charity and in respect of which a person has obtained relief for social investment.
- Condition F is that there are no benefits associated with the gift, or there are benefits associated with the gift but the restrictions on those benefits are not breached.

There is no minimum limit for gifts, instead the relief applies to any gift made by a donor who has sufficient income charged to UK tax. There is no maximum limit for gifts either. Gift Aid applies only to donations made to a charity established solely for charitable purposes. This does not include donations made for the benefit of charities as the case of *Odyssey (Tendercare) Ltd v Revenue & Customs Comrs* (TC 2215) [2012] UK FTT 539 (TC) illustrates.

If a gift qualifies for relief the donor is treated as having deducted income tax at the basic rate from his gift. The tax deemed to have been deducted by the donor can be recovered by the charity. If a taxpayer pays less income tax or capital gains tax than the amount recovered by the charity then the taxpayer will be assessed to tax on an amount equal to the difference. Care should be taken to ensure that a taxpayer has sufficient tax to pay to avoid a nasty surprise.

A simple form of certification is required under which the donor or an intermediary merely gives to the charity or its intermediary a gift aid declaration. This declaration can be given in writing, orally or by means of electronic communication and must contain the following:

(a)   the name and home address of the donor;
(b)   the name of the charity;
(c)   a description of the gift which may be a single gift or a series of gifts;
(d)   a statement identifying the gift or gifts to which the declaration relates; and
(e)   where the declaration is given in writing, a statement confirming that Gift Aid is to apply.

It should be noted that the regulations detailing the information to be contained in the statement still refer to the provisions in FA 1990 and not to the provisions in ITA 2007.

A declaration may cover gifts since 6 April 2000 and all future gifts.

Where an oral declaration is made (ie a Gift Aid donation is made by telephone) special rules apply. The charity must send a written record to the donor who will then have 30 days to change his mind. (Donations to Charity by Individuals (Appropriate Declarations) Regulations 2000 (SI 2000/2074)).

Election to carry back

[15.15] A donor may elect that qualifying donations be treated as if they were made in the previous year of assessment, provided that the donor's income or gains of the previous year would have covered the grossed-up amount of the gift (ITA 2007, s 426). Such an election must be made in writing within certain statutory time limits. Care needs to be taken to ensure that the claim for Gift Aid relief is made in the claimant's original return (ITA 2007, s 426(6)). In *Cameron v Revenue & Customs Comrs* [2010] UKFTT 104 (TC), [2010] SFTD 664 Mr Cameron made an election to carry back Gift Aid relief in an amended tax return. HMRC refused the claim saying that such a claim could only be made in the original return and not in an amended return. The Tribunal examined the relevant legislation but could not find anything that supported the taxpayer's claim that the return could be an amended return. Nor did it matter that the amended return had been submitted before the 31 January deadline. The relief was not allowable. This decision demonstrates that the most cautious approach should be adopted in all circumstances and the submission of a taxpayer's return be delayed until a firm decision has been made as to the utilisation of the tax relief. This clearly goes against the usual advice of submitting returns early in advance of the last minute rush.

Anti-avoidance provisions

[15.16] The definition of 'associated benefits' is found in ITA 2007, s 417. As mentioned above, relief may be denied if there are benefits associated with the gift and such benefits breach the restrictions found in ITA 2007, s 418 by satisfying either condition A or condition B.

Condition A is that the total value of the associated benefits exceed the variable limit which is:

(a)   25% of the amount of the gift, if the amount of the gift is £100 or less;

(b)   £25, if the amount of the gift is between £101 and £1,000;

(c)   5% of the amount of the gift, where the gift is in excess of £1,000.

Condition B is that the sum of the total value of the associated benefits and the total value of the associated benefits of each relevant prior gift is more than £2,500.

Small Donations Scheme

[15.17] The Gift Aid Small Donations Scheme provides that charities and Community Amateur Sports Clubs will be able to claim a top up equivalent to Gift Aid on up to £8,000 (previously the limit was £5,000) on small monetary donations, of no more than £20 each, made after 5 April 2013 without a Gift Aid declaration (Small Charitable Donations Act 2012). The important point to note about this scheme is that it is not a tax relief. Higher rate and additional rate taxpayers will not be able to claim tax relief on their donations.

Payroll deduction scheme

[15.18] The payroll deduction scheme provides that an employee wishing to make a gift to charity can authorise his employer to withhold any amount from his PAYE income. The deductions must be made pursuant to a scheme which is approved by HMRC or is of a kind approved by HMRC. The employer must pay the sums withheld to an HMRC approved agent. The agency must distribute the donations within 60 days of their receipt from the employer. The donor will then obtain tax relief as if the donations were allowable deductions of his employment provided the donations are not tainted charity donations (see **15.23**).

Gifts of shares and securities

[15.19] As mentioned above, Gift Aid payments must be payments of money. If a potential donor has shares pregnant with capital gains, it may be better to give the shares to the chosen charity which will be treated as a no gain no loss transfer, rather than sell the shares, pay capital gains tax and give the net proceeds to the charity. This is especially so because income tax relief is available on particular shares and securities (ITA 2007, s 431). Relief will be given on a gift of shares or securities which are listed on a recognised stock exchange or dealt in on any designated market in the UK, units in authorised unit trusts, shares in open-ended investment companies and interests in offshore funds (ITA 2007, s 432) given to charities provided the donor makes a claim.

The amount of the relief is allowed as a deduction in calculating the net income of the donor for the tax year in which the disposal is made. Where a claim is made, no income tax relief can be given under any other provision of the Income Tax Acts.

The amount of the relief on a gift is the net benefit to the charity (market value) plus any incidental costs of transfer less any benefits received by the donor or a connected person as a result of the transfer. Where there is a transfer at an undervalue, the amount paid by the charity is deducted from the tax relief (ITA 2007, s 434).

The rules for gifts of qualifying investments have been used in relation to tax avoidance strategies and so as a result the legislation provides that individuals cannot obtain tax relief in excess of the benefit received by the charity.

Where:

* the qualifying investment given to the charity (or anything from which the investment derives) was acquired within four years of the date of disposal;
* the acquisition was made as part of a scheme; and
* the main purpose, or one of the main purposes, of the individual entering into the scheme was to obtain tax relief or an increased amount of relief;

the amount of relief to the donor is adjusted to the lower of the market value and the acquisition cost of the gift to the donor (ITA 2007, ss 437–440). When a donor places an obligation on a charity that results in the value of the gift to the charity being less than the value of the gift to the donor, the income tax relief is restricted to the lower amount (ITA 2007, s 437).

It should be noted that if the gift was a tainted charitable donation then relief would not be available (see **15.23**).

Gifts of real property

[15.20] There is a relief from income tax, similar to that given in relation to gifts of shares and securities, where a qualifying interest in land is given to a charity (ITA 2007, ss 431 and 433). Therefore, where a potential donor has a qualifying interest in land on which there is an unrealised gain, it may be more tax efficient to give the property to the chosen charity rather than sell the property and give the proceeds to the charity.

A qualifying interest in land is defined as a freehold interest in land or a leasehold interest in land which is a term of years absolute where the land in question is in the UK (ITA 2007, s 433). Agreements to acquire a freehold interest and agreements for lease are not qualifying interests in land.

No relief is available if the land is situated outside the UK. Relief is calculated in the same manner as shares by way of a formula which uses the net benefit to the charity thus preventing an income tax advantage being secured on an amount in excess of the benefit received by the charity as discussed above (ITA 2007, ss 434, 437).

In order to claim the relief the taxpayer must have received a certificate from the charity containing a description of the qualifying interest in land, the date of the disposal and a statement that the charity has acquired the qualifying interest in land (ITA 2007, ss 431(4) and 441).

There will be a clawback of relief on the happening of a disqualifying event within the provisional period. A disqualifying event occurs if the donor or a person connected with him becomes entitled to an interest or right in relation to all or part of the land to which the disposal relates or becomes party to an arrangement under which he enjoys some right in relation to all or part of that land otherwise than for full consideration in money or moneys worth. There is no disqualifying event if a person becomes entitled to a right or interest as a result of a disposition of property on death. The provisional period is the period beginning with the date of disposal and ending with the fifth anniversary of 31 January following the end of the year of assessment in which the disposal was made (ITA 2007, s 444).

Example

> Cheryl has just received a significant dividend on her family company shares and has some development land on which she has recently obtained planning permission for residential properties. This land has a significant unrealised capital gain on which she will have to pay capital gains tax. She has decided that she has assets which she can afford to give away and so decides to make a gift of the land to a local charity. There will be no capital gains tax on the disposal nor will any stamp duty land tax be payable (FA 2003, Sch 8). Income tax relief will be available on the gift so her income will be reduced by the value of the land transferred.

Gifts made by a person carrying on a trade

[15.21] A person carrying on a trade is able to donate any items manufactured or of a class or description sold by the donor in the course of the trade to a charity, a registered club, certain designated bodies or a designated educational establishment without bringing its market value into account for tax purposes (ITTOIA 2005, s 108). It should be noted that special rules apply where the donor or a connected person receives a benefit in connection with the gift (ITTOIA 2005, s 109).

Relief will not be available if such a donation is a tainted charitable donation (ITTOIA 2005, 108(5)).

Capital gains tax

[15.22] TCGA 1992, s 257 provides that gifts to a charity, registered club or any bodies mentioned in IHTA 1984, Sch 3 are to be treated as disposals for a consideration producing neither a gain nor a loss. If income tax relief or corporation tax relief is available to an individual or company on the gift or disposal at an undervalue of a qualifying investment to a charity, the charity is treated as acquiring the investment for a consideration which is reduced accordingly (TCGA 1992, s 257(2A–2C)). Relief from capital gains tax will only be available provided the gift is not a tainted charitable donation (TCGA 1992, s 257A) (see **15.23**).

Anti-avoidance provisions

Tainted charitable donations

[15.23] Anti-avoidance legislation found in ITA 2007, Pt 13 Ch 8 (ss 809ZH–809ZR) provides that the usual tax reliefs are not available where a donor makes a relievable charitable donation after 31 March 2011 which is a 'tainted donation'. These rules are based on a purpose test and largely replace the substantial donor rules that applied to donations made up to 31 March 2013.

A relievable charitable donation

[15.24] A relievable charitable donation is a gift or other disposal which is made by a person to a charity and is eligible for tax relief. A gift or other disposal is eligible for tax relief (as defined) if (ignoring the tainted donations provisions) tax relief would be available in respect of it and/or the charity is entitled to claim a tax repayment in respect of it (ITA 2007, s 809ZI).

Tainted donations

[15.25] For a relievable charitable donation to be a tainted donation, conditions A, B and C must be met. These anti-avoidance provisions only apply to donations that are defined as 'relievable charitable donations'. Donations that are not so defined are not affected by these rules.

Condition A is that essentially the donation to the charity and the arrangements entered into by the donor are connected. ITA 2007, s 809ZJ(2) provides that condition A is satisfied where a linked person enters into arrangements and it is reasonable to assume that the donation would not have been made and the arrangements would not have been entered into independently of one another. A judgement has to be made as to whether it is reasonable to assume that a donation and the arrangements would or would not have been made independently of each other. HMRC's Guidance states at para 5.3 that a 'judgement must take into account the likely effects of the donation and the arrangements and/or the circumstances surrounding the donation and the arrangements entered into'. The making of a donation is not in itself an arrangement (HMRC Guidance, para 6.4). A 'linked person' is defined as the donor or a person connected with the donor at the 'relevant time' (ITA 2007, s 809ZJ(3)).

Condition B is satisfied if the main purpose, or one of the main purposes, of entering into the arrangements is for the linked person to receive a financial advantage directly or indirectly from a charity.

Condition C is that the donor is not a 'qualifying charity-owned company' or a 'relevant housing provider' linked with the donee charity (ITA 2007, s 809ZJ(6)).

Financial advantage

[15.26] The term 'financial advantage' is not defined in the legislation but it deems a financial advantage to be obtained in certain circumstances.

ITA 2007, s 809ZK outlines when a financial advantage is deemed to be obtained by a linked person (X). This occurs where:

(i)   the terms of the transaction are less beneficial to another person (Y) or more beneficial to X (or both) than those which might reasonably be expected in a transaction concluded between parties dealing at arm's length; or

(ii)   the transaction is not of a kind which a person dealing at arm's length and in place of Y might reasonably be expected to make.

Of course, the term is not limited to only those circumstances. It should be noted, however, that certain financial advantages which are listed in ITA 2007, s 809ZL are ignored for the purposes of this test.

The term 'transaction' is not defined in the legislation but examples are given at ITA 2007, s 890ZK(5) and CTA 2010, s 939D(5) and includes the sale or letting of property, the provision of services, the exchange of property, the provision of a loan or any other form of financial assistance and investment in a business.

Effect of tainting

[15.27] Where a donation is tainted, no tax reliefs are due to the donor (ITA 2007, s 809ZM). Where the donation, if it were not a tainted donation, would have been a qualifying donation under the Gift Aid scheme, the charity will still be able to make a repayment claim to HMRC. An income tax charge will, however, arise equal to the repayment of tax due to the charity (ITA 2007, s 809ZN). The donor, a connected person or any other potentially advantaged person in relation to the tainted donation, or the charity, is liable for any tax charge arising. HMRC state in its guidance at para 13.1 that it will 'look to the donor and any other financially advantaged person first'. No charge will arise, however, on the charity, unless the charity was party to, and fully aware of the arrangements.

Strategy for capital gifts

Lifetime gifts v transfers on death

[15.28] The timing of a would-be benefactor making a gift to a charity is important and depends on a number of factors, including the donor's personal circumstances, the assets to be given, the value of the remainder of his estate and his income tax and capital gains tax position. Since outright gifts to charity are exempt from inheritance tax, it is usually sensible for an individual to make lifetime gifts to his family (since these are not exempt *ab initio* although they may be potentially exempt) and to make any gifts which he wishes to make to charity in his will (given that he will probably need to retain some capital in his estate during his lifetime).

Example

Florence, a widow, has an estate of £500,000. Her children have already been well provided for. She decides that she would like £100,000 of her estate to go to charity and £400,000 to her children. She calculates that she can afford to give away £100,000 now. If she makes a potentially exempt transfer of £100,000 in favour of her children and survives for the following seven years, no tax would be payable on the potentially exempt transfer and she would leave a chargeable estate (assuming no change) of £300,000 on which no inheritance tax would be payable. If, on the other hand, she makes a lifetime gift of £100,000 to charity and leaves the whole of her estate to her children, she will leave a chargeable estate (assuming no change) of £400,000 on which inheritance tax at 2016/17 rates amounts to £30,000.

If an individual decides to make a lifetime capital gift to charity, he should consider making a direct gift of assets with large unrealised capital gains rather than a gift of cash, since the disposal of the assets will not result in any charge to capital gains tax (TCGA 1992, s 257) and will not reduce his cash resources. The charity, if it requires cash, can immediately sell the assets and realise a gain free of tax provided the proceeds are applicable and applied for charitable purposes (TCGA 1992, s 256). This is an important planning point, because small charities may sometimes be reluctant to receive donations in any form other than cash. If the would-be benefactor informs the charity that he can give them more in non-cash assets than he could if they would only take cash and reminds them that they can sell the assets free of capital gains tax the charity may be willing to receive a donation in a non-cash form. An income tax deduction is also available on gifts to a charity of qualifying investments or qualifying interests in land (ITA 2007, s 431).

If an individual wishes to make a gift of cash to a charity or a charitable trust he should consider making a Gift Aid donation within ITA 2007, ss 414 and 521 to obtain the income tax relief (see **15.14**). Of course, this is dependent on the individual paying sufficient income tax or capital gains tax. The gift will also be exempt from inheritance tax.

Getting tax relief on a lifetime gift has to be balanced against obtaining a lower inheritance tax rate on death (see **15.6**). Obviously this will depend on the individual facts of a case.

Gifts from inherited capital

[15.29] An individual may want to make a capital gift to charity because of a change in his personal circumstances. If he has inherited capital (by will or on intestacy) he should consider executing a deed of variation to give capital to the charity and making a statement under IHTA 1984, s 142 to have the disposition treated as if it had been made by the testator (provided the two-year period has not yet expired).

Example

Catherine dies leaving the whole of her estate of £412,000 to her son Ben (an only child). Inheritance tax on the estate at 2016/17 rates amounts to £34,800. Of the £377,200 which Ben receives he decides he would like to make a gift to charity of £25,000. If he makes a simple gift of £25,000 the gift will be exempt from inheritance tax and he will be left with £352,200. If, on the other hand, he executes a deed of variation of Catherine's will and makes a statement under s 142 to have the disposition treated as if it had been made by Catherine, he will transfer £25,000 to the charity but will be able to claim a repayment from HMRC of £10,000 (£25,000 at 40%) by way of overpaid inheritance tax, leaving himself with £362,200 (£377,200 – £25,000 + £10,000). No income tax relief under ITA 2007, s 414 would be available on the grounds that a benefit under s 416(7) had been received because the amount of inheritance tax payable on the estate had been reduced (*St Dunstan's v Major (Insp of Taxes)* [1997] STC (SCD) 212).). In that case, it was held that, because under Gift Aid rules a donor should not receive a benefit in excess of 2.5% of the gift (this has now been changed), relief was not available. This decision was considered by many commentators to be incorrect because only a benefit which flows from the charity should be able to disapply Gift Aid relief. The principle in *St Dunstans*, however, was followed by the First-tier Tax Tribunal in *Harris v Revenue & Customs Commissioners* [2010] UKFTT 385 (TC), [2010] SFTD 1159.

Where a gift of either quoted shares or an interest in land is made to a charity, there is a different rule relating to benefits to the donor. The rules operate in a different way and there is no mention of a defined percentage instead the amount of the gift is reduced by the value of any benefit received by the donor. It may therefore be sensible to have a deed of variation relating to the shares or land. In the above example, if a gift of quoted shares equal to £25,000 was made, the inheritance tax saving would be £10,000 and so the relievable amount is £15,000 (£25,000 – £10,000). That amount will be deducted from Ben's total taxable income for the year. As a higher rate taxpayer, Ben would have an income tax saving of £6,000. If he were an additional rate taxpayer, the income tax saving would be higher, namely £6,750.

Setting up your own charity

[15.30] An individual may wish to create his own charity which can be done in a number of different ways; for example, as a trust, a company limited by guarantee or a charitable incorporated organisation ('CIO').

Charitable trust

[15.31] A wealthy individual may wish to create his own charitable trust. If he is anticipating doing this by will, he should be careful to ensure that the trust will be a valid charitable trust, since if it fails it will be too late to take any remedial action once the testator has died. The gift would probably lapse as a result. However, it might be effective to create a valid non-charitable trust if the trust is not invalid for uncertainty of objects. Alternatively, the individual could set up a charitable trust with a small sum during his lifetime which is registered with HMRC in order to ensure that HMRC will accept that the trust is charitable. He could then make a substantial bequest to the charitable trust in his will.

Model documentation for charitable trusts can be found on the gov.uk website. Gift Aid will be available in respect of cash gifts made to such a trust. Relief will also be available for gifts of qualifying investments as outlined in **15.19**.

A disposal of a chargeable asset to a charitable trust is exempt under TCGA 1992, s 257 which is discussed in more detail in **15.22**. Gifts and legacies to charitable trusts are exempt transfers under IHTA 1984, s 23.

There is a specific exemption from SDLT for gifts of land to charitable trusts under FA 2003, s 68 and Sch 8, para 4. Stamp duty will not be chargeable on a gift of the shares to a charitable trust.

Charitable Incorporated Organisation

[15.32] A Charitable Incorporated Organisation (CIO) is a relatively new form of limited liability structure designed specifically for charities with income greater than £5,000. The process to register must be completed through the Charity Commission's pages on the gov.uk website and will have to go through the usual Charity Commission scrutiny as to public benefit and charitable status.

Alternatives to setting up your own charity

[15.33] For individuals who do not wish to incur the costs of setting up and running their own charitable organisations there are organisations which operate to allow individual donors to make contributions to a charity which are identified as the donor's so-called charitable pot. This charitable pot can then be used to make gifts to charities selected and chosen by the donor subject to certain due diligence. There are some organisations which specifically deal in a local area so donors can benefit their neighbourhood. Some offer an advisory service in that a donor may specify that he wishes to benefit sports facilities in the local area and the organisation will identify potential benefactors.

Charities Aid Foundation

[15.34] If an individual does not want to incur the costs and burden of creating a charity himself, a very convenient half-way house is offered by the Charities Aid Foundation ('CAF'). In many cases people would like to be able to earmark some of their salary for charity before the end of each tax year, but postpone payment until such time as they find charities they want to benefit and then divide the sums earmarked amongst whatever charities and in whatever amounts they care to choose. All these demands can be satisfied by the person involved making a Gift Aid payment to CAF. CAF receives the sums paid and reclaims the basic rate tax withheld at source by the payer. The sums paid (subject to a small deduction for administration) and the tax reclaimed are then held by CAF to be distributed to charities as the original payer directs. Donations can be made via the Internet, or using the charity voucher book. It is not an inapt analogy to think of CAF as a charitable bank with which the donor has an account, sums only being capable of being withdrawn from the account for payment to a charity. More details of the scheme can be obtained from www.cafonline.org.

General rules for charitable gifts

[15.35] The greatest tax saving from making charitable donations is generally achieved by the payments being made direct from the source from which the donor would derive the money with which to make the donation.

Example

> As outlined above the recipient of property by will, or on intestacy, might seek to make a capital donation by means of a deed of variation and a statement under IHTA 1984, s 142 to have the disposition treated as if it had been made by the testator.
>
> Similarly, a director and controlling shareholder of a company might authorise the company (assuming that it has power to do so under its memorandum and articles of association) to make charitable donations rather than give some of his own income to charity or make contributions under the payroll deduction scheme.

Within a family, the income and inheritance tax savings can be maximised by the family member who pays the highest rate of tax making the donations.

A further tax-efficient way to support a charity is for income to be paid from a discretionary trust assuming that the trustees have the power to make such a payment. The charity will be able to reclaim the relevant amount of income tax paid by the trustees on the sum given. This is because ITA 2007, s 497 enables the charity to reclaim a tax credit equal to the rate applicable to trusts (45% for 2016/17) applied to the payment grossed up by the tax credit. If a capital payment is made by the trustees, IHTA 1984, s 76 should ensure that there will be no inheritance tax charge on the property leaving the trust.

Drafting gifts to charity

[15.36] Care needs to be taken in drafting deeds of gift and wills containing charitable gifts as was illustrated in the case of *Harding (dec'd), Re, Gibbs v Harding* [2007] EWHC 3 (Ch), [2008] Ch 235, [2007] 1 All ER 747.

First, and most importantly of all, as mentioned at **15.1** above, when advising a client who wishes to make a significant gift to charity, an adviser should discuss with his client the form that the gift should take, particularly if a client wishes to leave a share of residue to a charity. There have been a number of cases where charities have challenged the interpretation of the wording of nil-rate band legacies (see **18.8**) and so it is important that this issue is discussed with a client. In some cases it might be more sensible for assets to be left on discretionary trusts together with a letter of wishes from the testator as to his chosen charities.

Secondly, the charity's correct name and address should be ascertained. It should be checked that the body or trust in question is in fact a charity. Some bodies which have members, such as the Prayer Book Society, are charities (or, as in the particular case of the National Trust, may be a specifically exempt body under IHTA 1984, s 25 and IHTA 1984, Sch 3); however, many are not.

Thirdly, when drafting a will it is advisable to include a 'mergers' clause, specifying that if the charity has been taken over, wound up or simply re-named, the gift shall be construed as a gift to the body which has taken over the charity or received the surpluses applicable for charitable purposes on the winding-up or the newly named body. Charities Act 2011, s 311 contains provisions allowing any merger of charities to be noted on a register of mergers with the result that any future legacies to the merged charities will automatically be passed on to the successor charity unless it is an excluded gift. Where no such clause is included, it may be possible to continue the charitable gift through an application to the Charity Commission for a scheme for the property to be applied cy-pres, ie to some other charitable purpose as nearly as possible resembling the original trusts.

Fourthly, when drafting a will it is helpful to include a receipt clause specifying that the receipt of the treasurer, or other proper officer for the time being of the charity, shall be a good discharge to the testator's executors who need be under no further obligation to see to the application of the moneys or assets given.

Temporary charitable trusts

[15.37] Mention should be made of funds which are held on charitable trusts for a specified period, following which the funds are held for non-charitable beneficiaries. This situation may occur unexpectedly, for instance if a site given for a school or village hall is no longer required and reverts to the descendants of the original donor.

Inheritance tax

[15.38] During the 'charitable period', there is an exemption from the decennial charge and the exit charge on distributions. Instead, a charge arises when the property ceases to be held on the charitable trusts and the rates of tax applicable are set out in IHTA 1984, s 70(6). The longer the charitable period, the greater the charge when that period ends, but subject to a maximum rate chargeable of 30% after 50 years.

Capital gains tax

[15.39] Under TCGA 1992, s 256, when property ceases to be held on charitable trusts, the trustees are deemed to have disposed of, and immediately reacquired, the property at its market value. Any gain not accruing to the trustees of the charitable trust is liable to capital gains tax, subject to a claim for hold-over relief under TCGA 1992, s 260. In addition, to the extent that the property at that time represents, directly or indirectly, the consideration for the disposal of assets by the trustees, any gain accruing on that earlier disposal (and previously exempt) is treated as not having accrued to the charity and capital gains tax is applied as if the exemption had never applied. A cumulative liability may, therefore, arise. An assessment may be made within three years of the end of the year of assessment in which the property ceases to be held for charitable purposes. Such an assessment seems to be able to be made even where the gain arising on the earlier disposal is outside the normal time limit for assessment.

Community Amateur Sports Clubs

[15.40] There are a variety of tax reliefs available to Community Amateur Sports Clubs ('CASCs') (CTA 2010, ss 662–665). A sports club can apply to HMRC for status as a CASC provided certain criteria are met as detailed in CTA 2010, s 658.

Gift Aid is available on donations made to a CASC (ITA 2007, ss 414 and 430). Whilst inheritance tax relief is available and gifts of assets are on a no gain/no loss basis for capital gains tax, no income tax relief is available on gifts of shares to a CASC.

Gifts for national purposes

[15.41] IHTA 1984, s 25 extends the s 23 exemption for gifts to charities to gifts to bodies named in Sch 3 to the Act. These bodies include UK national museums, local authorities, government departments and universities or colleges. The anti-avoidance provisions in IHTA 1984, s 23 (see **15.5** above) also apply to gifts for national purposes. Gifts to these bodies are also treated for capital gains tax purposes as disposals for a consideration producing neither a gain nor a loss (TCGA 1992, s 257). For a more detailed discussion on gifts of heritage property, see **CHAPTER 16 HERITAGE PROPERTY**.

Gifts to political parties

[15.42] A gift of any amount made either during a person's lifetime or on his death to a qualifying political party is exempt from inheritance tax (IHTA 1984, s 24).

A qualifying political party is defined in s 24(2) as one in respect of which, at the last general election preceding the transfer of value, two members of the party were elected to the House of Commons or one member was so elected and the party received not less than 150,000 votes overall. There are currently 11 qualifying parties.

Gifts to non-qualifying political parties do not qualify for any exemption or relief.

The anti-avoidance provisions in IHTA 1984, s 23 (see **15.5** above) also apply to gifts to political parties.

Chapter 16

Heritage Property

Introduction

[16.1] Encouraging the preservation of our national heritage through the giving of tax privileges is not a new concept. The Finance Act 1896 first gave the Treasury discretion to waive estate duty in respect of settled chattels considered to be of national, scientific or historical interest, such as paintings, books and other works of art. Although the legislation still refers to the 'Treasury', their functions were transferred to HMRC (FA 1985, s 95). From 15 September 2016, however, the function of approving new national institutions for IHTA 1984, Sch 3 (see 16.2) will be transferred from HMRC to the Treasury.

The current reliefs, encompassing inheritance tax, capital gains tax, income tax, stamp duty and stamp duty land tax aim to help in the preservation of our national heritage property. Generally, these reliefs tend to encourage continued private ownership of heritage property including land and buildings of outstanding interest as well as land essential for the protection of the character and amenities of an outstanding building and objects historically associated with such a building. This is illustrated by the availability of relief for 'maintenance funds' which are tax-efficient vehicles for providing funds for the upkeep of heritage property kept in private ownership. In addition, there are also specific reliefs which facilitate tax-free gifts or sales of heritage property to certain national bodies, including the Gifts to the Nation Scheme designed to encourage donations of pre-eminent works of art or historic objects to the nation in return for a tax saving.

The reliefs available can broadly be split into those which enable the property to be placed in some form of public ownership and those which do not. The two sets of reliefs interact and are discussed below.

Gifts for national purposes

Inheritance tax

[16.2] Transfers of property to various national and local bodies are exempt from inheritance tax (IHTA 1984, s 25). The bodies to which such gifts may be made are listed in IHTA 1984, Sch 3 and include the National Gallery, the British Museum and other national museums, the National Trust for Places of Historic Interest or Natural Beauty, any museum or art gallery maintained by a local authority or university, any university library, and any local authority or government department. A list of the qualifying bodies can be found in the HMRC Inheritance Tax Manual, para 11224.

Capital gains tax

[16.3] Disposals to certain national bodies within IHTA 1984, Sch 3 (IHTA 1984, s 25) qualify for capital gains tax relief under TCGA 1992, s 258. Relief is given by providing that the gain is not a chargeable gain.

Cultural Gifts Scheme

Inheritance tax

[16.4] This scheme, which came into effect on 1 April 2012, is to encourage taxpayers to donate pre-eminent objects, or collections of objects, to the nation. In return such taxpayers will receive a deduction in their tax liability based on a set percentage of the value of the object they are donating.

Operation of the scheme

[16.5] The scheme works as follows. A potential donor will offer property that they consider to be pre-eminent property as a gift to the nation together with a self-assessed valuation of the property. This offer will be considered by a panel of experts (which will include the panel of experts used in respect of the Acceptance in Lieu of Tax Scheme) who will determine whether the object is pre-eminent. If it is considered to be so, the panel will agree a valuation with the donor. If the donor wishes to proceed on the basis of the agreed valuation he will receive a tax reduction. This will be based on a set percentage of 30% for individuals (and 20% for companies) of the agreed value of the object that has been donated. Individuals will be able to allocate the tax reduction across a period of up to five years beginning with the tax year in which the object is offered.

The Department of Culture, Media and Sport (DCMS) has published guidance which can be found at www.artscouncil.org.uk.

Conditions to be satisfied

[16.6] In order for the tax benefit to be available, a qualifying gift must be made (FA 2012, Sch 14, para 3). A qualifying gift is defined as a gift made in the following circumstances:

(a)   the taxpayer offers to give pre-eminent property to be held for the benefit of the public or nation;

(b)   the taxpayer is both legally and beneficially entitled to the property and the property is not owned jointly with others;

(c)   the offer is made in accordance with the scheme;

(d)   the offer is registered in accordance with the scheme;

(e)   the offer, or part of the offer, is accepted in accordance with the scheme; and

(f)   the gift made pursuant to the offer, or the part of the offer, is accepted (FA 2012, Sch 14, para 1(2)).

Jointly held property cannot be the subject of a gift. Where, therefore, a husband and wife jointly own property, they cannot take advantage of the scheme. They could, of course, transfer the property into sole ownership without any tax charges arising but this is of little use unless steps have been taken to ensure that the tax liability rests with the spouse who has sole ownership of the asset.

Pre-eminent property

[16.7] Pre-eminent property is defined in FA 2012, Sch 14, para 22 and follows the definition found in the Acceptance in Lieu Scheme under IHTA 1984, s 230 (see **16.19**). The decision as to pre-eminence lies with the relevant minister, the Secretary of State for Culture, Media and Sport, unless the property has an interest related with either Scotland, Northern Ireland or Wales in which case a Minister in the relevant devolved administration will be involved in making the decision having been advised by the Arts Council. The legislation clearly states that there is no right or expectation that an offer which satisfies para 1 will be accepted (FA 2012, Sch 14, para 25).

Effect of the scheme

Basic rule

[16.8] The basic rule is that where a taxpayer makes a qualifying gift then part of his tax liability for a relevant year is treated as having been paid either as if he had paid the tax on the due date or on the date that the offer was registered (if the due date was earlier). Subject to agreement, the taxpayer may apply for a tax reduction against his income tax and/or capital gains tax liabilities in the tax year in which the offer was registered or any of the succeeding four tax years (FA 2012, Sch 14, para 3).

A qualifying gift of property under the scheme is exempt from inheritance tax (IHTA 1984, s 25) and will not be subject to capital gains tax on its disposal. A special rule applies where the taxpayer had received the property as a result of a potentially exempt transfer: no chargeable transfer will be made in the event that the person from whom the taxpayer received the object dies within seven years of making the PET.

Allocation of tax reduction

[16.9] The total tax reduction for an individual is 30% of the agreed value of the qualifying gift.

Example

Jasmine has a painting of which she is not overly fond which was given to her by her aged aunt over ten years ago. She knows the painting is valuable and of interest because she was constantly reminded of the fact by her aunt. It has increased significantly in value since it was given to her. Jasmine has recently realised a chargeable gain of £8 million on the disposal of some land.

She has decided to take advantage of the scheme and offers the painting to the nation. The painting is accepted and a value of £5 million is agreed.

Jasmine will receive a reduction in her tax liabilities of £1.5 million (30% of £5 million). Her tax liability will be £100,000 calculated as follows:

Capital gains tax	
(£8 million × 20%)	1,600,000
Tax reduction	
(£5 million × 30%)	1,500,000
	£100,000

No capital gains tax nor inheritance tax will be payable on the gift made by Jasmine.

The tax reduction can be allocated across more than one relevant tax year. A taxpayer may agree, pursuant to the scheme, that the total tax reduction amount is to be allocated across the five relevant tax years in whatever amounts they wish, and can include a nil amount for any of the years. In the event that no order is specified in the agreed terms, the tax reduction will be applied first to the individual's income tax liability and thereafter to any capital gains tax liability (FA 2012, Sch 14, para 5). In most cases it is impossible to state with certainty when liabilities will arise. There are special rules which apply where a taxpayer has previously made a gift of another pre-eminent object under the scheme. A taxpayer is not required to use the whole of the tax reduction available. It should be noted that if the relief is not used within five years then it will lapse. Similarly, if a taxpayer were to die before the income or capital gains arose against which he had specified that the relief was to be taken, the relief would be lost.

Effect on interest and penalties

[16.10] The legislation details the position in relation to late payment interest and late payment penalties. Where an offer of a gift is accepted under the scheme with the result that the taxpayer's tax liability is treated as having been satisfied, no late payment interest or penalties will be payable on the amount from the date of registration (that is, the date the offer is registered). In effect, therefore, interest and penalties will not be incurred during the negotiation period. In the event that there are multiple due dates for a particular tax year, the deemed payment will be allocated in a manner that minimises any late payment interest and penalties. A taxpayer will continue to be liable for any interest or penalties that accrue before the registration of the offer. Schedule 14 will not reduce those. In the event that a taxpayer's tax liability for a year subsequently changes, the portion of that tax liability for a relevant year (to which the tax deduction was applied) will be recalculated. In the majority of cases the effect of this provision is limited.

Deferment of tax

[16.11] Where an offer of a gift has been made by a taxpayer, he may make a request for payment of the tax to be deferred until the negotiations are concluded provided that:

(a)   the offer is registered in accordance with the scheme;
(b)   the offer includes a proposal of the agreed terms;
(c)   the taxpayer will be required to pay an amount of tax or on account of tax for a relevant tax year by a certain day (the due date);
(d)   the negotiations are not expected to conclude before that date (FA 2012, Sch 14, para 9).

Such a request must be made in writing to HMRC and sent with a copy of the proposal and any such other information as an officer of HMRC may reasonably require, at least 45 days before the due date.

The amount of tax that can be deferred cannot exceed the proposed tax reduction figure set out in the donor's proposal. It should be noted that this is only a request and HMRC is under no duty to agree to a deferment of the tax.

In considering such a request HMRC must have regard to all the circumstances of the case (including, for example, the creditworthiness of the potential donor) (FA 2012, Sch 14, para 9(7)). HMRC has the power to attach conditions or restrictions to such a deferment.

Where HMRC has agreed a deferment, late payment penalties will not accrue from the date of registration. Interest will, however, run from the date when the tax should have been paid.

Withdrawal of agreement to defer tax

[16.12] HMRC has the power to withdraw from the agreement to defer payment at any time whilst negotiations are continuing. In such circumstances, the taxpayer must pay the outstanding tax and late payment interest within 30 days of a notice being issued by HMRC (FA 2012, Sch 14, para 10). If payment is not made within 30 days, penalties will be imposed. Where a gift is withdrawn or the offer is rejected, the taxpayer will need to pay the outstanding tax including any interest that would have accrued on that portion since the tax was initially due within 30 days of the negotiations concluding. Again, if payment is not made within 30 days, penalties will be imposed.

Conclusion of negotiations

[16.13] When negotiations have been concluded and a qualifying gift is made then the actual tax reduction agreed will be applied to the tax amount that is being deferred as if the tax had been paid when it became due or on the date that the offer was registered (if the tax had become due before this date). If the actual tax reduction figure is less than the amount of tax that has been deferred, with the result that the taxpayer still owes tax to HMRC, the balance, together with any interest, is payable within 30 days of the negotiations concluding. If payment is not made within that 30-day period, the taxpayer will be liable to penalties. If negotiations are concluded in relation to only part of the offer, HMRC will apply the provisions of para 11 as far as it 'is reasonably practicable' so to do.

Clients should be advised that once the agreed terms are finalised they cannot be subsequently amended even if a taxpayer's circumstances have changed (FA 2012, Sch 14, para 7(2)).

Withdrawal of the tax reduction

[**16.14**] FA 2012, Sch 14, para 8 has the effect of withdrawing the tax reduction where the qualifying gift is set aside or declared void. In its Explanatory Notes, HMRC gives the example of a court order being made. In such circumstances the tax liability that has been treated as satisfied ceases to be treated as so and late payment interest and penalties treated as not having arisen now fall into charge. The taxpayer will be required to pay an amount representing the tax reduction together with any late payment penalties and interest up to and including the date of payment within 30 days of the date of the gift being set aside or declared void. Obviously, where the tax reduction has not yet taken effect, the normal due dates will apply.

Interaction with conditionally exempt property

[**16.15**] Where a person inherits a conditionally exempt object on the death of its previous owner, that person may give that object to the nation under the scheme within three years of the previous owner's death without triggering the inheritance tax recapture charge that would otherwise have become due on the death of the previous owner and without any need to renew its conditional exemption. In addition, a recapture charge will not be triggered on the death of the donor. Where a taxpayer makes a gift of a conditionally exempt object under the scheme, the gift will not be a chargeable event which would otherwise result in inheritance tax held over on the object becoming payable.

Effect on the remittance basis

[**16.16**] Special rules apply to those UK resident taxpayers who use the remittance basis of tax. Where property has been brought into the UK and been accepted under the scheme, there will be no charge to income tax or capital gains tax on the remittance of that property.

Capital gains tax

[**16.17**] No chargeable gain will arise on a disposal arising on the gift of pre-eminent property to the nation under the Gifts to the Nation/Cultural Gifts Scheme created by FA 2012, Sch 14 (TCGA 1992, s 258(1A)).

Points to note

[**16.18**] There is a limit on the total amount of tax reductions available between the Cultural Gifts Scheme and the Acceptance in Lieu of Tax Scheme.

The total reduction in tax liabilities under both schemes for each fiscal year must be within an annual £40 million limit. Each application will be considered on a first come, first served basis and so an application should be made earlier in the fiscal year as opposed to later.

It should be remembered that interest does not run from the date that the offer is registered. However, if the offer is not accepted, interest will have run from the due date even if a request for deferment has been made.

If a taxpayer makes a qualifying gift under the Cultural Gifts Scheme, he must be confident that he will realise the tax liabilities which he proposes to set off. If the tax reduction is not utilised within the five-year period, it will be lost. A client should also be advised that should he die before the tax reduction is utilised, it will also be lost.

Acceptance in lieu of tax

[16.19] HMRC has a discretion to accept particular heritage property in satisfaction of the payment of inheritance tax, estate duty or interest (IHTA 1984, s 230). It should be noted that the person liable to pay the tax and the offeror must be the same person. In addition, an offer cannot be made if the tax has already been settled, unless that payment is a payment on account of the liability. Where property is accepted in lieu of inheritance tax, neither capital gains tax (TCGA 1992, s 258(2)(b)) nor stamp duty land tax (where relevant) is charged.

Land can be accepted where it has been agreed between HMRC and the person liable to pay the tax. Objects can be accepted provided they are, or have been, kept in any building if:

(a)   the building is being or has been accepted in lieu of tax or estate duty;

(b)   the building or interest in the building belongs to the Crown, the Duchy of Lancaster, the Duchy of Cornwall, a Government Department or held for the purposes of a Government Department;

(c)   the building is under the guardianship of the Secretary of State under the Ancient Monuments and Archaeological Areas Act 1979;

(d)   the building belongs to any body listed in IHTA 1984, Sch 3;

and it appears to the Secretary of State desirable for the objects to remain associated with the building (IHTA 1984, s 230(3)).

Pictures, prints, books, manuscripts, works of art, scientific objects, other things or collections thereof which are considered pre-eminent can also be accepted.

The acquisition price is a matter for negotiation between HMRC and the taxpayer. The value at which property is accepted can be the value at the date of the offer or the value as at the date of acceptance but not the time of transfer. There is a financial incentive in using an arrangement known as 'the douceur'. The amount of tax is satisfied by agreeing a special price. A special price is usually the net value of the property (market value less the notional tax liability) plus a percentage of the value of the tax. The 'douceur' for chattels is generally 25%, and 10% for land and buildings of outstanding interest. An offer must be made to HMRC detailing certain information (para 11.14 of the Capital Taxation and the National Heritage Memorandum (the 'Memorandum').

Where the special price exceeds the liability to tax and interest, that excess cannot be reimbursed nor set against any future liability. If such a situation arose, there are two choices. Firstly, the excess amount is foregone, or secondly, a Schedule 3 body is identified which is prepared to fund the difference between the tax liability and the special price. This is known as a 'hybrid'. If such a hybrid offer is made, HMRC must be informed of the details.

Example

Honoria inherited her uncle's residuary estate which included a pre-eminent painting worth £500,000 for which she did not care. Below is a comparison of Honoria selling the painting or the painting being accepted in lieu of inheritance tax.

Open Market Sale

Sale price	500,000
Inheritance tax at 40%	200,000
Net sale proceeds	300,000

Offer in Lieu	
Agreed open market value	500,000
Less: notional inheritance tax (40% @ 500,000)	200,000
	300,000
Plus: 25% douceur of the inheritance tax	50,000
	350,000

Where the property has a latent estate duty charge, HMRC will use the estate duty rate to calculate the special price, assuming it is higher than the inheritance tax rate of 40%.

Using the example above, the painting inherited by Honoria had a latent estate duty charge of 80%:

Agreed open market value	500,000
Notional Estate Duty at 80%	400,000
Net value	100,000
Plus: 25% douceur of the tax paid	100,000
Special price credited to the estate	200,000

It should be noted that there is a limit on the total reduction of tax liabilities that can be given. The limit is currently £40 million but this is a joint limit with the Cultural Gifts Scheme. The annual limit runs from 6 April to 5 April and so therefore if an application is to be made it should be made as early as possible in the tax year.

Conditional exemption for heritage property

Inheritance tax

[16.20] The provisions allowing heritage property to be retained in private ownership are found in IHTA 1984, ss 30–35A which provide that a transfer of value of heritage property is exempt from inheritance tax provided certain conditions are met (the 'conditional exemption').

Conditions

[16.21] IHTA 1984, s 30 provides that a transfer of value is an exempt transfer to the extent that the value transferred is attributable to property which is:

(a)   designated by HMRC as falling within one of the categories listed in s 31; and

(b)   in respect of which a person the Board thinks appropriate in the circumstances of the case gives the undertakings required for that kind of property.

When does it apply?

[16.22] Exemptions may be given for transfers on death and lifetime gifts but the latter are only eligible if:

(a)   the transferor or his spouse or civil partner has been beneficially entitled to the property throughout the six years ending with the transfer; or

(b)   the transferor acquired the property on a death and the acquisition was itself a conditionally exempt transfer (IHTA 1984, s 30(3)).

Property held on trust may also qualify for conditional exemption in certain circumstances.

Transfers of value which are already exempt from inheritance tax because they are either gifts to charities or inter-spouse or civil partner transfers cannot also be conditionally exempt transfers (IHTA 1984, s 30(4)). Similarly, potentially exempt transfers cannot also be conditionally exempt transfers unless the transfer subsequently becomes chargeable due to the transferor dying within seven years. Conditional exemption can only be claimed after the transferor's death if the property has not been disposed of in the interim unless the disposal is to a body within IHTA 1984, Sch 3, is in satisfaction of tax under IHTA 1984, s 230 or the disposal is a gift under the Cultural Gifts Scheme and, in each case, the property has been or could be designated as heritage property under IHTA 1984, s 31 (IHTA 1984, s 26A).

Conditional exemption may also be claimed if the property has been disposed of by the donee provided the disposal was by way of gift and the new owner, is prepared to give the necessary undertakings. Therefore, conditional exemption may be claimed for transfers made on death, for lifetime transfers into a discretionary trust, for a lifetime transfer which was a PET when made if the donor dies within the following seven years, or where the donor has reserved the benefit which subsists until or is given up within seven years of his death.

Designation

[16.23] There is no definition of 'heritage property' in the legislation. IHTA 1984, s 31, however, states that the Treasury may designate:

(a)   a relevant object which is pre-eminent for its national, scientific, historic or artistic interest or a collection or group of relevant objects which, taken as a whole, is pre-eminent for its national, scientific or artistic interest. A relevant object is defined as a picture, print, book, manuscript, work of art or scientific object. The test of pre-eminence, which replaced the old test of 'museum quality', requires a higher standard to be reached;

(b)   land of outstanding scenic, historic or scientific interest;

(c)   buildings of outstanding historic or architectural interest;

(d)   land essential for the protection of the character and amenities of a building falling within (c) above; and

(e)   objects historically associated with a building falling within (c) above.

Guidance published in 2011 by HMRC found in the Memorandum explains what HMRC considers to be heritage property.

The Commissioners for HMRC are, of course, unable to determine themselves what objects, buildings and land should be designated as national heritage property. The HMRC Heritage Team (the 'Heritage Team'), which is responsible for designating property, therefore takes expert advice before deciding whether to designate a property. In reaching their opinion, they seek as territorially appropriate, the views of Natural England, English Heritage, Historic Scotland, Cadw, Countryside Council for Wales and other more specialist advisers such as the Royal Botanic Gardens (for rare trees), etc.

If a building is listed in England and Wales as Grade I or II* or Grade A in Northern Ireland and Scotland or is a scheduled monument, that is a prima facie indication that it will be accepted as outstanding. Land essential for the protection of the character and amenities of an outstanding building is also eligible for exemption. The factors to be taken into account here include 'the need to protect the views from an outstanding building (eg to landscaped parkland); the views of and approaches to it and the need to prevent undesirable development close to it'. HMRC states that 'the "essential" in "essential amenity land" must be viewed initially from the perspective of the claimant. That an expert might regard a larger area than that in claim as "essential" amenity land cannot in itself preclude conditional exemption for the smaller area' (para 6.2 of the Memorandum). The conditional exemption for amenity land will include the trees and underwood on the land provided they do not detract from the qualifying interest. There is no requirement that the land has to adjoin an outstanding building (para 6.3 of the Memorandum). Where the amenity land is separated from the outstanding building by other land, supportive undertakings in relation to that intervening land will be required. A claimant of the exemption will therefore need his neighbour's co-operation. Buildings on essential amenity land qualify for exemption in their own right if they are of outstanding historic or architectural interest. When they are not eligible for exemption in their own right, the exemption granted to such essential amenity land will none the less extend to buildings on it providing that they do not compromise the protection of the character and amenities of the outstanding building (para 6.4 of the Memorandum).

For 'objects' within categories (a) and (e), HMRC takes advice from Arts Council England. An object is considered to be 'pre-eminent' if it falls within one of the following:

- Does the object have an especially close association with our history and national life?
- Is the object of especial artistic or art-historical interest?
- Is the object of especial importance for the study of some particular form of art, learning or history?
- Does the object have an especially close association with a particular historic setting? (paras 4.1 and 11.23 of the Memorandum)

Foreign objects as well as British works may fall within the definition.

HMRC has issued guidance in relation to an object or a group of objects which it will regard as historically associated with a building. HMRC's guidance, found in App 15 of the Memorandum, requires a historical link between the object and the building itself. Examples that would qualify are:

- Objects with a direct relevance to the appreciation of the building such as original architect's drawings.
- Objects with a direct relevance to the appreciation of the history of the house such as portraits of previous owners where there is a demonstrably historical association with the building.
- Objects with a direct relevance to the appreciation of the building in a wider sense such as archival material relating to a major event which took place at the building.

Examples given by HMRC as unlikely to qualify include:

- Works of art commissioned by the owner specifically for the house so that they complement the architectural character of the house and existing collection.
- An item added to a specific collection enhancing the cultural value of the whole collection.

It is often preferable for an object to be the subject of an individual conditional exemption, rather than as part of a collection or group. This gives maximum flexibility for future disposals because if a painting was part of a collection, the sale of that painting might jeopardise the exemption for the other paintings.

Undertakings

[16.24] As mentioned above, undertakings will have to be given which will depend upon the particular nature of the property and facts of the case. The undertakings must be given 'by such person as [HMRC] think appropriate in the circumstances of the case' (IHTA 1984, s 30(1)(b)). Such a person can include a company. The undertakings may include matters such as the maintenance, repair and preservation of the assets, the management of any land, the conservation plans for buildings and their contents and the proposed public access and how it is to be provided and publicised. Although the legislation does not specifically refer to a Heritage Management Plan, it is a common requirement of HMRC that one is prepared which is incorporated into the undertakings. Such a plan is described by Natural England as 'a policy and priorities statement under which day-to-day management will operate and a frame of reference against which detailed working decisions will be taken by those managing the property.' The preparation of such a plan is a time-consuming and very costly exercise. HMRC has stated that a Heritage Management Plan should be agreed prior to the designation of the property. Therefore, conditional exemption will not be given until an agreed Heritage Management Plan is in place unless based on the facts it would be plainly unreasonable.

Public access

[16.25] All owners of exempt assets will have to provide a measure of 'open' access to those assets in accordance with the terms of the undertaking agreed with HMRC. 'Public access' must be reasonable and this will depend upon the nature of the asset. This will vary from property to property depending on factors such as features of interest, size, location, content and other individual circumstances. There is, therefore, 'no hard and fast rule' (para 6.13 of the Memorandum).

In the case of exempt buildings and their amenity land, HMRC at para 6.13 of the Memorandum states that:

'as a general guide,

- we seek access to the interior of a smaller building on at least one day a week plus public holidays during the spring and summer months amounting to 28 days (or 25 if appropriate in Northern Ireland, Scotland and Wales) each year but
- for some buildings, it might be appropriate to seek fewer days' access (or none at all) to the interior. Such buildings might include those of specialised interest, or whose structure, contents or decoration would suffer from excessive internal access. They might also include those whose historic interiors had been removed or destroyed or were of no intrinsic interest. The decision to allow more limited access is dependent solely on the nature of the building while
- for larger buildings likely to attract, and be capable of handling, larger numbers of visitors anything up to 156 days' internal access might be appropriate'.

In the case of land, the access will, in general, be 'to afford public access for walking and, if appropriate, riding on existing rights of way and permissive paths, supplemented where necessary by new access of either type' (para 5.6 of the Memorandum). It is recognised that for some land of scientific interest, it may be appropriate to impose restrictions with agreed closure periods for sporting activities, land management, nature conservation, etc. In most circumstances it will be open to the individual to charge a fee to view the exempt building but this must be reasonable. HMRC considers that such charges should be 'along the lines of those made by locally comparable sources, eg the National Trust' (HMRC IHT & Trusts Newsletter – December 2007).

For chattels exempt in their own right, 'open access' may be provided by displaying the objects at:

(a)   the residence of the individual or at the place the object is kept (and unless the building itself is tax exempt, access may be limited to the area of the building where the chattels are displayed);

(b)   a museum or gallery to which the public have access;

(c)   any other building open to the public, eg a local Records Office;

(d)   the appropriate European Heritage Open Days event (ie Heritage Open Days (England), Doors Open Days (Scotland), London Open House, and European Open Days (Wales and Northern Ireland); and

(e)   local, regional or touring exhibitions.

Objects may be loaned for display in public collections for special exhibitions and this period counts as 'open'. An owner must give an undertaking that an object will be kept permanently in the United Kingdom and will not leave the country temporarily except for an approved purpose and period, eg a temporary public exhibition abroad. An application must be sent to HMRC before applying for an export licence (in the case of objects more than 50 years old). Loans to public collections may be covered by the Government Indemnity Scheme to relieve the borrower of the need to take out commercial insurance.

Access should be given for a suitable period and time each year, and without the need for a prior appointment. HMRC states that it would not expect this annual period to be less than a month or so (or, where it suited an owner and an institutional borrower, a corresponding triennial arrangement). It is considered that only in very exceptional circumstances would gaps of three or more years be reasonable (Appendix 1A, para 9 of the Memorandum).

Historically-associated objects will normally be displayed in the building with which they have an historical association.

Publication of the terms of the undertaking

[16.26] Publicising access and undertakings is a requirement of conditional exemption for heritage assets. HMRC will expect the individual to make any undertaking available to any member of the public who asks to view it. The undertaking in relation to the building or exempt chattel may be displayed at the premises and will be displayed on HMRC's website database (www.gov. uk/tax-relief-for-national-heritage-assets). The information required for the website is:

•   a description of each object, group or collection;

•   the county (though not the full address) in which it can normally be seen;

•   viewing details including the dates the public can see it and, if applicable, the museum, gallery or other venue for its display;

- a contact point for information, for by appointment access and for loans for special exhibitions.

Owners of buildings open to the public will have their own publicity. The publicity for the attraction, together with HMRC's website publicity, will be sufficient. For items displayed in houses not normally open to the public, additional publicity will be necessary – in the local press or at a local tourist information centre and in a national publication or guide.

It is important that these details are renewed and updated annually to avoid an inadvertent loss of the exemption. Appendix 1A of the Memorandum contains HMRC's views of what it considers is acceptable or not and common problems encountered.

Owners of outstanding land or buildings will generally be required to make annual reports to HMRC about the maintenance of the assets and the provision of public access (see the Model Undertakings provided by HMRC included in the Memorandum). Exempt land and buildings will be inspected usually every five years (NE64 Conditional Exemption and Heritage Management Plans).

Making a claim

[16.27] Conditional exemption from inheritance tax depends upon the property being designated by the Commissioners for HM Revenue & Customs and appropriate undertakings being given by the relevant persons. There is no prescribed form for making a claim. In practice, HMRC states that a claimant should:

(a) provide a statement that the exemption is being claimed, specifying the event to which the claim relates;
(b) clearly identify each asset covered by the claim;
(c) provide a brief statement of why each asset is considered to qualify for the exemption, including a confirmation that proposals to provide public access will be made; and
(d) confirm that there is no present intention to sell the asset (para 3.5 of the Memorandum).

A written claim for relief from inheritance tax under IHTA 1984, s 30 must be made to HMRC within two years after the date of death or date of transfer. HMRC has the discretion to extend this period and has indicated that an oversight on an individual's part or his adviser's part, or the making of a post-death variation, will not normally by itself be an acceptable reason to allow a late claim (para 3.5 of the Memorandum). In the case of both lifetime chargeable transfers and transfers on death (including potentially exempt transfers which became chargeable as a result of death), a claim cannot be made until after the event. With lifetime chargeable transfers this was, perhaps, not such a problem but where the relevant transfer was as a result of death the procedural delays can cause significant problems for the executors as regards the administration of the deceased's estate.

Unfortunately, there is no formal advance clearance procedure. However, Natural England will usually give an informal indication of the likelihood of land qualifying for relief on the basis of it being of outstanding scenic interest. Where a claim is likely to be made, perhaps because of the poor health of the current owner, it is worthwhile seeking in advance informal advice from Natural England. This will, at least, allow alternative planning steps to be considered if the property is unlikely to meet the required standards.

There are only two occasions where a claim can be made in advance. First is the intended lifetime creation of a maintenance fund in support of an outstanding building, outstanding or amenity land and historically associated chattels (IHTA 1984, Sch 4 para 1(2)).

The second situation is in connection with the decennial charge arising under IHTA 1984, s 64. For decennial charges arising after 17 November 2015, a claim for conditional exemption must be made within two years of the decennial charge arising. HMRC does have the discretionary power to allow a late election.

Chargeable events

[16.28] By definition, conditional exemption from inheritance tax is not absolute. The deferred charge will become payable if one of the three 'chargeable events' found in IHTA 1984, s 32 occurs, namely:

(a)   the death of the beneficial owner of the property (with certain exceptions);

(b)   the disposal, whether by sale or gift, of the property (with certain exceptions); and

(c)   the failure of the relevant person to observe, in any material respect, an undertaking given to the Treasury or Commissioners for HM Revenue and Customs.

The exceptions to (a) and (b) above are, broadly, if the transfer of value on death or disposal by gift is itself a conditionally exempt transfer, the sale or disposal is to a body within IHTA 1984, Sch 3 or is in satisfaction of a tax liability under IHTA 1984, s 230, a gift of property is made under the Cultural Gifts Scheme, or the requisite undertakings under IHTA 1984, s 31 where required are given by such persons as HMRC considers appropriate in the particular circumstances. It is no longer acceptable for such replacement undertakings to simply correspond with the old undertakings.

HMRC does not regard an appropriation or allotment of conditionally exempt property in satisfaction of a legatee's entitlement, as a chargeable event provided the legatee does not pay an equivalent amount in money (para 7.2 of the Memorandum).

The legislation imposes a tax charge if the undertakings are not observed in a material respect (IHTA 1984, s 32(2)). There is little guidance as to what the phrase 'in a material respect' means in practice in the Memorandum, although the Memorandum does state that in certain circumstances one opportunity to remedy matters within a reasonable timeframe will be offered (para 7.3).

Meaning of 'disposal'

[16.29] There has been much debate about what constitutes a 'disposal' for the purposes of IHTA 1984, s 32. At one time there was concern that mortgaging the property as security for a loan would be treated as a disposal. Mortgaging a property to raise finance to restore it would not be treated as a disposal (para 7.3 of the Memorandum). Indeed, HMRC's view is that mortgaging a property is not a disposal of it for these purposes and nor is the grant of a lease. However, an adviser should ensure that any lease granted 'does not undermine the integrity of the lessor's undertakings as to amount to a failure to observe them in a material respect'.

If in doubt, the Heritage Team of HMRC should be consulted before any plans are made to grant leases or raise capital from the property by way of mortgage.

Calculating tax

[16.30] The inheritance tax charge is calculated according to the rules contained in IHTA 1984, s 33 which depend upon what triggers the charge and the market value of the relevant property at the time of the chargeable event. The value of the property will be taxed by reference to the transferor's rates of inheritance tax. Where an individual is still alive, his cumulative total of chargeable transfers is adjusted upwards by the amount of the value of the property on which tax is paid (IHTA 1984, s 34). Where this person is dead his estate will be similarly increased and this can affect the rate of tax applicable on the event of a second and subsequent chargeable event. The legislation provides that where property has been sold (with no intention to confer a gratuitous benefit on anyone), the value is taken to be the proceeds of sale (IHTA 1984, s 33(3)). Where the chargeable event is not a sale, the computation is more complex because two transfers could occur, on the gift and on the triggering of the deferred charge. Where the gift is a chargeable event (not including PETs), the tax payable on the gift is credited against the triggered deferred charge. Where the gift is a chargeable transfer but not a chargeable event and so no charge arises the credit will be available to be offset against future chargeable events affecting that property.

There are special rules which apply in respect of the interaction between the transferable nil rate band, the residence nil rate amount and the tax payable on a chargeable event under s 32 (IHTA 1984, ss 8C and 8M).

The rate of tax depends upon the relevant transferor. It should be noted that the lower rate of inheritance tax (36%) will not apply even if the 10% test was satisfied originally.

It is the responsibility of the owner of heritage property to notify HMRC Trusts & Estates of the ending of the conditional exemption. This should be done on Form IHT100 and IHT100F within six months from the end of the month in which the event occurs.

The rules applicable to maintenance funds are dealt with separately below.

Interaction with agricultural property relief and business property relief

[16.31] In the case of landed estates qualifying as heritage property, much of the land will also qualify for agricultural property relief at either 50% or 100%. The relief is given as a reduction in the value transferred by a transfer of value. In addition, there may be situations where property qualifies not only as heritage property but also for business property relief.

A chargeable event occurs if conditional exemption is forfeited on one of the three occasions mentioned above. A charge under IHTA 1984, s 32 will arise as explained above and also under the associated property provisions of IHTA 1984, s 32A. Under ss 32 and 33, tax is charged on 'an amount equal to the value of the property at the time of the chargeable event' (IHTA 1984, s 33(1)). There is no transfer of value (deemed or otherwise) and therefore any agricultural property relief or business property relief will not be available. It is usually better, therefore, to make a chargeable transfer subject to business or agricultural property relief rather than to claim conditional exemption.

Variations on undertakings

[16.32] Both existing and future undertakings may be varied by HMRC. At any time HMRC may propose a variation of the original undertaking to the owner for agreement. A judge sitting in the first-tier Tribunal (Tax) may direct that the proposed undertaking is to have effect from a specified date, which is not to be less than 60 days after his direction, if he is satisfied that:

(a)   the Board has made a proposal for the variation of such an undertaking to the person bound by the undertaking;

(b)   that person has failed to agree to the proposed variation within six months after the date on which the proposal was made; and

(c)   it is just and reasonable, in all the circumstances, to require the proposed variation to be made (IHTA 1984, s 35A).

In the case of *Re Applications to vary the undertakings of A and B* [2005] STC (SCD) 103 the Revenue's application was dismissed on the basis that the accumulated burdens placed on the owners as a result of the proposals would so outweigh the benefits to the public that it would not be just and reasonable to direct that they took effect. It was considered that the increased risks of theft and damage to the owners' possessions would go beyond what Parliament had in mind when empowering the inclusion of extended access requirements and publication requirements. The Special Commissioner listed seven principles in 'no particular order of importance' to be considered when determining whether proposed variations are reasonable.

HMRC is not able to seek adjustments to terms attaching to estate duty exemptions.

Capital gains tax

[16.33] Section 258 also gives capital gains tax relief for the gift of any asset which either has been or could be designated heritage property under IHTA 1984, s 31. This relief includes gifts to a settlement and disposals by trustees of property vesting absolutely. If no inheritance tax designation has actually taken place (for example, because the relevant asset was the subject of a potentially exempt transfer and the gift has not therefore created an immediate inheritance tax liability) then the equivalent undertakings required under IHTA 1984, s 31 must be given in order to claim the capital gains tax relief.

As regards heritage property falling within IHTA 1984, s 31, capital gains tax relief is given by deeming the gain not to be a chargeable gain. Any relief given can subsequently be clawed back by deeming there to have been a disposal at market value upon one of three occasions which broadly correspond to the occasions on which a chargeable event occurs for inheritance tax (see **16.28** above).

(a)   Where the property is sold and an inheritance tax charge arises under IHTA 1984, s 32.

(b)   Where an undertaking has not been observed in a material respect.

(c)   Where there is a disposal other than by way of sale and no new undertaking is given. This could apply, for example, where the new owner of the property subsequently dies and no new undertaking is given by the transferee. In this instance, the owner of the asset is treated as having immediately reacquired it at market value.

Therefore, where there is a clawback and the property has increased significantly in value, there will be a gain arising of not only the clawed back gain but also the gain accruing since the original disposal.

Where a capital gains tax charge arises due to the clawback of relief and inheritance tax is also chargeable, the capital gains tax payable is allowed as a deduction in determining the value of the asset for inheritance tax purposes (TCGA 1992, s 258(8)).

Maintenance funds

[16.34] The beneficial tax treatment afforded by the heritage property provisions outlined above may not alone be sufficient to enable a private individual or family to retain and maintain a substantial heritage property. By their very nature, many heritage properties are not income-producing or are unlikely to create sufficient income to be self-maintaining. Generally, other means of support are required.

Legislation designed to alleviate the problems facing the owners of heritage properties exists to exempt funds set aside to maintain the properties from capital taxes. Maintenance funds can be a useful tool in the preservation of heritage properties but they are not, however, always the best solution.

Statutory conditions

[16.35] A qualifying maintenance fund is one which falls within IHTA 1984, Sch 4, Pt I. Such funds are tax favoured as they attract inheritance tax reliefs, and to some extent, capital gains tax and income tax reliefs.

To qualify for relief, a fund should be for the benefit of land and/or buildings (and/or historically associated objects) which qualify, or could qualify, for conditional exemption and the fund must be held on the terms of a trust which are specified in IHTA 1984, Sch 4 para 3. In the first six years the trust fund must not be capable of being applied for a use other than for the maintenance, repair and preservation of, or making provision for public access to, heritage property, except that income not so applied and not accumulated can be paid to a qualifying charity or to a body included in IHTA 1984, Sch 3 (IHTA 1984,

Sch 4, para 3). The property comprising the trust fund must be of an appropriate character and amount. HMRC interprets the requirement that the settled property be of an appropriate character to include 'a propensity [sic] to produce an income but not necessarily investment in a high-yielding portfolio' (para 8.5 of the Memorandum). Assets whose own maintenance might make excessive demands on the fund are not considered by HMRC to be of an appropriate character. In respect of the requirement that the amount should be appropriate, HMRC says that it will 'have regard to other sources of upkeep available to the owner'. In practice, this means it must produce sufficient income to maintain the relevant heritage property. The trustees of the settlement must be approved by HMRC. The trustees or a majority of them should be UK resident and must include either a trust corporation, a solicitor or an accountant or a member of such other professional body (IHTA 1984, Sch 4, para 2). With regard to the trustees' powers, HMRC does not have a defined list of powers that must be included. Instead, it says that 'cases must turn on their own facts.' In the Memorandum HMRC does make some general comments about the trustees' powers.

Although the provisions are reasonably stringent, there is some scope for flexibility. In particular, funds can be withdrawn from the settlement after the initial 6-year period (subject to an inheritance tax charge) if it becomes apparent that they are required for other purposes or are excess to requirements. It is also possible to add further funds at a later date, for example, on the death of the settlor if this is found to be necessary.

Inheritance tax

[16.36] The maintenance fund is, in effect, a discretionary trust. Without any reliefs there would be an inheritance tax charge on transferring funds into the trust, a decennial charge and an exit charge in the event of trust capital being used to maintain or otherwise benefit the heritage property itself. However, there are inheritance tax reliefs which exempt such transfers of value from inheritance tax (IHTA 1984, s 27 and Sch 4).

A maintenance fund can be established not only for national heritage property which has already been subject to a claim for conditional exemption, but also prior to a claim for conditional exemption. HMRC can designate the relevant heritage property (ie confirm it believes it to be of sufficient national importance to qualify) and accept undertakings given by the current owner as if it had been the subject of a chargeable transfer. This allows the maintenance fund to be formed prior to, say, the death of the owner. This course of action is a means of testing whether heritage property is of an acceptable standard to be designated prior to claiming conditional exemption.

Additional property can be added to an existing maintenance fund, free of inheritance tax, by an individual. Under IHTA 1984, Sch 4, para 16, property held by a relevant property trust can be appointed to a maintenance fund without an exit charge arising under IHTA 1984, s 65. The property may pass either straight to the maintenance fund or via a beneficiary of the relevant property trust provided the beneficiary transfers the property to the maintenance fund within 30 days. The trustees of the maintenance fund must not have acquired an interest in the relevant property trust for money or money's worth or, where the property passes via an individual, that individual must not have acquired the property for money or money's worth.

On the death of a life tenant, property already in an interest in possession settlement can be transferred to a maintenance fund free of inheritance tax (IHTA 1984, s 57A). Where a person became entitled to an interest in possession after 21 March 2006, relief will not be available unless the interest was immediately before the person's death in one of the privileged trusts, namely an immediate post-death interest, a disabled person's trust, a transitional serial interest or a section 5(1B) interest in possession. The transfer must be made within two years after the death of the life tenant or within three years if a court order is required to change the terms of the settlement.

A claim for inheritance tax relief must be made within two years after the date of the transfer concerned or within such longer period as HMRC may allow.

If property leaves a maintenance trust for a purpose other than to repair, preserve or maintain the property and is not given to a qualifying charity or to a body falling within IHTA 1984, Sch 3, an exit charge arises (IHTA 1984, Sch 4, Pt II). Although property can be reclaimed from the maintenance fund after six years, there is a penalty for doing so. One notable exception to this charge is where the property is transferred to another qualifying maintenance fund (IHTA 1984, Sch 4, para 9) which again gives some flexibility to the arrangement.

Income tax

[16.37] The income of what is called in the legislation a 'heritage maintenance settlement' is taxed under the normal income tax provisions applicable to settlements, subject to the provisions contained in ITA 2007, ss 507–517. Where the settlor has retained an interest in the trust fund, even an indirect interest by virtue of his owning the heritage property which the trust is established to benefit, the income arising is treated as that of the settlor (ITTOIA 2005, ss 624–629). Such income taxed as that of the settlor will not be taxed again as a receipt of his trade or otherwise as his income under s 511.

It is, however, possible for the trustees to elect that the trust income, which would otherwise be taxable as the settlor's income, be taxable as if it were the trustees' own income (ITA 2007, s 508). As the election will result in the income from the maintenance fund being taxed on the trustees, ITA 2007, s 511 will not apply and so in certain circumstances there is a potential double tax charge. If a s 508 election is made, the trust's income will be taxable at 45%. If the settlor does not pay additional rate tax it will be better for the trust income to be taxed as if it were the settlor's and no election should be made. Should the settlor have losses available it may make it preferable for the income to be taxed on the settlor.

Where property of the maintenance fund (either capital or income in nature) is applied for a non-qualifying use, or the fund ceases to qualify or HMRC's direction is withdrawn, any income which has arisen since the establishment of the settlement and which has not been applied in the upkeep of the heritage property is, with certain exceptions, subject to an additional tax charge (ITA 2007, ss 512–513). This additional tax charge is at a rate equivalent to the difference between the additional rate of income tax and the trust rate. Because the trust rate and the additional tax rate are currently the same at 45%, no additional tax charge will be payable.

Capital gains tax

[16.38] A charge to capital gains tax on property being transferred to a maintenance fund may be held over under TCGA 1992, s 260(2)(b)(iii). The relief is available on the establishment of the maintenance fund, on the addition of further funds at a later date and on transferring funds from an existing maintenance fund to a new maintenance fund.

Special rules apply where the settlor has an interest in the settlement. Provisions in TCGA 1992, ss 169B and 169C prevent hold-over relief being available on transfers into a settlor-interested trust and provide for a clawback of the tax in certain circumstances. These provisions do not, however, apply to a disposal to the trustees of a settlement which is a maintenance fund for historic buildings, provided an income tax election under ITA 2007, s 508 has been made or could have been made (TCGA 1992, s 169D(1)).

Gains actually accruing to the trustees of a maintenance fund on the disposal of an asset by them are not exempt from capital gains tax. Where the settlor retains an interest under the trust, capital gains tax on the trustees' gains will be charged as if they are the gains of the settlor, unless there has been an election under ITA 2007, s 508.

Settled heritage property

[16.39] Historically, owners of heritage property have used trusts to ensure continuity of ownership and management and also to protect the property from improvident heirs.

Broadly speaking, property can be subject to the settled heritage property provisions in three circumstances.

(a)   Where the property is the subject of a chargeable transfer into trust.
(b)   Where an individual dies with a life interest in settled heritage property.
(c)   Where property is held on discretionary trusts and is therefore subject to the relevant property regime.

These three situations are dealt with in turn below, followed by a brief review of a number of problem areas encountered in practice.

Transfer of property into trust

[16.40] The lifetime transfer of property to a trust other than a privileged trust is a lifetime chargeable transfer unless a relieving provision makes it exempt. A claim is made in the normal way and, if conditional exemption is granted, the trustees will have to give the required undertakings.

Therefore, a lifetime transfer of heritage property to a trust other than a privileged trust, where conditional exemption is relied upon to mitigate the potential inheritance tax liability, can be an expensive strategy if conditional exemption is not, subsequently, granted.

Termination of life interest on death

[16.41] The termination of a life interest on death may be a chargeable transfer by the holder of the interest if the interest either existed before 22 March 2006 or was a privileged interest. If that is not the case, it may be an occasion of charge on property ceasing to be relevant property under IHTA 1984, s 65 because, for example, an individual becomes absolutely entitled to the trust property. In either circumstance, the charge may be avoided if the property is designated as heritage property in relation to that occasion.

Property held on trust

[16.42] A trust can be exempt from inheritance tax in respect of heritage property for the purposes of the decennial charge (IHTA 1984, s 79) and also when heritage property leaves the trust subject to certain ownership conditions (IHTA 1984, s 78).

Generally, the trust is exempt from the decennial charge if either the trust property has previously been the subject of a conditionally exempt transfer (and has therefore already been designated) or there has been an exempt disposal for capital gains tax purposes (also requiring designation). Alternatively, the trust property may be specifically designated as heritage property prior to the decennial charge to avoid tax on that event. As explained above, this is the only occasion the statute provides for advance designation of a property. For decennial charges arising after 17 November 2015 a claim for conditional exemption must be made within two years of the decennial charge arising.

Gifts with reservation

[16.43] Where heritage property is settled on trust and the original owner is included as one of the initial beneficiaries, the gifts with reservation provisions need to be considered regardless of whether the settlor actually receives any benefit. FA 1986, s 102(5) provides an exemption from the provisions for exempt transfers of property to maintenance funds but not for transfers of the heritage property itself. Presumably this is because the heritage property is conditionally exempt and should continue to be exempt provided the undertakings are not broken and, therefore, the gift with reservation provisions should not cause any difficulty.

Pre-owned assets

[16.44] A charge to income tax will arise on donors who continue to enjoy a benefit from property of which they have previously disposed. Where the arrangements put in place reserve a benefit to the original owner, there will be an exemption from the pre-owned assets charge. If, however, the original owner is excluded from the class of beneficiaries under the trust but later derives some benefit from the property, an income tax charge will arise. There is an exemption from the charge for transfers of property to maintenance funds for historic buildings although there is no exemption for transfers of the heritage property itself.

Strategy

[16.45] When considering the strategy for a particular set of circumstances, there are three main questions to be answered.

(a) Does the family wish to, and indeed is it able to, retain and finance the upkeep of the heritage property in future years?

If the answer is 'yes', then it is necessary to consider whether, and how best, to utilise the various heritage property reliefs. In some circumstances where one qualifies for conditional exemption, it may be beneficial not to claim it.

(b) Is a lifetime gift appropriate or should conditional exemption be claimed on death?

To some extent, lifetime gifts are encouraged by the inheritance tax legislation and heritage property is no exception. A gift on trusts under which neither an existing IIP nor a privileged interest subsists would be a chargeable lifetime transfer and conditional exemption may therefore be claimed. Other gifts will generally be potentially exempt transfers and may, therefore, escape the impact of inheritance tax altogether or, if the donor dies within seven years, conditional exemption may be claimed on death. Furthermore, a gain on a lifetime transfer is deemed not to be a chargeable gain for capital gains tax purposes where the property is either designated or could be designated as heritage property.

One potentially significant disadvantage of a lifetime gift is the loss of the tax-free capital gains tax uplift on death. This may be relatively unimportant where the property is to be retained by the family and can continue to be designated as heritage property or where the property is unlikely to appreciate significantly prior to the death of the transferor. However, if the property is ever sold, or conditional exemption lost for other reasons, the cost of losing the capital gains tax uplift on death may be substantial.

A lifetime gift on flexible trusts may be considered as it enables the choice of eventual heir to be left open and the transferor can oversee such matters as the provision of public access to the newly designated heritage property. However, there are problems as explained above with this strategy.

Waiting until the death of the current owner of potential heritage property before claiming conditional exemption may have its advantages. This enables the capital gains tax uplift on death to be utilised. However, it also means that the deceased's executors and family will have to make an application for conditional exemption.

(c) Should 'supporting property' (ie property to provide funds for the upkeep of the heritage property itself) be placed in a maintenance fund or not?

Maintenance funds do have advantages and they are flexible vehicles. In particular, a lifetime gift of property to a maintenance fund has the advantage that it requires the relevant heritage property to be designated even where no chargeable transfer of the actual heritage property has been made. The establishment of a maintenance fund can therefore be used to test whether the relevant property is of sufficiently high standard to be designated as heritage property. However, the use of property held in a maintenance fund is severely restricted for the first six years. This restriction will need to be weighed against the tax advantages of using a maintenance fund.

An alternative to a maintenance fund is to advance supporting property direct to the transferor's heir. Such a gift, during lifetime, would be a potentially exempt transfer and no inheritance tax would be payable if the transferor survives for seven years. However, this is risky as, if it fails, it is not then possible to obtain relief retrospectively by transferring the property to a maintenance fund and asking for the now chargeable potentially exempt transfer to be ignored. It is understood that HMRC is aware that this can cause a problem but does not consider the existing rules to be unfair. The income tax and capital gains tax advantages of maintenance funds are not huge and the motivation for using a maintenance fund will be almost purely inheritance tax driven.

The final decision as to whether to use a maintenance fund may well be determined on practical grounds, such as whether the family is comfortable with the supporting property being almost entirely alienated from their control for six years. The attractiveness of a maintenance fund from an inheritance tax perspective should not, however, be overlooked.

Chapter 17

Relationship Breakdown

Note. The non-fiscal laws, practices and procedures referred to in this chapter relate to England and Wales only and not to Scotland.

Divorce/dissolution

Establishing dates

[17.1] When a marriage irretrievably breaks down, it is necessary to determine the date when the parties permanently separated. This date will normally be fixed by mutual agreement and may be recorded in a deed of separation or court order. The date of separation is important for capital gains tax. That is because the capital gains tax exemption for transfers between spouses who are living together applies up to the end of the tax year in which a couple separate. In the limited circumstances where the husband is still entitled to a married couple's allowance (see **17.2** below), his entitlement will cease from the following tax year even if he voluntarily maintains his wife. By way of contrast, it is the date a divorce becomes final that is important for inheritance tax purposes, as will be seen later in this chapter. It may be in the interests of both spouses to defer the date of formal separation until the former matrimonial property has been transferred between them. Consideration should also be given as to whether separation can be deferred until after 5 April in any given year to mitigate any capital gains tax that might otherwise arise as part of the separation process.

Both parties to the marriage should notify HMRC that they have separated. HMRC will write to each party to determine the date of permanent separation. If the spouses give differing separation dates, HMRC will write to each party to try to agree a date. However, in some circumstances HMRC may allow different dates for each spouse in order to bring matters to a close. Where the separated spouses are still living in the same house, the Inspector will usually seek nothing more than a formal assurance that the separation is indeed permanent.

Personal allowances

[17.2] The married couple's allowance was abolished with effect from 6 April 2000 except where one of the spouses or civil partners was born before 6 April 1935. In the limited circumstances in which the married couple's allowance is still available and the couple separates, in the year of separation the husband and wife or civil partners will continue to receive the married couple's allowance that they were entitled to at the date of separation. For 2016/17, the maximum amount of married couple's allowance is £8,355 and the minimum is £3,220. If the marriage occurred before 5 December 2005 and at least one spouse was born before 6 April 1935, the husband can claim the allowance. If the marriage occurred on or after 5 December 2005 or there is a civil partnership and at least one spouse or partner was born before 6 April 1935, the person with the higher income can claim the allowance. The tax bill is reduced by 10% of the applicable allowance and the allowance is determined by reference to the husband's or claimant's income (as appropriate). If the income concerned is over £27,700 the allowance is reduced progressively from £8,355 down to the minimum of £3,220. The allowance is reduced by £1 for every £2 of income above the limit. The personal allowance can be reduced below the basic personal allowance where the income is above £100,000. If the couple have elected, prior to the start of the tax year in which the separation takes place, to split the married couple's allowance, this cannot be altered after the date of separation and remains in force until the end of the tax year. No married couple's allowance is due to either party for subsequent years although transitional rules apply where a married couple separated before 6 April 1990. In such a case, provided they are not divorced, and the husband continues to maintain his wife by *voluntary* payments, full transitional married couple's allowance can be claimed by the husband for years subsequent to the year of separation.

In years of assessment following the year of separation, the single personal allowance is due.

The recently introduced Marriage Allowance allows an individual whose annual income is less than £11,000 (excluding tax-free savings income) to transfer £1,100 of his personal allowance to his spouse or civil partner, provided the recipient's income is between £11,001 and £43,000 and neither spouse or civil partner was born before 6 April 1935. If these conditions are satisfied, a tax reduction of up to £220 can be made by the transfer of personal allowance between the spouses.

Procedure

[17.3] Part 7 of the Family Procedure Rules 2010 (SI 2010/2955) ('FPR 2010') and Practice Direction 7A contain the procedural rules for applications in matrimonial and civil partnership proceedings. Upon the irretrievable breakdown of a marriage or civil partnership, proceedings can be issued for divorce. If the divorce is undefended, the divorce process has three stages, commencing with the applicant (formerly called the petitioner) filing with the court or divorce centre an application (still known in practice as a petition) for a matrimonial or civil partnership order; upon the respondent acknowledging receipt of the application and acceding to it the applicant applies for the first decree of divorce, the decree nisi or conditional order. A decree nisi or conditional order is pronounced in open court, but the parties need not attend unless directed to do so. It is at this stage that a consent order concerning the division of finances can be filed for the court's approval; before the decree nisi or conditional order is pronounced the court is unable to seal any consent order agreed. Six weeks and one day after a decree nisi or conditional order is pronounced the applicant can apply for a decree absolute or a final order; only after a further three months can the respondent apply if the applicant has not done so.

To establish that the marriage has broken down irretrievably, the applicant must prove one of five facts set out in the Matrimonial Causes Act 1973, s 1(2) (MCA 1973). In the case of a civil partnership, the applicant must prove one of four facts (Civil Partnership Act 2004, s 44(5)). That is because adultery by the respondent is not one of the grounds for dissolution.

A decree absolute or the final order is the final decree and marks the conclusion of the marriage or civil partnership. Until the parties are divorced (or their civil partnership is dissolved), property will still pass on their deaths under the terms of any will and commonly, one spouse or civil partner will have bequeathed a substantial part of his or her estate to the other. Even where no will has been made, the rules on intestacy will apply and a large part of the intestate's estate will go to the spouse or civil partner. A separated spouse or civil partner may therefore inherit most of the deceased's assets unless action is taken at the time of separation to reverse the position by executing a new will or a codicil to the existing one.

Under the Law Reform Succession Act 1995 a divorced spouse or civil partner will be treated as if he or she predeceased the deceased person on the date of the divorce for all purposes. A gift in a will to a former spouse or civil partner will therefore lapse on divorce. This may possibly disinherit the children of the former marriage. Similarly, the appointment of the former spouse or civil partner as executor and trustee will be void unless the will provides otherwise. If there is a wish to leave property to a former spouse or civil partner, it should be borne in mind that the spouse or civil partner exemption does not apply to divorced spouses or civil partners and such a gift may be liable to inheritance tax.

Following the divorce, either or both former spouses may marry a new partner. Marriage revokes a will unless the will was made in contemplation of the new marriage. Similarly, the children of a new partner will have no rights under intestacy. However, if the children of a new partner are adopted, they will then rank equally with the children of the former marriage. This may well be in accordance with the wishes of those immediately concerned, but if other people, such as grandparents, have left property to 'the children of X' this will equally also include the adopted children.

The provisions of the Marriage (Same Sex Couples) Act 2013, which received Royal Assent on 17 July 2013, came into force at various times. The legislation enabled same-sex couples to marry, either in a civil ceremony or in religious premises. The legislation does not prevent same-sex couples from entering into civil partnerships, but since 10 December 2014 those in civil partnerships may convert their relationship to a marriage if they choose to do so. The conversion process involves attending a registry office, signing the register, and having the marriage listed on the index of converted marriages.

Nullity

[17.4] Nullity proceedings declare that the marriage or civil partnership was either void from the beginning or is voidable, meaning that the marriage or civil partnership is valid and subsisting until a decree or order of nullity is obtained. Where it has been held that the marriage is void or voidable then the parties to the suit for nullity are entitled to apply for all the financial orders which are available on divorce or dissolution. A voidable marriage will revoke a will made prior to it (again save where the will has been in contemplation of marriage). However, where it is held that the marriage was void it has no impact on a will. Irrespective of whether the decree or order of nullity is granted on the basis of the marriage or civil partnership being void or voidable it will have the same consequences for a then existing will as a decree of divorce. Such a decree or order also means that neither spouse or civil partner will be able to claim in the event of the other party's intestacy. Nullity cases are comparatively rare and require a hearing. It is therefore often more efficient to pursue a divorce.

Judicial separation

[17.5] Judicial separation does not dissolve the marriage or civil partnership but can be used in cases where for example religious beliefs prevent divorce. As a judicial separation does not dissolve the marriage or civil partnership it only releases the parties from a duty to live together and therefore does not affect existing wills. It is therefore important to advise clients to review their wills in light of any judicial separation. The same menu of financial orders is available on judicial separation as in divorce or dissolution proceedings.

Financial remedies

Overview

[17.6] In deciding how to approach the division of a couple's assets on divorce the court will rely on s 25 of the MCA 1973. Section 25(1) states:

> 'It shall be the duty of the court in deciding whether to exercise its powers under sections 23, 24 . . . above and, if so, in what manner, to have regard to all the circumstances of the case, first consideration being given to the welfare while a minor of any child of the family who has not attained the age of eighteen.'

The Act then provides in s 25(2) a list of eight relevant factors:

(a) The income, earning capacity, property and other financial resources which each of the parties to the marriage has or is likely to have in the foreseeable future, including in the case of earning capacity any increase in that capacity which it would in the opinion of the court be reasonable to expect a party to the marriage to take steps to acquire;

(b) The financial needs, obligations and responsibilities which each of the parties to the marriage has or is likely to have in the foreseeable future;

(c)   The standard of living enjoyed by the family before the breakdown of the marriage;

(d)   The age of each party to the marriage and the duration of the marriage;

(e)   Any physical or mental disability of either of the parties to the marriage;

(f)   The contributions which each of the parties has made or is likely in the foreseeable future to make to the welfare of the family, including any contribution by looking after the home or caring for the family;

(g)   The conduct of each of the parties, whatever the nature of the conduct and whether it occurred during the marriage or after the separation of the parties or (as the case may be) dissolution or annulment of the marriage, if that conduct is such that it would in the opinion of the court be inequitable to disregard it;

(h)   In the case of proceedings for divorce or nullity of marriage, the value to each of the parties to the marriage of any benefit (for example, a pension) which, by reason of the dissolution or annulment of the marriage, that party will lose the chance of acquiring.

Schedule 5 to the Civil Partnership Act 2004 (CPA 2004) echoes the factors set out in section 25(2).

How these factors are to be interpreted, including the relative weight to be attributed to each factor, are established by case law (see **17.31** below). There is no set formula for the division of assets. Case law has given a wide construction to the words of the statute, such that the advice of a matrimonial lawyer will be needed to assess the likely value of a matrimonial claim. In addition, the Family Justice Council has published 'Guidance on "Financial Needs" on Divorce' intended 'as a useful tool for the judiciary'.

The court is also to give regard, when exercising its powers, to whether 'it would be appropriate to exercise those powers so that the financial obligations of each party towards the other will be terminated as soon after the grant of the decree as the court considers just and reasonable.' A clean break may be imposed in relation to capital claims, income claims or both, but a court will not permit a clean break in relation to maintenance for a child.

The procedure for the issuing of a claim for financial remedies which includes all financial orders (formerly known as 'ancillary relief') is found in FPR 2010 Part 9. The overriding objective is to enable the court to deal with cases justly, having regard to any welfare issues involved. The main steps of a standard financial remedy process are as follows:

(1)   Issuing the appropriate form;

(2)   Preparing financial disclosure;

(3)   First Appointment hearing at court;

(4)   Financial Dispute Resolution hearing at court ('FDR');

(5)   Final hearing at court.

Settlement may be achieved at any time during this process and the timetable can be compressed. For example, it is possible for the First Appointment to be converted into an FDR.

Issuing the appropriate form

[17.7] A notice of intention to proceed with an application for a financial order which has been made in a divorce petition or answer must be made by notice in a Form A or an application for a financial order or financial remedy by a respondent must be made in Form A1. When the court receives Form A it will fix a First Appointment not less than 12 weeks and not more than 16 weeks after the date of the filing of the notice.

All applicants wishing to issue relevant family proceedings (for example, financial remedy applications) will need to show that they have attended a mediation and information assessment meeting ('MIAM') with a mediator, unless one of the limited relevant exceptions applies to those proceedings (see the Children and Families Act 2014).

Preparing financial disclosure

[17.8] Prior to the First Appointment Hearing, which is usually listed for 30 minutes of court time, both parties must file and simultaneously exchange their financial disclosure in a Form E, to which the parties will attach prescribed financial documents. At least 14 days before the hearing of the First Appointment each party must file with the court:

- a concise statement of issues between the parties;
- a chronology of important dates during the marriage and litigation;
- a questionnaire setting out by reference to the concise statement of issues any further information or documentation requested from the other party;
- a notice stating whether that party will be in a position at the First Appointment Hearing to proceed on that occasion to a FDR appointment.

In *NG v SG (Appeal: Non-Disclosure)* [2011] EWHC 3270 (Fam), [2012] 1 FLR 1211, [2012] Fam Law 394, Mostyn J set out the court's approach where the disclosure given by one party has been materially deficient and where adverse inferences may be drawn. The importance of full and frank disclosure was emphasised by the Supreme Court in the two cases *Sharland v Sharland* [2015] UKSC 60-1 and *Gohil v Gohil* [2015] UKSC 61 which were heard together. See also *Hutchings-Whelan v Hutchings* [2012] EWCA Civ 38, [2012] 1 FCR 339, [2012] 2 FLR 108, and *Arbili v Arbili* [2015] EWCA Civ 542. In more extreme cases of non-disclosure, the defaulting party may be held to be in contempt of court as was the case in *Young v Young* [2013] All ER (D) 91 (Jan).

First Appointment

[17.9] The FPR 2010 explains that the hearing of the First Appointment must be conducted with the objective of defining the issues and saving costs. The judge will consider whether directions are required to value assets, to obtain further disclosure and to seek expert evidence. The majority of cases will then be set down for a FDR Appointment.

FDR Appointment

[17.10] The FPR 2010 provides that the FDR Appointment must be treated as a meeting held for the purposes of discussion and negotiation. Regard should be had to the Family Justice Council's document 'Financial Dispute Resolution Appointments: Best Practice Guidance'. The consequences of ignoring this guidance are illustrated by *X v X (financial remedies: preparation and presentation)* [2012] EWHC 538 (Fam), [2012] 2 FLR 590, [2012] Fam Law 804.

At least seven days before the FDR Appointment, the applicant must have filed all offers and proposals. The judge at the appointment will indicate to the parties how he or she would deal with the case at a final hearing. This will often precipitate agreement, as the parties are able to hear a judicial opinion on the merits of their respective cases. If an agreement is reached at the FDR Appointment then the judge will consider that agreement, and if appropriate, will make a court order in the terms agreed.

Final hearing

[17.11] If the FDR Appointment does not result in settlement the judge who conducted the appointment will have no further involvement with the case. A final hearing will be listed, usually for at least 1 day of court time. Directions may be given for further evidence, such as statements, required to prepare the case for final trial. At a final hearing a judge will hear appropriate evidence from both parties as well as any third party or expert witnesses and submissions by their representatives. The judge will then hand down judgment. Expert evidence is restricted to that which in the opinion of the court is 'necessary' to assist the court to resolve the proceedings (see Part 25 FPR 2010). See *Cooper-Hohn v Hohn* [2014] EWCA Civ 896 and *J v J* [2014] EWHC 3654 (Fam).

Interim applications

[17.12] At any time during the financial remedies process, the parties can make interim applications, for example:

• to deal with interim maintenance provision, which is called maintenance pending suit (see **17.15** below);
• to freeze vulnerable assets and prevent them from being spent or transferred offshore, which is called a s 37 application;
• to seek the court's assistance in the disclosure process, for example, if a party is refusing to disclose documents.

Costs

[17.13] General rules about costs and specific provision about costs in financial remedy proceedings are found in FPR 2010 Part 28. At each court appointment the parties must provide the court with details of the costs they have incurred during the litigation. Offers can be made throughout the proceedings on an open or a without prejudice basis. Only open offers will be considered at the final hearing for the purposes of determining whether the other party should pay costs.

Generally the court will decide that there should be no order for costs, save where there is relevant conduct that should be taken into account. The case of *J v J* [2009] EWHC 2654 (Fam), [2010] Fam Law 329 provides guidance where the court is considering making a costs order (see **17.31** below). In the case of *J v J* [2014] EWHC 3654 (Fam), Mostyn J ordered the husband to pay £50,000 towards his wife's costs to reflect his delinquency in the litigation in addition to equalising the costs differential. In *Thiry v Thiry* [2014] EWHC 4046 (Fam) Sir Peter Singer awarded the wife's costs of £456,000 on a summary assessment together with £500,000 for the purpose of funding her costs of any future litigation in Belgium brought by the husband in light of his conduct. Mostyn J in *Fisher Meredith v JH and PH (financial remedy: appeal: wasted costs)* [2012] EWHC 408 (Fam), [2012] 2 FCR 241 [2012] 2 FLR 536 set out the principles applicable to wasted costs applications where negligence is alleged: the party alleging wasted costs must not only persuade the court to exercise its discretion to make such an order but must prove that the solicitors failed to act with the competence reasonably expected of ordinary members of the solicitors' profession and must show a causal link between the solicitors' conduct and the wasted costs. In *Ezair v Ezair* [2012] EWCA Civ 893, [2013] 1 FLR 281 the Court of Appeal held that wasted costs orders should be kept separate and should not be included within lump sum payments. For the costs treatment of third parties, see *Hashem v Ali Shayif and Radfan Ltd* [2009] EWHC 864 (Fam), [2009] 2 FLR 896, [2009] Fam Law 665; *Baker v Rowe* [2009] EWCA Civ 1162, [2010] 1 FCR 413, [2010] 1 FLR 761 and *KSO v MJO* [2008] EWHC 3031 (Fam), [2009] 1 LFR 1036, [2009] Fam Law 185.

In the case of *Young v Young* [2013] EWHC 3637 (Fam), [2014] 2 FCR 495, the husband's non-disclosure had been so great that the judge's initial view was that the wife should be entitled to her costs on an indemnity basis. This was, however, only to the extent to which Mr Justice Moor considered that the case should have cost had it been properly conducted, and not the full £6.4m actually incurred by the wife. Also see *M v M (costs)* [2013] EWHC 3372 (Fam), [2014] 1 FLR 499 and *W v W* [2015] EWHC 1652 (Fam). Regarding the application of FPR rule 28.3(8) on appeal, see also the commentary of Moor J in *WD v HD* [2015] EWHC 1547 (Fam), [2016] Fam Law 160.

Bundles

There is now a universal practice for dealing with bundles for any hearing before the Family Court or the High Court (Family Division). Failure to comply may result in cost penalties. The consequences of non-compliance with Practice Direction 27A are illustrated in detail by Mostyn J in the case of *J v J* [2014] EWHC 3654 (Fam) and also by Holman J in the case of *Seagrove v Sullivan* [2014] EWHC 4110 (Fam). The comments made in these cases received the support of the President of the Family Division in the case of Re L (a child) [2015] EWFC 15. See also *Davis Solicitors LLP v Raja* [2015] EWHC 519 (QB).

Powers of the court

Menu of Orders and their tax implications

[17.14] On the granting of a divorce, decree of nullity or judicial separation or on the dissolution of a civil partnership the court has wide statutory powers under MCA 1973 to redistribute the assets of the parties.

Often in determining whether assets belong to one of the parties, so as to be available for distribution, reference is made to other areas of law. In addition, consideration should be given to whether the family court is the appropriate forum for this dispute. In *Edgerton v Edgerton* [2012] EWCA Civ 181, [2012] 1 WLR 2655, [2012] 1 FCR 421 it was held that unless technical issues arise outside familiar family law territory, it is better for the family court to determine all issues. There are, however, limits to this principle as demonstrated by *KK v MA* [2012] EWHC 788 (Fam).

Maintenance pending suit and legal services orders

[17.15] The court may make an order for maintenance pending suit under MCA 1973, s 22 whose application procedure is governed by the FPR 2010 Part 18. The payments will be made periodically (weekly, monthly etc) for a term beginning with the date of presentation of the application for a matrimonial or civil partnership order (formerly petition) and ending on the grant of the decree absolute. This form of maintenance is available to a spouse to provide for immediate rather than capital or long-term needs.

An impoverished party can apply to the court for a Legal Services Payment Order ('LSPO') under MCA 1973, s 22ZA. A court has the power to order one party to the marriage to pay to the other an amount for the purpose of enabling the applicant to obtain legal services for the purposes of divorce, nullity, judicial separation and associated financial proceedings. These payments may be made as a one-off payment, in instalments or by way of a deferred payment. Similar to an application for maintenance pending suit, the applicant will need to show that without the LSPO the applicant would not reasonably be able to obtain appropriate legal services; and that they are not reasonably able to secure a legal loan or obtain legal services by granting a charge over the assets to be recovered in the proceedings. See the case of *TL v ML* [2005] EWHC 2860 (Fam) for general guidance and also *SJ v RA* [2014] EWHC 4054 (Fam) for the Court's view on litigation loans with very high interest rates.

If a divorce eventually proceeds in a foreign jurisdiction, the court has no power to order the refund of maintenance pending suit already paid, see *M v M* [2009] EWCA Civ 1427, [2010] 1 FLR 1413, [2010] Fam Law 335.

In *MET v HAT* [2013] EWHC 4247 (Fam), [2014] 2 FLR 692, Mostyn J acknowledged the court's power to award maintenance pending suit even where the jurisdiction of the court to pronounce a decree has been challenged. The case of *Chai v Peng* [2014] EWHC 750 (Fam), [2014] Fam Law 809, involved a wife's application for further maintenance pending suit. Mr Justice

Holman stated that, regardless of jurisdiction (there was a dispute as to the correct forum for divorce proceedings), the husband would have to make fair payment to his wife.

In *Rubin v Rubin* [2014] EWHC 611 (Fam), [2014] Fam Law 797 a wife was unsuccessful in seeking costs which she had already incurred by way of a LSPO, which Mostyn J described to be 'designated as an interim order'. Mostyn J also summarised the principles applicable where an order is sought to fund costs in proceedings under Schedule 1 of the Children Act 1989, the Inheritance (Provision for Family and Dependents) Act 1975 or Part III of the Matrimonial and Family Proceedings Act 1984 (see also *Makarskaya v Korchagin* [2013] EWHC 4393 (Fam) in which the wife was denied a further LSPO having been granted one, two weeks previously). In *BC v DE* [2016] EWHC 1806 (Fam), the judge distinguished Mostyn J's guidance about orders for legal costs funding as set out in *Rubin* and made an order for costs already incurred in proceedings including proceedings which had arguably been concluded.

Periodical payments

[**17.16**] This type of order, under MCA 1973, s 23(1)(a), is the one most commonly recognised as a 'maintenance' order. Either party can be ordered to make payments to the other for such term as may be specified. A periodical payments order can be made once the decree nisi has been pronounced and will take effect on decree absolute. The order may continue until the death of the recipient or the payer or, if earlier, the remarriage of the recipient (MCA 1973, s 28(1)(b)). The periodical payments may be ordered for an extendable term of years or alternatively for a term which, pursuant to MCA 1973, s 28(1A), may not be extended (see *L v L (Financial Remedies: Deferred Clean Break)* [2011] EWHC 2207 (Fam), [2012] 1 FLR 1283 and *Chiva v Chiva* [2014] EWCA Civ 1558). Case law has confirmed that the quantum of maintenance should be assessed on needs alone (*B v S (Financial Remedy: Marital Property Regime)* [2012] EWHC 265 (Fam), [2012] 2 FCR 335, [2012] 2 FLR 502). The case of *Matthews v Matthews* [2013] EWCA Civ 1211 provides a commentary on nominal periodical payments orders as opposed to clean break orders.

The case of *CR v SR* [2013] EWHC 1155 (Fam), [2014] 1 FLR 186, [2013] Fam Law 938 emphasised that orders made must be affordable, and must not result in an imbalance between parties' respective future financial positions. Maintenance orders cannot be based too heavily on estimates of future income which may turn out not to be achieved.

The case of *Walker v Walker* [2013] EWHC 3973 (Fam) is an example of where a husband appealed a first instance decision on the grounds that his own income needs after payment of periodical payments to the wife and children had not been taken into consideration.

The case of *H v W* [2013] EWHC 4105 (Fam), [2014] Fam Law 445 provides guidance on the treatment of a spouse's future bonus payments when deciding an award for maintenance. It was held that, due to the uncertain nature of bonuses, setting a cap on maintenance payments deriving from bonuses is essential, and such payments can only be expressed in percentage terms.

In the case of *SS v NS*[2014] EWHC 4183, Mostyn J set out summary guidance of the principles to be applied upon an application for spousal maintenance. The case of *Murphy v Murphy* [2014] EWHC 2263 (Fam) provides guidance as to when a "step down" in maintenance is appropriate as does *Wright v Wright* [2015] EWCA Civ 201, [2015] Fam Law 523 in relation to the payee achieving independence.

A periodical payments order can be varied by further application to the court under MCA 1973, s 31 (see *N v N (Re Financial Proceedings)* [2011] EWCA Civ 940, [2012] 1 FLR 622, [2011] Fam Law 1069). Upon a variation application, the court has jurisdiction to make lump sum, property adjustment and pension-sharing orders in discharge of the maintenance order (see *Pearce v Pearce* [2003] EWCA Civ 1054, [2004] 1 WLR 68, [2003] 3 FCR 178 and *Mullins (Grocholewska) v Mullins* [2014] EWCA Civ 148, [2014] Fam Law 444). Furthermore, in cases where maintenance has been awarded on the basis of a compensation argument, the court can order for periodical payments to be varied upwards (see *McFarlane v McFarlane* [2009] EWHC 891 (Fam)); *Hvorostovsky v Hvorostovsky* [2009] EWCA Civ 791, [2009] 3 FCR 650, [2009] 2 FLR 1574); and *Yates v Yates* [2012] EWCA Civ 532, [2013] 2 FLR 1070). The effect of subsequent cohabitation with another party by the payee was considered in *Grey v Grey* [2009] EWCA 1424, [2010] 1 FCR 394, [2010] 1 FLR 1764, approving *Fleming v Fleming* [2003] EWCA Civ 1841, [2004] 1 FLR 667, [2004] Fam Law 174. See also *AB v CB* [2014] EWHC 2998 (Fam), [2014] All ER (D) 152 (Sep) and *Hart v Hart* [2016] EWCA Civ 497 regarding the effect of the payee's cohabitation following divorce. Notwithstanding social changes, cohabitation is not to be equated with marriage. In assessing the impact of cohabitation the court should have regard to the overall circumstances, including its financial consequences and duration.

In the case of *Aburn v Aburn* [2016] EWCA Civ 72, the Court of Appeal emphasised that where the case is based around the needs of a party, any future increase in the level of periodical payments must be justified on an informed basis, having regard to the paying party's ability to pay and the receiving party's future needs at the time of any proposed variation.

Secured periodical payments

[17.17] Under MCA 1973, s 23(1)(b), the court can order the payer of the periodical payments under **17.16** above to set aside a fund from which such payments are to be made, or to earmark assets to secure payment thereof. The court can specify the term of the periodical payments, but if they are to the former spouse this will not extend beyond the remarriage or the death of the recipient (MCA 1973, s 28(1)(b)). Essentially, this represents an order for the transfer of income-producing assets to trustees with the income to be used to pay maintenance to the other spouse. Once the obligation to pay maintenance ceases, the trust ends and the property reverts back to the transferor.

The advantage of such an order is that it continues for the duration of the payee's life and will not cease on the death of the payer. Also, the order secures the source of the payments where the payer's other assets diminish or, in an extreme case, where the payer becomes insolvent (although in the latter case it is always necessary to consider the full implications of the Insolvency Act 1986).

Tax implications of paying and receiving maintenance

[17.18] As far as income tax is concerned, the payment of maintenance under a court order or an agreement does not confer any benefit on the taxpayer (save in certain circumstances where one spouse or civil partner was born before 6 April 1935) and the receipt of the maintenance does not create any tax liability in the recipient's hands. The income remains that of the payer throughout.

For inheritance tax purposes, the date of the decree absolute rather than the date of separation is relevant. Up until that date, transfers between spouses are covered by the spouse exemption provided that the recipient spouse is UK-domiciled for inheritance tax purposes (or both spouses are non UK-domiciled for those purposes). Transfers from a UK domiciled spouse to a non-domiciled spouse will be exempt up to the exemption limit which currently is £325,000 (although for transfers on death occurring after 5 April 2017 this may be supplemented by an additional 'main residence nil rate amount'). It does not matter for these purposes that the spouses may no longer be living together. It should also be noted that a non-UK domiciled spouse may elect to be treated as UK domiciled for inheritance tax purposes. This is explained further at **17.23** below and in CHAPTER 21 UK RESIDENTS WITH MULTI-JURISDICTIONAL AFFAIRS.

Where maintenance is paid to a spouse under a court order, the exemption for transfers which are not gratuitous should apply (IHTA 1984, s 10). In 1975, the Senior Registrar of the Family Division issued a statement with the agreement of HMRC.

Alternatively, it can be argued that the exemption for dispositions for family maintenance under IHTA 1984, s 11 applies. This exemption covers transfers of value by one spouse to another, or to a former spouse. It will also cover transfers to children of either spouse where the transfer is for the maintenance of the recipient or the maintenance, education or training of the child who must be either under 18 or, if older, in full-time education or training.

Maintenance payments will not be within the scope of inheritance tax where either of the above exemptions or the exemption for normal expenditure out of income applies. If the payments do not fall within any of the exemptions they will be potentially exempt transfers which will become chargeable if the payer dies within seven years, subject to the £3,000 annual exemption.

Maintenance payments on a voluntary basis to a former spouse or to a child after the decree absolute will be potentially exempt transfers unless they fall within the exemption for dispositions for family maintenance, the exemption for normal expenditure out of income, or the £3,000 annual exemption.

Lump sums

[17.19] Pursuant to MCA 1973, s 23(1)(c)–(d) and CPA 2004, s 5, Part 2, the court can order a party to pay to the other, or to a child of the family, a lump sum or sums. In doing so the court will be guided by the factors set out in MCA 1973, s 25(2), including in the first instance whether the payer has the resources to meet such payments. A lump sum order may specify payment by instalments. A lump sum order cannot be varied by the court, but the court can vary, suspend or even discharge the instalments of a lump sum (see *Hamilton v Hamilton* [2013] EWCA Civ 13, [2013] Fam 292, [2013] 2 WLR 1440 which outlines the court's discretion to vary an order for a lump sum paid in instalments over time). A lump sum order is frequently made in conjunction with an order dealing with the matrimonial home.

A spouse is entitled to apply for one lump sum order only (although as mentioned above, the court does have power on an application to vary a periodical payments order to make a second lump sum order for capitalisation of periodical payments). Lump sum orders are also available for children, although they are rare. They may, for example, be relevant in the case of a child who is disabled.

Property adjustment orders

[17.20] Under MCA 1973, s 24 the court can order one party to transfer property to the other party or to a child. A property adjustment order is final, only one such order can be made and it is not possible to vary these orders (save as referred to above, the court has power to make a further property adjustment order on a variation of a periodical payments order).

The most common options open to the courts in respect of the family home have been as set out below. The Finance Act 2006 has had an impact on the popularity of *Mesher* and *Martin* orders because such orders will now normally create relevant property settlements. Although they may not constitute chargeable transfers (being within IHTA 1984, s 10 or s 11) such settlements may be subject to decennial and exit charges.

(i)   *Outright transfer.* It is unusual for a court to order an outright transfer of the family home if it is the only family asset.

(ii)   *Mesher orders.* A court can order that the parties retain shares in the former home, but defer the sale of the house until the earlier of any number of negotiated terminating events, such as the youngest child reaching 18 or the wife co-habiting for more than six months, remarrying or dying. This is called a *Mesher order.* This type of order can leave the spouse who remains in the property very vulnerable if the house must be sold once the youngest child attains 18.

(iii)   *Martin orders.* A *Martin* order is often considered by the court to be fairer than a *Mesher* order. The conditions are generally the same with the important distinction that there is no requirement to move once the youngest child attains 18. The order takes the form of a settlement.

(iv)   *Charge back.* A variation on *Mesher* and *Martin* orders involves the outright transfer of the house to the occupying spouse, but the house is charged with a payment in favour of the other spouse, the charge not to be realised until a specified event. This charge-back can be on the basis of:

      •   a charge of a fixed percentage of the market value on sale;

- • a charge of a percentage of the net market value at the time of the order plus interest accrued at an appropriate rate; or
- • a charge of a percentage of the net market value at the time of the order, index-linked to a property-based index.

There are potential drawbacks to the first two of these bases. The first basis provides no incentive for the occupying spouse to improve the property and, in fact, the occupying spouse could allow the property to deteriorate (unless safeguards are added to the order). The second basis is arbitrary and takes no account of fluctuations in the property market. The third basis appears the fairest.

(v) *Order for sale.* This is commonly encountered where the former matrimonial home is large or more luxurious than is justified by the needs of the occupying spouse or the non-occupying spouse has greater need of the capital represented by the house. The order may contain consequential and supplementary provisions directing, for example who is to have conduct of the sale and how the price is to be fixed. In the rare circumstances where there is no realistic chance that either party would be able to obtain an outright transfer or a deferred sale in the financial remedy proceedings, the court can make an interim order for sale under the Trusts of Land and Appointment of Trustees Act 1996 (see *Smith (Miller) v Smith (Miller)* [2009] EWCA Civ 1297, [2010] 1 FLR 1402, [2010] Fam Law 142).

Tax implications of transfers between spouses

Capital gains tax

[17.21] While a husband and wife are living together, (as defined in TCGA 1992, s 288(3) and ITA 2007, s 1011) and before the decree absolute, transfers between them are deemed to be made for a consideration which gives rise to neither a gain, nor a loss (TCGA 1992, s 58). The transferee spouse takes over the base value. In effect, the transferee spouse steps into the shoes of the transferor spouse in relation to the asset for capital gains tax purposes. The no gain, no loss rule cannot be disapplied. Any actual consideration for the transfer is ignored. This relief applies for the years up to and including the tax year of separation but does not apply in subsequent years. While the spouses are separated but not divorced, they will be connected persons for capital gains tax. This means that transfers between them will be deemed to be at full market value. Once the couple divorce, they will normally cease to be connected and transfers will be for actual consideration, if any.

The matrimonial home will be exempt from capital gains tax provided it was the only or main residence of the transferring spouse throughout the period of ownership. TCGA 1992, s 225B provides that the home may be regarded as continuing to be the only or main residence of the transferring spouse from the date that spouse ceased to occupy the house until the date of transfer. However, certain conditions need to be satisfied:

- • the house must be transferred to the former spouse as part of the agreement made in contemplation of, or in connection with the dissolution or annulment of the marriage or civil partnership or a judicial separation;

- it must have remained the only or main residence of the former spouse; and
- the transferring spouse must not have elected in the meantime for some other house to be treated as his or her only or main residence.

It should be remembered that the last 18 months of ownership always count as a period of residence, even if a new qualifying residence has been acquired (TCGA 1992, s 223). Before 6 April 2014, the relevant period was 36 months. In certain circumstances (for example, where job-related accommodation is provided) other periods of absence are also ignored. In some cases, the house may be transferred after a period considerably in excess of 18 months after the transferring spouse leaves it, in which case a time-apportioned part of the gain will be assessable. This gain may, however, be covered by the annual exemption, which for 2016/17 is £11,100. If a house is jointly owned, both spouses must have resided in it throughout the period of ownership for the exemption to apply. If this is not the case, it should be noted that capital gains tax will be payable at a rate of either 18% or 28% (because it is a gain on residential property not qualifying for main residence relief).

In some cases, it may in fact be more advantageous not to claim relief under TCGA 1992, s 225B. If the transferring spouse has another property eligible for relief it may be better to make the transfer of the former home to the other spouse within 18 months of leaving the former matrimonial home. Otherwise, a proportion of the relief on the new house may be lost.

The transferring spouse may retain an interest in the matrimonial home being transferred. This may arise from a mutual agreement or an order of the court (see above). If the transferring spouse is to receive a specified sum (not exceeding his or her current entitlement), but postponed until the earliest of certain events, no capital gains tax liability arises when the sum is paid because main residence relief was due when the interest in the home was transferred to the remaining spouse. This would apply, for example, where the former matrimonial home is transferred to the remaining spouse in return for a cash sum paid from the proceeds of its eventual sale. However, if the non-occupying spouse holds a charge for a percentage of the equity on a future sale, a capital gains tax liability could arise when paid. Arguably, the deferred charge is a new chargeable asset for capital gains tax purposes (following the decision in *Marren (Inspector of Taxes) v Ingles*, [1980] 3 All ER 95, [1980] STC 500, HL) and the realisation of the charge will constitute a disposal. However, there is a contrary argument that such a secured charge is in reality a debt and, as such, no capital gains tax charge arises on its realisation. However, the issues are by no means clear cut and each case will turn on its own circumstances.

With regard to a *Mesher* order, HMRC considers that such an order creates a settlement for capital gains tax purposes (see Capital Gains Tax Manual para CG65365). At the date of the order the spouses are treated as disposing of the property to trustees at market value. Any gain would be exempt provided that no more than 18 months had passed since the non-occupying spouse left the family home permanently. When the *Mesher* order lapses there will be a deemed disposal and reacquisition under TCGA 1992, s 71 on termination of the settlement. However, an exemption may be available as the beneficiary will have occupied the property throughout the period of ownership by the trustees (TCGA 1992, s 225).

Inheritance tax

[17.22] As noted above, a *Mesher* order may be regarded as a settlement for capital gains tax purposes. It is likely that HMRC may also regard a *Mesher* order as a settlement for inheritance tax purposes which could have inheritance tax consequences for the trustees. The settlement of any property will be a settlement of relevant property unless the settlement falls within one of the categories listed in **6.8**. The settlement will be a chargeable transfer (subject to a 20% charge to inheritance tax) unless the exemption for transfers which are not gratuitous (IHTA 1984, s 10) or the exemption covering dispositions for family maintenance (IHTA 1984, s 11) applies. Decennial and exit charges may arise and therefore the funding of these charges will need to be agreed.

For inheritance tax purposes the transfer of the matrimonial home between separated, but not divorced, spouses falls within the spouse exemption. After the decree absolute has been made, transfers will be potentially exempt transfers unless it can be shown, as is generally the case, that either of the exemptions under IHTA 1984, s 10 or s 11 applies.

It would be prudent to ensure that all property transfers are effected prior to the decree absolute to take advantage of the spouse exemption.

Surviving spouses or civil partners will be able to claim the proportion of available nil rate band (£325,000 for 2016/17) unused by the first spouse or civil partner on their death provided they were married or in a civil partnership at the time of the first death. This may be supplemented, from 6 April 2017 by the additional 'residence nil rate amount' (RNRA) in relevant circumstances. The maximum RNRA will be £100,000 for 2017/18, £125,000 for 2018/19, £150,000 for 2019/20 and £175,000 for 2020/21.

If 100% of the nil rate band of the first to die is available, the nil rate band available to the survivor is effectively doubled. It is not possible to exceed this level of allowance, even in the case of a widow or widower remarrying. Separated couples are able to benefit from a transfer of the unused nil rate band. Divorce, however, will extinguish the ability for any unused nil rate band to be transferred. This is discussed in more detail in **CHAPTER 18 MAKING A WILL**.

Overseas aspects – capital gains tax and inheritance tax implications

[17.23] In a tax year following the year of separation, a spouse who is not resident in the UK who transfers property to his or her former spouse will generally not be liable to capital gains tax. However, non-resident capital gains tax may be payable on a disposal of UK residential property by a non-UK resident in respect of any gain arising from 6 April 2015 to the disposal date. Such disposals are reportable to HMRC and the tax is payable within 30 days. Where there is a disposal of UK residential property between a resident and a non-resident spouse the exemption under TCGA 1992, s 58 will apply. Main residence relief will be available to a non-resident owner of UK residential property, although the rules have been amended and require a minimum level of use (broadly 90 overnight stays in each tax year for which relief is claimed).

Being not resident in the UK can provide scope for tax planning depending on the nature of the assets which is considered elsewhere in this book.

Where the inheritance tax spouse exemption is in point, it is necessary to bear in mind that a transfer to a non-UK domiciled spouse by a UK-domiciled individual is only exempt up to the exemption limit which is currently £325,000. Together with the transferring spouse's own nil rate band of £325,000 (and ignoring other potential exemptions and reliefs), up to £650,000 of property may pass from a UK domiciliary to a non-UK domiciled spouse free of inheritance tax. A non-UK domiciled spouse is able to elect to be treated as UK domiciled for inheritance tax purposes (such that the spouse exemption becomes unlimited). The election is for inheritance tax purposes only. It takes effect from the date specified in the election notice (which can be the date of the election itself or up to seven years prior to a lifetime election though the couple need not have been married throughout the seven years). The election cannot be revoked (although it will automatically cease to have effect after a period of four successive tax years of non-UK residence by the electing spouse).

In some cases, where one or both spouses are beneficiaries of an offshore trust, it should be remembered that, depending on their personal circumstances, income tax or capital gains tax may be payable in respect of any payments made to them from the trust as part of the divorce agreement.

Stamp duty land tax and stamp duty

[17.24] Stamp duty is only chargeable under FA 1999, Sch 13 on instruments relating to stock or marketable securities. Stamp duty land tax is payable in relation to land.

There are exemptions from both stamp duty and stamp duty land tax on the conveyance or transfer from one party to a marriage to the other in certain circumstances (Stamp Duty (Exempt Instruments) Regulations 1987 (SI 1987/516) and FA 2003, Sch 3, para 3). There may however, be some circumstances where it is not clear if a transfer is for consideration or not and so care needs to be taken.

Council tax

[17.25] Where the original council tax demand has been issued in joint names, the departing spouse may be able to negotiate a cessation of joint liability with the local authority at the time he or she leaves the property on a permanent basis. Otherwise joint liability will cease on grant of the decree absolute.

Where a separation has taken place and the remaining spouse can prove himself or herself to be the sole adult occupant, a discount of 25% is available.

Transfers of other property

[17.26] The court can order property other than the matrimonial home or cash sums to be transferred between the spouses. Alternatively, this may be done by mutual agreement. In either event, the capital gains tax and inheritance tax implications will broadly be the same as those considered above except for the absence of main residence relief.

A transfer of assets between separated spouses (after the tax year of separation itself) will be a disposal which, because spouses are connected persons, will be deemed not to be a bargain at arm's length (TCGA 1992, s 18(2)). The disposal will therefore be deemed to take place at market value. If the recipient spouse gives no actual consideration for the acquisition of the asset (or gives consideration not exceeding the base cost of the asset), hold-over relief under TCGA 1992, s 165 may be available (relief under TCGA 1992, s 260 will not be available) but only if the asset is a business asset. It does not, therefore, relate to any other assets such as residential property or works of art. A business asset is defined as an asset or an interest in an asset used for the purposes of a trade, profession or vocation carried on by an individual or in partnership or by a company in which an individual claiming relief holds at least 5% of the voting rights, shares or securities not listed on a recognised stock exchange and shares in a company in which the individual holds more than 5% of the voting rights. Hold-over relief will be available on shares in a listed company where the individual owns more than 5% of the voting rights and on agricultural property for the purposes of inheritance tax. The availability of entrepreneur's relief may also be a relevant consideration where there are business assets.

It may not, however, be in the interests of the recipient spouse to join in a hold-over election because he or she will receive the assets at the transferor's original low base cost. The question arises as to whether consideration is given by the parties. The disposal of an asset from one spouse or civil partner to the other is, where there is no recourse to the courts, usually made in exchange for a surrender by the donee of rights which they would otherwise be able to exercise to obtain alternative financial provision. HMRC takes the view 'that the value of the rights surrendered represents actual consideration of an amount which would reduce the gain potentially eligible for hold-over relief to nil.' (HMRC Capital Gains Manual, para CG67192). Unless the parties are able to demonstrate that there was a substantial gratuitous element in the transfer so that no consideration passed in the form of surrendered rights, hold-over relief will not be available. It is HMRC's view that where assets are transferred between divorcing partners or civil partners of a dissolved civil partnership by reason of a court order the relief should not be restricted because actual consideration has been given by the transferee. There must however be a court order, which includes a consent order formally ratifying an agreement reached by the parties.

The capital gains tax liability is deferred and passes to the recipient which may be payable on a future disposal.

Where a court makes a financial remedy order under MCA 1973, including transfer of rights under a life assurance policy from one spouse to another, or formally approves an agreement reached by divorcing parties that includes a transfer of assets including a life assurance policy, then the transferee of the life assurance policy does not give consideration in money or money's worth for the transfer and, as a result, no chargeable event gain can arise on the transfer (see HMRC Insurance Policyholder Taxation Manual, para 7370).

Pension sharing orders

[17.27] Pension sharing orders can be made by the courts under the Welfare Reform and Pensions Act 1999 ('WRPA 1999'), s 85 where a petition for divorce or nullity is filed. This was extended to the dissolution of civil partnerships for same-sex couples following the introduction of the CPA 2004. Pension sharing orders are not available in judicial separation proceedings.

The courts have the ability to split an existing pension arrangement and divide it between parties following divorce, nullity or dissolution proceedings. The pension credit received by the payee can either be invested into the same scheme from which it came (an internal transfer), or alternatively it can be transferred to a new scheme (an external transfer).

The powers of the court extend to making 'one or more' pension sharing orders in relation to the marriage. MCA 1973, s 21A defines a pension sharing order as:

> 'an order which:
>
> (a)   provides that one party's—
>   (i)   shareable rights under a specified pension arrangement, or
>   (ii)   shareable State scheme rights,
>   be subject to pension sharing for the benefit of the other party, and
> (b)   specifies the percentage value to be transferred.'

Advisers have to consider:

(i)   the value of all those rights — the cash equivalent transfer value (CETV) and a percentage of that being transferred from one spouse to the other (WRPA 1999, s 29(2));

(ii)   what rights the recipient spouse can derive from the percentage transferred; and

(iii)   what rights will be left with the other spouse.

CETV is the sole method of valuation under WRPA 1999; in the case of a pension in payment the valuation is called the cash equivalent of benefits (CEB) (Pensions on Divorce (Provision of Information) Regulations 2000, reg 3). Only benefits at the 'valuation date' can be taken into account by the court. The rules for calculating CETV assume employees' service terminates on the valuation date and does not take into account projected increases to the pension fund for possible future service. The pension administrators will implement the pension share within four months of the decree absolute or court order, whichever is the later.

Pension sharing orders can be made over:

* personal pension plans;
* retirement annuity contracts;
* employer's pension schemes (whether money purchase or final salary schemes);
* small self-administered schemes;
* services pension schemes;
* pension plans which are the product of a pension sharing order from a previous marriage;
* pension schemes without HMRC approval (eg employers funded arrangements);
* pension in payment; and
* an annuity or insurance policy which provides pension benefits but not widows/dependants pension in payment.

The order must provide for a percentage of the pension to be shared. It is not sufficient to insert wording to describe a percentage which yielded a particular amount (*H v H* [2009] EWHC 3739 (Fam), [2010] 2 FLR 173, [2010] Fam Law 575).

The court does not have power to make a pension sharing order over a pension scheme which is:

(i)   subject to a pensions attachment order from a previous marriage; or
(ii)   subject to a pensions attachment order from the current marriage.

A pension provided by a pension sharing order has the same tax treatment as any other pension scheme. The recipient spouse will be entitled to a tax free lump sum on drawing benefits and will be taxed on the pension payable as income. Death in service benefits will pass outside the estate for tax purposes provided the right of nomination has been properly used or they are written in trust.

Generally speaking a pension sharing order made under an approved pension scheme will not be at risk of falling into the hands of the trustee in bankruptcy. Even if it is determined that a former spouse has made excessive contributions to a pension prior to the presentation of the bankruptcy petition then they are deemed to have been made from the bankrupt member's portion of the shared pension and should be recovered from that portion. However, if the bankrupt member's rights are exhausted, the trustee could then proceed against the spouse.

The Pensions Act 2014 has introduced significant changes to UK pensions, providing greater flexibility as to how and when benefits are taken including the ability to withdraw the entire fund in one lump sum. These changes have led to the family courts adopting a new approach to the treatment of pension rights in financial remedy cases. In larger money cases a trend has developed which has seen pensions treated as disposable cash assets (for example *SJR v RA* [2014] EWHC 4054 (Fam) and *JP v SL* [2015] EWHC 555).

Pension attachment

[17.28] The court still has the power to make immediate or deferred lump sum orders and/or periodical payments orders taking effect against any of the following benefits under a pension scheme:

- members retirement pension;
- lump sum commutation;
- death in service lump sum;
- guaranteed lump sum on death in retirement (MCA 1973, ss 25B–25D).

These are known as pension attachment orders (previously known as earmarking) and are less favoured by applicants than pension sharing orders. Unlike pension sharing orders, pension attachment orders are available in judicial separation proceedings. Orders made under MCA 1973, ss 25B–25D do not effect a true pension split - they merely attach the member's own benefits. The pension continues to be taxed as the member's income while the earmarked maintenance is tax free in the hands of the recipient. An earmarking order is one kind of financial provision order and, as in the case of maintenance, it lasts only during the joint lives of the parties or until the remarriage of the recipient.

Orders relating to children

[17.29] Currently there are two regimes covering financial provision for children. The Child Support Agency (CSA), which was previously the only regime, is currently being phased out in favour of the Child Maintenance Service (CMS). All new applications for maintenance calculations are dealt with by the CMS.

There are subtle differences between the CSA and the CMS, not least because the CSA and the CMS use different formulas in calculating the level of maintenance payable. The CMS is based on an assessment of the payer's gross (rather than net) income. It is designed to be a safety net for difficult cases where parents have been unable to agree the level of child maintenance. Using information from HMRC together with other data, CMS will calculate the amount of maintenance that should be paid by the non-resident parent. The CMS charge a £20 application fee in addition to their collection fee.

The methods of enforcement against non-paying parents include the ability to make a regular deduction order or a lump sum deduction order on the payer's bank account irrespective of whether it is a joint account to collect maintenance or record arrears, the imposition of a curfew and the ability to apply to the magistrates' court for an individual to be disqualified from holding or obtaining a passport or driving licence.

Further details can be found on the Child Maintenance Options website at www.cmoptions.org which has been set up to provide impartial information and support to help both parents make informed choices about child maintenance. There is also a child maintenance calculator which can be found at www.gov.uk/calculate-your-child-maintenance.

School and university fees

[17.30] School and university fees can be an important element in any financial settlement and a court has the power to make an order for payment of the school fees of a child. At first sight, it may appear sufficient to calculate a global figure for the maintenance of a child. However, the provision for fees can be more complex. For example, the level of fees will increase over time and the frequency of payments should be co-ordinated with the school's terms.

There is no tax advantage in having a school fees order.

Factors taken into account by the court

Case law

Equality

[17.31] In his leading speech in the House of Lords' decision in the seminal case of *White v White* [2001] 1 AC 596, [2001] 1 All ER 1, Lord Nicholls said (para 2):

> 'The Matrimonial Causes Act 1973 confers wide discretionary powers on the courts over all the property of the husband and the wife. This appeal raises questions about how the courts should exercise these powers in so-called "big money" cases, where the assets available exceed the parties' financial needs for housing and income.'

The judgment reasserts that the objective of the MCA 1973 is to achieve a fair outcome and, to achieve this objective, there must be no discrimination between a husband and wife on divorce. Lord Nicholls found that if a judgment does provide for an unequal distribution then the judge needs to check the decision against a yardstick of equality of division and provide articulated, good reasons for the departure, to try to avoid discrimination between the parties. However, the court shied away from a legal presumption of equal division of assets. It ended the reign of the test of reasonable requirements, which had effectively put an upper limit on the capital award payable, usually to the wife, once her reasonable requirements had been met. The court robustly addressed the question: 'where the assets exceed the financial needs of both parties, why should the surplus belong solely to the husband?' (para 35)

Over the next five years, the judiciary, practitioners and academics wrestled with the 'yardstick of equality' in interpreting the *White v White* judgment. Then in May 2006, less than six years after *White*, the House of Lords heard the cases of *Miller v Miller; McFarlane v McFarlane* [2006] UKHL 24, [2006] 2 AC 618, [2006] 3 All ER 1 from which the principles of needs, compensation and sharing have been distilled. These are now applicable to financial remedy cases. Many cases fall at the needs hurdle, when parties do not have the luxury of surplus funds to which the concepts of compensation and sharing should be applied (see *Tattersall v Tattersall* [2013] EWCA Civ 774, [2013] 3 FCR 453, [2014] 1 FLR 997 for a recent example).

Financial needs

[17.32] The Law Commission in their report published on 27 February 2014 recommended that the Family Justice Council provide guidance to clarify the law relating to 'financial needs', to ensure that the law is applied consistently by the courts and to assist those without legal representation. It also suggested investigating the possibility of a formulaic approach in calculating the financial needs to assist negotiations between the parties. Where there is a surplus, however, the courts will consider compensation to redress any economic disparity or 'relationship generated disadvantage' (para 140) and a sharing of the 'fruits of the matrimonial partnership' (para 141). As a result of the report, the Divorce (Financial Provision) Bill 2015 has been published which, at the time of writing has had its first reading in the House of Lords but the general debate on all aspects of the Bill is yet to be scheduled.

This continues to be a key area of debate for family law practitioners. The Family Justice Council has produced a publication entitled 'Guidance on "Financial Needs" on Divorce' dated June 2016, which provides guidance identifying the key points arising from the Law Commission's report.

The case of *Estrade Juffali v Juffali* [2016] EWHC 1684 emphasises the principle that in appropriate cases the court should assess its award on the basis that needs for housing and income should reduce in the future.

There are differing opinions amongst practitioners as to the continuing relevance of the principle of compensation in financial remedy cases. In the case of *SA v PA* [2014] EWHC 392 (Fam), Mostyn J set out guidelines as to the use of the principle of compensation. See also *H v H (Periodical Payments: Variation: Clean Break)* [2014] EWHC 760 (Fam) for the treatment of the principle and also *H v H* [2014] EWCA Civ 1523.

Inherited/gifted assets

[**17.33**] Uncertainty abounds until these concepts have been interpreted through practical application by the courts. As regards inheritance, which in *White* included 'property acquired during the marriage by one spouse by gift or succession or as a beneficiary under a trust' (para 41), this is likely to be labelled as 'non-matrimonial property' as opposed to 'matrimonial property' or 'matrimonial acquest'. The general view is that non-matrimonial property will have to be included in the pot of available assets if needs require this.

Turning to the case law in this area, further guidance is found in the Court of Appeal judgment in *Charman v Charman* [2007] EWCA Civ 503, 9 ITELR 913, [2007] 2 FCR 217 which held that consideration of the equal sharing principle need no longer take place at the end of the statutory exercise, but is instead the presumption from the start. To 'the extent that their property is non-matrimonial, there is likely to be better reason for departure from equality.' (para 66). Another illustration is provided by the decision in *L v L (Ancillary Relief)* [2008] Fam Law 12 where the sharing principle was applied but the judge found there was good reason to depart from equality based on the assets the husband had brought into the relationship and an inheritance he had received. In the Court of Appeal decision in *Robson v Robson* [2010] EWCA Civ 1171, [2011] 3 FCR 625, [2011] 1 FLR 751 (previously reported as *R v R* [2009] EWHC 1267 (Fam)) Ward LJ set out useful guidance as to how the courts should approach high net worth cases where a substantial proportion of the assets is inherited. Both the source and the nature of the inheritance are relevant and may provide a good reason to depart from the principle of equality.

The case of *AR v AR (Ancillary Relief: Inheritance)* [2011] EWHC 2717 (Fam), [2012] 2 FLR 1, [2011] 44 LS Gaz R 19 illustrates that inheritances and assets received by way of gift can be shared but otherwise, the fate of that asset, and the applicability of the sharing concept, depends on a whole raft of factors, including the length of marriage. In *Y v Y* [2012] EWHC 2063 (Fam), [2013]

2 FLR 924, [2013] Fam Law 535 where a needs-based award involved using inherited assets to cover the award. In *Davies v Davies* [2012] EWCA 1641, [2013] 1 FCR 459 the court had to determine what proportion of the assets was non-matrimonial property.

Special contribution

[17.34] In *Evans v Evans* [2013] EWHC 506 (Fam), [2013] 2 FLR 999, [2013] Fam Law 958, Moylan J noted that the husband's special contribution was a form of conduct, and so it would be inequitable for it to be disregarded by the court. Whether or not a party's contribution warranted a departure from equality should depend on a 'striking evidential foundation which so clearly stands out that the question almost answers itself'.

The case of *SK v TK* [2013] EWHC 834 (Fam) involved a husband who had done extremely well in business but nevertheless failed to persuade the Court of his "exceptional" contribution. In contrast, in the case of *Cooper-Hohn v Hohn* [2014] EWHC 4122 (Fam), the husband was described as a "genius" in his field and Roberts J ordered that there should be a departure from equality based on his special contribution. She did not define what could be classified as a special contribution, but set out a checklist of specific questions to answer in this scenario. In *Gray v Work* [2015] EWHC 834 (Fam), the Court of Appeal considered that a successful claim to a special contribution required an exceptional quality and that hard work alone did not meet this threshold. This decision has been appealed and it is understood that it will be considered by the Court of Appeal in February 2017.

In the case of *Robertson v Robertson* [2016] EWHC 613 (Fam), the husband was worth an estimated £219m. The judge rejected the husband's assertion of special contribution, emphasising that a special contribution must be un-matched and in this case the wife was an 'excellent home-maker'. This case suggests that contributions to the home are as valuable as financial endeavours.

Treatment of bonuses

[17.35] *Since Miller and McFarlane* the courts have sought to apply the reasoning expounded in those cases. In *H v H* [2007] EWHC 459 (Fam), [2008] 2 FCR 714, [2007] 2 FLR 548, Charles J addressed the distinction between matrimonial and non-matrimonial property in a case involving substantial bonuses. The judge concluded that matrimonial property should be assessed at the date when the 'mutual support' of a marriage is at an end and found in that case that a bonus was no longer matrimonial property. The judgment includes a detailed analysis of the law on this issue.

While the Law Commission in their Consultation Paper on Matrimonial Property, Needs and Agreements published in February 2014 made no recommendations on this issue, it did note that there is considerable uncertainty surrounding property such as post-separation bonuses, stating that such bonuses acquired during the marriage are generally regarded as matrimonial property and therefore shared, subject to the courts' discretion.

Post-separation accrual

[17.36] It is appropriate to take into account the increased value of a business post-separation if it represents latent growth (*Jones v Jones* [2011] EWCA Civ 41, [2011] 1 FCR 242, [2011] 1 FLR 1723 and *SK v WL* [2010] EWHC 3768 (Fam), [2011] 1 FLR 1471, [2011] Fam Law 339 and *Evans v Evans* [2013] EWHC 506 (Fam), [2013] Fam Law 958, 157 Sol Jo (no 12) 35). In *Cooper-Hohn v Hohn* [2014] EWHC 4122 (Fam), the assets had almost doubled in value between the date of separation and the final hearing. Although the husband's post-separation endeavours could not be ignored, it was not possible to identify a "bright line" delineating matrimonial from non-matrimonial property. The wife received a share of the post-separation accrual as part of her overall award. In *JL v SL (No 3) (post-judgment amplification)* [2015] EWHC 555 (Fam), [2015] 2 FLR 1220, [2015] Fam Law 521, Mostyn J identified three key principles in dealing with post-separation accruals.

In the case of *JS v RS* [2015] EWHC 2921 (Fam), [2016] Fam Law 17, there was a seven-year delay between the parties' separation and the application for financial remedy during which it was shown that there had been more than simply passive growth in the post-separation accrual. As a result, the court held that the husband's efforts should be reflected although the wife still had some entitlement to a share, resulting in a division of 60% to the husband and the remaining 40% to be shared equally between the parties.

See also the cases of *B v B* [2016] EWHC 210 (Fam) and *D v D* [2015] EWHC 1393 (Fam) dealing with the treatment of post-separation accrual.

Pre-marital assets

[17.37] The court will have regard to the nature of the assets when determining how they should be divided. One such consideration that has been examined at length in case law is the question of assets held prior to marriage, as opposed to assets acquired during the marriage. The argument that assets were held prior to the marriage may be used by those seeking to exclude such assets from division between the parties.

In *N v F (Financial Orders: Pre-Acquired Wealth)* [2011] EWHC 586 (Fam), [2012] 1 FCR 139, [2011] 2 FLR 533 Mostyn J felt that a two-step approach was appropriate to the treatment of pre-marital property, and whether the existence of pre-marital property should be reflected at all in the award would depend on factors such as the duration of the marriage and the intermingling of marital property with pre-marital property. The court should then determine how much of the pre-marital property should be excluded and how the remaining marital property should be divided equally between the parties. The fairness of the final award should be tested by reference to the overall percentage technique (adjusting the award from 50% of the total assets).

Mostyn J's analysis in *N v F* reflected the approach adopted by Wilson LJ in *Jones v Jones* [2011] EWCA Civ 41, [2011] 1 FCR 242, [2011] 1 FLR 1723. The case of *FZ v SZ (Ancillary Relief: Conduct)* [2010] EWHC 1630 (Fam), [2011] 1 FLR 64, [2010] Fam Law 1259 is a further example of Mostyn J's adoption of the two-stage approach to deal with a husband's pre-acquired assets. In the case of *Robertson v Robertson* [2016] EWHC 613 (Fam), Holman J considered the formulaic approach adopted in *Jones* as opposed to the exercise of broad judicial discretion under MCA 1973, s 25 and ultimately followed the latter approach.

It was decided by Sir Hugh Bennett in *AC v DC (No 2)* [2012] EWHC 2420 (Fam), [2013] 2 FLR 1499 that it would not be fair if none of a husband's pre-cohabitation wealth was excluded. The husband's shares had not been formally valued at the time of the marriage, however in a pre-nuptial agreement the shares had been given a value of £4 million. The husband was prohibited from resiling from that figure at the time of the proceedings.

The modest needs of the applicant husband in *K v L* [2011] EWCA Civ 550, [2011] 3 All ER 733, [2012] 1 WLR 306 impacted strongly on the Court of Appeal's decision to uphold an award of £5m in the context of a 20-year marriage and a total asset base of £59m. The wife owned shares in a family business which she had inherited nearly 20 years before the marriage and which had never been intermingled with the marital property. The value of the wife's share of the business represented over 95% of the total asset base yet the couple enjoyed a relatively modest lifestyle, living in a £300,000 house and spending £80,000 a year. The husband argued that following on from guidance in *Charman* a recognition of a 'special contribution' should not cause a departure from the equality principle of more than two-thirds/one-third. The Court of Appeal found that although non-marital property fell within the sharing principle, equal division was not the ordinary consequence of its application and that where the husband's needs had been met it was unnecessary to award him a significant share of the non-marital property. In the case of *S v AG (Financial Remedy: Lottery Prize)* [2011] EWHC 2637 (Fam), [2011] 3 FCR 523, [2012] 1 FLR 651, Mostyn J found that whilst a wife's lottery winnings were non-matrimonial property, the proportion of the winnings which had been used to purchase a matrimonial home had been converted into matrimonial property. However, the source of capital and the fact that the husband had only lived in the property for a short period justified a departure from equality.

The Law Commission in their Consultation Paper on Matrimonial Property, Needs and Agreements, without making any recommendations, said that the arguments for treating a solely-owned, pre-acquired family home as non-matrimonial property are at their strongest when that home is inherited (particularly when it has been in the family for generations).

Civil partnerships

[17.38] The case of *Lawrence v Gallagher* [2012] EWCA Civ 394, [2012] 1 FCR 557, [2012] 2 FLR 643 was the first reported case dealing with the treatment of assets on the dissolution of a civil partnership to reach the Court of Appeal. The Court of Appeal held that the criteria for calculating a financial settlement are identical to the matrimonial sharing principle used in divorce cases.

Set aside and Barder events

[17.39] If there is a significant and unforeseen supervening event in relation to the value of assets and/or circumstances since a financial remedies order was made, an application may be made for a Barder order under *Barder v Barder (Caluori Intervening)* [1988] AC 20, [1987] 2 All ER 440, HL. The impact of the recession on the value of assets whether shares or real property has not been considered to be a *Barder* event sufficient to revisit the original order. In *Myerson v Myerson* [2009] EWCA Civ 282, [2009] 2 FCR 1, [2009] 2 FLR 147 the Court of Appeal held that the fact that the husband's company shares had plummeted in value from £2.99 to 27.5p per share did not constitute a *Barder* event. In *S v S* [2013] EWHC 991 (Fam), [2013] 2 FLR 1598, [2013] Fam Law 960 the husband did not disclose that the company, of which he was a shareholder, was planning a stock market flotation (the sharing of this shareholding had been the issue in the case). The wife unsuccessfully sought to reopen proceedings because the court took the view that if proper disclosure had taken place the outcome would not have been substantially different. See also *Judge v Judge* [2008] EWCA Civ 1458, [2009] 2 FCR 158, [2009] 1 FLR 1287, and *Walkden v Walkden* [2009] EWCA Civ 627, [2010] 1 FLR 174, [2009] Fam Law 1023. In *Critchell v Critchell* [2015] EWCA Civ 436, the Court of Appeal restated the application of the principle in the *Barder* case and held that the husband's inheritance had invalidated the basis upon which the consent order in question had been made. The case of *WA v Executors of the estate of HA and Others* [2015] EWHC 2233 (Fam) illustrates the effect of the husband's suicide shortly after the making of a consent order.

In *MAP v RAP* [2013] EWHC 4784 (Fam) Mostyn J clarified the procedure to be used in applications to invalidate a consent order. Where there is no real challenge to the validity of the order (for example, for lack of capacity, as in this case), the procedure is a set aside application. Where the challenge relates to the content of the order (for example a *Barder* event or non-disclosure) the procedure is by way of appeal.

The cases of *Sharland v Sharland* [2015] UKSC 60, [2015] 3 WLR 1070, [2016] 2 FLR 1367 and *Gohil v Gohil* [2015] UKSC 61, [2015] 3 WLR 1085, [2015] 2 FLR 1289 were together considered by the Supreme Court. Both involved two wives' applications to set aside orders on the basis of their respective husbands' non-disclosure. In both cases, the Supreme Court unanimously allowed the wives' appeals and set aside consent orders obtained on the basis of the husbands' fraudulent non-disclosure. The importance of these judgments has been recognised in subsequent decisions, such as *AB v CD* [2016] EWHC 10 (Fam), [2016] 4 WLR 36. In this case, the judge found that, whilst there was not deliberate fraud and deception, the wife had failed to give full and frank disclosure and consequently the consent order should be set aside.

Strike out

[17.40] It is also possible to strike out claims (*G v G (Financial Remedies: Strike Out)* [2012] Fam Law 800). In *Vince v Wyatt* [2013] EWCA Civ 495, [2013] 3 FCR 1, [2014] 1 FLR 246, the wife sought financial remedy against her husband after having divorced him 18 years previously. At the time of the divorce both parties were impoverished, however the husband subsequently created a successful business estimated to be worth £90m. The Court of Appeal struck out the wife's claim because at the time when the wife should have brought her claim neither party had any money and both were in relationships with new partners. The wife successfully appealed to the Supreme Court (*Wyatt v Vince* [2015] UKSC 14) which provided guidance regarding the distinction between an application to strike out and an application for summary judgment and held the wife was free to pursue her application for a financial remedy as there is no time limit for bringing a financial application.

In the case of *Dellal v Dellal* [2015] EWHC 907 (Fam), the judge applied *Wyatt v Vince* and held that 'real prospect of success' has a limited meaning under the strike out rule, which is restricted to a claim which is legally unrecognisable. It was held that serious arguments about 'real prospects of success' should be reserved for summary judgment applications. For examples of cases in which applications to strike out have failed see *GN v MA* [2015] EWHC 3939 (Fam), [2016] Fam Law 439 and *T v R (Financial Relief) (Maintenance after Remarriage: Agreement)* [2016] EWFC 26, [2016] 4 WLR 95, [2016] Fam Law 955.

Appeals

[17.41] Of course, parties to financial remedy proceedings may be able to appeal the Court's decision. Moylan J in *CR v SR (Financial Remedies: Permission to Appeal)* [2013] EWHC 1155 (Fam), [2014] 1 FLR 186, [2013] Fam Law 938 considered the proper test in respect of applications for permission to appeal. He considered the words 'the court considers that (a) the appeal would have a real prospect of success . . . ' in light of case law. The applicable test was that set out in *Tanfern Ltd v Cameron-MacDonald* [2000] 2 All ER 801, [2000] 1 WLR 1311, CA: the use of the word 'real' means that the appellant must show the prospect of success to be realistic rather than fanciful. See also *NLW v ARC* [2012] EWHC 55 (Fam), [2012] 2 FLR 129, [2012] Fam Law 388 and *Karim v Musa* [2012] EWCA Civ 1332, [2013] Fam Law 16.

In *AB v CB* [2014] EWHC 2998 (Fam), Mostyn J expressed his dissatisfaction when the appellants sought permission to appeal not from him as first instance judge but directly from the Court of Appeal. The procedure was subsequently clarified by the Court of Appeal in *P v P* [2015] EWCA Civ 44 in which Jackson LJ confirmed that it remains 'good practice' for the appellant in the first instance to seek permission from the lower court although this is no longer mandatory.

In the case of *WD v HD* [2015] EWHC 1547 (Fam), the judge dealt with procedural issues relating to appeals and costs in an appeal against an order terminating a wife's spousal maintenance.

Add back

[17.42] Whilst the Court generally will not entertain arguments in relation to parties' conduct either during or after the marriage, it may take it into account if it would be considered inequitable to disregard such conduct. Examples of conduct which may be taken into account include non-disclosure, litigation misconduct and reckless or wanton expenditure of family assets. Guidance on the treatment of add back cases is provided by the Court of Appeal in *Vaughan v Vaughan* [2007] EWCA Civ 1085 and more recently by the High Court in *US v SR* [2014] EWHC 175 (Fam) and *MAP v MFP* [2015] EWHC 627 (Fam).

In the case of *JS v RS* [2015] EWHC 2921 (Fam), the judge emphasised that in a successful application for add back it must be shown that there was a 'wanton dissipation of assets'.

Media

[17.43] The Family Courts are open to the media, albeit subject to strict rules and restricted reporting as set out in the Family Procedure Rules 2010, SI2010/2955, Part 27 and PD27B. Guidance has been issued by the President of the Family Division on the transparency of the courts. In addition, the case of *Cooper Hohn v Hohn* [2014] EWHC 2314 (Fam) provides guidance as to the extent to which media should be permitted to report and the circumstances in which they should be excluded or reporting restrictions imposed. See also *Fields v Fields* [2015] EWHC 1670 (Fam), *DL v SL* [2015] EWHC 2621 (Fam) and *Appleton & Gallagher v NGN* [2015] EWHC 2689, *Wyatt v Vince* [2016] EWHC 1368 (Fam). In the case of *Veluppillai v Veluppillai* [2015] EWHC 3095 (Fam), the judge published his judgment without anonymisation to expose the husband's abysmal litigation conduct in order to highlight the scale of the problems that courts face when dealing with these issues.

Trust assets

[17.44] Assets held in trust are capable of being treated by the court as a 'resource' that a party 'has or is likely to have in the foreseeable future' within the meaning of MCA 1973, s 25(2)(a).

The Court of Appeal's view (post-*White*) on how to deal with trust assets on divorce was set out in *Charman v Charman (No 4)* [2007] EWCA Civ 503, 9 ITELR 913, [2007] 1 FLR 1246. In that the first instance judge held that it was acceptable for all of the trust assets to be considered as a resource available to Mr Charman and there was a likelihood that, if requested by Mr Charman, the trustee would advance all of the assets to him. The Court of Appeal agreed. The court reasoned that the likelihood of the assets being advanced was increased on the basis that the assets would be needed to meet the husband's legal obligations, ie to satisfy his liabilities to his ex-wife (para 53) as a result of the court order. Sir Mark Potter stated that it would have been an emasculation of the court's duty to be fair if the trust assets in that case had not been attributed to Mr Charman, and he encouraged the judiciary to carry out a balancing exercise to achieve an outcome that reflects the reality of the situation:

> 'Prior to the decision in White, the elaborate enquiry in the present case as to the attributability of the assets in a trust to a party as part of his or her resources would probably have been unnecessary. But, whenever it is necessary to conduct such an enquiry, it is essential for the court to bring to it a judicious mixture of worldly

realism and of respect for the legal effects of trusts, the legal duties of trustees and, in the case of offshore trusts, the jurisdiction of offshore courts.'

(para 57)

The House of Lords refused Mr Charman's appeal from the Court of Appeal's decision. The type of order made in Charman amounts to what is referred to as giving 'judicious encouragement' to trustees, ie not a variation of the terms of the trust (see below) but an order which all but requires them to exercise their powers in a certain way to enable the paying party to comply with an order made against that party personally.

In this area, the courts continue to have regard to the pre-*White* decision of the Court of Appeal in *Thomas v Thomas* [1995] 2 FLR 668. At para 677G, Glidewell LJ provided the following summary of the principles developed in earlier cases:

(a)   Where a paying spouse can only raise further capital, or additional income, as the result of a decision made at the discretion of trustees, the court should not put improper pressure on the trustees to exercise that discretion for the benefit of the other spouse.

(b)   The court should not, however, be 'misled by appearances'; it should 'look at the reality of the situation'.

(c)   If on the balance of probability the evidence shows that, if trustees exercised their discretion to release more capital or income to a spouse, the interests of the trust or of other beneficiaries would not be appreciably damaged, the court can assume that a genuine request for the exercise of such discretion would probably be met by a favourable response. In that situation if a court decides that it would be reasonable for a spouse to seek to persuade trustees to release more capital or income to him to enable him to make proper financial provision for his children and his former wife, a court would not, in so deciding, be putting improper pressure on the trustees.

In *C v C* [2009] EWHC 1491 (Fam), [2010] 1 FLR 337, [2009] Fam Law 920, the court considered as a preliminary issue whether a husband's reversionary interest in a trust fund was a 'resource' for the purposes of the computation of the pot available on divorce. The trust fund was valued at between £4m and £6.2m. On the husband's mother's death, he would receive one quarter of the trust fund. However, during her lifetime, the trustees had no power to benefit the husband without the consent of his mother, who had an unfettered discretion to grant or withhold her consent. Munby J decided 'without much enthusiasm' that the fund was a resource, although *very close to the outer extremity of what can properly be considered a financial resource*'. The difficulty was placing a current value, or making an immediate order, in relation to a future interest in property of an uncertain value at the time it was due to fall in. It was emphasised that while the judge at the final hearing should have regard to the husband's interest under the trust, the judge may decide it is inappropriate to make an order in relation to it.

In the Court of Appeal case of *Whaley v Whaley* [2011] EWCA Civ 617, 14 ITELR 1, [2011] 2 FCR 323 the husband sought to argue that the court had placed 'improper pressure' on the trustees as per the judgment in *Thomas v Thomas*. The first instance judge had found the parties' resources to be

£10.4m, including around £7m held in two trusts. He awarded the wife a lump sum of £3m and periodical payments. The husband could not comply with the order without recourse to trust assets. The Court of Appeal held that the judge had (properly) formed a view that the trust assets were a resource and that the trustees were likely to make assets available to the husband if requested (in fact the trustees and protector would do whatever the husband asked of them). The judge's choice of ancillary relief order, having made those findings, did not amount to improper pressure.

In *RK v RK* [2011] EWHC 3910 (Fam), [2012] 3 FCR 44, Moylan J, *reviewing Charman, Thomas* and *Whaley*, considered that 'resources held within a bona fide discretionary trust are a party's resources to the extent which, on the balance of probabilities, they are likely to be made available to that party either now or in the foreseeable future'. In that case, the court was satisfied that the trustees of the trusts of which the husband was a beneficiary could provide sufficient funds to the husband to meet the court's order without damaging the interests of the trusts or the other beneficiaries.

An alternative to seeking an order which applies 'judicious encouragement' is to seek to set aside a trust completely to return the assets to the ownership of the settlor because, for example, the trust is a sham. In *A v A* [2007] EWHC 99 (Fam), [2007] 2 FLR 467, [2007] Fam Law 791, Munby J noted that (consistent with the law of sham in other contexts) '[t]he only way, as it seems to me, in which a properly constituted trust which is not, *ab initio*, a sham could conceivably become a sham subsequently would be if all the beneficiaries were, with the requisite intention, to join together for that purpose with the trustees.' A transaction is a sham only if all of the parties have a common intention to 'appear' to create legal rights and obligations different to the actual rights those parties intend to create. A finding that there is a sham trust is therefore rare in practice.

In matrimonial cases involving trusts, and particularly discretionary trusts, there will be a conflict between the courts desire to impose a fair division of the assets of a marriage and the fiduciary duties of the trustees to act in the best interests of beneficiaries as a whole. Cases such as *TL v ML* [2005] EWHC 2860 (Fam), [2006] 1 FCR 465, [2006] 1 FLR 1263 and *Re C* [2007] EWHC 1911 (Fam), [2008] 1 FLR 625 have discussed the extent to which the court should make awards where there is a probability that, with or without judicial encouragement, the family trusts would in all likelihood 'come to the rescue' of the beneficiary when faced with a court order against them.

The court's willingness to take trust assets into account can cut both ways. In *G v G* [2012] EWHC 167 (Fam), [2012] 2 FLR 48, the husband was (on his current and future earning capacity) the financially stronger party. However, the wife was a beneficiary of several family trusts and the court held that it could take the wife's payments from the trusts (and which she could expect to receive in future) into account when calculating the level of the wife's expenditure the husband would have to fund in future.

The Family Procedure Rules 2010, at rule 19.2(6)B, provides that the court can add a party to the proceedings if it is desirable so that the court can resolve the matters in dispute. In some cases, the trustees may wish to join the proceedings voluntarily to ensure their views (on behalf of the other benefi-ciaries of the trust for example) are represented, but trustees should consider such a move very carefully before taking it, particularly if the trustees are resident in another jurisdiction.

There may also be issues over whether or not the trustees will provide financial or other information relating to the trust (particularly an offshore trust). The English court has power to order disclosure against non-parties if necessary (FPR 21.1). Enforcement of such an order against offshore trustees may, however, be problematic. Some offshore cases indicate that foreign courts are willing to encourage trustees to provide financial information to an English court and the spouses (even if the trustees are not joined) in order that an English court has a full understanding of the overall financial position. In recent years, however, some jurisdictions have strengthened their so-called 'firewall' legislation to limit the disclosure of confidential information relating to trusts outside of the jurisdiction to ensure that issues connected with those trusts are dealt with, insofar as possible, within the relevant jurisdiction itself. One method to obtain information other than a disclosure order, is to ask the court to issue what are known as letters rogatory (or 'letters of request'), by requesting examination of an offshore trustee by their local court. It is recommended that the party seeking the information takes advice from a local adviser to understand the range of options and their likely effectiveness.

So far we have discussed setting aside a trust completely, or applying 'judicious encouragement' to trustees. An English court order or agreement may also or alternatively require the establishment or variation of one or more trusts so as to make provision for one or more of the parties to the divorce. Where a settlement is either an ante or post-nuptial settlement, the court has power to vary the trust provisions under MCA 1973, s 24(1)(c). In order to qualify as a nuptial settlement, the settlement must have been made '*on the parties to the marriage*'. The issue of whether a trust may or may not fall within this category is regularly debated in the courts. There is no statutory definition of a nuptial settlement, but the following propositions emerge from the authorities:

- the disposition must make some form of continuing provision for both or either of the parties to a marriage with or without provision for their children;
- it is not necessary for the husband or wife to be the settlor, it can be a third party;
- the question of 'continuing provision' is one of construction; and
- generally the greater the connection of the trust and the family and the less the connection with outsiders, the stronger the case for arguing that a settlement is nuptial.

The Court of Appeal confirmed in the case of *Charalambous v Charalambous* [2004] EWCA Civ 1030, [2005] 2 WLR 241, [2004] 2 FCR 721 that, according to English law at least, the English court has jurisdiction to vary foreign trusts under MCA 1973, s 24(1)(c). It does, however, raise the question of whether an English court's decision is capable of enforcement in an offshore jurisdiction. Much may depend on the *situs* of the trust assets and indeed the specific provisions of the relevant offshore jurisdiction's trust and private international law. Most offshore jurisdictions have enacted 'firewall' legislation to prevent foreign court orders being enforced directly in their jurisdictions.

In the case of *Li Quan v Bray* [2014] EWHC 3340 (Fam), the parties had established a UK charitable trust relating to the protection of Chinese tigers. In that unusual context, the court considered whether the charity was a nuptial settlement (within MCA 1973, s 24) and, if not, the extent to which it was a resource (within MCA 1973, s 25). Coleridge J held that the mere fact that a trust was a fully discretionary trust capable of being varied to add other beneficiaries did not of itself make it a post-nuptial settlement. There must be an existing intention to benefit one or both parties, evidenced by an actual flow of benefits or receipts from the settlements. The judge also opined that a settlement which is non-nuptial at its creation could become a nuptial settlement if there was a flow of benefit from the settlement to one or both parties to the marriage. This view has been thrown into doubt by the more recent case of *Joy v Joy-Marancho* [2015] EWHC 2507 (Fam), where Sir Peter Singer reached the opposite view as, otherwise, 'every truly dynastic settlement, bereft of nuptial character at the outset but providing benefits for . . . either a husband or wife, would arguably become variable under s 24(1)(c) . . . '. The issue of whether a non-nuptial settlement can become a nuptial settlement, therefore, is still in some doubt.

If the settlement is an offshore settlement and the English court finds that it (i) is a nuptial settlement and (ii) should be varied, the aforementioned firewall legislation in the trustees' local jurisdiction is likely to result in the relevant party being unable to enforce the English court's order directly against the trustees, especially if the trust assets are also located in an offshore jurisdiction. There may be other methods of giving indirect effect to the order, such as where the trustees decide to act in a way consistent with the English court order (and may seek their local court's approval). If the trustees are uncooperative, however, this is likely to present significant difficulties in enforcing the order.

Company assets

[17.45] The case of *Prest v Petrodel Resources Ltd* [2013] UKSC 34, [2013] 2 AC 415, [2013] 4 All ER 673 provides some insight as to how the courts will deal with assets held in a corporate structure which is owned by one of the parties to the marriage. The court in that case considered whether such property should be treated as assets of the husband within the meaning of MCA 1973, s 24(1)(a). The husband contended that he had net liabilities of £48m; he consistently failed to adhere to court orders for financial disclosure of information; and was found to be an unreliable witness.

At first instance it was held that the husband was the 'only effective shareholder' and that the corporate structure was effectively the husband's 'money box' which he could use at will. The judge concluded that the husband was 'entitled' to the companies' assets by looking beyond the corporate ownership of the properties and determining that in reality they belonged to the husband and not the companies, thus piercing the corporate veil. Therefore the court could order the transfer of seven properties to the wife.

The companies appealed. The Court of Appeal overturned the decision of the court of first instance. It held that a company's assets belonged beneficially to the company itself and not to its shareholders. Those assets could not, therefore, be the subject of a financial provision order unless there were legitimate grounds for piercing the corporate veil; for example, if there had been impropriety. The court of first instance had not, however, found impropriety. Rimer LJ stated that 'a one-man company does not metamorphose into the one-man simply because the person with a wish to abstract its assets was his wife.'

The Supreme Court overturned the Court of Appeal's decision and held that the wife's appeal should succeed, on the basis that the properties in question were beneficially owned by the husband and held by the companies on resulting trust for him. As the properties were beneficially owned by the husband, the court could order that the properties be transferred to his wife. The corporate veil could only be 'pierced' in limited circumstances and no special or wider principle applied in matrimonial cases.

Applying these principles in *M v M* [2013] EWHC 2534 (Fam), 16 ITELR 391 a wife was awarded a property transfer to include UK properties held in complex offshore corporate structures. The husband was held to have been at all times the beneficial owner of the properties, which were found to be held on resulting and constructive trusts for him by the companies.

Use of trusts

[17.46] A trust often used to be an effective means of providing for a spouse or children of a former marriage. Typically they were used for the:

(a) settlement of assets on trust for the benefit of the children of the former marriage;

(b) settlement of the former matrimonial home on trust to enable the former spouse to remain in occupation until some specified event (for example, remarriage); and

(c) settlement of high-income-yielding assets to provide a fund for maintenance payments, effectively giving the transferor relief for maintenance by taking the income stream out of his or her hands.

Now, however, most new lifetime trusts will be subject to the relevant property regime. Although the establishment of a trust pursuant to a court order should qualify for the inheritance tax exemption applicable to transfers which are not gratuitous (IHTA 1984, s 10), thus avoiding an 'entry' charge, a trust within the relevant property regime will nevertheless be subject to decennial charges and exit charges on future distributions. Therefore, although trusts will continue to be a useful mechanism when making financial provision on separation or divorce, it is more important than ever to give careful prior consideration to the tax implications of using a trust in these circumstances before taking any action. The different types of trust and their tax treatment are considered in CHAPTER 6 CREATING SETTLEMENTS and CHAPTER 7 EXISTING SETTLEMENTS.

Inheritance (Provision for Family and Dependants) Act 1975 and spouses

[17.47] Where a person dies without making adequate financial provision their spouse (and a former spouse who has not remarried), amongst other categories of claimant, may have a claim under the Inheritance (Provision for Family and Dependants) Act 1975 (IPFDA 1975) (see **18.3**). Where there has been a divorce with a 'clean break' it is important that any final order contains a provision preventing a former spouse 'coming back for more' on death. Likewise, a former spouse receiving continuing maintenance payments may wish to have the possibility of making such a claim on the death of the paying party.

The difference between a spouse or civil partner and other categories of claimant under the IPFDA 1975 is that they can expect to be awarded 'such financial provision as it would be reasonable in all the circumstances of the case for a [spouse or civil partner] to receive, whether or not that provision is required for his or her maintenance' (IPFDA 1975, s 1(2)(a)(aa)) as opposed to 'such financial provision as it would be reasonable in all the circumstances of the case for the applicant to receive for his maintenance' (IPFDA 1975, s 1(2)(b)).

Further, the court will in the case of a spouse or civil partner 'have regard to the provision which the applicant might reasonably have expected to receive if on the day on which the deceased died [the marriage or civil partnership], instead of being terminated by death, had been terminated by a [decree of divorce or dissolution order]' (IPFDA 1975, s 3(2)). This means that the considerations set out above which apply on divorce, may also be relevant on death where a spouse or civil partner is concerned. It is noteworthy that for inheritance tax purposes, IHTA 1984, s 146 provides that where an order is made by the court under IPFDA 1975 the property directed to be paid to the claimant is treated as having devolved on death and is therefore subject to a 'reading back' provision similar to IHTA 1984, ss 142 and 144 but without the two-year deadline. These provisions can be used to construct a tax efficient settlement of such claims.

Financial relief after an overseas divorce

[17.48] The English courts have the power to make orders where no or inadequate financial orders are made after a foreign divorce provided there is a substantial connection with England and Wales (Matrimonial and Family Proceedings Act 1984, Part III). Jurisdiction can be established by one of the parties:

(a)   being domiciled in England and Wales on the date of the application for leave or was so domiciled on the date on which the divorce, annulment or legal separation obtained took effect in that country; or

(b)   being habitually resident in England and Wales, for one year prior to the application or the date of the foreign divorce, annulment or separation; or

(c)   having at the date of the application a beneficial interest in possession in a house in England or Wales which was the matrimonial home at some time during the marriage (Matrimonial and Family Proceedings Act 1984, s 15).

Leave of the court to bring the application must be obtained before an application is made (Matrimonial and Family Proceedings Act 1984, s 13). The Supreme Court, in *Agbaje v Akinnoye-Agbaje* [2010] UKSC 13, [2010] 1 AC 628, [2010] 2 All ER 877, considered for the first time the Matrimonial and Family Proceedings Act 1984, Part III and gave guidance on the application of the statute. Following *Traversa v Freddi* [2011] EWCA Civ 81, [2011] 2 FLR 272, [2011] Fam Law 464 there is no bar to applying under Part III for orders relating to capital and particularly the transfer of property if no capital orders have been made by a court of the European Union. For an example of the application of *Agbaje*, see *Golubovich v Golubovich* [2011] EWCA Civ 479, [2011] 2 FLR 1193, [2011] Fam Law 935. The case of *Abuchian v Khojah* [2014] EWHC 3411 (Fam) highlights the difficulties of setting aside the grant of leave under Part III.

In *Schofield v Schofield* [2011] EWCA Civ 174, [2011] 1 FLR 2129, [2011] Fam Law 570 it was held that the German divorce court did not have jurisdiction to make any pension sharing order in respect of a British Army Pension which had accrued to the husband during the marriage. In allowing the wife's appeal seeking leave to apply for an English pension sharing order, Mr Justice Thorpe said that:

' . . . whether the English courts will co-operate internationally to deal with English assets following a foreign divorce is particularly important where the foreign jurisdiction has made plain that it lacks jurisdiction to deal with the English pension and the claim has been deliberately severed and left for the English court to deal with. Plainly there should be judicial collaboration across state boundaries to ensure that the adjudication as between husband and wife is complete and comprehensive.'

In the case of *Juffali v Juffali* [2015] EWHC 1684, Roberts J provided a review of the current jurisprudence in the context of a case where the standard of living was described to be 'unimaginably high', which provides commentary of 'needs claims' in cases involving significant sums of money.

Cohabitation

[17.49] The options for cohabitees in relation to financial matters are somewhat limited. At present, a cohabitant cannot make a claim for periodical payments and is restricted, if there is a jointly owned property, to making an application under the Trusts of Land and Appointment of Trustees Act 1996 for an order declaring the nature or extent of his interest in the property.

Where there is a child, an application under the Children Act 1989, Sch 1 can be made for a periodical or secured periodical payments order, a lump sum order or for the settlement or transfer of property.

In *Stack v Dowden* [2007] UKHL 17, [2007] 2 AC 432, [2007] 2 All ER 929 the court provided guidance for establishing the beneficial ownership of a jointly owned property where there is no express declaration of beneficial interests. A conveyance into joint names indicates both a legal and beneficial joint tenancy unless and until the contrary is proved. The difficulty came in establishing the contrary and subsequent case law has dealt with such situations in differing ways thus creating uncertainty. The Supreme Court had the opportunity to consider *Stack v Dowden* in the case of *Jones v Kernott* [2011] UKSC 53, [2012] AC 776, [2012] 1 All ER 1265. It was held that an unmarried couple's share in property can be adjusted after they separate provided that there is evidence of a common intention to adjust ownership. Mr Kernott's decision to stop contributing to the mortgage and purchase another house indicated that his interest in the property crystallised at that point. See also *Graham-York v York* [2015] EWCA Civ 72, *Barnes v Phillips* [2015] EWCA Civ 1056, [2015] All ER (D) 206 and *S v J* [2016] EWHC 586 (Fam), [2016] All ER (D) 87.

On the breakdown of a relationship it is advisable that the financial arrangements of the parties are finalised at that time. Delaying such matters can cause more difficulties in the long term as the case of *Quigley v Masterson* [2011] EWHC 2529 (Ch), [2012] 1 All ER 1224, [2012] 1 FCR 541 illustrates.

In the case of *Curran v Collins* [2015] EWCA 404, [2015] All ER (D) 01, the Court of Appeal emphasised the need for claimants to produce evidence of detrimental reliance. In *Capehorn v Harris* [2015] EWCA Civ 955, [2015] All ER (D) 384, the Court of Appeal referred to established case law and set out the two stage analysis required in order to establish whether a common intention constructive trust arose. In *Ely v Robson* [2016] EWCA Civ 774, [2016] All ER (D) 140, the Court of Appeal highlighted that an oral agreement may be sufficient to establish a constructive trust.

The Law Commission reported in 2007 that reform of cohabitees' rights was necessary having found that existing law relating to cohabitees was uncertain and gave rise to unjust results. It made various proposals including financial relief for cohabitants who had had a child together or who had lived together for a minimum duration. The first reading of the Cohabitation Rights Bill [HL] 2016–17 has taken place, but at the time of writing the general debate on the bill is yet to be scheduled.

Insolvency

[17.50] The bankruptcy of a spouse creates difficult problems for matrimonial practitioners and leads to a situation where the other spouse and the creditors have to compete for the matrimonial assets. Historically, creditors have prevailed as a result of powers under the Insolvency Act 1986 to set aside 'transactions at an undervalue' when a party becomes bankrupt shortly after the making of a final financial order. In the case of *Haines v Hill* [2007] EWCA

Civ 1284, [2008] Ch 412, [2008] 2 All ER 901, the Court of Appeal redressed the balance and concluded that a property adjustment order made in the course of financial proceedings cannot be attacked as a transaction at an undervalue, finding that the right to apply under MCA 1973 was not only a right recognised by law but also had value.

The Insolvency Act 1986, s 281(5)(b) provides that on the discharge of a bankruptcy order, the bankrupt is not released from any bankruptcy debt arising under any order made in family proceedings save to such an extent and on such conditions as the court may direct. Should a spouse apply to be released from such an order, the court will have reference to all the relevant circumstances existing at the date the application is determined (*Hayes v Hayes* [2012] EWHC 1240 (Ch), [2012] All ER (D) 236 (Mar)).

Judge Pelling QC in *Hayes v Hayes* said that the 'discharge of the debt will be a disproportionate step to take unless the court can be confident that the applicant for relief under s 281(5) will never be in receipt of income or capital which will enable the debt to be discharged.' He further stated: 'This factor . . . in combination with the default position . . . is likely to provide an answer in many if not most cases.'

This case was considered in *McRoberts v McRoberts* [2012] EWHC 2966 (Ch), [2013] 1 WLR 1601, [2013] BPIR 77 in which Hildyard J said that all these factors should be taken into account and that a balance should be struck:

'between (a) the prejudice to the respondent/obligee in releasing the obligation if otherwise there would or might be some prospect of any part of the obligation being met and (b) the potential prejudice to the applicant's realistic chance of building a viable financial future for himself and those dependent upon him if the obligation remains in place.'

Property adjustment orders or lump sum orders cannot be made against a bankrupt except in respect of residue of sale proceeds or the estate following discharge of the bankruptcy. Pension sharing or attachment orders can be made. Periodical payments can be ordered against a bankrupt. These are, however, overridden by an income payments order made by the bankruptcy court although the income payments order must provide for the reasonable domestic needs of the bankrupt and his family.

Efforts must be made to check whether the bankruptcy is genuine. See *Paulin v Paulin* [2009] EWCA Civ 221, [2009] 3 All ER 88n, [2010] 1 WLR 1057. Any application to annul the bankruptcy must be made sooner rather than later (*Mekarska v Ruiz & Boyden* [2011] EWHC 913 (Fam), [2011] Fam Law 802).

The case of *Arif v Zar* [2012] EWCA Civ 986, [2012] All ER (D) 243 (Jul) relates to the unsuccessful attempt to transfer the hearing of an application for the annulment of a bankruptcy order to the Family Division. The case of *Young v Young* [2013] EWHC 3637 (Fam), [2014] 2 FCR 495 is an illustration of the court's treatment of assets on divorce belonging to an undischarged bankrupt spouse. The case of *Grant v Baker* [2016] EWHC 1782 (Ch), [2016] All ER (D) 108 (Jul) involved a postponement of the sale of a property whilst the respondent's disabled adult child remained living there.

Pre- and post-nuptial settlements

[17.51] Pre-nuptial settlements are formal written agreements entered into by some couples prior to getting married. Such agreements usually set out who will own what when they are married and what will happen if they divorce.

In many countries, pre-nuptial agreements are treated as binding and enforceable by the courts. In England and Wales, such agreements have historically been considered to be against public policy and therefore void. However, pre-nuptial agreements have gained recognition in a number of cases, culminating in the Supreme Court's decision in *Radmacher v Granatino* [2010] UKSC 42, [2011] 1 AC 534, [2011] 1 All ER 373 in 2010.

Following *Radmacher*, whilst pre-nuptial agreements cannot oust the jurisdiction of the court to make orders on the division of assets on a divorce, the court will attach great weight to them subject to certain requirements. Provided there is no unfair pressure and there is no material lack of information, disclosure or advice, then the guidance from the Supreme Court is that: 'The court should give effect to a nuptial agreement that is freely entered into by each party with a full appreciation of its implications unless in the circumstances prevailing it would not be fair to hold the parties to the consequences.' In *Z v Z (No 2) (Financial Remedies: Marriage Contract)* [2011] EWHC 2878 (Fam), [2012] 1 FLR 1100, [2012] Fam Law 136 the husband was not arguing that the pre-nuptial agreement quantified his wife's claim but rather he was arguing that it extended the sharing principle. The decision in *Z v Z* to uphold the pre-nuptial agreement in as far as it excluded sharing reflected the approach of the Supreme Court in *Radmacher* and in *V v V (Prenuptial Agreement)* [2011] EWHC 3230 (Fam), [2012] 2 FCR 98, [2012] 1 FLR 1315 Charles J confirmed that the decision in *Radmacher* meant a significant change to the impact of pre-nuptial agreements.

Before a pre-nuptial agreement is signed, it is good practice to ensure that there is full and frank disclosure of each party's financial position. It is sensible to have the document properly negotiated in good time before the marriage (21 days in advance as a general rule of thumb) and for both parties to have independent legal advice. Whilst *Radmacher* does not set down any specific procedural guidelines about timing, nor make it absolutely necessary for independent legal advice on both sides, it is helpful to be able to demonstrate that no pressure was applied by either party. Basic provision for the needs of the spouse and certainly for the children should be included to ensure the agreement is not viewed as unfair.

As for post-nuptial agreements, in *Kreman v Agrest (Financial Remedy: Non-disclosure: Post-Nuptial agreement)* [2012] EWHC 45 (Fam), [2012] 2 FCR 472, [2012] 2 FLR 414, when determining what weight should be attributed to the post-nuptial agreement Mostyn J used the factors identified by the Supreme Court in *Radmacher* in relation to pre-nuptial agreements effectively reducing the distinction between agreements made before and after marriage.

In *Kremen v Agrest*, although the wife had some idea of the husband's wealth no financial disclosure was made at the time the agreement was entered into.

The wife received some legal advice from her husband's cousin but that advice was not independent and was not sufficient to ensure that she understood what rights she would be losing under English law as a result of the agreement. Consequently, the wife could not be said to have entered into the Russian post-nuptial agreement with a full appreciation of its implications and it was accorded no weight. In *SA v PA (Pre-marital agreement: Compensation)* [2014] EWHC 392 (Fam), [2014] Fam Law 799 a husband contended that the parties were bound by a Dutch pre-marital agreement. Mostyn J determined that the wife was fully aware of the contents of that agreement (which had been witnessed and executed at a notary's office) and that it was clear the parties intended to enter into a binding agreement. The agreement in relation to the division of capital was therefore to be implemented as the parties had intended.

In *Y v Y* [2014] EWHC 2920 (Fam) (unreported) French spouses elected for a regime of separation of assets. The Judge gave the agreement reduced weight observing that while the wife intended the settlement to govern the parties' financial affairs during the marriage she had no understanding and was unaware (and therefore never intended) that its provisions should apply to a division of their marital estate in the event of divorce.

In *Luckwell v Limata* [2014] EWHC 502 (Fam) the court followed the propositions drawn from *Radmacher* but the judge decided that the pre-nuptial agreement should be overridden. Following *Radmacher*, the judge said that in the absence of vitiating factors such as duress or non-disclosure 'very great weight should be given to the agreements'. However, the judge went on to find that the husband was now in a "predicament of real need" while the wife enjoyed a 'sufficiency or more'. As a result, the pre-nuptial agreement (which provided nothing at all for the husband no matter how great his need at the time the marriage broke down) should be overridden and capital provision made for the husband on the basis of his needs in conjunction with his role as a father.

In *B v S (Financial Remedy: Marital Property Regime)* [2012] EWHC 265 (Fam), [2012] 2 FCR 335, [2012] 2 FLR 502 the judge specifically noted the difference between a negotiated pre-nuptial agreement made in contemplation of a divorce and an agreement made in a civil jurisdiction which adopts a particular marital property regime.

The case of *AH v PH* [2013] EWHC 3873 (Fam), [2014] 2 FLR 251 provides a commentary on the court's treatment of non-matrimonial property and the relevance of a marriage settlement.

The case of *L v M* [2014] EWHC 2220 (Fam), [2014] All ER (D) 100 (Nov) involved a separation agreement entered into some 20 years earlier which the first instance court considered to be of 'magnetic importance' because the parties had acted on and relied upon the agreement since it was entered into. The court therefore held that the agreement should be upheld. The wife's application for permission to appeal was refused. See also *L v M* [2014] EWHC 220 (Fam).

The case of *Hopkins v Hopkins* [2015] EWHC 812 (Fam) is a useful illustration of the application of *Radmacher*. In this case, a post-nuptial agreement was largely upheld on the grounds of fairness following the wife's case of vitiation by duress being rejected. The case of *WW v HW* [2015] EWHC 1844 (Fam), [2015] Fam Law 1060, 165 NLJ 7663 highlights the need for more certainty in the law of financial remedy and nuptial agreements.

On 27 February 2014 the Law Commission published a report on Matrimonial Property, Needs and Agreements, following the consultation papers published in 2011 and 2012. The report recommended that legislation be enacted to introduce 'qualifying nuptial agreements' (similar to pre/post-nuptial/civil partnership agreements) which would be enforceable contracts to enable couples to make binding arrangements for the financial consequences of divorce or dissolution. In order for an agreement to be a 'qualifying' nuptial agreement, certain procedural safeguards would have to be met. Qualifying agreements would not, however, be able to be used by the parties to contract out of meeting the 'financial needs' of each other and of any children. The report also introduced the 'Nuptial Agreements Bill' in draft form. At the time of writing the Government's final response regarding nuptial agreements is still awaited.

Chapter 18

Making a Will

Introduction

[18.1] A crucial element of estate planning for an individual is the preparation of a will, correctly drawn to ensure that the property remaining at his death is distributed among his family and dependants and other beneficiaries according to his wishes and in a tax-efficient manner. It is essential to this strategy to ensure that the testator's spouse or civil partner (and other dependants) are adequately provided for at the minimum tax cost in each case.

There is no certain formula for determining what will amount to adequate provision for dependants. It used to be suggested that a capital sum equal to ten times the husband's annual salary was required to provide adequately for his widow and family. Certainly, in smaller estates of less than £1,000,000 there may be little scope for anything but provision for the surviving spouse unless she has means of her own.

The importance of having a will, correctly drawn and regularly reviewed, is three-fold. First, it ensures that the deceased's estate devolves exactly as he desires and in as tax-efficient a manner as possible. If there is no will, then the statutory intestacy provisions will apply which may achieve a devolution in the deceased's estate in a manner which does not fulfil his wishes. These provisions are discussed in more detail at **18.2**. Secondly, it simplifies the administration of the estate thereby saving time and the expense to which an intestacy invariably gives rise. Finally, it enables the testator to choose suitable, competent executors to administer his estate, which is preferable to relying on the statutory order in the case of an intestacy.

An adviser must ensure that he or she has correctly understood the testator's intentions, made a detailed file note of all discussions with the testator, drafted a will reflecting those wishes, advised on the tax implications of the will, and ensured that it is correctly executed. The importance of this is illustrated by the case of *Marley v Rawlings* [2014] UKSC 2, [2014] 1 All ER 807, [2014] 2 WLR 213 where a couple accidentally signed each other's wills. The Supreme Court overruled the lower courts to allow the rectification of the wills.

Intestacy rules

[18.2] In the absence of a will the estate will pass on death under the intestacy rules which may, but much more likely will not, bring about the desired result in the distribution of the estate. The intestacy rules for England and Wales provide that where there is a surviving spouse or civil partner:

(i) if there are surviving children, a fixed sum of £250,000, together with the personal chattels pass to the surviving spouse or civil partner together with an absolute interest in one half of the residue of the estate. The other half of residue will pass to the children or their issue absolutely if they are over 18 and under a statutory trust if they are unmarried (and not parties to a civil partnership) and under the age of 18;

(ii) if there are no surviving children, the surviving spouse or civil partner receives the entire estate absolutely.

It should be noted that a surviving parent, sibling and their issue will not benefit on an intestacy where there is a surviving spouse, civil partner or issue.

In relation to (i) above, on the death of the first spouse, the only charge to inheritance tax on the estate that may arise is in respect of the one-half of the residue passing to the issue. On the death of the second spouse, however, a charge to inheritance tax will arise on his or her estate (reflecting the benefit of the deceased's personal assets and the fixed sum to the extent it is not spent in that spouse's lifetime) including, for inheritance tax purposes, the one-half share of residue of the deceased's estate which passes to the children on the second death.

A surviving spouse or civil partner may in certain circumstances by written notice require that the family home is appropriated in satisfaction of any absolute interest (Intestates Estates Act 1952, s 5).

Currently, the surviving partner of an unmarried couple or a couple not in a civil partnership has no right to any share of the deceased's estate under the intestacy rules. He or she may, however, have a claim under the Inheritance (Provision for Family and Dependants) Act 1975. At the time of writing, a Private Member's Bill, the Cohabitation Rights Bill 2016, has had its first reading in the House of Lords. This Bill provides that a 'qualifying cohabitant' will have the same rights as a spouse or civil partner on an intestacy. A person will only be a 'qualifying cohabitant' provided the deceased was not married or in a civil partnership immediately before death.

In relation to Scotland, the intestacy provisions are found in the Succession (Scotland) Act 1964 and the Family Law (Scotland) Act 2006, which provide that a surviving spouse or civil partner will be entitled to 'prior rights'. In addition, the surviving spouse and children or issue of a predeceasing child may claim their 'legal rights' in any moveable estate which is not distributed in terms of the 'prior rights'. Thereafter any estate which is not distributed in terms of the foregoing 'prior' and 'legal rights' is then distributed under the Scottish intestacy rules. It should be noted that a spouse or civil partner of the deceased rank below the deceased's parents and siblings.

A cohabitant can apply to the Court for a share of his cohabitant's estate (Family Law (Scotland) Act 2006, s 29). The Scottish Law Commission Report 'Report on Succession 2006' (Scot Law Com No 215) recommended that the intestacy rules be reformed and has been the subject of a consultation. Although, to date, no further information as to the timing of any reform has been given.

In addition, the provisions of the Succession (Scotland) Act 2016 should be taken into consideration. The Act has made significant changes to the law of succession generally in Scotland and applies to deaths after 31 October 2016.

Provision for family and dependants

[18.3] When advising a client who wishes to exclude a family member or dependant from his will, his attention should be drawn to the provisions of the Inheritance (Provision for Family and Dependants) Act 1975 (I(PFD)A 1975). Where a person dies domiciled in England and Wales and is survived by certain persons defined in s 1 of the 1975 Act, that person may apply to the court for an order on the ground that the deceased had not made reasonable financial provision for the applicant. Those defined persons are:

(i)   the deceased's spouse or civil partner;

(ii)   a former spouse or civil partner of the deceased who has not remarried or entered into a new civil partnership or any person who, for the whole period of two years ending immediately prior to the date of death, was living in the same household as the deceased and as the husband, wife or civil partner of the deceased;

(iii)   a child of the deceased;

(iv)   a person treated by the deceased as a child of the family in relation to any marriage or civil partnership of the deceased;

(v)   any person who immediately before the deceased's death was maintained (either wholly or in part) by the deceased. The deceased must have been making a substantial contribution in money or monies worth towards the reasonable needs of that person.

It is not always easy to determine whether a relationship will satisfy the criteria in (ii) above. In such a situation the courts will first examine the internal nature of the relationship to determine whether it was of long-life commitment and then will determine if that commitment was externally apparent. In *Harkinder Kaur v Sandeep Singh Dhaliwal* [2004] EWHC 1991 (Ch) the High Court held that despite the couple not continuously living together throughout the two-year period they had continued their relationship as if husband and wife and therefore the criteria were satisfied. In *Swetenham v Walkley & Bryce* [2014] WTLR 845, a couple had been together for 30 years but had not had sexual relations. They each had their own property although the deceased spent every day at his partner's house. They did not formally share any of their finances. The Court held that there was a bond of mutuality and support with each knowing and understanding the needs of the other and a claim could be brought by the applicant. In *Chekov v Fryer* [2015] EWHC 1642 (Ch) the applicant had been married to the deceased and under the terms of their divorce order neither party was entitled to claim against the estate of the other under I(PFD)A 1975 unless the partner shall remarry. Neither party remarried at the time of the deceased's death but they were living together. The applicant argued that the divorce order did not prevent her from claiming as a cohabitee, rather than a former spouse. The judge agreed with the applicant and found that it would be irrational if a person formally married to A, but since divorced and cohabiting with B would be able to make a claim against B's estate on his death. Similarly, a person formerly married to A then divorced but remarried would be able to make a claim; while such a person formally married to A and since divorced and cohabiting with him would not be allowed to do so.

In determining 'reasonable financial provision' a court has to take into account all the relevant factors listed in I(PFD)A 1975, s 3. One such factor is the deceased's net estate which is defined in the statute and which does not include joint property held as joint tenants. The court does have, however, under I(PFD)A 1975, s 9(4), a discretionary power to order that the deceased's severable share of jointly owned property is treated as part of his estate at its value immediately before death. In the case of *Lim (an infant) v Walia* [2014] EWCA Civ 1076, 164 NLJ 7622 a married couple had taken out a life policy under which a lump sum would either be paid on the first death or, if either spouse developed a terminal illness, at an earlier date (in which case no death benefit was payable). Mrs Walia developed such an illness but no claim was made. On her death, the death benefit was paid to her husband. A claim was made under I(PFD)A 1975. The Court of Appeal held Mrs Walia had a severable joint interest in a terminal illness benefit under an insurance policy immediately before her death. That interest, however, had no value because it would cease to exist if death occurred without a claim to that benefit being made. The decision seems to suggest that if a policy provides for terminal illness benefit to be paid to one policyholder only, rather than to both of them, the outcome may be different. It is advisable for advisers to consider the terms of such policies carefully.

One would wish to avoid litigation and in some cases a testator may leave a legacy to avoid his spouse or family members being involved in a contentious probate after his death. In some cases the testator may be adamant that he does not wish to make any form of provision. In such circumstances it is advisable that the testator details in a letter of wishes his relationship with the party concerned, any financial provision that had been made or not over the years and his wish for his executors to defend any claim brought. In addition, it is sensible that the testator advises the relevant party that he has not made provision for them under his will. In the case of *Ilott v Mitson* [2015] EWCA Civ 797, the testatrix had prepared such a statement but it was held not to be determinative. The court still considered that provision should have been made for her daughter despite the testatrix having been well advised and taking the actions mentioned above. It is understood, at the time of writing, that leave to appeal to the Supreme Court has been granted.

A testator may consider making a gift with an accompanying 'no-contest' clause, which would mean that if the individual does contest the will they will forego the gift.

As the case of *Lilleyman v Lilleyman* [2012] EWHC 821 (Ch), [2013] Ch 225, [2013] 1 All ER 302 illustrates, where a claim is made, all offers to settle should be given careful consideration. In this case the court held that the deceased had failed to make adequate financial provision for his second wife but the amount awarded by the court was less than the offer made by the defendants which was not accepted. As the wife had failed to accept the reasonable offer, she was liable for the defendants' costs from the date of the offer. So although the applicant was successful, she ultimately received far less than she would have, had she accepted the offer from the defendants.

Care does need to be taken in challenging the terms of a will, as a recent case, *Elliott v Simmonds & Tulip (Executor of the Estate of K W Jordan deceased)* [2016] EWHC 962 (Ch) demonstrates. The High Court made a costs order against a defendant who had no reasonable grounds to oppose the will, acted obstructively, caused delay and increased the costs.

EU Succession Regulation

[18.4] The EU Succession Regulation (EU 650/2012) (known as 'Brussels IV') was introduced with the aim of unifying succession laws in EU member states. This regulation applies to deaths after 16 August 2015. Although the UK has opted out of the regulation, it will still have an effect for anyone with a connection to a participating member, such as nationality, habitual residence, domicile or assets situated in any of those states. The regulation states that the law of succession of the member state where the deceased was habitually resident governs succession unless the deceased was 'manifestly more closely connected with another state'. An individual may, however, choose the law of his nationality to govern the succession of his estate under reg 22. This can be useful so as to avoid ambiguities and the application of the forced heirship rules.

Testamentary capacity

[18.5] Many probate disputes involve the question of testamentary capacity. The general rule is that at the time a will is executed the testator must have testamentary capacity. That is, he must understand the nature of the document, the property of which he is disposing, the persons who have a natural claim to provision from his estate, and the manner in which he provides for his estate to be distributed (*Banks v Goodfellow* (1869–70) LR 5 QB 549, [1861–73] All ER Rep 47).

There is an exception to this general rule which is known as the *Parker v Felgate* Rule ((1883) lR 8PD 171). The Rule provides that if a testator has lost capacity by the time he executes a will, it is sufficient that he understands that he is executing a will for which he has previously given instructions. This rule is at odds with the Mental Capacity Act 2005 as capacity has to be demonstrated at the material time. The *Parker v Felgate* Rule has been applied in a number of cases, including in *Perrins v Holland* [2010] EWCA Civ 840, [2011] Ch 270, [2011] 2 All ER 174 where the rule was upheld. This case illustrates the difficulty in the application of the rule as once instructions are given, an individual cannot change his mind when incapacity intervenes. The Rule was considered and confirmed more recently in *Burns v Burns* [2016] EWCA Civ 37. In that case, a will was upheld despite a documented decline in the testatrix's mental health at the time she executed her will.

When taking instructions for a will an adviser has to consider the 'Golden Rule' first formulated by Templeman J in *Kenward v Adams* [1975] CLY 3591 (and repeated in *Re Simpson* (1977) 121 SJ 224, [1977] LS Gaz R 187). In the case of an ageing testator or a testator who has suffered a serious illness, the making of a will by such a testator ought to be witnessed or approved by a medical practitioner who satisfies himself of the capacity and understanding of the testator, and records and preserves his examination and finding. The Golden Rule was cited in the case of *Key v Key* [2010] EWHC 408 (Ch), [2010] 1 WLR 2020, [2010] All ER (D) 155 (Apr) which illustrates that an adviser cannot afford to ignore the Golden Rule.

In certain situations it can be difficult for the Golden Rule to be complied with, particularly when preparing a will for a dying man. This difficulty was acknowledged by Norris J in *Wharton v Bancroft* [2011] EWHC 3250 (Ch), [2011] All ER (D) 84 (Dec) who made some helpful comments. Where it is not possible in the circumstances to obtain a medical opinion, it is extremely important that the solicitor addresses the question of capacity and makes a full note of the steps taken to ascertain capacity. In the case of *Burgess v Hawes* [2013] EWCA Civ 74, [2013] All ER (D) 220 (Feb) Mummery LJ said that:

> 'If, as here, an experienced lawyer has been instructed and has formed the opinion from a meeting or meetings that the testatrix understands what she is doing, the will so drafted and executed should only be set aside on the clearest evidence of lack of mental capacity. The court should be cautious about acting on the basis of evidence of lack of capacity given by a medical expert after the event, particularly when that expert has neither met nor medically examined the testatrix, and particularly in circumstances when that expert accepts that the testatrix understood that she was making a will and also understood the extent of her property.'

The Court of Appeal's remarks have influenced subsequent decisions such as *Greaves v Stolkin* [2013] EWHC 1140 (Ch), [2013] All ER (D) 51 (May) and *Re Ashkettle* [2013] EWHC 2125 (Ch), [2013] All ER (D) 202 (Jul) where the judge commented that among other things 'any view the solicitor may have formed as to the testator's capacity must be shown to be based on proper assessment and accurate information or it is worthless'.

Assessing capacity retrospectively does create difficulties as was illustrated in the case of *Cowderoy v Cranfield* [2011] EWHC 1616 (Ch), [2011] All ER (D) 191 (Jun). In that case, while there was some evidence of confusion on the part of the testatrix, the court held that when she gave instructions for the will, she was having a good day. The comments made in *Hawes v Burgess* gives support to the argument that an assessment of a testator's capacity by an experienced solicitor can carry as much weight (if not more) as an assessment made by a doctor, particularly where the doctor is giving his view 'after the event'.

The Law Commission has announced that it is to review the law of wills having identified four areas requiring reform, namely testamentary capacity, the formalities of a valid will, the rectification of wills and mutual wills. Preliminary work started in 2015 and a consultation document is expected in spring of 2017.

Mutual wills

[18.6] It is often the case that two spouses will execute wills on identical forms with reciprocal provisions as to the distribution of their estates and will agree that they will not revoke their wills. On the first death the survivor will hold the property on implied trusts (the ambulatory trust) for the beneficiaries to whom it was agreed it should be left. This is known as the doctrine of mutual wills. A common example is where the spouses leave everything to each other and thereafter to their children.

In the words of Dixon J in *Birmingham v Renfrew* (1936) 57 CLR 666, 43 ALR 520:

> 'The purpose of an arrangement [of this sort is] to enable the survivor during his life to deal as absolute owner with the property passing under the will of the party first dying . . . the object of the transaction is to put the survivor in a position to enjoy for his own benefit the full ownership, so that, for instance, he may convert it and expend the proceeds if he choose.'

The purpose of mutual wills is to ensure that the parties' estates devolve as agreed between them. The parties have voluntarily forgone their testamentary freedom which is a key feature of succession law. Mutual wills might be viewed as an agreement by which a person is obliged to bequeath their estate in a particular way and therefore similar to inheritance contracts which are a characteristic of other jurisdictions. Such agreements fall within the definition of 'agreements as to succession' contained in the European Union Regulation (known as Brussels IV). The UK has decided not to opt into Brussels IV but nevertheless it cannot be ignored by practitioners because it will apply to assets within the EU. Particular care is needed when advising clients who own assets in one or more EU member states to ensure that the potential effects of Brussels IV are considered.

Disputes can be avoided by the simple measure of recording whether wills are intended to be mutual wills. In order to prove the existence of mutual wills, the evidence has to establish:

(a)   prior agreement by the testators to make mutual wills, intending their agreement to become irrevocable on the first death; and

(b)   the making of the mutual wills pursuant to that agreement: *Fry v Densham-Smith* [2010] EWCA Civ 1410, [2010] All ER (D) 136 (Dec).

Both *Fry v Densham-Smith* and the case of *Charles v Fraser* [2010] EWHC 2154 (Ch), 13 ITELR 455, 154 Sol Jo (no 32) 30 illustrate the nature of the evidence that is required to show that the wills were intended to be mutual. To avoid litigation it is advisable that the wills state that they are intended to be mutual wills and are irrevocable. In addition, the adviser should keep a separate file note. An adviser should ascertain whether the testators intend the wills to be irrevocable and an explanation of its meaning given. If a will is not intended to be irrevocable a statement to that effect should be included in the wills. It should be remembered that mirror wills may not necessarily be mutual wills.

Use of exemptions and reliefs

[18.7] When a testator is considering his will and the terms thereof, regard should be had to ensure that any exemptions available on death are maximised. One needs to consider the spouse exemption, which is discussed in detail in CHAPTER 4 LIFETIME PLANNING: MAKING GIFTS, the nil rate band of £325,000, the transferable nil rate band and the residence nil rate amount for deaths after 5 April 2017.

Transferable nil rate band

[18.8] Before the introduction of the transferable nil rate band it had been the case that an essential element of estate planning was the utilisation of an individual's inheritance tax nil rate band. However, many wills of a husband and wife were drafted so that they each left everything to each other which meant that on the first death the nil rate band was unused. It is now possible for a nil rate band unused on a person's death to be transferred to the estate of their spouse or civil partner. In respect of deaths after 5 April 2017, a separate residence nil rate band will be available, which is discussed in detail in **18.16–18.26**.

The legislation is found in IHTA 1984, ss 8A–8D. In addition, HMRC has published 'guidance' which can be found in the HMRC Inheritance Tax Manual, starting at para 43000.

For spouses, the first death can have occurred at any time; indeed, the first death could have occurred under Estate Duty Rules. It should be borne in mind that there was no general spouse exemption under the estate duty provisions until 1972 when a £15,000 exemption was introduced with a complete exemption from 1974. As a result, nil rate bands were frequently utilised. The interaction of the transferable nil rate band legislation with some of the rules which apply to deaths which occurred under estate duty provisions has caused some confusion. For example, in relation to deaths of persons killed or missing in action before 12 March 1952 (see IHT Newsletter April 2009). For civil partners, however, the first death must have occurred after 4 December 2005 which was the date that the Civil Partnership Act 2004 became law. The parties to a legal relationship equivalent to civil partnership entered into before that date under the law of another jurisdiction are treated as having formed a civil partnership on 5 December 2005. Where there is a divorce or a dissolution of a civil partnership any unused nil rate band is not available to be transferred to the surviving former spouse or civil partner.

Where a marriage ceremony has taken place abroad it must meet the legal requirements of that country 'for the parties to the marriage to be regarded as "spouses" for TNRB purposes'. (HMRC Inheritance Tax Manual, para 43003).

As mentioned above, before the introduction of the transferable nil rate band, wills were drafted to ensure that both spouses' nil rate bands were utilised. This was usually done by creating nil rate band discretionary trusts (see **18.13**) which was sometimes done by defining the amount to be settled on trust as being 'the maximum sum that I can leave without inheritance tax becoming payable' in respect of this gift. This wording can now result in a maximum of £650,000 being settled on discretionary trusts. Whereas if the will stated that 'a sum equal to the upper limit of the nil percent rate band in the table of rates of tax (applicable on my death) in Schedule 1 of the Inheritance Tax Act 1984' is settled on trusts then an amount equal to a single nil rate band will be settled. This is an important issue as was illustrated in the case of *Royal Society for the Prevention of Cruelty to Animals v Sharp* [2010] EWCA Civ 1474, [2011] 1 WLR 980, [2011] STC 553.

In *Loring v Woodland Trust* [2013] EWHC 4400 (Ch), [2014] 2 All ER 836, [2014] WTLR 593 the testator left a legacy in her will 'equal to such sum as is at the date of my death the amount of my unused nil rate band for inheritance tax'. There was no evidence of the testator's intention available. The Court considered that the testatrix had understood that the size of the legacy at the date of her death could be different to that at the date of her will. The Court of Appeal held that the wording of the relevant clause meant that the legacy was equal to an amount that would not give rise to any inheritance tax being payable and in which case the legacy included both the testator's nil rate band and the transferable nil rate band. The interpretation of nil rate band legacies and trusts is being challenged in the courts and it is therefore important that this issue is discussed with a client to determine their wishes and that the will is drafted in accordance with those wishes.

Unused nil rate band

[18.9] The first issue to determine is whether there is an unused nil rate band. IHTA 1984, s 8A contains a formula to determine the question. A person has an unused nil rate band if:

$$M > VT$$

Where:

M is the maximum amount that could be transferred on the first death at 0%. Currently, this is therefore the nil rate band on the first death less the chargeable value of any lifetime transfers that use up the nil rate band first. For deaths after 5 April 2017, this may include an amount in respect of the residential enhancement (see **18.16**).

VT is the chargeable value of the transfer on death. This includes all non-exempt or relievable legacies passing under the will or intestacy, assets passing by survivorship, gifts with reservation chargeable at death and any settled property.

Where M is greater than VT, that amount is expressed as a percentage of the nil rate band available on the first death and is the amount by which the nil rate band on the second death is increased. That percentage is:

$$\frac{E}{NRBMD} \times 100$$

Where:

E is the amount by which M is greater than VT; and

NRBMD is a nil rate band maximum at the first death.

Example

Malcolm died on 1 November 2002, leaving an estate as follows:

Net estate	£300,000
Chargeable legacies	£100,000
Residue to Edna (his spouse)	£200,000

Malcolm had made no lifetime chargeable transfers. The nil rate band was £250,000 and so M was £250,000. The chargeable value (VT) was £100,000.

E is therefore £150,000 (£250,000 less £100,000). The percentage of nil rate band available to transfer is:

$$\frac{£\,150,000}{£\,250,000} \times 100 = 60\%$$

Edna died on the 16 September 2016 when the nil rate band was £325,000. On her death her nil rate band would be calculated as follows:

£325,000 + (60% of £325,000) = £520,000

Where the deceased dies with a cumulative total of lifetime transfers, the nil rate band is first set against those transfers.

Married more than once

[18.10] Special rules apply to limit the amount of the available nil rate band where a spouse or civil partner has been a party to more than one marriage or civil partnership.

Example

Sophie was married to Edward who died in 1988 leaving an estate of £200,000. Under his will he left £50,000 to their daughter and the remainder to his wife. At that time the nil rate band was £110,000. No tax was payable. In 1998, Sophie married Clive who died in 2005 leaving an estate of £300,000. Under his will he left £100,000 to a nephew and the remainder to Sophie. The nil rate band was £275,000.

Sophie died in June 2016.

On the death of Edward, 54.5% of his nil rate band was unused calculated as follows:

(110,000 – 50,000 therefore the unused nil rate band was 60,000/110,000) = 54.5%

On the death of Clive, 63.6% of his nil rate band was unused calculated as follows:

(275,000 – 100,000 therefore the unused nil rate band = 175,000/275,000) = 63.6%

On the death of Sophie the unused nil rate band is calculated as follows:

Although the amount of the unused nil rate band is £383,825 ((54.5% of 325,000 = 177,125) + (63.6% of 325,000 = 206,700)) = 383,825), the amount is limited to £325,000. Sophie will have a nil rate band available on her death of £650,000 (IHTA 1984, s 8A(5)).

To avoid the restriction on the amount of nil rate band available a discretionary trust can be used (see **18.13** below).

Simultaneous deaths

[18.11] Special rules apply where there are simultaneous deaths. The rules are different in England and Wales than to those which apply in Scotland and Northern Ireland. In England and Wales, where spouses and civil partners die leaving wills in circumstances rendering it uncertain which of them survived the other, there is a presumption that the elder person died first (the 'Commorientes Rule') (Law of Property Act 1925, s 184). IHTA 1984, s 4(2) provides that where it cannot be ascertained which of two people survived the other then it is assumed for inheritance tax purposes that both deaths occurred at the same time. This means that the property of the elder falls outside the charge to inheritance tax on the younger's death. HMRC's Guidance states that 'the younger person's estate could benefit from a double nil rate band and the assets accruing to their estate from the elder are excluded' (HMRC Inheritance Tax Manual, para 43040).

In Scotland and Northern Ireland, both spouses or civil partners are treated as dying at the same moment, so neither can inherit from the other. Each person's estate will pass to their heirs whether by will or under an intestacy. In the event that one spouse or civil partner had any unused nil rate band it is available to be transferred to the estate of the other, if required.

Example

Sebastian is 65 and Susan is 45 and both are resident in England. They both have estates worth £500,000. Under their wills each leaves his or her estate to the other survivor and, subject to that, thereafter to their son Augustus.

Unfortunately they are both involved in an accident and it is not possible to determine who died first.

If their wills did not contain survivorship clauses Susan is deemed to have survived Sebastian and so inherits his assets.

For IHT purposes Sebastian and Susan are assumed to have died at the same time. The spouse exemption will be available on Susan's inheritance from Sebastian. Because Sebastian's assets cannot have formed part of Susan's estate immediately before her death there is no inheritance tax payable on Sebastian's assets as a result of Susan's death.

Susan's estate is valued at the moment immediately before her death at £500,000. At that time she had not inherited Sebastian's assets and so his assets will not form part of her estate. As Sebastian had not utilised his nil rate band, Susan has a nil rate band of £650,000 to utilise. Augustus therefore inherits his parents' estates free of inheritance tax.

If Susan and Sebastian's wills had contained a 30-day survivorship clause their assets would have passed directly to Augustus. The inheritance tax payable on each estate would be as follows:

(500,000 – 325,000) x 40% = £70,000 resulting in a total inheritance tax liability of £140,000.

The above example illustrates that where both estates are in excess of the nil rate band a survivorship clause where the Commorientes Rule applies can produce an unnecessary tax charge.

Care should therefore be taken when considering a survivorship clause and its effects should be explained to the client.

Making a claim

[18.12] The transfer of an unused nil rate band must be claimed by the personal representatives of the surviving spouse within the permitted period (IHTA 1984, s 8B). This period is defined as two years from the end of the month in which the survivor dies or if it ends later, three months from when the personal representatives first act as such or such longer period as an HMRC officer may allow. The phrase 'first act as such' is not defined in the legislation and so follows the general law concerning acts done by the executors. HMRC gives examples in its guidance as to when it will permit a late claim (Inheritance Tax Manual, para 43009). If the personal representatives do not make an election, a claim can be made by any other person who is liable to the tax on the survivor's death within such later period as HMRC may allow.

When a claim is made various records should accompany it. These are listed in the Inheritance Tax Manual at paras 43006 and 43012.

It is important that records from the first death are retained to support a future claim. Obviously for some individuals records will not have been retained. The first death may have happened a considerable time ago. HMRC's Guidance states that 'provided the documents show the claim is valid and any tax due has been paid, you can release form IHT421/C1. You should then consider the risk to tax in deciding whether or not to accept the claim as offered. Where records don't exist, personal representatives are entitled to complete their claim to the best of their ability and based on the information available. Provided there is no evidence that any other assets were chargeable, you can accept the claim.' (HMRC Inheritance Tax Manual, para 43011). It would seem that there is not the same discretion where the first death happens after the 8 October 2007.

Once a claim has been submitted it can only be withdrawn within one month of its submission.

Nil rate band discretionary trusts

[18.13] There has been much written about whether the ability to transfer the unused nil rate band has made nil rate band discretionary trusts redundant. It is common for an individual in his will to leave a legacy equal to the nil rate band in force at his death (or equal to the unused amount of the band taking into account transfers within seven years of death) on discretionary trusts with the surviving spouse or civil partner as one of the objects of the discretion. It should be noted that the wording of the nil rate band legacy is important. It was often the case that wills provided for a cash sum to be settled of 'an amount equal to the largest amount that can pass without payment of inheritance tax'. Because it is now possible to 'transfer' the unused nil rate band of the first spouse to die to the other spouse, this wording might settle an amount equal to double the amount of the full inheritance tax nil rate band.

The trustees (given the appropriate guidance in a letter of wishes) might, in each year, exercise their discretion over the income, (and, where appropriate, the capital) of the fund in favour of the surviving spouse or civil partner. If there were minor children of the testator included in the class of beneficiaries, then the discretion over income might instead be exercised in their favour to utilise their income tax personal allowances in each year. The income so appropriated might be paid to the spouse or civil partner as guardian of the children to be used for the children's maintenance, education or benefit, thereby relieving the surviving spouse's or civil partner's own income from this burden. This is, of course, subject to the duty of the trustees to have regard only to the interests of the beneficial objects.

This route enables a surviving spouse or civil partner to benefit from the income of the testator's property whilst at the same time keeping it outside his or her estate. If the testator's widow or civil partner dies before the tenth anniversary of the testator's death, then the capital of the trust might be distributed to the children without incurring any inheritance tax charge regardless of the then value of the fund. This is because inheritance tax on a capital distribution before the first decennial is calculated by reference to the initial value of the relevant property in the settlement and related settlements (and certain other related property and values relating to same day additions) plus any chargeable transfers made by the settlor in the seven years before making the settlement. If that total does not exceed the nil rate band, no tax is payable. Before 22 March 2006, where a will established a nil rate band discretionary trust and an interest in possession for a spouse in the remainder of the estate, the interest in possession trust was not related property and was, therefore, ignored when considering the situation of the nil rate band discretionary trust. This will still be the case where a spouse or civil partner has an immediate post-death interest or a disabled person's interest after 21 March 2006. In calculating the inheritance tax on a capital distribution before the first decennial, where the value of the property transferred to the trust fund only fell within the nil rate band by virtue of the availability of business property relief or agricultural property relief, the initial value of the trust fund in these circumstances is the unrelieved value and a charge may therefore arise. If the widow is likely to survive the decennial, then a decision will have to be made as to whether it is better to break the trust before the anniversary or to pay the ten-year charge.

The nil rate band discretionary trust still has a large part to play in estate planning, particularly as the nil rate band is frozen at £325,000 until 2020/21.

The nil rate band discretionary trust allows the taxpayer to 'hedge his bets'. Taking advantage of a claim under IHTA 1984, s 8A capital can be appointed out to a surviving spouse or civil partner within two years of death. Alternatively, the chargeable transfer can simply be left in being with or without absolute appointments to beneficiaries.

Where an individual has children from their first marriage it may be preferable to set up a nil rate band discretionary trust under the will of the first spouse to die rather than relying on transferring the unused nil rate band on the death of the second spouse.

Example

> Robert has two children from his first marriage to Liz. He has recently married Elspeth and is concerned to ensure that his children benefit under his will whilst utilising his nil rate band. By including a nil rate band discretionary trust he will achieve his aim.

As discussed above there are restrictions on the amount of the unused nil rate band that can be transferred where there have been multiple marriages. Because there are no such restrictions on the number of discretionary trusts that can be created, the discretionary trust may be a useful tool in avoiding the restriction.

Example

> Winnie married Felix in 1984. He died in 1988 leaving his estate of £400,000 to Winnie. The nil rate band was £110,000. In 1993 Winnie married Augustus. He died in 2005 leaving his estate of £1m to Winnie. The nil rate band was £275,000.
>
> Winnie died in May 2016.
>
> On the deaths of both Felix and Augustus, 100% of their nil rate bands was unused. However, on Winnie's death the increase in her nil rate band is limited to 100% thus increasing her nil rate band by £325,000.
>
> If both Felix and Augustus had created nil rate band discretionary trusts for the benefit of Winnie and their children their nil rate bands would have been utilised on their deaths. Therefore £110,000 would have been transferred to a discretionary trust on Felix's death and £275,000 would have been transferred to a discretionary trust on Augustus's death making a total of £385,000. If Winnie had needed funds during her lifetime the trustees could have advanced funds to her. On her death these trusts would not have formed part of her estate on death and therefore would not have been subject to inheritance tax.

The use of nil rate band discretionary trusts can allow a husband and wife to reduce the impact of the relevant property regime.

Example

> Bonnie and Clyde are husband and wife both owning assets worth £325,000 each. Bonnie dies first leaving her assets to Clyde and so no tax is payable. When Clyde dies he leaves his assets on discretionary trusts to his children. Clyde uses his own and Bonnie's nil rate band which exactly matches the value of his estate of £650,000. Whilst no inheritance tax was payable on his death, future decennial charges on the discretionary trust will be based on the total value of the trust property (currently being £650,000) plus any capital growth. If Bonnie and Clyde had made separate nil rate band discretionary trusts, there would either have been no charge or only a very small one.

The nil rate band discretionary trust is also of benefit where there are assets with the prospect of high growth in their capital values. It can also be used as a means of losing the marriage value of various assets.

Relievable property

[18.14] Care should be taken where a nil rate band discretionary trust is being created on death and the estate includes assets which qualify for business property relief or agricultural property relief. It is advisable in such circumstances that the assets qualifying for relief are the subject of a specific gift. The case of *Brooke v Purton* [2014] EWHC 547 (Ch), [2014] WTLR 745 highlights the importance of considering the effects of standard precedents used in such situations.

A benefit or not

[18.15] The provisions allowing the transfer of the nil rate band are undoubtedly useful in that they allow the nil rate bands of both spouses to be utilised but the nil rate band discretionary trust is still of significance in many situations. The wording of any nil rate band discretionary trusts in an existing will needs to be reviewed to ensure that it still accords with the testator's wishes (see **18.8**).

There are, however, situations where the availability of a transferable nil rate band can cause difficulties which would not have occurred previously.

Example

> Bob was married to Bunty and had two children. They divorced in 1998 and he married Brenda. Brenda had also been married before and had one daughter. Brenda died in 2010. Under her will, Brenda left the residue of her estate on a life interest trust for Bob with remainder to her daughter. She did not use her nil rate band. In 2016, Bob made a gift of £650,000 to his two children and unfortunately he died later that year. To ensure that Brenda's nil rate band is utilised, Bob's executors will make a claim so that a nil rate band of £650,000 is available. This will be first set against the PET to Bob's children which has now become chargeable and so the entire £650,000 is utilised. The termination of Bob's IPDI under Brenda's will will be chargeable at 40%. This has therefore resulted in the benefit of Brenda's unused nil rate band being fully utilised by Bob's children and not by her own daughter. Before the introduction of the transferable nil rate band

this issue would not have arisen because Brenda would have had to have used her nil rate band on death to ensure that it was not lost.

Residence nil rate amount

Outline

[18.16] In addition to the nil rate band of £325,000 in respect of a death after 5 April 2017, a residence nil rate amount (RNRA) will be available if the deceased's interest in a property, which has been occupied as a residence of the deceased and is included in their estate, passes to a direct descendant on death, or where the deceased had downsized or ceased to own a residence after 7 July 2015 and other assets are passed on death to direct descendants (see **18.18**).

The RNRA will only be available to reduce the tax on death (IHTA 1984, s 8D). It will not be available to reduce the tax payable on lifetime transfers that become chargeable as a result of death. It will, however, be available where the property is treated as forming part of the deceased's estate on death because he made a gift subject to reservation during his lifetime.

The RNRA is used first. After the RNRA has been deducted, tax will be charged on the remainder of the chargeable estate after deducting the amount of any nil rate band remaining after taking into account the amount of previous chargeable transfers in the last seven years and then applying the rates applicable for transfers on death.

The RNRA will be the lower of:

(a) the value of the 'qualifying residential interest' that is 'closely inherited'; or

(b) the amount of the 'residential enhancement'.

The amount of the residential enhancement is to increase annually for four years as follows (IHTA 1984, s 8D(5)):

Year	RNRA £	Maximum relief for spouses £	Potential IHT £
2017/18	100,000	200,000	80,000
2018/19	125,000	250,000	100,000
2019/20	150,000	300,000	120,000
2020/21	175,000	350,000	140,000

After 6 April 2021, the RNRA will increase in line with the Consumer Prices Index.

Where the value of the deceased's estate after deducting liabilities (but before the value has been reduced by relief such as business property relief or agricultural property relief) exceeds £2 million, a form of taper relief is applied to reduce the amount of the residential enhancement. There will be a withdrawal of £1 for every £2 over the £2 million threshold. Again after 6 April 2021, this threshold amount will increase in line with the Consumer Prices Index.

Qualifying residential interest

[18.17] As mentioned above, the RNRA is only available where there is a qualifying residential interest in a person's estate. If there is no such interest the RNRA is nil. Section 8H defines a 'residential property interest' in relation to a person as 'an interest in the dwelling-house which has been the person's residence at a time when the person's estate included that, or any other, interest in the dwelling-house'. Where the person's estate immediately before his death includes a residential property interest in one dwelling-house, that interest is a 'qualifying residential interest'. It could include a property that had been a residence of the deceased which at the time of death was let, for example, if a person has moved into a care home but has retained the property. A property which was never the dwelling-house of the deceased will not qualify; for example, a property that has always been let by the deceased. If the person's estate included residential property interests in two or more dwelling-houses, the personal representatives are able to nominate one of them to be the 'qualifying residential interest' (IHTA 1984, s 8H(4)). A dwelling-house includes any land occupied and enjoyed with it as its garden or grounds, but does not include any trees or underwood in relation to which an election has been made under IHTA 1984, s 125.

Where a person's estate includes a dwelling-house and that person resides in job-related accommodation (as defined for capital gains tax main residence relief purposes) but intends to occupy the dwelling-house as a residence, that dwelling-house is treated as being occupied by the person as a residence at that time (IHTA 1984, s 8H(6)).

Closely inherited

[18.18] The qualifying residential interest must be 'closely inherited' (IHTA 1984, s 8K(1)(b)). A property is inherited by a person (B) if there is a disposition of the property by will, under the law relating to intestacy or otherwise to B (IHTA 1984, s 8J). Where the property becomes comprised in a settlement, B inherits the property only if he becomes entitled to an interest in possession, that is an IPDI or DPI, or if the property becomes held on trust for his benefit to which IHTA 1984, s 71A (Trusts for Bereaved Minors) or s 71D (Age 18-to-25 Trusts) apply (IHTA 1984, s 8J(4)).

No RNRA will be available in respect of trusts outside of these limited exceptions; for example, a discretionary trust or a trust for grandchildren who do not receive the property on the deceased's death.

Where a property was the subject of a lifetime gift but the reservation of benefit rules apply so that it is treated as forming part of the donor's estate on death, then the donee of the lifetime gift is treated as having inherited the property (IHTA 1984, s 8J(6)).

The legislation defines 'closely inherited' as a property inherited by a lineal descendant of the deceased (IHTA 1984, s 8K). A lineal descendant includes a step-child, adopted child, foster child or child under guardianship and grandchildren.

Calculation of RNRA

[18.19] To calculate the amount of the available RNRA, one must determine a person's 'default allowance' or, where the value of the estate exceeds £2 million, the 'adjusted allowance' (IHTA 1984, s 8D(5)). The default allowance is the amount of the residential enhancement at the date of death, together with any brought forward allowance. The adjusted allowance is the default allowance reduced by the tapering.

Estate is £2 million or less

[18.20] Where the value of the estate is less than the taper threshold (currently £2 million), the available RNRA is the lower of:

(a)   the default allowance; or
(b)   the amount of the qualifying residential interest that is closely inherited.

Where (b) is less than (a), the difference will be available to be carried forward to a surviving spouse or civil partner (IHTA 1984, ss 8E(2), (3)).

Estate is over £2 million

[18.21] Where the value of the estate exceeds the taper threshold (which is currently £2 million) the available RNRA is the lower of:

(a)   the adjusted allowance; or
(b)   amount of the qualifying residential interest that is closely inherited.

Where (b) is less than (a) the difference will again be available to be carried forward to a surviving spouse or civil partner (IHTA 1984, s 8E(4), (5)).

If either a person's estate does not include a qualifying residential interest or it includes a qualifying residential interest but that interest is not closely inherited, the amount of the RNRA is nil. An amount equal, however, to the default allowance (if the value of the estate before reliefs and exemptions does not exceed the taper threshold) or otherwise the adjusted allowance will be available to be carried forward (IHTA 1984, s 8F).

In 2017/18 an estate in excess of £2.2 million will not have the benefit of an RNRA. In 2020/21 that will be the situation with estates in excess of £2.35 million.

Downsizing

[18.22] In 2015, when the RNRA was first announced, concerns were raised in relation to individuals who had downsized to a less valuable residence or had sold their home, for example, to pay for nursing or care home fees. Legislation has been introduced in FA 2016 to provide that a downsizing addition is available when an individual downsizes from a higher value residence to a lower value one or ceases to own a residence and other assets are left on death to direct descendants. The provisions in IHTA 1984, ss 8FA–8FE will apply for deaths after 5 April 2017 where there has been a disposal after 7 July 2015.

Where a person has downsized from a more valuable residence and there is a less valuable residence in the estate on death, a downsizing addition will be available provided that conditions A to F are met (IHTA 1984, s 8FA):

- Condition A is that either there is a residence in the estate on death which qualifies for RNRA but the full amount is not due because the value of the residence or the proportion closely inherited is below the maximum RNRA available for that person or there is a residence in the estate on death but it is not closely inherited and the value of the residence is less than the RNRA available for that person.
- Condition B is that the value transferred by the chargeable transfer on death is more than the value of the person's qualifying residential interest.
- Condition C is that the person has a qualifying former residential interest, as defined in IHTA 1984, s 8H.
- Condition D is that the value of the qualifying former residential interest is more than the chargeable value of the person's qualifying residential interest in the estate at death.
- Condition E is that at least some of the other assets in the estate are closely inherited.
- Condition F is that a claim is made for the downsizing addition.

The amount of a downsizing addition would be equal to the lost relievable amount, which is effectively the lost RNRA. This is calculated in accordance with IHTA 1984, s 8FE. This amount is, however, limited to the value of other assets 'or a proportion of that value' which is closely inherited.

Where there is no residence in a deceased person's estate on death, a downsizing addition will be available provided conditions G to K are satisfied (IHTA 1984, s 8FB):

- Condition G is that, immediately before the death of the deceased, his estate does not contain a residential property interest.
- Condition H is that the value transferred by the chargeable transfer on death is greater than nil.
- Condition I is that the deceased previously had a qualifying former residential interest.
- Condition J is that at least some of the other assets in the estate are closely inherited.
- Condition K is that a claim is made for the downsizing addition.

The amount of the downsizing addition is equal to the lost relievable amount, calculated in accordance with IHTA 1984, s 8FE. The amount is, however, limited to the value of other assets 'or a proportion of that value' which is closely inherited.

Claim for brought forward allowance

[18.23] As mentioned above, any RNRA that is not utilised on the first death can be transferred to the surviving spouse or civil partner to be used in their estate on death. Rather than call this a transferable RNRA it is called a 'brought forward allowance'. The amount unused expressed as a percentage will be applied to uplift the surviving spouse or civil partner's entitlement based on the amount which applies on the second death. This allowance cannot exceed 100% of the residential enhancement amount on the second death.

Example

> Sebastian dies in 2017/18 leaving the family home, Floral Cottage, valued at £75,000 to his children with the residue of his estate to his wife, Annabel. Annabel moves from Floral Cottage to Glebe Cottage where she lives until her death in 2020/21. She leaves her entire estate to her children. Glebe Cottage at the time of her death is worth £300,000.
>
> £75,000 of Sebastian's RNRA of £100,000 will be set against the gift to his children and so he has used three quarters of his RNRA (£75,000/£100,000). On her death Annabel's default allowance is the total of the residential enhancement available on her death (£175,000) plus the brought forward allowance of £43,750 (25% of £175,000) if claimed. Her total default allowance is, therefore, £218,750. This is her RNRA because it is less than the value of her qualifying residential interest that is closely inherited: £300,000.

It does not matter if the death of the spouse or civil partner occurred before 6 April 2017 but special rules apply in calculating the brought forward allowance in such circumstances. Where the first death occurred before 6 April 2017 the result is, in essence, that the brought forward allowance on the second death will be 100% of the residential enhancement at that time unless, on the earlier death, the value of the person's estate exceeded £2 million in which case the carried forward amount is reduced (but not below nil) by:

RPE – £2 million / 2

Where RPE is the value of the person's estate

The brought forward allowance is only available if it is claimed (IHTA 1984, s 8L). The claim may be made by either the deceased's personal representatives or, if no claim is made by the personal representatives within the permitted period, by any other person liable to the tax chargeable on the person's death.

The permitted period in which the personal representatives may make the claim is the later of:

* two years from the end of the month of death;
* three months from the date that the personal representatives begin to act; or
* such a longer period as HMRC may allow.

Example

> Tim died in January 2011 leaving an estate of £2.1 million to his wife, Topsy. Topsy dies on 16 July 2019 leaving an estate of £1.5 million, including her home worth £400,000, to their daughter, Fenella.
>
> *Step 1: calculate the carry-forward allowance on Tim's death*

$$100,000 \ - \ \frac{(2,100,000 \ - \ 2,000,000)}{2} \ = £50,000$$

This is 50% of the residential enhancement (£100,000) on Tim's death.

Step 2: calculate Topsy's default allowance

Topsy's default allowance is calculated as follows:

Residential enhancement	150,000
Brought forward allowance (50% of residential enhancement)	75,000
	225,000

Therefore, the inheritance tax will be calculated as follows:

Estate		1,500,000
Less:		
Brought forward allowance	225,000	
Topsy's nil rate band	325,000	
Transferable nil rate band	325,000	
		875,000
		625,000

$$625,000 \ \times 40\% \ = £250,000$$

More than one earlier death

[**18.24**] If there has been more than one earlier death because, for example, a widowed spouse or civil partner has remarried or entered into another civil partnership, then it is necessary to calculate the percentage of the residential enhancement available for carry forward on each earlier death and add together the percentages. The brought forward amount is the total percentage (or 100% if it is less) multiplied by the residential enhancement available on the second death.

Conditional exemption

[**18.25**] There are special rules which apply where a residence qualifies for conditional exemption.

Planning

[**18.26**] Although these rules do not come into effect until 6 April 2017 they will need to be taken into account when considering planning for clients. Current arrangements ought to be reviewed to ensure that the RNRA is not wasted, which is of course dependant on the facts of each individual case.

For example, individuals who have or are likely to have estates with a value of slightly more than £2 million might consider making lifetime gifts to take the value of their estate below the threshold. It is important that the taper threshold is not exceeded on the second death so spouses should consider the division of their estates to avoid this. It is also important that a mortgage does not reduce the net value of the property to an amount below the amount of the available RNRA.

It would appear that, on current rates, it generally will not be better to use the RNRA on the first death because it will be worth more on the second. This, of course, may change after 2021.

Agricultural and business property

[18.27] Property which qualifies for agricultural or business property relief should, where possible, be given to non-exempt beneficiaries since the relief will be lost if given to a surviving spouse or civil partner who fails to satisfy the necessary conditions to obtain the relief on his or her death. Agricultural property relief is discussed in detail in CHAPTER 13 THE FAMILY FARM and business property relief is discussing in CHAPTER 12 THE FAMILY BUSINESS.

It is important that the property qualifying for relief should be the subject of a specific gift. If it is not, then the relief must be apportioned over the whole estate, including that part which is spouse exempt. The expression 'specific gift' is defined, somewhat inadequately, in IHTA 1984, s 42(1). The following points should be noted. An appropriation of business property in satisfaction of a pecuniary legacy does not count as a specific gift. A direction to pay a pecuniary legacy out of business property is likewise not a specific gift of that property (IHTA 1984, s 39A(6)). IHTA 1984, s 39A contains rules relating to the attribution of values to gifts in a will when part of the residuary estate is given to an exempt beneficiary and part of the residuary estate also qualifies for agricultural or business property relief. Any agricultural or business property relief is, in effect, apportioned between any specific gifts and the property in the residuary estate. Specific gifts of agricultural or business property are treated as gifts of the value of that property reduced by the relevant relief and if expressed to be free of tax the gifts will be grossed-up (see **18.41**).

HMRC's Inheritance Tax Manual at para 26104 contains an illustration of the application of s 39A which involves a six-step process. If necessary, a formula can be used to leave business property equal in value to the nil rate band after relief at 50% (where applicable). Leaving a specific gift to non-exempt beneficiaries means that a proportionately larger gift can be made for the same inheritance tax cost.

Example

A gift in the testator's will of a property which is valued at £650,000 on death and which is used by a company he controls is entitled to 50% business property relief. If given to his children or other non-exempt beneficiaries no inheritance tax will be suffered on the testator's death (provided he has made no chargeable transfers or potentially exempt transfers within seven years of his death).

Alternatively, it may be possible to obtain either business or agricultural property relief twice where one spouse leaves the property qualifying for relief to a discretionary trust in favour of his family including his spouse. On the first spouse's death, agricultural or business property relief would be available. Under the terms of his will, the first spouse would leave his investment assets to the other so no inheritance tax would arise on those assets. The surviving spouse could then purchase the agricultural or business assets at arm's length from the trustees of the discretionary trust. Provided she survives for two years after the purchase, the assets should also be eligible for agricultural or business property relief. In addition, the capital gains tax uplift on death will be available on both the agricultural and business property and the investment assets. The provisions of the GAAR will need to be considered to ensure that such an arrangement does not fall foul of them.

Charitable gifts

[18.28] Gifts by will to charities or registered clubs are exempt from inheritance tax (IHTA 1984, s 23). However, relief will be precluded where the gift to a charity or registered club only takes effect on the termination of any other interest, or depends on a condition which is not satisfied within 12 months of the death, or is for a limited period, is defeasible (s 23(2), (3)).

In addition, a lower rate of inheritance tax of 36% will be chargeable on the deceased's estate where there are charitable legacies of at least 10% of a testator's net estate. Therefore where an individual wishes to make some charitable legacies under his will it will be important to determine whether advantage can be taken of the lower rate of tax. If a testator intends to give 4% of his net estate to charity, his gift can be increased to 10% without the value of the benefits received by the chargeable beneficiaries being reduced. More discussion can be found in CHAPTER 15 GIFTS TO CHARITIES AND OTHER NON-PROFIT ORGANISATIONS.

The drafting of the clause will be essential. HMRC has included in its guidance a draft clause which it considers will satisfy the conditions of the relief. STEP have also produced a model clause which HMRC has confirmed satisfies the requirements of the legislation which can be found at www.step.org/step-model-clause-iht.

Gifts for the public benefit

[18.29] An exemption is also available for gifts to:

(a) political parties (IHTA 1984, s 24);
(b) certain bodies of national importance specified in IHTA 1984, Sch 3 (IHTA 1984, s 25);
(c) maintenance funds for historic buildings (IHTA 1984, s 27);
(d) Community Amateur Sports Clubs (FA 2002, Sch 18, para 9(2)); and
(e) housing associations (IHTA 1984, s 24A).

For further details, see CHAPTER 15 GIFTS TO CHARITIES AND OTHER NON-PROFIT ORGANISATIONS and CHAPTER 16 HERITAGE PROPERTY.

Limitations on reliefs available on death

[18.30]   Certain reliefs available in respect of lifetime gifts are not available on death (in some cases, for fairly obvious reasons). These are:

(a)   the annual exemption, currently £3,000;
(b)   the small gifts exemption, currently £250 per person;
(c)   the normal expenditure out of income exemption;
(d)   the exemption for gifts in consideration of marriage; and
(e)   the exemption for certain dispositions for the maintenance of a family.

One relief available only on death is limited to a person who is not domiciled and not resident in the UK immediately before his death. IHTA 1984, s 157 provides that the balance on any qualifying foreign currency account of such a person, or of the trustees of settled property in which he is beneficially entitled to an interest in possession, is to be left out of account in determining the value of the estate.

Gifts to a spouse or civil partner

Equalisation of estates

[18.31]   It may be thought that some measure of equalisation with regard to the values of the spouses' or civil partners' respective estates is of less significance now because unused nil rate bands can be transferred between the estates of spouses and civil partners. It is still, however, an essential element of estate planning. Equalisation will allow both spouses or civil partners to make potentially exempt transfers and gifts within the annual exemption. Such gifts between spouses or civil partners will generally not give rise to any inheritance tax, capital gains tax, stamp duty or stamp duty land tax liabilities. This equalisation of estates will also help to ensure that the survivor is provided for adequately.

The possible impact, however, of the related property provisions contained in IHTA 1984, s 161 should not be overlooked. Section 161 provides that where the value of any property forming part of the estates of both spouses or civil partners taken together is greater than the value of the spouses' or civil partners' respective shares or interests in the property when valued individually, then the value to be adopted is the appropriate proportion of the value of the property as a whole. Property which is or has within the preceding five years been the property of a charity or the property of a political party, housing association or national body, in either case typically as a result of a transfer by either spouse, will also be related property.

In *Arkwright v IRC* [2004] STC (SCD) 89 (SpC 392) it was successfully argued before the Special Commissioners that s 161(4) was intended to apply to the splitting of related property where the property had a distinct individual existence as a unit, such as unit trusts or a set of furniture but it did not apply to fractions of units such as freehold property held as tenants in common. Although this issue was not considered further when the Revenue's appeal against the decision was heard by the High Court, the Revenue claimed to have received legal advice that s 161(4) may apply to fractional shares of units. In Brief 71/07 HMRC stated that it will apply the apportionment method in s 161(4) when valuing shares of land as related property. The related provisions do not nullify the purpose of the equalisation of estates.

In *Price (executor of Price, dec'd) v Revenue & Customs Comrs* [2010] UKFTT 474 (TC), [2011] SFTD 52, [2011] SWTI 310 it was held that the deceased's one half interest as tenant in common in the marital home was to be valued for the purposes of s 161 on the basis of the price it would have fetched on the open market if offered for sale in conjunction with the surviving spouse's interest.

Where gifts are being made between spouses or civil partners, it is advisable that a deed of gift is used to record the gift so as to provide evidence that the donor intends beneficial ownership to pass to the donee.

Absolute gifts v life interests

[18.32] The question as to whether a surviving spouse or civil partner should be given property absolutely by the will, or be given a life interest only in the whole or part of the estate, is one often asked by clients. The spouse or civil partner who has an interest in possession which is an immediate post-death interest ('IPDI') will be treated as if he or she owns the underlying assets and tax is charged accordingly on his or her death (IHTA 1984, s 49(1A)). Therefore, the property given absolutely or on trust for life (which is an IPDI) by one spouse to another or between civil partners will be exempt from tax on the first death but on the second death will be taxed in some form or another. The decision may be made for personal rather than fiscal reasons. A testator who has confidence in his or her spouse or civil partner can give capital instead of a life interest. Where a testator is concerned that the surviving spouse or civil partner will fritter away or mismanage the estate so that there is nothing left for any children, then clearly the testator should consider only giving the spouse or civil partner a life interest, with the capital passing automatically on the spouse's or civil partner's death to the children. The survivor's life interest could also expressly be made to come to an end on any subsequent marriage or registration of a civil partnership.

A combination of a life interest, coupled with a power for the trustees (who may or may not, depending on the circumstances in which the gift is made, include the testator's spouse or civil partner) to release capital to the life tenant will produce a more flexible provision for the surviving spouse or civil partner whilst preserving part of the capital for future generations at no extra inheritance tax cost. The release of capital to the spouse or civil partner, who already has an interest in possession and is consequently treated for inheritance tax purposes as owning the assets provided the interest is an IPDI, will not give rise to a charge to tax (IHTA 1984, s 53(2)). However, depending upon the nature and value of the assets released, there may be a charge to capital gains tax on the release.

As mentioned above, in particular situations there are a number of advantages of an IPDI, namely:

(i)   It may be preferable to create an IPDI when making wills for elderly clients. If following the first death the surviving spouse is not able to make a gift by way of a potentially exempt transfer, the trustees may exercise their discretion by terminating the surviving spouse's interest;

(ii)   An IPDI may be advantageous in a second marriage situation. Although inheritance tax may be payable on the second death it can be avoided by the termination in whole or part of the IPDI provided the surviving spouse or civil partner survives by seven years. In the event that the spouse or civil partner does not survive the seven years, the step children will benefit from the second wife's nil rate band first (as shown in the example in **18.15**). This issue should be explained to the testator who may consider a discretionary legacy to address the burden of inheritance tax;

(iii)   An IPDI will be preferable if there are concerns about the surviving spouse or civil partner's insolvency;

(iv)   It is easier to control the level of income of the surviving spouse or civil partner with an IPDI when dealing with means tested benefits and care home fees.

An outright gift is, however, more simple and straightforward and for the majority of clients will be preferred. It is also preferable to an IPDI where both spouses or civil partners die within a two year period and a double death variation is required.

Gifts to children and remoter issue

[18.33] A gift may be either vested, that is the right to the gift is certain, or contingent, that is dependent upon an uncertain future event. A vested gift may be either vested in possession, that is of immediate effect, or vested in interest, that is coming into effect on a certain future event such as the expiry of a period of time.

Vested gifts

[18.34] Where a gift is vested in possession, no particular tax problems are usually encountered. If the vested gift is to a legatee who is a minor, the executors will on the completion of the administration hold as bare trustees until the minor attains 18 and can give them a valid receipt. Any income or capital gains arising will be taxed as those of the minor. In the absence of any contrary intention in the will the Trustee Act 1925, ss 31 and 32 will apply. For trusts created or arising before 1 October 2014, the trustees will be able to release the income for the minor's maintenance, education or benefit as the trustees may think fit and up to one half of the capital for his advancement or benefit (though it is usual to extend s 32 to enable the whole of the capital to be released). For trusts and will trusts created or arising after 30 September 2014 trustees are able to pay out up to the whole of the capital of the beneficiary's respective share.

Contingent gifts and gifts vested in interest

[18.35] Contingent gifts are more complex. In the absence of an express direction in the will, the general rule is that the gift will not carry the intermediate income unless it is a gift of residue or is a specific gift (Law of Property Act 1925, s 175). Therefore, the income of a contingent gift which does not carry the intermediate income (such as a general pecuniary legacy to a child of the testator upon attaining an age exceeding the age of majority) will be payable to the residuary beneficiaries until the contingency is attained. On the occurrence of that event the residuary beneficiaries' interests in possession in the contingent fund will be terminated. Whether or not a termination is a potentially exempt transfer will depend upon its nature (see CHAPTER 6 CREATING SETTLEMENTS and CHAPTER 7 EXISTING SETTLEMENTS).

On the occurrence of the contingency there may be a disposal by the trustees for capital gains tax if the gift is of chargeable assets. However, depending upon the nature of the assets a hold-over election under TCGA 1992, s 165 may be available. Where the gift does carry the intermediate income it may qualify as a trust for a bereaved minor or an 18–25 trust. In such circumstances hold-over relief under TCGA 1992, s 260 might be available, whatever the nature of the asset, provided the satisfaction of the contingency results in capital and income vesting contemporaneously.

For income tax purposes income which is accumulated or over which the trustees have a discretion will be subject to income tax at the trust rate (currently 45% or 38.1% on dividend income) unless the minor has a vested interest in the income in which case it will be taxed as his or her income.

There are effectively four options available in respect of gifts to children:

(i)   an outright gift. This is usually used for small amounts of cash or chattels;

(ii)   an immediate post-death interest (an 'IPDI') which is discussed in detail in **6.30**;

(iii)   a bereaved minors trust, discussed in more detail in **6.42**;

(iv)   an age 18–25 trust which is discussed in **6.44**.

In respect of both outright gifts and an IPDI, the beneficiary is treated as absolutely entitled to the assets. The advantage of an IPDI is that the underlying assets are ring-fenced. They will not be available for distribution in a matrimonial or insolvency matter. The disadvantage of an IPDI is that if capital is advanced to a beneficiary there will be a disposal on which a capital gains tax liability could arise unless hold-over relief is available under TCGA 1992, s 165. Hold-over relief under TCGA 1992, s 260 would, however, be available in respect of an 18–25 trust and a bereaved minor trust.

The choice of structure will depend on all the circumstances including the type of assets and their value, the ages of the children concerned and the flexibility required.

Generation skipping

[18.36] If the testator's children are sufficiently well provided for, then consideration should be given to skipping a generation in the will to provide for grandchildren, present and future. Even if the testator's children are not particularly wealthy, the advantages of enabling them to use the grandchildren's income tax personal allowances each year, which might otherwise be lost, may be a significant benefit to a child of the testator by relieving his own income from the burden of maintaining or educating his children.

Skipping a generation will ensure that property reaching the grandchildren will avoid at least one charge to inheritance tax which would otherwise have arisen on the death of the parent. Before 22 March 2006, such trusts would have been in the form of a gift to an accumulation and maintenance trust because of their flexibility and inheritance tax benefits. Such trusts no longer enjoy a favoured tax status. Although there is nothing preventing such trusts being created they will now be taxed in accordance with the relevant property regime. A gift under a will to grandchildren could be in the form of an interest in possession trust or a discretionary trust. An interest in possession trust for the benefit of grandchildren may be an immediate post-death interest ('IPDI') if it falls within IHTA 1984, s 49A. Such a trust will not be subject to decennial charges nor exit charges. Instead, on the death of the life tenant, the underlying assets will form part of the deceased's estate under IHTA 1984, s 49.

Where the trust is not an IPDI or other form of privileged trust, then the trust will be subject to the relevant property regime. Of course, a discretionary trust offers more flexibility and in many cases will be preferable.

The family home

[18.37] Very often a testator will ask for advice on giving away his matrimonial home or, where this is owned by both spouses or civil partners, for advice on giving away his share of it. A gift of a share of the home can only be made by will if the property is beneficially owned as tenants in common. In the case of a joint tenancy, the share of the property will automatically pass by survivorship. A discussion of property ownership can be found at **11.2**.

If the property is owned jointly as tenants in common, the property will be held by them in trust. They each have an interest in the proceeds of sale of the property and a right to reside there while it remains unsold. These rights will pass to a legatee if a share of the property is given by the will.

A discretionary will trust (see **18.39** below) often permits the surviving spouse or civil partner to continue to occupy the family home.

Where the testator is proposing a gift in his will of his interest in the property, other than to his wife, he will usually be concerned to preserve the ability for his wife to reside in the property. HMRC's view is that any right given to the wife for her to continue to reside there will create an interest in possession in favour of the wife in the testator's half of the property (based on the decision in *IRC v Lloyds Private Banking Ltd* [1998] STC 559 (Ch D), [1998] 2 FCR 41; *Woodhall (Woodhall's Personal Representative) v IRC* [2000] STC (SCD) 558 (SpC 261) and *Faulkner (Trustee of Adams, dec'd) v IRC* [2001] STC (SCD) 112 (SpC 278)). In *Judge v HMRC* 2005] STC (SCD) 863 the husband had owned the whole house and under a discretionary will trust had provided that the trustees should permit the use and enjoyment of the property 'for such periods as they shall in their absolute discretion think fit'. It was held that the wife did not have the right as against the trustees to occupy the property because the trustees had an absolute discretion as to whether or not they would permit her to exercise that right. Accordingly, she did not have an interest in possession. It should be noted that SP10/79 was not considered in the case. A termination of an interest will occur on the subsequent death of the wife or possibly on an earlier sale.

Where under the terms of a will, a property is left on discretionary trusts and the trustees permit the beneficiary to occupy the property, it is HMRC's view that there will be an interest in possession but the trust will be a relevant property settlement and not an IPDI. In correspondence between CIOT/STEP and HMRC, HMRC has said that where a discretionary trust is created and funded by a share in a property which the trustees permit a surviving spouse to occupy on an exclusive basis at their discretion on similar terms to those in *Judge*, the trust will not automatically be an IPDI but it will depend upon the terms on which the spouse occupies (Questions by STEP/CIOT and Answers from HMRC to Schedule 20, Finance Act 2006). Where the trust arises on a death and the spouse's occupation commences within two years of the death it is clear that if a spouse's occupation amounts to an interest in possession it will be an IPDI (IHTA 1984, s 144).

Similar considerations apply where the matrimonial home is in the sole name of one spouse. Should it be left to the surviving spouse alone, to the surviving spouse and children jointly or to the children alone? The testator's primary concern will often be the security of the surviving spouse but he may have to balance that security against the fact that if the home is left solely to the children and they allow their surviving parent to occupy it for the rest of his or her life, the gifts with reservation provisions will not apply. Of course, if the house is likely to be sold on the first death, different considerations will apply.

Where the joint owners are an unmarried couple living together, consideration should be given to the surviving cohabitee's position after the death of the first to die. Where a property is purchased by only one of the cohabitees, the purchaser may wish to make provision for the surviving cohabitee on his death. The tax consequences are discussed in detail in CHAPTER 11 THE FAMILY HOME AND OTHER RESIDENTIAL PROPERTY.

Survivorship clauses

[18.38] It is common practice to make gifts to individuals in wills contingent on them surviving the testator for a given period, usually three months. Such a survivorship clause can serve various purposes.

(a) It can prevent a double charge to tax where the legatee dies shortly after the testator.

(b)   In the case of a gift to a spouse or civil partner it can prevent a greater charge to inheritance tax arising than would otherwise have arisen on the death of the spouse or civil partner by preventing the deceased's property from passing to the surviving spouse or civil partner and being aggregated with his or her own estate.

(c)   It ensures that property will devolve, in the event of the second death occurring within the survivorship period, to a substituted legatee of the first testator's choosing and will not pass under the will of the second to die.

(d)   It avoids the same property having to be administered twice over in two different estates within a relatively short space of time.

IHTA 1984, s 92 provides that a survivorship clause for a period not exceeding six months is back-dated to the date of death for inheritance tax purposes and tax will be charged on the death depending on whether the legatee survives for the period or dies before the period expires.

In some instances it may be desirable that if a married couple die simultaneously, for example, in a car accident, that the survivorship period should not apply. In the situation where spouses die together and it is not certain who died first, the elder spouse is deemed to die first (Law of Property Act 1925, s 184). Therefore, if the survivorship period does not apply, the elder spouse's estate will pass to the younger. IHTA 1984, s 4(2) provides that where it cannot be ascertained which of two people survived the other then it is assumed that both deaths occurred at the same instant. This means that the property of the elder falls outside the charge to inheritance tax on the younger's death. Therefore, from the point of view of inheritance tax, a survivorship clause need not operate in the event of a common accident.

As illustrated in **18.11** above, the inclusion of a survivorship clause in a 'Commorientes' case can have a disastrous effect on the transferable nil rate band. Because of this, it is becoming accepted practice for a survivorship clause not to be included in wills for spouses or civil partners.

Survivorship clauses can cause severe cash flow problems (and worry) for a dependent spouse. For this reason, should the will have a survivorship clause it should contain a power for the executors to use either the capital or the income to maintain the spouse during the survivorship period. Alternatively, it should be coupled with a joint bank account or other similar arrangements so that the dependent spouse is not deprived of funds for a lengthy period.

Discretionary wills

[**18.39**]   Often, an individual wishing to make a will is, at the time, precluded by financial or family circumstances from making a decision as to how his property should be distributed on his death. When drafting his will a testator cannot be certain what resources he and his survivors will have at his death or indeed who will survive him. After his death it will be much clearer to the executors and the family to how assets should be divided between those whom he wishes to benefit and also whether there is scope to skip a generation. In these circumstances the appropriate solution may be to give the whole or the largest part of his estate to his executors to be held on discretionary trusts. A discretionary will confers on the executors an overriding power of appointment drafted in wide terms which is exercisable over their entire estate in favour of a specified class of beneficiaries (relying on IHTA 1984, s 144). The power of appointment must be exercised within two years of the testator's death. Such a will usually contains provisions that the testator wishes to take effect in default of an appointment. Whilst a discretionary will provides flexibility, the disadvantages should not be overlooked:

(1)   The circumstances which led the testator to delegate his testamentary responsibility to his executors may still exist at his death or at the end of the period of two years from his death – nonetheless, even if the uncertainties are not fully resolved, the executors/trustees will at least know the latest situation;

(2)   The executors may be at a disadvantage in as far as they are not as familiar with the circumstances of the family as the testator himself – but in such circumstances the executors will normally be either family members or long-established family advisers;

(3)   The testator must appreciate that he will have to rely on others to make decisions and judgements about his family over which he will have no control – he can guide his executors, however, by means of a letter of wishes and provide 'long stop' provisions within the will in the event that the executors cannot agree amongst themselves.

Despite these supposed disadvantages, it is still preferable to have a discretionary will rather than to rely on a possible variation of the will by the beneficiaries, following the death. The scope for a variation may be limited unless all beneficiaries are *sui juris* and willing to agree. In addition, it should be noted that the Chancellor in his Autumn Statement 2015 said that the use of Deeds of Variation for tax purposes will continue to be monitored. This might result in IHTA 1984, s 142 being amended so that the reading back of the variation into the will is restricted or prevented. Where a parent beneficiary confers a benefit on his relevant children (unless they are vulnerable beneficiaries) by a variation he will fall within the provisions of ITTOIA 2005, s 629 in relation to the income of the property. An appointment under a discretionary will is outside the provisions of that section. It has been argued, surely erroneously, that where the power is vested in the deceased's executors a surviving spouse, who is the sole executor (or even one of the executors) may be regarded as a settlor for the purposes of s 629 in exercising, or concurring in the exercise, of this power.

Discretionary wills are discussed in more detail at **19.38**.

Types of gifts and legacies

[18.40] A testator should expressly state in his will where the inheritance tax on a specific bequest is to fall. If there is no express provision, the general principle is that the tax on UK unsettled property is a testamentary expense payable from the residue. When drafting a will, it is advisable that there be express provisions stating whether bequests are tax bearing or free of tax.

Free-of-tax legacies: grossing-up

[18.41] Under IHTA 1984, s 38, where the residue of an estate is exempt from inheritance tax because, for example, it passes either to the testator's spouse or to charity, then any legacies and bequests given in the will 'free-of-tax' will be grossed-up to determine the amount of tax chargeable which is in respect of those legacies, and payable out of residue. The gross sum which, after deduction of tax at the rate applicable to the chargeable value of the estate, will provide the amount required to meet the legacies and bequests, and inheritance tax is then charged on this grossed-up value. Where gifts have been made within seven years of death, whether chargeable transfers or potentially exempt transfers, these will be aggregated with the value of the free-of-tax legacies and other chargeable property passing on the death to determine the rate at which tax is payable. Such lifetime transfers will have the benefit of the nil rate band in priority to the estate on death.

Where part of the residue is chargeable, and part is exempt, the grossing-up calculation involves a second stage in which the value of the chargeable residue as well as the value of the free-of-tax legacies (and the value of any transfers within seven years of the death) are included. If the calculated net value of the chargeable estate does not exceed the nil rate band at the death, grossing-up becomes irrelevant, and no tax is payable.

Grossing-up will be avoided if gifts to non-exempt beneficiaries are made subject to inheritance tax instead of free of it. This will result, however, in the non-exempt beneficiaries receiving a lower net sum which may not accord with the testator's wishes in every case. Of course, the testator could always increase the size of the legacy if the gift is to bear its own tax which will have a similar (if not identical) effect to the grossing-up provisions. Alternatively, if instead the legatees are given a share of residue to be divided between them, grossing-up will be avoided and some tax saved. However, such a gift is less precise, in that the sum which the legatee will receive often cannot be calculated accurately when the will is drawn up, but only on the distribution of the estate following the testator's death.

Where a will provides for half of the testator's estate to pass to an exempt beneficiary and the other half to a taxable beneficiary, will the estate be divided equally before inheritance tax or after it? In *Re Benham's Will Trusts, Lockhart v Harker, Read and the Royal National Lifeboat Institution* [1995] STC 210 (Ch D) the court decided that the division was after tax and therefore that the exempt beneficiary's after tax share was equal to the taxable beneficiary's. In *Ratcliffe, Re, Holmes v McMullan* [1999] STC 262, [1999] 11 LS Gaz R 70 on similar facts the court decided that the division was before tax so that the exempt beneficiary received a larger net amount than the non-exempt beneficiary. The decision distinguished *Re Benham's Will Trusts* on the basis that no general principle was to be applied but rather the intentions of the particular testator were to be determined from the construction of the will.

Where a will provides for free-of-tax legacies and at the same time there are one or more separate funds (eg settlements in which the deceased had an interest in possession on 22 March 2006) also chargeable to tax on the deceased's death, then HMRC accepts that the rate of tax applicable when grossing up free-of-tax legacies is that applicable to the free estate in isolation and not that applicable to the total value of all property chargeable on the deceased's death (reported in the Law Society's Gazette of 9 May 1990 on p 14; see *Tolley's Yellow Tax Handbook* and HMRC Inheritance Tax Manual, para 26121). This means that where, for example, a will contains free-of-tax legacies and provides for residue to pass to an exempt beneficiary (eg a surviving spouse or civil partner) and there is separately chargeable settled property, either there will be no grossing up if the legacies are less than the nil rate band or only one round of grossing up will be needed if the legacies are in excess of the nil rate band.

Incidence of tax: residue

[18.42] Whilst the tax attributable to any tax-free legacies will be borne by the whole of the testator's residuary estate (even if it includes exempt beneficiaries), the burden of tax on non-exempt residuary gifts cannot be shifted by the will on to exempt residuary gifts (IHTA 1984, s 41). Any such provision is void. Where the residue is divided between exempt and non-exempt beneficiaries the tax payable on the estate and attributable to residue will be borne wholly by the non-exempt slice. However, the gifts contained in the will can reflect this fact: for example, instead of gifts of one half of residue to the spouse (exempt) and one half to the children (non-exempt) the will could contain gifts of one third of residue to the spouse and two thirds to the children.

Incidence of tax: land

[18.43] IHTA 1984, s 211 provides that inheritance tax is a testamentary expense payable from the residue if it is attributable to the value of UK property which vests in the deceased's personal representatives and was not comprised in a settlement immediately before the death, and so long as there is no contrary intention in the deceased's will. Therefore, to ensure that a legacy whether of land or other property bears its own tax, the will must state so expressly. In respect of foreign property the position is unclear. It is the better view that foreign property bears its own inheritance tax unless the will states otherwise and is therefore borne out of residue.

Gift of tax payable on potentially exempt transfers, etc

[18.44] A donor of a potentially exempt transfer who dies within seven years of the gift may leave the donee with a problem of funding the tax, for example, where the gift was of private company shares or other assets which are not easily realisable. To avoid this problem the donor may provide in his will that the tax due is to be paid out of his estate. This is the equivalent of a legacy to the donee of a sum equal to the amount of the tax. Such a legacy, if given free of tax, will have to be grossed-up as explained above. Personal representatives are under a secondary liability to pay the tax on a potentially exempt transfer under IHTA 1984, s 199. Therefore, where a legacy of the amount of the tax is given, rather than expressing this as a gift to the donee of the original gift, consideration should be given to coupling with it a power for the executors themselves to use the sum given to discharge the inheritance tax liability on the potentially exempt transfer (or even imposing a binding obligation on them to do so). This ensures that the gift is used for its intended purpose.

Similar considerations apply to chargeable lifetime gifts, where additional tax will be payable in the event of the donor's death within seven years, and to gifts where the deceased has reserved a benefit which are therefore taxable on his death as part of his estate. Legacies of the sum equivalent to the tax or additional tax which is payable need not be limited to one particular gift but could be expressed in general terms to cover all gifts by the testator during his lifetime which become chargeable, or give rise to tax payable, as a result of the death.

Gift of annuities

[18.45] As a general rule, gifts by will of annuities are best avoided, because of their disadvantageous tax treatment.

For inheritance tax purposes, the setting aside of the annuity fund will be treated as a settlement and a charge to tax will arise on the death of the annuitant or on the termination of his or her interest in possession (IHTA 1984, s 50).

For income tax purposes, the whole of the annuity given by the will is taxable in the hands of the annuitant. An annuity payment under a purchased life annuity is charged to income tax as savings and investment income and not under the separate provision for annual payments generally (ITTOIA 2005, s 422). However, because an annuity payment contains an element of capital, the capital element is exempt from income tax (ITTOIA 2005, s 717). Where, however, there is a direction in a will to purchase an annuity there is no exemption (ITTOIA 2005, s 718(2)(b)). A gift of a capital sum, calculated by reference to annuity rates, coupled with a non-binding suggestion to a legatee that it should be used to purchase an annuity is likely to be within the exemption. An annuity left to a spouse or civil partner may be advantageous because the transfer will benefit from the spouse exemption and over time the capital fund will reduce.

Gift of chattels

[18.46] It is often appropriate for chattels to be the subject of lifetime gifts. If a donor wishes to wait, it is common to use a precatory trust giving chattels by the will to a legatee or even to the executors with a non-binding condition that they are distributed in accordance with the testator's last known wishes as expressed in any note or memorandum left by the testator at his death (whether written before or after the date of the will). If the distribution is made within two years of the death it is treated as if it was made by the testator in his will and no additional charge to inheritance tax arises on that distribution (IHTA 1984, s 143). Precatory trusts are discussed in more detail in **19.44–19.45**.

Capital gains tax

[18.47] A gift by a legatee will be a disposal for capital gains tax purposes. A charge to capital gains tax could arise but in practice it is unlikely to do so. In the case of chattels, HMRC considers that a chattel is anything which is tangible, moveable property (HMRC Capital Gains Manual, para 76550). The exemption in TCGA 1992, s 262 will be available where the chattel is worth £6,000 or less, and marginal relief may apply where the value exceeds that sum. Chattels which are wasting assets are exempt from capital gains tax under TCGA 1992, ss 44 and 45. Special rules apply, however, in relation to plant and machinery. All plant and machinery is regarded as having a predictable life of less than 50 years. Plant and machinery are not defined in the legislation and so are given their normal meanings. Machinery includes any machine or its parts. A machine is any apparatus which applies mechanical power. Therefore clocks, watches and guns are all machinery and exempt from capital gains tax.

Limitation

[18.48] The testator must appreciate that his wishes will not be legally binding on the legatee of the chattels, but assuming he is prepared to accept this risk, a 'memorandum of wishes' clause in a will provides a flexible and tax effective way of dealing with gifts of a large number of chattels to individual legatees. There is nothing in IHTA 1984, s 143 which limits the operation of the provision to chattels, although the use of the word 'bequeathed' may limit the operation of the section to personalty and not realty. It could equally well apply to cash, although generally testators are more prepared to put specific chattels at risk rather than sums of money.

Gifts for anatomical and therapeutic purposes

[18.49] At common law, a decedent has no ability to direct the disposition of their remains. The right to dispose of the remains passes to the next of kin. Directions in a will for the disposal of the body or organs are therefore only wishes of the testator. Nevertheless it is important for the spouse or next of kin to know whether the testator would be willing for his body and organs to be used for transplant purposes or for medical research. As very prompt action will be required if he would be willing for such use to be made of them, there may not be time to refer to the will. He should therefore record his wishes in writing and ensure that a copy is held by his doctor and his spouse.

Safe keeping and review of wills

Safe keeping and review of wills

[18.50] Once signed, a will should be kept safely where, following the death, it can be obtained easily. Banks will usually agree to release the will, following the death, to allow solicitors acting in the estate to make an application for probate. Those who will need to know of its existence should be informed of its location.

There is sometimes a tendency for a testator having made a will to forget about it. The testator should be encouraged to review it regularly at least every five years and, in any event, following the introduction of any new tax legislation or a significant change in his personal or family circumstances or in the assets in his estate. Because of the large number of changes to inheritance tax legislation in the last few years and the recent changes to the Scottish law of succession, it is essential that wills are reviewed.

Small changes in a will can simply be made by a codicil. Testators should, however, always bear in mind that after death a will and codicils are public documents and he or she may prefer to consolidate an earlier will as varied by subsequent changes into one document to avoid the testator's changing fortunes and/or whims being subject to public scrutiny.

Personal Asset Schedule

[18.51] Executors often face a difficult task in locating a will, or a possible will, and share certificates and other documents of title. The testator should be encouraged to complete and to maintain a personal assets schedule. This should contain full details of:

(a)   assets;
(b)   all insurance cover on the testator's life and assets;
(c)   the names and addresses of his banks, building societies and professional advisers (eg solicitors, accountants and stock-brokers);
(d)   a copy of his will, and the location of the original of his will; and
(e)   the lifetime transfers which he has made.

While the schedule cannot be expected to contain details of every liability of the testator, it should at least record details of contingent liabilities under guarantees or indemnities, for example, knowledge of which may be crucial to the executors but which may otherwise be late in being drawn to their attention.

Digital Assets and Accounts Schedule

[18.52] It is also advisable that an individual should keep an inventory of their online assets and accounts, including email, social networking, gaming and music sites, to make it easier for them to be dealt with after death. This inventory should be updated regularly. The Law Society's Will and Inheritance Protocol suggests clients keep a personal assets log. An individual may leave instructions as to how he wishes his executors to deal with his digital assets.

Even where express instructions are given in a letter of wishes, problems may arise where a service provider does not recognise the authority given in the letter. Many people are unaware that they do not own their online content and have only a licence to use a website's services. The terms and conditions of many service providers provide that the licence terminates on death and is non-transferable. It is becoming of increasing importance as individuals expand their online presence and use. With music and ebooks being purchased online, a collection of significant monetary value can accumulate. Bitcoin accounts can also be valuable.

Saga has a guide for dealing with digital assets which provides a useful explanation as to how various electronic accounts can be wound up.

An Apple iTunes licence allows the playing of digital recordings to be used on up to five computers, but is not transmissible. It would appear, however, that Apple will allow the transfer and closure of an account on presentation of a death certificate and grant of probate.

A Facebook account holder is able to appoint an 'online executor' to administer a Facebook page after his death.

Yahoo accounts are terminated upon notification of the death of an account holder.

Microsoft will, upon receipt of a death certificate and grant of probate, provide a copy of emails on a disc to the next of kin.

Google and Youtube both enable an account holder to set up an 'inactive account manager'. Google will notify up to ten chosen beneficiaries after an account has been inactive for a pre-determined period of time, who will have access to the deceased's account before it is terminated.

Where a service provider has a procedure which allows the account holder to determine what happens on his death, clients should be encouraged to use this.

It is also recommended that, where possible, digital assets stored solely in the Cloud should be backed up to an external hard drive.

Variation of the will after death

[18.53] Whatever provision the testator may make in his will, his beneficiaries, if they are *sui juris*, may rearrange the distribution of the estate by means of a deed of variation or a disclaimer or by an application to the court either under the Variation of Trusts Act 1958 or under the Inheritance (Provision for Family and Dependants) Act 1975. Any variation may result in different inheritance tax consequences. This should not prevent a testator making proper provision in his will as none of these routes can be relied upon to produce the result which the testator (and his beneficiaries) would wish and there is always a risk that those who survive him will be unwilling or unable to enter into a variation. In addition, any application to the court will inevitably deplete the value of the testator's estate. These matters are considered more fully in CHAPTER 19 POST-DEATH ESTATE PLANNING.

Death in service benefits and pension schemes

[18.54] For members of an approved death in service benefit scheme or pension scheme, it is important that any right of nomination or request in the form of a letter of wishes is exercised. These matters are considered fully in CHAPTER 10 PENSIONS.

Death-bed planning

[18.55] The scope for transferring assets only once it is clear that a person is dying is severely limited because there will be no mitigation of the inheritance tax payable on any lifetime gifts unless the donor survives for three years, when taper relief will commence (see **4.2**). In addition, the benefit of the valuable capital gains tax base uplift on death will be lost. There are, however, some exercises which may be carried out.

(a)   *The conversion of assets into excluded property.* Where persons are not domiciled in the UK and not deemed to be domiciled here, they can dispose of property situated in the UK in favour of property situated abroad. In the case of a person not resident in the UK any sterling bank accounts can be converted into foreign currency held in a qualifying bank account so that IHTA 1984, s 157 will apply. Alternatively, the purchase of exempt British government securities by persons non-resident and non-domiciled (any deemed domicile being ignored for this purpose) will be excluded property under IHTA 1984, s 6(2). While, for example, excluded property includes reversionary interests in settlements it will not include a reversion purchased for money or money's worth.

For individuals who are domiciled and resident in the UK the excluded property provisions do not offer any tax planning opportunities.

(b)   *Using up any unused lifetime exemptions such as the annual exemption and the small gifts exemption.* One should not forget that dispositions made for the maintenance, education or training of a testator's child are not transfers of value (IHTA 1984, s 11). A terminally ill person with young children could make substantial transfers from his estate tax free.

(c)   *Assets pregnant with gains.* An individual should not make death-bed gifts of assets pregnant with gains because, as mentioned above, the valuable capital gains tax uplift on death will be lost. Where, however, the individual is married and his spouse or civil partner owns assets which are pregnant with gains, these assets could be transferred to the individual (free of capital gains tax) and then bequeathed back to the spouse or civil partner by will. The spouse or civil partner would then obtain a new base cost for the assets, ie their market value at the date of death. The pre-owned assets income tax charge will not apply in such a situation as any gift to a spouse or civil partner is an excluded transaction. Of course, one has to consider the application of the GAAR.

(d) *Joint bank accounts.* The conversion of bank accounts from sole to joint accounts and the transfer of property into joint names will assist in avoiding the need to obtain probate (see below). This will also assist with the funding of the payment of any inheritance tax.

(e) *Charitable gifts.* Where an individual is intending to leave either a cash legacy, shares and securities or an interest in land to one or more charities, he could make the gifts whilst still alive so as to obtain an income tax advantage but this needs to be weighed against the advantage of the lower rate of tax at 36% being charged on his estate on death (see CHAPTER 15 GIFTS TO CHARITIES AND OTHER NON-PROFIT ORGANISATIONS).

(f) *Heritage property.* Where a donor has heritage property qualifying for conditional exemption for inheritance tax purposes he could sell the heritage property to his children. The crystallised charge would be conditionally exempt provided the children were willing to give the requisite undertakings (see CHAPTER 16 HERITAGE PROPERTY).

(g) *Conversion of assets to relievable property.* Where there is a possibility that the individual may survive for the requisite two-year minimum ownership period, the acquisition of business or agricultural property will be effective in reducing the amount of inheritance tax payable on the death. Buying a farm or woodlands would qualify for 100% relief provided the two-year period and the other criteria were satisfied. The acquisition of a balanced portfolio of securities dealt in on the Alternative Investment Market and qualifying for business property relief would provide relief at 100% although the individual must be willing to accept the risks inherent in such an investment. There are also other strategies that might be followed where an existing interest is held which is eligible for 100% relief. The aim would be to enhance the level of relief available.

(h) *Maximise business property relief.* Although there is a two-year ownership period, it is not a requirement that the property must have been relevant business property throughout that period. It may be possible to convert an investment company into a trading company shortly before one of the shareholders die. There would need to be clear evidence of the change in the character of the business, and there would need to be evidence of trading rather than an intention to trade.

Assets which do not currently qualify for business property relief but would qualify if they were used in the business of a trading company could be transferred to the company. One would have to consider the capital gains tax implications of doing so but hold-over relief under s 165 may be available. In addition, SDLT will need to be considered.

Funding the inheritance tax payable on death

The estate

[18.56] The personal representatives are accountable for the tax on the free estate passing on the death and must pay that tax on the application for the grant of probate or letters of administration. This is with the exception of instalments of tax which have not fallen due on any land or business property qualifying for the instalment option. This can create a number of difficulties as the personal representatives will often need to borrow from a bank to fund the tax. This problem is aggravated where the principal asset in the estate is a shareholding in a family company or some other asset which is not easily realisable. Borrowing from the bank to fund this tax, let alone the realisation of the asset to repay the bank loan, will be difficult. This burden of funding can be eased in a number of ways, for example, by the use of insurance policies held in trust or joint bank and building society accounts. Even joint share-holdings in quoted companies, all of which will pass to the survivor, can be realised before probate is granted. The survivor could then lend the proceeds to the personal representatives or purchase assets from the estate.

Funding through insurance

[18.57] Policies of insurance held in trust for the life assured's children are a useful vehicle for providing funds to pay the inheritance tax on death (see CHAPTER 9 INSURANCE). In the case of a married couple where the sole or main inheritance tax charge will fall on the death of the survivor, the policy should be taken out on a joint life last survivor basis. The policy proceeds, will be paid to the trustees (or direct to the children if they are of age) on production of a death certificate only and will be available for loans to the personal represen-tatives or for the purchase of estate assets. Ideally, the beneficial interests under the trusts should correspond to those under the will to avoid any question as to whether a loan by the trustees to the personal representatives will be in breach of trust.

Potentially exempt transfers and chargeable lifetime transfers

[18.58] In the event of the death of the donor within seven years of a lifetime chargeable transfer or a potentially exempt transfer, inheritance tax (which in the case of lifetime chargeable transfers will be additional inheritance tax) may be payable on that transfer. To determine the rate of tax payable on the death, the transfer will also be aggregated with the value of the donor's free estate at death and any other gifts made within the seven-year period. The donor's nil rate band will be applied to gifts within the seven-year period in the order in which they are made and any balance then remaining will be available in respect of his estate on death.

In addition to the nil rate band, potentially exempt transfers and chargeable lifetime transfers may have the benefit of taper relief. The relief (ranging from 20% where the death occurs in the fourth year following the gift to 80% where the death occurs in the seventh year following the gift) is given against the tax, and not against the value of the property, so that the full value of the gifts is aggregated with the estate throughout the seven-year period and the taper relief does not reduce the tax payable by the estate.

Tax on the gift

[18.59] Funding the tax on lifetime gifts which become taxable or subject to additional tax can cause problems for the donee, and for the personal representatives on whom a secondary liability falls. This is particularly the case if the subject matter of the gift is not easily realisable such as private company shares or land. The tax liability can be covered either by a seven-year decreasing term insurance policy effected by the donee on the life of the donor or by the donor effecting such a policy on his own life and assigning it to, or settling it in trust for, the donee. In the latter case any premium paid by the donor will be a gift but may be covered by the annual exemption or by the normal expenditure out of income exemption. Alternatively, the donor might pass funds to the trustees, which would be a potentially exempt transfer, leaving the trustees to pay the premiums themselves.

The cost of insurance will depend on the age, state of health of the donor and the sum insured. The decreasing sum payable under the policy in the fourth and subsequent years from the date of the gift should reflect the benefit of taper relief on the inheritance tax charge on the gift.

Additional tax on the estate

[18.60] Where the donor fails to survive for seven years after the potentially exempt transfer or a chargeable transfer is made, an increased charge to inheritance tax may arise on his estate. This is because the benefit of the nil rate band will be applied first to the chargeable lifetime gifts in the order in which they were made which may result in the estate paying a higher rate than would otherwise be the case. In addition, taper relief is only given against the tax on the gift and not against the value of the property given. Consequently, the risk of the higher amount of tax remains constant for the full seven-year term.

This additional tax can be funded by a seven-year term policy for a level sum rather than a decreasing one. The policy can be effected by the donor in trust for the beneficiaries of his estate or by the beneficiaries themselves. If the premiums are funded by the donor, such payments may again be covered by the annual exemption or normal expenditure out of income exemption, or may be potentially exempt.

If the policy is effected by the donor it should be written in trust for the beneficiaries. Otherwise, it will fall into the donor's estate and will be subject to inheritance tax on the death as part of that estate.

Methods of avoiding probate

[18.61] A grant of probate or letters of administration is necessary to prove the title of the executors or administrators to the assets of a person who has died in order that those assets may be collected in for the benefit of his estate. It is not required in respect of any assets where title automatically passes to someone else on the death. Where property is held in joint names the production of a death certificate will be sufficient. As a result considerable legal and other expenses may be saved.

There are other advantages as well. For example, in the case of a joint bank account, the survivor will have access to funds to meet immediate expenses and perhaps to meet some or all of the inheritance tax liability on the death.

Avoiding probate does not override the duty to submit an inheritance tax account of the property and to pay the relevant tax. Any liability to inheritance tax arising on the death will still have to be paid, even if all assets are in joint names and pass by survivorship. The duty to submit the account falls jointly upon the co-owner and the personal representatives and both are jointly liable for the tax although the incidence of tax falls on the deceased's share of the joint property (IHTA 1984, s 211(3)). Where, as often happens, the tax is borne by the estate in the first instance this can cause cash flow difficulties in the estate and this factor should not be overlooked.

Property held in joint names

[18.62] All property may be held in joint names. In the case of land, the maximum number of joint owners permitted by the Law of Property Act 1925, s 34(2) is four, and, in practice, a similar restriction is often applied to other types of property, for example, shares and bank and building society accounts. It should be remembered that because property is in joint names, and legal title passes to the survivor or survivors, the beneficial interest may not always pass in exactly the same way. The survivors may be holding as trustees. When property is first transferred into joint names some separate statement of the beneficial ownership will be desirable as evidence of the parties' intentions.

In the case of *Sillars v IRC* [2004] STC (SCD) 180, 148 Sol Jo LB 536 the issue arose as to whether the whole of a bank account in which the deceased owned a share as joint tenant was subject to inheritance tax on the basis that she had a general power to dispose of the entire account or, alternatively, whether she had made a gift subject to a reservation when she transferred the bank account into the joint names of herself and her daughters. The intention was to make an immediate gift to her daughters. All subsequent transfers into the account were made by, or derived from, the mother. Although the daughters operated the account on behalf of their mother when she was ill, it was held that they did not have a general power over the account. The mother and two daughters each included one third of the annual interest on the account in their respective tax returns. The Special Commissioners held that a tenancy in common had not been established and that the deceased had a general power over the whole account by virtue of which, under IHTA 1984, s 5(2), the whole amount was liable to inheritance tax. In order to establish a tenancy in common, it was held that accounts should have been kept of who owned the funds and the parties would have needed an understanding of how deposits and withdrawals were dealt with. The joint account was plainly not settled property. There was no accounting procedures to see whether the deceased was taking more than her share. This case highlights the importance, when transferring property into joint names, of setting out clearly the shares of each joint owner and establishing whether a tenancy in common is intended.

In *Taylor v Revenue & Customs Comrs* [2008] STC SCD 1159 a widow, B inherited two building society accounts from her husband. She subsequently put the accounts in the joint names of herself and her brother-in-law, P. The withdrawals made from the accounts by B were to give presents to her family. B died in 2004 leaving all her property on trust for the benefit of her two nieces. The Revenue argued that B had been beneficially entitled to the moneys in these two accounts or alternatively the disposal was a gift of property subject to a reservation and so it was deemed to be property to which B had been beneficially entitled. B's executrix argued that B held the accounts as trustee and that the money belonged to P. The Special Commissioner held that B had not held the accounts as trustee and that B had a general power which enabled her to dispose of the whole of the accounts within the meaning of IHTA 1984, s 5. She was therefore treated as having been beneficially entitled to the two accounts. If B had not required access to the accounts the problem could have been avoided if she had entered into a formal trust arrangement.

In *Matthews v Revenue & Customs Comrs* [2012] TC 2329 the deceased had transferred £94,000 to a joint account with her son. The Revenue sought tax on the full amount of the bank account. The FtT held that the deceased had a general power over the entire account and was taxable under IHTA 1984, s 5.

Benefits under death in service policies and pension schemes

[18.63] Such benefits can very often be paid to beneficiaries following production of a death certificate and without production of probate. This is the case where the trustees have a discretion to pay the proceeds among the dependants and are not required to pay them to the personal representatives. Where the proceeds are payable to personal representatives title must be proved by production of probate or letters of administration. The absence of a letter of wishes from the scheme member may lead to a delay and may tempt the trustees to avoid the issue of dividing the moneys between the dependants and to pay them to the personal representatives. In this case payment will be made when the grant is eventually produced some months later.

Care should be taken to ensure that the letter of wishes is lodged by the member with the scheme's trustees if this is required under the rules of the scheme or, if lodged elsewhere, can be obtained from safe custody and sent to the trustees without first having to obtain probate or letters of administration.

Insurance policies

[18.64] Life policies and personal accident policies can all be effected in trust for dependants and the proceeds paid to the named trustees on production of a death certificate and without production of probate. The Married Women's Property Act 1882, s 11 and the Civil Partnership Act 2004, s 70 provide a relatively simple route for creating a trust over policies effected by one spouse or civil partner on his life and expressed as for the benefit of a spouse or civil partner and/or children. More elaborate trusts, and trusts for beneficiaries other than spouse and children, will require individual drafting, although most life offices can provide standard trust wordings on request.

Policy documents, if lodged at a bank or elsewhere in safe custody, should be held jointly to the order of the life assured and some other person, preferably the policy trustees or the beneficiary. If they are deposited in safe custody to the order of the assured alone, a grant of representation may be necessary to obtain the release of the policy document and therefore the policy proceeds cannot be used to fund inheritance tax payable before the grant is issued.

Assets worth less than £5,000

[18.65] Certain assets, if valued at less than £5,000 each, may be collected in by personal representatives, or intending personal representatives, without production of a grant. The Administration of Estates (Small Payments) Act 1965 and the Co-Operative and Community Benefit Societies Act 2014 authorise building societies, trade unions and loan societies and other registered societies to pay over balances, etc held of less than £5,000 without production of a grant of representation (although increasingly they are asking for production of the grant). National Savings and Investments similarly permits balances on accounts, premium savings bonds, national savings certificates and government stock held on the department's register to be released without production of a grant where the total invested is not more than £5,000, although the Department reserves its right to require production of the grant. Where these are required to meet the inheritance tax due, there are procedures available through the Probate Registry and HMRC Trusts & Estates for most forms of national savings investments to be encashed prior to the grant being obtained.

Foreign assets

[18.66] Small holdings of directly owned foreign assets are usually best avoided in the absence of an overriding investment or recreational reason for acquiring such assets. Proving title to these assets on the death of the registered owner will often require the involvement of lawyers both in the UK and in the foreign country concerned as well as probate formalities (or the equivalent) in both countries because title in foreign countries will usually be established through title granted in the court of the place of domicile. Often the expenses involved do not justify collecting in an asset of modest value. Foreign death duties may be payable and foreign death duty returns will need to be submitted. There will usually be relief given against inheritance tax for foreign tax paid. In the case of land situated abroad, where there is a double tax treaty between the UK and the country where the land is situated, the credit is usually to be given in the overseas country for inheritance tax paid in the UK.

Ownership of foreign assets through offshore settlements or companies or through UK nominees may overcome difficult and expensive foreign probate requirements and may also avoid the payment of local death duties. These possibilities should be considered before a foreign asset is acquired, as should the disposal costs arising on death.

Where a testator is likely to die owning foreign realty, consideration should be given to the succession implications of the law of the country in which the land is situated. The law of the jurisdiction may specify how the property is to devolve on the death regardless of any will left by the deceased. It may also be sensible to have a separate will dealing solely with that particular asset drawn up by a local lawyer under the local law.

Ownership of foreign assets is considered in more detail in CHAPTER 20 UK DOMICILIARIES INVESTING ABROAD.

Lloyd's underwriting interests

Background

[18.67] Historically, all members of Lloyd's were sole-traders with unlimited liability. In response to market developments, Lloyd's has allowed existing names to trade through partnerships and/or companies. All new participants must now underwrite only through a limited liability partnership (LLP) or a company.

A member of Lloyd's may be an individual member or a corporate member. The term 'corporate member' includes limited companies (NameCos), Scottish Limited Partnerships (SLPs) and LLPs.

A member of Lloyd's carries on a trade of underwriting at Lloyd's and is taxed accordingly. Lloyd's operates a three-year accounting base.

Elements of an interest

[18.68] There are three distinct elements to a Lloyd's business interest which are taken into account in valuing the Lloyd's business:

- the pipeline Lloyd's underwriting results of the open years of account together with the result of any closed year of account not distributed before death;
- the value of syndicate capacity; and
- the value of assets held in a Fund at Lloyd's (FAL), which are also known as ancillary trust funds. FAL is the capital used to support the Lloyd's trade. FAL may consist of cash on deposit or shares or securities quoted on a recognised stock exchange and are valued according to the usual rules. Bank guarantees and letters of credit can also be used as FAL and are taken at face value or the value of the underlying security or collateral provided to the financial institution, if lower. The assets that can be used as FAL have to be in a form that is agreed by Lloyd's.

Unlimited members have been able to put profits into a special reserve fund (SRF) to pay future underwriting losses and which can be used as part of an unlimited member's FAL. The SRF cannot be used to support the underwriting of an SLP, LLP or a NameCo.

Unlimited members

[18.69] An unlimited member's membership of Lloyd's ceases on his death. Where a Name dies part way through the first 12 months of a year of account, ie on or before 31 December, they are treated as not having underwritten any business for that account. The account that ended 31 December before death is then the final account for which the deceased Name took new business. If for example an unlimited member dies in June 2017 then the final year of underwriting will be the 2016 year of account which would normally close at 31 December 2018 and be distributed in May 2019. In this example, the FAL cannot be released until all relevant years of account that the member had participated in close and the syndicate capacity would be sold in the 2017 auctions.

The value of the Lloyd's interest on death will include:

- syndicate capacity valued at the weighted average prices from the last syndicate capacity auctions before death;
- FAL including the SRF; and
- the pipeline underwriting results which are valued either on the Lloyd's audit basis as shown in the previous Lloyd's solvency test, which is the strict legal basis, or on the basis of the actual results. In either case, the value can be discounted to reflect the fact that the profits will not have been available to the estate until after the accounts have closed. An election by the personal representatives to use the actual results must be made within 12 months of the grant of representation. In practice, however, an election is not made and discounting is not used, because business property relief (BPR) at 100% is usually available.

Unpaid profits on a closed year of account are simply debts due to the unlimited member.

As an unlimited member is carrying on a qualifying trade business property relief will be available. The pipeline underwriting results and the syndicate capacity will normally be eligible for 100% business property relief. In HMRC's view FAL and the SRF will only be eligible for relief to the extent that those funds are 'commensurate with the amount of underwriting business that was being written by the Name'. In its *Lloyd's Manual* at para 8290, HMRC states that 'as a rule of thumb [we] would not normally seek to restrict business property relief if the value of FAL assets is not substantially greater than the minimum FAL requirement'. It would appear, however, that HMRC has changed its practice in this regard. HMRC is seeking to restrict business property relief to the figure detailed at part C of the last Lloyd's Release Test at the valuation date.

Business property relief is currently also available on the assets used to provide security for bank guarantees or letters of credit which form part of a Lloyd's deposit or reserve. The amount of relief 'cannot exceed the nominal value of the guarantee but will nevertheless be dependent on the market value of the collateral assets' *(Lloyd's Manual, para 8290)*.

HMRC's *Lloyd's Manual* at para 8290 says that 'there is no restriction of relief by reference to the nature of the underlying assets supporting the guarantee or letter of credit, but [HMRC] will treat the value of the underlying assets as reduced by the amount of the guarantee or letter of credit for the purpose of giving any other reliefs or exemptions'. In practice bank guarantees and letters of credit are usually secured against assets that would not qualify for either business property relief or agricultural property relief.

HMRC has recently sought to argue that a bank guarantee or letter of credit is a liability within IHTA 1984, s 162A. The effect being that where a member takes out a new bank guarantee or letter of credit after 5 April 2013 (or makes changes to an existing one), a liability is created which should be deducted from the member's Lloyd's underwriting assets, rather than from the assets which provide the collateral for the bank guarantee or letter of credit. It is understood that the matter is currently with HMRC's Solicitor's Office.

In addition to business property relief, the investments and cash in the deposits and reserves are also discounted to reflect the fact that they are unavailable until the date pipeline profits are paid and the dates when FAL and SRF assets are released to the estate. With business property relief at 100%, this further discount is not very important and is only likely to be relevant where the amount of FAL eligible for the business property relief is restricted.

The SRF cannot be released until all the unlimited underwriting years close. The release of the SRF will be treated as taking place and being taxable as a trading receipt of the final year in which underwriting profits are assessable on the Name personally (FA 1993, s 179A). That final amount cannot, however, be determined until the last open year closes. This income tax liability should be allowed as a debt of the unlimited member's estate for inheritance tax purposes.

Until the unlimited member's last year of underwriting closes his estate cannot be formally wound up. In practice this can take a minimum of three years and possibly up to five years. The position will also depend on whether the member has an Estate Protection Plan in place.

Members of an LLP or SLP

[18.70] In the case of an LLP or SLP, the death of a member will not bring about a cessation of the Lloyd's business.

The value of the member's interest in the LLP (or SLP) will include:

* syndicate capacity; and
* the pipeline underwriting results.

It is normal for the LLP (or SLP) agreement to provide that the FAL are held directly by the member and not by the LLP. Accordingly, the value of the member's interest in the LLP will need to include the value of the FAL provided by the member to the LLP, as well as their share of the syndicate capacity and pipeline underwriting results. The normal rules of valuation outlined above will apply equally to the LLP (or SLP) and its member.

As is the case, for unlimited members, bank guarantees and letters of credit are eligible for business property relief, subject to the other requirements being met and the outcome of the challenge being made by HMRC (see **18.69**).

Shareholders in a NameCo

[18.71] As a NameCo is a trading company, business property relief may be available in relation to the NameCo shares.

The value of the NameCo shares will be calculated, taking into account:

- the pipeline underwriting results;
- syndicate capacity;
- FAL owned by the NameCo; and
- any other assets net of liabilities of the company.

The normal valuation rules outlined above will apply to the Lloyd's assets of the NameCo.

Business property relief will not be available in relation to:

- loans made by the shareholder to the NameCo;
- FAL that is beneficially owned by the shareholder but made available to the NameCo; nor
- FAL that is in the form of the bank guarantee or letter of credit collateralised on assets owned by the shareholder.

It is usual practice for a NameCo to hold additional funds to cover future underwriting opportunities and potential unexpected underwriting liabilities. Whilst HMRC acknowledge that there may be commercial reasons for a member to carry surplus funds, it will expect to see evidence that the investment or funds were required for a specific purpose at the valuation date, on the basis of *Barclay's Bank Trust Co Ltd v Commissioners of Inland Revenue* (1998) SpC 158. The Special Commissioner said of the requirements of IHTA 1984, s 112(2)(b) that:

> 'I do not accept that "future" means at any time in the future nor that "was required" includes the possibility that the money might be required should an opportunity arise to make use of the money into, three or seven years' time for the purposes of this business. In my opinion and I so hold that "required" implies some imperative that the money will fall to be used upon a given project or for some palpable business purpose.'

Conversion by an unlimited member

[18.72] As mentioned in **18.67** many unlimited members have transferred their underwriting trade to an LLP, SLP or NameCo.

In 2014, Lloyd's allowed members of an LLP or SLP to transfer (convert) their underwriting interests to a NameCo, which involves two separate stages. The first is the transfer of syndicate capacity, and the second is the transfer of FAL once the pre-conversion underwriting years of account have closed.

The FAL of a converting member supports both the run-off of the pre-incorporation underwriting years as well as the post-conversion underwriting by the LLP, SLP or NameCo. This process is known as inter-availability.

If the member dies before his last pre-conversion underwriting year is closed then two valuations will normally be required; one for the unlimited underwriting business (or that of the LLP or SLP) and the second for the NameCo (or LLP or SLP). FAL that is inter-available to a NameCo is not eligible for business property relief except in as far as they are required to support the run-off of pre-conversion open years.

In the case of conversion by an unlimited member to an LLP or SLP there is no change in the beneficial ownership of the FAL and so there is no requirement to satisfy another two-year ownership period.

The position is slightly different in relation to the transfer of underwriting by an unlimited member, or a member of an LLP or SLP, to a NameCo. On the transfer of the syndicate capacity at stage one of the conversion process, the converting member has the choice as to whether the consideration for the transfer of the capacity is either an issue of NameCo shares or is left outstanding on a shareholder's loan account. As mentioned previously, business property relief will not be available on a loan with a NameCo, whereas the shares will be treated as a replacement asset.

Lloyd's and wills

[18.73] Depending on a member's personal and family circumstances the inheritance tax efficiency of a will can be maximised by leaving assets that qualify for 100% business property relief directly to the deceased's children (or other non-exempt person). If the assets are passed under the will to the spouse then business property relief would be wasted because of the spouse exemption.

It should be borne in mind that some part of the underwriting property, including unpaid profits on a closed year of account which are simply debts due to the member, may not qualify for business property relief.

If the will refers to a bequest of the member's Lloyd's underwriting business in general terms, then all the Lloyd's assets will pass to the beneficiary, whether or not business property relief is available. If it is the member's intention that only property which qualifies for business property relief is to be passed under that bequest, it is necessary to state this specifically in the will to ensure that any Lloyd's assets which do not qualify for business property relief are excluded.

If a member does not wish to leave their Lloyd's assets directly to their children then an alternative approach would be to leave those assets that qualify for relief on a discretionary will trust for the benefit of, say, their children, spouse and others. As the assets should be eligible for business property relief, no inheritance tax charge on the transfer into the trust should arise. If the trustees hold those assets for at least two years, the assets should qualify for business property relief and be treated as having no value for the purposes of calculating any decennial or exit charges. The surviving spouse would still be able to benefit from the trust if required and business property relief will have been fully protected.

It is important to ensure that, where the interest in Lloyd's is in the form of NameCo shares, the value is in the NameCo shares and not in assets that are held outside the NameCo, or in the form of loan to the NameCo. This may require some pre-death planning to ensure that:

- loans owed to a shareholder are either repaid or converted into ordinary shares in the NameCo; and
- FAL is transferred into the NameCo and not held by the shareholder in his own name.

If a bank guarantee or letter of credit is supporting the underwriting of a NameCo, the assets providing collateral are not eligible for business property relief. In this case it may be appropriate to see if the bank guarantee could be replaced by other assets that are owned by the NameCo.

In relation to an LLP the collateral supporting a bank guarantee or letter of credit that forms part of the LLP's FAL will be eligible for business property relief. If the asset providing the collateral is not to pass to the same beneficiary who is to receive the interest in the LLP, it may be necessary to reorganise the provision of FAL pre-death.

Specific provision in the will in relation to an interest in a Lloyd's business will provide certainty as to the testator's intentions and the future ownership and running of the Lloyd's business which will greatly assist the executors or administrators.

Chapter 19

Post-Death Estate Planning

Introduction

[19.1] Personal representatives do not have an easy task and the administration of an estate is made more complicated by the various options open to them and the beneficiaries of the deceased's estate, following the death, to mitigate the impact of inheritance tax and to take the estate planning steps which the deceased ought to have taken but failed (for whatever reason) to take during his lifetime. This is the case even where the deceased died intestate.

Considerations

Availability of reliefs

[19.2] If the estate is subject to inheritance tax, it will be important to identify any property which may qualify for any of the available reliefs to reduce the amount of inheritance tax payable (such as relevant business property within the meaning of IHTA 1984, s 105 or agricultural property within the meaning of IHTA 1984, s 115) and to ascertain whether or not the relief will apply in the particular circumstances of the estate.

Availability of lower rate of tax

[19.3] As discussed in **15.6**, an estate can benefit from a lower rate of inheritance tax of 36% where 10% or more of a donor's net estate is left to charity. It may be the case that after the testator's death the beneficiaries and personal representatives may wish to increase the amount left to charity to take advantage of the lower rate.

Heritage property

[19.4] If the estate includes any assets such as works of art or land and buildings which are pre-eminent for national, scientific, historic or artistic interest, then a claim under IHTA 1984, s 31 may be made to HMRC by the personal representatives to have the assets made exempt from tax. If the claim is allowed, an exemption will be granted, subject to various undertakings being given in relation to the preservation of the asset and the provision of public access to it. Therefore, no tax will be payable at death on the relevant assets but the exemption will be lost if there is a breach of one of the undertakings or if the asset is sold and so the tax will become payable at that stage. If an estate includes assets which might qualify for such relief, expert advice should be taken at an early stage to ascertain whether or not a claim should be made for an exemption and as to which assets should be included in the claim. (See CHAPTER 16 HERITAGE PROPERTY for a more detailed explanation of the rules.)

Payment by instalments

[19.5] The personal representatives should also consider whether the inheritance tax may be paid by instalments; and also establish upon whom the burden of the tax falls: for example, whether a legacy is to be paid subject to or free from inheritance tax.

Sale of assets

[19.6] The personal representatives should also consider that if any investments or land forming part of the deceased's estate are to be sold after the death and the values at the date of sale are less than the values at the date of death, then the sale price can be substituted for the value at death, provided that certain conditions are fulfilled. The timing of the sales is all important.

Submission of accounts

[19.7] IHTA 1984, s 216 imposes an onerous duty of inquiry in relation not only to the deceased's estate at death but also in relation to lifetime chargeable transfers. These onerous duties are reflected in the form IHT 400 on which personal representatives make a return of the deceased's estate. Anybody, but especially professional advisers, should consider carefully before accepting an executorship in view of their personal liability for a failure to comply with these duties. Penalties are imposed for continuing failure to file an account or notify HMRC of the inheritance tax payable under IHTA 1984, ss 245 and 245A.

By far the most important estate planning consideration for personal representatives and the beneficiaries of the deceased's estate will be their ability to vary the dispositions effected by the will or by the applicable intestacy rules so as to redirect parts of the estate to different members of the family. Such rearrangements may be solely tax-driven or they may arise from other personal or family considerations. The personal representatives will wish to draw this possibility to the attention of the beneficiaries at as early a stage as possible.

Post-death estate planning must be undertaken within strict time limits in order to be tax effective, which may be during a particularly stressful and difficult period for the beneficiaries. An adviser will need to establish his clients' requirements with sensitivity and care but without delay.

Reasons for a rearrangement

[19.8] In most cases the primary purpose of a rearrangement is to reduce the burden of inheritance tax. But there may be a secondary purpose which is to effect an equitable distribution of the deceased's assets between the beneficiaries and other members of the deceased's family.

There may be many personal or family reasons which prompt beneficiaries to surrender or redirect the whole or part of their entitlement under a will or on intestacy. It may be that a will does not provide adequately for a particular beneficiary. For example, a widow inheriting the whole of her late husband's estate may wish to make immediate provision for her children. Conversely, children who inherit under their father's will at the expense of their mother might wish to redirect part of their entitlement to her.

Occasionally, the personal representatives receive a claim under the Inheritance (Provision for Family and Dependants) Act 1975 (see **18.3**). This Act enables a person who was maintained by the deceased to make an application to the court for provision to be made for him out of the estate on the grounds that the deceased's will did not make reasonable financial provision for him. An order in favour of one or more members of the deceased's family and dependants will of necessity require rearrangement of the estate. If such a claim is anticipated, it might be preferable for the beneficiaries to reach an agreement with the potential claimants and to embody such an agreement in a written variation made within two years of the death without an application to the court.

Where the beneficiaries under a will are already wealthy, a generation might be missed out; this is known as 'generation skipping'. For example, a son of a deceased testator might wish to pass on a legacy bequeathed to him under his father's will to his own son. Once again, the desired result can be achieved by the testator's son entering into a written variation.

There are other non-tax motives which can sometimes prompt a rearrangement. For example, if a will is defective in some respect, perhaps because of a typing error or some mistake made by the testator in the description of an asset or beneficiary, it may be possible to avoid applying to the court for a remedy by rewriting that defective part of the will in the form of a variation which would save both time and expense.

A rearrangement can take many forms including a written variation by the following:

(i)   agreement;
(ii)   disclaimer;
(iii)   discretionary wills; and
(iv)   precatory trusts, all of which are discussed in this chapter.

There has been a concern in recent years that the tax treatment of deeds of variation will be amended. In July 2015, the Government published a document entitled 'Review looking at the use of deeds of variation (DoV) for tax purposes'. No action has been taken and in his Autumn Statement 2015, the then Chancellor said that he would continue to monitor the use of deeds of variation.

Variations

Inheritance tax

General

[19.9] The provisions of IHTA 1984, s 142 enable the beneficiaries under a will or on an intestacy to alter the dispositions of the deceased's estate effected by the terms of the deceased's will or by the intestacy rules.

The popular notion that one is 'varying' the terms of a will is a misconception, since the terms of a will can never be varied once the testator has died. Section 142 speaks of 'varying' the dispositions of the deceased's estate effected by his will and is directed at cases where the recipient of property from the deceased chooses to redirect it to other persons whether by way of an outright gift or a declaration of trust or a settlement. If the provisions of s 142 are satisfied then the redirection will, for inheritance tax purposes, be treated as if it had been effected by the deceased on his death and tax will be charged accordingly. There is a similar back-dating provision for capital gains tax which is considered below. It must never be forgotten, however, that this retroactive effect is a fiction imposed for tax purposes – as a matter of strict law any redirection takes effect when the instrument effecting the redirection (be it a deed of gift, a stock transfer form or a declaration of trust) is entered into and not from the date of death. Thus, the redirection does not alter the income tax treatment of any income arising before the redirection is made applying *Re Scadding* (1902) 40LR 632. The charge to income tax on pre-owned assets, does not apply to a disposition made under a variation provided that the disposition is not treated for inheritance tax purposes (under IHTA 1984, s 17) as a transfer of value by that person (FA 2004, Sch 15, para 16).

A variation must be made

[19.10] The variation must be made by an instrument in writing within two years of the death. There is no requirement that the variation be by deed as any instrument in writing which effectively transfers property, or an interest in property, will suffice (HMRC Inheritance Tax Manual, para 35022), although in some cases, a deed may be necessary to transfer the property. HMRC has published guidelines setting out the requirements that an instrument must satisfy (HMRC Inheritance Tax Manual, para 35021). The variation may be made not only in relation to the dispositions effected by a will but also in relation to those taking place under the intestacy rules. In addition, s 142 will apply to a redirection by a joint owner of the interest in property which automatically passes to him by survivorship on the other co-owner's death.

By virtue of IHTA 1984, s 142(5), an instrument of variation will not be effective for property comprised in a settlement in which the deceased had an interest in possession at his death. Thus, if the deceased had a life interest under a settlement and, under the terms of the settlement, his son takes an absolute interest therein on his death, his son cannot use the provisions of s 142 to redirect that interest in remainder elsewhere following the life tenant's death. Estate planning in relation to settlements therefore must be achieved during the life tenant's lifetime. There is nothing to prevent a variation being made in respect of a trust created by the will itself.

The subsection also ensures that property which is treated as forming part of the deceased's estate at the date of death because he has retained a benefit in it within the terms of FA 1986, s 102 (gifts with reservation) cannot be the subject matter of a post-death variation.

Inclusion of statement

[19.11] Section 142 will automatically apply provided the document contains a statement made by all the relevant persons to the effect that s 142 should apply to the variation. Relevant persons are defined in IHTA 1984, s 142(2A) and discussed in **19.14**. Such a statement should include the appropriate statutory references; an example of the wording can be found in the HMRC's Inheritance Tax Manual, para 35028. In *Wills v Gibbs* [2007] EWHC 3361 (Ch), [2008] STC 808 the statement had been omitted in the deed of variation and so an application for rectification was made. The High Court held that that rectification would be allowed as the deed did not give effect to the true agreement between the parties and the rectification was not solely intended to procure a beneficial tax consequence.

In *Vaughan-Jones v Vaughan-Jones* [2015] EWHC 1086 (Ch), the statement had been omitted. A claim for rectification on the grounds of mistake was successful but only in relation to inheritance tax.

Gifts made to charity

[19.12] A deed of variation redirecting property to a charity shall only be treated as having been made by the deceased provided it is shown that the appropriate person has been notified of the existence of the deed of variation (IHTA 1984, s 142(3A)). The appropriate person is the charity or registered club to which the property is given or the trustees of the charitable trust or registered club (IHTA 1984, s 142(3B)) (see **15.11**). There is no requirement for the charity or trustees to be a party to the deed of variation. Copies of the exchange of correspondence between the parties involved showing the charity or trustees are aware of the arrangements will suffice (HMRC Inheritance Tax Manual, para 35124). The execution of a deed of variation may result in the lower rate of inheritance tax of 36% applying to all or part of the deceased's estate because the requisite proportion of the estate has been left to charity.

No consideration

[19.13] For a variation to be effective the person entering into the variation must not receive any extraneous consideration for the variation as the provisions of IHTA 1984, s 142(1) do not apply to a 'variation . . . made for any consideration in money or money's worth other than consideration consisting of the making, in respect of another of the dispositions, of a variation . . . to which [s 142(1)] applies' (s 142(3)). An indemnity given by one party to the variation to another in respect of tax liabilities or legal costs could amount to such extraneous consideration, if making the variation is conditional upon giving the indemnity, as the indemnity is given as part of a single transaction with the variation.

The case of *Lau (executor of Lau dec'd) v Revenue & Customs Comrs* [2009] STC (SCD) 352 is an example of where it was held that consideration was given for a variation. In the case substantial cash gifts of £665,000 each made to the deceased's two daughters and stepson were redirected to the surviving spouse. Subsequently, each legatee received £1m from their mother. The daughters accepted that section 142(3) applied. The son, however, argued that the £1m gift represented the honouring of an earlier promise that his mother would finance his business venture and also contained an element of a wedding present. This was rejected as being 'incredible' and 'unreliable'.

It is understood that HMRC seems to accept that a deed which is entered into solely to avoid or compromise a claim under the Inheritance (Provision for Family and Dependants) Act 1975 will not be regarded as a deed having been made for consideration in money or money's worth unless the deceased died domiciled outside the UK (HMRC Inheritance Tax Manual, para 35100).

In the case of *Vaughan-Jones v Vaughan-Jones* [2015] EWHC 1086 (Ch) a rectification claim was successful. Although HMRC did not wish to be joined in the litigation it made it known that it would 'not agree to give effect to the deed as rectified'. This was because HMRC's view was that the deed was made for consideration in money's worth on the basis of the decision in *Lau*. Counsel for the claimants argued that *Lau* was a decision based on its own particular facts. It was submitted that the expression 'any consideration in money or money's worth' was a technical question that required a bargain which is sufficiently definite. It did not include a generalised intention to give sums of an indefinite amount at an indefinite time in the future which gave rise to no legally enforceable obligation and where the widow could, without adverse consequences to herself, change her mind at any time. The matter was not an issue to be decided by the present Court.

Parties to the arrangements

[19.14] The persons entering into the variation must be of full age and capacity and willing to act. If minor or unborn beneficiaries are involved, it may be possible to apply on their behalf to the court under the Variation of Trusts Act 1958 for the court's consent (embodied in a court order). However, in those circumstances to be effective the court order must be made within the 2-year period.

Section 142(2A) provides that the 'relevant persons' are:

'(a)   the person or persons making the instrument, and
(b)   where the variation results in additional tax being payable, the personal representatives.'

Personal representatives may decline to join in an election only if no, or no sufficient, assets are held by them in that capacity for discharging the additional tax.

This means that where additional tax is payable as a result of the variation, and the personal representatives are holding sufficient assets to discharge the liability, the personal representatives are necessary parties to the instrument and can be compelled to join in if they initially refuse to do so. However, where the personal representatives validly decline to join in the instrument, then IHTA 1984, s 142(1) will not apply to the variation, although it will be legally effective for all other purposes.

Where a discretionary will trust is being varied it may be the case that the potential beneficiaries cannot be identified or they are minors. In such circumstances it may be possible for the executors or trustees to appoint a portion of the trust fund to an adult beneficiary for him to make the variation (through the use of IHTA 1984, ss 144 and 142). Of course, trust law matters would need to be considered to ensure that there was no 'fraud on the power'.

Dead beneficiaries

[19.15] Where one of the beneficiaries (the 'second deceased') has died before a variation to a will is made, HMRC has stated that a deed entered into by the by the beneficiaries of the second deceased will be acceptable to it (HMRC Inheritance Tax Manual, para 35042).

Jointly held property

[19.16] In cases where the deceased held an interest in jointly held assets which passed on death by survivorship, HMRC has confirmed that s 142 will apply to a variation of that interest (HMRC Inheritance Tax Manual, para 35071). For both inheritance tax and capital gains tax the legislation provides that the rules apply not only to a disposition/inheritance arising under a will or the law of intestacy, but also to those effected 'otherwise' which includes jointly held assets passing by survivorship. This means that a surviving joint owner may enter into a written variation to give the deceased's joint interest to someone else to which s 142 will apply provided that the necessary conditions are met.

A variation in the 'real world'

[19.17] HMRC states that a variation must be implemented 'in the real world' (CTO Newsletter December 2001 and HMRC Inheritance Tax Manual, para 35042). IHTA 1984, s 17 expressly provides that a variation or disclaimer within IHTA 1984, s 142(1) is not a transfer of value. The instrument in writing should be more than an empty piece of paper. An example is given where A leaves a life interest in property to B with remainder to C. On B's death (but within two years of A's death) C makes a deed of variation which purports to vary A's will by redirecting B's interest to C. HMRC argues that, in the real world, B's interest does not exist at that time and there is nothing for the deed to do, so s 142 cannot apply. There has been much debate about this amongst commentators. Section 142 is artificial, in any event, as it retrospectively rewrites the will of the deceased and treats the retrospectively revised will as if the deceased had made different dispositions on his death to those he actually made. In the example given, the variation would not have been made by C alone. It would be made by B's executors and C. Certainly, there is no dispute that the executors can execute a deed of variation which itself makes the whole matter more artificial. However, that is the purpose of s 142. In the example, C is entitled to the assets both before and after the variation, the difference being the route by which he obtained them. One could argue that this was not an empty piece of paper because it could increase or decrease the amount of inheritance tax payable.

It is suggested that the deed of variation is ineffective under the general law, however, one must question the relevance of general law to this situation as s 142 is a deeming provision upon which a tax charge is based.

In their April/May 2002 Newsletter, the Revenue (as it was then) published its responses to two letters relating to the above.

'It would appear that in a situation where A dies leaving his estate outright to his widow B, who dies within two years leaving her estate to her children, your view is now that a deed of variation redirecting the estate to the children would be ineffective. Is this correct?

The example you give is one where an absolute interest is given to the survivor. On the death of the survivor, the property inherited on the first death still exists in the survivor's estate and it is therefore possible, in the real world, for those inheriting on the second death to redirect the estate of the first to die. Contrast this with the example given in our Newsletter where, on the first death, the survivor is given a life interest in property. That interest is extinguished on the death of the survivor, so that when, in the real world, those inheriting on the second death come to consider a variation, there is nothing for the variation to bite on.

You say that B's life interest does not exist because "there is nothing for the deed to bite upon". Surely:

- The interest exists until the variation, and
- It is a type of property which can be disposed of by B (or his personal representatives) at any time up to the deed of variation.

As the variation was made after the death of the life tenant, there was then no life interest in existence. Whilst such an interest is capable of disposition by the life tenant, the fact that it ceases on his death means that it is not capable of being disposed of after that has occurred.'

The Revenue's view received some support in the Special Commissioner's decision in *Souter's Executry v IRC* (SpC 325) [2002] STC (SCD) 385, SCD. In that case, under the will of Miss Souter, Miss Greenlees received a life interest in a property which had been the two ladies' residence. Miss Greenlees continued to live in the property after Miss Souter's death but died within two years of the death of Miss Souter. The executors and beneficiaries of Miss Souter's estate (including the executors of Miss Greenlees' estate) then entered into a deed under which they provided that Miss Souter's will was to take effect as if Miss Greenlees had not received the life interest. The Commissioners accepted the Revenue's contention that Miss Greenlees' executors could not have continued to enjoy the life interest after Miss Greenlees' death and therefore that they had nothing to vary. In order to satisfy s 142, the deed had to vary a disposition under Miss Souter's will and there could be no disposition following Miss Greenlees' death.

Compliance

[19.18] Where a deed of variation is made which results in additional tax being payable, the relevant persons must submit a copy of the instrument to

HMRC and notify it of the amount of additional tax payable within six months of the instrument being executed (IHTA 1984, s 218A). A penalty of up to £3,000 may be charged where failure to comply continues after the six-month anniversary for delivery of the instrument and notification of the additional tax payable (IHTA 1984, s 245A(1B)). The penalty will not be imposed where there is a reasonable excuse (IHTA 1984, s 245A(5)) and the instrument and amount of additional tax (if any) is delivered without unreasonable delay after the excuse has ceased.

More than one variation?

[19.19] There are occasions when it may be desirable for the beneficiaries to enter into more than one variation. Whilst this is clearly permissible with regard to different property in the estate, HMRC takes the view that an instrument would not fall within IHTA 1984, s 142 if it further redirected any property or any part of any property that had already been redirected under an earlier instrument of variation (HMRC Inheritance Tax Manual, para 35082). The case of *Russell v IRC* [1988] 2 All ER 405, [1988] 1 WLR 834 confirmed this view. It is HMRC's view that an election, once made, is irrevocable (HMRC Inheritance Tax Manual, para 35081).

Rectification of deed of variation

[19.20] It is possible for a deed of variation once executed to be varied but in limited circumstances. In *Lake v Lake* [1989] STC 565 it was held that a deed of variation can be rectified by the courts if the words mistakenly used mean that it does not give effect to the parties' joint intentions. It is immaterial that the rectification achieves a tax advantage or that it is made more than two years after the death. In *Wills v Gibbs* [2007] EWHC 3361 (Ch), [2008] STC 808 the deed of variation did not contain the statement that it was intended by the parties that s 142 should apply. This of course meant that the provisions in the deed of variation would not be treated as being made by the will. An application for rectification was made. It was held that a deed could be rectified to achieve the correction of a voluntary settlement so as to enable any mistakes in the settlement as executed to accord with the settlor's true intention when he executed it. The court allowed the deed to be rectified to include the requisite statement because the parties although not aware of the formalities of s 142 knew of the consequences of making such a deed. In *Ashcroft v Barnsdale* [2010] EWHC 1948 (Ch), [2010] STC 2544, 13 ITELR 516 a claim for rectification of a deed of variation was successful. In that case a deed of variation had been entered into to ensure that assets attracting agricultural property relief were left to a non-exempt beneficiary. Unfortunately the deed omitted the words 'subject to Inheritance Tax' which resulted in the residuary beneficiary having an increased tax burden. The evidence showed that it was clearly not a consequence intended by the parties. In that particular case, HMRC would not accept a deed of rectification without a court order. The court held that the rectification could be made because there was a common intention as to how the parties' fiscal objectives were to be achieved.

In *Giles v The Royal National Institute for the Blind* [2014] EWHC 1373 (Ch), [2014] STC 1631, 164 NLJ 7605 the High Court agreed to rectify a deed of variation. The case involved two sisters, Hilda and Ellen. Hilda died leaving a property to Ellen, together with the residue of her estate. Ellen died 19 months later leaving her estate to four charities. Inheritance tax of over £250,000 was due on Hilda's estate. If, however, her will was varied so that Ellen's entitlement was left to the four charities, the exemption under IHTA 1984, s.23 would be available and no tax would be due. A deed was executed which unfortunately did not reflect the parties' intention as it only referred to the residue and did not include the specific legacy. HMRC neither opposed the application nor wished to be joined as a party.

In *Vaughan-Jones v Vaughan-Jones* [2015] EWHC 1086 (Ch), the court allowed the deed to be rectified to include the requisite statement which had been omitted as discussed in **19.13**.

Capital gains tax

General

[19.21] TCGA 1992, s 62(1) provides that the assets of a deceased person's estate shall be deemed to be acquired on his death by his personal representatives for a consideration equal to their market value at the date of death but shall not be deemed to be disposed of by him on his death. Therefore, no capital gains tax is payable on the death.

The provisions of TCGA 1992, s 62(6)–(9), dealing with variations and disclaimers, correspond to those applicable to inheritance tax. Thus TCGA 1992, s 62(6) provides that:

> 'where within the period of 2 years after a person's death any of the dispositions (whether effected by will, under the law relating to intestacy or otherwise) of the property of which he was competent to dispose are varied, or the benefit conferred by any of those dispositions is disclaimed, by an instrument in writing made by the persons or any of the persons who benefit or would benefit under the dispositions —
>
> (a)   the variation or disclaimer shall not constitute a disposal for the purposes of this Act, and
>
> (b)   this section shall apply as if the variation had been effected by the deceased or, as the case may be, the disclaimed benefit had never been conferred.'

The above provisions apply only to property of which the deceased person was 'competent to dispose' as defined by TCGA 1992, s 62(10). Such property includes an interest under a joint tenancy but not property subject to a general power of appointment.

The statement

[19.22] Section 62(6) will apply provided that the instrument contains a statement by the persons making the instrument that they intend that s 62(6) will apply to the variation (TCGA 1992, s 62(7)). There is no longer a specified time period by which the instrument has to be submitted to HMRC. This is because: 'the Government . . . are content that the consequences of a variation should be considered, if necessary, by [HMRC] only if and when they become relevant to the capital gains tax liabilities of the beneficiaries'.

In most cases the inclusion of the relevant statement stating the intention of the parties for s 62(6) to apply will in any event be appropriate, regardless of whether the administration of the estate has been completed or not. Where, however, the value of the relevant asset has increased since the date of death and any gain would fall within the donor beneficiary's annual exemption or within the exemption for chattels, then the advantage of not including such a statement is that the donee will acquire the asset at a higher base cost. The same point would arise where the original beneficiary can obtain a tax-free uplift because of main residence relief. Where, on the other hand, the asset has fallen in value, not to include a statement for the operation of s 62 will create a capital loss for the donor beneficiary, but if the donee is a 'connected person' within TCGA 1992, s 286 (and he often will be), such a loss can only be set against a gain on another disposal to the same donee (TCGA 1992, s 18), so little will be gained from not including a statement.

Where a statement to the effect that it is intended that s 62 should apply is included, it provides that 'section 62(6) shall apply as if the variation had been effected by the deceased'. There are special rules which apply where property becomes settled property as a result of the variation (TCGA 1992, s 68C). In such a case, the person making the variation will be treated as the settlor for capital gains tax purposes.

Example

Marjorie, under her will, leaves quoted shares worth £300,000 to Marian absolutely. As Marian does not need the assets she decides to vary the will so that a discretionary trust is set up for the benefit of her grandchildren, Jasmine, Luke and Cory. Provided that s 62(6) applies, Marian will be treated as the settlor of the trust for capital gains tax purposes and not Marjorie.

Where property was already settled under the will or intestacy and then becomes comprised in another settlement as a result of the variation, the deceased person is treated as being the settlor and not the person making the variation.

Income tax

General

[19.23] The income tax legislation does not provide the reliefs which are available in the case of inheritance tax and capital gains tax following a variation of beneficial interests in a deceased's estate. Income arising between the date of death and the date of the variation is generally taxed as though it were that of the beneficiary entitled prior to the variation. Disclaimers, because of their legal nature (and because they are not a fiction of fiscal legislation as is the case with variations), are treated differently and relate back to the date of death for income tax purposes.

Subject to the express terms of the will, a general legacy will normally bear interest from one year after the date of death if it still remains unpaid. The interest is payable when the legacy is paid. Where such a legacy is varied the interest paid on the legacy should only be taxable in the hands of the new beneficiary under the variation, even though it covers a period prior to the variation. This is because the liability to income tax depends on actual receipt of the income and not receivability.

The main exceptions to the above rule are contingent legacies, which do not bear interest until the contingencies are fulfilled unless they are set aside for the benefit of the legatee, and certain legacies to minors, which bear interest from the date of death. In practice, these types of legacies are rarely subject to any variation.

Income from property which is the subject of a specific legacy is taxed in the hands of the legatee from the date of death. Where the property is redirected to another person by way of variation, the original legatee will only be taxable on the income arising up to the date of the variation.

ITTOIA 2005, ss 649 and 654 provide for the taxation of income paid to beneficiaries with limited interests in residue during the course of the administration of the estate. Sums paid over to the beneficiary during the course of administration are taxed as the income of the beneficiary for the year of assessment in which they are paid. Any amount that remains payable in respect of the limited interest on the completion of administration of the estate is deemed to have been paid to the beneficiary as income of the year of assessment in which the administration period ended.

Where there is an absolute interest in residue, the provisions of ITTOIA 2005, s 652 apply. The beneficiary is taxed on amounts he receives in any tax year to the extent that they do not exceed the residuary income for that year plus any residuary income of previous years on which he has not already been subject to tax. At the end of the administration period the residuary income for the whole period is aggregated and, where this aggregate exceeds the total amount on which he has already been taxed, the excess is treated as income paid to him immediately before the end of the administration period.

Where a person has a discretionary interest in residue, ITTOIA 2005, ss 649 and 655 provide that the beneficiary is taxed on any payments made in any tax year in exercise of the discretion in his favour.

There are specific provisions (ITTOIA 2005, ss 671–675) dealing with successive interests in residue such as might arise where a residuary gift is varied. The overall effect of these provisions is to ensure that each beneficiary is taxed on the amount to which he is entitled.

An instrument of variation will be a settlement within ITTOIA 2005, Pt 5 Ch 5 whereas a disclaimer will not. As a result, any variation by a parent in favour of a relevant child will fall within ITTOIA 2005, s 629 and any income paid to or for the benefit of any relevant children will be taxed in his hands. A relevant child is defined as either an unmarried minor or a minor not in a civil partnership (ITTOIA 2005, s 629). In addition, any variation which involves the legatee resettling property upon trusts under which he retains an interest may be caught by ITTOIA 2005, s 624 and, if so, the income of the trust will remain taxable in his hands.

Instruments of variation should expressly deal with the right to income accrued up to the date of the instrument as between the donor and the donee. It is usually appropriate to provide that the income should belong to the person who would bear the burden of paying income tax on it and this will usually be the donor.

Pre-owned assets charge

[19.24] The charge to income tax on pre-owned assets (**4.35**), imposed by FA 2004, will not apply to a disposition made by a person in relation to an interest in the estate of a deceased person if, by virtue of IHTA 1984, s 17, the disposition is not treated as a transfer of value by that person for inheritance tax purposes. This means that any disposition made by variation or disclaimer and any disposition falling within IHTA 1984, s 143 (dispositions made in accordance with a testator's wishes within two years of the testator's death) will not be caught by the pre-owned assets rules (FA 2004, Sch 15, para 16).

Stamp duty and stamp duty land tax

[19.25] An instrument of variation relating to land is exempt from stamp duty land tax provided certain conditions are satisfied (FA 2003, Sch 3, para 4).

An instrument of variation relating to stock or marketable securities is exempt from stamp duty under the Stamp Duty (Exempt Instruments) Regulations 1987 (SI 1987/516) provided it contains the required certificate.

Disclaimers

General

[19.26] A person cannot be made to accept a gift (whether lifetime or testamentary) if he does not wish to do so. He always has the right to decline the gift at any time before he expressly or impliedly accepts it but he will be treated as having accepted a gift once he takes any benefit from it or after a reasonable time has elapsed during which he could have disclaimed but failed to do so. A disclaimer is the refusal to accept a gift. It can be withdrawn but only if it has not been acted upon by any party relying upon it. While a legatee can accept one gift and refuse another, if they are separate and distinct, under the same will, he cannot in England and Wales accept only part of a gift and disclaim the remainder. (The law in Scotland is different.)

In the case of *Smith v Smith* [2001] 3 All ER 552, [2001] 1 WLR 1937 the High Court held that a disclaimer in advance of the death of the relevant estate owner was not valid because, since the estate owner was alive at the date of the disclaimer and could vary her will, there was no real interest which could be disclaimed.

IHTA 1984, s 93 provides that where a person who becomes entitled to an interest in settled property disclaims their interest, then provided the disclaimer is not made for money or money's worth, then the legislation applies as if he had not become entitled to that interest.

Effect

[19.27] The effect of a disclaimer is that the original gift becomes void *ab initio*. Thus, if a legacy or other bequest or devise is disclaimed, it falls into the residue of the testator's estate and, if the residue is not effectively disposed of by will, it will pass under the intestacy rules. If a residuary gift is disclaimed, that part of the residuary estate disclaimed will pass as on intestacy. To be a genuine disclaimer, the person disclaiming must simply refuse to accept the benefit being disclaimed and must not have any ability to decide its ultimate destination. Before, therefore, contemplating a disclaimer, one should look to see to whom the benefit to be disclaimed will pass under the operative rules of law.

For example, if residue is left to A, B and C in equal shares and A disclaims his share, that share will pass as on the testator's intestacy and will not accrue to B's and C's shares. The disclaimer of a life interest in residue will either accelerate the vesting of subsequent interests or create a partial intestacy of income if the doctrine of acceleration is not applicable. However, if an interest in remainder is disclaimed, this will (unless there are subsequent remainders) result in the trust property passing on the partial intestacy of the testator. Where on an intestacy one of a class of beneficiaries disclaims, his or her share passes to the remaining members of the class. Care needs to be taken by anyone considering a disclaimer of an interest under an intestacy because the rules can operate so as to pass over closer relatives in favour of remoter ones.

IHTA 1984, s 142 applies to disclaimers and thus the effect of a disclaimer for inheritance tax purposes is that the ultimate beneficiary is treated as having received the benefit in question from the deceased and not from the person disclaiming.

Formalities

[19.28] For s 142 to apply, the disclaimer must be in writing and made within 2 years of the deceased's death. However, there does not have to be an election or statement of intent to bring a disclaimer within the operation of s 142. Thus, in an appropriate case, where a disclaimer will achieve the desired result, it is a simple alternative to a written variation. Interestingly, there is no time limit in which a disclaimer should be made. Therefore, if the two-year time limit has passed and the beneficiary has taken no benefit from the assets, and it has not been made for consideration, it may be possible to take advantage of IHTA 1984, s 93. However, where such time has passed it can be expected that HMRC will examine the situation carefully (HMRC Inheritance Tax Manual, para 35165).

Stamp duty and stamp duty land tax

[19.29] A disclaimer is not liable to stamp duty nor stamp duty land tax, as it does not affect the transfer of any property.

Enquiry by HMRC

[19.30] HMRC Inheritance Tax Manual, para 35091 states that a variation should not be accepted as being within IHTA 1984, s 142 'until any investigation in accordance with [their] instructions on exploitation has been satisfactorily concluded'. Whether this is a prelude to an attack on the making of a potentially exempt transfer by the donee of property under a deed of variation by the application of the associated operations provisions contained in IHTA 1984, s 268 or on the basis that the dispositions under the will have not been varied, remains to be seen, but clearly an arrangement under which it is contemplated by all the parties that the beneficiary under a variation (eg a surviving spouse or civil partner) will return particular property by way of a potentially exempt transfer to the original legatee or beneficiary under a will (eg a child of the deceased) is vulnerable to an attack on these lines (HMRC Inheritance Tax Manual, para 35093).

If the subject matter of the variation and the subsequent gift are different assets, then the transaction will be strengthened but may still be susceptible.

As an alternative, the property could be settled on an interest in possession trust for the benefit of the surviving spouse, with their adult children having an interest in the remainder. The interest to the spouse would be an immediate post-death interest ('IPDI') trust. An IPDI is subject to the old rules that used to apply to interest in possession trusts. There will be no exit charge on property passing to a life tenant and there will be aggregation of the trust property with the beneficiary's free estate on death. Should the surviving spouse ultimately decide that she no longer requires the income, she could surrender her interest under the trust, thereby accelerating the interests of the children, or the trustees could exercise a power of appointment or advancement in favour of the children. The termination of her IPDI will be a potentially exempt transfer if the trust property is absolutely vested in her children. It is difficult, therefore, to envisage how HMRC might seek to challenge this.

If the trust deed had provided that no immediate vested right to income arose but rather that the property was to be held on trust for a beneficial class in which the children were included then the tax implications would be quite different. The termination of the spouse's interest would not be a potentially exempt transfer because the children would not immediately take an absolute interest and the interest would not have been terminated in favour of a trust for bereaved minors. Although the settlement would have been established by the will of the deceased parent and the age qualification would have been met there would still be a chargeable transfer.

Planning points

[19.31] The fact that a variation or disclaimer may be made within two years of a person's death should not be used as an excuse for not taking estate planning steps during his lifetime, particularly as the use of deeds of variation for tax purposes is being kept under review by the Chancellor. IHTA 1984, s 142 does provide, however, a two-year breathing space in which oversights may be corrected and account taken of changes in legislation since the will was made. The two-year period is also the appropriate time to review all the family's financial circumstances and in particular the needs of any surviving spouse or civil partner.

Use of nil rate band

[19.32] In the past, variations were often used to ensure that the nil rate band was utilised. It was used often where, for example, a widow who had inherited her husband's entire estate on death redirected sufficient sums to utilise her husband's nil rate band. With the ability to transfer nil rate bands between spouses and civil partners this is no longer required to the same extent although in certain circumstances it will still be appropriate.

Business and agricultural property relief

[19.33] Where property qualifying for business or agricultural property relief has been left to the surviving spouse or civil partner, consideration should be given as to whether it will still qualify as at the date of his or her death. If there is any prospect of the property not so qualifying (for example, if the property is likely to be sold) then the property might be redirected to non-exempt beneficiaries to ensure that the relief is not wasted. Any amount of property qualifying for 100% relief can be redirected at no tax cost. £650,000 of property qualifying for 50% relief may be redirected to children tax-free if the deceased died without having used any of the available nil rate band (see above). Where the surviving spouse requires the income from the property, consideration may be given to redirecting the property to a discretionary trust of which the surviving spouse is a beneficiary. The income can be distributed to the widow. If she dies before the tenth anniversary, the trust can be terminated. However, an exit charge may arise because in calculating the inheritance tax on a capital distribution before the first decennial, the initial value of the trust fund is the unrelieved value. The exit charge based on current rates will not be more than 6% which must be compared with a possible 40% rate on unqualifying property in the spouse's estate on death.

Increase in asset value after death

[19.34] Where the deceased's estate has significantly risen in value during the two-year period a deed of variation can be used to pass the gain element on to the next generation free of inheritance tax.

Example

Augustus leaves his entire estate worth £325,000 to his wife Abbie and 18 months after his death the estate has trebled in value.

If Abbie declares in writing that she will hold the estate upon trust as if she had been left a legacy of £325,000 with the residue passing to her children, the inheritance tax provisions will operate so as to attribute the value of the estate at death (ie £325,000) wholly to the legacy (which is exempt from tax by virtue of the spouse exemption) with the result that the remaining £650,000 ((3 × £325,000) – £325,000) passes to the children tax-free.

Gifts with reservation

[19.35] The interaction of IHTA 1984, s 142 with the gifts with reservation provisions contained in FA 1986, s 102 could provide useful possibilities regarding the matrimonial home. For example, a widow inheriting her late husband's house may decide to redirect the gift so that the house passes to her children. However, her children may allow her as their licensee to continue to occupy the property. Provided the variation has been entered into within two years and a valid instrument has been delivered where relevant, it will fall within IHTA 1984, s 142(1). IHTA 1984, s 142 overrides FA 1986, s 102 thus preventing the gifts with reservation provisions applying, which they clearly would have done had the widow simply given the house to her children but continued to live there. It would seem that HMRC accepts this interpretation (HMRC Inheritance Tax Manual, para 35151).

The POA charge will not apply to a disposition made under a deed of variation, provided that the disposition is not treated as a transfer of value by that person for inheritance tax purposes (FA 2004, Sch 15, para 16).

Potentially exempt transfers

[19.36] A gift qualifying as a potentially exempt transfer by a widow or other beneficiary should not be overlooked as an alternative to post-death variations of wills and other rearrangements. A potentially exempt transfer (of any amount or value) will be completely free from inheritance tax provided the transferor survives the transfer by seven years. Inheritance tax taper relief will apply if the transferor survives the gift by three years but not by the full seven. Thus, for example, a surviving spouse inheriting the deceased spouse's estate (free of inheritance tax) may wish to make lifetime gifts by way of potentially exempt transfers rather than become involved in varying the terms of the will especially if her life expectancy is greater than seven years.

Discretionary wills

Inheritance tax

[19.37] As discussed at **18.39**, some testators choose to execute discretionary wills. Under such a will the trustees are given a wide power of appointment by the testator exercisable in favour of a specified class of beneficiaries, leaving them to distribute the trust property or declare trusts of it following his death. If the executors exercise the power within two years of the death, and no-one has obtained an interest in possession within that time, then tax will be chargeable as if the gifts or trusts were made by the testator on his death, and the appointment will not be subject to the usual inheritance tax regime for discretionary trusts (IHTA 1984, s 144). It is not essential that the power of appointment be vested in the executors. It could instead be vested in, for example, the testator's spouse (although consideration would then have to be given to the possibility of the spouse predeceasing the testator).

The essential elements are as follows.

(a) The power of appointment must be exercised within two years of the death. To ensure that this is achieved it may be advisable that the will provides that the trust will automatically terminate at the end of the two-year period and contain a gift in default of the exercise of the power.

(b) The power must be exercised before privileged interest in possession subsists in the property; namely, before an IPDI or a DPI exists in the property.

(c) The will must give adequate power to the appointor to enable trusts, discretionary or otherwise, to be declared over the property, and to enable the appointor to confer whatever powers are needed or are appropriate, within the confines of the testator's overall requirements.

(d) An event occurs which would give rise to an exit charge or which would have given rise to such a charge were it not for relief given under IHTA 1984, ss 75 and 76 or Sch 4, para 16(1).

The 'back-dating' operation of s 144 only applies where, on a distribution from the trust, tax would otherwise have been charged. As a result, it used to be the case that if the discretion was exercised within three months of the death in favour of a surviving spouse or civil partner, section 144 would not apply because tax would not otherwise have been chargeable as illustrated by *Frankland v IRC* [1997] STC 1450 (CA) and *Harding (Loveday's Executors) v IRC* (SpC 140) [1997] STC (SCD) 321.

For deaths occurring after 9 December 2014, where an appointment is made within three months of the date of death, that appointment can be read back into the will. Where such an appointment is in favour of the deceased's spouse or civil partner, the spouse exemption under IHTA 1984, s 18 will apply.

Both pre and post-22 March 2006 appointments of IPDIs, TBMs and age 18–25 trusts may be made without a charge to inheritance tax and backdated to death (IHTA 1984, s 144).

Example

> Malcolm died in January 2012 and on his death his will created a flexible trust. In December 2013 the trustees appointed property to a trust for a bereaved minor. No charge was imposed when the property was transferred to the trust under IHTA 1984, s 71A. The appointment may be read back into the will.

One difficulty of varying a discretionary will trust is that some of the potential beneficiaries will be minors or indeed unascertainable. Such a variation would require consent of the court which of course is costly. It is suggested in a STEP Briefing Note that where the class of beneficiaries has not closed, the executors might appoint the trust fund to one or more of the objects with a view to them making the variation. HMRC has indicated that in its view such an arrangement will fall within both IHTA 1984, ss 142 and 144, although the executors will need to ensure that the arrangement did not constitute a fraud on the power (*Wong v Burt* [2005] WTLR 291, CA).

There are other financial consequences to be considered in relation to a discretionary will.

Payment of inheritance tax

[19.38] Inheritance tax will be payable on the application for a grant of probate on the value of the property subject to the discretionary power unless the power is exercised before the application is made. This is assuming that the property does not qualify for instalment relief in which case only those instalments which have fallen due at that date will be payable. In such cases, executors often have to fund this tax by bank borrowing which can be expensive. If the property is subsequently appointed to an exempt legatee such as a spouse or civil partner, the inheritance tax would be repayable.

Capital gains tax

Difficulties

[19.39] Capital gains tax complications may arise in respect of discretionary wills. TCGA 1992, s 62, which applies to variations within two years of death, does not apply to discretionary wills. An absolute appointment made under the trust is treated as a disposal under TCGA 1992, s 71. Hold-over relief under TCGA 1992, s 260 will not be available because any disposition of the trust assets within the two-year period will not be an occasion of charge to inheritance tax as IHTA 1984, s 144 prevents a charge arising. Hold-over relief under TCGA 1992, s 165 may, however, be available. If relief is not available, whether or not a chargeable gain results will depend on whether there has been any increase in value of the property appointed since the date of death.

If the appointment is not absolute but on continuing trusts it will be necessary to consider whether a new settlement has thereby been created or whether the trusts are a continuation of those established by the will, in accordance with the principles laid down in *Roome v Edwards (Inspector of Taxes)* [1982] AC 279, [1981] 1 All ER 736; *Ewart v Taylor (Inspector of Taxes)* [1983] STC 721, 57 TC 401; and *Bond v Pickford* [1983] STC 517. Where property was already settled under the will or intestacy and then becomes comprised in another trust as a result of the variation, the deceased person is treated as the settlor for capital gains tax purposes. The position is, however, less clear where a variation only amends or varies a will trust rather than transferring the property to a new settlement or where the person making the variation simply varies their own interest under the settlement. If a new settlement is created, a disposal to the new trustees will have taken place (although hold-over relief may be available). If the trusts are merely a continuation, there will be no disposal.

Chose in action

[19.40] A further complication will arise where an absolute appointment is made before the estate is fully administered, unless the assets which are the subject of the appointment have first been appropriated by the deceased's personal representatives to the trustees.

There is an argument that the subject matter of the appointment will be a chose in action in accordance with *Marshall (Inspector of Taxes) v Kerr* [1995] 1 AC 148, [1994] 2 All ER 106, HL, which will have a nil base cost and therefore a significant chargeable gain could arise. However, HMRC takes the view that where the trustees exercise their powers of appointment before the assets have vested in them, the assets are still held by the personal representatives at that time. When the assets vest, they will be treated as passing directly to the appointee (HMRC Capital Gains Manual, CG31432).

There is a disposal of the assets in question by the personal representatives to the person who benefits under the appointment but HMRC's view is that the exercise of the power of appointment is, however, read back into the original will. Thus, the beneficiary takes the asset as legatee and acquires the assets at probate value under the terms of the will (TCGA 1992, ss 62(4) and 64(2)). No chargeable gain will arise until the subsequent disposal of the asset by the beneficiary.

The result of this is somewhat surprising as the capital gains tax implications of an appointment prior to an assent or ascertainment of residue will be completely different from that of an appointment made after assent or ascertainment of the residue of the estate.

For example, where an asset has increased in value since the date of death, appointment of that asset following assent or ascertainment will result in a capital gains tax charge arising to the trustees on the appointment. Hold-over relief will only be available if the assets are business assets (see above).

However, if that asset were to be appointed to the beneficiary before assent or ascertainment, no chargeable gain will arise as HMRC will treat the beneficiary as if he received the asset at probate value under the terms of the will and no chargeable gain will arise until the subsequent disposal by the beneficiary (HMRC Capital Gains Manual CG31432).

This distinction should be considered carefully by trustees wishing to appoint assets to beneficiaries as it may be important for capital gains tax purposes to exercise the power of appointment prior to assent or ascertainment of the residue if an unwanted tax charge is to be avoided.

There has been correspondence between the Chartered Institute of Taxation and HMRC in respect of some further practical matters and changes were made to HMRC's Capital Gains Manual CG31432 to reflect the points made in the correspondence. HMRC has commented that the base cost to a beneficiary of rights under an unadministered estate will be their market value at the date of the appointment.

Income tax

[19.41] For income tax purposes the income arising under the discretionary trusts during the period from death to the exercise of the power will be taxed at the trust rate.

Conclusion

[19.42] In spite of the disadvantages discussed above, most of which may be overcome by a little forward planning, the flexibility offered by discretionary wills is such that most clients with estates in excess of £1 million should consider having wills in a discretionary form.

A discretionary will offers considerable opportunities for estate planning, more so than relying on a variation which can usually only be made by adult beneficiaries acting unanimously. After the testator's death the executors and the family will have determined the assets in the estate and can then consider to what extent assets should be divided between the surviving spouse and subsequent generations. In addition they can consider whether there is scope to skip a generation. It should be remembered that unlike a variation, a discretionary will can also avoid the income tax disadvantages under ITTOIA 2005, s 629 of a parental settlement.

There is no provision in the capital gains tax legislation corresponding to IHTA 1984, s 144. TCGA 1992, s 62(6) has no application to an exercise of the overriding power of appointment, because the variation will not be made 'by the persons or any of the persons who benefit or would benefit under the dispositions [made by the will]'. Consequently, if the power is exercised to make outright distributions of property to any beneficiary, a charge to capital gains tax may arise. There will usually only be a chargeable gain if the relevant assets have increased in value since the date of death because of the base cost uplift on the testator's death. Where a chargeable gain arises on business assets, it may be possible to make a claim under TCGA 1992, s 165 to hold-over the gain. Where the power is exercised before the administration of the estate is complete, HMRC takes the view that the beneficiary acquires the asset as a legatee under the will and there is no disposal by the personal representatives and therefore no capital gain can arise.

Precatory trusts

Inheritance tax

[19.43] So-called precatory trusts are not in fact trusts at all. They are outright gifts coupled with an expression of preference by the donor as to how he would like the donee to exercise his ownership which is not enforceable against the donee. They are commonly used to deal with the distribution of chattels within a class of beneficiaries. For example, a testator may give a collection of paintings to one of his sons with the wish that he distribute the individual paintings between all the children of the testator in a fair and agreed manner. However, as a matter of law, the named beneficiary is the owner of the bequest. This might have caused inheritance tax problems if the named beneficiary then distributed the property comprised in the bequest to the intended recipients in accordance with the testator's wishes as this would *prima facie* be a transfer of value by him. However, IHTA 1984, s 143 provides that, if the legatee transfers any of the property bequeathed to him in accordance with the testator's wishes within the period of two years of the testator's death, the property transferred will be treated as having been bequeathed to the transferee by the testator. It is probable that this relief will not apply to real property as the reference in s 143 is to property 'bequeathed' and not 'devised' and a bequest is a disposition by will of personal and not real property.

In *Harding (Loveday's Executors) v IRC* [1997] STC (SCD) 321 the Special Commissioners held that s 143 did not apply to an appointment in exercise of a fiduciary power under a discretionary will trust, that is, one where there was no interest in possession between the deceased's death and the appointment. It is arguable whether s 143 applies to a distribution in exercise of a fiduciary power where there has been an interest in possession between the deceased's death and the exercise of the power, because one of the grounds for the decision in *Harding* was that, because an event within s 143 is expressly declared not to be a transfer of value (IHTA 1984, s 17), s 143 only applies to events which would be transfers of value apart from that provision. An appointment out of a discretionary trust is never a transfer of value, whereas the termination of an interest in possession to which a person became beneficially entitled to before 22 March 2006 is deemed to be a transfer of value (IHTA 1984, s 52(1)) Similarly, a disposition after 21 March 2006 of an interest in possession to which a person became beneficially entitled on or after 22 March 2006 and which is an IPDI, DPI, TSI or a section 5(1B) interest in possession is treated as a transfer of value.

There was no debate in *Harding* as to whether s 143 was confined to gifts of personalty, although land does seem to have been comprised in the residuary estate which was appointed, and it may therefore be that the argument that s 143 only applies to personalty was not a point taken by HMRC.

Therefore, where it is intended that property disposed of by will should be distributed by the executors in accordance with the testator's wishes, at least where the property subject to such a gift will be valuable, it will be safer to provide that there is no interest in possession pending the executors' decision on how to distribute the property, so that s 144 can apply.

Capital gains tax

[19.44] No special capital gains tax reliefs apply to precatory trusts and so a capital gains tax charge could arise, although in practice they tend not to do so. This is because the property concerned will often fall within the exemption in TCGA 1992, s 262 for chattels valued at £6,000 or less.

Changes in value after death

Inheritance tax

[19.45] IHTA 1984, ss 178–198 provide relief for investments or land forming part of a deceased person's estate which are sold shortly after the date of death and have fallen in value. Although this section concentrates on personal representatives, it should always be borne in mind that these provisions will also apply to the trustees of a settlement following the death of a beneficiary entitled to a privileged interest.

It should be noted that the relief available for falls in value of qualifying investments and the relief for sales of land are entirely separate and are not aggregated for the purpose of the adjustment. Thus, a large gain on a sale of land will not reduce a loss on a sale of qualifying investments.

Qualifying investments

[19.46] Where an estate includes qualifying investments, such as quoted shares and securities and units in authorised unit trusts, which are sold within 12 months of the death for a sum less than the value at the date of death by the personal representatives or by the beneficiary if he is liable for the tax, they can apply to have the gross sale proceeds substituted for the value at the date of death for the purposes of inheritance tax (IHTA 1984, s 179). This will apply to all investments sold within the 12-month period. The lower value will be substituted for the probate value and the inheritance tax payable on the death will be recalculated accordingly. Unquoted shares and shares traded on AIM do not qualify for relief (HMRC Inheritance Tax Manual, para 34132).

The relief also applies to situations where qualifying investments:

(a) are cancelled, without being replaced, within 12 months after the date of death. These must be held immediately before cancellation by the personal representatives or by the beneficiary if he is liable for the tax (IHTA 1984, s 186A); or

(b) have their listing on a recognised stock exchange or dealing on the Unlisted Securities Market suspended at the date of the end of the 12-month period following the death and their value was at that time lower than at the date of death. The investments must be held at the end of the 12-month period by either the personal representatives or by the beneficiary if he is liable for the tax (IHTA 1984, s 186B).

These provisions deem qualifying investments within (a) above to have been sold for a nominal consideration of one pound and those within (b) to have been sold at their value at the end of the 12-month period following death.

It is important to note that where a claim is made all the investments sold within 12 months of the death have to be valued. The claim cannot be restricted to the investments which have fallen in value. Where some qualifying investments have risen in value since the date of death, but others have fallen, the personal representative should consider appropriating those that have risen in value to the relevant beneficiaries prior to selling the investments. This will enable a claim to be made only in relation to those investments which have fallen in value.

Land

[19.47] A similar relief applies to land forming part of the deceased's estate which is sold within three years (or four years in certain circumstances, see below) after the date of death (IHTA 1984, s 191). The relief for land will not apply if the sale price differs from the value at the date of death by less than £1,000 or 5% of the value on death, whichever is the lower. If HMRC is of the opinion that the sale was for an under-value, it can substitute the best consideration that could reasonably have been obtained for it at the date of sale. Where an interest in land which formed part of the deceased's estate on death is sold by the appropriate person and an election is made by that person, the value of that interest is its sale value and not its probate value.

Where there is more than one sale, the sale values must be substituted for all the sales of land and cannot be confined to one sale only.

It is many commentators' view that IHTA 1984, s 191 could apply where land is sold at a gain within three years of death, although this is not the view of HMRC (HMRC Inheritance Tax Manual, para 33026). It relies on the case of *Stonor (Dickinson's Executors) v IRC* (SpC 288) [2001] STC (SCD) 199, which is considered by many to be a poor decision which may in a later case be reversed by the courts.

Relief is not available if the sale is made to the beneficiary of the land under the will, a spouse or descendant or to the trustees of a settlement in which the beneficiary has an interest in possession by the personal representatives or trustees even if the sale is at an independent market value (IHTA 1984, s 191(3)(a)). The land can, however, be sold to the trustees of a discretionary trust of which the beneficiary is a potential object or to the parents of a beneficiary.

Date of sale

[19.48] For the purpose of each relief, the date of sale is the date of the contract for sale provided that the contract proceeds to completion, see *Jones (Balls' Administrators) v IRC* [1997] STC 358 (Ch D). There are special rules in relation to sales pursuant to the exercise of options and under compulsory purchase powers. Where the sale or purchase results from the exercise of an option, if the option is exercised not more than 6 months after the grant of the option, the material date is the date of grant (IHTA 1984, s 198(2)). In the event that the sale follows a notice under compulsory acquisition powers, the date of sale is generally the date on which compensation is agreed or otherwise determined or the date when the authority enters the land (if earlier) (IHTA 1984, s 198(3)). Where the sale is an acquisition under a general vesting declaration or a vesting order, the date of sale is the last day of the period specified in the declaration or the date when the vesting order comes into operation (IHTA 1984, s 198(4)).

Anti-avoidance provisions

[19.49] The object of the provisions is to grant relief where assets have been sold to meet tax and other liabilities. For this reason there are anti-avoidance provisions where investments or land are purchased within two or four months, respectively, of the last of the sales (IHTA 1984, s 192). This provision adjusts the amount of the relief that is available. Sales of land made in the fourth year after death are ignored for this purpose. However, a sale by the personal representatives followed by a cash distribution to the relevant beneficiary will enable that beneficiary to repurchase the investments sold without falling foul of these provisions.

If it is anticipated that qualifying investments or land which the personal representatives intend to sell in the course of administration, will have changed in value within the relevant period from the date of death, then it is essential that the sale of such assets is correctly timed to ensure that they receive the benefit of the relief provided for in these sections.

Making a claim

[**19.50**] A claim for relief must be made on form IHT35 in respect of shares and form IHT38 in respect of land by the appropriate person as defined by IHTA 1984, s 178(1), who is the person liable for the tax; that is, the personal representatives, trustees or the beneficiary. It is therefore essential that the personal representatives do not pay the inheritance tax and then assent the shares or land to the beneficiary who sells them at a loss because relief will not be available. A claim for relief on the sale of land or shares must be made within four years of the end of the appropriate period for qualifying sales. For sales of land this means that the claim must be submitted within seven years from the date of death and for sales of shares within five years.

In the case of *Stonor (Dickinson's Executors) v IRC* (Spc 288) [2001] STC (SCD) 199 the residuary estate was left to charities and the executors made a claim under IHTA 1984, s 191 so the higher property values on death could be used as base values for capital gains tax purposes. The legislation defines the 'appropriate person' as being the person liable for inheritance tax. The gifts to the charities were exempt transfers and so no tax was chargeable on them. There was only a liability for tax which was actually payable. As there was no tax payable, there was no person liable to pay the tax and accordingly the executors' claim was dismissed.

Capital gains tax

[**19.51**] Under TCGA 1992, s 274, the value of an asset as determined for inheritance tax purposes in charging a deceased person's estate is deemed to be the market value on death for capital gains tax purposes. Thus, where the value of land is amended under the above provisions, it is the amended value that applies for capital gains tax purposes. This is why an advantageous capital gains tax position can be obtained on sales within 3 years of death at an increased value. If, however, the assets will not bear inheritance tax (because, for example, the estate is less than the nil rate band) it is understood that HMRC's view is that no election can be made because of the decision in *Stonor (Dickinson's Executors) v IRC* (Spc 288) [2001] STC (SCD) 199. This used to be stated in HMRC's Capital Gains Tax Manual at paras CG 32461 and 32462; however, these paragraphs have now been deleted. It is now stated in HMRC Inheritance Tax Manual, para 33026. As regards qualifying investments, IHTA 1984, s 187 contains provisions for ascertaining the values for capital gains tax purposes of specific investments sold after death, which will usually be their respective sale values.

Where assets are sold after the death at a value lower than probate value and a claim for the relief is made, the result will be to reduce a capital loss for capital gains tax purposes. (There will still be a capital loss attributable to the difference (if any) between the gross sale proceeds and the net sale proceeds.)

Payment by instalments

[19.52] Tax chargeable on certain property passing on death may, while the property remains unsold, be paid in ten equal annual instalments (IHTA 1984, ss 227–229). The relief applies to:

(a)   land wherever situated;
(b)   a business or an interest in a business;
(c)   controlling shareholdings; and
(d)   unquoted shareholdings where either:
   (i)   the Board are satisfied that the tax attributable to their value cannot be paid in one sum without undue hardship; or
   (ii)   the tax payable on the shares represents not less than 20% of the tax payable by that person on the estate; or
   (iii)   the value of the shares is over £20,000 and they form not less than 10% of the capital of the company.

The first instalment of tax will fall due for payment six months from the end of the month in which the death occurs.

Interest on unpaid tax

[19.53] Interest accrues on unpaid tax from six months from the end of the month in which the chargeable transfer occurs (IHTA 1984, s 233(1)(b)). Where the chargeable transfer is death, the tax is due six months after the end of the month in which the death occurred. To determine the current rate of interest reference should be made to HMRC's website. However, tax payable by instalments, other than where attributable to certain securities or to land (which is neither a business asset nor attracts agricultural property relief), is not chargeable to interest provided each instalment is paid on the due date (IHTA 1984, s 234). Therefore, if paid on time, tax on each instalment is interest-free.

Repayments of overpaid tax carry with them the benefit of interest supplement (IHTA 1984, s 235(1)). Interest paid on unpaid tax is not deductible from the income of the estate for income tax purposes so that the beneficiaries receive no income tax relief in respect of it. However, the interest supplement is not taxable in the hands of the personal representatives or the beneficiaries (IHTA 1984, s 235(2)).

Capital gains tax exemption

[19.54] Personal representatives have the same annual capital gains tax exemption as an individual (£11,100 for 2016/17) for the tax year in which the death occurs and for the following two tax years (TCGA 1992, s 3(7)). When deciding whether to sell an investment and distribute the proceeds to a beneficiary or whether to distribute the investment in specie allowing the beneficiary to use his own annual exemption on the sale the annual exemption should be considered.

Where the beneficiary is not resident in the UK, consideration should be given to distributing assets in specie rather than selling and distributing the proceeds as the beneficiary will not be chargeable to UK capital gains tax on disposals of assets. That is unless the asset is a UK residential property interest. Advice on the beneficiary's liability to tax in the jurisdiction where he is resident must be taken, however, to ensure that his overall position is not worsened.

Death benefits under insurance policies and pension schemes

[19.55] Death benefits under death-in-service benefit schemes and pension schemes often provide for the trustees of the scheme with a discretion as to the person to whom the payment is to be made. If the deceased has, by letter of wishes, nominated someone to receive the moneys then the trustees will normally follow those instructions. If no such nomination has been made then the trustees will usually either make payment to the next-of-kin or to the deceased's personal representatives, having first consulted the family. The opportunity should be taken to arrange for the payments to be made to specific members of the deceased's family with a view to satisfying immediate financial needs and to minimising the inheritance tax burden on subsequent deaths. For a more detailed discussion see CHAPTER 9 INSURANCE and CHAPTER 10 PENSIONS.

Chapter 20

UK Domiciliaries Investing Abroad

Introduction

[20.1] An increasing number of individuals cross national barriers in business, in the employment of multi-national companies or in pursuit of a better life and so often acquire assets situated outside the UK. Improved worldwide communications and the varying fortunes of national economies and governments encourage individuals, even if firmly domiciled and resident in the UK, to spread assets and risks by investing internationally.

Whilst the network of double taxation treaties was developed largely to encourage the international operations of business, they also facilitate multi-national investment by individuals. The private international laws of national legal systems have also grown up in recognition of the increasing involvement of individuals in various legal jurisdictions.

Foreign investments may be made and retained by an individual in his own name. Direct ownership of those foreign assets can, however, present disadvantages such as the obligation to comply with local administrative procedures and succession laws on death and the payment of gift or death duties imposed by the country in which the assets are situated. In such circumstances consideration is often given to other means of ownership of foreign assets.

The planning steps which may be taken by an individual who is moving to or from the UK and by a foreign domiciled and resident individual in relation to the ownership of assets in the UK are examined in **CHAPTER 21 UK RESIDENTS WITH MULTI-JURISDICTIONAL AFFAIRS** and **CHAPTER 22 THE OVERSEAS CLIENT**. This chapter primarily considers the advantages and disadvantages of direct ownership of foreign assets by an individual domiciled and resident in the UK and the indirect ownership of those same assets through a nominee, a company or a trust.

Any tax or succession planning with overseas assets must be undertaken with care in order to avoid creating a continuing tax liability. Care must be taken to ensure that a charge does not arise under the pre-owned assets rules because for UK resident and domiciled individuals, those rules apply to their worldwide assets. These provisions are discussed in greater detail in **CHAPTER 4 LIFETIME PLANNING: MAKING GIFTS**.

Direct ownership

[20.2] An individual may hold assets in a foreign country in his own name. As a UK resident and domiciled individual he will be liable to income tax on income arising from those assets, capital gains tax on gains realised on the disposal of those assets and potentially, inheritance tax on any gift (whether made during his lifetime or on his death) of those assets; in addition, he may also be liable to income tax on those assets in respect of a charge arising under the pre-owned assets rules. Similar taxes may also be imposed in the country in which the assets are located. The existence of a double taxation treaty may alleviate the position in one of two ways. Either the profit or gain which the tax system of the country in which the asset is situated and the UK tax system both seek to tax may be exempted from tax in one of those jurisdictions (or the liability may be reduced); or credit may be given in one country for tax suffered in the other. Even where no double tax treaty exists between the UK and the country in which the asset is situated, relief may be given unilaterally by the UK. Relief may be given for tax suffered in the foreign jurisdiction against income tax or capital gains tax suffered on the same profits or for gift or death duties suffered in a foreign jurisdiction against inheritance tax chargeable in respect of the same assets.

Ownership of assets in a foreign jurisdiction will not only cause the UK individual to fall within that foreign country's tax net on his death but local administration procedures will apply. Title to the assets will have to be established by his personal representatives or beneficiaries. In some circumstances a UK grant of representation may be re-sealed by local authorities (as in, for example, most Commonwealth countries). In other jurisdictions (principally those governed by a civil code such as France and Spain) the concept of a personal representative does not exist and it may be necessary to arrange for title to pass directly to the beneficiaries of the property.

In addition to the conflicting formalities in foreign jurisdictions relating to the transfer of property to an individual's heirs on his death, succession to that property may also be governed by the law of the foreign country.

Succession to immovable property (ie land) will be governed by the law of the country in which that land is situated. Where a foreign country has particular rules relating to the devolution of a fixed portion of an individual's estate on death to his surviving spouse (or a civil partner equivalent) and/or children, any attempt to displace these rules by provision in his will, will be unsuccessful.

Even though succession to movable property (such as shares) situated abroad is usually governed (under the conflict rules of most foreign countries) by the law of the individual's country of domicile (or nationality) taxation difficulties may arise if the property is given by a will to personal representatives to be held for others. These difficulties stem from the fact that many civil law jurisdictions do not recognise the role and duties of a personal representative in relation to the deceased's assets and those beneficiaries for whose benefit he holds and administers the deceased's property. Therefore, if a UK domiciled individual were to leave all their movable assets to their executors to be held by them for their surviving spouse, some foreign jurisdictions would attempt to impose death duties on their movable property situated there as though the deceased's gift had been an outright gift to the executors.

The European Succession Regulation (EU) 650/2012 (known as 'Brussels IV') which apply to the estates of persons dying after 16 August 2015, is designed to ensure that succession to an estate is treated coherently. Essentially, the relevant jurisdiction and applicable law will be that of the testator's habitual residence at the time of death unless there is a jurisdiction to which the deceased was more closely connected or the deceased elected for the law of their nationality to apply. Transitional provisions permit a choice of law clause to be included in wills and testamentary documents executed before 16 August 2015. The choice of law stated in a will, therefore, is very important. The UK, together with Ireland and Denmark, has opted out of these regulations and so their effect is uncertain. It is difficult to see how it could apply to the UK when it was not a party to the agreement and so it is likely that the English doctrine of the conflict of laws will continue to apply.

In many countries, death duties are imposed at rates determined according to the proximity of the relationship between the deceased and those who take his property on his death, the lowest rates usually being charged on gifts to a spouse (or civil partner equivalent), higher rates on gifts to children and grandchildren and the most punitive rates on gifts to unrelated individuals. This is particularly affected by the variations between the recognition of unions between individuals of the same sex. Some countries do not give any legal recognition to such unions whilst some allow individuals of the same sex to marry.

Unless the foreign jurisdiction will accept that the 'gift' to the UK individual's executors is not a beneficial gift but, rather, an administrative measure, death duties may be imposed at the highest rates unless the deceased's executors are close relations. The provisions of an applicable double tax treaty may alter this position but these problems require investigation at the outset. An individual owning assets abroad (in particular, land) should consider if there is any significant advantage in making a will (in the local language), in accordance with the applicable laws of each of those countries where his assets are situated, to ensure that he achieves the transfer of those assets to his chosen heirs at the lowest possible cost.

When dealing with more than one jurisdiction a timing issue may arise where there is a delay in determining the tax liabilities in one country. In *Whittaker v IRC* [2001] STC (SCD) 61n (SpC 272) the Commissioners held that an executor could not validly appeal against an inheritance tax determination in respect of foreign property on the grounds that the Italian tax liabilities had not yet been determined.

Where an individual wishes to invest in stocks and shares of companies in various foreign jurisdictions and intends that those investments will be bought and sold over a period of time, it is likely to be impractical, expensive and burdensome administratively for him to investigate the taxation and succession laws of each country and to make a will under the laws of each of those countries. In these circumstances, the individual may wish to simplify his affairs by making his investment through another medium situated in the UK, such as a unit trust or investment trust or a unit-linked life policy, which in turn invests in foreign companies. This will avoid any problems with foreign succession laws and taxes on his death.

Some individuals enjoy foreign property by participation in a 'time share' arrangement rather than by owning foreign property direct. The procedural and succession rules applying to the transfer of the individual's rights of occupation to his heirs will depend upon the nature of the time share structure and the terms of the individual's rights. However, if the occupation rights are conferred by a trustee holding land for the benefit of members of a time share club and permitting those members occupation of the property on specified terms the individual's asset may be a chose in action against the trustee (ie an entitlement to enforce his rights against the trustee). If this is so, the chose in action is likely to be situate in the jurisdiction of residence of the trustee to which the individual would have to go to enforce his rights. Frequently, the trustee of a time share arrangement will be resident in a jurisdiction other than that in which the property is held (and often somewhere such as Jersey or the Isle of Man) where procedural and succession rules on the death of the individual may be more akin to those of the UK than those of the countries in which the land is situate.

Ownership by a nominee

[20.3] It may be possible for an individual to avoid local succession procedures and laws by holding assets in the joint names of himself and another if the local law permits beneficial ownership to pass automatically to the survivor of joint owners. A problem may still arise, however, on the death of the surviving co-owner.

Alternatively, assets may be held in the names of corporate nominees which can exist indefinitely. An individual investing abroad could set up his own nominee company in the UK specifically for this purpose. On the death of the beneficial owner of the assets, his personal representatives may need only to direct the nominee to hold to the order of the beneficiary to whom the asset devolves under the will. There may be no requirement for the legal ownership of the foreign assets to change. It should be borne in mind that the Small Business, Enterprise & Employment Act 2015 provides that information on individuals who ultimately own or control more than 25% of a UK company's shares or voting rights, or who otherwise exercise control over such a company or its management, will need to be kept on the Register of Persons with Significant Control.

This may avoid any local administrative procedures on death and also, if the local law does recognise the concept of a trust (which is what the nominee relationship is), both local succession laws and local death duties. That would be the case if the local law treats the nominee as the absolute owner of the assets and does not recognise any changes in the underlying beneficial ownership.

If the local laws do not recognise beneficial ownership then it may be necessary to ensure that any foreign assets are purchased in the name of the nominee since to transfer foreign assets into the name of the nominee may result in a charge to local gift taxes. A liability to gift tax might also arise on a transfer of the assets by the nominee company to any new beneficial owner or owners and if the rates of tax depend upon the proximity of relationship between the transferor and the transferee, the highest rates are likely to apply.

Another potential problem is that if the nominee were to transfer assets into the names of the deceased's heirs shortly after the death it might constitute itself an 'executor de son tort' if the local law recognised such a concept, with a resulting exposure to death duties on the assets in the jurisdiction. The case of *IRC v Stype Investments (Jersey) Ltd* [1982] Ch 456, [1982] 3 All ER 419 is a reverse illustration of this potential risk, where a foreign nominee owned UK situs assets.

In some countries (Switzerland, for example) it may be possible for an individual to give another person a power of attorney, valid under local law, to deal with the individual's assets in the event of his death. In such a situation, normally the attorney will acquire no beneficial interest in the assets but only the right to administer them. This may assist in relation to procedural matters but will not prevent the application of local succession laws or the imposition of local death duties.

Ownership by a company

[20.4] Ownership of foreign investments by a company, the shares of which are owned by the individual investor, may avoid local succession procedures and laws and duties on the death of the individual if that company is incorporated and resident outside the jurisdictions in which its investments are made. It will be necessary, however, to arrange the transfer of the shares of the company itself to the heirs of the deceased who will inherit the company's shares. The ownership of the underlying investments will remain unchanged.

The cost-effectiveness of this arrangement as a means of holding foreign assets will depend upon the value of the investments to be acquired (in view of the costs of setting up and administering the company), the tax liability of that company in its country of residence and in the countries in which its investments are made and the UK tax liability of the shareholder. Overall, some simplification of the administration of the deceased's estate may be achieved.

An individual resident and domiciled in the UK would not, by holding his assets through a foreign resident company, save any UK income, capital gains or inheritance tax. If he held foreign assets directly he would be charged to income tax on his foreign income. Dividends received from a foreign resident company interposed between the individual and his investments would be charged to income tax as savings and investment income. Under ITA 2007, ss 720 and 727, however, where the income from the foreign assets is rolled-up in the offshore company and not distributed by way of dividend, such undistributed income would be deemed to be the individual investor's for all purposes unless the individual could show that the transfer of assets abroad was not to avoid any liability to UK tax (ITA 2007, ss 736–742). This charge is on a current year basis. The individual would, however, receive the benefit of any rebates or reliefs under any double taxation treaties between the UK and the country in which an investment is situated (ITA 2007, s 746(2)).

It is common for foreign property, such as a holiday home which the individual uses for his personal use, to be held by a non-resident company which in turn is owned by a UK individual. There was a concern for some time, a concern reinforced by the decision in *R v Allen; R v Dimsey* [2001] UKHL 45, [2002] 1 AC 509, [2001] 4 All ER 768, that a benefit in kind charge under ITEPA 2003, Ch 5 may be imposed on such an individual who has a controlling interest in a non-resident company. ITEPA 2003, ss 100A and 100B, however, specifically exempts certain living accommodation outside the UK from the benefit-in-kind charge which might otherwise apply. The living accommodation must have been provided by a company for a director or other officer of the company ('D') or a member of his family or household. It must have been provided by a company which is wholly owned by D solely or by D and other individuals. The exemption is available both in relation to direct holdings of interests in such accommodation and to holdings through wholly owned subsidiaries. In relation to direct holdings, the interest must be the company's main or only asset and the only activities undertaken by the company must be ones that are incidental to the ownership of the interest. In relation to holdings in a subsidiary, the subsidiary must be wholly owned by the company and must meet the conditions set out in relation to direct holdings. Various exceptions apply to the exemption in ITEPA 2003, s 100A, the most important being that s 100A will not apply where living accommodation is provided in pursuance of an arrangement the main purpose, or one of the main purposes, of which is the avoidance of income tax, corporation tax or national insurance contributions. The legislation contains complex provisions relating to transactions with connected companies.

Whilst domiciled and resident in the UK, an individual will suffer capital gains tax on all gains realised on his worldwide assets. Even if assets are held beneficially by a non-resident company, gains realised by that company may be deemed to be an individual's by virtue of TCGA 1992, s 13. Where the provision applies, its effect can be unduly harsh. Losses made by a non-resident company cannot be used to reduce its gain before apportionment, nor can the losses as such be apportioned except to the extent that a shareholder has had a gain apportioned to him in that tax year and the apportioned loss would reduce the gain.

Any transfer *inter vivos* or on death of foreign assets or the shares of a foreign company through which foreign assets are held will be chargeable to inheritance tax because the individual is domiciled in the UK (IHTA 1984, ss 5 and 6).

In any situation where a company holds funds, one has to consider the issue of how to extract moneys in the most tax efficient manner. One possibility is that the company could be initially funded by way of a cash loan. This will enable capital to be extracted subsequently from the company tax-free by way of repayment of the loan. Alternatively, a special type of redeemable share capital could be used although that can cause difficulties with the rules concerning transactions in securities (ITA 2007, ss 682–685). Alternatively any income received by the company may be extracted by payment of a dividend. In practice, this may not give rise to an additional income tax charge for the investor if the amount of income has already been taken into account in charging the investor to income tax under ITA 2007, ss 720 and 727 (ITA 2007, s 743).

Ownership through other forms of entities

[20.5] It is common for overseas property to be held through entities other than companies and trusts. For example, a usufruct is a common way of holding property in France and also in Spain. When advising a client on a particular entity it is essential that the UK tax effects of the entity holding assets are considered. This is not always straightforward, as the inheritance tax implications will be more complex particularly where the entity has varying characteristics, resulting in more than one interpretation.

HMRC published its view in its April 2013 newsletter that it will usually treat a usufruct as an interest in possession trust for inheritance tax purposes under IHTA 1984, s 43(2), although the circumstances of each arrangement need to be considered carefully because the nature of a usufruct differs between jurisdictions. A number of commentators do not agree with HMRC's view on the basis that a usufruct cannot be characterised as similar to a settlement as defined in IHTA 1984, s 43(2). In its September 2015 newsletter HMRC confirmed that its view remains the same. It would appear that HMRC has had a small number of cases where an estate included a usufruct and, having applied its approach to the case, the difference in value reported by the taxpayer and that calculated by HMRC was not sufficient to warrant further pursuit. It would appear that HMRC in those cases adopted the tax-payer's value.

In addition, the UK treatment of an overseas entity can conflict with that of the other country. Double tax treaty protection is only available if the tax and the taxpayer is the same in both countries. The treatment can also change over time. It was formerly the case that a French société civile immobilière (SCI) was transparent for both UK and French tax purposes. Following *Memec plc v IRC* [1998] STC 754, 71 TC 77, 1 ITLR 3, CA, a French SCI is now classified by HMRC as opaque. Such an entity is liable to UK corporation tax on the sale of the property or distributions made resulting in double taxation.

Individuals sometimes create foundations to hold assets. Foundations may be established under the law of Liechtenstein, Austria, Switzerland, Panama, Malta, The Bahamas, Jersey, the Isle of Man and Guernsey amongst others. Broadly speaking, a foundation is a self-owning legal entity, separate from its founder, officers and beneficiaries (if any) which has a council board which is responsible for its administration. The foundation may hold assets in its own name, it is capable of suing and being sued and will usually have the rights, powers and privileges of an individual. This is in contrast to a trust which does not have a separate legal personality, does not beneficially own assets and cannot be made personally liable for trust debts.

A foundation does not need beneficiaries but, if it does have them, they will usually have no interest in the foundation's assets and will not be owed fiduciary duties by the foundation or the members of the foundation council. Indeed, a foundation council will owe fiduciary duties to the foundation in the way that a company's board of directors owes a fiduciary duty to the company and not to the shareholders.

Offshore settlements

[20.6] An individual might hold his foreign investments through an offshore settlement, although such settlements are unlikely to provide any UK tax advantages during his lifetime and may, indeed, create disadvantages in respect of UK tax. The terms of the settlement would normally be such that neither the settlor nor any other beneficiary can require the trustees to return assets to them. Nor should the settlor or any UK resident person have the power to direct how the trust fund should be invested.

Although no individual resident in the UK will usually be able, under the terms of the settlement, to enforce the distribution of assets from the settlement, whether to himself or others, sometimes under such trusts the settlor retains some say in the running of the settlement; for example, if its terms provide that any distribution of assets from the settlement can only be made by the trustees with his consent. To reverse the balance and repose a power of appointment in the settlor, but provide that it is exercisable only with the trustees' consent, is unusual.

Forms of settlement

[20.7] Before 2006, the most common form of settlement was one giving a life interest to the settlor (and his spouse or civil partner) under which the trustees had power to pay capital to the settlor at their discretion. Such settlements secured the division of ownership between the settlor and trustees whilst leaving the settlor almost in the same position as if he owned the assets directly. For inheritance tax purposes, it was the case that, provided the settlement conferred an interest in possession on the settlor, no inheritance tax charge would arise on the transfer of assets to the trustees since he would be treated as remaining the beneficial owner of all the settled property in which his interest subsisted (IHTA 1984, s 49). Since the changes made by FA 2006, most such settlements will now be relevant property settlements.

Where a UK domiciled settlor creates any trust (unless it is a privileged interest trust – see **CHAPTER 6 CREATING SETTLEMENTS**), he will suffer an inheritance tax charge unless an exemption or relief applies. As we have seen, where a settlor and beneficiaries are UK resident and domiciled there are no particular taxation advantages in holding assets including foreign property in a non-resident settlement during the settlor's lifetime.

Tax situation of trustees

[20.8] Where a trust is created by a settlor who is resident or domiciled in the UK, the body of trustees of a settlement will be regarded as not resident for UK income tax purposes (ITA 2007, s 475) and capital gains tax purposes (TCGA 1992, s 69) provided all the trustees are resident outside the UK. A non-resident trustee will be deemed to be resident when he acts as a trustee in the course of a business which he carries on in the UK through a branch, agency or permanent establishment.

Where the income of a settlement is payable to, or applicable for the benefit of, the settlor, his spouse or civil partner, that income will be treated for income tax purposes as the settlor's, and therefore will be subject to UK income tax. The UK resident settlor will, because of his interest in the settlement, be subject to capital gains tax on the gains realised by the trustees in the tax year they are realised (TCGA 1992, s 86, Sch 5).

For more detailed explanation of the taxation of non-resident settlements, see **CHAPTER 8 OFFSHORE TRUSTS.**

Chapter 21

UK Residents with Multi-Jurisdictional Affairs

Introduction

[21.1] This chapter deals with those individuals who take up residence in the UK or cease to be resident in the UK either in the long term or the short term. By far the greater part of this chapter deals with the position of a person taking up residence in the UK.

The chapter does not address the immigration rules applied by the Home Office to individuals resident abroad wishing to come to the UK to live or to work, or European Union law on the free movement of nationals of Member States. These aspects should be reviewed well in advance of the anticipated date of entry into the UK.

A substantial number of individuals coming to the UK will not be domiciled in the UK and may never become so.

A brief summary of the concept of domicile is also given in this chapter. The Government has proposed a number of charges to the taxation of non-UK domiciliaries which, at the time of writing, are the subject of a formal consultation, entitled '*Reforms to the taxation of non-domiciles: further consultation*'.

These proposed changes are due to come into effect on 6 April 2017. Whilst some draft legislation has been published with this consultation there are parts of the proposals where the Government are still in discussions with the professional bodies and various other interested parties.

The proposed changes include:

- the definition of deemed domicile being changed, which is discussed in detail in **21.11–21.14**;
- the concept of deemed domicile being extended to income tax and capital gains tax, which is discussed in detail in **21.15**;
- UK residential property interests held indirectly by non-domiciled persons, including trusts with non-UK domiciled settlors or beneficiaries being subject to inheritance tax, which is discussed in detail in CHAPTER 11 THE FAMILY HOME AND OTHER RESIDENTIAL PROPERTY;
- changes to the transfer of assets abroad provisions, which are discussed in CHAPTER 8 OFFSHORE TRUSTS and **21.80**; and
- changes to the taxation of settlors and beneficiaries of offshore trusts, which is discussed in CHAPTER 8 OFFSHORE TRUSTS and **21.75**.

Domicile

[21.2] Domicile is of fundamental importance in estate planning. There are two types of domicile: domicile under the general English law and an artificial deemed domicile which currently applies specifically for inheritance tax purposes. The Government proposes to introduce revised deemed domicile rules which will apply not only to inheritance tax (as is currently the case), but also to income tax and capital gains tax. These rules, which will take effect from 6 April 2017, are discussed in **21.10–21.15** below.

Domicile under the general law

[21.3] Under the law of England and Wales, every individual must at any time have a domicile in one specific country. There are three categories of domicile: those of origin, dependency and choice. Scotland also has a law of domicile which varies from the law of England and Wales in some aspects. The following is a description of the law in England and Wales.

Domicile of origin

[21.4] An individual is born with a *domicile of origin*, which if he is legitimate, will be that of his father at that time. An illegitimate child takes his mother's domicile. Where an individual is actually born has little to do with his domicile. It is therefore important when a client is claiming to have a foreign domicile of origin to determine his parents' situation both at the time of his birth and subsequently, bearing in mind that while under the age of 16 his domicile of origin will remain but if his father or mother's domicile changes depending upon which parent his domicile follows (while he is under 16) his domicile will follow that of his relevant parent and will be a *domicile of dependence*.

Domicile of choice

[21.5] Once an individual reaches the age of 16, he has the legal capacity to acquire an independent domicile in a different country – a *domicile of choice* (Domicile and Matrimonial Proceedings Act 1973, s 3). This is acquired both by actual physical presence in another country and by forming a definite intention (evidenced by all the circumstances surrounding the individual and his way of life) to make his home in that country permanently or indefinitely (*Udny v Udny* (1869) LR 1 SCD 441 (HL)). In *Bell v Kennedy* [1868] LR 1 SCD 307 (HL) it was said that the question to be considered was whether the appellant had 'determined to make, and had made, [the new country] his home, with the intention of establishing himself and his family there, and ending his days in that country'. If he does not acquire a domicile of choice in this way, he will retain his domicile of dependence, and if he loses that without acquiring a domicile of choice, his domicile of origin will revive.

Change of domicile

[21.6] An individual loses a domicile of choice (and a domicile of dependency) by leaving the country in question with the intention (supported by clear evidence) of ceasing to regard it as his permanent home. An individual may thereupon acquire a new domicile of choice, if the requirements mentioned below are met. If they are not, his domicile of origin will revive.

It is difficult to lose a domicile of origin. There must be clear and positive evidence that a change has been made. The intention to remain in the new country permanently or indefinitely has to be formed free of all external constraining factors. For example, in *F (Personal Representatives of F dec'd)* [2000] STC (SCD) 1 (Spc 219) the deceased moved to the UK from Iran for various reasons including religious persecution. He had maintained a settled intention to return but was unwilling to do so immediately because an exit bar meant that if he had gone to Iran he might have been prevented from leaving again. It was held that he did not acquire a domicile of choice in a country of the UK. An individual may be taken to have acquired a new domicile of choice for a period even if he later changes his mind and returns to his previous country of domicile. In practice, however, the evidence of the necessary intention at the outset will have to be very strong to convince HMRC that an individual has lost a domicile in a country of the UK and has acquired a domicile of choice in another country if he subsequently resumes residence in the UK. It has not been uncommon for Englishmen to spend many years in a foreign country (for example, in government service or working in the Far East), with the intention of leaving that country eventually, either to retire to England or some other country. In those circumstances, the individual will not acquire a domicile of choice in the foreign country regardless of the length of the period he resides there. This approach was confirmed in *Civil Engineer v IRC* [2002] STC (SCD) 72 (Spc 299).

Where a person maintains more than one residence as was the case in *Gaines-Cooper v Revenue & Customs Comrs* [2007] EWHC 2617 (Ch), [2008] STC 1665, he will have a domicile of choice in that country in which he has his chief residence.

In *Mark v Mark* [2005] UKHL 42, [2006] 1 AC 98, [2005] 3 All ER 912, a case concerning divorce, in which it was argued that someone in the UK illegally could not acquire a domicile of choice here. Baroness Hale, giving the leading judgment, held that domicile was a means of connecting an individual with a jurisdiction for certain purposes. Sometimes that connection would be to the individual's advantage and sometimes it would not. There was no reason why a person's residence in a country and his intentions should not determine his domicile in the normal way simply because that residence was illegal.

A finding as to domicile requires a careful evaluation of all the facts as was clearly demonstrated in *Cyganik v Agulian* [2005] EWHC 444 (Ch), 7 ITELR 831. In that case the individual's unbroken 30-year residence in the UK was not conclusive of an acquisition of a domicile of choice.

In *Barlow Clowes International Ltd v Henwood* [2008] EWCA Civ 577, [2008] BPIR 778, [2008] All ER (D) 330 (May), which was a non-tax case, the Court of Appeal considered the interaction of a domicile of origin with a domicile of choice.

The respondent, Mr Henwood, had a domicile of origin in England and Wales and later acquired a domicile of choice in the Isle of Man. In 1992, he left the

Isle of Man and moved to Mauritius. He also spent significant periods in France. It was argued by the respondent that his domicile of choice in the Isle of Man was replaced by a new domicile of choice in Mauritius. The Court of Appeal held that when the respondent abandoned his domicile of choice in the Isle of Man he did not acquire a new domicile of choice. As a result his domicile of origin in England and Wales revived and between then and 2005 he had not acquired a new domicile of choice. In the case Arden LJ held that when the court has to determine which of two jurisdictions represents an individual's chief residence, the court has to look at the quality of the residence in the two jurisdictions. It is not as simple as looking at which contains the individual's main home in terms of size or amenities or of the jurisdiction in which the individual spends most time. The key is to ascertain in which jurisdiction the individual intends to reside permanently.

The fact that an individual makes an application for naturalisation in another country does not of itself indicate a change of domicile (*Wahl v A-G* (1932) 147 LT 382, HL, and *F (Personal Representatives of F dec'd) v IRC* (SpC 219) [2000] STC (SCD) 1.

Married women

[21.7] It used to be the case that a woman on her marriage automatically took her husband's domicile as a domicile of dependence. A wife's domicile is now determined in the normal way (Domicile and Matrimonial Proceedings Act 1973, s 1). Where a woman already married on 1 January 1974 had acquired her husband's domicile as a domicile of dependence, that domicile is her domicile of choice until such time as she acquires a new domicile. A married woman can, therefore, have a different domicile to that of her husband. If an Englishwoman marries a man with a domicile of origin in New York and after the marriage the couple live in Europe for the time being (eg due to the husband's employment) she will not acquire a domicile of choice in New York. She will retain her English domicile. By way of further example, suppose a man with an English domicile of origin works for most of his life in Hong Kong. At the time of his retirement he marries a woman domiciled in California, and they decide to live in California for a while, but not necessarily permanently. His wife, having never lived in England and having no intention of doing so, remains domiciled in California, but the husband, at any rate initially, does not become domiciled in California. So they have different domiciles. The case of *IRC v Bullock* [1976] 3 All ER 353, [1976] 1 WLR 1178, CA, is authority for the proposition that a married couple (only one of whom already has an English domicile) may set up home in England on a permanent basis without the spouse with the foreign domicile necessarily thereby acquiring an English domicile of choice. If one spouse maintains links with his or her original country and demonstrates a clear intention (rather than 'a vague hope or aspiration') of returning there should he or she survive the other or in the event that the other were to agree to go and live in that original country, then that spouse will retain his or her domicile in that original country.

Determining one's domicile status

[21.8] Being able to plan one's future financial affairs may be dependent upon determining one's domicile status to a high degree of probability and yet, as we have seen, domicile is a complex concept which is determined by a detailed consideration of the factual background. One might have thought, therefore, that there would be a facility to obtain a ruling on one's domicile status from HMRC. There has never been a formal statutory procedure but for many years, in practice, it was possible to obtain a ruling which could be relied upon by submitting a DOM1 form to HMRC. HMRC will no longer provide an opinion on the domicile status of a taxpayer outside the normal enquiry process. Its current practice, set out in Revenue and Customs Brief 34/10, is that:

'... HMRC will consider opening an enquiry where domicile could be an issue, or making a determination of Inheritance Tax in such cases, only where there is a significant risk of loss of UK tax.

The significance of the risk will be assessed by HMRC using a wide range of factors. The factors will depend very much on the individual case but will include, for example:

- a review of the information available to HMRC about the individual on HMRC databases;
- whether there is a significant amount of tax (all taxes and duties not just Inheritance Tax) at risk.

HMRC does not consider it appropriate to state an amount of tax that would be considered significant, as the amount of tax at stake is only one factor. It should be borne in mind that HMRC will take into account the potential costs involved in pursuing an enquiry, and also those of potential litigation should the enquiry not result in agreement between HMRC and the individual; clearly such costs can be substantial.

Where HMRC does open an Inheritance Tax enquiry in any of these cases, it will keep the factors in view and may stop the enquiry at any stage if it considers the continuation of the enquiry is not cost effective. The outcome of such an enquiry may be that HMRC does not consider it appropriate to make a determination of the Inheritance Tax.

Individuals should also bear in mind that enquiries into domicile involve a detailed inquiry into all of the relevant facts and HMRC is likely to require considerable personal information and extensive documentary evidence about the taxpayer and the taxpayer's close family.'

As it is extremely difficult to obtain any form of determination as to an individual's domicile, it is advisable for an individual to retain as much information and documentary evidence on a continuing basis as is relevant to his domicile status. In the HMRC Residence, Domicile and Remittance Basis Manual at para 23080 there is a useful list of information that HMRC might request when an enquiry is raised in respect of an individual's domicile status. This information will prove very useful where domicile is being challenged on a death. It would appear that HMRC in opening its enquiries is now asking very detailed questions and so a client and his advisers should be prepared to give very full responses.

The case of *Gaines-Cooper v Revenue & Customs Comrs* [2008] STC 1665 illustrates the breadth of evidence that was presented to the court.

Deemed domicile

Current position

[21.9] Currently for inheritance tax purposes only, a person who is not domiciled in the UK under the general law will be deemed to be domiciled here at the relevant time if:

(a)   he was domiciled in the UK under the general law within the period of three calendar years immediately preceding that time; or

(b)   he was resident in the UK for income tax purposes in 17 of the 20 years of assessment ending with the year in which the relevant time falls (IHTA 1984, s 267).

The result of being deemed domiciled in the UK is that an individual will be liable to inheritance tax on their worldwide assets. In such a situation a person may pay inheritance tax not only in the UK but also in another country where they have property situated in that country. HMRC states that in such circumstances 'her estate can, of course, claim tax relief for any Inheritance Tax paid in another country' (Inheritance Tax Manual, para 13024). This is somewhat misleading as a claim for tax relief usually means some form of deduction from the amount chargeable to tax. IHTA 1984, s 159 provides an entitlement to a tax credit for the tax which has been paid in the other country. That of course is more valuable than a deduction for the foreign tax paid.

In determining whether the individual is resident in any year for the purposes of the rule, residence is determined as for income tax purposes (see **21.25** below).

Because of the deemed domicile rules, currently it is often the case that an individual is, under general principles, not domiciled in the UK but deemed to be domiciled in the UK for inheritance tax purposes. The deemed domicile rules may in certain situations be overridden (IHTA 1984, s 267(2)). If an individual is domiciled in a country which has a suitable double tax treaty with the UK, then assets held outside the UK will not be subject to UK inheritance tax provided they do not pass under a disposition governed by the law of any part of Great Britain. Such countries include France, Italy, India and Pakistan.

The proposed 2017 changes

[21.10] In his Summer 2015 Budget Speech, the Chancellor announced that the taxation of non-UK domiciliaries would be changed. There have been a number of formal and informal consultations, the most recent formal consultation being the publication of the *'Reforms to the taxation of non-domiciles: further consultation'*, published on 18 August 2016 (the '2016 ConDoc'). The following narrative is based on the draft legislation published with this consultation (the 'Draft Legislation'). It should be noted that the front page of the Draft Legislation states that 'the legislation published in this document is not intended to be complete and excludes some issues which will be included in the Finance Bill 2017'.

As mentioned in **21.11** currently the concept of deemed domicile applies only in relation to inheritance tax. It is proposed, however, that the concept will also apply, from 6 April 2017, to income tax and capital gains tax. It should be noted that the income tax and capital gains tax Draft Legislation is structured in a different way to the inheritance tax Draft Legislation. We shall first deal with the inheritance tax provisions.

Deemed domicile for inheritance tax purposes

[21.11] An individual who is not domiciled in the UK under the general law will be deemed for inheritance tax purposes to be domiciled here at the relevant time (the time at which the individual's domicile is to be determined) if:

(a)   they were domiciled in the UK under the general law within the previous three calendar years immediately preceding the relevant time (the 'Recently Domiciled Rule');

(b)   they are a formerly domiciled resident for the tax year in which the relevant time falls (the 'Formerly Domiciled Resident Rule');

(c)   they were resident in the UK for income tax purposes for at least 15 of the 20 tax years preceding the tax year in which the relevant time falls and resident for that tax year or if they were not UK resident in that tax year, they were resident for at least one of the four tax years immediately preceding that tax year (the 'Long-Term Resident Rule').

The Recently Domiciled Rule

[21.12] This rule remains the same as the current rule found in IHTA 1984, s 267. It operates by reference to former actual domicile in the UK and so the application of that rule will not be affected by the fact that the person concerned has been treated in a prior year as if they were domiciled in the UK. Because of that, a person who has not actually been domiciled in the UK even though they have been treated as so domiciled will not be subject to the Recently Domiciled Rule.

In the ConDoc published in September 2015 the Government suggested a rule which would treat a UK-domiciled individual as non-domiciled on the latter of the date that they acquire a domicile of choice in another country and the time when they have not been resident in the UK for six years. If a person, however, were to become non-resident and later lose his UK domicile after the end of the third fiscal year in which they were non-resident they would continue to be treated as if they were UK domiciled under the current version of the Recently Domiciled Rule after the end of his sixth year of non-UK residence. This seems to indicate that the Government intends to modify or abrogate the Recently Domiciled Rule.

In the most recent ConDoc, the 2016 ConDoc, it is stated that 'the Government will change the deeming rule so that where individuals become deemed domiciled under the Long-Term Resident Rule, that status will fall away once they have been non-resident for more than four consecutive years'. Again, it would seem to be implicit in this statement that the Recently Domiciled Rule will be modified or abrogated.

Formerly Domiciled Resident Rule

[21.13] A formerly domiciled resident is defined for the purposes of inheritance tax in the Draft Legislation (amended IHTA 1984, s 272) as a person:

(a) who was born in the UK;
(b) whose domicile of origin was in the UK;
(c) who was resident in the UK for that tax year; and
(d) who was resident in the UK for at least one of the two tax years immediately preceding that tax year.

The grace period of two years applies only for inheritance tax purposes. It does not apply for the purposes of income tax and capital gains tax (see **21.15**).

The introduction of this rule has been severely criticised by the professional bodies. It will result in radically different treatments of taxpayers according to the accidents of events which have happened decades in the past and which would not seem to result in any differences in their circumstances sufficient to justify a difference in tax treatment.

Example

Tim and Tom were brothers. In 1950, before their birth, their father, who was domiciled in the UK, went to work in Australia and became resident there. Tim was born in Australia in 1951. Tom was born in 1952, his mother having returned to the UK for the birth because of complications in her pregnancy which required treatment by a London specialist. She returned to Australia with her newly born son and until 1 June 2016 neither Tim nor Tom nor their parents ever set foot in the UK again. Their father gradually settled in Australia and acquired a domicile of choice there at the beginning of 1955.

In June 2016, Tim and Tom decided to visit their cousins in the UK for a couple of months but, unfortunately, whilst here they were both involved in a car crash and after a period in which they were in a coma they died on 10 December 2017. They were both resident in the UK under the statutory residence test for the fiscal years 2016/17 and 2017/18. Both had had domiciles of origin in the UK but had acquired domiciles of dependence in Australia which had become their domiciles of choice. Whereas Tim had not been born in the UK, Tom had. The result was that Tim's worldwide estate suffered no UK inheritance tax whereas Tom's was fully subject to it.

The Long-Term Resident Rule

[21.14] There has been a Long-Term Resident Rule for as long as inheritance tax has existed but the current version is that a person will be treated as domiciled in the UK at any particular time if he has been resident in the UK in 17 of the previous 20 years ending with the fiscal year in which the relevant time falls.

Applying the current or proposed Long-Term Resident Rule requires a person to have determined his country of residence over a period of 20 fiscal years. For the purposes of determining where a person is resident in the fiscal year 2013/14 and onwards the statutory residence test (SRT) applies (see **21.25**). In applying the SRT, it is sometimes necessary to determine a person's residence for a prior year in which the SRT did not apply. It is possible to make an election (the 'SRT Transitional Election') under FA 2013, Sch 45, para 154 (see **21.47**) to apply the SRT for this purpose to those prior years.

In respect of determining residence for years before 2013/14, however, one must apply the highly uncertain law which applied then. The professional bodies have recommended that a taxpayer should be able to make an election, similar to the transitional election under FA 2013, Sch 45, para 154, to apply the SRT provisions to all relevant years for the purposes of the deemed domicile rules. In the 2016 ConDoc the Government said that it would not do so.

For a client who has already been in the UK for more than 15 out of the previous 20 tax years but fewer than 17, they will be deemed, under the Long-Term Resident Rule to be domiciled in the UK from 6 April 2017.

Example

Costa was born in Tasmania. His parents were married at the time of his birth. His father was domiciled in Tasmania when he was born and so Costa acquired a domicile of origin in Tasmania. He came to school in the UK when he was 11 in September 2001 and continued his education in the UK until completing his Legal Practice Course in 2014. He obtained a training contract at a UK law firm, qualifying as a solicitor in September 2016. Assuming he remains living and working in the UK, under the proposed Long-Term Resident Rule, he will, on 6 April 2017, be deemed to be domiciled in the UK. This is because for the tax years 2001/02 to 2015/16 Costa has been resident in the UK for 15 years.

So he will satisfy the condition that he will have been resident in the UK for at least 15 of the 20 fiscal years preceding the tax year in which the relevant time falls. Under the current version of the rule, however, he would not be deemed to be domiciled in the UK because he would not satisfy the condition that he has been resident in the UK for at least 17 of the 20 fiscal years ending with the fiscal year in which the relevant time falls.

An oddity of the new rule is that minors who have a domicile of dependence, which, of course, will follow their father's domicile, may find that they are treated as having a different domicile to their father for inheritance tax, income tax and capital gains tax purposes. A child whose father loses his UK domicile under the general law but who continues to be treated as UK domiciled under the Long-Term Resident Rule, may be treated for tax purposes as domiciled in a different country from his father because the child cannot satisfy the Long-Term Resident Rule for the first 14 fiscal years of his life.

If a father acquires a foreign domicile during his son's minority but continues to be treated as domiciled in the UK under the Long-Term Resident Rule the son will acquire his father's foreign domicile as a domicile of dependence and he will not be treated as domiciled in the UK under the Long-Term Resident Rule until he has been resident in the UK for 15 years.

Conversely, however, where the father acquires a foreign domicile in the 15th or 16th fiscal year of his son's life it will be possible that the father will not satisfy the Long-Term Resident Rule whereas the son will do so. In that case, although he had his father's domicile of dependence in another country, the son would be treated as being domiciled in the UK whereas the father would not.

Applying the Draft Legislation the maximum period after ceasing permanently to be resident in the UK for which a person can be treated as domiciled here under the Long-Term Resident Rule, however, is five consecutive years. As we have said, however, the 2016 ConDoc says that the Government intends that deemed domicile under the Long-Term Resident Rule will 'fall away' after four years of non-residence.

Under the Draft Legislation, it would be possible for a person not previously treated as deemed UK domiciled who was not resident at any time after 5 April 2017 to be treated as domiciled in the UK from 6 April 2017 to 5 April 2021. The 2016 ConDoc says, however, that a person who is not resident in the UK after 5 April 2017 will not be subject to the Long-Term Resident Rule. Such persons will be subject to the current rules outlined in **21.9**. In addition, the Long-Term Resident Rule will not be relevant in determining the excluded property status of property added to a settlement before 5 April 2017.

Example

> Bambos is not domiciled in the UK. He became UK resident in 2000/01 and was UK resident in all years up to and including 2015/16. He ensured that he was not UK resident in 2016/17 so that he was not treated as domiciled in the UK for the purposes of inheritance tax in that year under the current legislation because he was not resident here for 17 out of the 20 fiscal years ending with the year (2016/17) in which his domicile was to be determined. In 2017/18, he continues not to be UK resident in that year. Although he will meet the Long-Term Resident Rule because he will have been resident in the UK in 15 of the last 20 fiscal years, if the 2016 ConDoc is to be relied upon, he will not be deemed to be UK domiciled because the Long-Term Resident Rule will not apply to Bambos because he is not resident after 5 April 2017.

Deemed domicile for income tax and capital gains tax purposes

[21.15] The income tax and capital gains tax Draft Legislation is structured in a different way to the inheritance tax Draft Legislation. A new section is to be inserted into ITA 2007 (s 835BA), which is to have effect only where it is specifically provided that it is to apply to particular provisions of the Income Tax Acts or other enactments. That means that one cannot simply assume that these provisions to treat non-UK domiciliaries as if they were domiciled in the UK will apply in respect of any particular provision of income tax or capital gains tax to which domicile is relevant. Instead, one will have to search in the provisions concerned for a specific provision applying the deemed domicile rule.

The draft s 835BA provides that:

'(2)   An individual not domiciled in the United Kingdom at a time in a tax year is to be regarded as domiciled in the United Kingdom at that time if –

    (a)   condition A is met, or
    (b)   condition B is met.

(3)   Condition A is that –

    (a)   the individual was born in the United Kingdom,
    (b)   the individual's domicile of origin was in the United Kingdom, and
    (c)   the individual is resident in the United Kingdom for the tax year referred to in subsection (2).

(4)   Condition B is that the individual has been UK resident for at least 15 of the 20 tax years immediately preceding the tax year referred to in subsection (2).'

This Condition A is the equivalent of the proposed Long-Term Resident Rule for inheritance tax. Condition B is the equivalent of the proposed Formerly Domiciled Resident Rule for inheritance tax. There appears to be no proposed equivalent for income tax and capital gains tax purposes of the Recently Domiciled Rule for inheritance tax purposes.

In Condition B, unlike its equivalent in the inheritance tax Draft Legislation, there is no condition as to UK residence in previous years so there will be situations where an individual is treated as if he were domiciled in the UK for income tax and capital gains tax purposes but not for inheritance tax purposes (see **21.11**). Because there is no condition as to prior residence for income tax and capital gains tax purposes, a person who was born in the UK and has had a UK domicile of origin will never be able to benefit from the remittance basis.

It should be noted that it seems that even under the 2016 ConDoc's proposals, an individual will have to be non-resident for six years in order to lose his deemed UK domicile status for income tax and capital gains tax purposes, whereas for inheritance tax purposes, it will be for a period of four consecutive years.

Action to be taken

[21.16] The proposed changes outlined in the 2016 ConDoc which are to take effect from 6 April 2017 will have a significant impact on non-UK domiciliaries. Such a person will wish to consider their UK tax situation before that date and take any necessary action. The difficulty for an adviser is that the Draft Legislation published is 'not complete and excludes some issues which will be included in the Finance Bill 2017'. The Government is still consulting on the detail of the changes and holding meetings with the professional bodies. Until the draft Finance Bill 2017 is published on 5 December 2016 the detail of the proposals will not be known and until it is enacted, they could change significantly.

In the meantime, a client and their adviser will need to react to the proposals as they develop and be prepared to take quick action when they have been sufficiently defined. Such clients should ensure that accounts and records are up to date so that prompt decisions can be made.

Where UK residential property is held through a company or similar entity, valuations should be obtained so that a decision may be made as to whether the UK residential property should continue to be held in this way or not and the likely tax costs of either proposal.

It is proposed that the rebasing of offshore assets to their market value at 5 April 2017 (see **21.66**) will only be available to those individuals who have paid the remittance basis charge. For a non-UK domiciled individual, therefore who has not paid the remittance basis charge in previous years, because, for example, their offshore income and gains were not sufficient to warrant payment of the charge, but who has substantial unrealised gains on directly owned foreign assets it might be advantageous for him to pay the charge in 2016/17 so as to rebase his assets.

An individual who will become deemed domiciled in the UK on 6 April 2017 because they satisfy the proposed Long-Term Resident Rule (15 years) and not the current 17-year rule, may consider settling a trust before 6 April 2017, which will be an excluded property trust. This will have to be balanced against benefitting from the tax-free rebasing as at 6 April 2017 (see **21.66**).

Advantage should also be taken of the ability to clean up historic mixed funds between 6 April 2017 and 5 April 2018 (see **21.67**).

It should be remembered that the proposed changes to excluded property trusts apply only to UK residential property. It does not apply to other assets; for example, UK commercial property.

For clients who may be considering becoming non-resident to avoid being deemed domiciled, or where there is a question as to their residence status for 2016/17 and later years, advice should be given now so as to leave sufficient time for that advice to be implemented.

Non-domiciled spouse election

General

[21.17] As mentioned in **4.15**, where the transferor is domiciled in the UK but his transferee spouse or civil partner is not so domiciled, there is a limited spouse exemption of £325,000 (before 6 April 2013 the limit was £55,000). There is no similar limitation on the spouse exemption given in relation to the income tax charge on pre-owned assets. Other inheritance tax exemptions may, however, apply to such transfers, such as the exemption in relation to dispositions between spouses for the maintenance of the other party (IHTA 1984, s 11(1)). This maintenance exemption would not normally be available where the transfer by the domiciled spouse is of an interest in a capital asset such as real property (*Phizackerley (Personal Representative of Phizackerley (dec'd)) v Revenue & Customs Comrs* [2007] STC (SCD) 328) (but see *McKelvey (personal representative of McKelvey, dec'd) v Revenue & Customs Comrs* [2008] STC (SCD) 944).

An election

[21.18] Under IHTA 1984, s 267ZA an election can be made for a non-domiciled spouse to be treated as domiciled in the UK for inheritance tax purposes. The election has the effect that any transfers from a UK domiciled spouse or civil partner to a non-domiciled spouse or civil partner will be exempt from inheritance tax but the previously non-domiciled spouse or civil partner's worldwide assets will fall within the scope of inheritance tax and will be fully chargeable. Such an election currently has no effect on the income tax or capital gains tax position of the individual.

Right to elect

[21.19] A person can make a lifetime election provided that at any time after 5 April 2013 and during the seven-year period ending with the date on which the election is made, the person had a spouse or civil partner who was domiciled in the UK (Condition A). At the time that the election is made the person making the election does not need to be married or in a civil partnership; nor do they have to be resident in the UK or domiciled outside the UK (HMRC Inheritance Tax Manual, para 13042).

A death election can be made by a person whose spouse or civil partner has died and during the period of seven years ending with the date of death, the deceased spouse or civil partner was domiciled in the UK (Condition B). An election can also be made by a personal representative. This will commonly occur where the person's UK-domiciled spouse or civil partner has also died, and where transfers between the couple were made at a time when the full spouse or civil partner exemption was not available under IHTA 1984, s 18(2).

Making the election

[21.20] A lifetime election can be made at any time. A death election must be made within two years of the death of the deceased, or in such a longer period as an officer of HMRC allows (IHTA 1984, s 267ZB(6)). HMRC states that it will apply the normal rules for allowing a late election found in HMRC Inheritance Tax Manual, para 43009. (HMRC Inheritance Tax Manual, para 13042.)

An election must be made to HMRC by notice in writing. There is no prescribed form of election but in its guidance at para 13043 HMRC states that the election should contain the following information:

(i)   'the full name and address of the person making the election, or for whom the personal representatives are making an election,
(ii)   their date of birth and, if appropriate, their date of death,
(iii)   the full name of their spouse or civil partner who is domiciled in the UK, and
(iv)   the date the election is to take effect from.'

The date from which the election is to take effect must be after 5 April 2013, and for a lifetime election be within a period of seven years of the date of the election, or for a death election, within seven years of the deceased's death (IHTA 1984, s 267ZB(4)).

The election is irrevocable (IHTA 1984, s 267ZB(9)). Once made, an individual during his lifetime will continue to be treated as UK domiciled until he has been resident outside the UK for income tax purposes for four consecutive tax years starting after the date of the election (IHTA 1984, s 267ZB(10)). This will remain the same when the proposed 2017 changes come into effect. Where an individual is living abroad and wishes for the election to remain effective he will need to renew it by the end of the fourth year.

Effect of making an election

[21.21] As mentioned above, the effect of an election is that the non-domiciled spouse will be treated as domiciled in the UK so that transfers to him from his spouse or civil partner will benefit from the spouse exemption. Of course, his entire worldwide estate will be brought within the scope of UK inheritance tax.

The election does not, however, affect the excluded property status of specific savings held by taxpayers domiciled in the Channel Islands, or the Isle of Man nor certain British Government securities that are exempt where the owner is domiciled abroad. In addition, an election is ignored when applying a Double Tax Treaty with France, Italy, India or Pakistan.

Should an election be made?

[21.22] As is usually the case, each situation will depend on its own facts. Putting his non-UK situs assets within the scope of UK inheritance tax may actually increase an individual's overall inheritance tax liability. Where a non-domiciled spouse is considering backdating the election it is essential that he consider the transfers that he has made. For example, any excluded property transferred into trust which originally would have been outside the scope of inheritance tax will be brought into charge if the election is backdated to include that event. A gift of non-UK assets to an individual would make that gift a potentially exempt transfer.

An individual could, however, transfer any non-UK situs assets to an excluded property trust before an election is made. Those assets held in the excluded property trusts will not be subject to UK inheritance tax even after the settlor elected to become UK domiciled. Of course, there may be a potential capital gains tax liability depending upon whether the remittance basis of assessment applies.

Where it is expected that a UK domiciled spouse will die first and the non-domiciled spouse will leave the UK and survive for a further period of four consecutive tax years, the non-domiciled spouse could make the election so the full spouse exemption was available on the death of the UK domiciled spouse. The election would then cease to apply after the surviving spouse has been non-UK resident for four complete tax years.

Where the surviving spouse disposes of their UK assets and invests the proceeds in non-UK situs assets after leaving the UK, the value of those assets will be outside the scope of inheritance tax when the election ceases to apply.

HMRC gives an example in its Inheritance Tax Manual at para 13047 where a husband transfers property to his foreign domiciled wife who subsequently settles some of her foreign assets on offshore trustees. The value transferred would be exempt as to the first £325,000, with the remainder being a potentially exempt transfer. In the event of her husband's death she could make an election to be treated as UK domiciled so that his gift to her is spouse exempt. By doing this, however, she will be treated as being UK domiciled and the transfer of her foreign assets to offshore trustees will no longer be a transfer of excluded property and will be a chargeable transfer. This example illustrates that where a domiciled spouse makes a transfer to a foreign domiciled spouse, the non-domiciled spouse has to be particularly careful in respect of subsequent transfers.

There is another anomaly in the provisions in respect of which particular care is required. If the husband had made the gift more than seven years before his death, it would have proved not to be a potentially exempt transfer but it might have been a gift with reservation unless the wife had excluded her husband from any benefit under the trust she had settled. The spouse exemption in the gift with reservation provisions in FA 1986, s 102(5) will only apply as to the first £325,000 of the value of the transfer. The subject matter of the gift may therefore be treated as forming part of the estate of the donor. There would be no spouse exemption on death because the assets would not pass on death. No election could be made to treat the recipient spouse as UK domiciled in respect of the transfer because, although an election can be made in respect of a failed potentially exempt transfer, this is not such a transfer. This illustrates the importance of professional advice being taken to ensure that all the consequences of an election being made are carefully considered before an election is made.

Interaction with IHTA 1984, s 267

[21.23] The election provisions found in IHTA 1984, ss 267ZA and 267ZB operate independently from the deemed domiciled provisions found in IHTA 1984, s 267. An election to be domiciled in the UK does not mean that a person is treated as being deemed domiciled under s 267. It is possible, however, that the person who has elected to be treated as domiciled in the UK may, whilst the election is in force, become deemed domiciled in the UK by meeting the conditions of IHTA 1984, s 267.

Residence

Background

[21.24] Until 6 April 2013 there was no statutory definition of residence and so advisers had to turn to the Taxes Acts to the extent that they provided particular rules, Revenue practice and case law.

HMRC's guidance found in HMRC6 was both deliberately vague and, in parts, of doubtful accuracy. The lacunae in the relevant case law and the inadequacy of the published guidance created great uncertainty which finally led to the introduction of the statutory residence test (the 'SRT').

The case law and Revenue guidance are still, however, of importance. First, there will still be open enquiries into clients' tax returns for prior years. Second, in order to determine an individual's residence status under the SRT for the fiscal years 2013/14 to 2017/18, his residence status for 2010/11 to 2012/13 will be of relevance.

In this edition of the book we discuss the SRT. For discussions of case law and revenue practice for those prior years, please refer to earlier editions of this book.

The statutory residence test

Outline

[21.25] The SRT, which is set out in FA 2013, Sch 45, determines whether an individual is resident or not in the UK. In addition, HMRC has issued its guidance, 'Guidance Note: Statutory Residence Test (SRT) (RDR3)' which, of course, should not be confused with the law. The rules apply in relation to 'relevant taxes' which are defined as income tax, capital gains tax and, so far as the residence status of an individual is relevant to them, inheritance tax and corporation tax (FA 2013, Sch 45, para 1(4)).

The SRT does not apply in determining whether or not an individual is resident or not resident in England, Wales, Scotland or Northern Ireland specifically, rather than in the UK as a whole (FA 2013, Sch 45, para 1(3)). The specific rules contained in the Scotland Act 1998 and the Government of Wales Act 2006 will determine whether an individual is a Scottish taxpayer or a Welsh taxpayer.

The test

[21.26] The basic rule is that an individual is resident in the UK for a tax year if he satisfies either:

(a)   the Automatic Residence Test; or
(b)   the Sufficient Ties Test.

If neither of these tests are met in the relevant year then the individual is not resident in the UK for that year (FA 2013, Sch 45, para (4)).

The Automatic Residence Test is met for a relevant year if an individual satisfies at least one of the Automatic UK Tests and none of the Automatic Overseas Tests (FA 2013, Sch 45, para 5(1)).

The flowchart below illustrates the Automatic Residence Test.

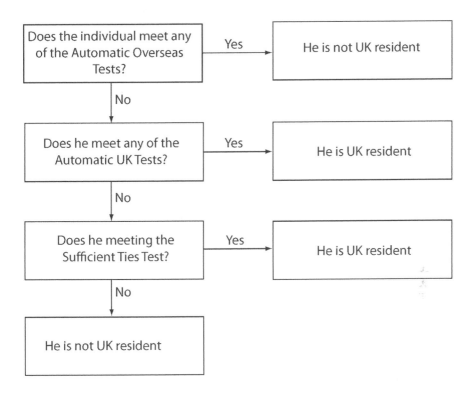

The Automatic UK Tests

[21.27] There are four automatic UK tests.

First Automatic UK Test

[21.28] The First Automatic UK Test is satisfied if an individual spends at least 183 days in the UK (FA 2013, Sch 45, para 7). If an individual is present in the UK at the end of a day, that day is considered as a day spent in the UK, subject to two exceptions and a deeming rule (FA 2013, Sch 45, para 22(1)). The first exception is the Transit Exception and applies where the individual arrives in the UK as a passenger on one day, leaves the UK the following day and between arrival and departure he does not engage in any activities that are to a substantial extent unrelated to his passage through the UK (FA 2013, Sch 45, para 22(3)). Unless the individual leaves the UK on the day after his arrival, the Transit Exemption cannot apply. So if an individual arrives for example on Tuesday evening and leaves early on Thursday morning, the Transit Exception will not apply even if there was no later flight which could have been taken to have allowed an onward flight to be caught out of the UK.

What constitutes 'activities that are to a substantial extent unrelated to [the individual's] passage through the UK'? HMRC has given its views in para 3.9 of RDR3 using a number of examples. Unfortunately, no reasons are given for its conclusions in the examples and so are of limited assistance.

The second exception is the Exceptional Circumstances Exception which applies where the individual would not be in the UK at the end of that day but for exceptional circumstances beyond the individual's control that prevent him from leaving the UK and he intends to leave the UK as soon as those circumstances permit (FA 2013, Sch 45, para 22(4)). Paragraph 22(5) then provides that:

> 'Examples of circumstances that may be "exceptional" are national or local emergencies such as war, civil unrest or natural disasters and a sudden or life-threatening illness or injury.'

To what extent can circumstances which affect other people and which indirectly prevent an individual from travelling be taken into account? For example, would the exception apply if a brother or close friend were suddenly taken ill or a spouse or adult child were injured in an accident? It is HMRC's view that the Exceptional Circumstances Exception is limited to circumstances primarily affecting a spouse, person with whom they are living as husband and wife, civil partner or dependent child (see RDR3, Annex B, paras B11 and B12) although there is no statutory basis for that limitation.

The SRT also imposes a statutory limit of 60 days per tax year that can be regarded as not spent in the UK as a result of exceptional circumstances. It is irrelevant whether the same or different exceptional circumstances exist (FA 2013, Sch 45, para 22(6)). This limit is particularly harsh because if someone is in the UK for more than 60 days because of exceptional circumstances beyond their control it will be because something is seriously wrong; for example, a serious accident or medical condition.

FA 2013, Sch 45, para 23(1) provides that if an individual is not present in the UK at the end of a day, that day does not count as a day spent by them in the UK. This is expressly subject, however, to a rule which deems certain days to count as days spent in the UK (the 'Deeming Rule'). This rule applies where the individual:

(a) has at least three UK ties for a tax year;
(b) the number of days in the tax year when he is present in the UK at some point in the day but not at the end of the day is more than 30; and
(c) he was resident in the UK for at least one of the three preceding tax years (FA 2013, Sch 45, para 23(3)).

Where para 23 applies, the excess of the number of days falling within (b) is counted as time spent in the UK (FA 2013, Sch 45, para 23(4)). The Deeming Rule does not apply in determining the number of ties that an individual has for the purpose of determining whether the Deeming Rule applies (FA 2013, Sch 45, para 23(5)).

The Second Automatic UK Test

[21.29] This test is satisfied if:

(a) the individual has a home in the UK during all or part of the tax year;
(b) that home is one where he spends a sufficient amount of time in that tax year;
(c) there is at least one period of 91 consecutive days in respect of which the following conditions are satisfied:

(i)   the 91-day period in question occurs whilst the individual has that home;

(ii)   at least 30 days of that 91-day period fall within the relevant tax year; and

(iii) throughout that 91-day period he has no home overseas or he has one or more homes overseas but is not present in them for more than 29 days during the tax year (FA 2013, Sch 45, para 8).

A 'sufficient amount of time' is at least 30 days in the relevant tax year on which the individual is actually present in the home on that day regardless of the length of time during the day when he is so present (FA 2013, Sch 45, para 8(4)).

Where the individual has more than one home in the UK, each home must be considered separately to determine if the test is satisfied (FA 2013, Sch 45, para 8(8)). Paragraph 25 provides limited definitional provisions in relation to the meaning of 'home'. Essentially, under the SRT:

(a)   a 'home' can be a building, a part of a building, a vehicle, vessel or structure of any kind (FA 2013, Sch 45, para 25(1));

(b)   a putative home which an individual uses periodically as nothing more than a holiday home or temporary retreat will not 'count as' a 'home' whether or not it is a 'home' in fact (FA 2013, Sch 45, para 25(3));

(c)   a place may count as a 'home' of an individual whether or not the individual holds any estate or interest in it (FA 2013, Sch 45, para 25(4));

(d)   something which has been an individual's home may cease to be his 'home' even if he continues to own an estate or interest in it (FA 2013, Sch 45, para 25(5)).

HMRC has provided its views as to what is a home through a number of examples found in Annex A to RDR3, but again because it has failed to give its reasons for its conclusions this guidance is of little value. Because 'home' is a word capable of such wide meaning it creates a major uncertainty at the heart of the SRT although, according to the government, the SRT is designed to be 'clear, objective and unambiguous'.

The Third Automatic UK Test

[21.30] This test is met if an individual works:

(a)   sufficient hours in the UK assessed over a period of 365 days;

(b)   during that period there are no significant breaks from UK work;

(c)   all or part of that period falls within the tax year; and

(d)   more than 75% of the total number of days in the 365-day period when the individual does more than three hours' work are days when he does more than three hours' work in the UK; and

(e)   at least one day which falls in both the 365-day period and in the tax year is a day on which he does more than three hours' work in the UK (FA 2013, Sch 45, para 9).

A significant break from UK work is a period of 31 days or more where there is no day on which the individual does more than three hours work in the UK or the reason for their absence is not because they were on annual leave, sick leave or parenting leave (FA 2013, Sch 45, para 29(1)).

Paragraph 9(2) details the steps to be taken to calculate whether an individual has worked sufficient hours in the UK.

'Work' is not actually defined in the legislation but FA 2013, Sch 45, para 26 defines when an individual 'is considered to be "working" (or "doing work")'. An individual is working at any time when he is doing something:

(a)   in the performance of duties of an employment held by him; or
(b)   in the course of a trade carried on by him (alone or in partnership).

'Employment' as defined by FA 2013, Sch 45, para 145 incorporates the definition found in ITEPA 2003, ss 4 and 5. The meaning of a 'trade' is extended to include:

(a)   a profession or vocation;
(b)   anything that is treated as a trade for income tax purposes; and
(c)   the commercial occupation of woodlands (FA 2013, Sch 45, para 145).

In determining whether something is being done in the performance of duties of an employment, one has to consider whether if the individual received value for doing the thing, it would fall within the definition of employment income in ITEPA 2003, s 7 (FA 2013, Sch 45, para 26(2)). Likewise, in determining whether something is being done in the course of a trade, one must consider whether, if expenses were incurred by the individual in doing the thing, those expenses would be deductible in calculating the profits of the trade for income tax purposes (FA 2013, Sch 45, para 26(3)).

Travelling time counts as time spent working provided that:

(a)   the cost of the journey, if it were incurred by the individual, could be deducted in calculating his earnings from that employment or in calculating the profits of the trade; or
(b)   the individual does something else during the journey that would itself count as work in accordance with para 26 (FA 2013, Sch 45, para 26(4)).

Time spent undertaking training counts as time spent working in certain circumstances (FA 2013, Sch 45, para 26(5)). In relation to an employee, the training time counts where the training is provided or paid for by the employer and is undertaken to help the employee in performing duties of his employment (FA 2013, Sch 45, para 26(5)(a)). For individuals carrying on a trade, training counts as work provided that the cost of the training could be deducted in calculating the profits of the trade for income tax purposes (FA 2013, Sch 45, para 26(5)(b)).

It should be noted that a voluntary post for which an individual has no contract of service does not count as an employment for the purposes of the SRT (FA 2013, Sch 45, para 26(8)).

FA 2013, Sch 45, para 27 provides a general rule that work is treated as done where it is actually done, regardless of where the employment is held or the trade is carried on, subject to two exceptions:

(a)   work done by way of or in the course of travelling to or from the UK by air or sea or via a tunnel under the sea is assumed to be done overseas even during the part of the journey in or over the UK;

(b)   travelling to or from the UK starts when the individual boards the aircraft, ship or train that is bound for a UK destination or overseas, and ends when the individual disembarks from that aircraft, ship or train.

So an individual travelling to the UK to attend a meeting in performance of the duties of his employment on a flight from Paris to Heathrow will be working overseas until he disembarks at Heathrow.

This rule does not apply to an individual with a relevant job on board a vehicle, aircraft or ship (FA 2013, Sch 45, para 27(4)).

The Fourth Automatic UK Test

[21.31] This test is satisfied if:

(a)   an individual dies in the relevant year;

(b)   who had for each of the previous three tax years been resident in the UK because he had satisfied the automatic residence test;

(c)   the preceding tax year would not be a split year for the individual even on the assumption that he was not resident in the UK in the relevant tax year; and

(d)   when he died his home was in the UK or he had more than one home and at least one of them was in the UK; or

(e)   if the individual had a home overseas during all or part of the tax year concerned, he did not spend a sufficient amount of time there in that year (FA 2013, Sch 45, para 10).

A 'sufficient amount of time' is at least 30 days in the relevant tax year when the individual was present in the home on that day regardless of the length of time during the day when he was present or he was present there for at least some of the time (regardless of the length of time) on each day of the tax year concerned, and including the day on which he died. The 30 days can be consecutive or intermittent days.

Where the individual has more than one home overseas, each home must be considered separately to determine if the test is satisfied.

The Automatic Overseas Tests

[21.32] An individual will be automatically non-resident if he meets any one of the five Automatic Overseas Tests.

The First Automatic Overseas Test

[21.33] The First Automatic Overseas Test is met if an individual was resident in the UK for at least one of the three tax years preceding the tax year concerned and the number of days spent in the UK is, in the year concerned, less than 16 (FA 2013, Sch 45, para 12). This test does not apply where the individual dies during the tax year.

The Second Automatic Overseas Test

[21.34] The Second Automatic Overseas Test is met if an individual was not resident in the UK in any of the three tax years preceding the tax year concerned and he spends less than 46 days in the UK in that year (FA 2013, Sch 45, para 13).

The Third Automatic Overseas Test

[21.35] The Third Automatic Overseas Test is met if the individual works sufficient hours overseas assessed over the relevant year without any significant breaks from that overseas work and:

(a)   the number of days in that year on which the individual does more than three hours' work in the UK is less than 31; and

(b)   the number of days spent in the UK in the relevant year is less than 91 (excluding deemed days) (FA 2013, Sch 45, para 14).

A significant break from overseas work is defined as any period of at least 31 consecutive days during which, on each of those days, the individual does no more than three hours' work overseas or would not have done so but for being on annual leave, sick leave or parenting leave (FA 2013, Sch 45, para 29(2)).

To determine whether an individual works sufficient hours overseas, a five-step calculation as laid out in FA 2013, Sch 45, para 14(3) needs to be followed.

This test does not apply to an individual who has a relevant job on board a vehicle, aircraft or ship at any time in the relevant tax year and at least six of the trips made by the individual in that year as part of that job are cross-border trips that either begin in the UK, end in the UK or begin and end in the UK (FA 2013, Sch 45, para 14(4)).

The Fourth Automatic Overseas Test

[21.36] This test is met where:

(a)   an individual dies in the relevant tax year; and

(b)   he was either:

(i)   not resident in the UK in either of the two tax years preceding death; or

(ii)   was not resident in the UK in the preceding year and the year before that was a split year within Cases 1, 2 or 3 (involving departure from the UK); and

(c)   he spends less than 46 days in the UK in the tax year (FA 2013, Sch 45, para 15).

The Fifth Automatic Overseas Test

[21.37] The Fifth Automatic Overseas Test is met where:

(a)   the individual dies in the relevant tax year;

(b)   he was not resident in the preceding two tax years because he met the Third Automatic Overseas Test for each of those two years or he was not resident in the preceding tax year by reason of meeting that test and the tax year before that was a split year within Case 1 (starting full-time work overseas); and

(c)   he would have met the Third Automatic Overseas Test in the tax year
of death if that test were modified so as to apply to a person who dies
during the year (FA 2013, Sch 45, para 16).

The Sufficient Ties Test

[21.38] If none of the Automatic UK Tests nor any of the Automatic Overseas
Tests are met by an individual, the Sufficient Ties Test must be considered. The
Sufficient Ties Test is met for a relevant year where the individual meets none
of the Automatic UK Tests nor any of the Automatic Overseas Tests but has
sufficient UK ties for that year (FA 2013, Sch 45, para 17). Whether or not an
individual has sufficient UK ties in a relevant tax year will depend upon
whether the person was resident in the UK for any of the previous three tax
years and the number of days the individual has spent in the UK in the relevant
tax year (FA 2013, Sch 45, paras 18 and 19).

Days spent in the UK in the relevant tax year	Number of ties that are sufficient where an individual has been UK resident in one of the three tax years preceding the relevant tax year	Number of ties that are sufficient where an individual has not been UK resident in one of the three tax years preceding the relevant tax year
More than 15 but not more than 45	At least four	
More than 45 but not more than 90	At least three	All four
More than 90 but not more than 120	At least two	At least three
More than 120	At least one	At least two

Special rules apply if the individual dies during the relevant year to reduce
proportionately the number of days in each row of the table.

UK Ties

[21.39] The legislation differentiates between what is a UK tie on the basis of
whether or not an individual was resident in the UK in one or more of the three
tax years preceding the relevant year. If they were so resident, the following are
UK ties:

(a)   a Family Tie;
(b)   an Accommodation Tie;
(c)   a Work Tie;
(d)   a 90-Day Tie; and
(e)   a Country Tie.

If that is not the case, the Country Tie is omitted and so only the following
count as UK ties:

(a)   a Family Tie;
(b)   an Accommodation Tie;
(c)   a Work Tie; and
(d)   a 90-Day Tie.

Family Tie

[21.40] Paragraph 32 provides that an individual has a Family Tie if in the relevant year there is a 'relevant relationship . . . at any time between [the individual] and another person' who is resident in the UK in the relevant tax year. An individual has a relevant relationship with:

(a)   their husband, wife or civil partner (unless they are separated at the time);

(b)   their partner if they are living together as husband and wife or as civil partners; or

(c)   their minor children (FA 2013, Sch 45, para 32(2)).

Special rules apply where a child is in full-time education in the UK at any time in the relevant tax year (FA 2013, Sch 45, para 33(3) and (4)).

A person does not have a Family Tie in respect of his child if he sees the child in the UK on fewer than 61 days in total in the tax year concerned or, if the child turns 18 during the tax year, in the part of that year before they do so (FA 2013, Sch 45, para 32(3)).

Accommodation Tie

[21.41] An individual has an Accommodation Tie in a relevant year if he has a place to live in the UK which is available to him for a continuous period of at least 91 days during that year and he spends at least one night at that place in that year or, if it is the home of a close relative, he spends at least 16 nights there during that year (FA 2013, Sch 45, para 34). A close relative is defined as a parent, grandparent, brother, sister, and a child or grandchild aged 18 or over. An individual is considered to have a place to live in the UK if he has a home, holiday home, temporary retreat or something similar in the UK, or accommodation is otherwise available to him where he can live when he is in the UK (FA 2013, Sch 45, para 34(3)). It is not necessary for the individual to hold an estate or interest in the accommodation or have any legal right to occupy it (FA 2013, Sch 45, para 34(4)). Where there are fewer than 16 days between the periods in which a particular place is available to the individual, that place is treated as being available to the individual for that period.

This can be a trap for those individuals who make regular trips to the UK staying at the same hotel or other place.

Work Tie

[21.42] An individual has a Work Tie if he works in the UK for at least 40 days in the relevant tax year (FA 2013, Sch 45, para 35). He is considered to work for a day if he does more than three hours' work in the UK on that day. Special rules apply to those individuals who have a relevant job on board a vehicle, aircraft or ship (FA 2013, Sch 45, para 36).

The 90-Day Tie

[21.43] An individual has a 90-Day Tie for the relevant tax year if he has spent more than 90 days in the UK in either the tax year preceding the relevant year, the tax year preceding that year or each of those tax years (FA 2013, Sch 45, para 37).

Country Tie

[21.44] An individual has a Country Tie for a relevant year if the country in which he meets the midnight test for the greatest number of days in that year is in the UK. In the event that he spends the same number of days in two or more countries in a year and that number is the greatest number of days spent by him in any country, he will have a Country Tie if one of those countries is the UK (FA 2013, Sch 45, para 38).

Split-year treatment

[21.45] Before the introduction of the SRT, a person who was resident at any time during a tax year was generally subject to income tax and capital gains tax on their worldwide income and gains subject to specific reliefs for persons who were either not domiciled in the UK or not ordinarily resident. In certain circumstances, however, when an individual came to, or left, the UK during a tax year, a concessionary treatment under ESC A11 enabled the tax year to be split into periods before and after arrival or departure. UK tax on most income and gains arising before a person had become UK resident or after they had ceased to be so resident was limited to the tax which, loosely, would have been due if the taxpayer had been non-resident throughout the year. FA 2013, Sch 45, Part 3 gives a statutory relief broadly similar to this concessionary relief.

This split-year treatment is available where the individual is resident in the UK for a year and they fall within one of eight Cases. Essentially, these cover situations where the individual leaves the UK part-way through a tax year or where he comes to the UK part-way through the tax year:

- Case 1 applies where an individual starts full-time work overseas (FA 2013, Sch 45, para 44).
- Case 2 applies where an individual is a 'partner' of someone who starts full-time work overseas and that person moves overseas to continue to live with that partner (FA 2013, Sch 45, para 45).
- Case 3 applies where an individual ceases to have any home in the UK (FA 2013, Sch 45, para 46).
- Case 4 applies where an individual comes to the UK and starts to have a home in the UK only (FA 2013, Sch 45, para 47).
- Case 5 applies where an individual comes to work 'full-time' in the UK (FA 2013, Sch 45, para 48).
- Case 6 applies where an individual comes to the UK and ceases to work 'full-time' overseas (FA 2013, Sch 45, para 49).
- Case 7 applies where an individual is a 'partner' of someone within Case 6 and moves to the UK to continue to live with that partner (FA 2013, Sch 45, para 50).

- Case 8 applies where an individual starts to have a home in the UK during the tax year and continues to do so until the end of the following tax year (FA 2013, Sch 45, para 51).

Anti-avoidance provisions

[21.46] Part 4 of the legislation contains anti-avoidance provisions said to be designed to prevent individuals from creating artificial short periods of non-residence to receive income or gains free of tax which would otherwise have arisen during a period of residence when it would have been liable to UK tax. The charge applies, inter alia, to income from closely controlled companies, lump sum benefits from employer financed retirement benefit schemes (EFRBS) and chargeable event gains from life assurance contracts. The provisions will apply if the period of temporary non-residence is five years or less (FA 2013, Sch 45, para 110).

Transitional election

[21.47] An individual considering his residence status for the tax years 2013/14, 2014/15, 2015/16 in respect of the First, Second and Fourth and Fifth Automatic Overseas Tests, the Fourth Automatic UK Test, the Sufficient Ties Test and the Split Year Rules will need to know his residence status for one or more of the three years prior to 2013/14. In addition, the application of the Split Year Rules in 2016/17 will be partly dependent upon an individual's residence status in 2011/12 and 2012/13 and in 2017/18 on his residence status in 2012/13.

An election can be made by an individual for the purposes of determining his tax residence for any of the years 2013/14 to 2017/18 to determine his residence status for one or more of the years prior to 2013/14 (a 'pre-commencement year') by reference to the SRT rather than in accordance with the prior law (FA 2013, Sch 45, para 154). The election will not change an individual's actual tax residence status for the pre-commencement year or years nor will it affect his tax liability in that year or those years.

The election must be made in writing and is irrevocable. It must be made within the specified time limit; that is, by the first anniversary of the end of that year in respect of which the election is to apply or, if the year is a split year, the first anniversary of the end of the 'relevant year' (FA 2013, Sch 45, para 154(3) and (4)). The relevant year is the year in respect of which the individual's residence is actually to be determined rather than the pre-commencement year to which, under the election, the SRT is to be applied only for the purposes of determining the individual's residence for the later, relevant year.

Example

Horatio wishes to make an election that his residence status for 2010/11 should be determined in accordance with the SRT for the purposes of determining his residence in 2013/14. He must make the election before 6 April 2015.

When applying the SRT to the tax years 2010/11–2012/13, the individual's residence status for 2007/08–2009/10 needs to be known. To apply the

SRT to 2007/08–2009/10 the individual's residence status for 2004/05–2006/07 needs to be known and so on, back to the year of his birth. An individual is able to apply the SRT to any, or all, of the years which are relevant to determining his residence status for the tax year in relation to which the election is made. It is not clear whether HMRC accept that this is the case (see RDR3, para 8.1).

As the election may be made in respect of any 'one or more pre-commencement years', it is possible to opt for a mixture of bases, applying the old rules to some years and the SRT to others according to which basis provides the more favourable result (FA 2013, Sch 45, para 154(3)).

Example

Alberto wishes to determine whether he is UK resident in 2014/15.

In 2014/15 he spent 60 days in the UK and has three UK ties. If he has been UK resident for any of the three years preceding 2014/15, he will be UK resident in that year because the number of ties which will be sufficient for him to meet the Sufficient Ties Test will be three. If he was not resident in any of those three preceding years, he will not be UK resident because the number of ties which will be sufficient will be four.

Alberto was not resident in the UK in 2013/14 under the SRT nor in 2012/2013 under the law in force in that year and would also have been non-resident in that year if the SRT had applied.

In 2011/12, however, he was actually resident in the UK but if the SRT had applied in that year, he would not have been UK resident provided he had not been resident in the UK for any of the preceding three years (2008/09, 2009/10 and 2010/11). In 2009/10 and 2010/11 he was actually non-resident and would also not have been resident had the SRT applied. In 2008/09, however, he was actually non-resident under the rules in force at that time but he would have been UK resident if the SRT had applied.

Alberto makes an election under para 154 in respect of all tax years from 2009/10 to 2012/13 but not in respect of 2008/09.

It might be thought that Alberto need only make the election in respect of 2011/12, being the only year in which he was actually resident in the UK but in which he would have been non-resident if the SRT had applied. Because of the uncertainties of the law ruling before the introduction of the SRT, however, it is very rare that applying the law as it was will give a result with the same degree of probability that arises from applying the SRT. It is therefore sensible to make the election in respect of years in which the two bases both result in the individual being non-resident.

Alberto must make his election before 6 April 2016.

Evidence

[21.48] The application of the SRT will depend upon the particular facts of the individual concerned. Therefore, it is essential that evidence is retained which is relevant to an individual's residence status. In section 7 of RDR3

HMRC lists information that it suggests helps to establish the relevant facts. This list illustrates the minimum detailed information which HMRC will now expect in residence cases. It has never been so important in respect of establishing one's residence status to retain relevant evidence.

Double tax treaties

[21.49] It is possible for an individual to be resident in more than one country at the same time. For this reason most countries concluded treaties with others to assign priority of taxing rights. Most are based to a greater or lesser degree on the OECD Model Tax Convention on Income and Capital which contains a provision to determine in which of the contracting countries an individual will be treated as being resident for the purposes of the treaty concerned, and most Double Tax Conventions contain some version of this provision. Historically, double tax treaties ('DTTs') have been of greater importance in UK taxation because they had a clearer definition of residence than UK domestic legislation and provided relief from double taxation in many circumstances. Although time will tell, this will, no doubt, remain the same because of the uncertainties of the SRT.

It should be remembered, however, that the definition of residence under a Treaty only applies for the purposes of the Treaty itself. It does not apply to determine a person's general tax status under UK tax law.

Overseas law

[21.50] For would-be immigrants to the UK it is important that they understand the extent to which they will continue to be affected by the revenue and other laws of their current country of residence when they come to the UK and how they will be taxed under UK law. Conversely, for those considering leaving the UK it is important for them to understand how they will be taxed under the law of their new country of residence and the extent to which they will continue to be affected by UK revenue and other law. This applies to both long-term and short-term residents. The individual, depending on his circumstances, should consider these matters and take any necessary advice in the appropriate country before taking any irrevocable steps. For example, the Civil Partnership Act 2004 recognises overseas relationships as falling within the definition of a civil partnership, whereas other countries may not recognise a UK civil partnership. Therefore, civil partners directly owning property in another country might find they were subject to that country's equivalent to the inheritance tax charge because they would not be eligible for the spouse exemption or its equivalent. Timing may be all-important, and the time to consider these matters is before departure, rather than when one is en route to the new country or on arrival.

Individuals coming to the UK

General

[21.51] It is essential that an individual considers his position well before the start of the UK tax year in which he plans to arrive, so that appropriate action may be taken.

In advising such an individual, the following factors should be taken into consideration:

(a) his age and the period for which he is coming to the UK;
(b) his domicile of origin and general background;
(c) his family circumstances;
(d) his employment or professional situation;
(e) the composition of his estate and his sources of income;
(f) his likely financial needs in the UK;
(g) the existence of any funds not required for actual expenditure in the UK;
(h) whether he has any intention of making gifts of capital assets to family members and others, the nature of those assets and the residence and circumstances of the donees;
(i) his intentions for his estate in the event of his death.

The short-term resident

[21.52] For the short-term visitor who becomes resident in the UK the following general points should be noted.

(a) They should ensure that their behaviour does not suggest that they are acquiring a domicile in the UK, otherwise they might be subjected to time-consuming enquiries from HMRC.
(b) They should keep theirhis assets in the UK to a minimum (ideally below the threshold for the actual payment of inheritance tax). For instance, their main bank account should be held abroad rather than in the UK.
(c) They may need to purchase accommodation in the UK. This can be arranged through a direct purchase in their own name or in the joint names of themselves and their spouse by means of a non-UK loan charged on the property. The loan (plus any accrued interest) should be repaid in a tax year after they have ceased to be resident in the UK. They should not repay any principal or interest on the loan while they are resident in the UK. Alternatively, they may consider purchasing a property, in their own name or in joint names, and effect life assurance (outside the UK) to provide funds to meet any inheritance tax liability which might arise in respect of the property either on their death or, if the property is in joint names, on the death of the survivor of themselves and their spouse. Historically such an individual would have been advised that residential property be held by a company or other corporate vehicle. With the proposed changes to the taxation of

non-domiciliaries in April 2017, the holding of UK residential property through a company is probably now to be avoided unless there is a significant non-tax reason for doing so.

(d)   Funds required in the UK should be obtained by remitting capital from abroad. Care should be taken, through separate capital and income bank accounts, to demonstrate that remittances have clearly been made from a capital source unless income can be remitted free of UK tax under a double tax treaty.

The short-term visitor will not be within the inheritance tax regime except in relation to UK assets. Even then, they may be protected under a double tax treaty. However, they will probably still be subject to the tax and succession laws of their home country in which case their scope for estate planning may well be constrained by those laws. They should, therefore, take advice in that country, as well as in the UK, before taking any steps whilst in the UK.

The long-term resident

[21.53] The following general points should be considered in relation to the long-term resident.

(1)   If a UK domicile is not acquired immediately upon, or within a short time after, arrival in the UK, any funds held abroad in the incoming individual's personal ownership representing foreign source income or the realised gains of foreign assets, may be used outside the UK for expenditure as appropriate (eg for travel, holidays or maintenance of a property abroad), without involving a liability to UK income tax or capital gains tax because neither income nor capital will have been remitted to the UK. The remittance basis will either apply automatically in certain circumstances (ITA 2007, ss 809D and 809E) or can be claimed without the individual having to pay the remittance basis charge until he satisfies the seven-year residence test (where he does not meet the 17-year residence test or the 12-year residence test but has been resident in at least seven of the preceding nine tax years), the 12-year residence test (where he does not meet the 17-year residence test but has been resident in the UK in at least 12 of the preceding 14 tax years) or he satisfies the 17-year residence test (that he has been resident in the UK in at least 17 of the preceding 20 tax years), (ITA 2007, s 809C).

(2)   Wherever possible, an incoming individual (not a temporary non-resident) should, in the tax year before becoming UK resident, sell and repurchase personally held capital assets to create new base costs for future UK capital gains tax purposes. The same applies to any trust property previously settled by him. This is to achieve a higher base cost for the trust assets before the trust comes within the scope of the capital payments charge (TCGA 1992, s 87) or the offshore settlor charge (TCGA 1992, s 86 and Sch 5). Special considerations apply, however, to UK residential property.

(3)   A rebasing election for trusts should be considered if one has not already been made. It is a common view that there is no disadvantage in making one where the beneficiaries have never been UK resident.

(4)   The would-be incoming individual should ensure that accrued income is realised before they become UK resident. So, for example, when the interest payment date on a bank account would fall after the change of residence, closing the account can ensure that the accrued interest is paid before the change.

(5)   Any foreign income arising from new sources should be kept outside the UK as far as possible.

(6)   An incoming individual should make a new Will. Probably, if they are going to be domiciled in the UK, this Will should be written under English law. If, however, they retain real property abroad it may (subject to local advice) be appropriate for them to make a Will under the local law to deal specifically with that property, leaving their new English Will to deal with UK situated assets. Care should be taken to ensure that a revocation clause does not revoke all former Wills made by the testator but only those relating to a particular country. For example, if an individual come to the UK from Spain having made a Spanish Will and makes a UK Will which contains a clause revoking all Wills made by them, their Spanish Will will be revoked.

Where a person comes to the UK with a settled intention of residing in the UK on a permanent basis, they will become UK domiciled as soon as they arrive. Where a person does not intend to settle in the UK permanently, they will not be domiciled in the UK until they form that intention. An incoming individual coming to the UK for the long-term should always consider the risk that HMRC will argue that he has acquired, or reacquired, a domicile within the UK under the general law upon their arrival if they intend to reside in the UK for a long time. As discussed earlier, it may be, however, that (following *IRC v Bullock* [1976] 3 All ER 353, [1976] 1 WLR 1178) one spouse of a married couple may be able to retain a domicile in his or her home country. There may be circumstances where an individual will not acquire a UK domicile until they have been here for a significant period of time. It may be possible to take advantage of his foreign domicile whilst resident in the UK by making gifts of foreign situated assets which will not be within the charge to inheritance tax. However, it is more sensible that such gifts are made before arrival in the UK.

As mentioned above, whilst an individual is non-UK domiciled, gifts can be made of foreign assets without liability to inheritance tax. As indicated above, however, it is dangerous to rely on the ability to do this, if there is any uncertainty as to the domicile status of the person concerned.

Remittance basis

[21.54] An individual who is resident in the UK but not domiciled here can claim to be taxed on the remittance basis. Where the remittance basis is available, an individual's relevant foreign earnings, foreign income and foreign chargeable gains are taxable only when they are remitted to the UK rather than when they arise. The intention of the legislation would seem to be that unless income or gains, loosely, are actually brought to or enjoyed in the UK, there is no tax charge. In fact, these rules are of such complexity and have been so poorly drafted that it is quite possible to make a technical remittance in circumstances which, in ordinary usage, would not be described as a remittance.

The remittance basis may be claimed by an individual who is UK resident in the tax year but is not domiciled in the UK in that year. Where that individual is aged 18 or over in that year and meets the seven-year residence test, the 12-year residence test or the 17-year residence test for that year, they will only be able to continue to benefit from the remittance basis if they pay the remittance basis charge. The charge if they satisfy the seven-year residence test is £30,000, £60,000 if they satisfy the 12-year residence test and £90,000 if they satisfy the 17-year residence test (ITA 2007, s 809C).

An individual meets the seven-year residence test for a tax year if they do not satisfy the 17-year residence test or the 12-year residence test for that year but have been UK resident in at least seven of the nine tax years immediately preceding that year. An individual meets the 12-year residence test for a tax year if they do not satisfy the 17-year residence test but have been UK resident in at least 12 of the preceding 14 tax years. An individual meets the 17-year residence test for a tax year if they have been resident in the UK in at least 17 of the preceding 20 tax years.

To benefit from the remittance basis an individual must make a claim through their self-assessment tax return (SA 109) except in two circumstances. The first exception is where the individual is not domiciled in the UK in that year, and their unremitted foreign income and gains for that year are less than £2,000. The remittance basis will not apply if he gives notice in this self-assessment tax return that the remittance basis is not to apply or that they are entitled to an exemption from income tax under ITA 2007, s 828A on their small amounts of employment income (ITA 2007, s 809D). The second exception is where the individual is not domiciled in the UK in that year, they have no UK income or gains for the year, or they have no UK income or gains other than taxed investment income of less than £100, they have not remitted any relevant income or gains to the UK in the year and either:

(a)   they have been UK resident in not more than six of the nine tax years immediately preceding that year; or

(b)   they are under the age of 18 throughout that year (ITA 2007, s 809E).

It should be noted that under the second exception such an individual can have any level of unremitted overseas income or gains. Minors can currently take advantage of the remittance basis without making a claim regardless of the time they have spent in the UK or their level of income or gains.

What is a remittance?

[21.55] What constitutes a remittance is governed by the provisions of ITA 2007, ss 809K–809Z6. The definition includes circumstances where money or other property is brought to or received or used in the UK or any services provided in the UK where it derives from foreign income or gains. Where a chattel is purchased with foreign income or gains outside the UK and then brought to the UK, there is a remittance even though no money will have been brought to the UK. There are exemptions from the remittance rule (see ITA 2007, s 809X) which include exemptions for clothing, footwear, jewellery and watches if they meet the 'personal use rule', assets brought into the UK for repair, assets which are in the UK for less than 275 days and property which satisfies the public access rule and for assets (or sets of assets) costing less than £1,000. Provided certain conditions are satisfied, there is not a remittance when exempt property that is brought into the UK is sold or otherwise converted into money in the UK (ITA 2007, s 809YA). This exemption will enable a non-domiciliary to bring art into the UK without an immediate charge to tax under the remittance basis. The exemption will not apply, however, if the sale is made as part of, or as a result of, a scheme the main purpose, or one of the main purposes, of which is tax avoidance.

Where exempt property is lost, stolen or destroyed whilst in the UK, a tax charge will not be treated as a remittance (ITA 2007, s 809Y(4A)). Any compensation payment made in respect of the theft, destruction or loss of such property will not be treated as a remittance provided such moneys are taken outside the UK or used to make a qualifying investment within 45 days of receipt.

Payments of the remittance basis charge using foreign income or gains do not constitute a taxable remittance provided they are paid directly to HMRC and certain conditions are satisfied (ITA 2007, s 809V). Where, however, the remittance basis charge is subsequently repaid because, for example, the individual decides not to claim the remittance basis, the money brought into the UK to pay the charge will be a taxable remittance. Where income or gains have been used to make a payment on account which relates to the remittance basis charge and the remittance basis is not claimed in the subsequent year, a repayment will be due to the individual. Such a repayment will not be treated as being remitted to the UK provided the moneys are taken offshore within the requisite time (ITA 2007, s 809UA).

Where foreign income or gains are alienated by a transfer to a relevant person, there will be a remittance by the donor if the donee remits the money to the UK. A relevant person is defined in ITA 2007, s 809M, and does not include an adult child. Therefore, a father could make a gift of non-UK interest to his adult daughter outside the UK which his daughter could bring into the UK without any charge arising on the father provided he does not benefit from the money in the UK. A man and woman living together as husband and wife or two people of the same sex living together as if they were civil partners will be treated as if they were married or civil partners respectively. In relation to welfare benefits, HMRC identifies a number of factors used to determine whether two people are living together as husband and wife or civil partners (Claimant Compliance Manual, para 15040).

Where a UK resident but non-domiciled individual has a foreign loan for use in the UK, any repayments of the principal amount out of foreign income or gains will be treated as a remittance. In addition, the payment of interest on a foreign loan will also be a taxable remittance. There are, however, grandfathering provisions in relation to qualifying loans that were in place on 12 March 2008 where interest is paid on such loans that are secured on UK residential property. Provided that the terms of such loans are not varied, no further advances are made and the loan continues to be secured on the same property, the payment of interest will not be a remittance. It is, therefore, important that there is no variation of the terms of the loan. HMRC has given its view of when it considers that a loan is varied which includes the changing of a variable rate to a fixed rate and the changing from one variable rate to another.

There has been some uncertainty about whether using foreign income or gains as collateral for such borrowing was a remittance. Where the loan was on commercial terms, HMRC did not treat the collateral as remitted. HMRC took the view that only the funds used to service and/or repay the loan were remitted. Many individuals structured their loan arrangements on the basis of that treatment. On 4 August 2014, however, HMRC announced a change in its practice and that its previous view would not be applied to new loans. Such new loans where foreign income and gains are used as collateral will be treated as a taxable remittance when the loan proceeds are received in the UK. If the loan is serviced or repaid from different foreign income or gains the repayments of capital and interest payments will be remittances so there is the potential for double remittances. In respect of existing loans, there was a limited transitional relief where the loan funds were remitted before 4 August 2014, provided:

(a) a written undertaking was given by 31 December 2015 that the loan would be reorganised and that the foreign income or gains used as security for the loan either has been, or will be, replaced before 5 April 2016 by security in the form of UK income or gains security; or

(b) the loan or the part of the loan that was remitted to the UK either has been, or will be, repaid before 5 April 2016.

In its Briefing Note dated 15 October 2015 HMRC announced that there was no longer a requirement to repay pre-4 August 2014 loans or replace foreign income and gains collateral with non-foreign income and gains collateral before 5 April 2016. Loans brought to or used in the UK before 4 August 2014 will benefit from HMRC's previous treatment.

Klaus Otto Pflum TC 2051 (unreported) is an interesting case on the treatment of joint bank accounts. The taxpayer and his girlfriend (later his wife) were both UK resident but had a joint bank account outside the UK. The taxpayer's foreign earnings, subject to the remittance basis, were transferred to their joint account which the girlfriend accessed in the UK using a debit card. HMRC was of the opinion that the bank account was held as joint tenants and when moneys were remitted to the UK they were to be regarded as remittances by the taxpayer as one of the joint holders of the account. The First-tier Tax Tribunal held that the essence of joint ownership of a bank account where withdrawals can be made without restriction by either party is that the sums belong to the party who withdraws them. When the girlfriend used the debit card, what was being remitted to the UK were funds solely owned by her and there was no remittance by Mr Pflum. HMRC argued that because the moneys were derived from Mr Pflum, he was to be regarded as not having alienated them, in the absence of clear evidence of severance of the joint tenancy, to confer beneficial ownership on Mrs Pflum. The Tribunal rejected this argument. This case will have application only where the other joint holder is not a relevant person.

Because of the very wide definition of a remittance, advisers need to pay careful regard to these rules to avoid their clients inadvertently making a remittance.

HMRC guidance on the statutory provisions is contained in the Residence, Domicile and Remittance Basis Manual and should be consulted. It should be remembered, however, that HMRC's Manuals merely state its view of the law and do not determine what is the law.

Care needs to be taken when giving instructions to a bank regarding the transfer of funds. In *Duke of Roxburghe's Executors v IRC* CS 1936 20 TC 711, the Court held that where, contrary to the customer's instructions, his bank remitted untaxed overseas income to him in error, there was no liability. Where it can be shown that specific instructions were given and the bank made a genuine error in processing the instructions, it would seem that HMRC accept that a bank may amend the transaction in accordance with the original instruction and treat the earlier transaction as never having taken place. This is, of course, dependent upon an individual having a record of his instruction and for that instruction to be clear and concise. Where an instruction is not clear or the individual himself makes an error, it is probable that HMRC will not accept that the remittance was made in error.

Making a claim

[21.56] Remittance basis claims are made on a year by year basis. Where the remittance basis is available only if an election is made, if no election is made the taxpayer will be taxable on a worldwide arising basis. Income or gains unremitted in a year in which the remittance basis applies which are subsequently remitted when the remittance basis is not claimed will be taxable in the UK.

It is therefore important for an individual to consider in advance (as far as he is able) any transactions and movement of funds or assets to minimise his overall tax liabilities.

Nomination of income and/or gains for remittance basis charge

[21.57] When making a claim, an individual must nominate the income or chargeable gains to which the special charge (under s 809H(2)) is to apply. The income nominated to be charged is chargeable on an arising basis whether or not it is remitted. To the extent that the tax charged on the nominated income is less than the remittance basis charge, an additional amount of income is deemed to arise under s 809H(4) so ensuring that the combined charge under s 809H will always be equal to the remittance basis charge. Where an amount which gives rise to an increase of tax more than the charge is nominated, then the remittance basis election is invalid.

The amount which is nominated is usually much less than the basic amount particularly where the credits for the charge are not to be claimed against tax in another country. This is because relief against foreign tax can generally only be claimed for the part of the charge which relates to actual income or gains. It is often the case that a nominated account generating a small amount of income is maintained which is kept separate from other funds.

US individuals resident in the UK paying the remittance basis charge are able to claim the foreign tax credit for US federal tax purposes but only on income which they nominate. Individuals paying the remittance basis charge who claim foreign tax credits on their US income on a paid basis may need to make an advance payment of the remittance basis charge by 31 December in the year in which the income is subject to US tax in order for it to be creditable.

Each year a decision has to be made as to whether it is beneficial to pay the charge for the privilege of the remittance basis.

In paying the charge care should be taken to ensure that an individual does not make an unnecessary taxable remittance. A payment of the charge will not constitute a taxable remittance provided the conditions of ITA 2007, s 809B are satisfied. The exemption will, according to HMRC's guidance, only apply where the payment is made by cheque directly to HMRC or electronic transfer direct from an overseas account (Residence, Domicile and Remittance Basis Manual, para 34020).

Effect of remittance basis claim

[21.58] Where the remittance basis is claimed, but not where it applies automatically, various personal reliefs from income tax are not available to the claimant. These are the personal allowance, the blind person's allowance, the married couples allowance and the relief for payments of life insurance. Similarly, no annual exempt amount for capital gains tax is available.

In effect, FA 2008 has imposed a cost on claiming the benefit of the remittance basis which, in the case of those who have been resident for at least 17 of the preceding 20 tax years is £90,000, £60,000 for those who have been resident for at least 12 of the preceding 14 tax years and £30,000 for those who have been resident for at least seven of the nine preceding tax years, plus the cost of being denied various allowances.

It should be noted that the provisions of certain double tax treaties will prevent the loss of those allowances.

Segregated funds

[21.59] It is best practice for UK residents who are not domiciled in a country of the United Kingdom to segregate the proceeds of capital disposals, clean capital and income. This will avoid the application of the statutory rules which apply to mixed funds (ITA 2007, ss 809Q–809S). Segregating capital from income is the traditional technique of remitting capital to the UK without triggering an income tax charge; it is still effective and is an important part of tax planning for a non-domiciliary.

It is important that such accounts are monitored on a regular basis to ensure that they are being used correctly and to avoid accounts being tainted.

Proposed FA 2017 changes

[21.60] As part of the changes proposed to the taxation of non-domiciliaries the 2016 ConDoc states that there will be a window of opportunity for an individual to rearrange his overseas mixed funds to separate out the different elements of those funds. This is discussed in more detail in **21.67**.

Business investment relief

[21.61] There is tax relief for foreign income and gains which are brought into the UK for the purposes of making a qualifying investment as defined in ITA 2007, s 809VC. In such circumstances, provided the relevant conditions are met, those foreign income and gains will not be taxed under the remittance basis. At the time of writing, the Government, as part of the proposed changes to the taxation of non-domiciliaries, is consulting on 'what changes might be made to [business investment relief] to increase its effectiveness as an investment incentive' and 'at the same time . . . ensure that the scheme is not used in a way that was not intended, in particular, as a means of tax avoidance'. The Government are asking for views as to whether the scope of the anti-avoidance provisions in relation to the relief is too wide.

Relevant event

[21.62] A relevant event will occur if money or other property is used by a relevant person to make a qualifying investment or is brought to or received in the UK in order to be used to make a qualifying investment. An investment must be made within a 45-day period beginning on the day on which the money or other property is brought to or received in the UK (ITA 2007, s 809VA(5)). In the event that the moneys are partially invested then the part to which the relief is given will be determined on a just and reasonable basis. The relief will not be available if the relevant event occurs, or the investment is made as part of, or as a result of, a scheme or arrangement the main purpose, or one of the main purposes, of which is the avoidance of tax (ITA 2007, s 809VA(7)).

Where foreign income or gains are remitted to the UK to repay a loan used to fund a qualifying investment, HMRC has stated to the CIOT that, in principle, relief would be available. This would be the case even where the remittance or repayment happens in a later year than the related investment.

It is possible for an individual to ask HMRC for its view as to whether their proposed investment will be a qualifying investment by using HMRC's Clearance Service.

A relevant person is defined in ITA 2007, s 809M.

Qualifying investments

[21.63] The legislation states that an investment is made if shares in a company are issued to a person or a loan (secured or unsecured) is made ('the holding') to a company ('the target company'). An investment will be a qualifying investment provided conditions A and B are met when the investment is made (ITA 2007, s 809VC(5)).

Condition A is that the target company is an eligible trading company, eligible stakeholder company or an eligible holding company (ITA 2007, s 809VD). An eligible trading company is a private limited company which is carrying on at least one commercial trade or is preparing to do so within the next two years and carrying on a commercial trade is all, or substantially all, it does or it is reasonably expected to do once it begins trading. 'All or substantially all' is not defined in the legislation. HMRC states in its Residence, Domicile and Remittance Basis Manual (at para 34345) that: 'Where carrying on a commercial trade accounts for at least 80% of a company's total activities, the company will generally be regarded as meeting this requirement'.

An eligible stakeholder company is defined as a private limited company which exists wholly for the purpose of making investments in eligible trading companies (ignoring minor or incidental purposes) and it holds one or more such investments or is preparing to do so within the next two years. An eligible holding company is a member of an eligible trading group or of an eligible group that is reasonably expected to become an eligible trading group within the next two years, that has a 51% subsidiary which is an eligible trading company in the group and, where it owns indirectly the ordinary share capital in the eligible trading company, each intermediary in the series is also a member of the group. A commercial trade is a trade conducted on a commercial basis and with a view to the realisation of profits (ITA 2007, s 809VE). A trade includes anything that is treated for corporation tax purposes as if it were a trade and also includes a business carried on to generate income from land. Therefore, businesses which develop or let commercial or residential property are also included in the definition of qualifying investment. Condition B is that no relevant person has directly or indirectly obtained or become entitled to obtain any related benefit and no relevant person expects to obtain any such benefit (ITA 2007, s 809VF). A benefit includes the provision of anything that would not be provided to the relevant person in the ordinary course of business, or would be provided but on less favourable terms. A benefit does not include the provision of anything provided to the relevant person in the ordinary course of business and on arm's length terms. The legislation defines when a benefit is related.

Clawback of relief

[21.64] There will be a clawback of the relief where a potentially chargeable event occurs after the investment is made and appropriate mitigation steps are not taken within the grace periods allowed.

A potentially chargeable event will occur where:

(a)   the target company ceases for the first time to be an eligible company;
(b)   the relevant person who made the investment ('P') disposes of some or all of the qualifying investment;
(c)   the extraction of value rule is breached; or
(d)   the two-year start-up rule is breached (ITA 2007, s 809VH).

The extraction of value rule is breached if:

(a)   value is received by or for the benefit of the relevant person who made the investment or any other relevant person;
(b)   the value is received from either an involved company or from anyone else in circumstances which are attributable to the investment or to any other investment made by a relevant person in an involved company;
(c)   the value is received other than by virtue of a disposal that is itself a potentially chargeable event.

The rule is not breached merely because a relevant person receives value which is treated, or would be so treated if that person were liable to tax, as income for tax purposes provided that the value is paid or provided on arm's length terms and in the ordinary course of business. An example would be the receipt of directors' remuneration provided it is treated as a receipt for income tax purposes and paid on arm's length terms in the ordinary course of business.

The two-year start-up rule will be breached if the target company is non-operational immediately after the end of the period of two years from the day on which the qualifying investment was made or if the target company becomes non-operational at any time after the end of this period.

Depending upon the type of a potentially chargeable event, ITA 2007, s 809VI outlines the appropriate mitigation steps that can be taken. Where the potentially chargeable event is a disposal of all or part of the holding, the proceeds arising from the disposal must be taken offshore or re-invested. In relation to any other potentially chargeable event, the individual must dispose of the entire holding and either take the proceeds offshore or reinvest them. The various grace periods allowed are set out in ITA 2007, s 809VJ, which are either 45 days or 90 days, although they can be extended in exceptional circumstances by HMRC (ITA 2007, s 809VJ). It is possible that part of the proceeds from a disposal of a qualifying investment be retained in the UK to meet a capital gains tax liability without being treated as remitted (ITA 2007, s 809VK).

A claim must be made

[21.65] In order for the relief to be available, a claim must be made on an individual's self-assessment return on or before the first anniversary of 31 January following the tax year in which the income or gains would have been regarded as remitted to the UK (ITA 2007, s 809VA). Where a reinvestment is made, a further claim for relief must be made.

CGT rebasing

[21.66] The 2016 ConDoc proposes that an individual who will become deemed domiciled in the UK on 6 April 2017 because they satisfy the Long-Term Resident Rule (see **21.14**) will be able to rebase their directly held foreign assets to their market value as at 5 April 2017.

This will have the result that any gain accruing before that date will not be subject to capital gains tax. This ability to rebase these assets will, however, only be available to individuals who have paid the remittance basis charge (see **21.54**) in any year before April 2017. Individuals who become deemed domiciled in years after April 2017 and those who become deemed domiciled under the Formerly Domiciled Resident Rule will not be able to rebase their foreign assets.

For a non-UK domiciled individual, therefore, who has not paid the remittance basis charge in previous years because, for example, their offshore income and gains were not sufficient to warrant payment of the charge but have substantial unrealised gains, it might be advantageous to consider whether to pay the remittance basis charge in respect of the tax year 2016/17, to take advantage of the ability to rebase their assets.

Cleaning up mixed funds

[21.67] The 2016 ConDoc proposes that an individual will have the opportunity to rearrange any overseas mixed funds to separate out the different elements of those funds.

An individual will be able to move his clean capital, foreign income and foreign gains into separate accounts and remit moneys from these accounts as they wish. There will be no requirement that a remittance must be made from the newly segregated accounts in any particular order or within a particular time limit. This ability to separate will only apply to mixed funds which consist of amounts deposited in bank and similar accounts and only where the individual is able to determine the component parts of his mixed fund. The 2016 ConDoc states that this treatment will be available to any non-domiciliary 'who was not born in the UK with a UK domicile of origin – it will not be restricted only to individuals [deemed to be domiciled under the Long-Term Resident Rule]'. An individual does not need to be UK resident in April 2017 to take advantage of this treatment.

An individual will have a period of one year from April 2017 to rearrange their mixed funds.

Excluded property trusts

Inheritance tax

Current situation

[21.68] IHTA 1984, s 6(1) provides that non-UK situs property is excluded property if the beneficial owner is domiciled outside the UK. Section 48(3) excludes from charge non-UK property (eg the shares in a non-resident company) held in a settlement made by an individual who was not domiciled in the UK at the date of settlement. Currently this rule applies even if subsequently the settlor becomes actually domiciled or deemed domiciled in the UK. Excluded property is not included in a person's estate on death. Settled property not situated in the UK in an excluded property trust will not be charged under the relevant property trust regime (IHTA 1984, s 58).

It has long been prudent advice for an individual not domiciled in the UK who wishes to avoid UK inheritance tax applying to their worldwide estate in the event that they acquire a UK domicile to establish a non-UK resident trust-based structure to hold a substantial proportion of their personal wealth. If such a structure with non-UK situs assets is established the trust property is excluded property and no inheritance tax will be chargeable on the assets held in the trust (IHTA 1984, s 48(3)).

That is still good advice. It is, however, essential that the effects of the proposed FA 2017 changes are considered before any action is taken. These proposed changes are discussed in **21.69**.

There are various anti-avoidance provisions which have been introduced over the years in response to various tax mitigation strategies involving the use of excluded property trusts and UK domiciled individuals. Property is not excluded property where a UK domiciliary has acquired, after 4 December 2005, an interest in possession in the property for a consideration in money or moneys worth (IHTA 1984, s 48(3B)). This provision was introduced to stop strategies which involved the sale of excluded property interests to UK domiciled individuals.

Provisions were introduced with effect from 19 June 2012 that, where a UK domiciliary acquires an interest in an excluded property settlement which has the effect of reducing their chargeable estate for inheritance tax purposes, and where the conditions in IHTA 1984, s 74A(1)(a)–(d) are satisfied, the property will not be excluded property under IHTA 1984, s 48(3D). The conditions to be satisfied are discussed in more detail in **7.35**. These provisions were introduced to prevent tax avoidance through a strategy under which a taxpayer acquired at full value an interest in an excluded property settlement which subsequently fell out of his estate for inheritance tax purposes thus saving tax at 40%.

There has long been uncertainty in relation to additions of property made to an excluded property settlement after the settlor has become UK domiciled or deemed UK domiciled. According to its Inheritance Tax Manual, para 27220, it is HMRC's view that the added property will not be excluded property. This issue was considered by the High Court in *Barclays Wealth Trustees (Jersey) Ltd v Revenue and Customs Commrs* [2015] EWHC 2878 (Ch), 165 NLJ 7677, [2015] WTLR 1675 where HMRC's view was upheld. The High Court concluded that the words 'the time the settlement was made' are capable of describing both the making of the original settlement and the subsequent addition of property to that settlement.

Proposed FA 2017 changes

[21.69] As mentioned above in **21.68**, the Government proposes to make various changes to the taxation of non-UK domiciliaries from 6 April 2017. These proposals will affect the effectiveness of excluded property trusts in certain situations. The 2016 ConDoc proposes that for a non-UK domiciliary who set up an offshore trust before becoming deemed domiciled in the UK under the proposed Long-Term Resident Rule, such excluded property trusts 'will have the same inheritance tax treatment as at present'. That will not be the case, however, in relation to UK residential property which is owned indirectly through an offshore structure. Such residential property will not be excluded property and will be subject to UK inheritance tax. This is discussed in detail in CHAPTER 11 THE FAMILY HOME AND OTHER RESIDENTIAL PROPERTY.

For trusts set up by a formerly domiciled resident (see **21.13**), it is proposed that any foreign assets will not be excluded property for a tax year in which the individual is resident in the UK. The property held in that trust will, therefore, be subject to UK inheritance tax. This proposal has been the subject of much criticism.

It is proposed that a non-domiciliary who has set up an excluded property trust before being deemed UK domiciled under the Long-Term Resident Rule 'will not be taxed on trust income and gains that are retained in the trust, or its underlying entities and such excluded property trusts will have the same IHT treatment as at present'. This is discussed in more detail in **21.75**.

Reservation of benefit

[21.70] Individuals who are not domiciled in the UK for inheritance tax purposes often establish discretionary trusts under which they retain a benefit. This is normally achieved by the settlor being either a beneficiary or a person who may be added to the class of beneficiaries (*Gartside v IRC* [1968] AC 553, [1968] 1 All ER 121, HL).

How does the rule in IHTA 1984, s 48(3), that non-UK situs settled property is excluded property if the settlor is not domiciled in the UK at the time the settlement was made, relate to the reservation of benefit rules? For a long time HMRC's position was confused. The confusion was largely resolved when para 14396 of the Inheritance Tax Manual was updated.

One has to be careful where either the settlor or his spouse has an initial interest in possession which is an IPDI or a DPI (see **Chapter 6 Creating Settlements**) (called a 'postponing interest') which is followed by an interest which is not a postponing interest. To ensure excluded property status, the individual must be both non-domiciled when the trust is created and on the termination of the postponing interest or the spouse's successive postponing interest.

Situs of assets

[21.71] When establishing an offshore structure, the inheritance tax rules as to situs should be considered as well as provisions in double taxation treaties which modify these rules for the purposes of the treaty concerned. Below is a brief outline of the rules.

(a)   *Land.* Immovable property is situated where it is actually located (*Johnson v Baker* (1817) 4 Madd 474).

(b)   *Registered shares and securities.* The general rule is that these are situated where they are registered or, if transferable upon more than one register, where they would normally be dealt with in the ordinary course of business.

(c)   *Government securities.* Here the situs is determined by the place of registration or inscription.

(d)   *Bank accounts.* A bank account is a debt and is situated at the branch of the bank at which it is kept. The denomination of the account is irrelevant in determining the situs of the account.

(e)   *Specialty debts.* These are debts under a deed. Their situs was regarded as being the place where the deed was kept. This is the position under common law and was acknowledged by HMRC in its Manual. It has now changed its view and believes that its previous approach 'may not be the correct approach in all cases involving speciality debts'. It is now HMRC's view that 'many such debts are likely to be located where the debtor resides, or where property taken as security for the debts is situated. Any cases involving situs and a specialty debt must be referred to Technical'. Different rules apply in Scotland. It is understood that the professional bodies are in correspondence with HMRC in respect of this change.

(f) *Simple debts.* Their situs is determined by reference to where the debtor resides (Inheritance Tax Manual para 27091). This rule might be changed because, under the Brussels 1 Regulation (Regulation (EU) No. 1215/2012), the general basis of jurisdiction is the defendant's domicile. Where, therefore, the debtor's residence produces an unfavourable result one might argue that it should be governed by the Brussels 1 Regulation. Where his residence produces a favourable result and the taxpayer has relied upon it to his detriment, he may be able to establish a legitimate expectation that HMRC would not depart from its stated practice, as set out in its Inheritance Tax Manual, para 27091.

The capital gains tax rules can be found in TCGA 1992, ss 275 and 275A which also apply for the purposes of ITA 2007, s 809W (consideration for certain services) but not for the remittance basis generally.

Where a trust, established by a settlor who was not domiciled in the UK, holds UK situs assets, that property will be within the UK inheritance tax regime. However, the use of a non-UK incorporated holding company can change the effective situs of the underlying assets for inheritance tax purposes, even if that holding company is itself resident in the UK (although corporation tax, capital gains tax and income tax issues would, of course, have to be addressed). A point to note is that the Government proposes that a UK residential property interest held by a company will be subject to UK inheritance tax from 6 April 2017, which is discussed in detail in **CHAPTER 11 THE FAMILY HOME AND OTHER RESIDENTIAL PROPERTY**. Where an individual is not domiciled in the UK for inheritance tax purposes and owns shares in a UK private company, it may be possible to arrange matters so that the situs of the asset is itself changed prior to inclusion in an offshore structure. Such steps, however, require careful planning.

Location of the trust

[21.72] For inheritance tax purposes it is not necessary for the trustees to be resident outside the UK for a settlement to be an excluded property settlement. A trust with trustees resident in the UK which contains trust property not situated in the UK will be as effective for inheritance tax purposes as a trust with trustees resident outside the UK. However, it is usual to establish the trust outside the UK (ie with all the trustees being non-resident) (TCGA 1992, s 69). This is to avoid capital gains tax being payable by the trustees in respect of their gains although capital gains tax will be charged on ATED-related gains arising on relevant high-value disposals of UK residential property where the consideration is more than £500,000 and on any disposals made by non-residents after 5 April 2015 of UK residential property. This is discussed in more detail in CHAPTER 11 THE FAMILY HOME AND OTHER RESIDENTIAL PROPERTY. It is important, however, to remember that, even though the foreign trustees may not be liable for capital gains tax on disposals of assets other than residential property, if the settlor later becomes domiciled and resident in the UK he will become taxable on all gains realised by the trustees if (broadly) either he or his spouse or civil partner or their children or their grandchildren or their spouses or civil partners might be benefited under the trust (TCGA 1992, s 86 and Sch 5).

The capital payments charge imposed by TCGA 1992, s 87 will apply to all settlements regardless of the domicile of the settlor.

What is more, an individual will normally also want to keep his trust completely offshore to obtain the benefit of the remittance basis for income tax on foreign source income and gains for as long as he can defer the acquisition of an actual domicile of choice in the UK under the general law or a deemed domicile under the Government's proposals that are due to come into effect in 2017.

Advisers should review trust arrangements on a continuing basis to ensure that the trust does not inadvertently become UK resident. In the majority of cases, however, where the trustee is an offshore trust company and all administration is done overseas, it will be clear that the trust is not resident in the UK.

Trustees and protectors

[21.73] In order to ensure that the trust is not resident in the UK it is prudent that, for UK tax reasons, neither the settlor nor his spouse or civil partner should be a trustee. This can sometimes cause difficulty for the proposed settlor in the selection of the trustees of his settlement. He may not have any non-resident friends or relatives whom it would be appropriate or fair to ask to act, and so usually professional trustees or a trustee organisation are appointed. The settlor will wish to appoint trustees whom he can trust and whose charges he finds acceptable. He may want to appoint a 'protector' to oversee in some respects the actions of the trustees. A protector is an individual or company, whose duty is to give or withhold consent to the exercise of certain powers by the trustees. A protector is appointed under the terms of the trust. Generally, the protector should take care that his appointment does not have any tax or other repercussions for him in his country of residence. Although the protector may give some comfort to the settlor over the running of the trust, care must be taken not to make his involvement too complicated and to avoid an unsatisfactory administration of the settlement in practice.

Capital gains tax

Current situation

[21.74] The taxation of non-UK resident trusts established by a settlor who later becomes resident in the UK and then domiciled here is subject to complex rules. Gains realised by offshore trustees currently cannot be attributed to a settlor until the settlor becomes both resident *and* domiciled in the UK (TCGA

1992, s 86 (the 'offshore settlor charge')). However, beneficiaries can be subject to the capital payments charge under TCGA 1992, s 87 (the 'capital payments charge') regardless of the residence or domicile status of the settlor. The offshore settlor charge and the capital payments charge are discussed in more detail in **CHAPTER 8 OFFSHORE TRUSTS**. Non-domiciled individuals who are resident in the UK can be assessed on their capital gains under the remittance basis. The remittance basis rules are adapted by TCGA 1992, s 87B to apply to gains treated as accruing under s 87.

For a settlor resident but not yet domiciled in the UK it is important that the trust assets be periodically rebased for capital gains tax purposes so that the base cost of the assets held is as high as possible prior to the settlor becoming domiciled in the UK. This is because currently, if the settlor has an interest in the settlement when he becomes domiciled in the UK, future gains will become immediately chargeable under the offshore settlor charge (TCGA 1992, s 86) rather than being chargeable under the capital payments charge (TCGA 1992, s 87) only when capital payments are made.

It is important to appreciate that the capital gains tax status of a trust can fluctuate over the course of time. Whilst the settlor is non-UK domiciled the trust is outside the offshore settlor charge. Once the settlor becomes both resident and domiciled in the UK the trust will be brought within that charge. After the settlor's death the trust will revert to being within the capital payments charge alone. Indeed, if the beneficiaries who receive capital payments are not resident in the UK, the trust gains may escape UK capital gains tax entirely depending on the type of asset being disposed of. Yet it is still important to bear in mind that, irrespective of the trustees' residence status, they will currently be subject to UK capital gains tax where they hold assets used in a UK trade undertaken on their behalf through a branch or agency there. This situation would arise, for example, where the trustees own farmland which is run on their behalf by a manager. In practice, there are a number of ways round this, including ensuring that the land is held by one legal entity, whilst being farmed by another. Alternatively, the entire farming business could be incorporated.

Trustees will also be subject to capital gains tax on the disposal after 5 April 2015 of a UK residential property interest. This is discussed in **CHAPTER 11 THE FAMILY HOME AND OTHER RESIDENTIAL PROPERTY**.

Proposed FA 2017 changes

[21.75] As mentioned at various points in this chapter the Government proposes to change the taxation of non-domiciliaries in various ways, including the taxation of non-resident trusts. At the time of writing, although Draft Legislation has been published as part of the 2016 ConDoc, discussions on the proposals are continuing between the Government and professional bodies. It is understood that the Draft Legislation will be significantly amended before being published in its final form.

The Government intends to extend the application of the Offshore Settlor Charge in TCGA 1992, s 86 'to apply to all those who are deemed-domiciled'. The legislation will not extend, however, to the settlor of a non-resident trust which was set up before he became deemed-domiciled where no additions of property have been made to the trust since that date. It is proposed that where property has been added to a protected settlement since the date on which the settlor became deemed-domiciled, the settlement will lose its protection. In effect, any addition after that date will taint the whole settlement so that it will lose its protection for that tax year and all future years. Where the settlement was created before 6 April 2017, only additions made on or after that date can 'taint' the settlement because that is the earliest date on which the settlor can become a long-term deemed-domiciliary. It is possible that in the future a person may fall in and out of long-term deemed-domicile status. In such cases, the settlement will be tainted by any additions made after the first occasion on which the settlor becomes a long-term deemed-domiciliary after the date of creation of the settlement. In addition, the settlor, their spouse, their minor children and/or stepchildren must not receive any actual benefits from the trust. If they do, the protection will not apply.

It is also proposed that the Capital Payments Charge under TCGA 1992, s 87 will apply to a UK resident and deemed UK-domiciled individual who receives capital payments or benefits from a non-resident trust or underlying entity regardless of where the benefits are received. A settlor who becomes deemed-domiciled will not be subject to the Capital Payments Charge. They will either be subject to the Offshore Settlor Charge under TCGA 1992, s 86 or, if the trust is protected, 'it will lose its protection once a benefit is paid out to them, their spouse or minor children resulting in the settlor being taxed on all gains arising'. The transitional rules introduced in 2008 relating to s 87 will continue to apply where the individual receiving the capital payment is deemed-domiciled but not where he is an individual born in the UK with a UK domicile or origin.

Income tax

Settlement provisions

Current situation

[21.76] The UK has a complex regime of anti-avoidance provisions aimed at nullifying any income tax advantages which might be obtained. Where a UK resident individual establishes a trust for his own benefit, or for his spouse or civil partner, or for his unmarried children under the age of 18, payments of income made to or for the benefit of a settlor's own unmarried infant child will be treated as the income of the settlor (ITTOIA 2005, s 629). The rule applies to settlements regardless of when they were made but where the total income paid to the child is less than £100 in any year it will not be treated as the settlor's income. If income is accumulated, the income is not treated as that of the settlor until it is paid out. In addition, where during a settlor's life any property subject to a settlement, or any derived property, can become payable to or applicable for the benefit of, the settlor, his spouse or civil partner, the income of the settlement is treated as the settlor's income for all income tax purposes (ITTOIA 2005, ss 624–628). A settlor who is taxed on the remittance basis cannot be taxed on foreign income accumulated overseas, even where he has an interest in the settlement. However, if that income is subsequently remitted to the UK in a tax year in which the settlor is UK resident, it will be treated as income arising in that year and chargeable to tax as the settlor's income (ITTOIA 2005, s 648). All UK source income will be assessed upon an arising basis. Where the income of a trust is not taxed on the settlor under ITTOIA 2005, s 624 or s 629, a capital sum paid directly or indirectly to the settlor, including loans made to the settlor, is treated as income of the settlor under ITTOIA 2005, s 633 to the extent that it can be matched to available trust income.

Proposed FA 2017 changes

[21.77] As discussed in **21.15**, the Government proposes to introduce provisions treating individuals who are not domiciled in the UK as if they were for income tax (and capital gains tax) purposes and to prevent such individuals from claiming the remittance basis. The 2016 ConDoc states that ITTOIA 2005, s 624 will not apply to a deemed-domiciled settlor in respect of foreign income arising to a non-resident trust set up before they became deemed-domiciled, provided the income is retained within the trust.

If, however, the settlor, their spouse, minor children or other relevant person receives a distribution of relevant foreign income arising in a year when the settlor was non-domiciled and the trust was protected, 'that distribution will be taxed on the settlor under ITTOIA 2005, s 624 to the extent that it can be matched against relevant foreign income arising in that year and in any other years when the settlement is protected and the settlor is a long-term resident non-domiciliary'.

Pre-owned assets charge

[21.78] The income tax charge on pre-owned assets does not apply in relation to any person in any year of assessment during which they are not resident in the UK. In such a case, a person's domicile is immaterial. The charge may still apply to a UK resident but non-domiciled person in certain circumstances, even if the individual has no other UK source income. In that case, the individual will be required to make an income tax return declaring the benefit. Where, however, such a person makes a transfer of property which is land or chattels or of intangible property comprised in a settlement which is not situated in the UK, the charge will not apply.

Example

Bruce is UK-resident for the tax year 2015/16 but is not UK domiciled (or deemed domiciled). Bruce has given his house in Sydney, Australia, to his son from which he derives a benefit. In 2001, Bruce gave his London flat to his daughter. He will be living in the flat in 2016 and intends paying rent to his daughter on an informal basis.

The pre-owned assets rules will not apply to the house in Sydney because the property is situated outside the UK. He will be subject to a charge to income tax on his occupation of the London flat from 6 April 2016 and subsequent tax years. As the rent paid by Bruce to his daughter is not under a formal agreement, it will not be deductible against the market rental value on which the income tax charge will be based.

There is an exemption for property which is excluded property for the purposes of IHTA 1984, s 48(3)(a) in relation to the person making the transfer. There is some uncertainty as to whether an individual is subject to the pre-owned asset charge when he becomes deemed domiciled in the UK. It is HMRC's view that:

> 'where a person who is domiciled outside the UK creates a settlement that contains overseas property, that settlement is an excluded property settlement for Inheritance Tax purposes . . . No regard is to be had to any such property for the purposes of the POA charge, FA04/Sch 15/para 12(3). This provision provides an exemption for individuals who subsequently become domiciled in the UK and continue to benefit from the settled property and who would therefore no longer be able to rely on the foreign domiciliary exemption.'

(HMRC Inheritance Tax Manual, para 44055).

Example

Xavier has been resident in the UK for ten years and he retains his French domicile of origin. In 1998, Xavier established a family discretionary trust and an offshore company to hold his Spanish residence that he occupies.

In 2015/16, he will not be subject to any income tax charge because he is not domiciled in a country of the UK. When he becomes deemed UK domiciled, in HMRC's view he will not be subject to an income tax charge on his occupation because the Spanish property is excluded from charge (Inheritance Tax Manual, para 44055).

Transfer of assets abroad

[21.79] ITA 2007, sections 720–730 are extremely widely drawn anti-avoidance provisions which seek to prevent the avoidance of income tax by individuals who are resident in the UK and who establish offshore structures to shelter income. These provisions are discussed in detail in CHAPTER 8 OFFSHORE TRUSTS.

Proposed FA 2017 changes

[21.80] The Government proposes to amend these provisions as part of its changes to the taxation of non-domiciliaries. The 2016 ConDoc says:

> ' . . . it will be necessary to partially dis-apply the part of the TOAA legislation at section 720 ITA 2007 that would apply to deemed-domiciled settlors who set up a non-resident trust before they become deemed-domiciled, to prevent them from being taxed on the foreign income of the trust or any underlying entity if it pays out dividends to the trust. If it doesn't, the income arising to the foreign company will still be taxed under section 720.'

The draft legislation detailing these amendments will, according to the 2016 ConDoc, be published later in the year.

The family home

General

[21.81] One of the main considerations of a non-resident proposing to take up long-term residence in the UK will be where he is going to live in the UK. This will normally be settled (at least in principle) before he arrives, even though the purchase of an actual property may not be completed until after his arrival. It is unlikely that an individual and his family will want to live with relatives or friends or in rented accommodation or a hotel for any appreciable period of time.

The straightforward solution will be for the individual to purchase a property in his own name or in the joint names of his wife and himself. This means that the property will on his death (regardless of domicile because it is a UK situs asset) be wholly within the scope of inheritance tax. If he leaves the property under his will (or his share in it as a tenant in common) to his wife, or if he and his wife are joint tenants, there will be no inheritance tax liability on the property until the death of the survivor of them. However, there will only be a limited spouse exemption of £325,000 if the surviving spouse or civil partner is not domiciled in the UK but the deceased spouse or civil partner was (IHTA 1984, s 18(2)) and no election is made under IHTA 1984, s 267ZA (see **4.15** and **21.17**). In such circumstances the property will be subject to inheritance tax on the first spouse's death, subject to the exemption. It may therefore be preferable for the property to be bought in the name of the non-domiciled spouse or civil partner and left by will to the domiciled spouse or civil partner.

Holding through a company

[21.82] In the past, a wealthy, non-domiciled individual was usually advised that UK property should be acquired by a non-resident company, the shares in which should be owned by a trust established by the individual. The trust would be created and funded before the individual took up residence in the UK and the property would subsequently be purchased. This arrangement was designed to convert the property into 'excluded property' for inheritance tax purposes under IHTA 1984, s 48(3) and therefore avoid inheritance tax.

This type of planning has been frustrated by the gradual introduction of a number of tax charges imposed on companies holding UK residential property, and most recently by the proposed changes to the taxation of non-domiciliaries from 6 April 2017. Trusts or individuals owning UK residential property through an offshore company, partnership or other opaque vehicle, will, from that date, be subject to inheritance tax on the value of such UK property in the same way as UK domiciled individuals. It would seem that this will apply to all UK residential property, regardless of whether it is occupied or let or, indeed, regardless of its value. These proposals are discussed in detail in CHAPTER 11 THE FAMILY HOME AND OTHER RESIDENTIAL PROPERTY.

Use of loans

[21.83] Loans have also been used as a way of mitigating UK inheritance tax. Property was purchased by an individual and financed by way of a loan charged on the property, the idea being that this would effectively reduce the initial value of the property to nil for inheritance tax purposes because the liability would be deducted against that asset. Non-domiciled individuals would often borrow against a UK situs asset to reduce its value for UK inheritance tax purposes and use the loan proceeds to fund the purchase of excluded property which would not be chargeable to UK inheritance tax. Any such loan will now be deducted against the value of the excluded property and not the asset against which it is secured following the introduction of legislation introduced in FA 2013 changing the treatment of liabilities for inheritance tax purposes. This is discussed in more detail in CHAPTER 3 LIFETIME PLANNING: AN OVERVIEW.

The long-term emigrant

Inheritance tax

[21.84] An individual leaving the UK is not in a position to make disposals of assets which are outside the scope of inheritance tax until he has lost his UK domicile and his deemed UK domicile. Even if he loses his domicile under the general law (ie he acquires an overseas domicile of choice) soon after leaving the UK, under IHTA 1984, s 267 he will currently have to wait for at least three calendar years (and, in most cases, three complete tax years) before his property will be excluded property. See under **21.9** above.

This period will be extended to more than four consecutive years under the Government's proposed changes to the taxation of non-domiciliaries from 6 April 2017 (see **21.12**).

The transfer of certain British Government securities ('exempt gilts'), however, may be made free of inheritance tax by a person not domiciled in the UK under the general law even if he is deemed to be domiciled here under IHTA 1984, s 267(1). It may be cost-effective to cover the inheritance tax liability which would arise if the emigrant died within the current relevant three-year period by entering into a term insurance policy written in trust for the benefit of his heirs.

A potentially exempt transfer made when a donor was domiciled in the UK will still be chargeable on his death within the seven-year period even if he is no longer domiciled in the UK at that time.

A relevant question in planning for the emigrant is where do the individual's heirs live? If they live in the UK, estate planning will still be substantially affected by inheritance tax and other UK taxes but generally it will be possible for a non-domiciled individual who has not been domiciled in the UK for at least three years to give or bequeath non-UK property to his heirs who are resident in the UK, or to set up an offshore trust for them, without creating a liability to inheritance tax. This period will change if the Government's proposals as to deemed domicile are enacted in the future.

It is very important for the emigrant to have a clear understanding of the tax regime of his new country before he leaves the UK. There may well be timing considerations and action might need to be taken before residence is taken up in the new country (for example, the creation of a discretionary trust to avoid taxes in that country). On the other hand, if such action is taken too soon it will involve an inheritance tax liability since the emigrant will not have shed his UK domicile. A temporary period in a 'third' country will probably not be helpful in that a domicile of choice will not be acquired there. It is often possible to have an arrangement which has advantages in both the UK and the new country, but each case must be considered carefully on its precise facts.

If the emigrant is a beneficiary under a foreign trust, there could be timing problems in obtaining distributions of income or capital from the trust. Generally, from the UK tax viewpoint, distributions should be delayed until he becomes non-resident, but by then he may be resident in another country and the distributions subjected to tax in that country. Again, every case has to be examined on its own particular facts.

Where a person is considering emigrating, it is often advisable to defer the setting up of any settlements until the UK domicile is lost so as to retain complete flexibility and to avoid locking the trust assets into the UK tax net.

Capital gains tax

[21.85] Where a person planning to emigrate has assets (other than UK residential property interests) pregnant with gains, he should wait until he is not resident in the UK before disposing of those assets. This is because currently a person is only chargeable to UK capital gains tax if they are resident in the UK during any part of the tax year in which the disposal is made. This is not the position in relation to a disposal of a UK residential property interest made after 5 April 2015 as such a non-UK resident is now chargeable to capital gains tax on this type of disposal. Obviously advice should also be taken on the tax position in the other country. No one can legislate for the future and so for some unforeseen reason a person might find themselves becoming resident again in the UK within a relatively short period of time. In such circumstances a person, having realised a substantial gain on the disposal of an asset whilst not UK resident, who returns to the UK within five years, will be charged to capital gains tax under TCGA 1992, s 10A (see **21.87**).

The short-term emigrant

Inheritance tax

[21.86] A person who ceases to be resident in the UK for a period – for example, through full-time employment abroad which lasts for a period including a full tax year – is likely to remain domiciled in the UK and therefore subject to the inheritance tax regime. Therefore, opportunities for estate planning generally are no greater than for a UK resident. It may be possible, however, for an individual working abroad and earning a large salary which is subject only to low local income tax to make substantial regular gifts out of his net income which would be exempt from inheritance tax under the 'normal expenditure' exemption (IHTA 1984, s 21). To take advantage of this exemption, it is advisable that the individual should not simply make regular voluntary gifts but instead create a commitment to do so (for example, by effecting life policies in trust involving regular premium payments or by entering into an agreement to make regular payments). However, consideration should be given to the individual's ability to continue to meet the payments when the individual returns to the UK and has a lower net surplus income.

Capital gains tax

Temporary non-residence charge

[21.87] An individual who leaves the UK might think that it would be sensible to dispose of any assets with gains before returning to the UK so as to avoid capital gains tax. It used to be possible to do this. However, TCGA 1992, s 10A provides that individuals who are temporarily non-resident, who have acquired assets before they leave the UK for a period of residence abroad of five or less years, will remain chargeable to capital gains tax on gains made on those assets while abroad. Gains made after the year of departure will be chargeable in the year of return. An individual will be treated as temporarily non-resident where:

(a)   for a residence period (called 'Period A') he has sole UK residence;
(b)   immediately after Period A one or more residence periods occur for which he does not have sole UK residence;
(c)   at least four out of the seven tax years immediately preceding the year of departure were either:
(i)   a tax year for which the individual had sole UK residence; or
(ii)   a split year that included a residence period for which he had sole UK residence; and
(d)   the temporary period of non-residence is five years or less (FA 2013, Sch 45, para 110).

A residence period is either a tax year (which is not a split year so far as the individual is concerned) or the overseas part or the UK part of a tax year that is a split year (FA 2013, Sch 45, para 111).

An individual has 'sole UK residence' for a residence period of an entire tax year if he is resident in the UK for that year and there is no time in that tax year when the individual is Treaty non-resident. If the residence period is part of a split year, then the individual has sole UK residence for that period if the residence period is the UK part of that year and there is no time in that part of the year when the individual is Treaty non-resident. The temporary period of non-residence is the period between the end of Period A and the start of the next residence period for which the individual has sole UK residence. A period of return is the first residence period after Period A for which the individual has sole UK residence.

Disposals of UK residential property interests

[21.88] Special rules apply where there is a disposal by a non-UK resident of a UK residential property interest after 5 April 2015. If, therefore, an individual disposes of such an interest when he is not resident he will be subject to the capital gains tax regardless of the period of time that he has not been UK resident. This tax is discussed in more detail in CHAPTER 11 THE FAMILY HOME AND OTHER RESIDENTIAL PROPERTY.

Income tax

[21.89] FA 2013, Sch 45, Part 4 provides that similar anti-avoidance provisions as discussed above will apply in relation to particular forms of income which are received when a person is temporarily non-resident. Again, a charge will arise in the tax year in which they return to the UK if they were temporarily non-resident.

Chapter 22

The Overseas Client

Introduction

[22.1] This chapter deals with a foreign individual who does not himself become resident or domiciled in the UK, but becomes involved with UK laws and with actual or potential liabilities to UK taxation through:

(a)   the ownership of assets in the UK; or
(b)   the wish to benefit persons resident in the UK.

It is assumed that the individual is and remains domiciled and resident outside the UK. For a consideration of the meaning of these terms, and the concept of 'deemed domicile' which currently applies only for inheritance tax purposes and for the purposes of the income tax charge on pre-owned assets, see CHAPTER 21 UK RESIDENTS WITH MULTI-JURISDICTIONAL AFFAIRS.

Tax considerations

Inheritance tax

[22.2] Where a foreign individual directly owns an asset in the UK, there may be an inheritance tax charge where there is a lifetime transfer of the asset or in the event of the individual's death. The nil rate band which is currently £325,000 will be available to a non-domiciled individual. In addition, one of the exemptions under IHTA 1984, Pt II may apply. Those exemptions include:

(a)   transfers between spouses. There is a limit of £325,000 on transfers from UK domiciled spouses to non-UK domiciled spouses. There is an election which can be made for a non-UK domiciled spouse to be treated as UK domiciled but that will bring their entire worldwide estate within the charge to UK inheritance tax. In some situations it might be advantageous to make the election and in others, not;
(b)   the annual exemption;
(c)   small gifts;
(d)   normal expenditure out of income;
(e)   gifts in consideration of marriage; and
(f)   gifts to charities or political parties or for national purposes or public benefit.

An asset may also be eligible for business property relief, agricultural property relief or relief on woodlands under IHTA 1984, Pt V. For further details see

CHAPTER 3 LIFETIME PLANNING: AN OVERVIEW (for exemptions), CHAPTER 12 THE FAMILY BUSINESS, CHAPTER 13 THE FAMILY FARM and CHAPTER 14 WOODLANDS.

It is often the case that an individual will have acquired a UK asset without much thought as to the possibility of UK inheritance tax being payable in the event of his death. That is no doubt because not all countries levy a charge to tax on death or, where they do, at rates as high as in the UK. Alternatively, foreign tax on death may operate as a true inheritance tax, under which it is the recipient of the bequeathed property who is charged to tax, rather than the estate. Because of the availability of the nil rate band, an individual can hold up to £325,000 of UK situs assets (or £650,000 of UK situs assets which qualify for business property or agricultural property relief at 50%) without UK inheritance tax being payable, provided he has not made transfers of other UK assets within seven years of death. Nevertheless, clients should be advised if they have a potential UK inheritance tax liability.

Currently, where an individual or a trust holds UK residential property through a non-UK resident company, the shares in that offshore company are excluded property and therefore not subject to inheritance tax. From 6 April 2017, it is proposed that inheritance tax will be chargeable on UK residential property held through such a structure. This is discussed in detail in CHAPTER 11 THE FAMILY HOME AND OTHER RESIDENTIAL PROPERTY.

Excluded property

[22.3] Currently, certain property situated in the UK is excluded from the scope of inheritance tax.

(a)   Under IHTA 1984, s 6(2), certain British Government securities (known as 'exempt gilts') are excluded property for inheritance tax purposes if they are in the beneficial ownership of a person resident outside the UK. Domicile is irrelevant for this purpose. Gilts can be currently used by individuals to avoid inheritance tax on their assets in the event that they die within the three years of their departure from the UK (IHTA 1984, s 267(1), (2)).

(b)   Under IHTA 1984, s 6(3) certain property owned by a person who is domiciled in the Channel Islands or the Isle of Man is exempt. The property so exempted consists of war savings certificates, national savings certificates, premium bonds, deposits with the National Savings Bank or a trustee savings bank and any certified SAYE savings arrangements within ITTOIA 2005, s 703(1).

(c)   Under IHTA 1984, s 6(1A), holdings in authorised unit trusts and shares in open-ended investment companies are excluded property, provided the person beneficially entitled to them is an individual domiciled outside the UK.

(d)   Under IHTA 1984, s 6(1B), a decoration or other award awarded for valour or gallant conduct which has never been the subject of a disposition for a consideration in money or money's worth is excluded property.

(e) Exemption from inheritance tax on death is given by IHTA 1984, s 157 to a qualifying foreign currency bank account, held at a bank as defined in Income Tax Act 2007, s 991 (ITA 2007), which is owned by a person who immediately before his death was not domiciled and not resident in the UK.

(f) Certain property owned in the UK by visiting forces and staff of allied headquarters and EU civilian staff (IHTA 1984, ss 6 and 155).

From 6 April 2017, it is proposed that the shares of a non-UK resident company holding UK residential property will not be excluded property. This is discussed in detail in CHAPTER 11 THE FAMILY HOME AND OTHER RESIDEN-TIAL PROPERTY.

Capital gains tax

General

[22.4] The disposal of an asset situated in the UK (other than a UK residential property interest) by an individual not resident in the UK will not generally give rise to a capital gains tax liability. This is because a person is chargeable to capital gains tax in respect of chargeable gains accruing to him in a year of assessment during any part of which he is resident in the UK (TCGA 1992, s 2(1)).

Carrying on a trade in the UK

[22.5] Taxation of Chargeable Gains Act 1992, s 10 provides that a person who does not satisfy the residence condition, for example, they are not resident in the UK *will* be chargeable to capital gains tax on gains accruing to them on a disposal, at a time when they are carrying on a trade in the UK through a branch or agency, of:

(a) assets in the UK used in or for the purposes of the trade at or before that time;

(b) assets in the UK used or held for the purposes of the branch or agency; and

(c) assets acquired for use by or for the purposes of the branch or agency. It would seem that on a strict reading of the legislation this charge applies whether or not the asset is situated in the UK. HMRC's view, however, appears to be that the charge applies only to UK-situated assets (HMRC Capital Gains Manual, CG25510).

A chargeable gain can arise in respect of such assets where the non-resident person ceases to carry on the trade, profession or vocation through the branch or agency or the assets become situated outside the UK (TCGA 1992, s 25). Generally speaking, the trading entity should be kept apart from the entity which holds the valuable asset likely to generate the gain. Farming activities would represent a typical example where land could be held by an entity other than the one which is going to farm it.

Capital gains tax on ATED-related gains

[22.6] Capital gains tax will be charged on gains arising on the disposal of interests in residential property by non-natural persons where the amount or value of the consideration exceeds a threshold amount, currently £500,000. This is discussed in more detail in CHAPTER 11 THE FAMILY HOME AND OTHER RESIDENTIAL PROPERTY. This charge only applies in relation to UK residential property and not to UK commercial property or other investments.

Non-resident capital gains tax

[22.7] Non-UK residents will now be subject to non-resident capital gains tax (NRCGT) on gains arising on disposals of UK residential property interests made after 5 April 2015. This is discussed in detail in. CHAPTER 11 THE FAMILY HOME AND OTHER RESIDENTIAL PROPERTY.

Income tax

[22.8] A foreign individual will be liable to UK income tax on income arising from a source in the UK. The income tax liability of a non-UK resident individual is limited to tax deducted at source or tax treated as deducted at source on income which is disregarded, and to tax at marginal rates on income which is not disregarded. Interest, dividends and stock dividends from UK resident companies are disregarded but rental income is not.

The income tax charge on pre-owned assets is only chargeable upon persons who are resident in the UK for the tax year in which the charge arises. Accordingly, a non-UK resident is outside the scope of the charge. The incidence of the charge on UK resident non-domiciliaries is discussed in further detail in CHAPTER 21 UK RESIDENTS WITH MULTI JURISDICTIONAL AFFAIRS.

Income tax will be chargeable on a non-UK resident person in relation to any profit or gain arising on a disposal of any UK land. It will also be chargeable on what might be called 'indirect disposals' (ITA 2007, ss 517D and 517E).

Annual tax on enveloped dwellings

[22.9] An annual charge will be imposed upon interests owned by non-natural persons in residential property where the taxable value of the interest is over £500,000. This is discussed in more detail at **11.26–11.29**.

Double tax agreements

[22.10] The liability of a foreign individual, or his estate, to inheritance tax, capital gains tax and income tax may be relieved or modified under a double tax agreement between the UK and his country of residence. For example, the provisions of TCGA 1992, s 10 (see above) do not apply to a person who under any relevant double tax agreement is exempt from income tax for the particular year of assessment in respect of his profits from the branch or agency. Nothing in the terms of any double tax agreement can be read as having effect to prevent a tax charge under TCGA 1992, s 10A. Relief will be given in the usual way in respect of any foreign tax paid in respect of any gains arising.

Generally, the small number of double tax agreements which cover inheritance tax, deal with its interaction with similar taxes in other jurisdictions by determining the domicile of an individual for the purposes of the agreement and allowing primary taxing rights to the country in which the individual is so domiciled. Certain old double taxation agreements contain their own rules for determining domicile and for resolving the issue where both countries claim domicile. HMRC accepts that domicile determined under the double tax agreements with France, Italy, India and Pakistan override deemed domicile, although if a person is domiciled under the general law in those countries, the deemed domicile rules can apply to chargeable lifetime transfers (HMRC Inheritance Tax Manual, para 13024). Charges on the basis of situs are usually restricted to land and business property. There are currently ten double tax agreements applying to, or capable of applying to, inheritance tax. These are between the UK and the Irish Republic, France, India, Italy, the Netherlands, Pakistan, South Africa, Sweden, Switzerland and the United States of America. It should be noted that Pakistan has no tax on death and India has no effective inheritance tax. Therefore if the domicile of an individual is determined under the treaty with either Pakistan or India as being outside the UK, any property which is situated outside the UK will not be subject to UK inheritance tax and it will not be subject to an equivalent tax in Pakistan or India.

It is understood that the Government is considering amending legislation to provide that, in relation to UK residential property, double tax agreements do not override the deemed domiciled provisions. At the time of writing, no legislation has, however, been published.

In the absence of a relevant double tax agreement, HMRC will allow unilateral relief by way of credit for a foreign tax similar in character to inheritance tax which has been imposed on property upon a disposition or event on which inheritance tax is chargeable in respect of the same property (IHTA 1984, s 159).

Planning points

[22.11] Is it possible to avoid any of the liabilities to UK taxation discussed above for a foreign individual who wishes, for whatever reason, to own assets in this country?

It is possible for inheritance tax to be avoided on a UK asset if it is owned by a company incorporated outside the UK rather than by a foreign individual directly. This arrangement ensures that the individual holds a non-UK asset (his shares in the foreign company) rather than the UK asset directly. The shares will be 'excluded property' (by virtue of IHTA 1984, s 6(1)). This has typically been the method by which UK residential property was held by non-UK domiciliaries. Of course, the imposition of the annual ATED charge and ATED related capital gains tax charge on the disposal of residential property worth in excess of £500,000 (see **CHAPTER 11 THE FAMILY HOME AND OTHER RESIDENTIAL PROPERTY**) will have deterred many from this course of action. Not satisfied with this, the Government proposes that UK residential property held through an offshore company, partnership or other opaque vehicle will, from 6 April 2017, be subject to inheritance tax. This is discussed in detail in CHAPTER 11 THE FAMILY HOME AND OTHER RESIDENTIAL PROPERTY. These provisions apply only in relation to UK residential property. It is still, however, a suitable structure for commercial property and other forms of assets.

Inheritance tax will not be payable on a UK asset owned by an individual who is not domiciled in the UK if it passes to his spouse on his death, either under his will or under the relevant succession laws or through the right of survivorship under a joint tenancy.

An individual may consider it worthwhile to take out life assurance to provide funds to meet an inheritance tax liability in respect of UK assets in the event of his death. Any such policy should either be effected outside the UK or written in trust to avoid the proceeds being treated as part of his taxable estate in the UK.

Other considerations

Probate

[22.12] If an individual dies owning assets in the UK, it will usually be necessary for a grant of probate or letters of administration to be obtained in this country. This will normally be an ancillary grant to the administration of the deceased's estate in his home country, issued to the person(s) entitled to administer the deceased's estate under the law of his home country. The procedure involves submitting an account of the UK assets to HMRC, together with a statement giving the reason why it is considered that the deceased died domiciled in a foreign country. No grant will be issued until all the tax due is paid. All this can involve time and expense, which may be disproportionate to the size of the UK estate. For example, the proceeds of a UK bank account will not be released by the bank without production of a UK grant of probate. It is also unwise for any UK assets to be disposed of or transferred abroad without production of a UK grant and without the tax position having been settled, since the person so disposing of or transferring the asset may be treated as an executor *de son tort* and accountable for any inheritance tax payable (*New York Breweries Co Ltd v A-G* [1899] AC 62).

A will in respect of which a grant of probate has been issued is a public document which can be inspected by anyone. Double tax agreements usually permit the exchange of information between two revenue authorities. The administration of the UK estate of a foreign individual can result in the exchange of information between the relevant authorities. Therefore, where UK assets are owned, consideration should be given to making a will governed by UK law dealing solely with those assets.

There are generally no ways of avoiding these considerations for a foreign individual who wishes to own UK assets beneficially himself. The use of a UK nominee to hold the assets on his behalf will not avoid the need to obtain a grant of probate (or letters of administration) nor the payment of UK taxes. The use of a foreign nominee may avoid the need for a grant of probate although the nominee may itself constitute an executor *de son tort* if it deals with the assets following the death (see *IRC v Stype Investments (Jersey) Ltd* [1982] Ch 456, [1982] 3 All ER 419, [1982] 3 WLR 228). This structure does not avoid the obligation to submit an account of the assets for inheritance tax purposes, and to pay the tax due.

Where the only UK asset is a joint bank account, on the death of one of the owners its ownership will automatically pass to the survivor. The bank will normally only want to see the death certificate and not a UK grant of probate. If, however, the survivor is not the deceased's spouse there will be a duty to submit an inheritance tax account and pay any liability due (unless the account is a qualifying foreign currency bank account which is exempt from inheritance tax, see under **22.3** above).

The safest way to avoid the need to obtain a UK grant of probate is for the non-UK domiciled individual to incorporate a company outside the UK to own the property as discussed earlier in the chapter. In the event of the death of the owner of the company a grant of probate would not be necessary as the company's shares would not be UK *situs* assets.

For foreign investors wishing to invest in shares in UK companies, there are various types of offshore collective investment schemes which avoid the problems of directly owning assets located in the UK.

Benefitting persons resident in the UK

Outright gifts

[22.13] The simplest way in which a non-UK domiciled individual can benefit a person resident in the UK is to make a gift to such a person of non-UK assets, eg foreign currency or foreign investments, which are subsequently remitted to the UK by the donee as desired. A gift made in this way will not involve any UK inheritance tax liability. For capital gains tax purposes, the donee will have acquired the asset given to him on the date of the gift at its market value on that date.

It is important to ensure that any gift of cash is made in a way which avoids the gift being of a UK asset and therefore liable to inheritance tax. A payment made from a bank account situated in the UK will be liable to inheritance tax as will a gift of the beneficial ownership of the whole or a part of the balance on the account. Conversely, a payment made from a bank account held outside the UK or the gift of the beneficial ownership of the whole or part of the balance on the account will not be so liable regardless of whether or not the account is denominated in sterling.

Offshore settlements

[22.14] If a non-UK domiciled and non-UK resident donor does not wish to make outright gifts to his beneficiaries in the UK, or his objective is to benefit his beneficiaries in the most tax efficient way, he may consider establishing a trust with trustees who are not resident in the UK. Assuming that he settles non-UK assets whose value is not derived from UK residential property, the creation of the trust will not involve any UK tax liability. During its life the trust will not usually attract any liability to inheritance tax, assuming that its funds continue to consist entirely of foreign assets. This applies regardless of the type of trust used. Disposals of foreign situs assets by the trustees resident outside the UK will not be liable to UK capital gains tax. The capital payments charge, however, will apply, subject to the remittance basis, where capital payments are made to beneficiaries who are resident in the UK when the gain is deemed to accrue to them (TCGA 1992, s 87).

The disposal of a UK residential property interest by non-UK resident trustees will be subject to NRCGT on any gain accruing since 5 April 2015. This is discussed in detail in CHAPTER 11 THE FAMILY HOME AND OTHER RESIDENTIAL PROPERTY.

The ATED-related capital gains tax charge on disposals of UK residential property where the amount or value of the consideration on the disposal exceeds £500,000 does not apply to non-UK resident trustees.

It should be noted, however, that the Government proposes that with effect from 6 April 2017, shares in offshore close companies and similar entities will not be excluded property if and to the extent that their value is derived directly or indirectly from UK residential property. This is discussed in more detail in CHAPTER 11 THE FAMILY HOME AND OTHER RESIDENTIAL PROPERTY.

If income is distributed to UK resident beneficiaries, they will be liable to income tax in the normal way, unless they are non-UK domiciled and the remittance basis applies. If benefits, which are not otherwise liable to income tax, are given by the trustees to a beneficiary resident in the UK, he will be liable to income tax to the extent that the value of the benefit falls within the 'relevant income' of the trust, but only if UK tax avoidance is the motive for the transfer (ITA 2007, s 731). This will catch, for example, capital payments to a beneficiary resident in the UK, if income has been accumulated in the trust (or in any underlying foreign company) rather than distributed. This is subject to relief being given for a non-domiciled beneficiary where there has been no remittance of the relevant income to, and the benefit was not received in, the UK.

With regard to the trustees, provided at least one trustee is resident outside the UK, *all* of them will be treated as resident outside the UK for income and capital gains tax purposes provided the settlor is non-resident or non-domiciled in the UK at the time he made the settlement (ITA 2007, s 475). In that case they will only be liable to tax on UK source income.

UK settlements

[22.15] It may also be worth considering a trust with UK resident trustees. Inheritance tax may be avoided if non-UK assets are settled and retained throughout the life of the trust.

Income Tax Act 2007, s 731 has no application to a trust with UK resident trustees. However, the trustees will be liable to UK income tax on all trust income in the normal way. Income of most UK resident trusts will be liable to tax at 45% subject to the special rate of 38.1% on dividends. An offshore trust will not normally be so liable (assuming it does not have UK source income) but income tax liabilities may arise under ITA 2007, s 731. Care is required in particular where an offshore trust subject to ITA 2007, s 731 is imported into the UK.

Conclusions

[22.16] For the wealthy foreign individual it may be appropriate to have both a trust in the UK and a trust abroad, both of which might include UK residents as beneficiaries. The former would be regarded as a 'spending' fund (ie the capital and income would be paid out to the beneficiaries as necessary), and the latter would be a 'roll-up' fund with neither capital nor income being remitted to the UK except in emergency situations.

The foreign individual who wishes to benefit beneficiaries resident in the UK should take advice in his home country regardless of the type of structure proposed to ensure that he is aware of the tax and other implications of his proposed action in that country as well as the UK.

The foreign individual who on his death wishes to benefit persons resident in the UK should also be advised to consider setting up, by his will, a continuing trust (probably outside the UK) rather than making outright bequests which would bring the property bequeathed into the UK tax net. The trust could either be contained in the will itself or be established by the individual during his lifetime, with his will simply directing the relevant assets into the trust.

Chapter 23

Disclosure of Tax Avoidance Schemes

Introduction

[23.1] It was announced in the March 2004 Budget that a disclosure measure was to be introduced under which 'accountancy firms and those promoting schemes' were required to disclose them to HMRC. Originally, only arrangements which conferred income tax, capital gains tax or corporation tax advantages and which were either connected to employment or involved financial products were required to be disclosed. Over time these rules have been amended so as to apply to arrangements which enabled a person to obtain an advantage in respect of income tax, corporation tax, capital gains tax, inheritance tax, annual tax on enveloped dwellings, stamp duty land tax, stamp duty reserve tax and petroleum revenue tax (FA 2004, ss 306 and 318). Separate but similar regimes govern value added tax and National Insurance.

This Chapter is primarily concerned with the disclosure of arrangements in relation to inheritance tax.

It should be noted that, at the time of writing, the government has published draft regulations, the Inheritance Tax Avoidance Schemes (Prescribed Descriptions of Arrangements) Regulations 2016 (the 'Draft IHT Dotas Regulations 2016'), which will significantly broaden the DOTAS Regime applying to inheritance tax. These proposed regulations have been sharply criticised by the professional bodies as being too wide and uncertain (see **23.39**). The consultation period closed in July 2016 and a response document will be published later in 2016. It is understood that the government intends to lay revised regulations in 2016. It is not known when these regulations will come into effect but, if and when they do, advisers will have to give careful attention to whether their advice falls within the extended rules.

The DOTAS Regime has significant consequences that were not envisaged at the time when the regime was initially designed. Firstly that HMRC has the power to issue a taxpayer with an accelerated payment notice (an 'APN') requiring the taxpayer to pay the amount of understated tax before the closure of an enquiry into a tax return or a final decision on appeal, where a taxpayer has entered into arrangements that are disclosable under the DOTAS regime. Of course, there is unlikely at present to be many APNs issued in relation to inheritance tax but HMRC may do so in the future and so clients need to be made aware of the possibility. In relation to other taxes HMRC has used its power to issue APNs and 'expect to issue around 64,000 notices by the end of 2016.'

Secondly, a Consultation Document 'Strengthening Tax Avoidance Sanctions and Deterrents: A Discussion Document', published on 17 August 2016, proposes that sanctions are imposed on those who enable or use tax avoidance arrangements that are later defeated, which include arrangements that are notifiable under the DOTAS Regime.

A flowchart designed to determine whether a disclosure needs to be made in relation to inheritance tax can be found at para 12 of the Guidance – 'Disclosure of Tax Avoidance Schemes' – (the 'DOTAS guidance'). This chart, like all HMRC's guidance, should be used with caution for, as is explained below, the guidance cannot be relied upon to be an accurate summary of the law.

HMRC has extensive powers to obtain information which are discussed in **23.44–23.49** as well as by way of an application to the tribunal. Whilst a discussion of these powers is outside the scope of this book, an adviser should be aware of HMRC's powers. HMRC can apply for an order that a scheme be treated as notifiable (FA 2004, s 306A), an order that a promoter provide further information and documents (FA 2004, s 308A), an order where HMRC has requested information under s 310A and a person has failed to provide it (FA 2004, s 310B), an order requiring a person to provide specified information or documents in support of a statement of reasons explaining why a disclosure was not required (FA 2004, s 313B), and an order enforcing disclosure (FA 2004, s 314A).

There are provisions designed to target what are termed 'high risk promoters'. HMRC has the power to issue promoters with a conduct notice where certain conditions are satisfied (FA 2014, s 237). It also has the power to issue promoters with a monitoring notice where the promoter has failed to comply with a conduct notice (FA 2014, s 242). A monitored promoter is subject to particular disclosure obligations and is required to inform clients of its promoter reference number ('PRN') and advise them that it is monitored (FA 2014, s 249). The names of monitored promoters may be published. HMRC is now able to issue follower notices to taxpayers who have implemented a scheme which is defeated in another party's litigation to the effect that they should amend their tax return or incur a tax-geared penalty unless they have a reasonable basis for not doing so.

HMRC has the power to publish information about notified schemes (for which a scheme reference number is allocated, see **23.47** below) and their promoter. Finance Act 2004, s 316C outlines the information that can be published, such as information about judicial rulings relating to the scheme and whether HMRC has or may issue an APN in relation to the scheme. HMRC is not able to publish information that reveals the identity of a scheme user unless he is also a promoter. Promoters are to be given 'reasonable opportunity to make representations about whether it should be published' but there is no right of appeal in such a situation.

The form of the legislation

[23.2] The primary legislation found in FA 2004, s 306 provides only a framework for the Disclosure Regime and a series of powers for the Treasury to make secondary legislation by way of statutory instrument. That ensures that the disclosure rules mostly escape detailed parliamentary scrutiny. The bulk of the legislation is, therefore, found in Regulations which have been amended piecemeal.

The Regulations governing inheritance tax are the Tax Avoidance Schemes (Prescribed Descriptions of Arrangements) Regulations 2006 (SI 2006/1543) (the '2006 Regulations'), the Inheritance Tax Avoidance Schemes (Prescribed Descriptions of Arrangements) Regulations 2011 (SI 2011/170) (the '2011 Regulations') and the Tax Avoidance Schemes (Information) Regulations 2012 (SI 2012/1836). These regulations are poorly drafted with the result that their scope is uncertain. HMRC have attempted to correct this faulty drafting through inaccurate and inadequate guidance found in the DOTAS guidance. The practitioner is, therefore, placed in the position of having to decide to what extent he can rely on HMRC's statements as to the effect of the law where many of those statements are inaccurate and, where they are not, present what is only one tenable view amongst many as if it were the only possible view. Unfortunately, the DOTAS guidance is often so imprecise that the practitioner will not know whether or not he falls within its terms. Even if he does fall within its terms, where the DOTAS guidance conflicts with the law he will only be able to rely on it to the extent that he can anticipate establishing, in Judicial Review proceedings, that he has a legitimate expectation that the guidance will be applied.

Because the IHT Disclosure Regime is an extension of the existing regime, it fits within an extensive compliance system which has been developed since 2004. In this Chapter by way of background the general provisions are discussed and a more detailed discussion is made of the Regulations dealing with inheritance tax.

Sections 308–310C of FA 2004 impose a duty of disclosure on promoters of notifiable proposals and on persons entering into transactions forming part of notifiable arrangements. The term 'promoter' is very widely defined and will include most providers of taxation advice in respect of notifiable proposals. As the definition of promoter is fundamental to the duty to make a disclosure imposed by FA 2004, s 308, and also in determining whether arrangements are grandfathered (see **23.20**), the definition of a promoter is discussed first.

'Promoter'

[23.3] In respect of a notifiable proposal, a person is a promoter:

' . . . if, in the course of a relevant business, the person ("P")–

(i) is to any extent responsible for the design of the proposed arrangements,
(ii) makes a firm approach to another person ("C") in relation to the notifiable proposal with a view to P making the notifiable proposal available for implementation by C or any other person, or
(iii) makes the notifiable proposal available for implementation by other persons,'

In respect of notifiable arrangements, a person is a promoter if in the course of a relevant business, he is to any extent responsible for the design of the arrangements or the organisation or management of the arrangements.

This is, of course, an extremely wide definition and barristers, solicitors, accountants, chartered tax advisers, financial advisers and other advisers whose work includes an element of tax advice are likely to fall within its scope. The width of the definition is, however, restricted by the Tax Avoidance Schemes (Promoters and Prescribed Circumstances) Regulations 2004 (SI 2004/1865) which exclude certain classes of persons who would otherwise be promoters. There are exclusions for employees (except for employees of a non-UK promoter) and for companies within corporate groups. A person who acts solely as an intermediary between a scheme provider and a potential scheme user is not a promoter. There are also three general exclusions which apply to persons who would otherwise be promoters under FA 2004, s 307(1)(a)(i) or (b)(i). Those three exclusions are given labels in HMRC's guidance. In spite of the rather misleading nature of those labels we shall use them here because they are commonly used as a shorthand. They are:

(a)   the Benign Test;
(b)   the Non-adviser Test; and
(c)   the Ignorance Test.

The Tests

'The Benign Test'

[23.4] The Benign Test is satisfied:

' . . . where, in the course of providing tax advice, a person is not responsible for the design of any element of the proposed arrangements or arrangements (including the way in which they are structured) from which the tax advantage expected to be obtained arises.' (SI 2004/1865, reg 4.)

In respect of this the DOTAS guidance says:

'for example, a promoter marketing or designing a scheme may consult a second firm to provide advice in relation to a particular element of it. This second firm will not be a promoter, despite being involved in the design of the overall scheme, so long as any tax (or NICs) advice does not contribute to the tax (or NICs) advantage element of it.' (DOTAS guidance, para 3.4.1.)

But it is not the advice which has to contribute to the tax advantage but rather the element on which the advice is given. So if, for example, it is essential to the tax advantage of arrangements that an investment should qualify as an authorised unit trust, a financial services specialist who provides advice to ensure that that is the case, will not, in spite of the apparent meaning of the DOTAS guidance's example, be exempt under the Benign Test. The guidance seems to recognise that because it goes on to provide a very much narrower view of the scope of the Benign Test:

'For example, a promoter may seek advice from an accounting or law firm on whether two companies are "connected" for any purpose of the Taxes Act. Provided the advice goes no further than explaining the interpretation of words used in tax legislation, it would be benign; as would advice on general compliance requirements and so on.' (DOTAS guidance, para 3.4.1.)

It is true that mere advice on the construction of legislation will not make a person a promoter in respect of a notifiable person. It would not fall within the basic provisions of FA 2004, s 307(1)(a).

The Non-adviser Test

[23.5] The Non-adviser Test is satisfied where:

'(a)   a person, in the course of a business that is a relevant business for the purposes of section 307 by virtue of subsection (2)(a) of that section, is to any extent responsible for the design of the proposed arrangements or arrangements; but

(b)   does not provide tax advice in the course of carrying out his responsibilities in relation to the proposed arrangements or arrangements.' (SI 2004/1865, reg 4(3).)

Finance Act 2004, s 307(2)(a) provides:

'In this section "relevant business" means any trade, profession or business which—

(a)   involves the provision to other persons of services relating to taxation . . . .'.

The Ignorance Test

[23.6] A person will not be a promoter where he or she:

'(a)   is not responsible for the design of all the elements of the proposed arrangements or arrangements (including the way in which they are structured) from which the tax advantage expected to be obtained arises; and

(b)   could not reasonably be expected to have—

(i)   sufficient information as would enable him to know whether or not the proposal is a notifiable proposal or the arrangements are notifiable arrangements; or

(ii)   sufficient information as would enable him to comply with section 308(1) or (3).' (SI 2004/1865, reg 4(4).)

This will absolve from being a promoter those firms which provide tax advice in respect of some limited part of the arrangements but are not responsible for the overall design of the arrangements and do not make the arrangements available for implementation by others. It will only do so, however, if they are acting in circumstances where they cannot be expected to understand the nature of the overall arrangements governing the elements on which they are giving advice. That must be a very limited class of advisers, particularly in view of the modern professional's need to guard against becoming involved in money laundering arrangements.

HMRC has specific powers to deal with promoters who have failed to comply with various disclosure requirements. It may issue a conduct notice imposing conditions to address the offending behaviour. If a promoter fails to comply with the conduct notice, HMRC may apply to the tribunal for a monitoring notice to be issued that imposes extensive obligations on the promoter. Such a promoter will have to notify specified persons of this and provide a promoter reference number ('PRN') to them.

'Made a firm approach'

[23.7] A firm approach is defined in FA 2004, s 307(4A) as follows:

'(4A) For the purposes of this Part a person makes a firm approach to another person in relation to a notifiable proposal if the person makes a marketing contact with the other person in relation to the notifiable proposal at a time when the proposed arrangements have been substantially designed.

(4B) For the purposes of this Part a person makes a marketing contact with another person in relation to a notifiable proposal if—

(a) the person communicates information about the notifiable proposal to the other person,

(b) the communication is made with a view to that other person, or any other person, entering into transactions forming part of the proposed arrangements, and

(c) the information communicated includes an explanation of the advantage in relation to any tax that might be expected to be obtained from the proposed arrangements.

(4C) For the purposes of subsection (4A) proposed arrangements have been substantially designed at any time if by that time the nature of the transactions to form part of them has been sufficiently developed for it to be reasonable to believe that a person who wished to obtain the advantage mentioned in subsection (4B)(c) might enter into—

(a) transactions of the nature developed, or

(b) transactions not substantially different from transactions of that nature.'

Notifiable proposals

[23.8] A notifiable proposal is ' . . . a proposal for arrangements which, if entered into, would be notifiable arrangements (whether the proposal relates to a particular person or to any person who may seek to take advantage of it)' (FA 2004, s 306(2)).

Notifiable arrangements

[23.9] Notifiable arrangements are central to the duty of disclosure, as it is only such arrangements which can give rise to a notifiable proposal. Notifiable arrangements are any arrangements which:

(a) are within any description prescribed by the Treasury by regulations (the hallmarks);

(b) enable, or might be expected to enable, any person to obtain an advantage in relation to any tax that is so prescribed in relation to arrangements of that description; and

(c) are such that the main benefit, or one of the main benefits, that might be expected to arise from the arrangements is the obtaining of that advantage (FA 2004, s 306(1)).

Before looking at those elements of this definition which are prescribed by regulation, the meanings of 'arrangements', 'advantage' and 'main benefit' will be considered.

Arrangements

[23.10] FA 2004, s 318(1) provides that the meaning of 'arrangements' for this purpose 'includes any scheme, transaction or series of transactions'. It will be noticed that the definition is inclusive rather than exhaustive. In the context of the definition of a settlement for the income tax provisions found in ITTOIA 2005, Pt 5 Ch 5 the term 'arrangement' has been held to be a wide one. See for example *Burston v IRC (No 1)* [1945] 2 All ER 61, 28 TC 123; *Halperin v IRC (No 2)* [1945] 2 All ER 61; *IRC v Prince-Smith* [1943] 1 All ER 434, 25 TC 84; *Young (Inspector of Taxes) v Pearce* [1996] STC 743, 70 TC 331; *IRC v Pay* [1955] 36 TC 109, 34 ATC 223; *Crossland (Inspector of Taxes) v Hawkins* [1961] Ch 537, [1961] 2 All ER 812, CA; *Vandervell v IRC* [1967] 2 AC 291, [1967] 1 All ER 1, HL; *IRC v Wachtel* [1971] Ch 573, [1971] 1 All ER 271. It is likely that the courts will take a similarly wide view of the meaning of 'arrangements' in the DOTAS Regime. Certainly it is clear from s 318(1) that 'arrangements' can include a single transaction. As we shall see, however, HMRC seems to assume erroneously that a single transaction cannot be within the meaning of 'arrangements' for this purpose.

Tax advantage

[23.11] For the DOTAS Regime to apply, the arrangements must enable or be expected to enable an advantage to be obtained and such an advantage must be either the main, or one of the main, benefits expected to arise' (FA 2004, s 306(1)). An 'advantage' in relation to any tax is defined in s 318(1) as:

'(a) relief or increased relief from, or repayment or increased repayment of, that tax, or the avoidance or reduction of a charge to that tax or an assessment to that tax or the avoidance of a possible assessment to that tax,

(b) the deferral of any payment of tax or the advancement of any repayment of tax, or

(c) the avoidance of any obligation to deduct or account for any tax;'

The definition is based on the definition in the transactions in securities legislation found in ITA 2007, Part 13 Chap 1 which has been considered by the courts in a number of cases. Although the exact meaning of that definition is uncertain, its scope is certainly extremely broad. In the DOTAS guidance, HMRC say:

'where the scheme is expected to result in tax being avoided or reduced then the long-standing judgement of Lord Wilberforce in *CIR v Parker* (1966 AC 141) applies and the existence of a tax advantage is tested on a comparative basis'. (DOTAS guidance, para 13.4.1.)

CIR v Parker concerned the transactions in securities provisions. It is perhaps a reasonable assumption that the courts will have regard to the case law on the meaning of 'tax advantage' in that legislation in construing the phrase in the DOTAS Regime.

In another transactions in securities case, *Emery v IRC* [1981] STC 150, 54 TC 607, it was held that a tax advantage is obtained where a person receives something in a non-taxable form which, if received in another way, would have been taxable even though it might also have been received in a third way which was non-taxable. By extension, the view might be taken that a tax advantage arises where a result might have been obtained by a route which results in a tax charge but is actually obtained by another route which results in no, or a lesser, tax charge.

What is more, in respect of the transactions in securities rules, the courts have applied a wide latitude in identifying a hypothetical receipt to which to compare the actual receipt. In *Cleary v IRC* [1968] AC 766, [1967] 2 All ER 48, HL, a company repurchased its own shares. In determining whether there was a tax advantage, a comparison was made with the situation which would have ruled had the company paid a cash dividend equal to the purchase consideration. Of course, a shareholder who sells shares suffers a diminution in his rights over the company whereas one who receives a dividend does not. In spite of that, the court was able to regard the receipt of sale proceeds as being the same for the purpose of the comparison as a hypothetical receipt of a dividend.

There is a very great difference between the sort of transactions which are subject to the transactions in securities rules and those which are undertaken for inheritance tax planning purposes. Where a transfer into trust is made, the transfer will not be a benefit to the transferor except in an intangible manner by satisfying his wish to provide for those whom he loves and for whom he feels responsibility. If we look at all of the parties concerned, the settlor and the beneficiaries, there will not be any net change in their wealth.

How will the courts decide which hypothetical transactions they are to regard as comparable to the actual transactions taking place in the arrangements? If the end result of two alternative sets of transactions is exactly the same and the actual and hypothetical transactions are only differentiated by the inclusion of intermediate steps in the actual transaction, it is likely that the courts will find the two sets of transactions, actual and hypothetical, to be equivalent.

Example

If a father who wishes to make a discretionary settlement for his daughters instead gives money to his wife in the hope and expectation that she will settle the money on discretionary trusts on identical terms to those on which he would have settled it, it would be easy for the court to decide that the hypothetical arrangement to which the actual arrangements are to be compared is the direct settlement. Even here, however, the effects of the two are not exactly the same. For example, if the wife were to become insolvent within two years of the settlement being made, it could be set aside whereas, in such circumstances, a settlement made directly by the husband could not (Insolvency Act 1986, s 339).

What, however, if the wife is subject to gift and succession taxes in another country and, by reference to the taxation laws in that country, makes a significantly different settlement from the one which the husband would have made? Will the courts then still see the actual and hypothetical transactions as equivalent? If they were to follow the wider approach adopted in the transactions in securities cases no doubt they would but would they do so in relation to the very different provisions relating to the disclosure of inheritance tax arrangements?

So it will often be difficult to determine what hypothetical transaction should be the comparator with which the taxpayer's actual transaction is to be compared.

Example

A father is contemplating settling shares in an investment company on discretionary trusts for his daughters. Because the shares are worth more than his unused nil rate band he decides first to reorganise the share capital of the company so as to create preference shares with a market value equal to his unused nil rate band and ordinary shares whose value is equal to the value of the whole company in excess of that amount. He then settles the preference shares on discretionary trusts and makes an outright gift of the ordinary shares. In determining whether a main benefit of the arrangements consisting of the re-organisation, gift and settlement is the obtaining of a benefit in relation to a relevant property entry charge, does one compare his actual transactions with a simple settlement of the original shares on discretionary trusts? The effect of the actual transactions will be very different from that of the transactions which the father originally contemplated which might be taken to be the appropriate comparator.

The DOTAS guidance provides no useful commentary at all on these difficult issues.

Main benefit

[23.12] Condition (c) of s 306(1) raises the difficult question of when a benefit is a 'main benefit'. The *Oxford English Dictionary* defines 'main' as 'chief or principal' and specifically in relation to 'an action, a quality etcetera' as meaning 'very great in degree, value etcetera; highly remarkable for a specified quality; very great or considerable of its kind'.

It should be clear from this definition that there can only be more than one main benefit of a thing where those main benefits may all be fairly described as chief or as very great in degree or highly remarkable, etc. Where one benefit is of greatly more importance than all the others, the absolute pre-eminence of one benefit precludes any other benefit from being a main benefit. One might, however, be cautious in the light of the Special Commissioner's decision in *Snell v Revenue & Customs Comrs* [2008] STC (SCD) 1094 which concerned the meaning of 'main benefit' in the transactions in securities legislation. The Special Commissioner found that, although a sale was undertaken for a bona fide commercial purpose, it also had another main purpose of conferring a tax advantage. This, in spite of the fact that the tax benefit of the transaction was just 7% of the total transaction value.

It should also be noted that in contrast to FA 2004, s 306(1)(b), s 306(1)(c) looks at the expected benefits of the actual arrangements concerned. So in deciding whether the benefit consisting of the advantage is a main benefit one is making a comparison with the other benefits expected to arise under the actual arrangements rather than arising from another set of hypothetical arrangements.

The DOTAS guidance gives no help in understanding the ambit of condition (c). It makes the point that the test is objective rather than subjective which is only partially true: as we have seen, although condition (c) does not look at an actual person's expectation it is still concerned with expectation, that of an hypothetical person. Apart from that all it says is:

'In our experience those who plan tax arrangements fully understand the tax advantage such schemes are intended to achieve. Therefore we expect it will be obvious (with or without detailed explanation) to any potential client what the relationship is between the tax advantage and any other benefits of the product they are buying . . . '. (DOTAS guidance, para 13.5.)

It will be noticed that in sub-sections (b) and (c), the definition is not concerned with actual benefits but rather with benefits which might be expected to arise. The use of the conditional 'might' implies a hypothetical person whose likely expectations are to be considered. One presumes that this is a hypothetical reasonable man. The question of whether the condition in FA 2004, s 306(1)(c) applies, therefore, must depend upon whether a reasonable man would consider one of the main benefits of the arrangements to be the obtaining of a tax advantage. It will often be the case that the 'promoter' of the arrangements asserts that they will have the desired taxation effects whereas HMRC, when it becomes aware of them, assert that they do not. In considering whether s 306(1)(c) is satisfied, however, it is the probable expectations of the reasonable man that matter who may share the opinion of either the 'promoter' or of HMRC or of neither.

Arrangements: prescribed descriptions

[23.13] The actual description of the arrangements which fall within FA 2004, s 306(1) are prescribed by the Treasury in Regulations. Each set of regulations prescribes one or more descriptions in respect of particular taxes. A description in respect of inheritance tax is currently prescribed by the Inheritance Tax Avoidance Schemes (Prescribed Descriptions of Arrangements) Regulations 2011 (SI 2011/170) (the '2011 Regulations') and the Tax Avoidance Schemes (Prescribed Descriptions of Arrangements) Regulations 2006 (SI 2006/1543) (the '2006 Regulations'). It should be noted that the Draft DOTAS Regulations that the government intend to lay will repeal the 2011 Regulations (see **23.39**).

2006 Regulations

[23.14] It is only since 23 February 2016 that particular provisions of the 2006 Regulations have applied to arrangements involving inheritance tax. The 2006 Regulations do not have effect for the purposes of: the duties of a promoter in relation to notifiable proposals, if the relevant date falls before 23 February 2016; or the duties of a promoter in relation to notifiable arrangements, if the date on which the promoter first becomes aware of any transaction forming part of notifiable arrangements falls before 23 February 2016; or the duties of a scheme user where the promoter is resident outside the

UK, or where there is no promoter, if the date on which any transaction forming part of notifiable arrangements is entered into falls before 23 February 2016.

The 2006 Regulations provide that arrangements which fall within a description contained in reg 5(2) (a 'hallmark') are prescribed arrangements. The hallmarks which now apply to inheritance tax are the confidentiality hallmark and the premium fee hallmark.

Confidentiality hallmark

[23.15] The confidentiality hallmark found in the 2006 Regulations, reg 6 provides that:

'(1)   Arrangements are prescribed if–

(a)   any element of the arrangements (including the way in which the arrangements are structured) gives rise to the tax advantage expected to be obtained under the arrangements; and

(b)   it might reasonably be expected that a promoter would wish the way in which that element of those arrangements secures, or might secure, a tax advantage to be kept confidential from any other promoter at any time following the material date.

(2)   The promoter would, but for the requirements of the Regulations, wish to keep the way in which the element of these arrangements that secures, or might secure, the tax advantage confidential from HMRC at any time following the material date, and a reason for doing so is to facilitate repeated or continued use of the same element, or substantially the same element, in the future.'

The test under (1)(b) 'it might reasonably be expected' is a hypothetical question which widens the scope of the application of the rules. The test in (2) is a question of what the actual promoter would wish to do in the absence of any requirement to make an early disclosure. A common factor in both tests is the desire for confidentiality to exist at any point in the period from the date of the first transaction in the scheme to the date when the first tax return to be affected by the arrangements is submitted.

It is HMRC's view that the test requires a person with a duty to disclose to ask themselves:

'Might it reasonably be expected that *any promoter* of the arrangements would wish the way in which any element of those arrangements (including the way in which they are structured) gives rise to and secures, or might secure, the expected tax advantage to be kept confidential from *any other promoter*, at any time following the material date?'

It would seem that HMRC takes the view that the test is whether *any promoter* would want to keep the arrangements (or an element of them) confidential. The attitude of the particular promoter to confidentiality is not, in HMRC's view, a defining factor.

Where a taxpayer gives an undertaking as to confidentiality before any details of the arrangements are given, would seem to indicate that the test under (1)(b) has been met, if such an undertaking might be expected to be required by the hypothetical promoter. An undertaking, however, need not necessarily have that effect. In its DOTAS guidance, HMRC states that 'if the scheme is reasonably well known in the tax community, the confidentiality test is not met'.

In connection with the test under (2) the DOTAS guidance emphasises that a promoter is expected to ask itself whether they wish to keep the arrangements, or an element of them, confidential and whether that confidentiality is desired at any time from the first transaction being implemented to the submission of the tax return. There is, however, a further question, which is whether the promoter wishes to keep an element of the arrangements confidential in order to enable continued use of the element expected to give the tax advantage or for some other reason. It would appear from its guidance that HMRC accepts that a promoter would wish to keep an element of the arrangements confidential from it for other reasons and that in such a case the arrangements would not be 'hallmarked' and so no disclosure would be required (DOTAS guidance, para 7.3.3). Unfortunately, HMRC provides no guidance as to what those other reasons are.

Premium fee hallmark

[23.16] The premium fee hallmark in the 2006 Regulations, reg 8 provides that:

> '(1) Arrangements are prescribed if they are such that it might reasonably be expected that a promoter or a person connected with a promoter of arrangements that are the same as, or substantially similar to, the arrangements in question, would, but for the requirements of these Regulations, be able to obtain a premium fee from a person experienced in receiving services of the type being provided.
>
> But arrangements are not prescribed by this regulation if–
>
> (a) no person is a promoter in relation to them; and
> (b) the tax advantage which may be obtained under the arrangements is intended to be obtained by an individual or a business which is a small or medium-sized enterprise.
>
> (2) For the purposes of paragraph (1), and in relation to any arrangements, a "premium fee" is a fee chargeable by virtue of any element of the arrangements (including the way in which they are structured) from which the tax advantage expected to be obtained arises, and which is–
>
> (a) to a significant extent attributable to that tax advantage, or
> (b) to any extent contingent upon the obtaining of that tax advantage as a matter of law.'

It is difficult to understand how a fee for any element of the arrangements could be anything other than 'attributable to the tax advantage', if the entire objective of the arrangements is to generate that tax advantage. HMRC would appear to agree but emphasise the need for the attribution to be 'significant' (DOTAS guidance, para 7.5.3). The words 'premium fee' in normal usage suggests a fee that is at a higher level than fees for the equivalent amount of time spent on more routine work. The regulations do not contain a quantitative test and HMRC's guidance makes it clear that the size of the fee might be influenced by factors which would not of themselves make the fee a 'premium fee'. These factors include the location of the hypothetical promoter, the urgency of the advice needed, the experience of the adviser, and the size, complexity and availability of the advice (DOTAS guidance, para 7.5.3).

Where the fee is payable to the hypothetical promoter would normally be contingent on success; the arrangements are hallmarked and must be notified.

2011 Regulations

[23.17] Regulation 2(2) and (3) of the 2011 Regulations provides:

'(2)   Arrangements are prescribed if –

(a)   as a result of any element of the arrangements property becomes relevant property; and

(b)   a main benefit of the arrangements is that an advantage is obtained in relation to a relevant property entry charge.

(3)   In this regulation –

"property" shall be construed in accordance with section 272 of the Inheritance Tax Act 1984;

"relevant property" has the meaning given by section 58(1) of the Inheritance Tax Act 1984;

"relevant property entry charge" means the charge to inheritance tax which arises on a transfer of value made by an individual during that individual's life as a result of which property becomes relevant property;

"transfer of value" has the meaning given by section 3(1) of the Inheritance Tax Act 1984.'

Any element of the arrangements

[23.18] It will be seen that currently arrangements will not be prescribed under the 2011 Regulations unless 'as a result of any element of the arrangements property becomes relevant property'. What is an 'element' of the arrangements? If a father gives property to his son and he in turn settles the property on trust for his daughter, is the settlement a result of an element of the arrangements if:

(a)   at the time when the father makes up his mind to make the gift, he and his son plan together that the son should make the settlement; or

(b)   they do not plan the son's settlement but he is enabled to make the settlement by the gift because he has no other assets with which to do so; or

(c)   they do not plan the son's settlement and he would have been able to make the settlement whether or not the gift proceeded but he feels morally obligated to share his good fortune with his daughter?

The answer is by no means clear. Tentatively, we should expect a Court to find Regulation 2(2)(a) satisfied in relation to (a) and, possibly, (b) but not in respect of (c).

A relevant property entry charge

[23.19] It can be seen that currently for the condition in regulation 2(2)(b) to be satisfied, the advantage must be obtained 'in relation to a relevant property entry charge' and that 'a relevant property entry charge' means 'the charge to inheritance tax which arises on a transfer of value made by an individual during that individual's life as a result of which the property becomes relevant property.' What is the effect of the opening indefinite article? It surely requires there to be an actual relevant property entry charge arising under the arrangements rather than merely referring to the abstract concept of the relevant property entry charge. So, under this construction, if no benefit is obtained in relation to an actual relevant property entry charge the arrangements will not be prescribed. So, if it were possible to place property in a relevant property settlement without giving rise to a relevant property entry charge, regulation 2(2)(b) would not be satisfied even if there were an alternative way of achieving the same result under which such a charge would arise. It does not appear that HMRC accepts that this is the case.

Paragraph 13.4.3 of the DOTAS guidance says:

'Where there are:

- arrangements which result in property becoming relevant property
- there is no transfer of value; but
- in the absence of other intervening steps in the arrangements there would have been a transfer of value

Disclosure may be required. This is because the arrangements, have, by definition, resulted in an advantage in respect of the relevant property entry charge whether disclosure is required will depend on the grandfathering rules.'

Paragraph 13.8 of the DOTAS guidance says under the heading 'Examples of arrangements not exempted from disclosure':

'Examples of arrangements which would not be excluded from disclosure include arrangements where property becomes relevant property and an advantage is obtained in respect of the relevant property entry charge:

- where the claim that there is no transfer of value relies on a series of transactions where, in the absence of all other intervening steps, there would have been a transfer of value and a relevant property entry charge;'

So it seems that, in HMRC's view, a benefit may be obtained where no relevant property entry charge actually arises but one would have arisen had the same result been obtained by different transactions.

It may be that HMRC has reached this view because it has overlooked the significance of the indefinite article in regulation 2(2)(b). In the passage quoted above from the DOTAS guidance, para 13.4.3 and in the following passage from para 13.4.1, for example, HMRC substitutes the definite for the indefinite article:

'It is important to note that under the Regulations a scheme is only disclosable if there is a tax advantage in respect of _the_ [emphasis added] 'relevant property entry charge' (see paragraph [13.4.2] below). Where a scheme provides a tax advantage but that advantage is not in respect of _the_ [emphasis added] "relevant property entry charge" then disclosure will not be required under the Regulations'.

If it is HMRC's view that regulation 2(2)(b) may be satisfied where there is no actual relevant property entry charge, its view is incorrect. If HMRC were correct in its view, however, it would not be necessary for arrangements to include a transfer of value for them to be notifiable arrangements. That is because, if that view were correct, it would be sufficient for property to have become relevant property as a result of the arrangements and that a relevant property entry charge would have arisen on alternative transactions even if one did not actually arise. The DOTAS guidance, however, says at para 13.4.3:

> 'Where there is no transfer of value and no wider arrangements then no advantage can be obtained in respect of a transaction which results in property becoming relevant property.'

Grandfathering

Restriction

[23.20] The guidance states that regulation 3 of the 2011 Regulations is designed to restrict disclosure to those schemes which are new or innovative by exempting schemes which are the same or substantially the same as arrangements made available before 6 April 2011 (DOTAS guidance, para 13.6).

Regulation 3 provides that:

> 'Arrangements are excepted from disclosure under these Regulations if they are of the same, or substantially the same, description as arrangements -
>
> (a)   which were first made available for implementation before 6th April 2011; or
>
> (b)   in relation to which the date of any transaction forming part of the arrangements falls before 6th April 2011; or
>
> (c)   in relation to which a promoter first made a firm approach to another person before 6th April 2011.'

The DOTAS guidance refers to this as 'grandfathering'. In order to understand the scope of this exclusion, the meaning of the following words and phrases needs to be understood:

(a)   ' . . . substantially the same . . . description';
(b)   'made available for implementation';
(c)   'promoter';
(d)   'made a firm approach'.

It should be noted that the draft IHT DOTAS Regulations 2016 do not provide for any form of grandfathering but rather provides for four types of excepted arrangements. This has been criticised by the professional bodies as discussed in **23.39**.

' . . . Substantially the same . . . description'

[23.21] In the DOTAS guidance, HMRC say:

> 'in our view a scheme is no longer substantially the same if the effect of any change would be to make any previous disclosure misleading in relation to the second (or subsequent) client.' (DOTAS guidance, para 14.2.3.)

It is tentatively suggested that the key to deciding whether arrangements are substantially the same as other arrangements is whether tax would be charged in the same manner on the two sets of arrangements. That would seem to follow both from the purpose of the provisions and from their concentration on whether a tax advantage is obtained. If that is the case, HMRC's assertion that arrangements (it should be noted that the DOTAS guidance does not use the statutory word 'arrangements' but substitutes the pejorative word 'scheme') will not be substantially the same if they have been adjusted to take account of 'changes in the law or accounting treatment' is only an approximation to the true position. For example, if the strategy involves the acquisition by trustees of shares qualifying for business property relief and the contractual terms of the acquisition are altered in order to take account of changes in Financial Services legislation, that would surely not prevent those arrangements being regarded as substantially the same as the arrangements before the alterations were made.

Determining when arrangements are substantially the same as grandfathered arrangements will often be difficult. Consider for example, if the changes made by FA 2006 to the inheritance taxation of trusts had been made shortly after the time when the IHT DOTAS Regime came into effect. Before the change, arrangements often involved using a discretionary trust because the designer wished the trust to be within the relevant property regime. After the change, arrangements which were otherwise the same often used interest-in-possession trusts because such trusts were for the first time within the relevant property regime and beneficiaries usually prefer to have a vested interest in income. Would that change have resulted in the arrangements being not substantially the same as arrangements prior to the introduction of the IHT DOTAS Regime? One would not have thought so. The DOTAS guidance contains no useful commentary on such matters.

'made available for implementation'

[23.22] The date when a promoter makes a notifiable proposal available for implementation is important in determining when a disclosure must be made to HMRC. It is obviously generally in the promoter's interest for that date to be as late as possible. In respect of the grandfathering provisions, however, it is in the promoter's and the client's interests for the date at which the same or substantially the same arrangements have been made available to be before 6 April 2011. The DOTAS guidance in respect of inheritance tax arrangements simply incorporates HMRC's general material as to when arrangements are made available for implementation. That material is obviously designed to draw the date back as early as possible.

The *Shorter Oxford English Dictionary* defines 'available' as 'able to be used . . . obtainable'. If a plan is available when it is 'able to be used', a person to whom it is available must be able to implement it and that must mean that he has all of the information available to him to allow him to do so. A tax planning scheme which has been described in sufficient detail to allow the client to decide whether or not he wishes to enter into it will not have been made available for implementation, if, for example, the client has not been given the documents which will enable him to implement it. HMRC's guidance, however, says that:

'a scheme is made available for implementation at the point when all the elements necessary for implementation of the scheme are in place and a communication is made to a client suggesting the client might consider entering into transactions forming part of the scheme, but it does not matter whether full details of the scheme are communicated at that time.' (DOTAS guidance, para 14.3.2.)

It is difficult to see how arrangements can be made available for implementation to a person who is in fact incapable of implementing them because he lacks some essential information such as the wording of an appropriate document. Yet such a person would be quite capable of understanding the expected tax advantages of an arrangement and of deciding whether or not to enter into it.

The guidance

General

[23.23] Paragraph 13.7 of the DOTAS guidance is headed 'list of grandfathered schemes and schemes that are not within the Regulations'. The guidance explains:

'A list of schemes which HMRC regards as being "grandfathered" may be found below . . . To be as extensive as possible, the list includes arrangements which do not fall within the regulations because, for example, property does not become relevant property.'

The DOTAS guidance again refers to 'schemes', a term which is not used in the legislation which is concerned with 'arrangements'. As the DOTAS guidance explains, the list does not just include grandfathered arrangements but also other arrangements which do not fall within the basic provisions of regulation 2. How a list of grandfathered arrangements can be made 'as "extensive" as possible' by mixing it up with other sorts of arrangements is not immediately apparent.

The DOTAS guidance also says:

'If there is any doubt as to whether a scheme ought to be disclosed then a disclosure should be made'. (DOTAS guidance, para 13.7.)

It will be apparent from the analysis that follows that in relation to much, possibly most, inheritance tax advice there will be uncertainty as to whether or not the scheme ought to be disclosed. If advisers were to follow the advice in the DOTAS guidance, HMRC would be inundated with disclosures in respect of perfectly routine inheritance tax planning. It is difficult to see how that is consistent with the guidance's statement that: 'One of the aims of the extension of the disclosure rules to Inheritance Tax is to restrict disclosure to those schemes which are new or innovative.' (DOTAS guidance, para 13.6.)

Of course, a liability to disclose can only arise in respect of arrangements which fall within the statutory definition but it will be prudent for advisers to err strongly on the side of caution in deciding whether or not to make disclosures, particularly because of the penalties that can be imposed where there is a failure to make a required disclosure. Penalties are discussed in **23.50–23.53.**

List of grandfathered schemes and schemes that are not within the Regulations

[23.24] The list of grandfathered schemes and schemes that are not within the regulations can be found in para 13.7 of the DOTAS guidance and includes:

(A)   Arrangements where property does not become relevant property;
(B)   Arrangements that qualify for relief/exemptions;
(C)   The purchase of business assets with a view to transferring the assets into a relevant property trust after two years;
(D)   The purchase of agricultural assets with a view to transferring the assets into a relevant property trust after the appropriate period;
(E)   Pilot Settlements;
(F)   Discounted Gift Trusts/Schemes;
(G)   Excluded property trusts; disabled trusts; employee benefit trusts which satisfy s 86 and a qualifying interest in possession trust;
(H)   Transfers on death into relevant property trusts;
(I)   Changes in distribution of deceased's estates;
(J)   Transfers of the Nil Rate Band every seven years;
(K)   Loan into trust;
(L)   Insurance Policy trusts;
(M) Making a chargeable transfer followed by a potentially exempt transfer;
(N)   Deferred shares;
(O)   Items of national importance;
(P)   Pension death benefits;
(Q)   Reversionary interests;
(R)   Transfers of value;
(S)   Gifts to Companies.

Arrangements which HMRC say do not fall within regulation 2

[23.25] Some of the items on this list are merely anodyne (for example, Item A) whereas others are obscure, inaccurate and contradictory (for example, Item B).

Item B Arrangements that qualify for relief/exemptions

[23.26] The guidance says at Item B that:

'(a)   A single step that qualifies for a relief or exemption (where there are no other steps in order to gain an advantage) will not require disclosure.
(b)   Where the arrangements lead to qualification for:
   •   multiple reliefs or exemptions;
   •   more than one application of the same relief or exemption;
   •   a single relief or exemption where there are further steps in order to gain an advantage,
   Then disclosure will not be required where the arrangements can be shown to be covered by the grandfathering rule.

When considering whether arrangements which qualify for a relief or exemption require disclosure, it is important to remember that the arrangements must result in property becoming relevant property for the Regulations to apply.'

If HMRC's apparent view is correct that regulation 2(2)(b) may be satisfied when no actual relevant property entry charge arises but one might have arisen in an alternative transaction, the statement in the guidance at Item B is clearly incorrect.

Example

> Luke, who has utilised his entire nil rate band, wishes to settle property worth £100,000 on discretionary trusts. Rather than settling £100,000 from his bank account he settles £100,000 of property qualifying for business property relief.
>
> This settlement is an arrangement because it is a transaction (FA 2004, s 318(1)). The arrangements satisfy the condition of regulation 2(2)(a) because as a result of the transfer, property becomes relevant property. There is an alternative way of achieving the same result or substantially the same result under which Luke would have suffered a relevant property entry charge. If HMRC's apparent view that regulation 2(2)(b) can be satisfied without an actual relevant property entry charge arising were correct, Luke would have gained an advantage in relation to such a charge and 2(2)(b) would be satisfied. So the settlement would be a notifiable arrangement unless it were 'grandfathered' by regulation 3.

The listed bullet points above must be alternative rather than cumulative so the implication is that where arrangements consisting of a single transaction lead to qualification for multiple reliefs or exemptions (the first bullet point) there do not need to be further steps in order for the arrangements to be disclosable. That implies that HMRC thinks that arrangements consisting of a single step can be disclosable in which case there appears to be a contradiction between Item A and Item B. So, for example, if Luke had not used his annual exemption in our example above, the settlement would have qualified for relief under IHTA 1984, s 19 as well as for relief under IHTA 1984, s 104. It would seem to fall within HMRC's first bullet point and, under the view of the law set out in the DOTAS guidance, would have been disclosable had it not been clearly covered by the grandfathering rule.

Item H Transfers on death

[23.27] The guidance says at Item H:

> 'A transfer into a relevant property trust made under the terms of a person's Will or paid into a relevant property trust on a person's death will not require disclosure.'

This is true if the arrangements have to involve an actual relevant property entry charge but is not true if they do not.

Example

> Septimus is considering setting up a relevant property settlement. He could do so during his lifetime or under his will. He decides to do so under his will because he has made previous chargeable transfers which are likely to drop out of cumulation if the settlement is not made until his death. It is clear that the creation of a settlement under the Will constitutes arrangements under the definition in FA 2004, s 318. As a result of an element of the arrangements, property becomes relevant

property. So regulation 2(2)(a) is satisfied. It appears that there is a tax advantage in respect of a relevant property entry charge because there is an alternative way of achieving the same result which would result in an inheritance tax charge. If regulation 2(2)(b) can be satisfied without an actual relevant property entry charge arising, then regulation 2(2) is satisfied in respect of the arrangements consisting of the settling of property under a will.

Item I Changes in the distribution of a deceased's estate

[23.28] In respect of changes in the distribution of a deceased's estates, the guidance says at Item I:

'S.17 prevents there from being a transfer of value where there is:

(i)   a variation or disclaimer to which s.142(1) applies;

(ii)   a transfer to which s.143 applies; ...

(iv) the renunciation of a claim to legitim or rights under s.131 of the Civil Partnership Act 2004 within the period mentioned in s.147(6)

Where property becomes relevant property but s.17 applies to the transaction then disclosure will not be required.

In addition, where distributions are made from property settled by Will to which s.144 applies then disclosure will not be required.'

If it is correct, as HMRC appears to think, that regulation 2(2)(b) can be satisfied where there is no actual relevant property entry charge, it is not clear why arrangements to which IHTA 1984, s 17 applies would not satisfy the criteria set in regulation 2(2). They will have resulted in property becoming relevant property and there are alternative transactions under which the same result could have been achieved which would have incurred a relevant property entry charge.

Example

Luke is left a legacy of £300,000 under Mr Tumble's will. Luke has been considering settling £300,000 of cash on trust for his sister and brother. He has previous chargeable transfers exceeding the nil rate band so were he to do so he would suffer a relevant property entry charge. Instead he enters into a Deed of Variation of Mr Tumble's will (containing a statement under s 142(2)) under which the executors are to transfer the legacy to trustees on trust for his siblings.

It seems clear that there is an alternative transaction with the same result as the actual transaction which would give rise to a higher relevant property entry charge. It is not clear, however, that the same point would apply to transfers under IHTA 1984, ss 143 and 144 because, crucially, those sections apply automatically where such transfers are made.

Item P Transfer of pension death benefits

[23.29] At item P the guidance says:

'The transfer of pension scheme death benefits into a relevant property trust where the scheme member retains the retirement benefits will not in itself require disclosure. However, where the transfer is part of arrangements which enable an advantage to be obtained in respect of the relevant property entry charge then disclosure may be required. This will depend on whether it can be shown that the arrangements are within the exceptions to disclosure outlined in Regulation 3.'

Presumably HMRC's view in the first sentence is based on the proposition that if the pension scheme death benefits are of value they will give rise to a relevant property entry charge on their value. If such a charge does not arise, it is because any diminution in the settlor's estate will be covered by the combination of the annual exemption and the settlor's unused nil rate band. The succeeding sentences make the guidance here all but valueless.

Items which HMRC consider are not disclosable because they fall within the grandfathering provisions

Items C and D Business and agricultural property

[23.30] In respect of business and agricultural property, it is stated in Items C and D that the purchase of such property with a view to holding it for two years prior to transferring it to a trust (and thereby qualifying for relief under IHTA 1984, s 105 or s 116) 'is not disclosable provided that there are no further steps in the arrangements as the grandfathering rules will apply' and this is so 'whether or not they are insurance backed.'

That at least is moderately helpful but what is the force of the proviso? Obviously, the purchaser will want in due course to actually transfer the assets into the trust. That is a further step. Read literally the DOTAS guidance does not cover arrangements which include that further step although one might infer that this is only the result of inaccurate drafting.

Item F Discounted Gift Trusts

[23.31] The DOTAS guidance says at Item F:

'Discounted gift schemes/trusts where the residual trust is a bare trust would not require disclosure as there is no property becoming relevant property.

Where, in relation to a discounted gift trust/scheme, property becomes relevant property then disclosure will not be required where the grandfathering provisions apply.'

Arrangements involving insurance often involve making settlements of death benefits arising under insurance policies, the market value of which is conventionally arrived at by applying a discount, determined actuarially, to the expected amount of the benefit payable on death. It is to be supposed that the DOTAS guidance here refers to such arrangements but it does not in words say so and the term discounted gift schemes/trusts (which is reversed in the second paragraph which refers to 'a discounted gift trust/scheme') is insufficiently precise to indicate the arrangements to which it refers. It would be a brave adviser who relied on this Item to refrain from disclosure.

Item J Transfers of the Nil Rate Band every seven years

[23.32] In respect of transfers equal to the nil rate band made at seven-year intervals, the guidance says at Item J:

'The transfer of the settlor's nil rate band into a relevant property trust every seven years (provided there is no other step or steps to the arrangements which enable an advantage to be obtained in respect of the relevant property entry charge) will not be disclosable as the grandfathering provisions will apply.'

At least that seems to be unequivocal but then one would hardly have thought that such arrangements would require disclosure.

Item K Loan into trust

[23.33] In respect of loans and trusts the guidance says at Item K:

'A transfer into a relevant property trust by way of loan where, other than the establishment of the trust, it is a single step transaction, will not be disclosable as the grandfathering provisions will apply.'

Presumably a 'transfer into a relevant property trust by way of loan' actually means a payment of money by way of loan, but the guidance is, perhaps, useful here subject to that. It is surely unusual for a payment under a loan to be a single step transaction, however, because the loan would normally be made in order that the moneys lent should be expended on something. If one lends money to the trustees of a relevant property trust for them to acquire a property to be occupied by a beneficiary, for example, and they do so, are the arrangements within HMRC's statement? It appears that they are not. Of course, it is likely that they will actually fall within regulation 3 whether HMRC agrees that that is the case or not.

Item L Insurance Policy trusts

[23.34] In respect of insurance policy trusts the guidance says at Item L:

'A transfer of the rights to the benefits payable on death into a relevant property trust will not be disclosable even where other benefits, for example, critical illness benefits are payable to the settlor as the grandfathering provisions will apply.

The payment of premiums on a policy settled into a relevant property trust paid by the settlor or other person will not be disclosable as the grandfathering provisions will apply.'

Item M A chargeable transfer followed by a PET

[23.35] The guidance also says at Item M that, because the grandfathering provisions will apply, arrangements under which a settlor makes a chargeable transfer prior to a potentially exempt transfer to ensure that the full nil rate band is available on the chargeable transfer are not disclosable 'unless there are further arrangements so as to allow an advantage to be obtained in respect of the relevant property entry charge.'

Item N Deferred shares

[23.36] At Item N the guidance says that 'the transfer of deferred shares into a relevant property trust in itself is not disclosable.' It goes on, however, to say that: ' . . . where the transfer is part of arrangements which enable an advantage to be obtained in respect of the relevant property entry charge then disclosure may be required. This will depend on whether it can be shown that the grandfathering provisions will apply.' So the initial, apparently useful statement, is so caveated as to be of no use at all.

Item Q Reversionary interests

[23.37] At Item Q there is a similarly valueless comment in respect of reversionary interests:

'Where property is transferred into a relevant property trust and the settlor retains a reversionary interest then the transfer will not require disclosure as long as it can be shown that the grandfathering rule applies.'

Summary

[23.38] The list in the guidance of arrangements which HMRC currently accepts fall within the grandfathering provisions of regulation 3 is only of the most minor use to advisers trying to decide whether a disclosure is required. The adviser, therefore, will have to rely on preserving evidence that the grandfathering provisions of regulation 3 applies to their advice.

Grandfathering will disappear once the Draft IHT DOTAS Regulations 2016 come into effect.

Proposed 2016 changes

[23.39] As already mentioned, the provisions in the Draft DOTAS Regulations 2016, if and when they are introduced, will extend the extent to which the DOTAS regime applies to inheritance tax. Arrangements will no longer be notifiable only when property becomes relevant property and a main benefit of its becoming so is that an advantage in relation to the relevant property charge is obtained or where the arrangements fall within the confidentiality or premium fee hallmarks. The Draft DOTAS Regulations 2016 will extend the application of the DOTAS regime to arrangements that seek to avoid inheritance tax, either on death or on lifetime transfers.

The Draft DOTAS Regulations 2016 provide that an arrangement will be prescribed if it would be reasonable to expect an informed observer, having studied the arrangements and having regard to all relevant circumstances, to conclude that the main purpose, or one of the main purposes of the arrangements is to enable a person to obtain an inheritance tax advantage (Condition 1) and:

- the arrangements are contrived or abnormal; or
- the arrangements involve one or more contrived or abnormal steps, without which the inheritance tax advantage could not be obtained (Condition 2).

Condition 1 refers only to an advantage in relation to inheritance tax being reasonably expected. It is not restricted to inheritance tax avoidance or to abusive arrangements.

There are certain arrangements that are excepted from the DOTAS regime. These are:

'1.   Loan trusts. The transferor ("S") establishes a settlement or bare trust of which S cannot be a beneficiary. S lends the trustees a cash sum interest free and repayable on demand. The trustees invest in a single premium insurance bond or capital redemption bond. Encashments of the bond may be used to repay the loan in whole or in part. The outstanding loan remains in S's estate for inheritance tax.

2.   Discounted gift schemes. The transferor ("S") establishes a settlement or bare trust of which S cannot be a beneficiary. S assigns to the settlement one or more contracts of life insurance or capital redemption policies. S retains specified rights to future payments, if S is alive at the date the payment falls due (the "retained rights"). The payments may be fixed cash sums, the maturity proceeds of individual policies or specified benefits under a policy. The retained rights cannot be varied and they remain in S's estate for inheritance tax.

3.   Flexible reversionary trusts. The transferor ("S") establishes a settlement or bare trust of which S cannot be a beneficiary. S assigns to the settlement one or more contracts of life assurance or capital redemption policies. S retains specified rights to future payments, if S is alive at the date the payment falls due (the "retained rights"). The payments may be fixed cash sums, the maturity proceeds of an individual policy or specified benefits under a policy. The retained rights can be defeated or varied by the trustees before the payments fall due.

4.   Split or retained interest trusts. The transferor ("S") establishes a settlement or bare trust which holds a single premium insurance bond or capital redemption bond. S retains specified rights to either a cash sum or a percentage of the bond (normally referred to as the "retained fund"). S has no right to the remaining property (normally referred to as the "gifted fund"). S may withdraw an amount of the retained fund at any time, which reduces the value of the retained fund. The retained fund remains in S's estate for inheritance tax.'

The first two exceptions relate to the discounted gift trusts (see **9.32**) and gift and loan trust arrangement (see **9.40**). It seems strange that the regulations except arrangements involving insurance products and loan products but do not except simple lifetime planning. It should be noted that there will be no form of grandfathering (see **23.20** above) as there is under the current regime with the result that more arrangements will be notifiable to HMRC which concern routine planning which has been used for many years which is well known to HMRC.

At the time of writing, there have been, to date, two consultation documents relating to inheritance tax and DOTAS. At both stages, the professional bodies have severely criticised the proposals and warned that mainstream estate planning would fall within the DOTAS regime, but whether they are amended remains to be seen. If they are not, even the most straightforward arrangements are likely to be disclosable.

The duty of disclosure

Duties of a promoter

[23.40] A person who is a promoter (see **23.3**) in relation to a notifiable proposal or notifiable arrangements must provide the Board with prescribed information relating to the notifiable proposal within the prescribed period (which effectively is within five days of the relevant date) (FA 2004, s 308(1)). HMRC can apply to the Tribunal for an order requiring a promoter to provide further information where it believes that the promoter has not provided all the prescribed information (FA 2004, s 308A). In addition, HMRC can require persons who have provided prescribed information in compliance or purported compliance within s 308 to provide further information or documents (FA 2004, s 310A).

Dealing with non-UK promoters

[23.41] Non-UK promoters fall within the scope of the DOTAS Regime but it can be difficult to enforce compliance. Therefore where a person enters into a transaction forming part of notifiable arrangements where the promoter is resident outside the UK and there is no promoter resident in the UK, it is the person entering into the arrangements who must make a disclosure unless the promoter has made a disclosure previously (FA 2004, s 309). In addition, HMRC can require persons who have provided prescribed information in compliance or purported compliance within s 309 to provide further information or documents (FA 2004, s 310A).

Duties of parties to notifiable arrangements not involving a promoter

[23.42] Any person who enters into any transaction forming part of notifiable arrangements as respects which neither he nor any other person in the UK is liable to comply with the duties of a promoter, or of a person dealing with a promoter outside the UK, must give prescribed information to HMRC within the prescribed time (FA 2004, s 310).

HMRC can require persons who have provided prescribed information in compliance or purported compliance within s 310 to provide further information or documents (FA 2004, s 310A).

Legal professional privilege

[23.43] A person who is prevented by reason of legal professional privilege from disclosing information which he would otherwise be required to give, is not treated as a promoter (FA 2004, s 314 and SI 2004/1865, reg 6). In such cases, the obligation to make a disclosure becomes the obligation of the client (FA 2004, s 310 and SI 2004/1864, reg 4(5A)). The Law Society has issued a practice note on this matter which can be found on their website.

The disclosure by promoters

[23.44] Once a decision has been taken that a disclosure should be made, it is usually the promoter who has to make the disclosure although, as we have seen, in certain circumstances it is the client's duty to do so (see **23.41–23.43**).

Time limits

[23.45] A promoter must make a disclosure within the prescribed period after the relevant date which is the earliest of the day on which he:

(i)   makes a firm approach to another person in relation to a notifiable proposal;

(ii)   makes a notifiable proposal available for implementation by any other person;

(iii)   becomes aware of any transaction forming part of the notifiable arrangements implementing the notifiable proposal (FA 2004, s 308(1) & (2));

The prescribed period is the period of five days (the Tax Avoidance Schemes (Information) Regulations 2012 (SI 2012/1836), reg 5(4)). Non-business days under the Bills of Exchange Act 1882, s 92 (loosely, weekends and bank holidays) are not counted in calculating the five days (The Tax Avoidance Schemes (Information) Regulations 2012 (SI 2012/1836), reg 2(3)).

Special provisions found in FA 2004, s 308(4)–(4C) apply to co-promoters. Where two or more persons are promoters in respect of the same, or substantially the same, scheme, whether or not it is made available to the same person, a single disclosure can be made. Use of these rules is optional by the parties.

A promoter is only required to disclose the same scheme once (FA 2004, s 308(3)). HMRC says that minor changes need not be disclosed 'providing the revised proposal remains substantially the same' (DOTAS guidance, para 14.2.3). It is HMRC's view that a scheme is no longer substantially the same 'if the effect of any change would be to make any previous disclosure misleading in relation to the second (or subsequent) client' (DOTAS guidance, para 14.2.3).

Making the disclosure

[23.46] A disclosure must be made on the relevant AAG form. The disclosure can be made online or by completing the hard copy version of the relevant form and sending it to HMRC.

The Tax Avoidance Schemes (Information) Regulations 2012 (SI 2012/1836), reg 4(1) sets out the information required, including:

(a)   the promoter's name and address;

(b)   details of the provision of the Arrangements Regulations, the ATED Arrangements Regulations, the IHT Arrangements Regulations or the SDLT Arrangements Regulations by virtue of which the arrangements or the proposed arrangements are notifiable;

(c)   a summary of the arrangements or proposed arrangements and the name (if any) by which they are known;

(d)   information explaining each element of the arrangements or proposed arrangements (including the way in which they are structured) from which the tax advantage expected to be obtained under those arrangements arises; and

(e)   the statutory provisions, relating to any of the prescribed taxes, on which that tax advantage is based.

When making a disclosure, a promoter may also provide HMRC with details of a co-promoter of the same or substantially the same scheme thus exempting him from having to make a disclosure.

The scheme reference number

[23.47]   Having submitted a disclosure HMRC may issue a scheme reference number (an 'SRN'), which is an eight digit number within 90 days.

If an SRN is issued, it is given to the person who made the disclosure; for example, the promoter or the scheme user and any co-promoters notified in the disclosure (DOTAS guidance, para 17.1). Where a promoter receives such a number he must provide it to any person to whom he provides, or has provided, services in connection with the notifiable arrangements (FA 2004, s 312). This must be done on a form AAG6(IHT) within 30 days of being provided with the number or becoming aware of any transactions forming part of the scheme, whichever is later.

The person who enters into any such arrangements must include the SRN on his form IHT100 or on a form AAG4(IHT) and also state the tax year in which or the date on which the advantage is expected to be obtained (FA 2004, s 313 and the Tax Avoidance Schemes (Information) Regulations 2012 (SI 2012/1836), regs 9(5) and 10(6)). The relevant forms must be submitted within 12 months of the end of the month in which the first transaction forming part of the notifiable arrangements was entered into. Such a duty does not apply in prescribed circumstances which will be defined in regulations yet to be published (FA 2004, s 313(6)).

Clients must also provide the promoter with certain prescribed information (FA 2004, s 312B) which will be reported to HMRC by the promoter.

HMRC has the discretion to withdraw SRNs. A promoter is under no obligation to notify clients and intermediaries of the withdrawal. HMRC states in its guidance that the withdrawal of an SRN does not 'relieve any obligation that may have existed prior to the date of withdrawal' (DOTAS guidance, para 17.10). The issue of withdrawals of SRNs is important, particularly in relation to the accelerated payments regime which may apply where an SRN has been issued.

Where a promoter is required to provide an SRN to a client and certain other parties under FA 2004, s 312(2) or 312A(2) or (2A) HMRC may specify additional information which must be given to recipients. This additional information is information supplied by HMRC, for example, information about the implications of entering into tax planning arrangements (FA 2004, s 316A).

Client lists

[23.48] Promoters are required to provide to HMRC lists of their clients to whom they have issued a reference number during that calendar quarter (FA 2004, s 313ZA and SI 2012/1836, reg 13). The information must be provided within 30 days of the end of the calendar quarter (counting weekends and Bank Holidays). A promoter should also include details of clients who take a first step to implement the arrangements but later withdraw.

HMRC has the power where it suspects that someone other than the client is or is likely to be a party to the arrangements to require a promoter to provide prescribed information about that other person provided the promoter might reasonably be expected to know his identity (FA 2004, s 313ZB).

Updated information

[23.49] Where an SRN has been issued a promoter must inform HMRC of a change in the name by which the notifiable arrangements or proposed notifiable arrangements are known or a change in the name or address of the promoter within 30 days of the change (FA 2004, s 310C).

Penalties

[23.50] The penalties imposed under the DOTAS Regime fall into three categories:

(a) disclosure penalties which apply where a scheme has not been disclosed;
(b) user penalties which apply where there has been a failure by a scheme user to report a scheme reference number to HMRC;
(c) information penalties which relate to all other failures to comply, with the exception of those mentioned above.

Disclosure penalties

[23.51] A Tribunal may impose a penalty of an amount not exceeding £600 per day during the initial period for the following failures:

(i) a failure by a promoter to notify a scheme under FA 2004, s 308(1) & (3);
(ii) a failure by a scheme user to notify a scheme under FA 2004, ss 309(1), 310 and 310A (TMA 1970, ss 98C and 100(2)(f)).

It should be noted that it is only a Tribunal that can impose these penalties and not HMRC.

The 'initial period' begins with the 'relevant day' which effectively is the first day following the end of the period prescribed in which the scheme should have been disclosed (TMA 1970, s 98C(2ZA)). In each case the initial period ends with the earlier of:

• the day on which the Tribunal determines the penalty; or

- the last day before the day on which the scheme is disclosed, thereby ending the failure.

In determining the amount of the penalty, the Tribunal must take into account all relevant considerations including the desirability of its being set at a level which appears appropriate for deterring a person from similar failures to comply on future occasions having regard to:

- in the case of a failure to disclose by a promoter, the amount of fees received, or likely to have been received by the promoter in connection with the notifiable proposal or arrangements;
- in the case of a failure to disclose by any relevant person, the amount of the tax advantage gained, or sought to be gained (TMA 1970, s 98C(2ZB)).

The Tribunal has the power to impose a higher penalty than the maximum penalty imposed under s 98C(I)(a) where that penalty 'appears inappropriately low after taking account of those considerations' (TMA 1970, s 98C(2ZC)). The Tribunal can impose a penalty of up to £1 million under this provision.

In addition, where the failure continues after a penalty has been imposed by the Tribunal, HMRC may impose a daily penalty of up to £600 for each day after the day on which the Tribunal imposed a penalty until the failure is remedied (TMA 1970, s 98C(I)(b)). HMRC states that 'in such cases we will normally begin by imposing a daily amount that is proportionate to the amount imposed by the Tribunal, compared to the maximum. If the failure continues, HMRC will consider increasing the amount, up to the maximum' (DOTAS guidance, para 23.5.2.)

Penalties can also be imposed where the Tribunal has made orders determining that a scheme is notifiable.

There is a right of appeal to the Tribunal against penalties imposed by HMRC (TMA 1970, s 100B).

User penalties

[23.52] Where a scheme user fails to report an SRN and related information to HMRC, he shall be liable to a penalty of the 'relevant sum' (TMA 1970, s 98C(3)). The relevant sum is:

(1) £5,000 for each scheme to which the failure relates for a first occasion;
(2) £7,500 per scheme on the second occasion within three years;
(3) £10,000 per scheme on the third and subsequent occasions (TMA 1970, s 98C(4)).

These penalties are imposed by HMRC (TMA 1970, s 100) but, again, there is a right for the penalised person to appeal to the First Tier Tribunal under TMA 1970, s 100B.

The penalties in relation to the failure to report are the same as those where a client and a monitored promoter (see **23.51**) fails to notify HMRC of any PRN that has been issued.

Information penalties

[23.53] Penalties may be imposed where information has not been provided by the due date and in the form and manner specified. The Tribunal may impose an initial penalty of up to £5,000 (TMA 1970, s 98C(1)(a)(ii)). In addition, HMRC may impose a daily penalty not exceeding £600 for each day the failure continues (TMA 1970, s 98C(1)(b)).

Where a notification order has been made by the Tribunal under FA 2004, s 306A or a disclosure order has been made, the maximum daily penalty increases to £5,000 per day.

Reasonable excuse

[23.54] Where a person has a reasonable excuse, they have no liability to a penalty (TMA 1970, s 118(2)). HMRC does not consider that the fact that a person has obtained legal advice stating that a scheme is not disclosable 'in itself' provides a reasonable excuse (DOTAS guidance, para 23.5.3). HMRC considers that 'the proper test . . . is whether it was reasonable for a particular person to rely upon the particular advice received in relation to the particular facts of the case'. It has produced a list of factors that it will consider which are found in DOTAS guidance, para 23.5.3.

HMRC's position on the ambit of reasonable excuse in respect of penalties generally was criticised by the First Tier Tribunal in *N A Dudey Electrical Contractors Ltd v Revenue & Customs Comrs* [2011] UKFTT 260 (TC), [2011] SWTI 1909 and in *Buxton Rugby Football Club v Revenue & Customs Comrs* [2011] UKFTT 428 (TC). In *Buxton* the Tribunal Judge said:

> '34. In the recent decision of *N A Dudley Electrical Contractors Ltd v R&C Comrs* [2011] UKFTT 260 (TC) (*"Dudley"*), the Tribunal explicitly rejects HMRC's formulation of the "reasonable excuse" defence, saying:
>
> > "HMRC argues that a 'reasonable excuse' must be some exceptional circumstance which prevented timeous filing. That, as a matter of law, is wrong. Parliament has provided that the penalty will not be due if an appellant can show that it has a 'reasonable excuse'. If Parliament had intended to say that the penalty would not be due only in exceptional circumstances, it would have said so in those terms. The phrase 'reasonable excuse' uses ordinary English words in everyday usage which must be given their plain and ordinary meaning."
>
> 35. I too consider that HMRC's formulation of the "reasonable excuse" defence is too narrow and reflects neither the normal and natural meaning of the term (per *Dudley*), nor the earlier *dicta* of this Tribunal quoted above.'

It should be noted that a higher standard of reasonable excuse will apply to monitored promoters and their clients.

Conclusion

[23.55] The costs of non-disclosure are substantial and cannot be ignored. Where a busy practice is delivering many pieces of advice to large numbers of clients they could, inadvertently, incur daily penalties of many thousands of pounds. It is essential, therefore, that practices delivering inheritance tax planning advice should have procedures under which every piece of advice is reviewed in order to consider whether a disclosure is required.

They should record their reasoning and append to this record the evidence on which they have relied in reaching that conclusion which will be drawn from published material, or from their own client files or from both. When recommending a strategy created by a third party, the adviser should make enquiries as to whether a disclosure has been made to HMRC and ask for a copy of that disclosure.

It is clear that most inheritance tax planning now bears a significant additional cost. At the margin, that makes some inheritance tax planning uneconomic which would otherwise have been cost effective.

Chapter 24

A Lifetime of Planning – A Case Study

In this chapter we provide an example of estate planning throughout an adult life. All statutory references are to IHTA 1984 unless otherwise stated. For the sake of simplicity it is assumed that tax legislation will remain unchanged over the period covered by the example and in particular that the nil rate band will remain at £325,000. Inflation is ignored. These assumptions are of course unrealistic. Taking account of likely legislative changes and changes in the value of assets and of money is an important element of inheritance tax planning. In an example dealing with tax planning over the whole of an individual's adult life, however, it would be entirely artificial to attempt to guess at the legislative changes which will be made over that period.

In respect of all of the tax planning set out below, one will have to consider the General Anti-Abuse Rule in FA 2013, Part 5. To what extent would a court regard it as involving arrangements ' . . . the entering into or carrying out of which cannot reasonably be regarded as a reasonable course of action, having regard to all the circumstances . . . '? None of the tax planning techniques discussed below seem particularly out of the ordinary or controversial but how is anyone to predict how the courts will apply such a vague test? For the purposes of our example we shall assume that the General Anti-Abuse Rule will not apply to them.

Early adulthood

Family

[24.1] Henry Clerestory is the eldest son of David and Eleanor Clerestory. He was born on 30 June 1990. He has just completed an internship with an environmentalist think-tank after coming down from University and is about to start work in an environmental consultancy.

Henry's father, David, was born on 30 January 1940 and is therefore 75 years old. David is a widower and has two other children, Richard and Caroline who are one and two years younger than Henry respectively.

Assets

[24.2] Henry has no substantial assets of his own but he has an interest in a settlement.

Interests in settlements

David Clerestory's birthday settlements

[24.3] On 1, 2 and 3 March 2007, David Clerestory had settled £100,000 each on three trusts each earmarked for one of his three children. The trusts gave the child concerned an interest in possession subject to a wide power of appointment exercisable by the trustees in favour of a beneficial class consisting of the children and their issue. Each settlement was named after the child concerned. In respect of each settlement, the trustees immediately took out a set of unit linked whole of life policies on the life of the child for whom the settlement was earmarked, with Insco Plc, and paid premiums of £100,000 in respect of the policies in each settlement. Insco Plc was a non-UK insurer and the law under which the policies were issued did not require the person to whom the insurance policies were issued to have an insurable interest in the life assured.

Each policy was in the conventional form. That is, it matured on the death of the life assured and could be surrendered, in whole or in part, at any time. The premiums paid under the policy were notionally invested in assets of Insco accounted for as 'units'. The surrender benefits were to be calculated as the amount which would be realised on a disposal of these units and the maturity benefit was 101% of the amount which would have been paid on a surrender taking place at the time of maturity. The contract provided that additional premiums could be paid by any person at any time up to the time of the maturity or final surrender of the policy.

The trusts made by David Clerestory are existing IIPs. David Clerestory was a wealthy man and, in 2014, although he was in good health he had been conscious that his life expectancy was quite short. He therefore decided to make some transfers in favour of his children but he did not want them to have unfettered control of large amounts of money. On 30 November 2014 he paid additional premia of £100,000 each in respect of the three policies with Insco held on the trusts of the three settlements.

These payments were transfers of value by David Clerestory because they reduced his estate.

Each of the insurance contracts satisfied the conditions of s 46A, because:

(a)   each settlement commenced before 22 March 2006;

(b)   each contract of insurance was entered into before that day;

(c)   each added premium was payable under the contract on or after 22 March 2006;

(d)   immediately before 22 March 2006 and at all subsequent times up to the payment of the premium, there were rights under the insurance contract which were comprised in the settlement and those rights were settled property in which a transitionally protected interest subsisted. That was because the same person had had an interest in possession in the contract continuously since before 22 March 2006;

(e)   enhanced rights under the contract have become comprised in the settlement by reference to the premium because the premium increases both the surrender and maturity benefits payable under the policy;

(f) there has been no variation of the contract, or if one argued that the payment of the premium was a variation, it was one that increased the benefits secured by the contract and was an allowed variation. That is, the payment of the premiums took place as a result of the exercise of rights conferred by provisions which formed part of the contract immediately before 22 March 2006.

Because s 46A applied to the insurance contract held by the settlement the payment of the premium did not prevent the rights under the contract from being treated for inheritance tax purposes as having become comprised in the settlement before 22 March 2006 and the beneficiary from being treated as having been entitled to his interest in possession since before 22 March 2006. The result of that, of course, was that the beneficiary's interest in the insurance contract was an existing IIP and therefore s 49 applied to it so that the beneficiary was also treated as beneficially entitled to the contract. In turn, that resulted in David Clerestory's transfers of value being treated as gifts to other individuals (by virtue of section 3A(2)) to the extent that, by virtue of the transfer, the estate of the beneficiary had been increased. That extended to the whole of the transfer of value because the premium immediately enhanced the surrender value by an amount almost equal to the premium.

The policies were also 'protected settlements' under section 62C.

Henry makes a will

[24.4] Although Henry has no significant assets outside his trust interest he makes a will because he appreciates that he is likely to accumulate assets in the near future. As his parents would have no need of any assets which he had accumulated in the event that he were to die, he makes a simple will leaving his assets equally to Richard and Caroline. If he had had substantial assets he would have made a will creating flexible life interest trusts for his siblings. In the event of his death, those life interests would have been IPDIs and so the inheritance tax consequences of his death would have been the same as for outright gifts. The advantage of creating flexible life interest trusts, however, would have been to allow flexibility for the future.

Marriage

[24.5] On 20 July 2020, when he is 30 years old, Henry marries Polly who was born on 1 October 1998 and who is therefore, 22 years old.

Henry's career has progressed and his wealth increased

[24.6] Henry has been successful in his career and he is now a director of Caring for the Planet Inc. He has inherited a share portfolio from a bachelor uncle. His major assets and liabilities are:

	£000
Shares in ISAs	80
Other Shares	1,000
Flat in Wimbledon	750
Less: mortgage	(200)
Pension fund	100
Venture Capital Trust shares	200
Cash at bank	70
	2,000

The inheritance tax liability which would arise were he to die is:

	£000	£000
Assets	2,000	
Less: pension fund value written on discretionary trusts	(100)	
Free estate		1,900
Interest in possession in 'David Clerestory Insurance Settlement for Henry Clerestory'		429
Taxable estate		2,329
Less: nil rate band		(325)
Subject to inheritance tax at 40%		2,004
Inheritance tax thereon at 40%		£802

Pension fund death benefit

[24.7] The pension fund death benefit is held on discretionary trusts under the rules of the scheme. A scheme member can nominate any person or persons to be a member of the beneficial class other than himself. Once a nomination is made he can remove any person from the beneficial class provided that there shall always be at least one member of that class. In default of such a nomination the death benefit is held on trust for the member absolutely. Henry has nominated Richard and Caroline, any issue of his born during the trust period and any person who is at the time concerned his wife. He now gives the pension fund trustees a letter of wishes in which he asks them, in exercising their discretion, to take account of his wish that, if his wife survives him, she should benefit from the trust and not his siblings subject to whatever is appropriate for tax planning purposes.

Liability for the inheritance tax

[24.8] That amount of the total charge which is proportionate to the property held on the trusts of the David Clerestory Insurance Settlement in which he has an interest in possession would primarily be a liability of the trustees of the settlement concerned.

Henry makes a new will

[24.9] On Henry's marriage his will is revoked by operation of law. He therefore makes a new will under which he creates a flexible life interest trust for his wife and, subject to that, a broad discretionary trust for his issue, his brother and sister and their issue and his father. The trustees are to be his wife and an old friend, who is now his solicitor.

Although there is a large potential liability which would arise on Henry's death if he were to be predeceased by his wife, he is not particularly concerned about it. The life interest trust he establishes for his wife on his death would be an IPDI and therefore his estate would receive the spouse exemption if she were to survive him. He has no children or other dependants and Henry takes the attitude that, after their father's death, Richard and Caroline, who would be the principal beneficiaries of his discretionary will trust after his wife's death, are likely to be very well provided for and so he need not worry about any inheritance tax which would arise on the discretionary trust in the somewhat unlikely event that his wife predeceased him before he changed his will again in response to changing circumstances.

Henry insures his life

[24.10] Polly is currently working part time in an art gallery and does not have a large income. Henry is concerned that, if he were to die suddenly, Polly would not have a very high standard of living.

On 15 July 2020, in preparation for his marriage therefore, he took out whole of life assurance on his own life for a level sum assured of £1m which he wrote on discretionary trusts for a beneficial class consisting of Polly, his brother Richard, his sister Caroline, his issue, Richard's issue, Caroline's issue and any spouses of Richard or Caroline. The aggregate annual premia paid for this assurance were £14,000.

The assurance is constructed as a bundle of 100 separate policies.

In spite of the large sum assured the current market value of the policy is insignificant because it is not likely to mature for many years due to Henry's young age. The trustees of the policy are himself and his wife. He has a power to appoint new trustees and of requiring trustees to retire. He gives the trustees a letter of wishes in which he sets out his requests as to the principles which he would like to govern their exercise of their discretion under the settlement.

Henry will pay the premiums out of his income. So Henry's payment of the premiums will be exempt as normal expenditure out of income. The settlement will be a relevant property settlement but because of the insubstantial value of the property within the settlement and the fact that Henry has made no previous chargeable transfers it is likely that any decennial and exit charges in the early years would be at 0%.

His father makes a gift of £300,000 to help towards the purchase price of a house. This gift is a potentially exempt transfer. Henry sells his Wimbledon flat and half of his share portfolio, takes out a larger mortgage loan of £450,000 and buys a house in the same area for £2.0m.

Henry becomes a father

[24.11] In rapid succession Henry and Polly have three children, Simon, who is born on 27 May 2021, Charity who is born on 20 June 2022 and Prudence who is born on 15 November 2023.

Henry revises his will

[24.12] Henry makes a new will. Having considered whether it is necessary to do so in view of the transferrable nil rate band provisions of s 8A, he provides for a discretionary will trust over a legacy equal to the nil rate band at the time concerned less the aggregate chargeable transfers made in the 7 years before his death. The beneficial class of this trust includes his wife, his issue, his brother, sister and father. As he contemplates the responsibilities of becoming a father, Henry begins to worry about the inheritance tax liability which would arise if he and Polly were both to die prematurely.

Henry insures his life again

[24.13] On 30 April 2021, Henry takes out joint life last survivor policies on the lives of himself and his wife for a level sum assured of £1m written on similar trusts to those governing the previous policies. Although Henry is older than when he took out the previous policies, because the new policies are is written on a last survivor basis, the premiums are primarily determined by reference to Polly's life expectancy, which, because she is both female and considerably younger than Henry, is significantly longer than his. The annual premiums are, therefore, only £11,000 in aggregate. Again, Henry pays these premiums out of income and so they are covered by the normal expenditure out of income exemption. The settlement is a relevant property settlement but because of the low immediate value of the policies it is apparent that decennial and exit charges will not arise in the near future.

David Clerestory makes a further gift

[24.14] With the birth of his third grandchild, David is keen to help Henry acquire a larger house in the country. He is concerned to treat his three children equally, taking account of their different circumstances. David gives Henry £500,000 as an outright gift and tells Richard and Caroline, who are recently married but, as yet, childless, that he will do the same for them when they become parents.

Henry sells his house in Wimbledon for £3.55m, maintains his mortgage of £450,000 and buys a country house in Sussex for £4.0m.

David Clerestory's death

David's taxable estate

[24.15] David Clerestory died on 20 December 2030 when he was 90 years old. Under his will £1m is bequeathed to the Prayer Book Society and the residue of his estate is to be divided equally between Henry, Richard and Caroline. His estate at death was as follows:

	£000
Clerestory Court	8,000
Clerestory Farm qualifying for agricultural property relief	12,000
Shares in Clerestory's Ecclesiastical Outfitters Ltd ('CEO Ltd'), qualifying for business property relief	5,000
Share portfolio	2,025
Cash at bank	3,000
	30,025
Less: agricultural and business property relief (Clerestory Farm and shares in CEO Ltd)	(17,000)
Total taxable estate	13,025
Less: charitable legacy	(1,000)
	12,025
Less: nil rate band	(325)
	11,700
Tax thereon at 40%	£4,680
Tax rate on estate 15.6%	

It will be seen that tax is chargeable on his gross estate at an average rate of only 15.6% because a large amount of the property in David Clerestory's estate qualifies for business and agricultural property relief or is bequeathed to charity.

Division of David Clerestory's estate

[24.16] Henry and Richard are executors of their father's will. Richard is now managing director of Clerestory's Ecclesiastical Outfitters Ltd and he wishes to take all of the shares in that company. Caroline is anxious to make as clean a break as possible between her affairs and the family's.

It is agreed, however, that they should avoid selling the farmland if possible. Clerestory Court is surrounded by grounds of 30 acres. The house and grounds are surrounded by Clerestory Farm which has been let to a variety of tenants for many years. Although the land is let and an agent is engaged to manage the lettings, the land requires the owner to be involved on a regular basis in a variety of decisions. Henry has been very successful financially over the last few years and so he is able to agree to take Clerestory Court with the farmland being held equally between the three siblings on bare trusts under which he is to be responsible for the management decisions in relation to the land for as long as the property is held in trust. Henry makes an equalisation payment to his siblings in respect of Clerestory Court on which stamp duty land tax is charged. The trustees' decisions in relation to the land, other than in relation to its management, are to be taken unanimously. In this way, the land could not be sold without Henry's consent and, until it is sold, he would be in a position to take the day to day management decisions in relation to it with the help and advice of the family land agent.

Henry considers making an application for conditional exemption for Heritage Property on Clerestory Court (an outstanding Grade I listed Jacobean house) but decides that the public access requirements are likely to be too onerous.

Henry, Richard and Caroline realise that if they enter into a deed of variation of David Clerestory's will to increase the amount passing to charity to 10% of the net estate, they will actually increase the net amount which they receive. They increase the charitable donation to the Prayer Book Society from £1,000,000 to £1,270,000; that is, 10% of the net estate (£12,025,000 – £325,000 + £1,000,000) (see **15.6** above). The taxable estate after deduction of the nil rate band becomes £11,430,000 (£13,025,000 – £1,270,000 – £325,000) resulting in an inheritance tax liability at 36% of £4,114,800. The total amount of the estate applied to tax and the charitable donation is decreased from £5,680,000 (£4,680,000 + £1,000,000) to £5,384,800 (£4,114,800 + £1,270,000) increasing the residue to be divided between the siblings by £295,200.

Henry sells his family home for £8,950,000 and repays the £450,000 mortgage on it. His gain on the sale of the home is exempt from capital gains tax as it is the sale of his Main Residence. Although the home has garden and grounds of five acres the whole of the gain relating to this area is exempt because the whole of the garden and grounds are required for the reasonable enjoyment of the dwelling house.

After his father's death Henry takes stock

[24.17] Henry is 40 years old on the death of his father. He takes stock of his financial position. His free estate now consists of the following.

	£000
A shareholding in EnviroEthics Group Plc	5,000
ISAs	250
Share portfolio	5,500
Venture Capital Trust shares	2,500
Portfolio of shares qualifying for EIS relief which are listed on the Alternative Investment Market and which are business property for inheritance tax purposes	1,500
Cash at bank	500
Clerestory Court	10,000

	£000
One third interest in Clerestory Farm	4,000
	29,250

Interests in settlements:

	£000

	£000
Existing life interest in insurance policies held by David Clerestory Settlement. The fund value is:	510
Pension fund	1,000

In addition the following settlements hold assets on discretionary trusts for beneficial classes including his wife Polly and their children—

The Henry Clerestory Insurance Trust No 1

Holds whole of life policies on Henry Clerestory's life for a level sum assured of £1m for annual premiums of £14,000. These policies have an insignificant market value	0

The Henry Clerestory Insurance Trust No 2

Holds joint life, last survivor policies on the lives of himself and his wife for a level sum assured £1m for annual premiums of £11,000. These policies have an insignificant market value	0

Henry has the following income:

	£000

	£000
Net dividend income from free estate (a small proportion of dividends are not subject to income tax)	200
Interest income	25
Director's emoluments	1,000
Share of rents from share of Clerestory Farm	50
	1,275

His annual expenditure is £850,000. This total includes taxation but excludes his regular investments which are deductible from income for taxation purposes (VCTs, pension contributions and EIS shares) and his payments of life insurance premiums.

The inheritance tax liability which would arise if he were to die immediately, followed shortly by the death of his wife Polly, would be as follows:

	£000
Free estate	29,250
Interests in existing qualifying IIPs	510
	29,760

	£000
Property qualifying for BPR:	(1,500)
Less: EIS portfolio	
Property qualifying for APR:	(4,000)
Less: interest in Clerestory Farm	
Less: nil rate band utilised by Henry's legacy on discretionary trusts	(325)
Less: nil rate band utilised on Polly's death	(325)
Subject to inheritance tax at 40%	23,610
Inheritance tax thereon at 40%	9,444

Henry's pension fund death benefit has continued to be held on discretionary trusts. Although his pension fund is £1m the value of the death benefit is very low. This is both because Henry is still a comparatively young man in good health and because, when Henry reaches the age of 55, he will have the ability to deplete the fund (and thus the death benefit) by opting to take his pension.

Henry is alarmed at the size of the potential inheritance tax liability on Polly's death. He therefore decides that he will also make regular additional gifts out of income in favour of his children. Although these gifts out of income will not be immediately chargeable, gifts into relevant property trusts of a significant size would create inheritance tax charges on the decennials of the trusts. He therefore decides that he will make gifts on bare trusts for his three children absolutely. He has no wish, however, to place large amounts of money into the hands of his children on their 18th birthday.

He therefore takes out with an insurance company a group of 100 identical unit-linked policies written on the joint lives of himself and Polly on a last survivor basis so that the policies will mature on the death of the last of them to die.

An unusual feature of the policies is that they have no surrender value. In that way they do not offer the immediate ability to realise spendable cash. The policies are not, however, a complete answer to the problem of giving beneficial ownership of assets to children at an age before they are fully financially responsible. Immediately on reaching an 18th birthday, the beneficiary of the bare trust could require the trustees to pass the trust property to him and, even though the insurance policies could not be surrendered, they could be sold for a capital sum or used to secure borrowing. Accepting these drawbacks, Henry enters into the policies.

Although the policies only require an initial premium to be paid, they allow the payment of additional premiums. Henry plans to pay aggregate annual premiums of £400,000; that is £4,000 per policy per year, being the surplus of his income over his annual expenditure and the premiums which he pays in respect of the insurance policies which he has previously taken out (£1,275,000 – £850,000 – £14,000 – £11,000).

From age 40 to age 60

[24.18] Between the ages of 40 and 60 Henry continues the pattern of transfers that he has established. There are also the following significant developments.

Henry requests the trustees of his pension fund death benefit to exercise their discretionary powers to hold the death benefit for his three children in equal shares absolutely. That is the occasion of an exit charge but because the value of the death benefit was less than the nil rate band at the last decennial, the rate of charge is 0%.

Henry continues to prosper, becoming the Chief Executive of EnviroEthics Group Plc and subsequently its chairman.

As Henry's, Richard's and Caroline's lives develop, Richard and Caroline become increasingly dissatisfied at having a substantial amount of capital tied up in Clerestory Farm which produces a very low income and which enhances Henry's enjoyment of Clerestory Court but does not similarly benefit them. Henry therefore buys their interests at their current market value of £6m each.

As each of his children comes down from university, he buys that child a flat for £2,000,000. When each reaches his or her 25th birthday he makes a gift to that child of £1,000,000 to provide an investment fund for them. All of these gifts are PETs.

Henry reaches 60 and retires

[24.19] When Henry reaches his 60th birthday on 30 June 2050 he retires after a long and profitable career in environmental lobbying and consultancy. He feels that it is time once again to take stock of his position. Simon is engaged to be married, although Charity and Prudence are showing no particular signs of settling down.

Disinvestment from EnviroEthics Group Plc

[24.20] His shareholding in EnviroEthics Group Plc has continued to increase in value significantly, although he has been making regular sales of shares accepting the capital gains tax charge which arises on the sale at an effective rate of 20%.

Assets and income

[24.21] In spite of the substantial gifts he has made, his assets have increased significantly and his wife Polly has inherited assets from her father. Their joint estates are now as follows:

	Henry £000	Polly £000	Total £000
ISAs	1,500	200	1,700

	Henry £000	Polly £000	Total £000
Pension fund	0	0	0
VCTs	5,000	0	5,000
Portfolio of shares qualifying for EIS Relief which are listed on the Alternative Investment Market and which are Business Property for inheritance tax purposes	5,000	500	5,500
Cash at bank	1,000	300	1,300
Clerestory Court	25,000	0	25,000
Clerestory Farm	20,000	0	20,000
Portfolio of shares, bonds and gilts	25,000	2,000	27,000
	82,500	3,000	85,500

Henry's pension fund has not performed well and is still valued at £1,200,000. He is very conscious that, now that he has retired, his income will have reduced substantially. He estimates that his and his wife's incomes will now be:

	Henry £000	Polly £000	Total £000
Dividends from ISAs	45	5	50
Dividends on VCT and EIS shares	50	5	55
Bank interest	40	10	50
Rents from Clerestory Farm	200	0	200
Other net dividends	500	50	550
Other interest	250	10	260
	1,085	80	1,165

Henry has not drawn down his pension and does not intend to do so in the near future.

Henry and Polly estimate their annual expenditure including taxation but excluding his payment of annual premiums on life assurance policies at £915,000 per annum.

Annual insurance premiums

[24.22] Henry realises that he can no longer pay all of the insurance premiums which he has been paying out of his surplus income which is now only £250,000 (£1,165,000 – £915,000). He decides to continue to pay the premiums on the policies held by the Henry Clerestory Insurance No 1 and No 2 Trusts amounting to £25,000 per annum. Of the 100 policies taken out in 2030 he reduces the amount of additional premiums which he pays from £400,000 per annum to £225,000; an amount which he can afford to pay from his surplus income.

Potential inheritance tax on Henry's and Polly's estates

[24.23] The inheritance tax liability which would arise if he were to die immediately followed shortly afterwards by his wife, Polly, would be as follows:

	£000
Aggregate free estate of Henry and Polly	82,500
Interests in existing IIP's David Clerestory Settlement for Henry	1,500
	84,000
Property qualifying for BPR:	
Less: EIS shares	(5,500)
Property qualifying for APR:	
Less: Clerestory Farm	(20,000)
Less: nil rate band utilised by Henry's legacy on discretionary trusts	(325)
Less: nil rate band utilised on Polly's death	(325)
Subject to inheritance tax on Polly's death at 40%	57,850
Inheritance tax thereon at 40%	23,140

Henry is once again appalled at the idea of so much of the family wealth being expropriated by the government.

Simon has just obtained an appointment in New York with Carbon Reduction Plc that he will take up immediately after his honeymoon. He will be out of the country for at least six UK fiscal years and expects to be non-resident throughout this period.

The trustees of the David Clerestory Settlement have made no withdrawals from the policies on the life of Henry which were taken out at the time the settlement was made. If the policies were to be encashed by the trustees, who are now Henry and Polly, the trustees would be chargeable on substantial chargeable event gains. The trustees decide to advance the policies to Simon. That is a potentially exempt transfer and is not a chargeable event for the purposes of ITTOIA 2005, Pt 4 Ch 9. If Simon were to surrender the policies whilst he was not resident in the United Kingdom, the chargeable event gain would be realised free of taxation provided his period of non-residence was more than five years. Simon subsequently does so receiving £1,100,000.

Henry reaches his 70th birthday

[24.24] By 2060 when Henry reaches his 70th birthday, Simon is married to Emma and has three children, James, John and Julia. Charity is married to Fergus and has one child, Angus. Prudence has been married, is divorced and is childless.

Gift of Clerestory Court

[24.25] Henry has reorganised his investments reducing his holdings in VCTs and increasing his investments in Enterprise Investment Scheme companies qualifying for business property relief.

Simon is now settled in this country again and, although he continues to travel internationally on business, he thinks it is unlikely that he will again reside for long periods abroad. It is agreed that Simon and his family will occupy Clerestory House with Henry and Polly and that Henry will give a 99% interest in the house, which is now worth £40m, to Simon. In the expectation of preventing a reservation of benefit arising Henry will pay his proportionate share of the expenses of the house. It appears that it may be HMRC's view that FA 1986, s 102B, which provides, *inter alia*, that there is not a reservation of benefit in land where a gift is made of an undivided share in the land, the donor and the donee occupy that land and the donor does not receive more than a negligible benefit from the donee, does not apply where the donor's and donee's interests in the land after the gift are unequal (see HMRC Inheritance Tax Manual, para 14332). That is the situation in respect of Henry's gift of a share in Clerestory Court to Simon. If that is HMRC's view of the construction of FA 1986, s 102B, HMRC is incorrect in its view.

Simon takes on the burden of managing Clerestory Farm relieving Henry of this responsibility.

Hope of development on Clerestory Farm

[24.26] A change of planning criteria has had the result that it is now hoped that an area of some 50 acres (the 'Ciborium Land') of Clerestory Farm, which is situated near Ciborium village and which forms that part of the farm which is furthest away from Clerestory Court, will be zoned for development. It is hoped that it will be possible, subsequently, to obtain planning permission for its development. Simon decides that he will instigate a policy of bringing the Ciborium Land in hand employing a professional farm manager. He does this for two reasons.

First, so that the land will qualify for business property relief. Although it already qualifies for agricultural property relief, any excess of its value over its agricultural value would not receive APR. Second, because any purchaser of the land for development will require vacant possession as a condition of the sale.

Henry's pension fund

[24.27] Annuity rates are particularly good, so Henry decides that his pension fund should purchase an annuity. The result of this is that on his death there will be no assets remaining in his fund.

Henry's charitable donation

[24.28] Henry wished to make a substantial charitable donation to the Prayer Book Society (registered charity number 1099295). He was considering making this donation under his will but decided that he could maximise the tax relief on it by making annual gift aid donations. He therefore made an interest free loan to the Society of £2m and determined to make payments under gift aid of £100,000 per year which the Society would apply in reducing the loan. He makes a new will providing that the balance of the loan outstanding at his death should be written off. At the same time he provides that Polly and Simon should be the executors of his will.

The death of Henry

[24.29] Henry died on 30 June 2075 when he was aged 85. He had made no chargeable transfers seven years before his death. All of the transfers he had made within seven years of death were either covered by the annual exemption or by the exemptions for normal expenditure out of income or for charitable gifts. His estate on death and Polly's estate on that date were as follows:

	Henry's estate on death £000	Polly's estate £000
ISAs	5,000	500
1% interest in Clerestory Court	500	0
Portfolio of shares on which EIS relief was given and qualifying as business property	10,000	1,000
Cash at bank	1,500	500
Clerestory Farm excluding the Ciborium Land	10,000	0
Ciborium Land	50,000	0
Portfolio of shares	30,000	0
Gilts and bonds	25,000	3,000
	132,000	5,000

The Ciborium Land

[24.30] Simon had been successful in freeing the Ciborium Land from the tenancies to which it had been subject and the land was now farmed in hand. Planning permission had been obtained on the land in 2073 and a number of offers from property development companies had been received for the land since that time. Henry had been in poor health for the last two years of his life and he had therefore determined to reject these offers so as to obtain the uplift to market value in the value of the land on his death for his children.

The land qualified for business property relief.

No discretionary will trust

[24.31] Henry had not changed his will since 2060. He had, however, reviewed it regularly.

His will provided for a legacy on discretionary trusts ('Henry's Nil Rate Band Trust') of an amount equal to the nil rate band less the amount of any lifetime transfers within seven years of his death. Because Henry had not made any chargeable transfers in the seven years before his death, the discretionary legacy was of the full £325,000. The residue of his estate was left on trusts ('Henry's Trust of Residue') conferring a life interest on Polly, subject to flexible powers for the trustees to defeat that interest, create new interests and to advance trust property absolutely.

Charitable legacy to the Prayer Book Society

[24.32] Henry had made 15 annual gift aid payments of £100,000 each to the Prayer Book Society with the result that the outstanding balance on the loan he had made to it was £500,000. The writing off of this outstanding balance under the terms of his will was a charitable donation which was exempt from inheritance tax. By making gifts of £1,500,000 under gift aid David had, in effect, received tax relief at 67%. He had received 45% income tax relief on his gift aid donations and, because, had he not made those donations his net income would have increased his estate at death, he had in effect received a further 40% inheritance tax relief on the net payments after 45% income tax relief.

No inheritance tax chargeable on Henry's estate

[24.33] The EIS shares and the Ciborium Land received 100% business property relief. Clerestory Farm, excluding the Ciborium Land, received 100% agricultural property relief. The will trust arising under the nil rate band legacy on discretionary trusts used Henry's nil rate band. Henry's Trust of Residue was an immediate post-death interest with the result that IHTA 1984, s 49 applied to it. The bequests and devises to the trust were therefore relieved from inheritance tax by virtue of being transfers to a spouse.

The advance from the will trust

[24.34] Polly decided that her own personal assets were sufficient to meet her living expenses and so it was decided to advance the assets arising under Henry's Trust of Residue to Simon, Charity and Prudence in equal shares. The Ciborium Land was advanced jointly to Simon, Charity and Prudence and the trustees appropriated the 1% interest in Clerestory Court and remaining Clerestory Farm land to Simon in part satisfaction of his remaining share. The EIS shares and the Ciborium Land again received 100% business property relief. Clerestory Farm again received 100% agricultural property relief. The advance of the remaining trust assets was a potentially exempt transfer by Polly which would only become chargeable if she were to die within seven years of the advance.

Sale of the Ciborium Land

[24.35] Simon, Charity and Prudence sold the Ciborium Land for a price roughly equal to its probate value to developers a few months after Henry's death. The land having passed free of inheritance tax on Henry's death, no chargeable gain was now realised on the disposal of the land because of the uplift of its base cost to market value on Henry's death. The effect of the sale was that business property relief would not be available on the trustees' previous advance of the land if Polly were to die within seven years of the advance so that her potentially exempt transfer would, in that event, become chargeable.

Relevant property settlements; planning for the decennial charges

Relevant property settlements; decennial charges

[24.36] Henry had been either the settlor or a beneficial object of various relevant property settlements. They had been dealt with by the trustees in the following ways.

At Henry's death, there were two relevant property settlements in existence the assets of which were earmarked for Henry's family. These were the insurance trust which Henry made on 15 July 2019 and the further insurance trust which he made on 30 April 2020.

In calculating decennial charges, one posits a hypothetical transfer by a transferor who has aggregate chargeable transfers equal to the chargeable transfers made by the settlor in the seven years preceding the settlement and the amounts on which exit charges had been made in the ten years preceding the decennial. Therefore, exits made in the ten years before the decennial will increase the rate of tax charged on that decennial. In order to minimise decennial and later exit charges therefore, trustees need to anticipate the growth in value of the trust assets not only to the next decennial but to the following one as well. The trustees of these three settlements had done so, carefully advancing amounts to the beneficiaries so as to ensure that the decennial charges arising on each decennial were at 0%.

The death of Polly

[24.37] Polly lived a further 11 years to the age of 88 and so the potentially exempt transfers resulting from the exercise, by the trustees of Henry's Trust of Residue, of their discretion to advance assets to Simon, Charity and Prudence absolutely proved not to be a chargeable transfer.

After Henry's death no more additions were made to the policies which Henry had established in 2030. Thereafter, on Polly's death the insurance policies matured. The aggregate maturity value of the policies at that time was £72m, premiums of £15.36m in total having been paid over the life of the policies. No chargeable event gain arose, however, because the policy did not have a surrender value immediately before death (ITTOIA 2005, s 493(7)).

Over his lifetime, and on his death, the following advances, gifts, devises and bequests had been made from the property which either did, or were deemed to, form part of Henry's estate for inheritance tax purposes without any inheritance tax being payable whatsoever.

Year	Event	Comment
2020	Henry takes out whole of life assurance on his life for a level sum assured written on discretionary trusts for his family and paying annual premiums of £14,000.	The trustees advance 25 policies each to Simon, Charity and Prudence during Henry's life. On his death £250,000 is received by the discretionary trust and £250,000 each is received by his children.
2021	Henry takes out life assurance on the joint lives of himself and Polly on a last survivor basis written on discretionary trusts for his family and paying annual premiums of £11,000.	The trustees advance 25 policies each to Simon, Charity and Prudence during Henry's life. On his death £250,000 is received by the discretionary trust and £250,000 each is received by his children.
2030	Henry takes out a group of policies on bare trusts for his children paying annual premiums out of income which initially amount to £400,000 per year.	On Polly's death Henry's children share £72m between them premiums of £15.36m having been paid under the policies.
2042–2048	Henry gives each of his three children a flat worth £2,000,000 and money to invest of £1,000,000 so that he makes gifts of £9.0m in all.	These gifts were PETS which proved not to be chargeable transfers.
2050	The trustees of the David Clerestory Settlement defeat Henry's life interest in the fund advancing the settlement assets to Simon absolutely.	Simon surrenders the capital redemption bonds advanced to him whilst he is non-resident realising £1.1m.
2060	Henry gives a 99% interest in Clerestory Court which is now worth £35m to Simon absolutely.	This was a PET which proved not to be a chargeable transfer.
2060–2075	Henry makes charitable donations totalling £1,500,000 under gift aid.	These are exempt transfers and receive income tax relief under Gift Aid.
2075	Under his will, Henry leaves a charitable legacy of £500,000.	This is an exempt transfer.

Year	Event	Comment
2075	£325,000 is held on the trusts of Henry's Nil Rate Band Trust. The trustees of Henry's Trust of Residue advance assets with a value of £132m less the nil rate band advance, to the children.	The transfer to the discretionary trust is within the nil rate band. The transfer by the trustees of Henry's Trust of Residue receives APR and BPR of £70m and is a potentially exempt transfer as to the balance. The potentially exempt transfer does not become chargeable.

Index